THE LEGACY OF YOGA IN BHAGAWAD GEETA

THE LEGACY OF YOGA IN BHAGAWAD GEETA

[The classical text of Srimad Bhagawad Geeta in Sanskrit, its romanized transliteration, English translation, Lucid commentary and Indexes]

Translation & Commentary by :
PRABHA DUNEJA

Publisher :
GOVINDRAM HASANAND
DELHI, INDIA

ISBN : 81-7077-007-6
First Edition : Delhi, July, 1998
Second Edition : Jan., 2005

Translation and Commentary by :
PRABHA DUNEJA
2822, Camino Segura
Pleasanton, CA 94566, U.S.A.
Tel. : 925-484-5411; Fax : 925-417-5946
e-mail : duneja@aol.com
website : www.holygeeta.com

Editors :
Swami Jagdishwaranand Saraswati
A renowned Vedic Scholar and Master of Sanskrit Grammar
Dr. Baldeo Sahai
Writer, Journalist and Fellow of Indian National Science Academy
Sh. P.N. Bhargawa
A senior proof reader in The Hindustan Times for over 25 years

Publisher :
GOVINDRAM HASANAND
4408, Nai Sarak, Delhi-110 006 (INDIA)
Tel. : 91-11-23977216
e-mail : ajayarya@vsnl.com
Web : www.vedicbooks.com

ACKNOWLEDGEMENTS

I want to express in few words my heartfelt gratitude to the holy sages of past and present and to other several Geeta-scholars, commentators, philosophers and poets whose teachings have inspired me for writing this book.

I feel immensely indebted to my husband Amritji and our son Anshuman for their genuine encouragement and sincere support in the completion of this noble work. I am especially grateful to my respected grandparents Sri & Smt. Ganga Ramji and my parents Dr. & Mrs. Manohar Lalji and my uncle Professor Nand Lalji who initiated me in the study of Vedic literature and Bhagawad Geeta at the early age of eight. I am extremely grateful to Mr. Baldeo Sahaiji, a renowned scholar, to go through the pages of this commentary. A fellow of the Indian National Science Academy, member of Indian Information Service, a journalist, poet, art critic and author of several books, he has also been good enough to give a Foreword to the volume. I want to thank sincerely Mrs. Manorama Iyer, who worked very patiently and enthusiastically in typing my handwritten work into a computer processed manuscript. Special thanks to Mrs. Neera Sekhri for her help in typing; and to Mr. Raj Iyer, Anshuman, Ajay Arya, Vijay Kumar Jha and Dharmesh Bhanabhai for their valuable technical help in processing the preliminary work.

—Prabha Duneja

ŚRĪ KṚṢṆA ARPAṆAM ASTU

तवदीय गीतं गोविन्दं तुभ्यमेव समर्पये

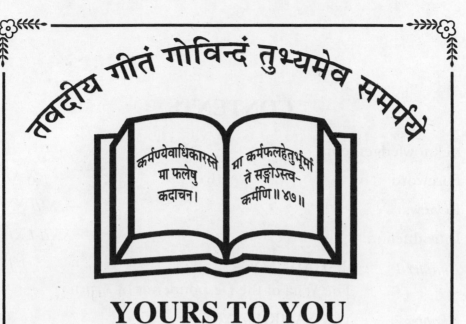

YOURS TO YOU

"...Vasūdeva Sutam Devaṁ
Kaṅs Chaṇur Mardanaṁ
Devaki Parmanaṅdaṁ
Kṛṣṇaṁ Vaṅde Jagatguruṁ..."

I salute to Lord Kṛṣṇa, the son of Vasūdeva, the destroyer of Kaṅsa and Chanura, the supreme bliss of Devaki and the teacher of the Universe.

CONTENTS

Acknowledgements		*V*
Foreword		*X-XII*
Reviews		*XIII-XXI*
Introduction		*XXII-LXIV*
Chapter 1 :	VISHADA YOGA The Yoga of the Despondency of Arjuna	*1-17*
Chapter 2 :	THE SAMKHYA-YOGA The Yoga of The Transcendental Knowledge	*18-79*
Chapter 3 :	KARMA YOGA The Yoga of Action	*80-117*
Chapter 4 :	JNANA-KARMA YOGA The Yoga of Action and Knowledge	*118-155*
Chapter 5 :	KARMA-SANNYASA YOGA The Yoga of Action and Renunciation	*156-177*
Chapter 6 :	DHYANA YOGA The Yoga of Meditation	*178-218*
Chapter 7 :	JNANAVIJNANA YOGA The Yoga of Wisdom and Knowledge	*219-242*
Chapter 8 :	AKSARABRAHMA YOGA The Yoga of the Imperishable Brahman	*243-271*
Chapter 9 :	RAJAVIDYA-RAJAGUHYA YOGA The Yoga of the Sovereign Science and Sovereign Secret	*272-300*

Chapter 10	:	VIBHUTIYOGA The Yoga of The Divine Manifestations	*301-341*
Chapter 11	:	VISVARUPADARSANA YOGA The Yoga of The Vision of the Universal Form	*342-374*
Chapter 12	:	BHAKTI YOGA The Yoga of Devotion	*375-403*
Chapter 13	:	KSETRA-KSETRAJÑA-VIBHAGA-YOGA The Yoga of the Knowledge of the Field and the Knower of the Field	*404-440*
Chapter 14	:	GUNA-TRIYA-VIBHAGA YOGA The Yoga of the Division of the three Gunas	*441-465*
Chapter 15	:	PURUSHOTTAMA YOGA The Yoga of the Supreme Person	*466-489*
Chapter 16	:	DEVASURSAMPATTI VIBHAGA-YOGA The Yoga of the Distinction between the Divine and Demoniac Endowments	*490-511*
Chapter 17	:	SRADDHATRIYA VIBHAGA YOGA The Yoga of the Threefold Division of the Faith	*512-536*
Chapter 18	:	MOKSHA-SANNYASA YOGA The Yoga of Liberation through Renunciation	*537-607*
Shloka Index			*608-617*
Word Index			*618-637*

FOREWORD

The Geetā is an intimate dialogue between God and man. The God-incarnate is Lorḍ Kṛṣṇa and man is represented by the *Mahabharata* hero Arjuna. It is intimate because the esoteric wisdom imparted therein, says the Lorḍ is "is more secret than secrecy itself" (XVIII. 63).

A great battle is to ensue between the two royal clans of Kauravas and Pandavas. Arjuna requests Kṛṣṇa, who is acting as his charioteer, to take him between the two standing armies so that he may have a look at those who have gathered to fight with him. There Arjuna is overcome with grief and refuses to raise his bow against his respected gurus and elders, and other kith and kin. At this critical juncture Lorḍ kṛṣṇa explains to him what is right and what is wrong, and how by adhering to dharma a person can earn the highest virtue.

Every human heart is like a battlefield of good and evil forces. At times a person is not able to decide the right course of action. He is deluded and confused. When confronted with such a situation, he can turn to the Geetā; it will not fail him. The book therefore is of universal appeal which offers satisfactory solution to basic human problems. Whatever page you turn, and whichever verse you read, it is bound to elevate and inspire. It is not the book of a particular race or religion but the common heritage of the entire mankind.

The recurring emphasis in the Geetā is on the gospel of selfless unattached action, performed with perfect equanimity, and with full awareness of the Divinity within. The dialogue begins with the sorrowful lamentation of Arjuna. 'O Lorḍ, I know as a Kśatriya, it is my bounden duty to wage a righteous war but I would rather beg to earn a living than to acquire a Kingdom by killing my relations and disturb the focal point of so many families. A noble thought indeed. His difficulty was not to choose between dharma and adharma but between dharma and a still higher dharma as he perceived it.'

The general theme of the dialogue is the realization of the

Supreme-Self through the constant practice of Yogic unity. Śrī Kṛṣṇa declares that those who strive, endowed with the spirit of selfless action, Yajña and Yoga, perceive the Lorḍ dwelling in the self. Śrī Kṛṣṇa gives a definite promise of His grace in the words, *"sarvadharman parityajya māmekaṁ śaraṇaṁ vraja, ahaṁ tvā sarvapāpebhyo mokśayiṣyāmi mā śucaḥ"*—resigning all the Dharmas, seek refuge in Me alone. I shall liberate you from all sins Grieve not.

Thus, the Geetā shows the path of attaining permanent peace and perfect bliss. The path is that of Yoga to be achieved through the performance of Yajña (selfless action). Yoga literally means 'union', a special type of union between the individual soul and the Supreme Soul. Yajña signifies sacrifice-briefly the offering of every little act at the altar of the Divine.

The Geetā recognises that the peoples have different tendencies. Therefore it puts forward a number of ways to achieve Yoga—the mystic union. Broadly, there is Karmayoga, the Yoga of Action; Bhaktiyoga, the Yoga of Devotion and Jñanayoga, the Yoga of Knowledge. The paths seem to be different to suit different natures, but the goal is the same, to attain union with the Divine Spirit.

These are mixed concepts, therefore a number of commentaries on the Geetā have been written to explain the implications of various Yogas. Śrī Adi Śaṅkara emphasises the knowledge aspect, while Shridhara prefers devotion and Bal Gangadhar Tilak is all for action to achieve the ultimate goal. There are other commentaries written by saints, sages and scholars.

To these has been added an elaborate and comprehensive commentary by Mrs. Prabha Duneja. It is a district contribution to the Geetā literature. She profusely draws upon the wisdom of Indian writers and relates their views with those of western thinkers like Aldous Huxley and Schumacher. This has been possible on account of her erudite scholarships of eastern and western philosophy, association with the Geetā since early childhood, and a passion for popularising the message of the Geetā at religious workshops and Vedic satsangs.

The author is a strong advocate of the path of devotion.

Throughout her commentary there is a running refrain to remain in constant awareness of the Divine. It is only when a person is attached to God that he can be detached from the world and all his actions will be purified in the 'fire' of Yoga of Knowledge. Living in a state of "perpetual connectedness" with the Indweller, she says, is far better than all the austerities, performance of rituals and scriptural knowledge. The author presents the concept of Yoga in a conspicuous manner. She has given a clear, concrete and comprehensive explanation of Yoga with her experiential knowledge, enlightened insight and authority.

In preface, the author has encapsulated the gist of each of the 18 chapters of the Geetā. The explanations of verse are elaborate and elegant and will also satisfy those who may not be quite familiar with the Indian ethos. Laced with inspiring anecdotes, it is a remarkable commentary which will enlighten the learned as well as the laymen, in India and also in foreign lands.

June 27, 1998
New Delhi

BALDEO SAHAI
Fellow, Indian National
Science Academy

REVIEWS

The Legacy of Yoga In Bhagawad Geeta is a valuable addition to the existing literature on the Bhagawad Geeta. Mrs. Prabha Duneja has presented the universal and timeless message of the Geeta in a scholarly yet practical way. For busy people in the world today, a manual outlining the science and yoga of action is most welcome.

—Swami Prabuddhananda
Vedanta Society of Northern California

Prabha Duneja's The Legacy of Yoga in Bhagawad Geeta is extraordinary. Combining a fresh, accessible translation with judicious use of rich and varied scholarship, and keen insight into the heart of the Geeta, Duneja has produced a wonderful resource for both personal and scholarly study. For those seeking spiritual truth, Duneja's book is a wonderful guide. Her writing is lucid, offering not only abundant insight into the nature of ultimate reality but also thoughtful reflection on the yogic practices which are central to the Geeta's message. Her understanding of inter-religious matters is clear as the book skilfully bridges not only linguistic and cultural chasms but philosophical ones as well, thus making it valuable for persons from all faiths. Students seeking to understand the message carried within the Geeta will be well served by this volume. I have been using it in my classes for a number of years now and happily report that students find her commentary—both explaining the text and expanding upon it—to be of immense value as it brings clarity to the most delicate and difficult of concepts. The Legacy of Yoga in Bhagawad Geeta is a unique scholarly achievement and one which will greatly benefit all who encounter it. I heartily recommend it.

Duneja's writing is vibrant—it touches not only the mind but the heart, soul and spirit as well. Her writing is alive.

—Prof. Norris W. Palmer, PhD
Saint Mary's College of California, U.S.A.

After having read the translations of Swami Prabhupada, Barbara Stoler Miller, Eliot Deutsch, and now by Prabha Duneja, I take the risk of admitting my debt to Duneja's work, which she calls the labour of love. Except for the style of writing, there is not much deviation from one translation to the next in terms of meaning. Sanskrit is a rich language. However, its meaning does not get lost in translation if one knows the language very well. Obviously, all of the translators know Sanskrit and hence have translated the text as best as it can be translated. However, there is a difference in the translation of Duneja's Geeta. Her work is accompanied by commentaries at the end of each chapter. Although this is also the case with Swami Prabhupada's monumental work, his work has the hallmark of a missionary quality, which may not be suitable in an academic setting.

I find Duneja's book extremely valuable, because she writes from her personal experience in very simple and plain language without using academic jargons such as epistemology, ontology and soteriology most books on religion are full of. She proves that one can still write a book and convey the meaning of profound wisdom without using terms that seldom relate to the general reader. It is clearly a book written for the general readers, whether that reader is from the East or from the West. As long as the reader is genuinely interested in learning the meaning of the Geeta this is the book I would recommend highly.

—Deepak Shimkhada, Ph.D.
Professor of Religious Studies
Department of Philosophy and Religion
Claremont McKenna College CA

From the moment I picked up Prabha Duneja's translation of the Bhagawad Geeta, I knew that this was an inspired work. Not only is her rendition an academic contribution in clear English but it retains the power of the original Sanskrit. Her commentaries further enhance this edition for both beginning students as well as for scholars. I immediately called to order this book for my world religion classes at Yuba College. It was just what I was looking for. I am grateful to Prabha Duneja for bringing forth this wonderful work.

—Dr. Sujan Burgeson, Ph.D.
Professor, Yuba College, CA.

I am struck by the universality of Prabha Duneja's elucidation of the Lord Krsna teachings. My own intention as a scientist is to understand the whole of nature, including both physics and humanity, and then to define a beneficial and harmonious role that I should play. Prabha's descriptions of constant awareness and focused, intent concentration are a rich and personal description of the processes of observation and integration that I would like to master. For her this yogic activity is fundamental to the development of knowledge and the determination of right and selflcss action, and is the key to harmony and the ultimate universal unity, or for me, being in accord with my personal and the grander universe. Prabha's exegesis is detailed and scholarly, but also personal, readable, and modern. She gives very helpful instructions on the process of meditation. She discusses selflessness and its essentialness in achieving unity with the ultimate universal principles. She discusses the senses, which can discern or distract, and the mind, which can chatter like a monkey or find calmness and knowledge. She leaves no doubt that attaining the goals of yoga, considering our humanness, requires constant effort, but she also finds in the Geeta that we can define destiny and affect good. Since I have heard Prabha speak, the words that I hear when I read her writings are her soft and intelligent voice encouraging me to selflessness and harmony.

—Thomas J. Gilmartin, Ph.D.
Senior Fellow,
Centre for Global Security Research,
University of California,
Lawrence Livermore National Laboratory.

The Legacy of Yoga in the Bhagawad Geeta is a true spiritual treasure. I so admire the spirit revealed in your work—a scholar who loves and honours the word the Lord combined with the spirit of a true pastor who loves and honours all people. The constant invitation to Divine Union which I find in the pages of your book is leavened with common sense, clear explanations of very complex concepts, and highly evolved philosophical observations all together. I particularly appreciate the tremendous compassion for human nature and the human condition that I find both in the Geeta itself and in your commentary on it. I believe that this book would serve as a fit companion for a lifetime. It is a monumental work, the fruit of a good and wise life spent in our Creator's service. I am filled with awe at the beauty and sense I find within it, and am deeply honoured to know you as my friend. Thank you for sharing such a treasure with me. I know I will be studying it for many years to come.

—The Rev. Carol L. Cook
M.A., M. Div.
Episcopal Priest, C.A.

Prabha's work on the Bhagawad Geeta is insightful in its commentaries and detailed in its explanations. Although scholarly, her book contains a wealth of practical information to inform and assist all people on their spiritual journeys. One need not follow an established religious tradition, either eastern or western, to understand and apply the wisdom contained both in the basic text and in Prabha's comments. For example, the text contains instructions on some basic meditation practices such as how to sit and how to concentrate. In addition Prabha gives her own thoughts and suggestions for leading a productive meditative life.

Later in the text, the question is raised about the relative values of the two spiritual paths, faith in the incarnate God or living a pure life and seeking the "Unmanifest", "Self" within. Sri Krsna states that the former is better, but the latter will also lead to Him. Prabha adds that as "the worshipper advances in spiritual growth from less awareness to increased awareness the 'One' being worshipped also changes until the individual reaches the divine within his ''own self." In other words, both paths lead the dedicated one to the same place, at one with God.

The basic text can be read as a guide on how to lead one's life. Additionally Prabha's comments provide practical answers to many of life's concerns. They also may satisfy the more ardent spiritual seeker's curiosity regarding the text's more difficult points.

I would recommend this book to anyone who would like some assurance that peoples from different countries and of different faiths have a wonderful commonality of spirit.

—Paul Thompson
President, Astro Business Technologies

Mrs. Duneja's *The Legacy of Yoga in the Bhagawad Geeta* is inspiring. If a student of religions were only to read one book on the Bhagawad Geeta, this should surely be it. Its commentary reads as an act of scholarly devotion. Any journey into a land as rich as the Bhagawad Geeta requires a guide. With Prabha's commentary and translation at your side, your journey promises to be a rich one, indeed.

—The Rev. Eric H. Meter
Unitarian Universalist Church
President, Tri-Valley Interfaith Council

I was very impressed by the immense amount of scholarship that has gone into your translation and commentary of *The Legacy of Yoga in Bhagawad Geeta*. The commentary is especially helpful in explaining each chapter to those of us who are not acquainted with the Bhagawad Geeta. There is so much knowledge in the book about the mystery of life and death, a subject that everyone on earth has to contemplate. I was struck by the similarity of philosophy in this book to the American Indian philosophy of living. The goal of Native American is to live a peaceful and harmonious life, just as it is presented in this book.

—Mary Puthoff
American Indian Educator
Member of the Lakota Nation

One does not have to fully understand the various aspects of Yoga to sense and appreciate Prabha's deep convictions of the existence of a Benevolent Creator of the universe, and the divine nature and brotherhood of mankind. The logic and consistency of her comments throughout the book demonstrates her keen understanding of the subject matter. Her writings reveal a belief that we are sent to earth to learn how to truly love and serve others, and thus to become more divine ourselves. Only in this way can we become celestialized beings, capable of living in pure harmony with our creator and His crea-tions. We have holy writings, and can have special messengers from God when needed to assist us in achieving these righteous goals. The various aspects of Yoga are designed to help bring our inner souls into closer harmony with the Divine Creator.

The thoughts that I glean from these writings are in complete harmony with my Christian beliefs.

—The Rev. Val Black
The Church of Jesus Christ of Latter Day Saints

Profound and eternal spiritual truths become accessible and practicable in *The Legacy of Yoga in Bhagawad Geeta* by Prabha Duneja. I was deeply moved by the warmth and sincere devotion that is expressed throughout the book. Her very extensive knowledge of philosophy and spirituality, that goes beyond Indian philosophy, allows her to express these truths in ways everyone can understand and appreciate regardless of religion or belief. I consider this book to be a very valuable asset for my spiritual growth and enlightenment.

—Pat Fleischman
Northern California Chairwoman
Woman's Federation for World Peace, USA

As a Christian minister I am delighted that Prabha Duneja's book *The Legacy of Yoga in Bhagawad Geeta* has been added to the tools of devotional life. Many Christians (and people of other faiths) see the Geeta as a wonderful story but do not have the tools to unlock its meaning for their own spiritual work. *The Legacy of Yoga in Bhagawad Geeta* allows the eighteen yogas to become words of wisdom for the soul's nourishment as well as disciplines for the tranquillity of the spirit. By giving voice to illustration of the eight steps of yogic discipline in Sri Krsna's conversation with Arjuna in her discourse on the Yoga of Action and Renunciation Prabha Duneja brings the yogic discipline to life for anyone wanting to find a deepening of his devotional life. I found this chapter's handling of the harmony between knowledge, work and renunciation especially helpful in my own devotional life. The cosmic dimension one is led to experience through her writing in chapter eleven when she describes the Yoga of Vision of the Universal Form is a great aid in giving a person deep, spiritual perspective about the sublime connection we share with all that is, and patience with all that unfolds about us.

Each of the discourses on the eighteen yogas as they relate to the Geeta brings similar wisdom and insight to people of all religious faiths who are seeking truth with open minds. I am grateful for the great work Prabha Duneja has done for people of all faiths.

—The Rev. William E. Nebo
Sr. Pastor, First Presbyterian Church,
Livermore, California, U.S.A.

The Geeta, to me, is universal and eternal—a confluence of possibilities, yet leaving the choice to you for your path for spiritual realization. It is like a bouquet of flowers—a harmony of different colours, pleasing fragrance, unique individual character, inviting attractiveness, and radiant beauty. Each is complete and perfect in itself. You pick the one that appeals you. Sri Krsna gave to humanity a very broad, liberal, inclusive and accepting philosophy: "Whatever be the path of worship of men, I accept them in all paths as they lead to Me", (BG iv, 11), "whatever form a devotee wishes to worship with faith, I give strength to his faith", (BG vii, 21). It is beautiful, it is rich, it is profound, it is enlightening, and it offers opportunity for discovery of our true self.

Prabha, I strongly believe you have done a remarkable job in very ably and succinctly presenting the concept of Yoga sutras in your book—*The Legacy of Bhagawad Geeta*. It certainly is an innovative approach to present synthesis of philosophy and spirituality to achieve balance and fulfilment in life. Your book is truly a reflection of your earnest effort in combining scholarship and relevance. It reads well, flows well, and connects well with the reader in search of meaning in and of life. I commend you immensely for bringing home the complexity of the concepts of the life of renunciation, the control of prakriti or nature on our actions and behaviour, and the indestructibility of our spiritual self—the Atman—through impressive use of metaphors and illustrative examples. I am sure the readers will find your book that makes Geeta meaningful for them as well those who want to dwell into the deeper aspects of the inner self. I commend you for your intellectual understanding of Geeta and it shines through the book.

—Mohan K. Sood, Ph.D.

Dean Emeritus, Northeastern Illinois University

In her translation of the classical text of Bhagawad Geeta and a lucid commentary thereon, Mrs. Prabha Duneja leads the modern man and woman gently but firmly to the state of Yogic bliss. She, on behalf of the Lord bequeathes the legacy of love through yoga to the readers and enables them to delve deep into the realm of Bliss. Indeed, blessed

is he who is helped by the authoress to become a beneficiary of *The Legacy of Yoga in Bhagawad Geeta.* **—Brigadier Chitranjan Sawant**
VSM

To many non Indians, the religion that we refer to as Hinduism often appears to be highly intellectual, involving the giving up of daily life, and commitment to rigorous austere practices, a demanding guru, and endless mysterious rituals.

I found that reading *The Legacy of Yoga in Bhagawad Geeta* helped me to correct that view. In her translation of and commentary on the "Geeta" Prabha Duneja opened a way for me to understand something of how many sincere Indian Hindus practice their faith. As Prabha Duneja emphasizes, the "Geeta" teaches that God or Divinity is found primarily within one self and that loving devotion to a benevolent power or God joined with a compassionate attitude toward the world is a superior (and more accessible) spiritual path than extreme ascetic practices, rituals, or giving up one's will to a human guru.

The "Geeta" is not a long document and along with its central focus, has much to say about meditation, prayer, ethics and the organization of society. It's brevity helps to make it accessible to the student of spiritual truths. **—The Rev. Lois F. Rose**
United Church of Christ, Great Barrington, MA

Prabha Duneja's translation and commentary in *The Legacy of Yoga in Bhagawad Geeta* is full of wisdom and rich with experience. It is written with sincere heart-felt devotion. Her clarity and style will be enjoyed by the common man and will satisfy the yearning in the intellect of the scholar. As for devotees already following the Lord, their minds will easily flow along the melodious stream of Sri Krsna's words, leaving their hearts and souls free to soar towards the Lord's loving embrace... **—Bettie Littie**
A Devotee of Bhagwan Sri Krsna

The present work reveals the stupendous scholarship, positive approach and mastery of Indian philosophical and religious thought of Mrs. Prabha Duneja. Designed both for general philosophical readers and for specialists in Indian thought, the work sets forth in a readable and concise manner the principal arguments, and views put forward by the leading commentators, Indologists, great leaders of the world and the renowned scholars about Geeta and its relevance. This book definitely and purposely explains the principles and practices of the gospel of inspired action. Her commentary on Bhagawad Geeta is in fact a very competent work, perhaps the best of its kind. To me, Prabha appears to be a receiver and transmitter of the voice of Bhagawan Sri Krsna.

—Dr. K.K. Sharma
Ph.D., U.W., U.S.A.

It is not surprising that within a few years of its publication, the 600 page book by Prabha Duneja—***The Legacy of Yoga in Bhagawad Geeta***—has gone through a second edition, which testifies to the popularity of the book.

There are many commentaries on the Holy Book by learned saints, sages and scholars from Adi Sankaracharya of the eight century to Vinoba Bhave of the twentieth. The beauty of this book lies in its being an updated commentary echoing the heart-heat of a modern man. On account of her long sojourn in America, and being an active member of interfaith organizations, Duneja has profusely drawn from the works of not only Indian scholars but also of western philosophers. Thus her commentary has a contemporary flavour and goes very well with an international audience.

The liberal use of stories and anecdotes picked up from Indian and western saints, as also from Sufies and Persian poets, to elucidate an abstruse esoteric point, is another charm of the book and ensures easing reading. There is hardly a page of the commentary which does not contain an illuminating anecdote. As pointed out by Dionysius : it is "philosophy learned from examples".

As the author has been soaked in the teachings of Geeta since childhood, her writing is not merely theoretical but has a ring of sincerity and personal experience. I am sure the book shall go into many more editions and benefit the readers.

—Dr. Baldeo Sahai
Founder President
Upanisad Society, New Delhi

INTRODUCTION

Bhagawad Geeta is the most luminous dialogue in the legacy of Vedic literature. The holy poem has been upheld as one of the *Prasthana-traya*—the three authoritative books of the *Sanatan Vedic* religion. The first one is the *Vedic Prasthana* called the *Upanisads*, the second is the philosophical *Prasthana*—the *Brahma Sutra*; the third *Prasthana* is the Bhagawad Geeta. These three holy books constitute the final authority on scriptural matters. Geeta is a unique scripture which summarizes almost all the essential teachings of the *Vedic* literature. It has been a perennial source of spiritual inspiration for the entire mankind. The message of the holy dialogue has been held in deep reverence by the sages, philosophers and learned scholars all over the world. The teachings of Geeta are universal, broad and sublime meant for the welfare of entire creation. Bhagawad Geeta is one of the most well-known and revered texts among the other scriptures of the world. It is a compendium of spiritual wisdom and the most appropriate guide for living a harmonious life in all respects. There are hundreds of commentaries on Bhagawad Geeta—both in Indian and in many foreign languages. This is perhaps the most widely translated scriptural text of the world. In the words of Dr. Radhakrishnan, "for centuries people have found comfort in this great book which sets forth in precise and penetrating words the essential principles of a spiritual religion which are not contingent on ill-founded facts, unscientific dogmas or arbitrary fancies. With a long history of spiritual power, it serves even today as a light to all who will receive illumination from the profundity of its wisdom which insists on a world wider and deeper than wars and revolutions can touch. It is a powerful shaping factor in the renewal of spiritual life and has secured an assured place among the world's greatest scriptures."

The message of the holy Geeta is indeed phenomenal and timeless. It is an anthology of spiritual wisdom which guides the individual into the mysteries of self-realization and God-realization. It analyses almost all the various levels of human psychology and trains the person into living a productive, joyful, balanced and creative life. The message of Geeta synthesizes almost all the well-known teachings of ancient scriptures of the world and it is addressed to the entire mankind. In the words of Dr. Annie Besant, "Among the priceless teachings that may be found in the great Hindu poem of the *Mahabharata,* there is none so rare and precious as this "The Lord's Song". Since it fell from the divine lips of Srī Kṛṣṇa on the field of battle, and stilled the surging emotions of the disciple and friend, how many troubled hearts has it quietened and strengthened, how many weary souls has it led to Him! It is meant to lift the aspirant from the lower levels of renunciation, where objects are renounced, to the loftier heights where desires are dead, and where the Yogi dwells in calm and ceaseless contemplation while his body and mind are actively employed in discharging the duties that fall to his lot in life. That the spiritual man need not be a recluse, that union with divine life may be achieved and maintained in the midst of worldly affairs, that the obstacles to that union lie, not outside us, within us, such is the central lesson of the Bhagawad Geeta."

The message of Geeta presents a profound insight into the working of human nature and provides the most appropriate guidance which is needed in almost every field of life in order to live in perfect harmony with our own self and with others. The dialogue provides an understanding into the mystery of the Supreme-soul and how every individual can restore himself to the Supremacy of his essential nature. Ever since the teachings of Geeta have become known to the people in Europe and America, it has quickly won the interest and admiration of millions. Many philosophical and religious groups in foreign countries hold the same respect for Geeta as the people in India. About the popularity of Geeta, Mahatma Gandhi has written that during one of his visits to England he went to a big library and inquired from the librarian about the most popular religious book which was in greatest demand. The librarian informed him that it was indeed the Bhagawad Geeta. Dr. Paul Brunton, a great British scholar, has written about the glory of Geeta in these words: "This ancient book can satisfy the modern needs. Nearly every literate yogi in India carries with him a small edition of this inspired and profound classic, the Bhagawad Geeta. If this gospel of contemplation combined with action had been understood in the land of its birth as it should be understood, India would today shed the radiance of her spiritual illumination to the far corners of the world and provide a masterly pattern of a balanced material-spiritual existence for all other countries to witness. The Geeta summarizes various approaches to the Overself and also describes the latter. Srī Kṛṣṇa not only represents the embodied spiritual teacher, He is ultimately the Overself within man, the God within who can illuminate all dark corners and answer all questions. At the end of the dialogue after hearing all the teachings, the pupil's mind becomes peaceful. He says indeed: "My doubts are dispelled. Destroyed are my illusions." By what magic was this mental change accomplished? Through both the guidance and grace received from his teacher and his own inner growth in striving for insight. The difficulties one meets in modern life can be met and overcome after we gain such insight. Wisdom means the ability to negotiate all the circumstances of life adequately, correctly and with spiritual success. The deep spiritual comfort emanating from the teachings of the Geeta is peculiarly needed at this stage of the world's affairs."

The great educationist and philosopher of India, Mr. Madan Mohan Malaviya, has written about Geeta in these words: "I believe that in all the living languages of the world, there is no book so full of true knowledge, and yet so handy as the Bhagawadgeeta". The well known professor of religion at Oxford University, Mr. Zaehner, has written about the glory of the sacred song in these words, "Geeta is a first-hand guide to the ancient roots of Vedic religion. Although in *Shevatsara Upanisad* the transcendence of the personal God has been affirmed to some extent—with Geeta has come the devotional religion". The great respect and appreciation for Geeta has been voiced by Warren Hastings, the first British Governor General of India, in year 1773. He has said, "The work as the Geeta would live long after the British Empire in India has ceased to exist". The Song Celestial by Sir Edwin Arnold describes the greatness of Geeta in these words, "In plain but noble language it unfolds a philosophical system which remains to this day the prevailing *Brahmanic* belief, blending as it does the doctrines of *Kapil*a, *Patanjali*, and the *Vedas*. So lofty are many of its declarations, so sublime its aspirations, and so pure and tender is its piety". Sir Edwin Arnold has called Geeta the incomparable religious classic of India. Similarly, Mr. Von Humboldt, Maxmuller, Emerson, Franklin Edgerton and Aldous Huxley and many other scholars and educationists of the world have taken Geeta as a text for the exposition of their thoughts. In the words of Aldous Huxley, "Bhagawad Geeta is perhaps the most systematic spiritual statement of the perennial philosophy."

Śrīmad Bhagawad Geetā has been designated as *Yoga Sastra*. The word yoga has been derived from Sanskrit root word *yuj* which literally means to bind, combine and join together the psychic energies in order to experience a union and communion with the indwelling Supreme-Self. It is an art which helps the individual to bring his scattered thoughts together into a reflective and meditative state of mind in order to comprehend the presence of the Divinity within. Yoga is the unity of the individual-soul (*Jivatma*) with the Supreme-Soul (*Paramatma*). The *yogic* practice helps the individual to accelerate himself to the state of consciousness in which his egoistic individuality is dissolved. It teaches the techniques of directing the attention from the gross body to the nerves and the senses; from the senses to the mind and from the mind to the intellect and the Supreme-Self. Philosophically, Yoga means union with the Supreme-spirit. The ancient scriptures describe *Yoga-chitvriti-nirodha*—means yoga is to control all the mental modifications. It is an art which persuades an incoherent and scattered mind into a reflective and coherent state. The Yoga system was first collated and written down by the sage *Patanjali* in his *Yoga Sutra* which consists of one hundred and ninety-five sutras divided into four chapters. The first part deals with the theory of Yoga; the second part describes the art of Yoga and the initiation into practice. The third illustrates the method of comprehending the inherent powers and the fourth deals with inner unity and freedom from the identification with the physical body. The *Yoga Sutra* of *Patanjali* also describes the eight steps of self-discipline which prepare the individuals for the ultimate experience of union and communion with the Supreme-Self. Yoga practice is not only a means to a certain end, it is indeed both the means and the end.

The eight steps of *yogic* discipline are—*Yama, Niyama, Asana, Pranayama, Pratyhara, Dharna, Dhyana* and *Samadhi*. In *Geeta Sastra* Srī Kṛṣṇa has given a vivid illustration of all these *Mahavratas* during his conversation with Arjuna. For example, the practice of *yama* which stands for the collective, universal and moral commandments like non-violence, truth, continence and non-stealing has been described at length in chapters thirteen, sixteen and seventeen. The practice of these *Mahavratas* in daily life accelerates and purifies the day-to-day emotions of the individual towards the pursuit of higher goals in life. The *Niyamas* are the rules adopted by the aspirants for self-purification. These include the various types of austerities and the study of scriptures which has been described in Geeta chapters third, fourth, fifth, sixth, sixteenth and eighteenth.

The next steps in *Yogasutra* are *Asanas* and *Pranayama. Asanas* are the physical exercises which purify the body and tune the senses of perception, action and mind into developing a unity with the indwelling-soul. The appropriate posture in *yogic* meditation helps the individual to eliminate the harmful toxins from the body and make the embodied-self more receptive to the voice of the inner-Self. *Pranayama* means a conscious control of breath. It is an act of rhythmic inhalation, retention and exhalation. In order to attain mastery in *yogic* communion, *Pranayama* plays a significant role. It is an art of breathing which helps the aspirant to monitor his quality, quantity and direction of thoughts. The necessity of the accurate posture in meditation and also the techniques of *Pranayama* have been described in chapter six from verses ten to fifteen in Bhagawad Geeta. The next step in *yogic* meditation is *pratyahara* meaning a conscious control of the senses which has been emphasized by Srī Kṛṣṇa throughout his dialogue. The other three steps are *Dharna, Dhyana* and *Samadhi. Dharna* is one pointed concentration with faith and determination. It integrates the thinking faculty and helps the individual to move into the serenity of *Dhyana* which means settled contemplation. In the meditative state of *Dhyana* the aspirant remains aware of the body, breath and mind; in *Samadhi* the outer consciousness starts fading and a blissful state of inner tranquillity is experienced. It is the method of rising to the state of consciousness wherein the egoistic individuality is dissolved and the embodied-self resumes his unity with the Supreme-Self. *Samadhi* is deep meditation; it is a blissful experience of *yogic* communion and unity with the indwelling-Self.

Śrīmad Bhagawad Geetā has been designated as the *Yoga Sastra* because it explains the theoretical knowledge of the Supreme-Soul and also the techniques to perceive and experience that Absolute Reality. The sage Ved Vyasa has declared *Geeta Shastra midam punyam yah pathet prayat puman vishnoh padam vapnoti bhaya shoka divarjitah*— any one who is genuinely devoted to the study of *Geeta Sastra*, he is liberated from all types of fears and sorrows; and attains the Supreme abode of Lord Vishnu. In words of Dr. Radhakrishnan, "The Geeta gives a comprehensive *Yoga-Sastra*, large, flexible and manysided which includes various phases of the soul's development and ascent into the Divine. The different *yogas* are special applications of the inner discipline which leads to the liberation of the soul and a new understanding of the unity and meaning of mankind. Everything that is related to this discipline is called a yoga such as *Jñana-yoga* or the way of knowledge, *Bhakti-yoga* or the way of devotion, *karma-yoga* or the way of action." The concept of Yoga as described in *Geeta Sastra* is very vast, subtle and broad. Here the aspirant is initiated to live his entire life in the awareness of the Divine and perform all his duties through the perpetual guidance of unity in Yoga. It is to live a life which is firmly grounded in eternal union with the Supreme-Soul and to work with the consciousness of the indwelling-self.

Nitya-yoga of Geeta is the perpetual unity with the absolute Divinity. Srī Kṛṣṇa has used many expressions in order to explain the subtle meaning of yoga such as *Nityayoga, Samatvayoga, Buddhiyoga, Karmayoga, Bhaktiyoga, Jñanayoga, Rajayoga, Jaapyoga, Karmasanyasyoga*, *Abhyasyoga*, and *Dhyanyoga* etc. The aim of *Geeta Sastra* is to initiate the individual into a life of *yogic* unity with the Supreme-soul, which upholds, supports and guides mankind into a higher, systematic, peaceful, creative, productive, joyous and balanced lifestyle irrespective of nationality, race, class and faith. In the words of Mahadev Desai, "Arjuna too had probably heard of yoga before, but he now finds it presented to him in a new light. If yoga means the forgetting of all fruit, all attachment, then it means detaching oneself from the lower self and identification with the Supreme Self. One has to disjoin oneself from the impermanent to join oneself to the Permanent. But so long as the Self is encased in the impermanent tabernacle, one cannot disjoin oneself from it, except by purifying it, spiritualizing it, by making the not-Self work in tune with the Self. Yoga is thus both means and end". Yoga of Bhagawad Geeta is to live in unity with the Supreme-soul and work in unity with the Supreme-soul. The verses such as *tasmat sarvesu kalesu mam anusmara yudha ca* and *mayy arpitamanobuddhir mam evai syasy asamsayah* mean therefore at all times remember Me and fight; with your mind and reason thus absorbed in Me, thou shalt surely come to Me.

The Yoga of Geeta demands the most sacred form of discipline, the toughest, purest and the highest form of discipline which is nurtured by living in the constant awareness of the Divine. The message of Geeta declares that the unity in Yoga is not merely a practice in isolation; it is the discipline of living in the consciousness of the Self. It is the manifestation of inner unity in every day life, it is a transcendental experience and also the ability to act efficiently in the world. The yogic unity with the indweller can be practised at almost each and every station of life—in office, at home, with family, while walking and while performing the most serious duties in the world. The yogic communion is to learn to live into the higher dimension of life and pursue each and every activity in unity with the indweller. It is the experience of living in Bliss which comes to the individual with a disciplined daily practice and grows in intensity from moment to moment. In the words of Swami Chinmayananda, "In all Hindu philosophies there are two distinct sections: one explaining the theory and the other describing the technique of practice. The portion that explains the technique of living the philosophy and coming to a close subjective experience is called the *Yoga Sastra*. Since the Geeta is called a *Yoga Sastra*, we must expect to discover in the Song of the Lord, not only airy philosophical expositions of a Truth too subtle for the ordinary man to grasp, but also instructions by which every one of us can, from this present state of imperfection, hope to reach, step by step, the giddy heights of the Divine pinnacles, that stand eternally swathed in the transcendental glory of Absolute Perfection".

The *Geeta Sastra* comprises seven hundred Sanskrit verses divided into eighteen chapters. Each chapter has been designated as a specific type of *Yoga.* The most luminous dialogue in Bhagawad Geeta opens with *Vishad Yoga* or the yoga of despondency. *Vishad* means deep sorrow, pain and despondency when the individual mind sinks in delusion, distress, dejection, depression, emotional conflicts and loneliness. *Yoga* means union with the indwelling-self. *Vishad Yoga*—means the unification of the individual soul with the Supreme-soul in moments of deep depression and dejection. Despondency is the dejected state of mind when everything in life appears to be unsettled, emotionally confused, fragmented and disintegrated. In moments of loneliness, when the individual soul feels helpless and depressed; he is persuaded to seek help from the over-self and take refuge in the realm of the Supreme-soul. It is indeed a fact that when the person feels dejected and cries out from the depth of his heart, the help is felt within the ever renewing current of life. Every individual has to experience the depth of *vishad* (depression) in order to experience the Bliss of *prasad* (grace). He has to pass through and cross over the self-created egocentric circles in order to be receptive to the love and blessings of the indwelling-self. The experience of inner unity purifies the individual and clears his mind from all kinds of emotional conflicts. It restores the embodied-self to the clarity of illuminated understanding and inner quietude. Any painful or serious and traumatic experience of life brings internal guidance which helps the individual to release the painful past and move on in life with a renewed concept of truth. In the experience of inner unison when the individual resorts to the benevolence of the indwelling Supreme-soul the veil of his egocentric thoughts disperses and disseminates momentarily and the person becomes receptive to the voice of the Supreme-Self. An honest surrender of the individual soul to the benevolence of the Supreme-soul in pain, honesty and innocence is indeed the *Vishadyoga*. In the words of Swami Tapasyananda, "the first chapter depicting Arjuna's grief is meant to show under what conditions a man opens himself to the voice of the spirit. A crisis is often required to make him turn his eyes to the spiritual reality. Often it is the impact of death, loss, disease, faithlessness of man or any other such bitter experience of life that causes the awakening".

The second chapter has been entitled the *Samkhya Yoga* meaning the yoga of the transcendental knowledge or communion through transcendental knowledge. The second discourse is very enlightening in which Srī Kṛṣṇa declares the immortality of soul and also introduces to Arjuna the most reverend doctrine of the gospel of selfless action. In this chapter Srī Kṛṣṇa explains to Arjuna some of the most useful aspects of *Samkhya* philosophy. The *samkhya* concept has been brought down to us by the ancient sages of vedic religion. *Samkhya* philosophy, as the name itself is self-explanatory, is an analytical study of the matter, mind and the Supreme-Soul. In the analytical process of *samkhya* knowledge, every aspect of learning goes through some hypothesis, formulas and conclusion. Almost all the sciences of modern world have originated from the *Samkhya* philosophy. It is experimental and also the experiential knowledge of the Supreme-Soul. In this chapter Srī Kṛṣṇa tells Arjuna that there is one unchanging reality that pervades the entire universe. It is the Supreme consciousness, the Supreme-Soul and the essential being of every one and everything. He draws Arjuna's attention towards the comprehension of the essential difference between the *sat* and *asat*—existent and nonexistent, real and unreal. The real always remains the same while the unreal changes every moment. Everything which is seen manifested in the world, it comes into existence; it is sustained for a while and then it perishes. The changing world is pervaded by the unchanging reality—the Supreme-Soul. He tells Arjuna that the wise sage who remains firmly grounded in the consciousness of the Divine, he has the experiential knowledge of both existent and non-existent.

Srī Kṛṣṇa explains Arjuna that the indwelling-soul is eternal, non-changing, imperishable and immutable. The soul of everyone existed in the past, is existing in the present and will exist in the future. The embodied-self changes merely the form and shape. The embodied-soul goes from one body to another; forced by the residual impressions which have been accumulated during the lifetime. The individual-soul retains its individuality from one stage to another and also from one life to another. The destruction of the gross body can never cause any destruction in the continuity of the indestructible soul. There is a mantra in *Rig Veda* which explains this truth : *yatha purva makal divim cha prithavi chantariksha mayo*—everything comes into existence just as before. He tells Arjuna that there is nothing in the world which becomes totally lost and loses its essentiality. Everything continues to exist in one or the other form. The entire universe is constantly evolving. It is only the spiritual insight which helps the individual to understand the continuity of life from the past—through the present and into the future. The person who remains grounded in the truth of the deepest awareness, to him the transmigration of the soul is merely like changing garments.

The chapter three has been entitled *Karmayoga* which is communion with the indwelling-soul through the performance of work. The word Yoga means a union and communion with the indweller; so *Karmayoga* literally means the type of actions, those help the individual to develop a union with God. *Karmayoga* is the art of living and acting through the uninterrupted consciousness of the Supreme-soul. As a matter of fact, the action itself becomes its reward when it is performed intelligently, diligently and devotedly. The discipline of Yoga is a practice of living in constant unity with the Supreme-soul. This inner discipline and inner unity transforms the psychological level of the individual and makes him receptive to the voice of the Supreme Lord within. The unity initiates the individual into self-surrender, self-realization and God-realization. It is the consciousness of the yogic unity which eventually transforms the performance of every activity into the yoga of action. Srī Kṛṣṇa assures Arjuna that even the highest achievement of transcendental unity is possible through the yoga of action because in this discipline the individual works in constant communion with the Divine. The constant practice of yogic unity in the performance of action enables the person to discover his sublime centre of ever luminous consciousness within his own self. When he becomes settled in that field of awareness, the concept of unity becomes his abiding heritage under all circumstances. It is a well known fact that the highest goal of life can be realized, when the person is unassailably established in yogic unity and when he himself becomes aware of the truth that he is living in it. Living a life in the consciousness of the Divine, and performing all work with the consciousness of the Divine is *Karmayoga.* It is the realization of God through the performance of actions.

Anyone who performs work with unity in yoga, he is eventually released from the bonds of birth-death and rebirth. He attains to the blissful state of immortality. In this chapter Srī Kṛṣṇa has explained the term *yajña* with its expanded meaning and contents. He presents the subtle meaning of *yajña* with reference to the mutual interaction, of activities. *Yajña*, a well known religious term of the vedic tradition literally means the act which helps the individual to live in harmony with everybody and everything. The performance of *yajña* is to perform all the activities as a worship and as an offering to the Supreme. *Yajña* transforms all work into yoga. The spirit of *yajña* conveys the idea of interdependence, continuity and the survival of the creation. It is the network of the services performed selflessly by human beings, gods and mother Nature. Srī Kṛṣṇa illustrates the process of God-realization through the work which is performed as *yajña* (sacrifice). Srī Kṛṣṇa suggests that every activity becomes a cause of bondage unless it is performed with the spirit of *yajña* meaning the ideology of *swadharma*. Srī Kṛṣṇa makes it more clear in verse eleven by declaring "fostering each other disinterestedly and by supporting each other with the spirit of *yajña*, one can attain the highest good in life". It is indeed the performance of every activity with the spirit of *yajña* which helps the individual to accomplish the highest goal of attaining unity in yoga. Srī Kṛṣṇa tells Arjuna that it is the duty of every individual to respect the spirit of sacrifice (*yajña*) which makes the life prosperous, auspicious, harmonious and peaceful. He says that the person who lives only for himself and holds his own selfish interests upfront, who accumulates wealth only for his sensual enjoyments, depriving others of their due share, he lives a sinful life. *Yajña* is an expression of virtue, purity, kindness, giving and sharing. In order to understand the meaning of ethical harmonious living, it is very important to understand the definition of *yajña*. In the words of B.G. Tilak, "The message of Geeta, that the individual's whole life should be turned into *yajña*, contains the essence of the entire *Vedic* religion". The spirit of *yajña* creates harmony in the entire universe. The performance of work in the spirit of *yajña* helps people to understand the ideals of selfless action.

In chapter four, Srī Kṛṣṇa declares that the revolutionary concept of *Karmayoga* is not new; it has been taught to the *Vivasvan* (sun-god) at the beginning of creation and later it has been imparted to *Manu* and the king *Ikshavaku* the first ruler of the sun dynasty. He tells Arjuna that the royal sages have been very well acquainted with the yoga of selfless action. This chapter has been entitled *Jñana-karma-yoga*—the Yoga of Action through Knowledge. It explains the union and communion with the indwelling Supreme-Self through the proper knowledge of performing actions. The nature of *Karmayoga* has been discussed from various angles and the importance of proper knowledge has been emphasized in the performance of action. It explains the philosophy about the nature of actions and also the wisdom which initiates the person into the practice of *Karmayoga*. Srī Kṛṣṇa tells Arjuna that the yoga of selfless action is not a new concept. This discipline of action came with the creation and it has always existed since the time immemorial. It is the perennial wisdom which has assisted the sustenance of life in this universe in all respects. The whole creation functions through the spirit of mutual exchange. It is a network of services performed selflessly.

In this chapter Srī Kṛṣṇa announces that whenever there is a decline of *Dharma* and the rise of *Adharma,* I manifest myself in order to re-establish the values of righteousness and to protect the virtuous people. The word *Dharma* derives its root from the word *Dhar* meaning to uphold and maintain. *Dharma* means the code of conduct which is supported by the voice of the inner-self. Srī Kṛṣṇa is declaring in these verses that whenever there is a decline of righteousness, moral values, I manifest Myself as God-incarnate, in order to uphold the righteousness and to restore the orderliness on earth. *Dharma* is a unique system of values which is determined by the inner-self; which guide the individual to perform his duty by keeping in mind the welfare of others. *Dharma* is the golden message of God, " treat others as you would like to be treated by them". It is a guidance from the Higher-self; devoid of all the external pressures from society. It is an inner awakening that enlightens the person to differentiate between the desirable and undesirable acts. *Swadharma* is the experiential realization of the Supreme-soul. Any activity which is carried on with the awareness of the indwelling light it becomes a source of peace for everybody, because in that lies the manifestation of God Himself. Any duty performed in this manner protects the rights of others and implies to the general well-being. So any type of dealing one undertakes and the advancement one proposes it should be in consideration to the well-being of others.

In any society where people become very materialistic, the existential fear increases. When each individual is led single-mindedly, in the pursuit of wealth, the spirituality is usually pushed to the very far end. With the negligence of spiritual values people become selfish, self-centred and ignore *swadharma.* When the feeling of jealousy, greed, envy and peer pressure of every kind increases in society, there comes the distortion of moral values, restlessness of mind and decline in ethics everywhere. Any type of material progress and happiness which is preferred over ethics, becomes another form of misery. Accepting the presence of the Divine and performing every bit of work with the guidance of the Divine is *Dharma*; on the other hand, conscious separation from the Divine and living a life against the voice of the Supreme-soul is *Adharma. Dharma* brings people together while *Adharma* disintegrates. The decline of *Dharma* (righteousness) starts at the individual level and gradually spreads throughout the community and nation causing a downfall of the entire human race. Decline of *Dharma* is the decline of morality, virtuosity and spiritual values everywhere. The decline of spiritual and moral standards generally happens due to the loss of self-respect and due to the loss of respect for God. The lack of faith in one's own self is also due to lack of faith in God. When people lose their conscious touch with God, they lose touch with themselves and with everybody and everything around. People become very insensitive, selfish, corrupt and self-centred. This is what Srī Kṛṣṇa means to say in the verse seven—Whenever there is the decline of righteousness and the rise of unrighteousness, O'Bharata, then I incarnate Myself; for the protection of the virtuous, for the destruction of the wicked and for the re-establishment of the righteousness.

Srī Kṛṣṇa enlightens Arjuna that the world is a vast field of mixed actions. People driven by their innate nature choose the kind of work that suits their liking and aspirations. These innate inclinations of people have brought into existence the fourfold work-order in society. The word caste is self-explanatory; it means the role one has been assigned to play in his lifetime. Although all men look alike on the surface, yet their intellectual and physical abilities do differ from one another in so many different ways. People have always divided themselves into four different classes. The people in each class have always performed their duties, guided by their *svabhava* (innate nature). Even today we can observe this division of work in almost all the developed cultures of the world. For example, the teachers, philosophers, scholars form the first; the second one is administrators, managers, leaders, soldiers; and the third class is businessmen, industrialists whereas the fourth is workers, servants and the labourers. The caste system has been based on the *swabhava* meaning the inborn nature which is expressed in the type of work one chooses to perform. The self-imposed classification of people in the society has always helped the community in the proper distribution of work according to the innate choice of every man. In the words of Swami B.V. Tripurari, "This social structure is called *varnashrama*. The Sanskrit word *varna* literally means 'colour', but it refers to the 'color' of the mind, or one's temperament, and not to the body. It therefore implies a standard of conduct or mode of occupation that naturally corresponds with one's mental disposition or karmic tendency. The *varnashrama* social system divides human effort into four classes of occupation by determining one's karmic leaning, not by what family one takes birth in. It first takes into consideration one's spiritual status and then determines one's material propensity".

In this chapter Srī Kṛṣṇa has emphasized that all types of spiritual services and the *yajñas* become beneficial only if performed with proper insight. These purificatory actions become the means of liberation, if co-ordinated with the knowledge of the Self. Therefore each and everyone who seeks emancipation and peace in the present life, must make appropriate efforts to illuminate the understanding which can enlighten the process of performing actions. He declares that there is nothing else in the world which can equal the purifying power of the transcendental wisdom. The individual, who is settled in *yogic* communion, experiences it in due time. As a matter of fact, the person's relationship with the Divine is primordial and perennial, but one experiences the grace only in proportion to the degree of one's faith, reverence and devotion. Strong faith and loving devotion can make even the impossible to be possible. The word *sradha* has been pronounced out loud in many ways by Srī Kṛṣṇa. *Sradha* is indeed the basis of spiritual life. Revelation of the Supreme is really difficult without the ardent faith, love and reverence. *Sradha* is an unwavering, most sincere and ardent form of faith which enables all the inner beauties of the Supreme-self to be revealed to the individual. It is like going into the most intimate and honest relationship with the Supreme-Soul, which gives strength and inner integrity. *Sradha* originates at the heart-centre by consciously living in the awareness of the Divine and gradually takes hold of the entire being. *Sradha* is indeed the dynamic force that nourishes the spiritual ideals. It illuminates the understanding of the scriptural knowledge and changes it into integral wisdom.

The fifth chapter of Bhagawad Geeta has been entitled as *Karma-samnyasa-yoga*—the Yoga of Action through Renunciation. In this chapter the chief features of *Karmayoga* and *Jñanayoga* have been reaffirmed, to round off the theme into *Karma-samnyasa-yoga*. The fullness of Yoga of action which rises out of the Yoga of knowledge becomes transformed into the yoga of *Karma-samnyas*—the communion through the renunciation of the fruit of action. This chapter describes the harmony between knowledge, work and renunciation. It explains the theoretical knowledge of the Supreme and also the techniques to experience that reality. The subtle message about the gospel of selfless action in vedic philosophy has been restated in this chapter. In these verses Srī Kṛṣṇa expounds the meaning of *Sannyasa* (renunciation). He tells that renunciation and the performance of actions in *Yoga* both lead to the highest good; but of the two the Yoga of Action is indeed superior. In general the word *Samnyasa* is related to complete renunciation of the world. It is an act of self-purification. The real renunciation is an awakened state of mind, wherein one comprehends the prime truth, and abandons the worldly enjoyments out of dispassion. Srī Kṛṣṇa presents the most luminous gospel of selfless action in the surest, clearest and most approachable manner. A *Karmayogi* always remains firmly grounded in the nature of the Supreme-Soul, he does everything selflessly because of his perpetual connectedness with the Self. Performance of actions with an attitude of detachment yields the rewards of *Karma-samnyasa.* Srī Kṛṣṇa calls that individual a perpetual *samnyasi*, who has risen above the dualities of life and remains detached towards the fruits of actions. *Sruti Bhagwati* also describes the state of genuine renouncer in these words "although engaged in the performance of duties, the one who maintains his balance and has no attachment to anything; whose work is characterized by the attitude of service and devotion to the God, he is surely a *Samnyasin*, even before (renouncing the world) following the path of *Samnyasa-yoga*."

Srī Kṛṣṇa tells that the individual of childish and immature understanding consider the Yoga of knowledge and the Yoga of action to be distinct and separate. A man of wisdom fully understands the subtlety of the concept and does not see any distinction between them. He synthesizes the essence of both. The essential knowledge of both is indeed complimentary to one another and makes the pursuit of the blissful state very easy and enjoyable. The Yoga of knowledge and the Yoga of action are indeed inseparable; following either brings the reward of both. Srī Kṛṣṇa indicates that following the path of renunciation from world, without proper knowledge of *Karmayoga,* can be dangerous and harmful in certain respects. A person cannot become a renunciate by merely giving up the family life or by running away from his duties out of frustration and failures. This type of renouncer loses self-respect, and becomes a ridicule for himself and for everybody else. *Karmayoga* is definitely much more rewarding than *Karma-samnyasa* (renunciation of actions).

It is the performance of actions in Yoga that prepares the individual for renunciation. The person who is devoted to selfless action, he becomes pure-minded and attains the status of a *samnyasin* in due time. The sage *Yajñavalkya* has described the concept of *Karma-samnya-yoga* in these words. He writes that even a family member who has devoted himself to the attainment of the knowledge of the Self and who is celibate and truthful; who remains detached to the fruits of his actions—he should be considered a *samnyasi* who attains liberation in due course of time. In these verses Srī Kṛṣṇa glorifies the magnificence of the unity with the Supreme-soul which forms the basis of genuine renunciation. He explains to Arjuna that by living in constant awareness of the Supreme, one develops an intimate relationship with the Divine. The individual learns to live in the ardent love of the Divine and takes pride in offering all his work as a service to the Divine. As the bond of love and reverence grows stronger, the detachment and renunciation from the world dawns automatically. The yogic unity helps the individual to develop detachment from worldly desires and the fruits of his actions. The inner purification, renunciation and liberation—this is a process of step by step progress towards self-realization and the attainment of *Brahman-Nirvana, Moksha* or the Absolute liberation.

Chapter six has been designated as *Dhyana-yoga* i.e. yogic union and communion with the indwelling-Self through meditation. Meditation on the Supreme indweller is the ecstasy of being in Yoga and being in close contact with one's own self. *Dhyana-yoga* refers to the tranquil state of mind in which the perennial unity is experienced with the indweller. Meditation is combination of two words, meditation—which exactly means to attend to the thoughts with attention and intention. It is one of the greatest arts of life in which the individual learns to live in the consciousness of the indwelling Supreme-Self. In meditation session the individual learns to attend, watch, observe and behold the movement of his thoughts, aspirations and dreams. He educates himself in monitoring the movements of his thoughts and learns to direct them into the quietness of the Self. It is the highest form of discipline which is cultivated by the practice of living in the consciousness of the indwelling Supreme-Soul, and with the help of specific meditative techniques. The techniques which are used by the yogis, saints, seers, mystics and the householders do vary to some extent but in general everyone follows similar guidelines. All the prescribed techniques are generally meant to induce a contemplative mood that would assist the person for inner integration, peace and tranquillity. The advance meditators do experience the ecstatic trance and occasionally enter into the state of prime unity with the Lord. Meditation is not just a religious practice. It is for sure a necessity of life. It helps the individual to live in perfect harmony with himself and with others. In the description of *Dhyana-yoga,* Srī Kṛṣṇa explains step by step the procedure of going into the state of deep meditation. First of all it is important to find a quiet place for meditation. A quiet place has been highly recommended because during the meditation period, when the nerves are being trained to go into peace, even the slightest disturbance can create imbalance and harm the sensitive nerves. The crosscurrents can create jerks and discomfort. If the individual meditates inside the room, it should be properly ventilated and detached from all strong smells. Even the incense burners should not be used; because any strong smell can disturb the flow of energy and can easily distract the mind. It is also important to choose a specific spot in the house and try to practise everyday at the same spot. It renders quick progress. The reason is because that particular spot of meditation becomes energized with positive vibrations. In regular practice, when the person resumes at that particular spot, and takes his seat making a certain posture, the flow of thoughts automatically begins to flow in an unbroken current towards the goal in meditation. In order to make the meditation session relaxed and enjoyable, a comfortable cushion has been recommended. It should be placed above the ground. A four-folded blanket provides enough padding in order to support the hips and buttocks. Actually if one elevates the buttocks with a low cushion, that helps in keeping the spine straight and relieves the unnecessary pressure on the lower back. This position locks the spine immediately and aligns the neck and head automatically.

The most popular, ideal and recommended posture in meditation is indeed the *padmasana*. The *padmasana* is the full lotus position. *Padmasana* is stretching the right foot and placing it over the left thigh and the left foot over the right thigh, with the soles of the feet pointing upward, and heels touching the pelvic bone. For a beginner in meditation this posture is slightly difficult, so it is appropriate to start with the simple posture, the crossed legs position with a cushion supporting the buttocks area. This simple posture is called *Sukhasana*. *Sukhasana* is an ideal posture for the beginners, wherein the right foot is placed over the left thigh and the left foot under the right thigh. Hands are placed over the knees with head, neck and back properly aligned. Another well recommended posture is *Sidhasan*a which helps the spinal steadiness and makes the meditation session very productive for a long time. This posture helps the person to develop an extra control over the sensual desires. This posture has a remarkable calming effect over the entire nervous system. With gradual and regular practice one learns to move from *Sukhasana* to *Sidhasana* and from *Sidhasana* to *Padmasana*, the full lotus posture.

The recommended posture for meditation definitely requires the proper alignment of lower back, neck, shoulder, trunk and head. The vertical column should be erect and at ninety degree from the ground. Perpendicular position of the vertebral column helps the proper functioning of the nervous system. It helps in the relaxation of the muscles and withdrawal from the physical body. It harmonizes the breathing rhythm and calms down the mind in all respects. When the head, neck and the spinal cord become vertical, the gaze can be easily concentrated on the tip of the nose or between the two eyebrows. This spot between two eyebrows is called *bhrumadhya*. Directing the vision inward towards the bridge of the nose helps in concentration. It is at this spot between the two eyes from where the breath control starts and one experiences the light between the two eyebrows. By meditating at this point the individual can clearly visualize the white rays emanating from the centre. One feels the entire body being revitalized from this centre, giving a conscious control over all the muscles of the body, and the breathing system.

There is a very subtle and powerful relationship between breath and the thinking faculty. The stability of mind is closely related to the breathing pattern and the other functions of the body. That is why it is indeed essential to observe the breathing rhythm and bring it under conscious control. The irregular and fast breathing pattern indicates stress and tension in mind and body; while a deep rhythmical breathing pattern signifies tranquillity and a peaceful state of mind. Breath awareness helps in maintaining the emotional tranquillity and equanimity in all respects. It is indeed an essential aspect of concentration and also for developing a conscious control over the mind and body.

Srī Kṛṣṇa suggests that the first and foremost duty of every individual is to learn to meditate and to become re-established in a communion with the indwelling divinity. He should perform his day-to-day activities of life through unity in Yoga. The Supreme-Self is not just a fantasy or a vague aspiration. God is indeed a reality that can be experienced and enjoyed. It is as real as the air we breathe, feel and touch. *Yunjann-evam* literally means getting in touch with that and feeling the close association with that. It is the experience of touch, unity and connectedness that guides one into identifying with Brahman. It is the *samasparsa*—the touch of the Supreme Divinity, which is expressed as the deep ecstasy arising from the depths of inner tranquillity. *Samasparsa* is being in the ecstatic unity in transcendence. Sri Sankara interprets the *Brahma Samasparsa* as the unity with the

Brahman, Sri Ramanuja interprets it as the experience of the *Brahman* and Srinivasan as contact with the *Brahman*. Although it involves tremendous courage and determination to start the inward journey towards the exploration of the Supreme-Soul, but as the individual moves ahead it really becomes the most enjoyable adventure. The silence of the bliss, which is experienced at the innermost levels of consciousness, manifests itself in the individual's behaviour and daily activities. Towards the end of chapter six, Srī Kṛṣṇa glorifies a yogi and exhorts Arjuna to become a devoted yogi. The word yoga as described earlier, has been derived from the Sanskrit word *yuj*, which literally means union, communion and communication with the supreme. Yoga is living in the consciousness of the inner self. It is like living a life totally soaked in the nature of the Divine. Srī Kṛṣṇa considers this state of perpetual connectedness with the indweller, to be far better than all austerities, scriptural knowledge and performance of all rituals. He tells Arjuna to become a yogi and act like a yogi. The practice of concentration and contemplation on God must manifest itself in the day-to-day activities of life. Living in yoga and working through the unity in yoga is indeed the most valuable spiritual discipline of life.

The seventh discourse is *Jñana-vijñana-yoga*—the Yoga of Wisdom and Knowledge. In seventh chapter, the essential nature of Supreme person has been discussed in detail. Srī Kṛṣṇa unfolds to Arjuna the knowledge of the Self along with the knowledge of the manifested Divinity. He emphasizes the fact that the Divine and the manifestation of the Divine are not separate from one another. Both of them are very intimately connected. It is the knowledge of the Supreme-Self which unfolds the mysteries about other branches of knowledge such as the physical self, the psychological self and the spiritual self. A similar kind of statement has been made by Rishi Uddalaka to his son Savetaketu: 'Know, by knowing which everything else is known'. Srī Kṛṣṇa uses the terms *Jñana* and *Vijñana—Jñana* is the spiritual knowledge which is attained through the study of the sacred books and also through the lessons imparted by an accomplished teacher. This is called *Paroksha Jñana*. *Vijñana* is *Visesha Jñana*—the experiential knowledge obtained through inner intuitional wisdom and self-realization. *Vijñana* is also called the *Aparoksha Jñana*. Srī Kṛṣṇa declares that when an aspirant takes refuge in the Supreme-Soul, the individual is blessed with the knowledge of real and unreal; also the nature of unmanifest and manifest Divinity.

The Supreme-Self, the essence of all life, is indeed the creator, the sustainer and the annihilator of the entire creation. Srī Kṛṣṇa declares that O'Arjuna there is nothing beyond Me, and besides Me. The entire creation is threaded in Me, on Me and around Me like the rows of beads. He declares Himself to be the thread which runs through the entire creation. In other words, everything manifest or unmanifest is essentially of the nature of the Divine. The entire universe is held together by the Supreme-Lord Himself. As the thread running through the cluster of beads remains unseen, so is the Supreme Lord, while holding and sustaining everything remains unseen to the mortal eyes. In order to comprehend the omniscience of the Lord, the individual has to understand the nature of both the material and the spiritual-self. It is only with the proper understanding of both, the individual can understand the distinction between them and learn to identify himself with the real. The omniscience of the Supreme Lord is the only truth that prevails at the heart of the entire creation.

The message is concluded with the declaration *Vasudeva sarvam iti*—means Vasudeva is all. Here, Vasudeva stands for the Supreme consciousness which presides over the cause, space and time; and also transcends all that. The God-realized individual comprehends the fundamental essentiality that the omniscience of the Lord is the only truth, which lies at the heart of the entire creation. He seeks refuge in Vasudeva—pursues Him as the highest goal and also the means to attain his goal. The consciousness of the cosmic-self (*Vasudeva sarvam iti*) is an experience, crystallized by the individual in two distinct ways. In one, he reduces his individual-self zero and merges into the oneness of the universal-self; and in the other, he encloses within himself the entire universe.

The eighth chapter has been entitled as *Akasara-Brahman-Yoga*—the Yoga of Imperishable *Brahman*. This chapter gives a detailed description of the *Aksara-Brahman* and also the process of realization. Srī Kṛṣṇa enlightens Arjuna about the essential practice in day-to-day life, which helps the individual to concentrate, meditate and contemplate on the *Aksara-Brahman* alone at the final hour of departure from the world. This chapter has been called the *Abhyas-yoga* also; because it describes the techniques of communion with the indwelling-soul through the practice of the holy syllable *AUM—Pranava*. The word *Aksharam* means the imperishable, immutable, indestructible and eternal—the Supreme-Brahman. The entire world is rooted in *Brahman.* Everything in the world is experienced, grasped and perceived through the *Brahman.* The multiplicity of the world is revealed through the medium of one imperishable reality. *Brahman* is the *sanatan* principle of all existence. In *Taittriya Upanishad,* Bhrigu, the son of Varuna, requests his father to enlighten him about the nature of *Brahman.* The father replied O' dear son, that from which everything emanates, by which everything is sustained and into which everything enters eventually is *Brahman.* The Rishi explains that Brahman is the substratum of the universe and can be perceived only with penances and disciplinary observances—*Brahma-vijñana-sadhana.* During the process of tough penances, as the aspirant moves from one perceptual experience to another he determines for himself that there is only one eternal principle of consciousness which exists as the essence of the entire universe. The Supreme Brahman is the power behind matter and life, mind and intelligence which controls each one of them. The nature of *Brahman* is indeed inexplicable. The son of the Rishi finally experiences for himself the spiritual ecstasy of the infinite principle. The final vision satisfies all the inquiries of the aspirant. After the experience of the ultimate reality everything becomes self-evident, nothing remains to be known any more. *Anando Brahmeti Vyajanti* means Bliss is Brahman. All the beings are born from Bliss, they are sustained by Bliss and into Bliss they enter, upon attaining salvation.

Srī Kṛṣṇa assures that yogic communion with the supreme is indeed possible for each and every individual, provided the person is ready to go through the essentials of self-discipline, and steadfastness in practise. In order to experience the transcendental state of Supreme Divinity at the time of death, the individual has to practice meditation regularly. In this chapter Srī Kṛṣṇa glorifies the greatness of *AUM*, and emphasizes the necessity of concentration on the sound of *AUM* at the heart centre. Meditation on this mystic syllable *AUM* is the most beneficial austerity practised during the life time which makes the hour of death a blessed experience. The reason why Srī Kṛṣṇa suggests to concentrate on the sound at the heart-centre is because the sound of the holy syllable can be experienced originating from the *Anahat Nada*. It perpetually resounds from there. There are seven well known psychic centres in human body called the seven *chakras*. These psychic stations are located along the *Sushumna Nadi*. In yoga meditation the awareness is guided through these stations with full consciousness to the *Anahat chakra* and later to the *Ajña chakra* located between the two eyebrows. The heart *chakra* can be felt to be located between the two breasts almost at the level of the physical heart. In meditation it is experienced inside the spine and also behind the breast bone. *Anahat,* as the word itself explains, means unstruck sound. At this centre vibrates a celestial sound which can be very clearly heard in deep meditation. When the meditator withdraws his attention from all other external sounds of the sensory organs, this celestial sound can be heard automatically. The sound of *AUM* is difficult to capture but the person who practises regular meditation on it, he captures the sound effortlessly. The individuals who have trained themselves in *nadayoga,* for them a quick absorption in the sound of the holy syllable becomes very easy; they also know how to channelize the life force with the sound of *AUM* at the time of death. Srī Kṛṣṇa explains to Arjuna two paths; from the path of fire and light one attains salvation, and from the path of darkness the person comes back to the world of mortals. The path of light is travelled by the man of inner integrity. The yogi who is ever connected with the Lord in Yoga, who acts in Yoga, thinks and moves in Yoga, he leaves his body in the light of Yoga. The inner integrity helps his mind to be one-pointed towards the goal and enables him to leave his mortal body with a clarity of vision. The yogi who lives in unity with *Brahman* he is naturally directed towards the oneness with *Brahman* at death. He doesn't have to make any special effort for proper alignment. The person who knows the art of living, he definitely knows the art of dying. Srī Kṛṣṇa wants Arjuna to understand the importance of yogic unity in life.

The title of chapter nine is *Rajavidya-Rajaguhya-Yoga*—The Yoga of the Sovereign Science and Sovereign Secret. The specific use of expressive words the *Rajavidya* and *Rajaguhyam* indicates the Supremacy of sovereign knowledge and sovereign mystery as described in this chapter. Srī Kṛṣṇa declares that the yoga of devotion is a self-sufficient means for the realization of the Supreme. He considers it to be the noblest, most practical and the most rewarding method. When the Supreme Lord is approached in the spirit of ardent devotion, he becomes revealed to the devotee quite instantly and immediately. The expression *Pratyaksavagamam* means to be experienced and realized by direct communion and communication.

The yoga of devotion has been called the Supreme purifier because it is fulfilment in itself and at the same time also a means for increased fulfilment. It removes all the blemishes from the heart of the individual in the process itself. It is pleasurable to practise and its enjoyment renews every minute. Srī Kṛṣṇa declares that those who overlook the subtle power of devotional services to the Divine, and remain involved in the structural explanations of the tough and dry reason, they generally remain deprived of the true experiential knowledge of the Self. The words of assurance in verse twenty-two of this chapter have moved the hearts of millions around the world. The expression indicates the most intimate, compassionate and caring concern of the Lord towards his devotees. The language is simple, precise and heart-touching. Here is a powerful message, reflecting the profound assurance from the Divine. Srī Kṛṣṇa has declared to the entire mankind: "Have faith in Me, I will always take care of you". The word *ananya* has been mentioned earlier also but here it means more than just undivided devotion; here it means perpetual unification. *Ananya-bhava* literally means the total identification with the object of devotion. Lord being the ruler of all situations glorifies the work of his devotees by providing for all their needs and taking care of whatever is already in the possession of the devotees. Faith with profound reverence is what explains "*Nityabhiyuktanam*".

As a matter of fact, living in yoga has its own measure; the ceremonial worship, prayers and rituals can't tip its scale. It is like living in the transcendental consciousness and working through it. In this case, the individual resorts completely to the gracious unity with the Supreme-Self. He works through the Lord living a life in the perpetual consciousness of the Lord.

Srī Kṛṣṇa suggests to the entire mankind to inculcate a strong faith in God and purify the heart with faith and devotional service. A purified heart becomes receptive to the voice of the innerself and can distinguish between the real and the unreal, the transitory and the permanent, the embodied-self and the transcendental self. To love is a natural instinct. When the feelings are saturated with love of the Divine, it is called devotion. The love for God initiates the individual into a close friendship with God, and also into developing a most intimate relationship with God. When the bond with the Self strengthens in close intimacy the individual becomes fully dedicated to the Lord in his thoughts, words and deeds. He lives in the thoughts of the Divine and works through the consciousness of the Divine. The process is easy and within the reach of everyone. There is nothing new to learn, because every individual is born with this natural instinct of 'Love'. Just a shift in awareness renders the marvellous results.

The tenth discourse is *Vibhuti Yoga*—the Yoga of the Divine Manifestations. The word *Vibhuti* stands for magnificence in several different ways. *Vi* stands for *Vishesha* meaning special and *bhut* means beings. Another illustration of the word is majestic appearance or special Divine expression. *Vi* + *bhu* means appear, expand, and manifest. The entire universe is an expression of the power and the majesty of the creator. *Vibhutayah* literally means the glorious manifestations of the Lord by which the Supreme-Soul permeates and pervades the entire universe. These are the expressions of the Divine power. The Divine potency is indeed holding everything together and also reflecting through everything. In the words of Swami Chidbhavanananda, "Lord is expressing Himself. Whatever catches our imagination, draws our attention, sends us into raptures and infuses bliss into us, that is none but the glory of the God." It is indeed so difficult to comprehend the infinitude of the supreme; the human understanding can catch only a small fraction of it, so it is just enough to know and remember that the Lord is everything. The *Ramayana* declares, *"Prbhu ananta Prabhu ki leela ananta."* By giving a short glimpse of the eighty-two attributes and majesties (Majestic manifestation) Srī Kṛṣṇa intimates to Arjuna that any type of glory, achievement, name or fame that comes to the individual should be considered to be the manifestation of the Supreme. One should not get deluded by the masks and should learn to appreciate and see the splendour of the Divine behind all masks. It helps one to feel the omnipresence of the Omnipresent; within and without, from the minutest to the grossest. In the entire creation whatever is expressed as unique and special in the form of learning, austerity, virtue, beauty, valour and victory, splendour and glory, mighty and meritorious, knowledge and intelligence, wisdom and intuition etc. presents itself as the attribute of Supreme Lord. This is the truth that needs to be accepted, recognized and practised in order to prepare the mind for contemplation and yogic communication.

Chapter eleven has been entitled *Visva-Rupa-Darsana-Yoga*—the Yoga of the Vision of the Universal Form—meaning union and communion with the Divine through contemplation and meditation on the cosmic form. It is in the yogic state of transcendence, wherein the individual-self is awakened to the universality of the cosmic-self and he experiences his own essentiality and wholeness. The individual accelerates himself from the limitations of his personal, physical body and identifies with the total physical bodies of the entire universe. It is the union of the embodied-soul with the cosmic-soul wherein the individuality vanishes and the *I-ness* dissolves. It is like going into the field of yogic unity and to catch the first hand experience of the Lord's immanence, magnificence and infinity. The divine vision is the expansion of the individual self, from the individual identity into the cosmic identity, from the boundaries of time, space and cause into the timeless infinity. Being blessed with the Divine vision is to be awakened into the field of pure consciousness. It is an ability to freeze time in present and perceive the past, present and future all together. Srī Kṛṣṇa has been initiating Arjuna to see into the distant future and calculate the proper strategy of the situation at hand. In the words of Swami Sivananda, "The vision of the cosmic form is not the ultimate goal; if that were so, the Geeta would have ended with this chapter. The vision of the cosmic form is also one more in a series of graded experiences." Srī Kṛṣṇa wants Arjuna to realize that he is a co-worker with God in the mammoth work of eliminating the negativity and destroying the wicked and vicious people. The establishment of morality and *Dharma* is a co-operative enterprise of God and man. In reality the great war has been a Divinely executed plan for the destruction of the evildoers and the harmful agents in society and also for the re-establishment of *Dharma*. The intimacy of Arjuna, which has been expressed in the verses fifteen to thirty, reflects the primordial relationship which exists between *Nara* and *Narayana* (the Supreme-soul and the individual-soul). These verses express the purity of relationship which lies between the Lord and his genuine devotee. He feels that the Lord has possessed him at every level of his consciousness. He realizes for the first time that his life is indeed meant to serve the Lord. The intimacy, that the individual develops in ardent devotion, gradually blossoms into ineffable unity with the Lord. This is what Srī Kṛṣṇa expounds in verse fifty-four "*jñatum drastum ca tattvena pravestum*"—with unswerving devotion one understands Me, perceives Me in essence and gradually enters into Me and becomes a part of Me. This is what the *Vedas* have declared as "Being-Becoming and Bliss." It is indeed through loving adoration and perpetual dedication that the individuality of the embodied-soul finally gets absorbed into the totality of the Supreme, and the individual enters into a blissful transcendence.

The chapter twelve of Bhagawad Geeta has been designated "*Bhakti-yoga*" or the Yoga of devotion meaning communion in transcendence through a loving devotion for the Lord. This discourse highlights the ideals of undeviated and ardent devotion. *Bhakti*, a Sanskrit word, has been derived from the root word *Bhaj* which literally means to serve the Supreme Lord. *Bhakti yoga* initiates the individual in developing a most intimate relationship with the indwelling-Self. The *Narada Bhakti Sutra* has described it in these words, *sa tvasmin paramaprema rupa—Bhakti* is intense love for God. When a person goes into intimacy with God, he experiences inner unity. *Narada* has described it as *Amrta-svarupa ca*—Divine love is immortal Bliss. According to Sri Ramanuja, "The fundamental theme of Geeta is the doctrine of *Bhakti* which leads to the attainment of the highest Reality". In the first few verses of this chapter, there is a description about the two types of devotees—the worshipper of the personal God and the devotees of the impersonal Absolute Omniscient Lord. Arjuna expresses his desire to know the comparative relevance of both. Actually through the words of Arjuna the great Sage Vyasa has voiced the most pertinent question which is usually brought forward by many aspirants during the pursuit of their spiritual evolution. It is indeed very difficult to draw a line between the worship of *Saguna* and the meditation on *Nirguna*. In the process of worshipping *Saguna,* the person actually meditates upon *Nirguna* who hides behind the *Saguna*. So by being devoted to either, the individual worships both at the same time. The Supreme Divinity and His manifestations cannot be separated. It is after performing the worship of *Saguna* for many years, the individual educates himself to live in the consciousness of *Nirguna* and rises to the 'ideal' behind the 'idol'.

For example, in some states of India, especially Maharashtra and Bengal, there is a *Visarjana* ceremony which forms the culmination of worship. Around the *Navratra* time people worship various forms of gods and goddesses made of clay. After the worship for nine days all the deities are taken in a procession to the Ganga or to the nearby sea coast for *visarjana*. The *visarjana* means giving up the concept of forms and names. It is like rising above the concept of *Saguna* to *Nirguna*, from idol to the ideal, from less awareness to the increased awareness. In the process of worship for ten days the individual is expected to understand the transitory nature of form and move into the reality of formless. Similarly, when the ardent devotee gets closer to the experiential knowledge of the indwelling-Self, he needs less and less help in the form of signs and symbols for concentration. The aspirant rises above the personal God to the impersonal, immutable, omnipresent dwelling in the heart of his own self. He realizes the essential truth behind the *Saguna* and *Nirguna*. The reason why Srī Kṛṣṇa expresses the concept of *Saguna* and then immediately after that the concept of *Nirguna* is that he knows that in the process of spiritual growth it is a natural progression, to move from one concept to another. The aspirant switches from one to another at various stages of his spiritual advancement. Although *Saguna* worship may take place at first, ultimately one slips into *Nirguna* otherwise the goal is not achieved. For example, Uddhava, a great devotee of Srī Kṛṣṇa, has worshipped his Lord in *Saguna* and *Nirguna* both at the same time. Srī Kṛṣṇa has explained the methods of attaining unity with the indwelling Supreme-Soul in these words, "*mayy eva mana adhatsva mayi buddhim nivesaya*", just fix your mind on Me alone and let your intellect dwell in Me—then you will live in Me, there is no doubt about it. The assurance of Srī Kṛṣṇa in verse eight presents an encouraging insight into the spiritual pursuit. Perfection in yoga is attained through the practice of perpetual absorption in the Supreme Lord. Again, while describing the hallmarks of a genuine devotee, Srī Kṛṣṇa declares *mayyarpita-manobuddhir*—with the mind and intellect totally dedicated to Me. The activities of a true devotee are centred around the consciousness of the Divine. In the last verse of this chapter Srī Kṛṣṇa declares that living a life in conformity with the voice of the Supreme-Self is indeed living by the code of *Dharma*. Srī Kṛṣṇa declares that anybody who is endowed with strong faith and understands the meaning of living a life which is constantly united with the consciousness of the Higher-self, he definitely knows his *Dharma*.

Chapter thirteen has been entitled as *Ksetra-Ksetrajana-Vibhaga-Yoga*—The Yoga of the Knowledge of the Field and the Knower of the Field. Srī Kṛṣṇa opens the conversation with the words *Idam Sariram Kaunteya Ksetram iti abhidhiyate*—means this body is a field. The modern physicist describes the field as an abstraction which expresses the influence of the forces of nature. According to a physicist everything in the universe expresses itself in some kind of field. There are many fields of forces such as the gravitational field, the electromagnetic field and the quantum field. Any type of force becomes manifested through a field only. So the field can be described as an abstraction, which takes any form and shape in respect of cause, effect and time. The word field that a present century physicist is using to describe the most well known forces of nature, has been used by Srī Kṛṣṇa in relation to the forces which express themselves through the bodies of all beings. The physical body is a field which is a manifestation of the forces of nature, the mind, intellect and ego. When Einstein was trying to describe the unified field from where all other fields draw their power wrote, "My religion consists of an humble admiration of the illimitable, superior spirit who reveals Himself in the slightest detail we are able to perceive with our frail and feeble mind."

While using the word field for the body, Srī Kṛṣṇa intends to enlighten Arjuna about the distinction between the field and the knower of the field. He wants Arjuna to pursue the validity of the knower of the field, and become introduced with that. He wants Arjuna to be awakened from the systematic self-deceptive logical explanation and engage into the subtlest adventure of experiencing the one beyond the boundaries of existent and nonexistent. The *para Brahman* is beyond and above the boundaries of mind, speech and intellect. The Supreme consciousness transcends all the levels of personal experiences; words cannot describe that and the sense of perception cannot experience that. In the words of Swami Sivananda, "It is one without a second. It is not the object of senses. It is beyond the reach of mind and the senses. It is actionless. It is the great transcendental and unmanifested absolute. It is always the witnessing subject in all objects." He explains to Arjuna that whatever comes into existence moving or unmoving, it emanates from the union of the field and the knower of the field. Although the field of matter is insentient but when the spirit plays through the field, it energizes the field. On the surface it may appear that the Supreme Spirit has become the field but in essence it maintains its essential separateness. The field and the knower of the field both exists in a very mystical union. Einstein, the well known scientist, has written "the observer enters into every observation. All the experiences of everything in creation are coupled with experiencing the Self because both are indeed inseparably fused in each and every perception." In verse twenty-three, Srī Kṛṣṇa says that the one who understands the truth concerning the material nature and the indwelling spirit together with the qualities, in whatever condition he may be at present, he surely attains liberation. Such a person lives an emancipated life, regardless of his present duties; and he attains freedom from the ever revolving cycle of birth, death and rebirth.

Srī Krṣṇa is emphasizing that with proper knowledge of the Supreme Spirit and the primordial nature one attains the discriminating ability which helps him to separate the real from the unreal, the conditioned from the unconditioned, and mortal from the immortal. He performs his duties in the light of the knowledge of the Self and in perfect co-partnership with God. He lives his life as a witness and as an onlooker to his own mind and body. This enlightened individual lives his life which is totally centred to the core of his being and his identification with body, mind and ego vanishes in due time. The Supreme reality has to be apprehended personally and directly. The *Upanisads* have declared this truth "the Self is revealed to the individual by *adhyatma yoga* meaning the unity with the indwelling-Self; and *jñana-prasadana* meaning by the knowledge of the Self, which comes to the individual as a *prasada* (grace) of the Divine. Srī Krṣṇa assures in this verse that the one who contacts the indweller and understands the distinction between the body and the master of the body, he becomes liberated in due time.

Chapter fourteen has been entitled as *Guna-Triya-Vibhaga-Yoga*—The Yoga of the Division of the Three *Gunas*. This discourse explains about the communion with the Supreme-Soul through the knowledge of transcending the three *gunas*. The three *gunas* are the attributes of the primordial nature and almost all the embodied beings live under the control of these modes. This chapter describes the characteristics and the functions of the three *gunas* and how the imperishable soul becomes imprisoned within the play of the *gunas*. As described in chapter seven and in thirteen, it is the One and the only ultimate reality which manifests itself in the innumerable forms and shapes, within various grades of potentialities bound by their own latencies. The Matter is indeed the cosmic mother of the entire spectacular universe and *Ishwara* is the cosmic Father. The multitude of beings comes into existence from the union of matter and the Supreme Spirit. It is the union of the spirit with the matter which actually vitalizes the matter and gives life to inert matter. The *gunas* are the primary constituents of Nature. And are responsible for the rise and fall of *jivatma* in the world. These modes of nature definitely create confusion for *jivatma* and the latter forgets its true identity. The involvement with these essential qualities of nature becomes the cause of slavery to the material world and also the cause of birth, death and rebirth.

Srī Kṛṣṇa explains the essential characteristics of these modes of nature, and how they interact with everything in the world. He also expounds upon the process in which the pure imperishable Self becomes enslaved and bound and how he can transcend the *gunas* and attain liberation in life. The realization of the Supreme-soul beyond the *gunas* is realized when the individual soul re-establishes his conscious relationship with the indweller and identifies himself with the Divinity within. That is the state of self-realization and inner awakening. In the process of self-revelation the individual-soul is reminded of his pure essentiality and the primordial relationship with the Supreme-soul. A self-realized individual rises above the trap of the *gunas*, and the tricks of mind. He remains grounded in the essential nature of the Divine and becomes settled in Yoga of undivided devotion. He surely attains a positive control over the triad of the *gunas* and becomes free from the bondage of all sufferings, old age, death and rebirth. It is only in human life that the individual-soul gets an opportunity for self-examination, transformation and liberation. It should be the endeavour of every individual to learn to live a life which is consciously connected with the awareness of the Divine. Human life should become a means of redemption. As dictated earlier in chapter six verse five by Srī Kṛṣṇa "*uddhared atmana tmanam na tmanam avasadayet atmai va hy atmano bandhur atmai va ripur atmanah*"—let a man lift himself by his own Self; let him not degrade himself; for he himself is his own friend and he himself is his own enemy.

Chapter fifteen has been called the *Purushotama-yoga*—the Yoga of the Supreme Person meaning communion through the realization of the Supreme-*Purusha*. In this chapter Srī Kṛṣṇa has declared that the Supreme-spirit transcends both the *ksetra* and *ksetrajña*, the *ksara* and the *Aksara,* the body and the embodied-self; the person who understands this truth—for him, nothing else remains to be known and he is designated as the God realized yogi. In the words of Adi Sankara, "Though the entire Geeta has been held to be a *Sastra*, this chapter by itself is styled as *Sastra* eulogistically. In fact the entire message of Geeta has been summed up in this chapter. Not only the import of the Geeta but also the entire meaning of the *Vedas* has been summarized in this chapter". This discourse is one of the rarest pieces of scriptural knowledge in the religious literature of the world. It contains the quintessence of the Geeta, the *Upanisads* and the *Vedas.* This discourse comprises the teachings from chapter two, seven, nine, ten, eleven, thirteen and illustrates the philosophy of *Purusottama* with excellent brevity, clarity and profundity. Srī Kṛṣṇa declares that *jivatma* is an eternal fragment of Myself in the world of mortals. The word *jiva* literally means *jiv* a Sanskrit word which means to breathe. *Jivatma* means the *Atma,* who identifies with *jiva. Jivatma* (embodied-soul) is perennially one with the *Atma* (Supreme-soul) but appears to be separate because of its separate assumed identity.

According to the *Samkhya* theory of multiplicity, it is the only one Supreme soul in the entire creation which becomes manifested in many modes at many levels. An eternal *amsa* or fragment or part of the Supreme-soul permeates into everything. According to Swami Chidbhavananda, "*Jivatma* is never an entity separate or independent of the paramatma. As a wave is ever part of the sea, the individual soul is eternally a part and parcel of Iswara." In the *Ramayana*, the same truth has been described in these words "*Iswar ansa jiv avinasi, cheitana amal saheja sukrasi*". In essence the embodied-soul is a fragment of the Supreme-Soul, primordial and imperishable. It is only due to ignorance that the embodied-soul forms a separate identity and feels alienated. In the words of Sri Ramsukdhas, "The soul having assumed its affinity with the body, senses, mind, and life breath—which are the evolutes of nature—has become the *jivabhutah* which is like an actor in a play". The experience of alienation occurs because of duality; but when the individual-soul dives deep in the subtle layers of consciousness from the gross to the subtlest realms of awareness; it realizes its true identity and feels a part of the super-soul again. In this chapter once again Srī Kṛṣṇa has declared the human heart to be the shrine of the Lord. Although the Supreme consciousness is the essence of life and resides in each and every little molecule of the body but can be perceived, intimated and experienced only at the heart centre. The realization of the Supreme Lord at the shrine of the heart is easy and the most rewarding experience of life. It is easy because the individual is not seeking something distant, not something foreign and alien; it is very much known, familiar and one's own indwelling-self. The contemplation at the heart centre has been highly recommended in almost all the religious traditions of the world. It is indeed in the most subtle realms of consciousness, at the *anahat chakra,* where the aspirant can perceive and experience the presence of the spirit within. When an ardent devotee concentrates at the heart centre and makes effort to grasp the sound waves of the eternal *nada (AUM).* He goes into yogic unity with the indwelling-soul. The spiritual experience of the proximity with the Divine at the heart centre prepares the individual for devotional love of the Lord. It is in the depths of the heart wherein the psychological and spiritual transformation takes place and the person is remade. Jesus has also written "discover the Lord in your heart and then in the heart of thy neighbour". It is at the heart centre, the act of purification starts and the spirit of surrender takes place. It is at the heart centre where the love for the Lord is awakened and the presence of the Divine is personally experienced.

In this chapter Srī Kṛṣṇa explains in detail the concept of *Purushottam Yoga* which literally means an introduction and communion with the Supreme-self. The word *ksarah* stands for the perishable manifestations in the world. This includes all the movables and immovables from the grossest to the tiny blade of grass. This is the material world which is composed of five gross elements. Everything which is seen and perceived by the eyes and the senses and comprehended by the mind comes under the vast territory of *ksarah* (perishable). This is the manifestation of the Divine potency in the field of space and time. The entire realm of matter is perishable, while the conscious principle that shines through the matter is indeed imperishable. The expression *dvavimau Purushau loke ksaras ca ksara eva ca* means there are two kinds of *purushas* in the world, the perishable and the imperishable. The Supreme-soul which is called the Higher Self is distinct and stands above the perishable and also the imperishable. The *Uttama purusha* is greater than the mutable and also greater than the immutable. The Supreme power is *anyah* meaning the other than these, which is known and perceived by the senses and mind. That power just observes and witnesses everything which takes place in the ever changing world. The *Purushottama Yoga* is the ultimate identification of the embodied-soul with the Supreme-soul. It is the most difficult status to be achieved in spiritual progression.

It is the most enlightened status in which the aspirant perceives the essential nature of both, perishable and imperishable quite separately and distinctly. Although the Geeta is the cream of all the *Sastras* (religious scriptures) chapter fifteen has been called a *Sastra* by Srī Krṣṇa. The very first verse describes the nature of the universe. The next few verses present a description about the nature of the *jivatma* (embodied-soul) and also the reasons of its bondage. The declaration of *Purushottma* combines together all the three and assimilates them into a clear and distinct statement.

Chapter sixteen has been named as *Devasur-Sampativibhag-yoga*—The Yoga of the Distinction Between the Divine and the Demoniacal Endowments which means the attainment of unity with the indwelling-soul through the distinct knowledge of the Divine and the demonic characteristics. The theme of the chapter is to trace the difference of the *Daivi Sampati* and the *Asuri-Sampati. Deva* literally means the one who knows how to give and share. The other word which is used for *Deva* is *Sura*—it is a Sanskrit word. *Sura*, as the word itself explains, means the one who is consciously in tune with the Supreme-soul. The *Asura* means the one who is not consciously in tune with the Supreme-soul. *Devas* are endowed with the divine traits; their nature expresses the purity, humanity, clarity, honesty, truthfulness and spontaneity of spiritual awareness. On the other hand, the *Asuras* are endowed with demonic traits and their behaviour expresses the conscious misalignment with the Higher-Self. Although every individual-soul (*Jivatma*) is potentially divine and a fragment of the Supreme-Soul; but when the embodied-soul seeks expression of its latencies and memories, he becomes entrapped. When the soul takes upon the human body, he becomes possessed with two strong desires. The individual-soul likes to enjoy everything in the material world; but being a fragment of the Divine, the embodied-soul likes to remain in the proximity of the Supreme-Soul. In human body, the embodied-soul becomes confused and enshrouded by various contradictions. The spiritual impulses give warmth, serenity, tranquillity and make the goal of his life spiritually oriented and stable, while the primitive impulses and materialistic desires make him restless, weak and distorted. An individual has the potential to rise to the greatest heights of spirituality in life and work in a co-partnership with God but if he becomes enslaved to the material comforts of the world, he falls into the ditches of degradation. He can become the crown of creation, but if he acts against the voice of the Supreme-Self, he becomes the scandal of the world. Although all the embodied-souls are essentially spiritual, but the degree of spiritual awareness differs from one person to another. In general people divide themselves in two categories; the men of divine traits and the men of demonic traits. This statement of Srī Kṛṣṇa has been also repeated by Viktor Frankl in his book *'Man's Search for Meaning'*. He writes, "There are two races of men in the world, but only these two—the race of a decent man and the race of the indecent man—both are found everywhere; they penetrate into all groups of society. No group consists entirely of decent or indecent people." In general, the entire creation falls into these two categories, the *Deva* and the *Asur*a or the gods and the Titans.

Srī Kṛṣṇa tells Arjuna that the divine qualities have been recognized to be conducive to liberation and emancipation while the demonic qualities become a great obstacle towards the path of liberation. The demonical nature becomes the cause of suffering and bondage. In verse twenty-one, Srī Kṛṣṇa declares the desire, anger and greed to be the triple gates of hell; that brings about the degradation of the embodied-soul. These Hi-three are indeed very destructive in all respects and the foremost cause of man's total ruin and disaster. These three traits of human behaviour act in close co-partnership with each other and do appear as uninvited comrade. In this chapter Srī Kṛṣṇa has emphasized upon the elimination of behaviour, which is characterized by these 'Hi-three' evils—'lust, anger and greed'. These are very destructive emotions and have to be renounced and shunned in all respects. Victory over these three gates of hell prepares the individual for inner enlightenment and liberation. Towards the end of this chapter, Srī Kṛṣṇa declares about the superiority of scriptural knowledge which should be used as the beacon light for living a balanced and harmonious life. The four holy *Vedas* and the other scriptures written on the basis of these such as the *Manu Smriti*, the *Puranas* and Epics; all of these have been called the *Sastras* by learned scholars. Every human being must follow the instructions of the scriptures at every step in life, until he becomes fully tuned to the voice of the indwelling Supreme-Lord. The ancient authentic scriptures should be respected, read intelligently and assimilated very diligently.

Chapter seventeen has been called the *Sradha-Triya Vibhag-Yoga*—The Yoga of the Threefold Division of the Faith. It is indeed a well established fact that "As a man's faith is, so is he". All the achievements of a person's life revolve around the kind of faith he holds. It is the person's faith and attitude which motivates the entire field of his diverse activities and the various kinds of pursuits. It is the faith that colours the entire field of choices he makes, the likings and dislikings, and also the acceptance and the rejections. The essential characteristics of the faith of an individual are generally determined by the degree of his self-awareness. The quality of faith directly correspond to the innate nature or *swabhava* of the person. *Swabhava* comprises two words. *Swa* means the indwelling light and *bhava* means the personal thinking. So *swabhava* means the personal thinking of the embodied-self. It also means the individualized comprehension of the indwelling-self. An enlightened person is generally distinguished by his respective adherence to the truth and untruth.

Srī Kṛṣṇa tells Arjuna that, in general, people are influenced by the three inherent qualities of mother nature, and categorize themselves in three types of *swabhava*—the *sattvic* (pure), *rajasic* (passionate) and *tamasic* (ignorant). He tells how the innate-disposition (faith) of a person determines the object of his worship. The *sattva* stands for purity, honesty and clarity. The *sattvic* people are spiritually awake and enlightened. They seek inner fulfilment from their inner connectedness with the Divine. The *sattvic* people perform all kinds of worships merely for self-purification and for the maintenance of orderliness in life. The people of *rajasic* (passionate) temperament are generally very ambitious. They worship the *Yakashas* and *Rakshasas*. The worshipper of *Rakshasas* pursue power—both physical and material. The *tamasic* people worship the evil spirits and the vicious powers for sense-gratification. These superstitious people are very selfish and seek only their personal comforts while ignoring the laws of *swadharma*. They make impure resolves in their worship in order to fulfil their selfish desires. Sometime these deluded people engage themselves in forming a cult and do misguide others into committing some heinous crimes. These deluded people of meagre understanding do create a lot of confusion in the society and disturb the peace and harmony. In this chapter Srī Kṛṣṇa tells Arjuna that the men, who practice violent austerities which are not enjoined by the scriptures, torture their bodies and also hurt Me, who dwells within the body. These deluded egoists engage themselves in the practice of severe penances which are against the laws of *swadharma*. The performance of their austerities reflects the lack of knowledge and proper insight. In general, their approach is very unreasonable and unauthentic. These types of penances have not been approved by the holy scriptures because these are against the laws of nature and the voice of the inner-self.

Srī Kṛṣṇa asserts that self-discipline and self-restraint should not be confused with physical torture of the body. The practice of self-mortification is painful and unworthy, it should not be followed at all. Towards the end of this chapter, Srī Kṛṣṇa enlightens Arjuna about the subtle power of *Aum-Tat-Sat* which transforms each and every act into the purity of *sattvikta. AUM TAT SAT* has been known to be the threefold appellation of the Absolute. These three words stand for the pure energy of the Supreme Divinity. The pronunciation of these three together arouses the latent Divinity and the person feels himself to be a part of the universal cosmic energy. The power of creation emanates from this mantra *AUM TAT SAT. AUM* is the primordial holy syllable that envelops the entire creation. The word *Tat* stands for the supreme reality in essence. It expresses the universal truth, the absolute truth in essence. The expression *AUM TAT SAT'* denotes that in essence everything is *AUM*. It is recommended in *Sastras* that all types of worship, *yajña,* and austerity should commence with the holy syllable *AUM* and the completion of worship should be dedicated with the recitation of the trifold sentence *AUM TAT SAT*. The offering of service with the words *Aum Tat Sat* declares that the Supreme Lord is indeed the substratum of the universe and pervades everywhere in everything. The worship has been initiated by the Supreme Divinity and is dedicated in the service of the Supreme Divinity. The worship and penance which commences with the holy syllable *AUM* and which is dedicated to the Lord with the utterance of *Tat* becomes sanctified and a means for emancipation and liberation. Here the word *Tat* signifies Brahman. It is specially uttered with *AUM* by the performer towards the completion of an offering.

Chapter eighteen has been entitled *Moksa-Sannyasa-Yoga*—The Yoga of Liberation Through Renunciation. The literal meaning of both words *sannyasa* and *tyaga* is to renounce; and both the words are used in the sense of relinquishment, but *tyaga* is slightly different from *sannyasa*. Renunciation is the abandonment of all desire-prompted actions, while relinquishment is the abandonment of the fruits of all ordinary and extraordinary activities. It is the renouncement of all anxieties related to the enjoyment of the fruits of actions. A genuine renunciate performs all the assigned duties in the spirit of *yajña* in order to maintain the orderliness in the community and society. He attempts every action with zeal and enthusiasm, and offers all the work as a service to the Supreme Lord. The performance of his duties becomes educational for him which transforms his each activity into *yajña* and helps him to overcome the shackles of all kinds of bondage. He always maintains his spirit of *tyaga* through the abandonment of the fruits of actions and gradually attains the tranquillity of *Sannyasa*. In this chapter Srī Kṛṣṇa declares once again that the renunciation of the obligatory actions is not proper. He tells that the renunciation of *Niyatam Karma*, merely out of ignorance, is considered to be *tamasic*. The obligatory actions include both the performance of the daily duties at the individual level and also the special duties which a person is expected to undertake as a member of the family and the society in which he lives. If a person ignores his obligatory duties and refuses to accept his responsibility in the community which supports his living and protection, his renunciation is considered to be *tamasic*. The individual who neglects his obligatory duties, disturbs the continuity of action in nature and brings about chaos in the society. His relinquishment is marked as an escapism from the realities of life. This type of renunciation brings more pain than any fulfilment or peace in the long run. A genuine relinquishment is that which guides the individual into the acceptance of higher moral values with greater responsibilities. It leads the individual into deeper satisfaction, inner fulfilment and one's own completeness.

Srī Kṛṣṇa declares that by being devoted to one's own duty, a man attains the highest perfection and spiritual competency in all respects. The Supreme Lord of the universe should be worshipped through the dedicated performance of one's own duty. It is for sure the attitude of sincere devotion to one's duty which reveals the presence of the Supreme through the execution of work. The performance of a duty definitely becomes a means of inner growth and perfection when it is determined from within and carried out as an offering to the Divine. When the individual makes himself a conscious instrument in carrying out the work of the Divine in society, he can transmute his work into a means for the highest spiritual perfection and freedom. To worship the Lord through performance of a duty is to transform the whole life into a sacrifice. A genuine renouncer is the one who remains soaked in the nature of the Divine while performing his day-to-day activities of life. He develops an identity with the Supreme-Self and with the community in which he lives. His work itself becomes his worship and qualifies him for the higher pursuits in spiritual life. The pure and sincere duty oriented attitude uplifts the individual and he lives like a yogi in the midst of worldly affairs. Such an individual cultivates valuable work ethics, and through the practice of *Karmayoga,* he becomes eligible for the majesty of going in complete *sannyasa*. The expression *aham tvam sarva-papebhyo* is a most exhilarating assurance from Srī Kṛṣṇa; it indicates that the Supreme Lord personally takes care of all the problems and the sins of that person who willingly takes refuge in Him and co-operates unconditionally. In these words Srī Kṛṣṇa's love for Arjuna has become more explicit. The affectionate expressions such as—always 'stay close to My heart', 'Have faith in Me', 'I promise I will always take care of you' and 'take refuge in Me, I will liberate you from all types of sins'—are indeed the gestures of intimacy, compassion, kindness and generosity. These terms are very significantly worded, very compassionately expressed and also indicate the ultimate truth that the Lord's help and assurance is always there for human beings.

Towards the end of the Holy dialogue, Arjuna feels totally re-oriented to a absolutely new concept of life. His entire outlook is changed for the better. He feels confident and integrated in all respects. The words *karisye vacanam tava* indicate the feelings of total acceptance with willingness and faith. Arjuna gives up his separate existence and identifies himself with the work of the Lord. A revelation of this magnanimity is indeed the prerogative of each and every individual. This rediscovery of one's own essential nature is possible for everyone, only if the person surrenders himself to the grace of the indweller. The grace of the Supreme-Lord lies perpetually within the various sheaths of one's own awareness. It lies veiled beneath one's own individualized egocentric limitations. In the act of total surrender, when the person resorts to the grace of the Lord, the purity and the essentially of his own divine nature unfolds itself and becomes available to the individual. Arjuna's experience of grace indicates his feeling of inner peace and tranquillity, in contrast to the turmoil of his previous emotions. He feels stabilized, confident, integrated, firm and motivated in carrying out the command of Srī

Kṛṣṇa. His expression *karisye vacanam tava* indicates his assurance to Srī Kṛṣṇa that now he will follow His instructions and guidance very devotedly, intuitively and spontaneously. Arjuna speaks these words of surrender from the purity of his heart and from the wisdom of inner unity. There is an identical expression in the *Ramayana, Nath kripa mama gatha sandheha, Ram charan upajehu nava neha*—the grace of the Lord has eliminated my doubts and delusions, now I feel totally surrendered to the majesty of the Lord. It is a very personal experience of the indwelling Divinity at the exalted level of inner awakening. It is the communication of the *nara* with his eternal companion *Narayana*. It is the transcendence of the individual soul into the majesty of the Supreme-Soul. It is the transmutation of the limited identification into the unbounded cosmic identification. The individual-self, who was enshrouded earlier in *vishad*, is now awakened into the attainment of *prasad*. When the individual-self surrenders into the wholeness of the Divine, the emotional turmoil and the *vishad* is transformed into *prasad* of the Lord. When the embodied-soul becomes awakened into the consciousness of the Supreme-soul, his individual *dharmas* are relinquished into the nature of the Divine for pure, clear and uncontaminated guidance from the indwelling Lord (the primordial *Dharma*).

Sanjaya concludes that wherever there is the contemplative wisdom and the yogic power of Srī Kṛṣṇa, and the practical efficiency of Arjuna in performing the work, there are prosperity, success, victory, glory, unfailing righteousness and indeed everything else. The implementation of the yogic power, and the contemplative wisdom under the guidance of the Higher-Self is surely required for any kind of success and victory. When the individual-self becomes united with the Supreme-self, then the yogic power of the Lord descends upon the individual and blesses him with the inner poise and appropriate balance of mind. It gives the capacity to work with a integrated attitude of mind and with immovable faith in one's own Self. When a person performs all his work in perfect conformity with the grace of the Supreme Lord, the results are definitely rewarding and spontaneously beneficial.

The performance of action is only a medium for the revelation of the Divine power and the yogic integrity. The victory, success and the glory are the expression of the Divine grace, kindness and generosity. Excellency in the performance of every action lies in direct proportion to the connectedness of the individual in yogic unity. The individual who resorts in the yogic unity of the Supreme-self, and performs all his actions with the guidance of the infinite Divinity, he is rewarded with excellency in work and liberation in life here and hereafter. The concluding word of the dialogue is *mama* while the opening word has been *Dharma.* The message of the entire dialogue is enclosed in these two words *mama Dharma* meaning My *Dharma.* The life on earth becomes peaceful, prosperous and instrumental for liberation only if the individual understands the meaning of My *Dharma. Dharma* of every individual is to remain united with the indwelling Divinity and perform all activities in perfect harmony with the voice of the Supreme-Self. Living in Yoga and working through Yoga is the *Dharma* of mankind.

All the eighteen yogas, described in the eighteen chapters, are further summarized in three—*Karmayoga, Bhaktiyoga* and *Jñanayoga.* The ancient sages have declared that spiritual progression of a person begins with the Yoga of action, evolves around Bhakti (devotion) and matures into the Yoga of knowledge. Srī Kṛṣṇa intends to enlighten Arjuna about the concept of each separately and then combines them all in order to seek unity with the indwelling-soul. Yoga is the conscious unification of the individual-soul with the Supreme-soul. Srī Kṛṣṇa wants Arjuna to combine all the three concepts of Yoga, in order to seek union with the Divine through the devoted performance of actions. Knowledge without action and action without knowledge cannot help anybody. Proper knowledge devotion and action must be intermingled in order to attain self-realization and God-realization. The word Yoga means a union and communion with the indweller; so the *Karmayoga* literally means the type of actions which help the individual to develop union with God. Similarly, the knowledge that guides the person in developing unity with the Divine is called *Jñanayoga* (Yoga of knowledge). The mode of ardent devotion which helps the individual to maintain constant union with the inner-self is called the *Bhakti Yoga* (yoga of devotion). In the practice of devotion-cum-action the individual experiences a spontaneous flow of inner awareness into the work of the day-to-day life, which prepares him for the direct experience of the Supreme. Srī Kṛṣṇa declares throughout the discourse that the success in the practice of *Karmayoga* and *Jñanayoga* is attained through the undeviated and unconditioned devotion to the Supreme-Self. The discipline of yoga is practice of living in constant unity with the Supreme Lord. It is the consciousness of the indwelling-self in yogic unity which transforms every action into the Yoga of Action. It is indeed the practice of *Bhaktiyoga* (devotion) which combines both the *Karmayoga* and *Jñanayoga* into harmonious whole. An ardent devotion to Lord initiates the individual into the experiential knowledge of the Self, and the knowledge of the Self initiates the person into the gospel of selfless action; this is how all the yogas blend into one another and set the pathway for the attainment of the ultimate goal in life. Srī Kṛṣṇa intends to teach Arjuna that he should pursue the path of *Karmayoga* with proper insight, wisdom, integrity, devotion and dedication. It is the proper understanding of the three yogas which initiates the individual into the performance of all actions with proper knowledge and gives him peace, happiness and liberation.

The great *Mahavakya* of the *Vedas—Tat-Tvam-Asi* (That thou art) is also wrapped in the verses of the *Geeta Yoga Sastra*. The entire dialogue elucidates the meaning of this great sentence. The philosophy of *Karmayoga* which has been discussed in the first six chapters of Geeta describes *Tvam* in *Mahavakyam. Tvam* or thou stands for the individual-soul. These chapters describe the limitations of the individual-self and the cause of his bondage. The nature of *Karmayoga* and its applications for the purpose of liberation has been also discussed in the beginning. The second part *Tat* or that has been discussed in chapters from seven to twelve. The path of loving devotion for God and the essential nature of Supreme-Self has been elucidated in these chapters. The third *pada Asi* or art covers the last six chapters. The knowledge of the embodied-soul and the Supreme-soul has been discussed in deep detail in the last six chapters of Bhagawad Geeta. The full meaning of *Mahavakya—Tat-Tvam-Asi* which means that you are essentially the Divine, immortal, imperishable and eternal—has been discussed in an unparalleled style. Each chapter of Bhagawad Geeta ends with a unique message with the words—*Aum tatsaditi Srimadbhagawadgeetasupanisatsu brahmavidyayam yogasastre sriKṛṣṇarjunasamvade* which means *AUM TAT SAT*. Thus in the *Upanishad* of the glorious Bhagawad Geeta, the science of the Brahman (Absolute) the scripture of yoga, the dialogue between Srī Kṛṣṇa and Arjuna, *Aum-Tat-Sat* has been declared to be the trifold designation of the Absolute. These three words indicate one or the other aspect of the Absolute Divinity. In the recitation of *AUM TAT SAT* the worshipper pledges himself to constancy, detachment, truth, beauty and goodness. These Holy words have some specific spiritual powers that give sanctity and purity to the worship and also initiates the individual into a detached, dedicated and respectful performance. Srī Krsna recommends that every type of worship and austerity should revolve around the holy formula *AUM TAT SAT*.

Bhagawad Geeta has been designated as an *Upanishad*. It is a scripture of Yoga on the science of *Brahman*. The dialogue reveals the mysteries of the Divine and leads the aspirant from lcss awareness into increased awareness, from the gross to the subtle into the experiential knowledge of the Supreme-Soul. The holy dialogue is the conversation between the individual-soul and the Supreme-soul. The topic of yoga which is very mysterious, broad and complex has been discussed in great detail. In the words of Swami Prabupada, "One will find in Bhagawad Geeta, all that is contained in other scriptures but the reader will also find those things which are not to be found elsewhere. That is the specific standard of Geeta. It is the perfect theistic science because it is directly spoken by the Supreme personality of Godhead Lord Srī Krsna". There are hundreds of revered commentaries on Bhagawad Geeta. The most ancient commentary on Geeta has been written by Sri Sankaracharya in 800 AD, although he refers to many previous ones, those were written in the past by other seers and sages. The traditional commentary of Sri Sankaracharya is indeed a great contribution and has always served as the most valuable guide for many commentators. The other revered commentators of the past have been Sri Ramanuja, Sri Madhvacharya, Sridhara and the great sage Sri Jñaneshwarji. Sri Ramanuja's work became available in the eleventh century AD. He declares the celebrated doctrine of Bhakti (devotion) to be the essential theme of Bhagawad Geeta. Sri Jñaneshwar's commentary and the work of Sri Madhavacharya came to the attention of public in 13th century AD. There are hundreds of other commentaries on Bhagawad Geeta. The most well known of the modern time are by Sri Bal Gangadhar Tilak *(Geeta Rahasya)*, Sri Aurobindo, Mahatma Gandhi, Swami Sivananda, Jayadayal Goyandaka, Swami Tapasyananda, Swami Chidbavananada, Swami Vivekananda, Mahrishi Mahesh Yogi, Sri Ramsukdhas, Sri Vinobhaji, Swami Chinmayananda, Swami Rama, Swami Prabhupada, Dr. S. Radhakrishnan, and the most celebrated work of Sri Satwalekar.

Among the Persian writers the famous translations on Bhagawad Geeta has been done by Darashikoh and Khwaja Dil Mohammed. The Bhagawad has been translated into French by Burnouf, into Latin by Lassen, into Italian by Stanislav Gatti, into Greek by Galanos, and into English by Mr. Thomson and Mr. Davies. Among the foreign commentators on Bhagawad Geeta the famous commentaries have been written by Charles Wilkins, Dr. Annie Besant, Aldous Huxley, Kant, Mr. Brook, Max Muller, Franklin Edgerton, Edwin Arnold and many other German and Russian scholars. All of these are worthy of great respect, veneration and appreciation.

The present commentary is only a humble addition to the work which has been accomplished by the previous Geeta scholars and commentators. This work combines the ancient wisdom of the Vedic philosophy with the contemporary thoughts and ideas of the west. It is a systematic guide which can help the individual to enhance his experiences of contentment, creativity, peace and inner fulfilment. It makes me feel so blessed that the message of Geeta which I have enjoyed sharing with others for so many years, is finally going to be presented as a commentary to the admirers of Geeta. This has been indeed, one of the most challenging, enlightening and rewarding experience of my life. This book is a *prasad* to the readers from the ever renewing grace of the Supreme Lord. I hope this work will initiate people into the subtle understanding of Geeta and also guide them into the practice of the science of yoga as explained in this book. The whole purpose of writing this commentary is to share my awakening with others and to pass on the legacy of Yoga in Bhagawad Geeta to the coming generations.

Śrī Kṛṣṇa Arpanamastu

Yata Kṛṣṇastato Dharmo Yato Dharmastato Jaya

Where there is Śrī Kṛṣṇa, Dharma or righteousness is there; and where there is righteousness victory is assured.

10th May, 1998 **—*Prabha Duneja***
Pleasanton, CA, U.S.A.

Chapter One

VISHĀDA YOGA

THE YOGA OF THE DESPONDENCY OF ARJUNA

धृतराष्ट्र उवाच

धर्मक्षेत्रे कुरुक्षेत्रे समवेता युयुत्सवः।
मामकाः पाण्डवाश्चैव किमकुर्वत सञ्जय॥ १॥

dharmakṣetre kurukṣetre samavetā yuyutsavaḥ
māmakāḥ pāṇḍavāścaiva kimakurvata sañjaya

Dhritarashtra said :

(1) On the holy field of Kurukshetra, assembled together and eager to fight the battle, what did my sons and the sons of Pandu do?, O' Sanjaya.

संजय उवाच

दृष्ट्वा तु पाण्डवानीकं व्यूढं दुर्योधनस्तदा।
आचार्यमुपसङ्गम्य राजा वचनमब्रवीत्॥ २॥

dṛṣṭvā tu pāṇḍavānīkaṁ vyūḍhaṁ duryodhanastadā
ācāryamupasaṅgamya rājā vacanamabravīṭ

Sanjaya said :

(2) Having seen the army of the Pandavas arrayed in the battle, Prince Duryodhana then approached his teacher Dronacharya, and spoke these words.

पश्यैतां पाण्डुपुत्राणामाचार्य महतीं चमूम्।
व्यूढां द्रुपदपुत्रेण तव शिष्येण धीमता॥ ३॥

paśyaitāṁ pāṇḍuputrāṇāmācārya mahatīṁ camūm
vyūḍhāṁ drupadaputreṇa tava śiṣyeṇa dhīmatā

(3) Behold O'Teacher, this mighty army of the sons of Pandu, arrayed by the son of King Drupada, thy wise disciple.

अत्र शूरा महेष्वासा भीमार्जुनसमा युधि।
युयुधानो विराटश्च द्रुपदश्च महारथः॥४॥

atra śūrā maheṣvāsā bhīmārjunasamā yudhi
yuyudhāno virāṭaś ca drupadaśca mahārathaḥ

धृष्टकेतुश्चेकितानः काशिराजश्च वीर्यवान्।
पुरुजित्कुन्तिभोजश्च शैब्यश्च नरपुङ्गवः॥५॥

dhṛṣṭaketuścekitānaḥ kāśirājaśca vīryavān
purujit kuntibhojaśca śaibyaśca narapuṅgavaḥ

युधामन्युश्च विक्रान्त उत्तमौजाश्च वीर्यवान्।
सौभद्रो द्रौपदेयाश्च सर्व एव महारथाः॥६॥

yudhāmanyuśca vikrānta uttamaujāśca vīryavān
saubhadro draupadeyāśca sarva eva mahārathāḥ

(4, 5, 6) Here are the heroes, the mighty archers, who are equal in warfare to Bhima and Arjuna—Yuyudhana, Virata and the great chariot-warrior Drupada. Dhristaketu, Cekitana, and the valiant King of Kasi; Purujit, Kuntibhoja, and Saibya, the best among men; the mighty Yudhamanyu, the valiant Uttamauja, Abhimanyu, the son of Subhadra and the five sons of Draupadi are also there. All of them are the well-known chariot-warriors.

अस्माकं तु विशिष्टा ये तान्निबोध द्विजोत्तम।
नायका मम सैन्यस्य सञ्ज्ञार्थं तान्ब्रवीमि ते॥७॥

asmākaṁ tu viśiṣṭā ye tānnibodha dvijottàma
nāyakā mama sainyasya sañjñārthaṁ tānbravīmi te

(7) Know also O'noblest of the twice-born! the distinguished warriors of our side, the generals of my army. I will name them for your information.

भवान्भीष्मश्च कर्णश्च कृपश्च समितिञ्जयः।
अश्वत्थामा विकर्णश्च सौमदत्तिस्तथैव च॥८॥

bhavānbhīṣmaśca karṇaśca kṛpaśca samitiñjayaḥ
aśvatthāmā vikarṇaśca saumadattistathaivaca

(8) Yourself and Bhishma, Karna and also Kripa who is ever victorious in battle; Ashwatthama, Vikarna and Saumadatti, the son of Somadatta.

अन्ये च बहवः शूरा मदर्थे त्यक्तजीविताः।
नानाशस्त्रप्रहरणाः सर्वे युद्धविशारदाः ॥ ९ ॥

anye ca bahavaḥ śūrā madarthe tyaktajīvitāḥ
nānāśastraprahraṇāḥ sarve yuddhaviśāradāḥ

(9) And there are many other heroes, who are ready to give up their lives for my sake; they are equipped with many kinds of weapons and all of them are skilled in the strategy of warfare.

अपर्याप्तं तदस्माकं बलं भीष्माभिरक्षितम्।
पर्याप्तं त्विदमेतेषां बलं भीमाभिरक्षितम् ॥ १० ॥

aparyāptaṁ tadasmākaṁ balaṁ bhīṣmābhirakṣitam
paryāptaṁ tvidameteṣāṁ balaṁ bhīmabhirakṣitam

(10) This army of ours, which is guarded and marshalled by Bhishma, is insufficient; while their army, which is marshalled by Bhima is sufficient.

अयनेषु च सर्वेषु यथाभागमवस्थिताः।
भीष्ममेवाभिरक्षन्तु भवन्तः सर्व एव हि ॥ ११ ॥

ayaneṣu ca sarveṣu yathābhāgamavasthitāḥ
bhīṣmamevā'bhirakṣantu bhavantaḥ sarva eva hi

(11) Therefore, all of you, stationed in your respective positions, in every division, must guard Bhishma in particular by all means.

तस्य सञ्जनयन्हर्षं कुरुवृद्धः पितामहः।
सिंहनादं विनद्योच्चैः शङ्खं दध्मौ प्रतापवान् ॥ १२ ॥

tasya sañjanayanharṣaṁ kuruvṛddhaḥ pitāmahaḥ
siṁhanādaṁ vinadyoccaiḥ śaṅkhaṁ dadhmau pratāpavān

(12) Then the revered grandsire (Bhishma) the oldest of the Kauravas roaring like a lion, blew his conch in order to cheer up Duryodhana.

ततः शङ्खाश्च भेर्यश्च पणवानकगोमुखाः ।
सहसैवाभ्यहन्यन्त स शब्दस्तुमुलोऽभवत् ॥ १३ ॥

tataḥ śaṅkhāśca bheryaśca paṇavānakagomukhāḥ
sahasaivābhyahanyanta sa śabdastumulo'bhavat

(13) Then conches, kettledrums, tabors, drums and cow-horns blared forth all at once and the noise became tumultuous.

ततः श्वेतैर्हयैर्युक्ते महति स्यन्दने स्थितौ ।
माधवः पाण्डवश्चैव दिव्यौ शङ्खौ प्रदध्मतुः ॥ १४ ॥

tataḥ śvetairhayairyukte mahati syandane sthitau
mādhavaḥ pāṇḍvaścaiva divyau śaṅkhau pradadhmatuḥ

(14) Then seated in the magnificent chariot, yoked with white horses, Srī Kṛṣṇa as well as Arjuna blew their celestial conches.

पाञ्चजन्यं हृषीकेशो देवदत्तं धनञ्जयः ।
पौण्ड्रं दध्मौ महाशङ्खं भीमकर्मा वृकोदरः ॥ १५ ॥

pāñcajanyaṁ hṛṣīkeśo devadattaṁ dhanañjayaḥ
pauṇḍraṁ dadhmau mahāśaṅkhaṁ bhīmakarmā vṛkodaraḥ

(15) Srī Kṛṣṇa blew His conch named Panchajanya, and Arjuna blew his conch called Devadatta, while Bhima the doer of terrific deeds blew his mighty conch, Paundra.

अनन्तविजयं राजा कुन्तीपुत्रो युधिष्ठिरः ।
नकुलः सहदेवश्च सुघोषमणिपुष्पकौ ॥ १६ ॥

anantavijayaṁ rājā kuntīputro yudhiṣṭhiraḥ
nakulaḥ sahadevaśca sughoṣamaṇipuṣpakau

(16) The King Yudhisthira, the son of Kunti, blew his conch Anantavijaya and Nakula and Sahadeva blew their respective conches, the Sughosa and the Manipuspaka.

काश्यश्च परमेष्वासः शिखण्डी च महारथः ।
धृष्टद्युम्नो विराटश्च सात्यकिश्चापराजितः ॥ १७ ॥

kāśyaśca parameṣvāsaḥ śikhaṇḍīca mahārathaḥ
dhṛṣṭadyumno virāṭaśca sātyakiścā'parājitaḥ

द्रुपदो द्रौपदेयाश्च सर्वशः पृथिवीपते।
सौभद्रश्च महाबाहुः शङ्खान्दध्मुः पृथक् पृथक्॥ १८॥

drupado draupadeyāśca sarvaśaḥ pṛthivīpate
saubhadraśca mahābāhuḥ śaṅkhāndadhamuḥ pṛthak-pṛthak

(17, 18) The King of Kasi, an excellent archer; Sikhandi, the great chariot-warrior, Dhristadyumna and Virata and the invincible Satyaki, the King Drupada as well as the five sons of Draupadi and the mighty-armed Abhimanyu, the son of Subhadra, every one of them blew their respective conches.

स घोषो धार्तराष्ट्राणां हृदयानि व्यदारयत्।
नभश्च पृथिवीं चैव तुमुलो व्यनुनादयन्॥ १९॥

sa ghoṣo dhārṭarāṣṭrānaṁ hṛdayāni vyadārayat
nabhaśca pṛthivīṁ caiva tumulo vyanunādayan

(19) The tumultuous uproar has pierced the hearts of Dhritrashtra's sons resounding through the heaven and the earth.

अथ व्यवस्थितान्दृष्ट्वा धार्तराष्ट्रान् कपिध्वजः।
प्रवृत्ते शस्त्रसम्पाते धनुरुद्यम्य पाण्डवः॥ २०॥

atha vyavasthitāndṛṣtvā dhārtarāṣṭrānkapidhvajaḥ
pravṛtte śastrasampāte dhanurudyamya pāṇḍavaḥ

हृषीकेशं तदा वाक्यमिदमाह महीपते।

hṛṣīkeśaṁ tadā vākyamidamāha mahīpate

(20, 21) Then looking at the people of Dhritrashtra's sons, standing arrayed in battle and about to commence with their weapons; Arjuna, the son of Pandu, whose flag ensign was monkey, he lifted his bow and said the following words to the Lord of the earth.

अर्जुन उवाच

सेनयोरुभयोर्मध्ये रथं स्थापय मेऽच्युत॥ २१॥

senayorubhayormadhye rathaṁ sthāpaya me'acyuta

यावदेतान्निरीक्षेऽहं योद्धकामानवस्थितान्।
कैर्मया सह योद्धव्यमस्मिन्रणसमुद्यमे॥ २२॥

yāvadetānnirīkṣe'haṁ yoddhakāmān avasthitān
kairmayā saha yoddhavyamasmin raṇasamudyame

Arjuna said :

(21, 22) O'Achyuta (Srī Kṛṣṇa)! Please place my chariot between the two armies, so that I may see all those, who stand here desirous of war with whom I have to fight this battle.

योत्स्यमानानवेक्षेऽहं य एतेऽत्र समागताः।
धार्तराष्ट्रस्य दुर्बुद्धेर्युद्धे प्रियचिकीर्षवः॥ २३॥

yotsyamānān avekṣehaṁ ya ete'tra samāgatāḥ
dhārtarāṣṭrasya durbuddheryuddhe priyacikīrṣavaḥ

(23) I want to see those who are assembled here with an intent to fight and are desirous to please in battle, the evil minded son of Dhritrashtra (Duryodhana).

संजय उवाच

एवमुक्तो हृषीकेशो गुडाकेशेन भारत।
सेनयोरुभयोर्मध्ये स्थापयित्वा रथोत्तमम्॥ २४॥

evamukto hṛṣīkeśo guḍākeśena bhārata
senayorubhayormadhye sthāpayitvā rathottamam

भीष्मद्रोणप्रमुखतः सर्वेषां च महीक्षिताम्।
उवाच पार्थ पश्यैतान् समवेतान्कुरूनिति॥ २५॥

bhīṣmadroṇapramukhataḥ sarveṣāṁ ca mahīkṣitām
uvāca pārtha paśyaitān samavetānkurūniti

Sanjaya said :

(24, 25) O'descendant of Bharata (Dhritrashtra), thus addressed by Gudakesa (Arjuna), Hrishikesha (Srī Kṛṣṇa) having placed the magnificent chariot in the middle of the two armies; in front of Bhisma and Drona and all the other kings said, "O'Arjuna, behold these Kurus assembled here."

तत्रापश्यत्स्थितान्पार्थः पितॄनथ पितामहान्।

tatrā'paśyat sthitānpārthaḥ pitṛnatha pitāmahān

आचार्यान्मातुलान्भ्रातॄन्पुत्रान्पौत्रान्सखींस्तथा ॥ २६ ॥
श्वसुरान्सुहृदश्चैव सेनयोरुभयोरपि।

ācaryān mātulān bhrātṝn putrān pautrān sakhīnstathā
śvasurān suhṛdaścaiva senayorubhayorapi

(26) There, Arjuna beholds, stationed between both the armies; his uncles, granduncles, teachers, maternal uncles, brothers, cousins, sons, grandsons, fathers-in-law and friends as well.

तान्समीक्ष्य स कौन्तेयः सर्वान्बन्धूनवस्थितान्॥ २७ ॥
कृपया परयाविष्टो विषीदन्निदमब्रवीत्।

tān samīkṣya sa kaunteyaḥ sarvān bandhūnavasthitān
kṛpayā parayāviṣṭo viṣīdannidamabravīt

(27) Looking at all the kinsmen, thus assembled there, Arjuna feels overwhelmed with deep compassion and speaks these words.

अर्जुन उवाच

दृष्ट्वेमं स्वजनं कृष्ण युयुत्सुं समुपस्थितम्॥ २८ ॥

dṛṣṭvemaṁ svajanaṁ kṛṣṇa yuyutsuṁ samupasthitam

सीदन्ति मम गात्राणि मुखं च परिशुष्यति।
वेपथुश्च शरीरे मे रोमहर्षश्च जायते॥ २९ ॥

sīdanti mama gātrāṇi mukhaṁ ca pariśuṣyati
vepathuśca śarīre me romaharṣaśca jāyate

गाण्डीवं स्त्रंसते हस्तात्त्वक्चैव परिदह्यते।
न च शक्नोम्यवस्थातुं भ्रमतीव च मे मनः॥ ३० ॥

gāṇḍīvaṁ sraṅsate hastāt tvakcaiva paridahyate
na ca śaknomyavasthātuṁ bhramatīva ca me manaḥ

Arjuna said :

(28, 29, 30) O'Kṛṣṇa, at the sight of these kinsmen, thus arrayed here, eager for battle, my limbs have become feeble and my mouth is parched, my whole body quivers and my hair stand on end. The Gandiva is slipping from my hands and my skin is burning all over. I am not able to stand firmly and my mind seems to reel.

Commentary—After having a close inspection of the armies, Arjuna feels overwhelmed with deep sorrow, pain, anxiety, doubt and insecurity. He feels very unsteady, confused, agitated, bewildered and unable to control his mind and body. These are typical symptoms of an individual, who is caught in the web of blind attachment, self-doubt, anger and self-pity. The inner conflict does reflect in the physical body. Any turmoil which occurs in thinking faculty, immediately involves the nervous system and expresses itself in physical body, in the form of irregular heart beat, dryness of salivary glands and blurred vision. The deep feeling of anxiety creates such an imbalance in the body that the person loses his ability to examine anything, clearly and intelligently.

निमित्तानि च पश्यामि विपरीतानि केशव।
न च श्रेयोऽनुपश्यामि हत्वा स्वजनमाहवे॥ ३१॥

nimittāni ca paśyāmi viparītāni kesava
na ca śreyo'nupaśyāmi hatvā svajanamāhave

(31) And I see very inauspicious omens, O'Kesava (Srī Kṛṣṇa); I do not perceive any good in killing my kinsmen in the battle.

न काङ्क्षे विजयं कृष्ण न च राज्यं सुखानि च।
किं नो राज्येन गोविन्द किं भोगैर्जीवितेन वा॥ ३२॥

na kāṅkṣe vijayaṁ kṛṣṇa na ca rājyaṁ sukhāni ca
kiṁ no rājyena govinda kiṁ bhogairjīvitena vā

(32) O'Kṛṣṇa, I do not desire any victory, nor kingdom, nor pleasures. What is the use of kingdom to us, O'Govinda, or the luxuries or even life itself.

येषामर्थे काङ्क्षितं नो राज्यं भोगाः सुखानि च।
त इमेऽवस्थिता युद्धे प्राणांस्त्यक्त्वा धनानि च॥ ३३॥

yeṣāmarthe kāṅkṣitaṁ no rājyaṁ bhogāḥ sukhāni ca
ta ime'vasthitā yuddhe prāṇāṅ styaktvā dhanāni ca

(33) Those, for whose sake we desire kingdom, enjoyments and pleasures, are standing poised for battle and ready to give up their lives and wealth.

आचार्याः पितरः पुत्रास्तथैव च पितामहाः ।
मातुलाः श्वशुराः पौत्राः श्यालाः सम्बन्धिनस्तथा ॥ ३४ ॥

ācāryāḥ pitaraḥ putrāstathaiva ca pitāmahāḥ
mātulāḥ śvaśurāḥ pautrāḥ śyālāḥ sambandhinastathā

(34) The teachers, uncles, sons and grandfathers, maternal uncles, fathers-in-law, grandsons, brothers-in-law, and other relatives as well.

एतान्न हन्तुमिच्छामि घ्नतोऽपि मधुसूदन ।
अपि त्रैलोक्यराज्यस्य हेतोः किं नु महीकृते ॥ ३५ ॥

etānna hantumicchāmi ghnato'pi madhusūdana
api trailokyarājyasya hetoḥ kim nu mahīkṛte

(35) These, I do not want to kill, even though they may kill me, O' Slayer of Madhu (Kṛṣṇa); even for the sovereignty of the three worlds—how then just for the sake of the earthly lordship?

निहत्य धार्तराष्ट्रान्नः का प्रीतिः स्याज्जनार्दन ।
पापमेवाश्रयेदस्मान् हत्वैतानाततायिनः ॥ ३६ ॥

nihatya dhārtarāṣṭrān naḥ kā prītiḥ syājjanārdana
pāpamevāśrayed asmān hatvaitānātatāyinaḥ

(36) By killing the sons of Dhritrashtra, what pleasure can be ours, O'Kṛṣṇa? Only the sin will accrue to us by slaying these desperadoes.

तस्मान्नार्हा वयं हन्तुं धार्तराष्ट्रान् स्वबान्धवान् ।
स्वजनं हि कथं हत्वा सुखिनः स्याम माधव ॥ ३७ ॥

tasmān nārhā vayaṁ hantuṁ dhārtarāṣṭrān svabāndhavān
svajanaṁ hi kathaṁ hatvā sukhinaḥ syāma mādhava

(37) Therefore, it is not appropriate for us to kill our relatives, the sons of Dhritrashtra. For, if we kill our kinsmen, how can we be happy, O'Madhva (Kṛṣṇa)?

यद्यप्येते न पश्यन्ति लोभोपहतचेतसः ।
कुलक्षयकृतं दोषं मित्रद्रोहे च पातकम् ॥ ३८ ॥

yadyapyete na paśyanti lobhopahatacetasaḥ
kulakṣayakṛtaṁ doṣaṁ mitradrohe ca pātakam

कथं न ज्ञेयमस्माभिः पापादस्मान्निवर्तितुम्।
कुलक्षयकृतं दोषं प्रपश्यद्भिर्जनार्दन॥ ३९॥

kathaṁ na jñeyamasmābhiḥ pāpādasmān nivartitum
kulkṣayakṛtaṁ doṣaṁ prapaśyadbhir janārdana

(38, 39) Although these people, whose minds are blinded by greed, do not perceive evil in the destruction of their own race, and the sin, in treachery to friends; why shouldn't we have the wisdom to turn away from this crime, we can clearly see the sin which is involved in the destruction of the family, O'Janardhana (Kṛṣṇa)?

Commentary—Arjuna continues speaking in utter depression and agony. His deep feeling of anxiety, helplessness and insecurity has been portrayed in many words. He tells Srī Kṛṣṇa that he is perceiving the omens of catastrophe and misfortune all around. It is indeed a very natural response of the person who is in a stressful situation. Since the mind, the physical body and the material world around are very closely interconnected, people do experience their thoughts and feelings reflected in nature. The material world, as it appears, is indeed a projection of senses. Human mind has the phenomenal capability to assume any form, of any size, of anything in the field of cosmic energy. A person can construct the mental image of a spider, an owl, a cat, a thunderstorm, fire, and the striking stars against one another. He can extend his imagination in any direction to any extent knowingly and unknowingly. Anything which is seen in space or experienced in space and time, is indeed the orchestration of the senses of perception. It is definitely through the trick of senses that every projection of the mind becomes palpable, touchable, visible, and audible.

The human mind and the material world definitely work in close cooperation with each other. Every single event which takes place in the universe, initially originates in the mind and then it becomes materialized in the physical world. Every person lives in a world of his own making and is able to infer the existence of things and events from his own sensory impressions of the world. If a person feels disturbed inside, he perceives everything in the world to be unsettled, fearful and inauspicious. The individual who feels restless and disturbed; he surely perceives all types of disturbances in nature, and the one who is at peace within himself, he experiences peace everywhere. Similarly, Arjuna has not seen so far any evil omens, while he has been preparing for war, but now because of his depressed mood he has started seeing all kinds of inauspicious omens in nature. The twilight looks to him like the storm of fire, dreadful and devouring. He perceives the appearance of inauspicious stars, striking against each other. In the words of Swami Ram Sukhdas, "Whatever Arjuna is regarding as omens are not omens in reality. These are the defects of his senses, mind and intellect."

When the individual is depressed and agitated, his mind becomes deluded, and he gives very irrational and irrelevant proposals. Srī Kṛṣṇa knows very well that all the arguments of Arjuna are superficial. His arguments against fighting are based upon his blind attachment and the egoistic deluded state of his mind; wherein he has completely forgotten the cherished purpose of waging a righteous war. The war he has to wage is not for any personal loss or gain, it is for the re-establishment of righteousness and for the welfare of the entire mankind. In the words of Swami Rama, "When one is attached, he isolates himself from the whole and thus deprives himself from listening to the voice of his conscience and to his preceptors. The faculty of discrimination does not then function, and one rationalizes to justify his emotional state". Srī Kṛṣṇa knows that Arjuna has to analyze the present situation by rising above his personal bonds of attachments. It is indeed the illusory attachment to the world which creates emotional conflict and bondage. A deluded and confused person who is disintegrated, sometimes makes lofty statements according to his point of view, which are generally self-contradictory and do reflect his disintegrated and frustrated state of mind. The suggestions of such an individual carry no importance because his words come only from his lips and not from the depth of his discriminating faculty. Arjuna is definitely slipping from his most cherished ideals of a warrior because of his delusions and misconceptions. He has been repeating over and over again the same fearful negative images and ideas which simply perpetuate the state of depression and withdrawal. He has surely enclosed himself in the vicious circle of self-suggestions, self-pity, and self-defence.

कुलक्षये प्रणश्यन्ति कुलधर्माः सनातनाः ।
धर्मे नष्टे कुलं कृत्स्नमधर्मोऽभिभवत्युत ॥ ४० ॥

kulakṣaye praṇaśyanti kuladharmāḥ sanātanāḥ
dharme naṣṭe kulaṁ kṛtsnamadharmo'bhibhavatyuta

(40) With the destruction of a family, the ancient religious traditions are destroyed; with the disappearance of the religious traditions, the unrighteousness takes hold of the entire family.

अधर्माभिभवात्कृष्ण प्रदुष्यन्ति कुलस्त्रियः ।
स्त्रीषु दुष्टासु वार्ष्णेय जायते वर्णसंकरः ॥ ४१ ॥

adharmābhibhavāt kṛṣṇa praduṣyanti kulastriyaḥ
strīṣu duṣṭāsu vārṣṇeya jāyate varṇasaṅkaraḥ

(41) With the prevalence of unrighteousness, O'Kṛṣṇa, the women of the family become corrupt; when the women become corrupt, O'Varsneya (Kṛṣṇa) there arise the intermixture of castes.

संकरो नरकायैव कुलघ्नानां कुलस्य च ।
पतन्ति पितरो ह्येषां लुप्तपिण्डोदकक्रियाः ॥ ४२ ॥

saṅkaro narakāyaiva kulaghnānāṁ kulasya ca
patanti pitaro hyeṣāṁ luptapiṇḍodakakriyāḥ

(42) The confusion of castes leads to hell the entire clan itself and its destroyers; for the spirits of the ancestors fall, deprived of their offerings of rice and water.

दोषैरेतैः कुलघ्नानां वर्णसङ्करकारकैः ।
उत्साद्यन्ते जातिधर्माः कुलधर्माश्च शाश्वताः ॥ ४३ ॥

doṣaireteiḥ kulaghnānāṁ varṇasaṅkarakārakaiḥ
utsādyante jātidharmāḥ kuladharmāś ca śāśvatāḥ

(43) By these evil deeds of the destroyers of the family which create confusion of Varnas, the ancient laws of the caste and family are destroyed.

उत्सन्नकुलधर्माणां मनुष्याणां जनार्दन।
नरकेऽनियतं वासो भवतीत्यनुशुश्रुम॥ ४४॥

utsannakuladharmāṇāṁ manuṣyāṇāṁ janārdana
narake'niyataṁ vāso bhavatītyanuśuśruma

(44) For those men, in whose families, the ancient religious traditions are destroyed, a place in hell is ordained, O' Kṛṣṇa, we have heard it so.

अहो बत महत्पापं कर्तुं व्यवसिता वयम्।
यद्राज्यसुखलोभेन हन्तुं स्वजनमुद्यताः॥ ४५॥

aho bata mahat pāpaṁ kartuṁ vyavasitā vayam
yadrājyasukhalobhena hantuṁ svajanamudyatāḥ

(45) Alas! We have resolved to commit a great sin in which we are prepared to kill our own kinsmen, merely out of our desire for sovereignty and enjoyments.

यदि मामप्रतीकारमशस्त्रं शस्त्रपाणयः।
धार्तराष्ट्रा रणे हन्युस्तन्मे क्षेमतरं भवेत्॥ ४६॥

yadi māmpratīkāramaśastraṁ śastrapāṇayaḥ
dhāratarāṣṭrā raṇe hanyus tanme kṣemataraṁ bhavet

(46) It will be better for me if the well-armed sons of Dhritrashtra do kill me in the battle, while I am unarmed and unresisting.

Commentary—Arjuna is literally grieving and expressing his deep sorrow at the painful memories of past and at the coming calamities of the future. The moment he finishes one statement, he brings up another in support of the previous one. It is indeed a fact, that when the individual contemplates upon the past continuously, he interferes with the normal flow of his present life. The memories of his past do create a blockade and distort the present. Anybody who carries the past on his shoulders for too long, he definitely becomes depressed and disintegrated. Arjuna knows very well that the opponents are the proclaimed desperadoes; and they definitely deserve punishment, but unfortunately the felons are his own kith and kin. A stream of endless thoughts, images, catastrophes are passing through his mind. He is making endless speculations about future and endless reconstructions over the painful memories of past. He feels absolutely trapped in the unfortunate circumstances. In the past, a war like this never seemed to be a big challenge to Arjuna. He has been the victorious hero of many terrible battles. The present situation has become challenging for him because of his strong bonds of attachment for his family and friends. His blind attachment for the elders of his family and teachers has bewildered his understanding, and overshadowed his spirit of duty.

In the words of Shri Vinobaji, "When a man with a sense of duty is caught in illusion, even then, he cannot bear to face the naked fact of his lapse from duty. He usually covers it up with an enquiry into principles". All the statements given by Arjuna so far do support the code of conduct from the ancient scriptures, and it has been for that reason only that the war has become mandatory. The major reason to wage the war has been to re-establish the codes of ethics and righteousness for the well-being of the society. The downfall of the society has already started with the selfish attitude of Dhritrashtra and his son Duryodhana. When the ruler of a country becomes selfish and deluded, selfishness spreads throughout the empire. When the government is corrupt, the corruption spreads throughout the kingdom. In some previous verses Arjuna himself has called Duryodhana, *durbudhie*—means the one with deluded understanding. Arjuna surely feels very angry at the insensitive attitude of his elders and teachers—but the dilemma, which he is confronting is that he is still very attached to them. Arjuna's objection to fighting is due to his over-attachment to his kith and kin. All his arguments are self-contradictory because he is speaking in a state of confusion and deep depression. Deep down in his heart Arjuna is well aware of the chaos in the country and knows very well that his relatives and their allies are insensitive and they definitely deserve to be punished but he does not have the inner integrity to accept the truth. In the previous conversation with Srī Kṛṣṇa, he himself has called them desperadoes and vicious minded people. According to Vasistha-smriti and Manu-smriti there is no sin in killing a desperado. A felon or a desperado is the one who sets fire, who poisons to kill somebody, who seizes someone's wealth, who commits a murder, who usurps a kingdom by treachery and the one who insults, kidnaps and abducts a woman. In the state of utter depression and delusion Arjuna has been overlooking the disappearance of ethical values in the community. He has completely forgotten the purpose of a righteous war which has become mandatory. A change in social structure with a revived concept of morality and ethics has become necessary for the healthy and sound functioning of society.

Srī Kṛṣṇa remains silent throughout the long lecture of escapism given by Arjuna. He doesn't show any sign of appreciation, sympathy or criticism at all. Srī Kṛṣṇa knows very well that Arjuna is speaking in a state of utter confusion and depression. Arjuna has been quoting the words of social ethics from scriptures and the most cherished sermons of morality; while totally ignoring his own perception of truth and *swadharma.* He has been overlooking the fact, that the battle he is about to fight is being waged for the protection of justice, Dharma, virtue, ethics and morality which demands a lot of personal sacrifice from him. In the words of Dr. S. Radhakrishnan, "The establishment of the Kingdom of God on earth is a cooperative enterprise between God and man. Man is a co-sharer in the work of creation."

संजय उवाच

एवमुक्त्वार्जुनः सङ्ख्ये रथोपस्थ उपाविशत्।
विसृज्य सशरं चापं शोकसंविग्नमानसः ॥ ४७ ॥

evamuktvārjunaḥ saṅkhye rathopastha upāviśat
visṛjya saśaraṁ cāpaṁ śokasaṁvignamānasaḥ

Sanjaya said :

(47) Having spoken thus, in the middle of the battlefield, Arjuna puts away his bow and arrows and sinks down on the seat of his chariot, with his mind overwhelmed with grief.

Commentary—Sanjaya tells King Dhritrashtra that Arjuna is overwhelmed with grief and is feeling very miserable. He has kept aside his bow and arrows and has decided to sit quietly in the back of his chariot. Sanjaya emphasizes the word *sokasamvigna manasah,* that is, with a mind distressed with deep pain and sorrow. This feeling of loneliness, helplessness, depression, disintegration, mental agony and confusion is called *vishad.* It is in this state of mental agony and mental crisis when a person turns inward for help. The unification of the individual soul with the Supreme-soul in moments of deep depression is called *vishad-yoga.*

Depression and despondency is the dejected and confused state of mind when everything in life appears to be unsettled and disintegrated. In the moments of dejection when the individual feels lonely and helpless, he is persuaded from within to seek refuge in the realm of the Indweller. The experience of unity with the indwelling divinity brings transformation. It clears the mind from all types of emotional conflicts and restores the individual-self to the clarity of illuminated understanding and enlightenment. When the person enters into the benevolence of the over-self; the veil of egocentric thoughts disperses and disseminates momentarily. The individual becomes receptive to the voice of the Supreme Indweller and the grace of the Lord flows from within. This is indeed the most essential step for any type of awakening in life. In the words of Dr. S. Radhakrishnan, "No one is so close to God as oneself, and to get at Him we require only an ardent heart, a pure intention. Arjuna stands naked and alone without intermediaries opposite his God. There is perpetual communion between the God and man, the dialogue proceeds until complete harmony of purpose is reached". It is a fact that when the dejected individual cries out for help, from the depth of his heart, from the purity of his heart; then guidance and help is experienced from within, from the God in us. Any painful, serious and traumatic experience of life brings the internal guidance which helps the individual to release the painful past and move on in life with a renewed concept of truth. It is like making progress from one stage to another, from darkness to light, from less awareness to increased awareness. The individual has to experience the depth of depression in order to experience the heights of reality. He has to pass through the self created egocentric boundaries of 'I and Mine' in order to comprehend the bliss of his immortal Self. It is in the state of *vishad* when a person makes contacts with the Supreme-Self; it is in the state of *vishad,* when a person is remade from within. As a matter of fact *vishad* is indeed a blessing in disguise and the Lord's unique way of preparing the individual for inner enlightenment.

ॐ तत्सदिति श्रीमद्भगवद्गीतासूपनिषत्सु ब्रह्मविद्यायां
योगशास्त्रे श्रीकृष्णार्जुनसंवादेऽर्जुनविषाद-
योगो नाम प्रथमोऽध्यायः ॥ १ ॥

'Aum' tatṣaditi Srīmadbhagawadgeetā sūpaniṣatsu
brahmavidyāyām yogaśāstre Śrīkṛṣṇārjunasamvāde-
Arjuna viṣādayogo nāma prathamo'dhyāyaḥ

'AUM TAT SAT'—Thus, in the Upanishad of the glorious Bhagawad Geeta, the science of the Brahman (Absolute) the scripture of yoga, the dialogue between Srī Kṛṣṇa and Arjuna—thus, ends the chapter one entitled *'Viṣād-yoga'*.

इति श्रीमद्भगवद्गीतासु प्रथमोऽध्यायः ॥ १ ॥

Chapter Two

THE SĀMKHYA-YOGA

THE YOGA OF THE TRANSCENDENTAL KNOWLEDGE

संजय उवाच

तं तथा कृपयाविष्टमश्रुपूर्णाकुलेक्षणम्।

विषीदन्तमिदं वाक्यमुवाच मधुसूदनः ॥ १ ॥

taṁ tathā kṛpayāviṣṭamaśrupūrṇākulekṣaṇam

viṣīdantamidaṁ vākyamuvāca madhusūdanaḥ

Sanjaya said :

(1) To him, who was thus overwhelmed with pity, whose eyes were filled with tears and was agitated, Madhusudana (Śrī Kṛṣṇa) spoke these words.

Commentary—This chapter opens with the words of Sanjaya, who describes Arjuna's depressed, deluded and discouraged state of mind. Arjuna recoils from his assigned duty and feels totally impoverished within. He feels overwhelmed with self-pity and sorrow. Self-pity is the wounded cry of a heart which is ruled by fear and confusion. It is an expression of emotional weakness, which generally perpetuates the situation and the individual ends up making a fool of himself. The dramatization of self-pity is an immature and emotional display of the false identification. The individual draws upon himself the veils of various delusions and feels imprisoned within his own-self. He becomes preoccupied with trivial matters which appear to be very valid and important to him but in reality are not. Arjuna, a well-known archer, has also been a great devotee of the Lord. Śrī Kṛṣṇa has always loved and respected Arjuna for his bravery, valour, enthusiasm, loving devotion and purity of heart. He has expected some of this emotional turmoil from Arjuna and that is why the morning, when the war was about to start, Srī Kṛṣṇa has advised the latter to purify himself by meditating on the power of the goddess Durga. The goddess had blessed Arjuna and had also reassured him about his victory in these words : "O'son of Kunti, you will surely conquer your enemies, because you have Vasudeva Himself to help you; the victory is certain, wherever Vasudeva Kṛṣṇa is". The Lord's intention as expressed through the revelation of the goddess Durga, was intended to enlighten Arjuna about his real identity, as a fragment of the Divine Himself. Srī Kṛṣṇa has wanted Arjuna to become united in Yoga and do realize his duty as a co-worker in the re-establishment of Dharma (righteousness) on earth. Besides, every time life renews itself, it is surely from the unification with the inner resources and with the grace of the Divine; but unfortunately, Arjuna has failed to perceive the entire message of his meditative worship.

श्रीभगवानुवाच

कुतस्त्वा कश्मलमिदं विषमे समुपस्थितम्।
अनार्यजुष्टमस्वर्ग्यमकीर्तिकरमर्जुन ॥ २ ॥

kutastvā kaśmalamidaṁ viṣame samupasthitam
anāryajuṣṭamasvargyamakīrtikaramarjuna

The Blessed Lord said :

(2) From where has come to you this despondency, O'Arjuna in this hour of crisis? It is unfit for a noble man and is indeed very disgraceful. It neither leads to heaven nor to any worldly fame and glory.

क्लैब्यं मा स्म गमः पार्थ नैतत्त्वय्युपपद्यते।
क्षुद्रं हृदयदौर्बल्यं त्यक्त्वोत्तिष्ठ परन्तप॥ ३ ॥

klaibyaṁ mā sma gamaḥ pārtha naitat tvayyupapadyate
kṣudraṁ hṛdayadaurbalyaṁ tyaktvottiṣṭha parantapa

(3) Yield not to this unmanliness, O'Arjuna. It does not befit you. Shake off this petty faint heartedness and stand up, O'Scorcher of the enemies.

Commentary—In these two verses Srī Kṛṣṇa expresses his great surprise at the unusual behaviour of Arjuna, whom he had known for so many years. He wonders at Arjuna's deviation from his heroic temperament and tells him that such cowardliness is shunned by the noble men of cherished values. He uses three strong words in one line such as *anāryajuṣṭam, asvargyam* and *akīrtikaram,* and reminds Arjuna about the three important goals of life—benediction, pleasures of heaven and the worldly name and glory. He warns the hero that his delusion is going to deprive him of all kinds of happiness on earth and also in heaven.

It is the inner integrity and wisdom which helps the individual to enjoy life on earth and in the life hereafter. The person who becomes overwhelmed by infatuation and faint heartedness is indeed a loser in all respects. A disintegrated person staggers between earthly pleasures and also the comforts of the heaven. The Vedas have declared *nai Atman balheen labhya*—the person who lacks faith in God and in his own-self becomes a poor victim of distractions and delusions. A dissipated mind lacks discrimination and will power. A person who is weak and feeble can never attain any success in worldly life as well as in the life hereafter. Inner integrity, courage, fearlessness, and self-confidence are the keys; these open the door of peace and fulfilment in life. Anyone who lacks inner integrity, he cannot cultivate the ability to contemplate and the one who cannot contemplate and reflect cannot develop the discriminating ability of choosing between the right and wrong. Srī Kṛṣṇa calls Arjuna, *anārya* means undeserving to be called a cultured and civilized person as an Arya (refined man of decency). By addressing Arjuna with the word *anārya*, Srī Kṛṣṇa reminds him of his great heritage. He points out to Arjuna's heroic nature and reminds him that he has been raised as an Aryan fighter to help and protect the people of the community. An Arya means a cultured, virtuous and educated person who respects and upholds the most cherished values of *swadharma*. The Aryans developed a most civilized culture that has excelled in the learning of the Vedas. The language and script of the Aryans has been Sanskrit and their literature has been very rich in science, art, commerce, mathematics, geometry, biology, astronomy, sociology and military science. Aryans have been highly respected for their nobility, generosity, heroism, and excellence in almost every field of knowledge.

In these verses Srī Kṛṣṇa is trying to enlighten Arjuna about his true identity. He addresses Arjuna by several different names in order to remind him of his great heritage, strength and valour. He points out to the heroic innate nature of Arjuna, who has been raised as an Aryan fighter in order to help and protect the community. He wants Arjuna to integrate his scattered energy and be aware of his heroism so that he can prepare himself to the demands of the occasion. Srī Kṛṣṇa out of his love for Arjuna addresses him as Partha, reminding him of his heroic mother Pritha, the queen Kunti who has been encouraging Arjuna to re-establish his claims over the lost empire, Indraprastha. The word Partha conveys Srī Kṛṣṇa's intimacy for His dear friend Arjuna and reminds him that such cowardliness does not behove the great hero. While reminding Arjuna of his great heroism, Srī Kṛṣṇa addresses him as *parantapa,* which means the scorcher of the enemies. Srī Kṛṣṇa is trying to pull Arjuna from his deep slumber of ignorance and forgetfulness, by stimulating his various levels of consciousness. He persuades him to integrate his scattered feelings towards the realization of his duty as an Aryan hero, who has always respected and adored chivalry. He tells Arjuna that the feeling of pity for others in war is another form of self-indulgence and very shameful for a warrior. The involvement in self-pity is indeed the most ignoble and disgraceful trait for an Aryan soldier. Srī Kṛṣṇa reminds Arjuna that he is indeed indestructible, eternal and infinite in his essential nature, and a great Aryan warrior in his relative nature. He ignores all the arguments presented by Arjuna and simply orders him to arise, awake and get ready for the battle, for which he has been preparing for many years.

अर्जुन उवाच

कथं भीष्ममहं सङ्ख्ये द्रोणं च मधुसूदन।
इषुभिः प्रतियोत्स्यामि पूजार्हावरिसूदन ॥ ४ ॥

kathaṁ bhīṣmamahaṁ saṅkhye droṇaṁ ca madhusūdana
iṣubhiḥ pratiyotsyāmi pūjārhāvarisūdana

Arjuna said :

(4) O'Kṛṣṇa, how can I fight in the battle with arrows against Bhishma and Drona? They are worthy of my respect and reverence, O'destroyer of the foes.

गुरूनहत्वा हि महानुभावान् श्रेयो भोक्तुं भैक्ष्यमपीह लोके।
हत्वार्थकामांस्तु गुरूनिहैव भुञ्जीय भोगान् रुधिरप्रदिग्धान्॥ ५ ॥

gurūnahatvā hi mahānubhāvān
śreyo bhoktuṁ bhaikṣyamapīḥ loke
hatvārthakāmāṅstu gurūnihaiva
bhuṇjīya bhogān rudhirapradigdhān

(5) It is better to live on alms in this world than to slay these venerable teachers, because even after killing them we will enjoy only bloodstained wealth, pleasure and worldly enjoyment.

न चैतद्विद्मः कतरन्नो गरीयो यद्वा जयेम यदि वा नो जयेयुः।
यानेव हत्वा न जिजीविषामस्तेऽवस्थिताः प्रमुखे धार्तराष्ट्राः॥ ६ ॥

na caitadvidmaḥ kataranno garīyo yadvā jayema yadi vā no jayeyuḥ
yāneva hatvā na jijīviṣāmaste'vasthitāḥ pramukhe dhārtarāṣṭrāḥ

(6) We do not know which is better, whether we should conquer them or they should conquer us. The sons of Dhritarastra, by killing whom we don't even wish to live, are arrayed against us.

कार्पण्यदोषोपहतस्वभावः पृच्छामि त्वां धर्मसम्मूढचेताः।
यच्छ्रेयः स्यान्निश्चितं ब्रूहि तन्मे शिष्यस्तेऽहं शाधि मां त्वां प्रपन्नम्॥ ७ ॥

kārpaṇyadoṣopahatasvabhāvaḥ
pṛcchāmi tvāṁ dharmasammūḍhacetāḥ
yacchreyaḥ syānniścitaṁ brūhi tanme
śiṣyaste'haṁ śādhi māṁ tvāṁ prapannam

(7) My heart is overpowered by the weakness of pity and my mind is confused about my duty; I request Thee, to tell me for certain, which is decidedly good for me. I am your disciple. Teach me, who has taken refuge in You.

न हि प्रपश्यामि ममापनुद्याद् यच्छोकमुच्छोषणमिन्द्रियाणाम्।
अवाप्य भूमावसपत्नमृद्धं राज्यं सुराणामपि चाधिपत्यम्॥ ८ ॥

na hi prapaśyāmi mamāpanudyād
yacchokamucchoṣaṇamindriyāṇām
avāpya bhūmāvasapatnamṛddhaṁ rājyaṁ
surāṇāmapi cādhipatyam

(8) I don't see any means, that can dispel this grief which is drying up my senses; even if I attain undisputed sovereignty and an affluent kingdom on this earth or even the Lordship over the gods.

Commentary—In answer to Srī Kṛṣṇa's command, Arjuna approaches Him in words of self-defence. He tells Srī Kṛṣṇa that he is not trying to escape from the situation but definitely he finds it very difficult to wage a war against his own kinsmen. By using the word *iṣubhiḥ* Arjuna is trying to prove his point that Bhisma and Drona are definitely worthy to be worshipped with flowers and not with arrows. They are both honourable. He uses the word *mahānubhāvān,* for the teachers like Dronacharya, Kripacharya and other noble elders arrayed in the army of Duryodhana. Arjuna, who has always followed very high ethics in his life, surely finds it very inappropriate to wage a war against his teachers and the respectable elders of the Kuru family. He attempts to speak in support of his refusal and tries to justify his point of view. Among the ancient Vedic tradition, the Guru-disciple relationship has always been very special and respectable. A Guru helps the aspirant to explore the best of his abilities. As the pot maker moulds the clay into a vessel of utility, as the goldsmith moulds the chunk of gold into some gold ornaments of beauty and appreciation, similarly the Guru with his teachings moulds the personality of his students. So when Arjuna thinks about his revered teacher Dronacharya, who has granted him the boon of excelling in military science, he definitely feels helpless in fighting against him. He does not understand why the elders should be killed although in the depth of his heart he knows that they have been supporting an unjust cause. He fully understands that according to the ethical code of sacred books, the Guru who supports unrighteousness and unjust activities, deserves to be abandoned. Bhisma and Drona both, in spite of their being aware of the fact that they have been fighting for the unjust cause, have still decided to support Duryodhana. So both of them had lost their venerability and adorability. Arjuna has known his duty all along as a member of the warrior class but his attachment has clouded his vision. He has been ignoring the fact, that his sympathy and compassion towards Kauravas' would definitely mean the victory of *adharma* (unrighteousness), injustice and terrorism. On the other hand, the victory of the Pandavas will surely bless the kingdom with a legitimate righteous ruler who will bring peace and prosperity to the Kuru dynasty as well as to the entire nation. Arjuna knows the truth, but he is very confused and has wrapped himself in the middle of the two extremes.

These verses indicate the feeling of helplessness of the great archer of all time. The expression *kārpaṇyadoṣopahata-svabhāvaḥ* indicates the truth that Arjuna is aware of his delusion and faint heartedness. He admits his weakness. *Kārpaṇya* literally means spiritual poverty and the lack of intuitive wisdom. Arjuna who wants to find a solution for his problem, cries for help. He accepts Srī Kṛṣṇa as his spiritual Guru and requests Him for guidance. He says "tell me that which is decidedly good for me—I am your disciple and totally surrendered to you. Please teach me and guide me into my well being". Arjuna realizes his confusion and also understands that his conflict is very serious. He feels that he needs some help which will integrate him within and will make him receptive to comprehensive consciousness. The acceptance and the acknowledgment of one's confusion and bewilderment is in itself the most important step taken by the disciple, who requests for help and is ready to listen. This by itself opens the doorway towards self-enlightenment. A complete surrender from the disciple leaves a great responsibility on the master. Surrender is an individual's request for help and assistance to the awakened. In the words of Maharsi Mahesh Yogi, "When Arjuna surrenders as a disciple, the Lord accepts him and it is from this point that Srī Kṛṣṇa's teaching commences. Faith makes the student a good assimilator of knowledge. Devotion sets him free from resistance, and that influences the heart of the master." A total surrender from the disciple leads towards the total acceptance from the master and eventually blossoms into perfect alignment with the Supreme-self. Self-surrender is the bridge that helps the disciple to move across the ocean of egocentric thoughts. The complete surrender connects the individual to the source of his being, and makes him receptive to the voice of *swadharma*.

संजय उवाच

एवमुक्त्वा हृषीकेशं गुडाकेशः परन्तप।
न योत्स्य इति गोविन्दमुक्त्वा तूष्णीं बभूव ह ॥ ९ ॥

evamuktvā hṛṣīkeśaṁ guḍākeśaḥ parantapa
na yotsya iti govindamuktvā tūṣṇīṁ babhūva ha

Sanjaya said :

(9) Having thus spoken to Srī Kṛṣṇa, Arjuna—the conqueror of sleep and the destroyer of foes—said "I will not fight" and became silent.

तमुवाच हृषीकेशः प्रहसन्निव भारत।
सेनयोरुभयोर्मध्ये विषीदन्तमिदं वचः ॥ १० ॥

tamuvāca hṛṣīkeśaḥ prahasanniva bhārata
senayorubhayor madhye viṣīdantamidaṁ vacaḥ

(10) Then, O'Dhritarastra, to him who was despondent in the midst of the two armies, Srī Kṛṣṇa spoke the following words with a smile on His face.

Commentary—While listening to the self-contradictory statements of Arjuna, a wave of friendly smile runs across the face of Srī Kṛṣṇa. He gives the smile of a concerned, well-wishing friend and teacher. Srī Kṛṣṇa perceives easily that Arjuna is indeed confused and trapped in a great turmoil but he doesn't want to admit it. On one hand Arjuna cries for help and on the other, without waiting for Srī Kṛṣṇa's advice, he quickly declares his decision : "I'll not fight" and becomes silent. This is a well-known example of the person who feels trapped in conflicting emotions and the web of multiple identities. Srī Kṛṣṇa knows very well that Arjuna has created the problem for himself and he has to solve it. He also knows that Arjuna has not been paying any attention to the voice of his own inner Self. He has been creating self-contradictory images and surely feels imprisoned in the net of negative self-judgments. The expression 'smilingly' indicates a gesture of friendliness. Srī Kṛṣṇa smiles at Arjuna's honesty, simplicity and straightforwardness. At this juncture, Srī Kṛṣṇa would have suggested Arjuna to do whatever the later wanted to do; but being the most sincere companion and guide of all times, He perceives His devotee's inner turmoil and goes forward to help. So instead of paying any attention to Arjuna's resolution "I'll not fight", Srī Kṛṣṇa starts His gospel from the verse eleven. He begins the dialogue in a little angry tone but with words full of love and affection for His friend. He knows that ultimate guidance and support has to be revealed to Arjuna from his own inner resources, which will make him feel confident, assertive and fearless. Srī Kṛṣṇa takes up the role of a Guru and starts telling his disciple about the immortality of the soul.

श्रीभगवानुवाच

अशोच्यानन्वशोचस्त्वं प्रज्ञावादांश्च भाषसे।
गतासूनगतासूंश्च नानुशोचन्ति पण्डिताः॥ ११॥

aśocyānanvaśocastvaṁ prajñāvādānśca bhāṣase
gatāsūnagatāsūnśca nānuśocanti paṇḍitāḥ

The Blessed Lord said :

(11) O'Arjuna, you grieve for those who should not be grieved for; yet you speak the words of wisdom. The wise men do not grieve for the dead or for the living.

न त्वेवाहं जातु नासं न त्वं नेमे जनाधिपाः।
न चैव न भविष्यामः सर्वे वयमतः परम्॥ १२॥

na tvevāhaṁ jātu nāsaṁ na tvaṁ neme janādhipāḥ
na caiva na bhaviṣyāmaḥ sarve vayamataḥ param

(12) There was never a time when I or you or these rulers of men did not exist; nor will there be any time in future when all of us shall cease to be.

देहिनोऽस्मिन्यथा देहे कौमारं यौवनं जरा।
तथा देहान्तरप्राप्तिर्धीरस्तत्र न मुह्यति॥ १३॥

dehino'smin yathā dehe kaumāraṁ yauvanaṁ jarā
tathā dehāntaraprāptirdhīrastatra na muhyati

(13) Just as in this body, the embodied-soul, passes through childhood, youth and old age; so too it passes into another body. The man of integral wisdom is not deluded by this.

Commentary—In these verses Srī Kṛṣṇa draws Arjuna's attention to the real nature of the Self and the nature of the transitory world around. He declares that the soul is immortal, permanent and non-changing. He explains to Arjuna that the entire manifestation represents the real and the unreal, the changing and the non-changing, the mortal and the immortal, the embodied-self and the Supreme-self. The real is immutable, eternal, permanent and imperishable and the unreal is ever changing and perishable. It has beginning and an end. The mundane world keeps changing and vanishing every minute of life, so the man of wisdom who understands the true nature of the unreal, he does not grieve for the living and for the dead. In the words of Swami Rama, "one is called the Absolute reality and the other is called the apparent reality. They are like light and shadow." The infinite consciousness is not an object of observation, nor is it different from the observer. It reflects itself within itself and conceives of itself as duality. The Supreme-soul is beginningless, eternal and unmanifested; yet it exists in all, and appears to be manifested. The entire universe exists within the infinite consciousness just as a statue exists in a big piece of marble. It holds within itself another world. There is nothing outside of this, although it appears to be outside itself. The Supreme-soul is the only reality which is *Purna*—fullness as described in the Vedas. Everything in the creation springs forth from the fullness, it is sustained by the fullness, the fullness fills the fullness and also in the fullness, it is perennially established.

Srī Kṛṣṇa tells Arjuna that the Self is eternal, non-changing, imperishable and immutable. The soul of everyone has existed in the past, is existing in present and will exist in future. The embodied-self changes merely the form and shape. There is a mantra in the *Rigveda* which describes *surya chandra masau dhatha yatha purva makal payat divim cha prithavi chantariksha mayo*—the sun, moon and earth and other planets keep coming into existence just as before. In verse twelve, Srī Kṛṣṇa makes reference to the pre-existence and post-existence of the beings. He tells Arjuna that 'He Himself', Arjuna and all the other kings have always existed in the past and will also continue to exist hereafter. The different terms like 'I', 'You' and 'These' are being used by Srī Kṛṣṇa in order to explain the truth about the existence of the Supreme-soul which is beyond time, cause and space. Srī Kṛṣṇa perceives that Arjuna has been grieving over the transitory changes of the mundane world and definitely fails to comprehend the ultimate truth about the essentiality of the Supreme-soul. He tells Arjuna about the absolute reality of the Supreme-soul, which forms the substratum, basis and background of the entire apparent panorama in the universe. The Supreme-soul is omnipresent, it is the invisible thread which connects everything and everybody in the entire creation with one another. Just as gold is considered to be the reality in all types of gold ornaments, just as water is considered to be the reality in bubbles, waves and tides, similarly the Supreme consciousness is the only reality of whatever appears to be manifested in the world. The entire manifested world comes into existence, it is sustained for a while and dissolves into the origin, to be created once again. There is nothing in the world which becomes totally lost and loses its essentiality. Everything continues to exist in one or the other form. The entire universe is constantly evolving. It is only the spiritual insight of the individual which helps him to understand the continuity of life from the past, through the present and into the future. As Rabindranath Tagore has mentioned in Gitanjali : "Thou hast made me endless, such is thy pleasure. This frail vessel Thou emptiest again and again, and fillest it ever with fresh life."

Srī Kṛṣṇa tells Arjuna that the different stages of body such as childhood, youth and old age indicate the changes only in the physical body. The body goes through all kinds of growth and changes but the one who witnesses the entire change that (soul) ever remains the same. As the embodied-self, while dwelling in the body, experiences childhood, youth and old age, so also he experiences death and passes into another body. In the words of Adi Sankara, "In the present body there is childhood in early age, youth in middle age, old age in the stage of disintegration. These three stages of life are distinct. At the end of the first stage the self does not perish. At the beginning of second stage, it is not born. It passes unchanged into the second and third stages. So also the self passes unchanged into another body. The wise are not bewildered by this." The soul is immortal, and indestructible. The bodies have a beginning and an end. The Supreme-soul resides in the body as the embodied-soul. In due course of time when the body disintegrates the soul gets out of the body and carries with it all the thoughts, desires and aspirations in the form of *samskaras*. The embodied soul goes from one body to another; forced by the residual impressions which have been accumulated during the life time. The individual soul retains its individuality from one stage to another and also from one life to another. All the changes do take place only at the physical level and the unchangeable soul remains untouched. The destruction of the gross body can never cause any destruction in the continuity of the indestructible soul. The *Atharva Veda* gives a description similar to this: *utaisham pitot waputra asha mutaisham jyashtha uta va kanishtha, akohadevo manasi pravistha, prathamo jata uho garbho anta.* "The soul at one time becomes someone's father, at another time, the son, the elder brother and at another time the younger brother. One soul dwelling within the mind has gone through many births before, and keeps entering into the new wombs."

मात्रास्पर्शास्तु कौन्तेय शीतोष्णसुखदुःखदाः।
आगमापायिनोऽनित्यास्तांस्तितिक्षस्व भारत ॥ १४ ॥

mātrāsparśāstu kaunteya śītoṣṇasukhaduḥkhadāḥ
āgamāpāyino'nityās tāṅstitikṣasva bhārata

(14) The contact of the senses with their objects, gives rise to the feeling of cold and heat, pleasure and pain, etc., these are transitory and fleeting. Therefore learn to endure them patiently, O'Arjuna.

यं हि न व्यथयन्त्येते पुरुषं पुरुषर्षभ।
समदुःखसुखं धीरं सोऽमृतत्वाय कल्पते ॥ १५ ॥

yaṁ hi na vyathayantyete puruṣaṁ puruṣarṣabha
samaduḥkhasukhaṁ dhīraṁ so'mṛtatvāya kalpate

(15) The man who is not tormented by these, O'Arjuna, to whom the pleasure and pain are alike—that steadfast man becomes eligible for immortality.

Commentary—Srī Krṣṇa is addressing Arjuna as *purusharshabha* means the most heroic and the strongest among men, in all respects. With the use of this compound adjective, Srī Krṣṇa intends to remind Arjuna of his great valour and heroism. He explains to Arjuna that the man of wisdom, who lives in complete awareness of the Self, he has the ability to rise above the dualities of life, and develop a very balanced state of mind. He declares that all the experiences of pleasure and pain are deeply rooted in the contacts between the senses and their objects. These feelings are very natural for every individual who identifies himself with his body and mind. It is the mind that prints all the impressions of the three worlds; it is the mind that creates the feeling of pleasure and pain, love and hate, fragmentation and division. The human mind can make even a moment to appear more like an epoch, and can make the minor problem to appear to be the most difficult. When the individual screens reality, through the ideas, those are conditioned with some fixed notion; his creativity suffers and his fulfilment in life becomes a far off dream. All the feelings of love and hate, pleasure and pain, do arise from false identification and they continue to exist until the dawn of self-realization. When the individual identifies himself with the Supreme-Self he develops the discriminating insight and liberates himself from the deep psychological conditioning of mind; he rises above the pairs of opposites and becomes established in the blissful state of equanimity. Srī Krṣṇa alerts Arjuna about the conditioned experiences of the senses, in relation to the material world. He tells that the perceptual experiences of the senses are transient and impermanent. He should ignore them and also learn to endure them; otherwise these experiences do delude the mind and create confusion for the individual. In the words of Swami Sivananda : "Identification of the Self with the body is the cause of pleasure and pain. The more you are able to identify yourself with the immortal, all-pervading Self, the less will you be affected by the pairs of opposites (*dvandas*, pleasure and pain, etc.)

नासतो विद्यते भावो नाभावो विद्यते सतः।
उभयोरपि दृष्टोऽन्तस्त्वनयोस्तत्त्वदर्शिभिः॥ १६॥

nāsato vidyate bhāvo nābhāvo vidyate saṭaḥ
ubhayorapi dṛṣṭo'ntas tvanayostattvadarśibhiḥ

(16) The unreal has no existence and the real never ceases to be; the essential truth about both of these is perceived by the seers of truth.

अविनाशि तु तद्विद्धि येन सर्वमिदं ततम्।
विनाशमव्ययस्यास्य न कश्चित्कर्तुमर्हति॥ १७॥

avināśi tu tadviddhi yena sarvamidaṁ tatam
vināśamavyayasyāsya na kaścit kartumarhati

(17) Know that to be imperishable by which all this is pervaded. No one can bring about the destruction of the indestructible.

Commentary—In these verses Srī Kṛṣṇa draws Arjuna's attention towards the comprehension of the essential difference between the *sat* and *asat*—existent and non-existent, real and unreal. The real always remains the same while the unreal changes every moment. Everything which is seen manifested in the world, it comes into existence, it is sustained for a while and then it perishes. Srī Kṛṣṇa tells Arjuna that there is one unchanging reality that pervades the entire universe. It is the supreme consciousness, the Supreme-soul and the essential being of every one and everything. In the words of Jaydayal Goyandka, "Sat or the real connotes the Supreme Spirit, which is all pervading and eternal. The words 'it never ceases to be' convey the idea that at no time and under no circumstances the soul undergoes any change or ceases to exist." The *asat* or unreal is within the comprehension of human mind, that's why the mind interprets everything in the world in relation to unreal. Everybody lives his life, with the notion of accepting unreal to be real, and the transitory to be permanent. The ordinary human mind with its finite powers can't grasp the difference between the *sat* and *asat*. But the wise sage who lives in the consciousness of the Divine, he has the experiential knowledge of both existent and non-existent. He transcends the limitations of the mind and body and lives in the blissful state of Sat-Chit-Anand. He understands perfectly that whatever passes through the birth-death and rebirth that has to be unreal; it is only the soul that exists as permanent and unchanging through all the changing circumstances and modifications. There is one unchanging reality which is imperishable, immutable and omniscient. In the words of Srī Jñaneswari, "Just as the swan separates water from the milk, the goldsmith segregates the pure gold by heating the alloy or one takes out the butter skilfully by churning the curd, so when the wise man cognates upon the creation, the world disappears and there remains only the Self". The man of wisdom doesn't assign any reality to the transitory, ever changing things of the mundane world because he has realized the essence of both.

अन्तवन्त इमे देहा नित्यस्योक्ताः शरीरिणः।
अनाशिनोऽप्रमेयस्य तस्माद्युध्यस्व भारत॥ १८॥

antavanta ime dehā nityasyoktāḥ śarīriṇaḥ
anāśino'prameyasya tasmād yudhyasva bhārata

(18) These bodies of the embodied-self are perishable while the Self is eternal, imperishable and incomprehensible. Therefore O'Arjuna, fight the battle.

य एनं वेत्ति हन्तारं यश्चैनं मन्यते हतम्।
उभौ तौ न विजानीतो नायं हन्ति न हन्यते॥ १९॥

ya enaṁ vetti hantāraṁ yaścainaṁ manyate hatam
ubhau tau na vijānīto nāyaṁ hanti na hanyate

(19) He who considers the soul to be the slayer and who thinks that this is slain; both of them fail to perceive the truth. The soul neither slays nor is slain.

न जायते म्रियते वा कदाचिन् नायंभूत्वा भविता वा न भूयः।
अजो नित्यः शाश्वतोऽयं पुराणो न हन्यते हन्यमाने शरीरे॥ २०॥

na jāyate mriyate vā kadācin nāyaṁ bhūtvā bhavitā vā na bhūyaḥ
ajo nityaḥ śāśvato'yaṁ purāṇo na hanyate hanyamāne śarīre

(20) The soul is neither born nor does it ever die; having come into being once, it never ceases to be. It is unborn, eternal, permanent

and primeval. It is not killed even when the body is killed.

वेदाविनाशिनं नित्यं य एनमजमव्ययम्।
कथं स पुरुषः पार्थ कं घातयति हन्ति कम्॥ २१ ॥

vedāvināśinaṁ nityaṁ ya enamajamavyayam
kathaṁ sa puruṣaḥ pārtha kaṁ ghātayati hantikam

(21) He who knows the soul to be indestructible, unborn, unchanging and immutable; how can such a person slay anyone, O'Arjuna or cause any one to slay?

Commentary—Here in these verses Srī Kṛṣṇa declares to Arjuna that the soul is indeed imperishable. He intends to enlighten his disciple about the real nature of the self—and the perishable and ever changing nature of the body. The body is composed of the material components which undergo many changes between birth and death but the Supreme-self remains unchanging and immutable. It is indeed due to the false identification of the embodied-self with the mind and body that the individual becomes disconnected from the eternal truth; and he forgets the real nature of his own essential being. He becomes weak, fearful, and disintegrated in all respects. People are afraid of death because of their own ignorance of identifying themselves with the body. Most of the worries and fears of life can be eliminated if the individual could ever perceive and experience the immortality of his essential being. The individual's identification with his body deprives him from the rich experience of his being ageless, timeless and imperishable. The transcendental field of pure consciousness is without beginning and without any end. The above principle has been described in *Kathopanisad—na jayate mriyateva vipashich nyayam kuthashchin babhuva kashicht, ajo nitya shashvatoham purano na haneyate hanyamane shareere*. The soul never takes birth nor dies; the soul is beginningless, unborn, eternal, primeval and ancient. It is not killed even when the body is killed. Srī Kṛṣṇa intends to intimate Arjuna about the immortality and immutability of the soul with many words and with many kinds of explanations, such as *ajah, nityah, sasvatah* and *purnah.* With the realization of this distinction between the body and the soul, the person becomes acquainted with his true nature, the essence of life. The knowledge of the Supreme-self brings freedom to the embodied-self, from the limitations of his conditioned boundaries.

A person who is settled in the Self he naturally becomes settled in righteousness, truth, justice and universal unity. After the attainment of the knowledge of one's own essential being, the person becomes enlightened about the reality of the transitory world. The experience of knowledge of his own immortality makes him very fearless and courageous. It is the understanding of the essential nature of the Self which enables the person to understand his expanded field of relationship which lies beyond the boundaries of I-ness. He becomes enlightened about his appropriate role as a member of the family and as a responsible member of the community and country at large. The individual who remains centred in the unity with the Supreme-self, he follows the guidance of the Supreme, and the laws of *swadharma*. The *Rigveda* describes it in these beautiful words: *yadagne syamaham tvam tvam va va sya ahem sayuste satya ehashis*—living in harmony with the universal soul, should be your most cherished prayer. Rise above the personal egoistic-self and merge in cosmic-self. Living in harmony with the transcendental consciousness is indeed the real fulfilment of human efforts. Srī Kṛṣṇa advises Arjuna to recollect his true identity and re-educate himself about the true nature of the soul and his own essential Divine nature. He wants Arjuna to re-evaluate the entire situation on the basis of his connections with the indwelling soul and not from the viewpoint of his limited identification with the body. The individual soul which is only an infinitesimal unit of the Supreme-soul is indeed endowed with all the powers, qualities and capacities of the Supreme. Srī Kṛṣṇa wants Arjuna to wake up to the reality of his essential being and realize the nature of the indwelling-self, which is immortal and immutable. He persuades him in examining his attitude once again with renewed understanding. He wants the later to be acquainted with the unconditioned ever-luminous purity of the Supreme-Self and be fearless, unattached and integrated. Srī Kṛṣṇa wants Arjuna to understand and realize the secret of performing his duty with inner peace, tranquillity, integrity and joy which is indeed the art of living in yoga.

वासांसि जीर्णानि यथा विहाय नवानि गृह्णाति नरोऽपराणि।
तथा शरीराणि विहाय जीर्णान्यन्यानि संयाति नवानि देही॥ २२॥

vāsāṅsi jīrṇāni yathā vihāya navāni gṛhṇāti naro'parāṇi
tathā śarīrāṇi vihāya jīrṇānyanyāni saṅyāti navāni dehī

(22) As a person casts off the worn-out garments and puts on the new ones; likewise the embodied-soul discards the worn out bodies and enters into the new ones.

नैनं छिन्दन्ति शस्त्राणि नैनं दहति पावकः।
न चैनं क्लेदयन्त्यापो न शोषयति मारुतः॥ २३॥

nainaṁ chindanti śastrāṇi nainaṁ dahati pāvakaḥ
na cainaṁ kledayantyāpo na śoṣayati mārutaḥ

(23) Weapons cannot cut the soul, nor can fire burn it. Water can not wet it nor wind can make it dry.

अच्छेद्योऽयमदाह्योऽयमक्लेद्योऽशोष्य एव च।
नित्यः सर्वगतः स्थाणुरचलोऽयं सनातनः॥ २४॥

acchedyo'yamadāhyo'yamakledyo'śoṣya eva ca
nityaḥ sarvagataḥ sthāṇuracalo'yaṁ sanātanaḥ

(24) The soul is uncleavable and incombustible. It can be neither wetted nor dried. It is eternal, all-pervading, unchanging, immovable and primordial.

अव्यक्तोऽयमचिन्त्योऽयमविकार्योऽयमुच्यते।
तस्मादेवं विदित्वैनं नानुशोचितुमर्हसि॥ २५॥

avyakto'yamacintyo'yamavikāryo'yamucyate
tasmādevaṁ viditvai'naṁ nānuśocitumarhasi

(25) This (soul) is said to be unmanifest, unthinkable and unchanging. Therefore, knowing it as such, you should not grieve.

Commentary—In these verses Srī Kṛṣṇa introduces Arjuna to the essential nature of the soul and the transmigration of the soul. The word *sharīrāṇi* means the embodied-self. The soul keeps migrating from one body to another and remains in the rounds of birth-death and rebirth because of its identification with the body. The cycle goes on until the individual-soul identifies itself with the Supreme-soul and merges in it for liberation. Srī Kṛṣṇa is trying to introduce one fact at a time and does not want to confuse Arjuna. He intimates his disciple with the truth that the death is not an end in itself, it only marks the time for change and a new beginning. Tagore has described this truth very beautifully in *Gitanjali*, "Even so, in death the same unknown will appear as ever known to me. And because I love this life, I know, I shall love death as well. The child cries out when from the right breast the mother takes it away, in the very next moment to find in the left one its consolation." The ancient sages have believed and have emphasized upon the truth that with increased awareness one develops the intuitive ability of looking into the past and the previous births.

The process of reincarnation requires no explanation. Even the modern psychologists have started showing an increased interest in these doctrines. Many doctors all around the world have brought forward many specific case histories suggestive of reincarnation. For example, in one particular case, a doctor has written about a five-year old boy who could remember his immediate previous birth and even the one before that. In that case the doctor took some special efforts and contacted the families. He was totally amazed with the actual facts related by the five-year old boy. The little boy could even recall the two different languages which were spoken by him in the previous life. The theory of reincarnation can be actually verified by only few people those have been blessed with increased intuitive ability. In the words of Swami Chinmayananda, "There was no great thinker in the past who had not, nor anyone in the present, who has not accepted, expressly or tacitly, these logical conclusions about the doctrine of reincarnation. Buddha constantly made references to his previous births. Virgil and Ovid regarded the doctrine as perfectly self-evident. Josephus observed that the belief in reincarnation was widely accepted among the Jews of his age. Solomon's *Book of Wisdom* says : 'To be born in sound body with sound limbs is a reward of the virtues of the past lives.' He further adds 'the prodigy Mozart is a spectacular instance, this genius wrote Sonatas at the age of four, played in public at the age of five, composed his first Opera at the age of seven!'"

The process of understanding the nature of *Atman* is very subtle and difficult. The nature of the soul can't be described in words. It is inexplicable. In the words of Jaydayal Goyandka, "The soul cannot be cognized by any of the senses, therefore, it is called unmanifest, nor it can be conceived by the mind therefore it is unthinkable". In these verses Srī Kṛṣṇa presents only those examples which are within the comprehension of the human sensory organs. By giving the simile, "that the fire can't burn it, water can't make it wet and weapons can't cut it," Srī Kṛṣṇa presents to Arjuna some symbolic terms, in relation to the description of the nature of the soul. The soul is beyond the boundaries of form and thought. Shape and forms do change but the one which is present behind the changes that remains permanent. In the words of Srī Ramanuja, "What is born must die some day, and death does not mean total extinction of the being but only the assumption of a new condition of being. Such a succession of states does not imply either the creation or destruction of the substance, whose states they are, but merely its passage from one specific condition of actuality to another condition of actuality. Such is the true view of causation. The fundamental material is unoriginated and indestructible. It passes through varied conditions of existence."

There is an interesting incident from the life story of Socrates. When he was asked as how his death sacraments should be performed, he had replied amusingly, "in any way you like, but first you must catch 'me', the real 'me'. He further stated after all you will be burying only my dead physical body; you could do with that, whatever is appropriate". The words of Socrates do assert the truth behind the theory of reincarnation—he always taught his followers about the immortality of the soul. The saints and the philosophers constantly live in the awareness of the Supreme Soul, for them death is only a change; in which the embodied soul casts off the worn out physical body and enters into another which is new. For an enlightened person death is not a complete annihilation. It is only a transmigration. They always live in the consciousness of the truth, that the physical body was meant to exist only for a limited time between the two events—

the birth and the death. The journey of the soul is ever-renewing on the path of eternity.

अथ चैनं नित्यजातं नित्यं वा मन्यसे मृतम्।
तथापि त्वं महाबाहो नैवं शोचितुमर्हसि॥ २६॥

atha cainaṁ nityajātaṁ nityaṁ vā manyase mṛtam
tathāpi tvaṁ mahābāho naivaṁ śocitumarhasi

(26) Even if you regard the soul as being continually taking birth and continually dying; even then, O'Arjuna, you should not grieve.

जातस्य हि ध्रुवो मृत्युर्ध्रुवं जन्म मृतस्य च।
तस्मादपरिहार्येऽर्थे न त्वं शोचितुमर्हसि॥ २७॥

jātasya hi dhruvo mṛtyurdhruvaṁ janma mṛtasya ca
tasmādaparihārye'rthe na tvaṁ śocitumarhasi

(27) For, death is certain of the one who is born, and also the rebirth is certain of the one who is dead; therefore you should not grieve over the inevitable.

अव्यक्तादीनि भूतानि व्यक्तमध्यानि भारत।
अव्यक्तनिधनान्येव तत्र का परिदेवना॥ २८॥

avyaktādīni bhūtāni vyaktamadhyāni bhārata
avyaktanidhnānyeva tatra kā paridevanā

(28) O'Arjuna, all the beings are unmanifest in their beginnings, they become manifested in the middle state and unmanifested again in the end. What is there in this, for lamentation?

Commentary—In these verses Srī Kṛṣṇa intends to enlighten Arjuna about the eternal principle of life. The entire world is going through constant change, and ultimately everything ends in death, in order to be born again. For example, the hidden desire of a seed is to become a tree, for that it goes through different forms and shapes, and different stages of growth. In the first stage it appears on the ground as a baby sprout, then as a small plant and later it becomes a tree; the hidden desire of every tree is to become a seed again. Civilizations come and go, kingdoms rise and fall, stars and planets keep breaking every minute to move towards the inevitable end. There is a very interesting dialogue in the *Mahabharata* where Yaksha asks a question to Yudhishtra. O'Yudhishtra, what is the greatest surprise on earth? Yudhishtra answers very assuringly "O'Yaksha! Every minute we see that people are dying around us, and yet every one hopes and thinks that he is going to live for ever." That is indeed the greatest surprise in this world. The phenomenon of the cycle of birth-death and rebirth has been going on since antiquity, still nobody wants to accept it. Everything in nature is going through an evolution and trying to get back to its origin. Everything in the physical world is in a process of transformation. This process is active in macrocosm as well as in microcosm. For example, every cell in the human body obeys the same law of creation, evolution and dissolution as an atom does in the material universe. Every single cell that dies is replaced by a similar type of another one. As estimated by the molecular biologists, millions and trillions of reactions take place in human body in almost every single minute of life. In the words of Vinobaji, "Modern scientists say that in seven years the whole body changes, and that not even a drop of the old blood remains. Our ancestors believed that the old body dies in twelve years. That is why they fixed the period for penance *(prayaschitta)*, austerity *(tapascharya)* or study *(adhyayana)* as twelve years". Creation and dissolution is an ongoing process into the stream of life which renews itself every single minute. The death is certain for the one who is born and rebirth is also certain for the one who dies. This is an inevitable law and well known to everybody, still nobody wants to accept it.

There is an illustration in the literature of Buddhist teachings, where Mahatma Buddha consoles the mother who had lost her son. Buddha requests the mother, who was in deep pain, to go into the town and bring some rice from a family where nobody had died so far. The lady went from one house to another and could not find a single family that had escaped the all-devouring grips of death. She instantly understood the inevitability of death and consoled herself. The man of wisdom who knows the kaleidoscopic nature of the material world, he never makes the mistake of identifying with it. The man of wisdom perceives and experiences the unchanging reality in the transition of all changes. He knows that there is only one unchanging reality behind the changing phases of life which remains untouched and undisturbed while one grows from childhood to youth and old age. The realization of this truth does enlighten the individual and he rises above the dualities of the transitory world. Everybody and everything in the world is unmanifested to the human senses in its origin, and also becomes unmanifested at the end. It is manifested only in the intermediate state and in that too, it changes, distorts and disintegrates constantly. The entire manifested world has its roots in the unmanifested. In the words of Srī Ramanuja, "All beings arise out of an antecedent condition of non-manifestation, manifest themselves for some time in the middle and then relapse into non-manifestation."

आश्चर्यवत्पश्यति कश्चिदेनमाश्चर्यवद्वदति तथैव चान्यः।
आश्चर्यवच्चैनमन्यः शृणोति श्रुत्वाप्येनं वेद न चैव कश्चित्॥ २९॥

āścaryavatpaśyati kaścidena-
māścaryavavadati tathaiva cānyaḥ
āścaryavacainamanyaḥ śṛṇoti
śrutvāpyenaṁ veda na caiva kaścit

(29) One perceives the soul in great wonder, likewise another speaks of it in wonder; still another hears of it in great wonder; and even after hearing of it, hardly any one understands it.

देही नित्यमवध्योऽयं देहे सर्वस्य भारत।
तस्मात्सर्वाणि भूतानि न त्वं शोचितुमर्हसि॥ ३०॥

dehī nityamavadhyo'yaṁ dehe sarvasya bhārata
tasmāt sarvāṇi bhūtāni na tvaṁ śocitumarhasi

(30) O'Arjuna, the soul dwelling in the body of every one is eternal and indestructible. Therefore, you should not grieve for any creature.

Commentary—In these verses Srī Kṛṣṇa proceeds to tell Arjuna about the magnitude of the Supreme-soul. He says that it is very difficult to find some one who has the perceptual and the experiential knowledge of the cosmic-soul; or the one who has understood the essential nature of it by reading and by hearing about it. The nature of the soul is very hard to comprehend and indeed very difficult to describe in words. It is not just marvellous, it is much more marvellous than the human mind and intellect can describe. He enlightens Arjuna step by step into the subtleties of the spiritual knowledge *(Samkhya Yoga).* The characteristics of the soul has been very surprising and astonishing to everybody since times immemorial. The absolute truth is beyond the comprehension of human mind, that is why it has been called unthinkable and inexplicable. The human understanding of the world is based upon the information of the sensory organs and also upon the knowledge which has been experienced and dictated by the learned sages. The description of a phenomena both at the physical and at the psychological level depends upon the perceptual experiences of the five senses. The functions of these senses are finite and so is the information reported by them. For example, while giving the description of a rock candy, the eyes can tell only the colour and shape of the candy, the tongue can describe its taste, the sense of touch can describe how hard it is; none of these sensory organs can give a complete description of the candy. Human sensory organs take in a limited, minute fraction of information of a certain object in the physical world as well as in others. The infinity of the soul can't be perceived and described by the finite sensory organs. In order to understand the infinite character of the soul one has to transcend the finite realms of mind and body and move into the field of infinite consciousness. Even when the individual transcends to that level of infinity, he experiences only a infinitesimal part of it and also finds it very difficult to describe the experience in words. As described in *Chhandogya Upanishad,* "The transcendental state of consciousness, wherein one beholds nothing else, hears nothing else, perceives nothing else, that is infinite; but where one sees something else, hears something else, understands something else, that is finite. The infinite is surely the immortal and finite is mortal. The infinite is perennially established in the Supreme-soul."

The absolute truth about the soul is veiled in many layers of consciousness and is indeed very difficult to comprehend. When an individual transcends the boundaries of mind and intellect and experiences the subtlety of the soul; he finds his experience to be totally inexplicable. The comprehension of the ultimate reality which has been ushered by the indweller of the body makes it possible for the individual to experience his own immortality that underlies the visible mortality of the body. So from that field of transcendental awareness, when the individual enters into the vicinity of the body, he looks upon the life to be merely a shadow. The one who remains grounded in the truth of the deepest awareness, to him the transmigration of soul is merely like changing garments. An enlightened person looks upon the physical body like any other material object in the physical world; to him the functions of body are merely the play of molecules. He perfectly understands that although his body is confined to space and time but his true identity as the immortal soul is not bound at all. He remains grounded in his deepest awareness and looks upon the creation as a play of matter and energy which flickers here and there creating new shapes and forms. He beholds the changes governed by the law of creation and the dissolution in the physical body and accelerates himself to the level of realization which is not touched by any type of change.

The knowledge of the soul is experiential which can be shared only to a certain degree, and not completely. The *Kathopanishad* explains it like this : "*shravanayapi bahubhiryo na labhya shrunavanthopi bahavo ya na vidhu.* The Supreme-soul is not easy to be heard; many who proclaim and explain, even they don't fully understand." This is a fact that the investigators into the mysteries of the Supreme-soul are very few. This realm of unified field is very subtle and mysterious and indeed remains unapproachable to many. The aspirant remains amazed while inquiring, experiencing, reflecting, thinking and even talking about it. The character of the soul can't be described like the other objects, formulas and theories. The description transcends the world of matter, forms, shapes and words.

It is indeed very difficult to educate some one about the knowledge of the Soul. Although each and every person is an eligible candidate for the experiential knowledge of the Divine, still only few are blessed with it. The reason is, that, only few in many billions are actually willing to pursue the path of God-realization. Only few in many millions have the genuine urge, courage, determination and an insatiable desire to comprehend the essentiality of the Supreme-soul. The realization of the soul becomes quite confirmed and real for a genuine aspirant who endeavours to live in the consciousness of the Supreme-soul. Any one who experiences himself as the Soul, he never loses his contacts with the source of Bliss even in the middle of experiencing everything in the world; for him the presence of soul becomes the only reality to be meditated upon.

स्वधर्ममपि चावेक्ष्य न विकम्पितुमर्हसि।
धर्म्याद्धि युद्धाच्छ्रेयोऽन्यत्क्षत्रियस्य न विद्यते॥ ३१॥

svadharmamapi cāvekṣya na vikampitumarhasi
dharmyāddhi yuddhācchreyo'nyat kṣatriyasya na vidyate

(31) Besides, in consideration of your own duty as well, it does not befit you to waver. For, to a kshatriya, there is nothing else better than a righteous war.

यदृच्छया चोपपन्नं स्वर्गद्वारमपावृतम्।
सुखिनः क्षत्रियाः पार्थ लभन्ते युद्धमीदृशम्॥ ३२॥

yadṛcchayā copapannaṁ svargadvāramapāvṛtam
sukhinaḥ kṣatriyāḥ pārtha labhante yuddhamīdṛśam

(32) Happy (fortunate) are the kshatriyas, O'Arjuna, those who are called upon to fight in a battle like this, that comes of itself as an open door to the heaven.

अथ चेत्त्वमिमं धर्म्यं सङ्ग्रामं न करिष्यसि।
ततः स्वधर्मं कीर्तिं च हित्वा पापमवाप्स्यसि॥ ३३॥

atha cettvamimaṁ dharmyaṁ saṅgrāmaṁ na kariṣyasi
tataḥ svadharmaṁ kīrtiṁ ca hitvā pāpamavāpsyasi

(33) But, if you do not fight this righteous war, you will be turning away from your assigned duty and respectable position. You will definitely incur sin.

अकीर्तिं चापि भूतानि कथयिष्यन्ति तेऽव्ययाम्।
सम्भावितस्य चाकीर्तिर्मरणादतिरिच्यते॥ ३४॥

akīrtiṁ cāpi bhūtāni kathayiṣyanti te'vyayām
sambhāvitasya cākīrtir maraṇādatiricyate

(34) Besides, people will speak derogatory words about you; and for the one who has been always honoured—dishonour is worse than death.

भयाद्रणादुपरतं मंस्यन्ते त्वां महारथाः।
येषां च त्वं बहुमतो भूत्वा यास्यसि लाघवम्॥ ३५ ॥

bhayād raṇāduparatam mansyante tvāṁ mahārathāḥ
yeṣāṁ ca tvaṁ bahumato bhūtvā yāsyasi lāghavam

(35) The great chariot-warriors will think that you have withdrawn from the battle in fear. Those men, who always held you in high esteem, will also show their disrespect.

अवाच्यवादांश्च बहून्वदिष्यन्ति तवाहिताः।
निन्दन्तस्तव सामर्थ्यं ततो दुःखतरं नु किम्॥ ३६ ॥

avācyavādāṅśca bahūn vadiṣyanti tavāhitāḥ
nindantastava sāmarthyaṁ tato duḥkhataraṁ nu kim

(36) Your enemies, slandering your prowess, will speak many disgraceful words. What can be more distressing than that?

हतो वा प्राप्स्यसि स्वर्गं जित्वा वा भोक्ष्यसे महीम्।
तस्मादुत्तिष्ठ कौन्तेय युद्धाय कृतनिश्चयः॥ ३७ ॥

hato vā prāpsyasi svargaṁ jitvā vā bhokṣyase mahīm
tasmāduttiṣṭha kaunteya yuddhāya kṛtaniścayaḥ

(37) If killed in the battle, you will attain heaven; or, if victorious you will enjoy sovereignty of the earth. Therefore, stand up O'Arjuna, resolved to fight.

सुखदुःखे समे कृत्वा लाभालाभौ जयाजयौ।
ततो युद्धाय युज्यस्व नैवं पापमवाप्स्यसि॥ ३८ ॥

sukhaduḥkhe same kṛtvā lābhālābhau jayājayau
tato yuddhāya yujyasva naivaṁ pāpamavāpsyasi

(38) Regarding alike the pleasure and pain, gain and loss, victory

and defeat; get ready for the battle. Thus, you will not incur sin.

Commentary—After declaring the soul as indestructible, immutable, omnipresent and ever existent, Srī Kṛṣṇa draws Arjuna's attention towards his own *swadharma* and the purpose of life. The word *swadharma* combines two words. *Swa*—means the indwelling (light), and the word *Dharma*, which derives from the root word *dhar*—means to hold or to maintain. *Swadharma* means to hold and maintain the constant identity with the Supreme-Self. *Swadharma* is a unique system of values, determined and dictated by one's own inner self, which guides the individual to perform his duties by keeping in mind the global welfare and harmony. The practice of *swadharma* helps the individual to realize the purpose of his life, while living in perfect harmony with his fellow beings. It awakens the individual and guides him in doing what is right and checks him from doing whatever is wrong. Even if the external pressures from the society does force the individual to behave in a particular way, the person who is fully established in *Swadharma*, he will always comply, only if his actions do correspond with his inner self. The notion of *Swadharma* in the *Geeta* indicates that this world is a *Dharmakshetra*. All activities of daily life must correspond to the maintenance of the world order. Every one should inculcate a sense of responsibility towards his own duty. When the person fails to perform one's *Dharma,* the result is indeed pain, misery, unhappiness and turmoil at the individual level and also at the universal level. The obedience to *swadharma* helps the individual to grow in all dimensions and fulfil the purpose of life.

In these verses Srī Kṛṣṇa reminds Arjuna of his *swadharma*, who has been raised to be a great warrior. He knows that Arjuna has always loved and liked archery. Since childhood, he has aspired to become the greatest warrior of the world. He has enjoyed being a soldier and work for the safety of his kingdom and his citizens. Arjuna has been given the name Dhananjaya because he has replenished his empire with all kinds of riches and prosperity. He has been given the fire chariot and the celestial conch Devadatta by Indra for fighting against demons in order to maintain peace on earth. A soldier who has been raised with the high ideals of service, he surely feels contented when he finds an opportunity to fight for the well-being of others. He fights like a respectable soldier and performs his role in the battle with respect and dignity; and even if he dies in the battle field, he dies like a free person, who has performed his duty in accordance with the laws of *swadharma*.

In these verses, Srī Kṛṣṇa draws Arjuna's attention towards his duty as a soldier, who has been trained to live and die for the welfare and protection of his kingdom, justice and righteousness. Srī Kṛṣṇa tells Arjuna, that if he recoils and decides against fighting the battle, he would deprive himself of the most desirable opportunity of attaining inner contentment and worldly honour. Turning away from *swadharma* will haunt him for the rest of his life. He will always condemn himself in future and will continue to live in guilt and shame. Srī Kṛṣṇa counsels Arjuna to perform his duty with a balanced state of mind and transcend the feelings of both pleasure and pain, loss and gain, victory and defeat. His approach towards the war should be totally selfless. His resolve should be focused and devoid of all fears and anxieties regarding the result of the war.

Srī Kṛṣṇa reminds Arjuna that he has been called upon to fight the battle in the spirit of service to his countrymen. If he fights with the tranquillity and equanimity of mind, he will definitely do the right thing at the right moment. Arjuna has to remind himself that he is not only an important member of the family, he is also a very important member of the community and an honourable citizen of the country. The performance of his duty should come with enthusiasm and inspiration from within and also as a necessity and command from his kingdom. He must learn to rise above the conflicting emotions and must learn to endure both love and hate, victory and defeat. He enlightens Arjuna about the fact that the interpretation and the experience of pleasure and pain exists in direct relation to the notion of what is important to that person under certain type of circumstances. It is attachment to that notion or idea which becomes the cause of pleasure and pain. So when the individual acts in response to *swadharma*, he rises above personal obsessions. Srī Kṛṣṇa tells Arjuna that if he is not obsessed with the idea of victory, in that case even the defeat should not hurt him. The only way to rise above the anxieties of life is to perform the duty in a detached, skilful and harmonious manner. It is identification with the *swadharma* which helps the individual to perform his duty by rising above the fixed personal realities. *Shruti Bhagawati* declares that the performance of one's duties with the purity, morality, virtuosity and a balanced state of mind, leads the individual to peace and happiness in life and emancipation hereafter.

एषा तेऽभिहिता साङ्ख्ये बुद्धिर्योगे त्विमां शृणु।
बुद्ध्या युक्तो यया पार्थ कर्मबन्धं प्रहास्यसि॥ ३९॥

eṣā te'bhihitā sāṅkhye buddhiryoge tvimāṁ śṛṇu
buddhyā yukto yayā pārtha karmabandhaṁ prahāsyasi

(39) This which has been declared to you so far is the wisdom of the Samkhya; now listen to the wisdom, in regard to yoga (Karmayoga). Endowed with this knowledge, O'Arjuna, you will get freedom from the bondage of karma.

नेहाभिक्रमनाशोऽस्ति, प्रत्यवायो न विद्यते।
स्वल्पमप्यस्य धर्मस्य, त्रायते महतो भयात्॥ ४०॥

nehābhikramanāśo'sti pratyavāyo na vidyate
svalpamapyasya dharmasya trāyate mahato bhayāt

(40) In this, there is no loss of effort, nor is there any fear of contrary result. Even a little practice of this discipline (Dharma) protects the individual from great fear.

व्यवसायात्मिका बुद्धिरेकेह कुरुनन्दन।
बहुशाखा ह्यनन्ताश्च बुद्धयोऽव्यवसायिनाम्॥ ४१॥

vyavasāyātmikā buddhirekeha kurunandana
bahuśākhā hyanantāśca buddhayo'vyavasāyinām

(41) O'Arjuna, in this path, the resolute intellect is one pointed; whereas the intellect of the irresolute is scattered in many directions and is endlessly diverse.

Commentary—From these verses onward Srī Kṛṣṇa proceeds to teach Arjuna the techniques of Karma-yoga. The word Yoga has been derived from the Sanskrit word 'Yuj'—which literally means to bind, join, and yoke the psychic energies, in order to experience a union and communion with the indwelling soul. Yoga is a technique of spiritual practice which leads the individual to a very special type of blissful experience of inner unity. The ancient scriptures describe *'yogah-chittavritti-nirodhah'*—means yoga is to control all the mental modifications. It is an art which brings an incoherent and scattered mind into a reflective and coherent state and helps the individual to experience the presence of divinity within. The yogic practice helps the individual to accelerate himself to the state of consciousness in which his egoistic individuality is dissolved; and the person moves from ignorance to light, from the fear of death to immortality and eternal unity. Yoga is the conscious unification of the individual-soul with the Supreme-soul. Samkhya system of spiritual progress and God-realization is more theoretical while the yogic method is more practical.

Srī Kṛṣṇa wants Arjuna to combine the Samkhya and Yoga in order to seek union with the Divine through the devoted performance of his actions. The knowledge without action and action without knowledge cannot help anybody. Proper knowledge—devotion and action—must be intermingled in order to attain self-realization and God-realization. The word yoga means a union and communion with the indweller; so the Karmayoga literally means the type of actions which help the individual to develop a union with God. Similarly, the knowledge that guides the person in developing unity with the Divine is called *Jñanayoga* (yoga of knowledge). The mode of ardent devotion which helps the individual to maintain a constant union with the inner-self is called the *Bhaktiyoga* (yoga of devotion). The discipline of yoga is a practice of living in constant unity with the Supreme-soul. This inner discipline and inner unity transforms the psychological level of the individual and makes him receptive to the voice of the Supreme Lord within. The unity initiates the individual into self-surrender, self-realization and God-realization. It is the consciousness of the yogic unity which eventually transforms the performance of every activity into the yoga of action.

In these verses Srī Kṛṣṇa tells Arjuna that it is not just the knowledge of the Supreme-self, that brings liberation and peace in life, it is the assimilation and application of that knowledge which helps in establishing a yogic unity with the Divine. It is the knowledge of the Supreme-self, combined with actions, which helps the individual to develop a unity with the indwelling-self and inspires the individual into the gospel of selfless action. It is the spirit of performing every single activity, quite skilfully, selflessly and harmoniously. In the words of Swami Tapasyananda, "Having reminded Arjuna of the real nature of man as the eternal Spirit, Srī Kṛṣṇa now proceeds to declare the disciplines by which one could gradually realize this Divinity inherent in oneself. For, it is a matter of realization, and not mere talk. Srī Kṛṣṇa tells Arjuna about the doctrine of communion with God through work." The Karmayoga of Geeta is to perform each and every activity with proper insight and with an attitude of loving devotion to God. The proper knowledge of the Self initiates the intellectual ability to be resolute, firm and one pointed, which helps the individual to perform his work in a very skilful and detached manner. A life which is lived without unity in yoga is definitely confused, bewildered and fragmented.

Srī Kṛṣṇa declares the concept of yoga to be in perennial unity with the Divine. It brings inner strength and unity consciousness. It helps the thinking faculty to get settled in the Divine and makes the mind very resolute and determined. In these verses Srī Kṛṣṇa assures Arjuna that even the highest achievement of transcendental unity is possible through the Yoga of action; because in this discipline the individual works in constant unity with the Divine. The person becomes very determined and resolute. Since he works with integral wisdom and stability, the results of his work are unparalleled. A yogi works wonders because of his inner peace and one-pointedness of intellect. His work is always performed meticulously well. The unity in Yoga opens the door of inner intelligence to intuitive knowledge and to the transcendental experience of the Supreme-soul. The constant practice of yogic unity in the performance of actions enables the person to discover his sublime centre of ever luminous consciousness within his own self. When he becomes settled in that field of awareness, the concept of unity becomes his abiding heritage under all circumstances. It is a well known fact that the highest goal of life can be realized when the person is unassailably established in yogic unity and when he himself becomes aware of the truth that he is living in it. The Yoga of action is experienced and perceived in the complete cessation of all desires for the fruit of actions and all mental anxieties and agitations. It is the most efficacious means for the attainment of liberation. Srī Kṛṣṇa makes it very clear to Arjuna that the performance of duty with the consciousness of the Divine, definitely brings freedom to the individual. The duties performed in a co-partnership with God, and with the guidance of God, are naturally dedicated to God and surely bring deliverance from all kinds bondage. Srī Kṛṣṇa insists upon Arjuna to become aware of the activities of mind and screen the reality through his unity in yoga. He wants him to be fully conscious of the yogic unity with the indweller before engaging into action. Buddhi is intelligence. It is the faculty of distinguishing the appropriate from the inappropriate. When the Buddhi is united with consciousness of the Supreme-self and rests joyously in the majesty of the Supreme-soul, it surely functions under the direct guidance of the transcendental awareness. In that respect the Buddhi becomes resolute, one pointed, determined and free from all external pressures of mind.

यामिमां पुष्पितां वाचं प्रवदन्त्यविपश्चितः ।
वेदवादरताः पार्थ नान्यदस्तीति वादिनः ॥ ४२ ॥

yāmimāṁ puṣpitāṁ vācaṁ pravadantyavipaścitaḥ
vedavādaratāḥ pārtha nānyadastīti vādinaḥ

(42) Flowery speech is uttered by the unwise, those who take delight in the eulogizing hymns of Vedas, O' Arjuna, saying, "there is nothing other than this".

कामात्मानः स्वर्गपरा जन्मकर्मफलप्रदाम् ।
क्रियाविशेषबहुलां भोगैश्वर्यगतिं प्रति ॥ ४३ ॥

kāmātmānaḥ svargaparā janmakarmaphalapradām
kriyāviśeṣabahulāṁ bhogaiśvaryagatiṁ prati

(43) Those who are obsessed by desires, who consider heaven as their Supreme goal, they are led to new births as the result of their actions. They perform various rituals for the sake of pleasure and power.

भोगैश्वर्यप्रसक्तानां तयापहृतचेतसाम्।
व्यवसायात्मिका बुद्धिः समाधौ न विधीयते॥ ४४॥
bhogaiśvaryaprasaktānāṁ tayāpahṛtacetsām
vyavasāyātmikā buddhiḥ samādhau na vidhīyate

(44) Those who are deeply attached to pleasure and power, whose minds are carried away by such flowery speech; they are unable to develop the resolute will of a concentrated mind in meditation.

Commentary—In continuation of the verse forty-one, here Srī Kṛṣṇa proceeds further to enlighten Arjuna about the unfailing rewards of the yoga of selfless action. He tells that the person who performs actions with the desire for fruit, his personality becomes very disintegrated and dissipated. Such an individual is constantly engrossed in the anxiety of fulfilling his dreams and desires. He allows himself to be deceived by the multiplicity of rewards and that is why his intelligence becomes weak and deluded. The performance of rituals, which is directed towards the fulfilment of worldly desires and heavenly enjoyment, surely distracts the mind from the most cherished goal of human life and that worship is quite unfit for yogic meditation. Srī Kṛṣṇa reiterates the overriding importance of the knowledge of the Supreme-soul and performance of all work with the awareness of the Divine. He further explains that the performance of rituals which is carried on without proper insight does not bring the essential peace and happiness. Any person who performs the rituals of *Vedas* without proper knowledge, gets trapped into the web of many desires. The individual of meagre understanding rolls constantly into the whirlpool of fulfilling his worldly desires, and so he loses the insight of thinking anything beyond that. In the ritualistic portion of the *Veda,* people perform the prescribed rituals for the attainment of worldly desires, pleasures, power and fortune. In this process they get trapped in desires and can never develop a determined intellect for self-realization because the illusive nature of desires keep distracting the mind from the final goal. The word 'Veda' exactly means the knowledge of the Divine. The ultimate goal of reciting the vedic hymns, and performing the vedic rituals is self-purification, self realization and God-realization. In the words of Jaydayal Goyandka, "The primary aim of the four Vedas is to propound upon the reality of God, who forms the essence of life. It is because of the ignorance of this truth, the people become attached to the rituals for the satisfaction of the worldly desires and miss the important message". Srī Kṛṣṇa declares those people to be ignorant and unwise, who practise spirituality merely for the attainment of earthly pleasures and lordship. These people become devoted to the ritualistic section of the *Vedas*, in which the prayers are addressed towards the fulfilment of worldly enjoyments and comforts of heaven. These people become enchanted by the glamorous promises and remain engrossed in the performance of actions which satisfy their desires. They fail to realize that the performance of these rituals is only a means, and not an end in itself. Srī Kṛṣṇa tells Arjuna in verse forty-four that the person who is attached to the enjoyments of life, his mind remains charged with many desires and he loses the steadiness of mind. He is always restless and definitely lacks the poised understanding. For him, even the meditation routine is performed as a ritual which renders hardly any peace and tranquillity. In the words of Srī Ramanuja, "In performing obligatory and occasional rituals, all fruits—primary and secondary—promised in the scriptures, should be abandoned, with the idea that release or salvation is the only purpose of all scripture-ordained rituals. These rituals should be performed without any thought of selfish gains."

त्रैगुण्यविषया वेदा निस्त्रैगुण्यो भवार्जुन।
निर्द्वन्द्वो नित्यसत्त्वस्थो निर्योगक्षेम आत्मवान्॥ ४५॥

traiguṇyaviṣayā vedā nistraiguṇyo bhavārjuna
nirdvandvo nityasattvastho niryogakṣema ātmavān

(45) The subject matter that deals with the triple attributes of nature in the *Vedas*, be Thou above those three attributes, O'Arjuna. Liberate yourself from the pairs of opposites and ever abide in the Sattva. Being free from the feeling of acquisition and preservation, stay established in the Supreme-self.

यावानर्थ उदपाने सर्वतः सम्प्लुतोदके।
तावान्सर्वेषु वेदेषु ब्राह्मणस्य विजानतः॥ ४६॥

yāvānartha udapāne sarvataḥ saṁplutodake
tāvān sarveṣu vedeṣu brāhmaṇasya vijānataḥ

(46) To a knower of Brahman, the *Vedas* are of as much use, as is a small reservoir of water in a place which is flooded with water on all sides.

Commentary—These two verses are the continuation of the same concept of Karmayoga as described in the last two verses. The ritualistic worship which is performed without proper knowledge and insight, that definitely becomes a source of bondage. This is indeed a fact that as long as the individual continues to identify his happiness with the fulfilment of worldly desires, he definitely remains bound, ignorant and lost in diversity. He becomes very ambitious and undertakes many kinds of projects which are mutually contradictory. His dream of securing enjoyments becomes so inordinate that only those things escape his grasp which are beyond his reach. The hopes and aspirations of such an individual gallop ahead of his mind and his desires remain unsatisfied even if he traverses the entire universe. Most of the human desires are prompted from the triad of nature—the three aspects of the gunas. Somehow, people in general are anxious to achieve what appeals to them fascinating and also worry to preserve whatever they have already achieved. The entire life span goes round and round in accumulating the material comforts and then safeguarding them. The anxiety and fear robs the individual of all peace and happiness. Although a certain part of the *Vedas* gives a vivid description about the performance of rituals, for the fulfilment of desires, but these rituals are meant for self-purification only. The purpose of the vedic rituals is to bring happiness and prosperity in the present life and in the life hereafter. The performance of these rituals does inspire the individual to live in perfect harmony with nature and with the inner-self.

The purpose of performing these rituals is to connect the day-to-day life of the individual with the awareness of the Supreme-self. It is essential to perform rituals for inner purification and in order to harmonize the diverse constituents of the physical, psychological and spiritual levels. For example, the performance of the vedic *samskaras* have been highly recommended for self-purification of the individual. There are sixteen *samskaras* as described in the ancient scriptures—*Garbhadana, Punsavanam, Simantonnayana, Jatakarma, Namakarna, Niskraman, Annaprashana, Chudakarma, Karnavedha, Upanayana, Vedarambha, Samavartana, Vivaha, Grahasthashrama, Vanaprastha, Sanyasa,* and *Antheshti*. The word *samskara* literally means thought and memory. The closest English word which has been used for the performance of *samskaras* is the sacraments or the purificatory ceremonies. These rituals are performed in order to give sanctity and purification to the human thoughts. The performance of the first *samskara* starts right from the day when the child is conceived and the last one is performed when the person dies, for the peaceful journey of the soul into the life hereafter. These are the purificatory rituals for the individual to shine in all respects and to live a balanced, healthy, respectful and blessed life. The validity of the performance of these ceremonies can't be denied. These rituals should be performed as a mode of guidance from less awareness to increased awareness, from darkness to light.

The second line in the verse forty-five indicates the special message in which Srī Kṛṣṇa tells Arjuna to recognize the essentiality about the modes of Prakriti and become firmly grounded in the nature of Sattva. Arjuna is advised to direct his attention to the presence of the Supreme reality within and become fully established in the bliss and the beatitude of the transcendental-soul. The term *nityasattwastho* literally means being perennially established in the purity of Sattva, and the term 'Atmavan' means firmly grounded in the Supreme-self. Srī Kṛṣṇa suggests to Arjuna to educate and train himself to be alert and observant. He tells him to become aware of his relationship with the Supreme indweller and of the guidance that comes from within. He should constantly try to remain awakened, in the consciousness of the Divine and avoid all the emotional involvements which are inconsistent with his resolve. When the individual rests in the pure transcendental state of consciousness; his desires of acquiring and accumulating do fade away automatically, and he feels settled in peace, contentment and the serenity of the Supreme-Self. In that state of self-realization, the qualities of nature also become supportive and help the individual to perform his work effortlessly, desirelessly and selflessly.

कर्मण्येवाधिकारस्ते मा फलेषु कदाचन।
मा कर्मफलहेतुर्भूर्मा ते सङ्गोऽस्त्वकर्मणि ॥ ४७ ॥

karmaṇyevādhikāraste mā phaleṣu kadācana
mā karmaphalahetur bhūr mā te saṅgo'stvakarmaṇi

(47) Your right is to perform your work only and not at all to its fruit; let not the fruit of action be your motive, nor let your attachment be to inaction.

योगस्थः कुरु कर्माणि सङ्गं त्यक्त्वा धनञ्जय।
सिद्ध्यसिद्ध्योः समो भूत्वा समत्वं योग उच्यते ॥ ४८ ॥

yogasthaḥ kuru karmāṇi saṅgaṁ tyaktvā dhanañjaya
siddhyasiddhyoḥ samo bhūtvā samatvaṁ yoga ucyate

(48) O'Arjuna, perform your actions, being steadfast in Yoga. Renounce all attachments and be balanced in success and failure. Evenness (equanimity) of mind is said to be Yoga.

दूरेण ह्यवरं कर्म बुद्धियोगाद्धनञ्जय।
बुद्धौ शरणमन्विच्छ कृपणाः फलहेतवः ॥ ४९ ॥

dūreṇa hyavaraṁ karma buddhiyogād dhanañjaya
buddhau śaraṇamanviccha kṛpaṇāḥ phalahetavaḥ

(49) Action with attachment is far inferior, O'Arjuna, to that action which is performed with the Yoga of wisdom. Seek refuge in integral wisdom; for pitiful are those who crave for the fruits of their actions.

बुद्धियुक्तो जहातीह उभे सुकृतदुष्कृते।
तस्माद्योगाय युज्यस्व योगः कर्मसु कौशलम् ॥ ५० ॥

buddhiyukto jahātīha ubhe sukṛtaduṣkṛte
tasmādyogāya yujyasva yogaḥ karmasu kauśalam

(50) Endowed with wisdom, one liberates oneself in this life, from virtues and vices. Therefore devote yourself to yoga. Yoga is skill in action.

कर्मजं बुद्धियुक्ता हि फलं त्यक्त्वा मनीषिणः।
जन्मबन्धविनिर्मुक्ताः पदं गच्छन्त्यनामयम्॥ ५१॥

karmajaṁ buddhiyuktā hi phalaṁ tyaktvā manīṣiṇaḥ
janmabandhavinirmuktāḥ padaṁ gacchantyanāmayam

(51) The wise sages, who are endowed with integral wisdom, having relinquished the fruits of their actions, become liberated from the bondage of rebirth. They attain the blissful Supreme state.

Commentary—The exposition of Karmayoga has been continued in these verses. Srī Kṛṣṇa concludes the message of selfless action with a declaration : "your right is to work only, and not at all to its fruit. Let not the fruit of action be your motive." The Karmayoga is the art of living and acting through the uninterrupted consciousness of the Supreme-soul. The success and satisfaction in any work lies in the attitude of performing it without all anxieties, fears and expectations. For example, an artist can produce an outstanding masterpiece of art, only if he becomes totally absorbed in his work; without being worried about the possible fear of failures and rejections. As a matter of fact, the action itself becomes its reward when it is performed intelligently, diligently and devotedly. In the words of Srī Mahadev Desai, "He who is ever brooding over result, he often loses his nerve in the performance of his duty. He becomes impatient and then gives vent to anger and begins to do unworthy things; he jumps from action to action never remaining faithful to any." The gospel of selfless action inspires the individual to the performance of work with proper attention, accuracy, and punctuality, which are the principal qualities required for any kind of success in work. The concentrated energy enables the person to force his way through the irksome, drudgery and dry details, and guides him onward in every station of life. He accomplishes his goals without any disappointment and peril. The practice of working through the unity of yoga enables the person to accomplish a great amount of work in the shortest span of time. The concentrated effort, diligence and skilfulness is surely the key to all success and satisfaction in work. On the other hand, the person who is always anxious about the fruits of his action and worries over the results he definitely wastes his time and dissipates his energy.

Srī Kṛṣṇa advises Arjuna to make the best use of the present without being involved in the anxieties for the rewards in future. The gospel of Karmayoga recommends to perform one's duty with the best of his ability without desiring any reward. In the words of Srī Vinoba, "Behind a man's action are generally two types of attitudes. One is the assured feeling, 'I shall enjoy the fruit of my action. I've the right to it'. On the contrary, there is feeling, 'If I'm not to enjoy the fruit of my action, then I'll not act at all'." The Geeta tells us of yet another attitude of mind or way of life, which says, "You must of course act but don't think that you have a right to the fruit".

The desire for the fruit of action interferes with the quality of the performance of action and it is also the root cause of many problems in life. There are thousands of people who are deeply plunged in grief and pain because of their expectations from all kinds of work which is undertaken in day-to-day life. It is a fact that anybody who depends upon the fruit of action for self-gratification, he eventually find himself bound and miserable. As it is noticed, in general people live in bondage because of their own self-imposed restrictions and limitations. For example, whenever somebody does a little favour to someone, he expects rewards in the form of appreciation and some words of thanks. This way, the person definitely imprisons his happiness and lives upon the mercy of other people. He depends upon other people's response for his personal satisfaction and happiness.

In this connection, Dale Carnegie relates a true incident in his famous book *How To Stop Worrying And Start Living*, "I recently met a businessman in Texas, who was burned up with indignation. I was warned that he would tell me about it, within fifteen minutes after I met him. He did. The incident about which he was angry, had occurred eleven months previously, but he was still burned up about it. He could not talk of anything else. He had given his thirty-four employees, ten thousand dollars in Christmas bonuses—approximately three hundred dollars each—and no one had thanked him. "I am sorry," he complained bitterly, "that I ever gave them a penny!" In continuation of this incident he further writes, "Instead of wallowing in resentment and self-pity, he might have asked himself why he didn't get any appreciation. May be he had underpaid and over worked his employees. May be they considered a Christmas bonus not a gift, but something they had earned. May be he was so critical and unapproachable that no one dared or cared to thank him. May be they felt he gave the bonus because most of the profits were going for taxes, anyway. May be this or may be that."

The truth is that actually no one has any control on what other people think, what their responses are going to be in a particular situation. These thoughts of expectations are the ghosts which haunt people day and night. These thoughts of resentment and bitterness usually destroy all the peace and happiness of life. These feelings of pain and resentment have caused a lot of torture to mankind throughout the history. People live in self-torture and die in ignorance. That's why Srī Kṛṣṇa repeats again and again to Arjuna the golden rule, "Your right is to perform your work only and not at all to its fruit; let not the fruit of action be your motive". The desire for rewards makes the individual weak, frustrated and anxious. It saps energy and drains away a whole lot of the best of one's ability. The people who constantly expect and desire the fruit of their action, for them, Srī Kṛṣṇa has used these words, *kṛpaṇaḥ phalahetavaḥ* means deluded and miserable are those who crave for the fruit of their action. In the words of Jaydayal Goyandaka, "Freedom of will is allowed to human beings only. Therefore, if through the performance of duty, and renouncing the attachment to action and fruit, a person carries out injunction of God, he can easily succeed in God-realization." He further adds the one who makes, "the best use of this opportunity, he gets liberated from bondage of Karma and attains the Supreme state." Living a life in the consciousness of the Divine, and performing all work in the consciousness of the Divine is Karmayoga. It is the realization of God through the performance of actions. In other words, the actions which help the individual to maintain his conscious unity with the Supreme-self is defined as Karmayoga.

Srī Kṛṣṇa tells Arjuna to remain established in Yoga i.e. to be in a constant contact with the Divine, which will help him to rise above all emotional conflicts. The transcendent state of yogic unity is devoid of all types of conflicts and anxieties of results. Once the individual becomes settled in that realm he automatically becomes free from all the desires of acquisition, preservation, rewards, name and fame. In that state of realization the attitude of selfless action becomes a second nature to the individual. Since the false sense of selfish individualism is dissolved, the person works very effortlessly and graciously. In the consciousness of inner unity and enlightenment, the individual's life becomes contented and his activities become fulfilling and rewarding in all respects. The well known key to the door of bliss in life is to be established in the unity of yoga and perform all work in the unity of yoga. It renders clarity of vision, and the awareness of working in a co-partnership with God. In the words of Maharishi Mahesh Yogi, "Yoga is the basis of integrated life, harmony of inner creative silence and outer action. A man can't remain balanced in loss and gain unless he is in a state of lasting contentment. Yoga is that eternal, balanced and never changing state of transcendental consciousness which sets the mind free to participate in activity without being involved in it." Skill in action manifests itself from the equipoise, tranquillity and placidity of mind, and the placidity of mind is possible only when the mind is settled in the Divine. Srī Kṛṣna tells Arjuna: *Yogaḥ karmaśu kausalam*—yoga is skill in action. The performance of work through unity in yoga is indeed the key to perfection in work. Any one who performs work with unity in Yoga, he is eventually released from the bonds of birth-death and rebirth. He attains the blissful state of immortality.

यदा ते मोहकलिलं बुद्धिर्व्यतितरिष्यति।
तदा गन्तासि निर्वेदं श्रोतव्यस्य श्रुतस्य च॥५२॥

yadā te mohakalilaṁ buddhirvyatitariṣyati
tadā gantāsi nirvedaṁ śrotavyasya śrutasya ca

(52) When your intellect will cross the mire of delusion, then you will gain the indifference to what has been heard and what is yet to be heard.

श्रुतिविप्रतिपन्ना ते यदा स्थास्यति निश्चला।
समाधावचला बुद्धिस्तदा योगमवाप्स्यसि॥५३॥

śrutivipratipannā te yadā sthāsyati niścalā
samādhāvacalā buddhis tadā yogamavāpsyasi

(53) When your intellect, which is confused by hearing the conflicting doctrines, will become firm and steadfast in meditation, you will attain the vision of the Supreme-Self in yoga.

Commentary—Srī Kṛṣṇa knows that Arjuna needs re-orientation into the concept of Karmayoga which is initiated from the unity with the Supreme-soul. When the individual becomes enlightened from within, he gains the insight into the philosophy of Karmayoga and performs his work selflessly and effortlessly. There are two different methods which help the individual to become enlightened in life. One source of enlightenment is tuition which is learning from teachers and accumulating knowledge from books etc. But there is another source of enlightenment from within that is called intuition. Intuition is the revelation from within which comes to the individual from his constant association with the Supreme-self. Intuition is the reward of living in yoga. This is not something to be acquired, it needs to be revealed from the grace of the Indwelling-Self. It comes in the form of inner understanding which provides the individual a tremendous discriminating ability. It is the unmanifested stream of knowledge which becomes manifested to the individual. According to our holy sages, the intuition is inner awakening, it is the inner guidance and the inner wisdom. In some cases the individual becomes blessed with it in a flicker of a moment; but in other cases it takes years and years of selfless service and the practice of ethical discipline. Whenever there is an honest desire for enlightenment, the individual receives it from his own source of life.

The knowledge of the Supreme-soul is experiential. It is not revealed to the person at random, it comes in a very systematic order. It emerges from the individual's deepest awareness and moves through the various levels of consciousness. When the mind is purified in yoga, the *Atma-jñana* is revealed from within. The inner chambers of the subconscious mind start opening one by one and the change takes place in the person's personality step by step. According to Rishi Patanjali, there are various stages of inner awakening, when the intuitive knowledge is perceived by the aspirant. He describes it as *Jñana, taraka, vivekaja, pratibham, prajana* and *ṛtambhara.* These are the various stages in yogic unity wherein the person moves from less intuitive ability to increased intuitive ability. The knowledge of the Self becomes revealed to the person's conscious plane from his subconscious or his subliminal-self. Gradually he starts becoming awarre of it and expresses its grandeur in his day-to-day life. His relationship with others becomes pleasant and harmonious. The perfect peace that reigns within his own self is expressed in his external harmony with the world in which he lives. For example, the saints and sages are usually very bright, intelligent, wise and very knowledgeable in all respects. The reason is that knowingly or unknowingly they are always settled in the deepest awareness of the Divine. In the verse fifty-two, Srī Kṛṣṇa enlightens Arjuna about this truth. He tells Arjuna that when the intellect becomes firmly grounded in the Divine, the individual develops inner intuition. He gets guidance from the Supreme-self, which helps him to go beyond the mire of delusion. The individual derives a sharp sense of discrimination between the real and unreal. This inner guidance disperses his confusion about the conflicting doctrines. The person becomes steady, he feels integrated and determined within. He feels confident and self-reliant. He himself experiences the presence of the higher power and becomes receptive to its guidance and instructions. He enjoys in being united in yoga and work through yoga with the indweller. Srī Kṛṣṇa is emphasizing that in order to be in touch with the inner guidance and grace the person has to turn inward to his own resources and has to take refuge in the Supreme-self.

अर्जुन उवाच

स्थितप्रज्ञस्य का भाषा समाधिस्थस्य केशव।
स्थितधीः किं प्रभाषेत किमासीत व्रजेत किम्॥५४॥

sthitaprajñasya kā bhāṣā samādhisthasya keśava
sthitadhīḥ kiṁ prabhāṣeta kimāsīta vrajeta kim

Arjuna said :

(54) O'Kṛṣṇa—what are the marks of the man of steadfast

wisdom, who is established in transcendental meditation? How does a man of integral wisdom speak, how does he sit and how does he walk?

Commentary—In this verse, Arjuna inquires about the characteristics of a person who becomes enlightened and who is firmly established in the consciousness of the transcendental awareness. He requests Srī Kṛṣṇa to describe the hallmark of that man who has become steadfast in the essential nature of the Supreme-self. *Sthitaprajñasya* means the one who is firmly established in the *para-jñana*—the knowledge of the Supreme-self. *Jñana* means the knowledge. *Parą-jñana* means the knowledge of the transcendental-Self. In other words, intelligence and wisdom may appear synonymous, but these two words definitely differ in their meanings. According to our holy scriptures intelligence stands for *Buddhi* and wisdom stands for *Dhee,* which literally means cultured intelligence. When *Buddhi* stays connected with the transcendental-Self, it becomes transformed into *Dhee* and later into *Medhaa* and *Prajñana*. It is the faculty of intuition. It is the purest manifestation of the self. The indwelling consciousness evolves and expresses itself at various levels. These are known by different names as the different states of inner awareness. The individual who is firmly grounded in the knowledge of the transcendental-Self, he is called *sthitaprajñasya.* Any one who has the experiential knowledge of the transcendental-Self, he definitely manifests that grace of his inner connectedness in his day-to-day life. A man of integral wisdom, who is ever united in the Self he makes quick, firm, impartial and very determined decisions. Such an individual is highly intuitive and his discriminating ability is unparalleled. His decisions come from the depth of his heart. His lifestyle becomes a beacon light for others in society. The eloquence of his speech and the careful analysis of his words manifest the serenity of his mind because he remains ever connected with the source of integral wisdom. There is a word in the prayer of the great Gayatri mantra—*dheemahi*—which means Let us meditate on *dhee*—the steadfast wisdom, the indwelling transcendental consciousness. Let's live in the awareness of the Supreme-Lord in order to be blessed with *prajñana*—the knowledge of the transcendental-Self.

श्रीभगवानुवाच

प्रजहाति यदा कामान्सर्वान्पार्थ मनोगतान्।
आत्मन्येवात्मना तुष्टः स्थितप्रज्ञस्तदोच्यते ॥ ५५ ॥

prajahāti yadā kāmān sarvān pārtha manogatān
ātmanyevātmanā tuṣṭaḥ sthitaprajñastadocyate

The Blessed Lord said :

(55) When a man abandons all the desires of his mind, O'Arjuna; when he feels satisfied in the Self, by the self, then he is said to be established in transcendental wisdom.

दुःखेष्वनुद्विग्नमनाः सुखेषु विगतस्पृहः।
वीतरागभयक्रोधः स्थितधीर्मुनिरुच्यते ॥ ५६ ॥

duḥkheṣv anudvignamanāḥ sukheṣu vigataspṛhaḥ
vītarāgabhayakrodhaḥ sthitdhīrmunirucyate

(56) He whose mind remains unperturbed in the midst of sorrows, who has no longing for pleasures, who is free from passion, fear and anger, he is called a sage of steadfast wisdom.

यः सर्वत्रानभिस्नेहस्तत्तत्प्राप्य शुभाशुभम्।
नाभिनन्दति न द्वेष्टि तस्य प्रज्ञा प्रतिष्ठिता ॥ ५७ ॥

yaḥ sarvatrānabhisnehas tattatprāpya śubhāśubham
nābhinandati na dveṣṭi tasya prajñā pratiṣṭhitā

(57) He, who is unattached in all respects, at receiving good or evil, who neither rejoices nor hates, he is surely settled in transcendental wisdom.

यदा संहरते चायं कूर्मोऽङ्गानीव सर्वशः।
इन्द्रियाणीन्द्रियार्थेभ्यस्तस्य प्रज्ञा प्रतिष्ठिता ॥ ५८ ॥

yadā saṅharate cāyaṁ kūrmo'ṅgānīva sarvaśaḥ
indriyāṇīndriyārthebhyastasya prajñā pratiṣṭhitā

(58) When like a tortoise, which withdraws its limbs from all sides (into the shell), he withdraws his senses from the objects of the senses,

then his wisdom becomes firmly set.

Commentary—In these verses Srī Kṛṣṇa enlightens Arjuna about the characteristics of a person who becomes fully established in the consciousness of the Supreme-self. He starts with the word *kāmān* which stands for the cravings of the mind in the form of *vasanas, sprha, iccha* and *trishna*. These are the various kind of desires and cravings for the possession of riches, comforts, woman, honour name and fame. When the mind of a person is haunted by these desires, it wanders in many directions and becomes very restless and unsteady. The person of inner instability becomes busy in taking up new plans and projects. His desire of one thing leads to another. When the individual continues to identify himself with worldly desires and inclination, he gradually loses his conscious connections with the transcendental-Self. As he drifts away from the indwelling light, he becomes contaminated by ignorance. The conscious separation from the inner wisdom is indeed the cause of inner instability and restlessness. Srī Kṛṣṇa tells Arjuna that the man of steadfast wisdom is very enlightened. He has the ability and strength to withdraw his mind from the cravings of the worldly desires. The man who becomes satisfied in the tranquillity of the transcendental-Self; he rises above the slavery of the desires. He lives in the consciousness of the Divine and works through that source. All his thoughts and activities become centred in the awareness of the Supreme Spirit. Since he has no desire for the fruits of his actions he works very fearlessly and skilfully.

The man of integral wisdom becomes a source of bliss and carries that bliss wherever he goes. His enlightened state of mind works like a *dehelideepakaanya*—a lamp, placed on the threshold, which connects many rooms. This one lamp provides light to all the rooms. A person established in the inner wisdom reflects the peace and integrity of the transcendental-Self into each and every type of work he undertakes. The nature of the Divine becomes reflected in every bit of the work he performs, and in every single word he speaks. Such a person becomes an embodiment of peace and contentment. He is free from all attachments, fears and anger. He has the strength to remain unperturbed in auspicious or inauspicious circumstances. To live in the enlightened state of mind is like living in eternity. Such an individual knows how to maintain his balance while facing the dualities of life. He does not feel arrogant about his own state of being illuminated and also does not worry if he is not rewarded for his deeds. The illuminated one regards pleasure and pain, loss and gain, honour and dishonour as the passing phases of life. He beholds the tragedies and the comedies of life with an attitude of undisturbed tranquillity.

In relation to this there is an incident from *The Life Story Of Ramakrishna* written by Christopher Isherwood. He writes that, "one time Srī Ramakrishna who was the chief priest at the Kali temple, Calcutta, made some mistakes during the Durga Pooja. The Managing Committee of the temple decided to get rid of him. Accordingly, one of the temple officials came to Ramakrishna and ordered him to leave at once. Without the least sign of resentment or dismay, Ramakrishna picked up his towel, slung it over his shoulder, and walked unprotestingly out of the room, which had been his home for the past twenty-six years. He had almost reached the gate of the compound when the temple officials came running after him crying, "Please Stay! We beg of you to stay!" At this, Ramakrishna smiled; turned around, without saying a word, went back to his room, sat down, and continued the conversation he had been having with some of his devotees, as if nothing unusual had happened." This is how the man of steadfast wisdom acts in his day-to-day life. He lives his life in perennial tranquillity of the self. A perfect calmness in attitude, self-mastery and righteousness do characterize the life of a self-integrated and self-realized saint.

The man of integral wisdom becomes very purified and remains perennially settled in the luminosity of the transcendental self. His life is very disciplined, regulated and organized. His intellectual faculty acts in perfect harmony with the indweller and his mind functions very concentratedly and effectively. Endowed with such stability and inner contentment, even if he takes an active interest in the world, or totally renounces the world, that becomes a matter of his personal choice. For example, Rishi Yajvalkya chose to retire to the tapovana (place of penances) while King Janaka ruled his great empire. The King lived and ruled his kingdom as an embodiment of the Divine. He has been called *Vedehi*—the one who lived a life which was totally soaked in the nature of the Lord. King Janaka always considered his body only a temple of God and a vehicle to perform the worldly activities. It is indeed immaterial where a self-integrated person decides to live or what he decides to do—all his activities are perennially centred in the consciousness of the Supreme-Self. He knows how to enjoy the serenity of his silent moods and he also knows how to deal with the turbulent waves of his mind. He lives in total vigilance of the self and stays very alert about all the information which is fed by the senses of perception to the mind. He knows very clearly and intelligently as what to see with his eyes and what to avoid. He knows what to eat and what not to eat and also what to accept and what to reject. His life becomes very disciplined. He has the strength to withdraw himself from the sense objects and their enjoyments.

Here Srī Krṣṇa gives a very appropriate illustration of the tortoise who instinctively withdraws his six limbs—four legs, a tail and a forehead into its shell for the protection against any visible danger. Similarly a person, who lives in the full awareness of the Self, can ingeniously withdraw his senses of perception and action from all kinds of desires for self-protection and purity. He holds total control over his thoughts and aspirations, those arise from the sense objects and knows how to withdraw them within, whenever he wants to. In the words of Srī Aurobindo, "As the tortoise draws his limbs into the shell, so these into their source, quiescent in the mind, the mind quiescent in intelligence, the intelligence quiescent in the soul and its self-knowledge, observing the action of Nature, but not subject to it, not desiring anything, which the objective life can give." A man of integral wisdom has the strength to divert the flow of his outgoing thoughts into the indwelling-self and direct his attention into the stability of the Supreme-soul. His life becomes very pure, enlightened and tranquil; and he carries that peace and radiance wherever he goes.

विषया विनिवर्तन्ते निराहारस्य देहिनः ।
रसवर्जं रसोऽप्यस्य परं दृष्ट्वा निवर्तते ॥ ५९ ॥

viṣayā vinivartante nirāhārasya dehinaḥ
rasvarjaṁ raso'pyasya paraṁ drṣṭvā nivartate

(59) The objects of the senses, cease to exist for the man who does not enjoy them but the taste for them persists. This lingering taste also disappears for the man of steadfast mind, on seeing the Supreme.

यततो ह्यपि कौन्तेय पुरुषस्य विपश्चितः।
इन्द्रियाणि प्रमाथीनि हरन्ति प्रसभं मनः॥ ६०॥

yatato hyapi kaunteya puruṣasya vipaścitaḥ
indriyāṇi pramāthīni haranti prasbhaṁ manaḥ

(60) O'Arjuna, the turbulent senses do forcibly carry away the mind of even a wise man who is practising self-control.

तानि सर्वाणि संयम्य युक्त आसीत मत्परः।
वशे हि यस्येन्द्रियाणि तस्य प्रज्ञा प्रतिष्ठिता॥ ६१॥

tāni sarvāṇi saṅyamya yukta āsīta matparaḥ
vaśe hi yasyendriyāṇi tasya prajñā pratiṣṭhitā

(61) Therefore, having controlled them all, one should remain firm in Yoga, regarding Me as the Supreme; for he, whose senses are under control, is surely settled in transcendental wisdom.

Commentary—Here Srī Kṛṣṇa alerts Arjuna that in general when a person withdraws himself from the worldly enjoyments, the sense objects may seem to turn away temporarily but still the taste for them lingers for a long time. The desires may seem to vanish momentarily, but still the wish to enjoy the sensual pleasures stays dormant in the subconscious mind. This taste lingers in the memory like the light of the twilight, long after the moment itself is gone. So it is very important to live in constant awareness of the Self in order to monitor the direction of thought. As in the words of Buddha, "Those who respect themselves must be on constant guard, lest they yield to evil desires. To conquer one's own self is a greater victory than to conquer the thousands in a battle." Srī Kṛṣṇa calls the senses to be turbulent which can forcibly disturb the thoughts of a disciplined aspirant. Even the slightest attachment to the taste of the sensual enjoyments can disperse the rewards of the most difficult austerity which was undertaken for many years. A little inclination to the enjoyment of the sensual objects can agitate and provoke the thoughts of a person who has been striving for self-control. Srī Kṛṣṇa tells Arjuna that although the springing up of these desires in the mind is quite natural but the individual's involvement in their fulfillment is very personal. He alerts mankind and suggests to remain perpetually vigilant in this respect. In the words of Maharishi Mahesh Yogi, "Withdrawal of senses doesn't necessarily mean that the senses don't experience outside objects, but that they are not totally engrossed in them to the extent that they transfer to the mind impressions deep enough to become the seed of future desires. When the mind is mainly identified with the inner being the senses don't identify with the objects." In the verse sixty-one, Srī Kṛṣṇa suggests that after having restrained the senses from the sensual objects, the aspirant should seek refuge in the Supreme indweller. The unity in yoga replaces the old habits with the newer ones and the inward joy of being surrendered in the Self blossoms in all respects. Through the incessant, persistent and unremitting practice of self-discipline, the individual becomes established in the serenity of the steadfast wisdom.

ध्यायतो विषयान्पुंसः सङ्गस्तेषूपजायते।
सङ्गात्सञ्जायते कामः कामात्क्रोधोऽभिजायते॥ ६२॥

dhyāyato viṣayān puṁsaḥ saṅgasteṣūpajāyate
saṅgāt sañjāyate kāmaḥ kāmāt krodho'bhijāyate

क्रोधाद्भवति सम्मोहः सम्मोहात्स्मृतिविभ्रमः।
स्मृतिभ्रंशाद् बुद्धिनाशो बुद्धिनाशात्प्रणश्यति॥ ६३॥

krodhād bhavati sammohaḥ sammohāt smṛtivibhramaḥ
smṛtibhraṅśād buddhināśo buddhināśāt praṇaśyati

(62, 63) The man who broods over the objects of the senses, he develops attachment for them; from attachment springs up desire, the desire (unfulfilled) ensues anger. From anger arises delusion, from delusion the confusion of memory; from the confusion of memory the loss of reason and from the loss of reason, he goes to complete ruin.

Commentary—In the continuation of the previous verses, here Srī Kṛṣṇa proceeds to tell Arjuna that the downfall of a man starts when he becomes engaged and perennially occupied with the gratification of the sensual pleasures of the world. These two verses of the holy dialogue present a new insight to the understanding of life, which becomes primarily subjected to the fulfilment of the worldly desires. Srī Kṛṣṇa tells Arjuna that the person who constantly thinks about the objects of senses, he gradually develops a strong attachment for them. The attachment grows into a longing desire and infatuation. When the infatuation for something starts disturbing the peace of mind, the individual feels very confused and deluded. So whenever there comes an obstacle in the fulfilment of that desire; the person becomes very frustrated and angry. He feels weak and insecure and also unable to judge the pros and cons of the situation. He goes ahead very strongly to acquire the desired object, without paying any attention to the consequences. An angry man becomes stupefied and also insults other people. He uses harsh, undesirable words and acts in a very demoralizing style without being aware of it. The delusion of mind leads him to the confusion of memory and the loss of reasoning ability. With the loss of reason he perishes. In the words of Swami Ramsukhdas, "Though it takes time to describe this order yet the rise of these propensities leading to the destruction of man are as fast as death caused by an electric shock." These two verses unfold a rational survey, which penetrates into the basic psychological aspects of human nature. The message unfolds that the downfall of a man is indeed rooted in his infatuation for the worldly temptations. As E.F. Schumacher writes in his book *Small Is Beautiful*, "A man driven by greed and envy, loses the power of seeing things as they really are; of seeing things in their roundness and wholeness, and in that case his very successes do become his failures. If the whole society becomes infected by these vices, they may indeed achieve astonishing things but they become increasingly incapable of solving the most elementary problems of everyday existence."

It is true that a person's contemplation on the object of the senses is unavoidable, on account of his latencies and impressions. The coming up of the worldly desires in human mind is very natural but the person's involvement in the gratification of these desires is very personal. In this context, there is an illustration given by a saint, "One day a man, while he was coming back from his office, looked at a beautiful car in a parking lot. Immediately, the desire of having that car flashed through his mind. Gradually the idea of possessing that car became an infatuation. Every night before going to bed, he looked at his bank balance. The bank statement clearly showed that he could not buy the car. Later on, he decided to apply for a loan; unfortunately the loan application was turned down by the bank. The rejection notice made him very angry, and his desire to possess that car became stronger than before. In the delusion of insecurity and ignorance, he decided to rob the car. In the act of robbery, he was caught and sent to jail." It is a fact, that when an angry man becomes attached to something, his urge to possess that object becomes an obsession. The burning desire to possess that particular thing deludes his thinking faculty and the individual loses the power of discrimination which itself becomes the cause of his self-degradation and self-destruction. In the words of Adi Sankara, "Man can be called Man, only when he retains his competency to discriminate between right and wrong, do's and don'ts. When that competence fails, man is totally lost and utterly ruined. Man perishes and becomes unfit to realize the meaning of human existence".

रागद्वेषवियुक्तैस्तु विषयानिन्द्रियैश्चरन्।
आत्मवश्यैर्विधेयात्मा प्रसादमधिगच्छति ॥ ६४ ॥

rāgdveṣaviyuktaistu viṣayānindriyaiścaran
ātmavaśyairvidheyātmā prasādamadhigacchati

(64) But a self-controlled man who moves among the objects of the senses with his senses under control and free from attraction and repulsion; he attains serenity of mind.

प्रसादे सर्वदुःखानां हानिरस्योपजायते।
प्रसन्नचेतसो ह्याशु बुद्धिः पर्यवतिष्ठते ॥ ६५ ॥

prasāde sarvaduḥkhānāṁ hānirasyopajāyate
prasannacetaso hyāśu buddhiḥ paryavatiṣṭhate

(65) With the attainment of this inner serenity, all his sufferings come to an end; and soon the intellect of such a person of tranquil mind becomes firmly established in the Bliss of the deepest awareness.

नास्ति बुद्धिरयुक्तस्य न चायुक्तस्य भावना।
न चाभावयतः शान्तिरशान्तस्य कुतः सुखम्॥ ६६॥

nāsti buddhirayuktasya na cāyuktasya bhāvanā
na cābhāvayataḥ śāntiraśāntasya kutaḥ sukham

(66) There is no knowledge of the Self for the one who is not united within. The transcendental meditation is not possible for the unsteady, and to the unmeditative there can be no peace. To the man who has no inner peace, how can there be happiness?

इन्द्रियाणां हि चरतां यन्मनोऽनु विधीयते।
तदस्य हरति प्रज्ञां वायुर्नावमिवाम्भसि॥ ६७॥

indriyāṇāṁ hi caratāṁ yanmano'nu vidhīyate
tadasya harati prajñāṁ vāyurnāvamivāmbhasi

(67) For, when the mind yields to the wandering senses, it carries away the discrimination of the man, just as the wind carries away the ship on the water.

तस्माद्यस्य महाबाहो निगृहीतानि सर्वशः।
इन्द्रियाणीन्द्रियार्थेभ्यस्तस्य प्रज्ञा प्रतिष्ठिता॥ ६८॥

tasmād yasya mahābāho nigṛhītāni sarvaśaḥ
indriyāṇīndriyārthebhyastasya prajñā pratiṣṭhitā

(68) Therefore, O'Arjuna, he, whose senses are withdrawn from their objects, he becomes firmly established in the transcendental wisdom.

या निशा सर्वभूतानां तस्यां जागर्ति संयमी।
यस्यां जाग्रति भूतानि सा निशा पश्यतो मुनेः॥ ६९॥

yā niśā sarvabhūtānāṁ tasyāṁ jāgarti saṅyamī
yasyāṁ jāgrati bhūtāni sā niśā paśyato muneḥ

(69) That which is night to all beings, in that state the self-controlled man remains awake. When all beings are awake, that is the night for the muni, who sees.

Commentary—After describing to Arjuna about the terrible fall of an individual, who broods over the pleasures of the sensual objects, Srī Kṛṣṇa proceeds to tell Arjuna about the lifestyle of a disciplined man. Self-discipline is the key to peace, happiness, self-realization and God-realization. The cultivation of this quality is of greatest importance in life which transforms every possibility into reality. Self-discipline forms the foundation of all types of progress in material life as well as in spiritual. It is astonishing how much a disciplined and a regulated person can accomplish by methodical working and by the careful use of his time; because he holds sound discretion, quick perception and firm determination in the execution of his plans. A self-disciplined person accomplishes the maximum amount of work with the minimum use of physical energy. The execution of his work is always very enjoyable and pleasant. Such an individual develops within himself the very precious faculties of analyzation, determination and one-pointedness of concentration. A disciplined person lives in yoga and works through the wisdom of yoga. A man of steadfast wisdom who is disciplined in all respects, he knows how to reconcile the various currents of conflicting emotions in his mind. He lives and moves among the various objects of the senses with a very detached attitude of mind. He has neither any special attraction nor aversion for anyone of the worldly enjoyment. It is by the practice of constant self-control, he cultures within himself a new and awakened lifestyle which operates under the direct guidance of the indwelling Lord. His entire span of work functions from the core of his essential being. He performs his duties very regularly, efficiently and relapses back into the stream of transcendental bliss whenever he wants to. In the words of Jñanashwariji, "Even as a tortoise spreads his limbs in joy and withdraws them when it desires; similarly, when one's senses remain under one's control and do whatever one wishes to, then one's wisdom has attained steadiness." A self-disciplined individual is always at peace with himself. The cultivation and practice of self-discipline may appear a long and laborious process to an ordinary person, but for an individual who remains firmly grounded in the integral wisdom of the Supreme-self; for him this practice comes very naturally.

Srī Kṛṣṇa has used the word *prasāda* in the verse sixty-four, which literally means the grace of the indwelling Divinity. Grace means the manifestation of the inner connectedness. It is the love of the Lord being expressed through the individual. When the grace of the Lord descends upon the person, he is said to be established in the serenity of the transcendental soul. In the words of Howard Thurman, "Whence comes this power which seems to be the point of referral for all experience and the essence of all meaning? No created thing, no single unit of life can be the source of such fullness and completeness. For, in the experience itself a man is caught and held by something so much more than he can ever think or be that there is but one word by which its meaning can be encompassed—God. Hence the Psalmist says that as long as the Love of God shines on us undimmed, not only may no darkness obscure but also may we find our way to other hearts at a point in them beyond all weakness and all strength, beyond all that is good and beyond all that is evil. There is nothing outside ourselves, no circumstance, no condition, no vicissitude, that can ultimately separate us from the love of God and from the love of each other. And we pour out our gratitude to God that this is so!" It is indeed the benign grace of the Supreme Lord wherein the individual secures his strength to overcome the feelings of attractions, aversions, envy, hate, anger and lust.

In the verse sixty-six, Srī Kṛṣṇa glorifies the practice of self-discipline once again and tells Arjuna that the person who has not controlled his mind and who is unsteady, he surely lacks the meditative ability and his unity with the integral wisdom. The man who can not concentrate his mind in meditation, he can never experience the tranquillity of the transcendental-self; and the one who lacks the experiential knowledge of the indwelling Lord, he definitely finds it very difficult to attain any peace and happiness in life. In order to attain happiness and fulfilment in life the quietude of mind is very important; and the quietude of mind becomes possible only by the practice of the self-control and self-discipline. It is the self-restraint, born of constant vigilance and austerity which brings about the blissful state of transcendental tranquillity and quietude. In the verse sixty-seven, Srī Kṛṣṇa speaks about the calamity that befalls upon the person who does not practise self-control and inner discipline. He tells Arjuna that when the person's mind follows the sway of the wandering senses, his discriminating ability is carried away by them as the wind carries away the ship upon the water. The pleasures of the objects of the senses do allure the individual with the false promises of happiness; those eventually become the cause of intensified delusion, disintegration, pain and misery. Such an individual is constantly busy in catching the froth and foam on the surface of the sensual enjoyments and wishes to enjoy as many pleasant sensations and thrills as he can manage to get. In the words of Swami Chinamayananda, "the life gets capsized and the individual drowned, if his mind is unanchored and left to be carried hither and thither by the uncertain buffets of passionate sense-storms. Therefore, the senses are to be controlled if man is to live a better and more purposeful life, designed and planned for enduring success. He alone is a man of wisdom, rooted in joy and bliss, who has completely restrained all his senses from their wild roamings among their sense-objects."

In the verse sixty-nine, Srī Kṛṣṇa gives the description of the sage who becomes fully awakened and who remains fully established in the awareness of the transcendental-Self. The Muni, who has attained his full control on the sensations of his mind, stays awake in the light of the Supreme consciousness; which remains obscured to the ignorant person, who is constantly awake in experiencing the pleasures of the senses. A self-realized Muni remains awake in the light of the transcendental bliss, which is like a night for the self-deluded person. So the wakefulness of the undisciplined and ignorant man is surely like the dark night for the sage. The hidden idea in this verse is that when the worldly person is busy in useless gossip, flirtations, eating, drinking, indolence, dandyism and debauchery, the self-controlled Muni remains indifferent to that and ignores as if he is in deep sleep. He does not pay any attention and gives no importance to any one of these activities. He remains aloof and witnesses the people who are roaming in darkness and heading further into the pitch of inner ignorance. The enlightened sage maintains the equipoise in honour and ignominy, in auspicious and inauspicious and feels sorry for the one who becomes angry and disturbed at the trivial things of day-to-day life. By using the analogy of day and night, Srī Kṛṣṇa brings out the implicit comparison between the man of self-discipline who lives his life in the light of the Self; and the undisciplined individual, who lives his life in inner darkness. In the words of Swami Sivananda, "The worldly-minded people are in utter darkness as they have no knowledge of the Self. What is darkness for them is all light for the sage. The Self, Atman or Brahman is night for the worldly-minded persons. But the sage is fully awake. He is directly cognising the supreme Reality, the Light of lights. He is full of illumination and Atma-jñāna or knowledge of the Self." Srī Kṛṣṇa has used the word 'Muni' for the self-enlightened sage. *'Mana'* (mind) is a state of consciousness. When *'mana'* becomes liberated from the false identifications, and returns to its source; it takes refuge in the awareness of the transcendental-self, and becomes silent. When the *'mana'* settles into a *'mouna'*, the person is called a *'mouni'* or *'muni'*.

आपूर्यमाणमचलप्रतिष्ठं समुद्रमापः प्रविशन्ति यद्वत्।

तद्वत्कामा यं प्रविशन्ति सर्वे स शान्तिमाप्नोति न कामकामी ॥७०॥

āpūryamāṇamacalapratiṣthaṁ samudramāpaḥ praviśanti yadvat

tadvat kāmā yaṁ praviśanti sarve sa śāntimāpnoti na kāmakāmī

(70) As the water of the rivers enter the ocean which though full, remains undisturbed; likewise the man in whom all desires merge themselves, he attains peace, and not the one who longs after the objects of desire.

विहाय कामान्यः सर्वान्पुमांश्चरति निःस्पृहः।

निर्ममो निरहङ्कारः स शान्तिमधिगच्छति ॥७१॥

vihāya kāmānyaḥ sarvān pumāṅścarati niḥspṛhaḥ

nirmamo nirahaṅkāraḥ sa śāntimadhigacchati

(71) He who has abandoned all his desires, and moves free from attachment and without the feeling of I and Mine, he attains the Supreme peace.

एषा ब्राह्मी स्थितिः पार्थ नैनां प्राप्य विमुह्यति।

स्थित्वास्यामन्तकालेऽपि ब्रह्मनिर्वाणमृच्छति ॥७२॥

eṣā brāhmī sthitiḥ pārtha naināṁ prāpya vimuhyati

sthitvāsyāmantakāle'pi brahmanirvāṇamṛcchati

(72) This is the state of transcendental unity *(brāhmīsthiti)*

O'Arjuna. Having attained this, he overcomes the delusion. Being established in this state, even at the time of death, he attains the Supreme Blissful state (Brahma-Nirvana).

Commentary—In these verses, Srī Kṛṣṇa gives the simile of the ocean, while illustrating the calmness and stability of a self-realized sage. The analogy of ocean illustrates the spiritual depth, and the unfathomable tranquillity of the person, who lives in the awareness of the Supreme Divinity. As the noisy turbulent rivers merge into the serenity of the ocean, the ocean absorbs everything in it; similarly, the turbulent desires and passions merge into the serenity of a self-realized sage, and he absorbs each one of them, without being disturbed at all. The person who remains established in the ecstasy of the infinite, he absorbs the pains and disturbances of even other people, with perfect calmness and tranquillity. He handles every moment of life as it comes with a balanced state of mind. In the words of Madusudana Saraswati, "Though the ocean receives the flow of rivers, it is majestic and changeless. The wise and stable intellect is similar; desires don't modify its stability." The awakened state of self-realized person is like an ocean which absorbs all types of disturbances without exhibiting any particular change. The man of steadfast wisdom performs all his duties at home, business and community but nothing ever disturbs his emotional equilibrium. The person of integral wisdom, who identifies his happiness in yogic unity with the Supreme-self, he maintains his perennial peace—but the person who identifies his happiness with the passions and the worldly desires, he definitely lives a very disturbed and disintegrated life.

The human nature holds within itself many kinds of conflicting emotions, desires and passions; those manifest themselves in the conscious or the unconscious behaviour. People in general live more by their emotions than by their reason. The ebb and flow of these desires drives people voluntarily and involuntarily into all kinds of temptations and make their life restless. The pursuit of worldly desires, which generally passes unchecked by reason, is definitely one of the greatest cause of human unhappiness on earth. It is a fact that the worldly desires do corrupt the thinking faculty and delude the intellect.

As Buddha has described, "Each thing comes into existence because of prior existence of something else and with the cessation of one link in the chain of existence the entire chain would fall apart. The desire, the craving is the key link in the chain. It binds us to misery which is inevitably associated with the revolving wheel of birth-death and rebirth." Srī Kṛṣṇa asserts that the individual can attain peace and happiness in life only when he rises above the notion of his identification of happiness with the worldly desires; and takes refuge in the tranquillity of the indwelling soul. When the person becomes accustomed to live his life in the consciousness of his ampler Divinity, he naturally becomes contented and fulfilled within. There is a famous saying, *chaha gayee chinta miti manava beparvah, jisko kuch nahin chahiye vohi shenashah*—which means that the person who has abandoned all of his desires and cravings of the mundane world, he is indeed the richest and the most blessed person on earth.

In the verse seventy-one, Srī Kṛṣṇa makes it very clear that the individual who has renounced his desires and moves about in the world without any attachment and without the feeling of I and Mine—he surely attains peace. The first line of the verse indicates the necessity of relinquishing all desires and attachments and the second explains the abandonment of the illusive sense of individualized separate existence. The sense of I-ness and My-ness is indeed the cause of bondage and is a great bane in the pursuit of self-realization. The egocentric emotions and the feeling of I and Mine forms a curtain which obscures the vision and the experiential knowledge of the pure indwelling-Self. As Paul Brunton writes, "In delusions of the ego, and its ignorance of true nature behind, that which expresses itself in the personal and vertical pronoun I, are the source, both of the evil it does and the ignorance it shows. In its unchecked selfishness is mankind's worst advisor." In order to overcome the pressure of the egocentric thoughts the individual has to seek refuge in the Divine. As the veil of ego lifts itself, the person enters into the realm of purity, wherein the feeling of 'I and Mine' is replaced by 'Thou and Thine'. A person who takes refuge in the awareness of the Supreme-soul, with complete surrender; he spontaneously becomes free from the feelings of 'I and Mine'. The individual-self becomes awakened to the joyousness of its completeness and wholeness. In the words of Mahatma Gandhi, "Moksha is liberation from egocentric thoughts, which is possible only with the God's grace, and the God's grace comes through ceaseless communion with Him and complete self-surrender. This communion may in the beginning be just a lip repetition of His name, even disturbed by impure thoughts; but ultimately whatever is on the lips will possess the heart." It is indeed a very difficult task to accomplish in one lifetime but not impossible for sure. The Supreme Lord's grace is all powerful and self-surrender is the best way to achieve it.

The quality of humility and the negation of 'I-ness' has been emphasized in almost all the religious traditions of the world. There are some beautiful lines by Thomas Kempis, "God walks with the humble; he reveals himself to the lowly; he gives understanding to the little ones; he discloses his meaning to pure minds, but hides his grace from the envious and proud". A complete surrender in to the graciousness of the Divine, is the only way to enjoy the totality of life and to enter into the totality of the Infinite Bliss at the time of departure from the world. Srī Kṛṣṇa has used the word *Brāhmīsthitiḥ* which literally means the state of super-consciousness, in which the mind becomes firmly established in Brahman. It is the oneness with Brahman or the Brahman-hood. It is the consciousness of experiencing the Divinity within one's own self. It is the state of awareness in which the individual soul recoils back to its true identity and resumes its original status, as the Supreme-soul. In the last verse of this chapter, the word Nirvana has been used which literally means the individual-soul merging into the Supreme-soul. A fragment merging into the wholeness, an individual drop dissolving into the serenity and the unfathomable depth of the great ocean. Nirvana is the freedom from all the false identifications. Nirvana is going back to the essential nature of the Supreme-soul, which makes the individual identical with Brahman. Nirvana means total Bliss.

ॐ तत्सदिति श्रीमद्भगवद्गीतासूपनिषत्सु ब्रह्मविद्यायां
योगशास्त्रे श्रीकृष्णार्जुनसंवादे सांख्ययोगो
नाम द्वितीयोऽध्यायः ॥ २ ॥

'Aum' tatsaditi Srīmadbhagawadgeetā sūpaniṣatsu brahmavidyāyām yogaśāstre Śrīkṛṣṇārjunasamvāde sāmkhyayogo nāma dvitiyodhyāyaḥ

'AUM TAT SAT'—Thus, in the Upanishad of the glorious Bhagawad Geeta, the science of the Brahman (Absolute) the scripture of yoga, the dialogue between *Srī Kṛṣṇa* and Arjuna thus, ends the chapter two entitled *"Samkhyayoga"*.

इति श्रीमद्भगवद्गीतासु द्वितीयोऽध्यायः ॥ २ ॥

Chapter Three

KARMAYOGA

THE YOGA OF ACTION

अर्जुन उवाच

ज्यायसी चेत्कर्मणस्ते मता बुद्धिर्जनार्दन।
तत्किं कर्मणि घोरे मां नियोजयसि केशव॥ १॥

jyāyasī cet karmaṇaste matā buddhirjanārdana
tatkiṁ karmaṇi ghore māṁ niyojayasi keśava

Arjuna said :

(1) If you consider that knowledge is superior to action, O'Kṛṣṇa, then why do you ask me to engage in this terrible action?

व्यामिश्रेणेव वाक्येन बुद्धिं मोहयसीव मे।
तदेकं वद निश्चित्य येन श्रेयोऽहमाप्नुयाम्॥ २॥

vyāmiśreṇeva vākyena buddhiṁ mohayasīva me
tadekaṁ vada niścitya yena śreyo'hamāpnuyām

(2) With an apparently conflicting statement, you seem to confuse my mind. Therefore, please tell me decisively that 'One', by which I may attain the highest good.

Commentary—In these two verses, Arjuna expresses his confusion with honesty. He feels that if the attainment of knowledge and unity in yoga is the only means to the realization of the Self, then how one can accept the idea that the genuine devotion to the performance of work leads to it. Arjuna lacks experiential knowledge and that is why he finds it very difficult to comprehend the complete meaning of Samkhya-yoga and Karmayoga. He requests Srī Kṛṣṇa for further explanation which will help him to understand clearly the meaning of both. Arjuna's confusion is indeed genuine and reflects his mixed state of mind. He pleads for help in determining the most appropriate course of activity for attaining the highest good in all respects. He wants to know for certain, that 'One' path by which he can attain the beatitude and Supreme blessedness.

श्रीभगवानुवाच

लोकेऽस्मिन्द्विविधा निष्ठा पुरा प्रोक्ता मयानघ।
ज्ञानयोगेन सांख्यानां कर्मयोगेन योगिनाम्॥ ३॥

loke'smin dvividhāniṣṭhā purā proktā mayānagha
jñānayogena sāṅkhyānāṁ karmayogena yoginām

The Blessed Lord said :

(3) O'Arjuna, in this world a twofold path has been declared by Me earlier; the path of knowledge of the Samkhyas and the path of 'Karmayoga' of the yogins.

न कर्मणामनारम्भान्नैष्कर्म्यं पुरुषोऽश्नुते।
न च संन्यसनादेव सिद्धिं समधिगच्छति॥ ४॥

na karmaṇāmanārambhān naiṣkarmyaṁ puruṣo'śnute
na ca sannyasanādeva siddhiṁ samadhigacchati

(4) Not by abstention from work, does a man attain liberation from action; nor by mere renunciation does he attain perfection.

Commentary—In these verses, Srī Kṛṣṇa explains to Arjuna that in this world there are two types of spiritual disciplines, practised by people, in order to achieve the highest good in life. Both the methods are equally valuable and highly adorable. The yoga of knowledge and the yoga of action may appear different due to the different use of terms but both lead towards the same goal. The word yoga has been derived from the Sanskrit word *yuj* which literally means union and communion with the inner-Self. Yoga is an art which helps one to bring the scattered thoughts together to a reflective and meditative state of mind. In Samkhya yoga the embodied-soul aims at identifying with the Supreme-Soul; on the other hand in Karmayoga (yoga of action) the same goal of identification with the Supreme-Soul is attained through the spirit of selfless action. A Karmayogi performs all his work as a devotional ritual and offers it to the Supreme-Soul. All his activities are centred around the worship of the Divine. Samkhya yoga is the intellectual and intuitive examination of the scriptural knowledge for the purpose of self-realization; while the yoga of action is the devoted performance of actions which eliminates the psychological and egoistical obstacles and makes the yogic union possible in all respects. In the practice of devotion-cum-action the individual experiences a spontaneous flow of inner awareness into the work of the day-to-day life, which prepares him for the direct experience with the Śupreme. Dr. Radhakrishnan has explained this concept in these words, "The teacher distinguishes, as modern psychologists do, two main types of seekers—introverts whose natural tendency is to explore the inner life of spirit and extroverts whose natural bias is towards work in the outer world. Answering to these, we have the yoga of knowledge, for those whose inner being is bent towards flights of deep spiritual contemplation, and the yoga of action for energetic personalities with love of action. But this distinction is not ultimate, for all men are in different degrees both introverts and extroverts."

Srī Kṛṣṇa tells Arjuna that the person has to blend both the methods in order to achieve the highest fulfilment in any activity. Both the methods of yoga are indeed interdependent. The individual needs the proper knowledge of both in order to attain perfection in either of them. For example, without going through the process of self-purification and self-discipline one can't achieve the final goal on the path of Samkhya yoga. The path of renunciation is not simply the abstention from all the worldly activities. In the words of Swami Prabhupada, "The renounced order of life can be accepted only, when one becomes purified by the discharge of the prescribed form of duties; without purification one can't attain success by abruptly adopting the fourth order of life". The yoga of action as suggested by Srī Kṛṣṇa is to do all work with proper knowledge and with the attitude of non-attachment. So renunciation is not an escape from the world, it is not an escape from the riddles of life; it is the renunciation of attachment to the fruits of action. In order to understand this concept of renunciation one has to understand the gospel of selfless action. Both Samkhya yoga and Karmayoga revolve around the performance of action selflessly and skilfully. In both the methods a great deal of sacrifice and self-discipline is mandatory.

न हि कश्चित्क्षणमपि जातु तिष्ठत्यकर्मकृत्।
कार्यते ह्यवशः कर्म सर्वः प्रकृतिजैर्गुणैः॥ ५॥

na hi kaścit kṣaṇamapi jātu tiṣṭhatyakarmakṛt
kāryate hyavaśaḥ karma sarvaḥ prakṛtijairguṇaiḥ

(5) For no one can remain even for a moment without performing action; everyone is made to act helplessly indeed, forced by the impulses born of nature.

कर्मेन्द्रियाणि संयम्य य आस्ते मनसा स्मरन्।
इन्द्रियार्थान्विमूढात्मा मिथ्याचारः स उच्यते॥ ६॥

karmendriyāṇi saṅyamya ya āste mansā smaran
indriyārthān vimūḍhātmā mithyācāraḥ sa ucyate

(6) He who controls his organs of actions and sits brooding over the objects of senses, he is said to be a self-deluded hypocrite.

यस्त्विन्द्रियाणि मनसा नियम्यारभतेऽर्जुन।
कर्मेन्द्रियैः कर्मयोगमसक्तः स विशिष्यते॥ ७॥

yastvindriyāṇi manasā niyamyārabhate'rjuna
karmendriyaiḥ karmayogamasktaḥ sa viśiṣyate

(7) But, he who controls his senses by the mind, O'Arjuna, and engages himself in the Karmayoga; with the organs of action, without any attachment—he definitely excels.

नियतं कुरु कर्म त्वं कर्म ज्यायो ह्यकर्मणः।
शरीरयात्रापि च ते न प्रसिद्ध्येदकर्मणः॥ ८॥

niyataṁ kuru karma tvaṁ karma jyāyo hyakarmaṇaḥ
śarīrayātrāpica te na prasiddhyed karmaṇaḥ

(8) Therefore, you must perform your assigned work, for action is superior to inaction; and even the maintenance of your physical body cannot be possible for you, without action.

Commentary—These four verses are the continuation of the answer to Arjuna's question in regard to the twofold path of spiritual discipline. Srī Kṛṣṇa tells that whichever the path one decides to follow, no one can ever remain inactive even for a moment. Breathing in and out, wakefulness, sleep and sound sleep or even in unconscious state the person is constantly involved in some activity or the other. All activities of the physical body, subtle body and at the subtlest level of the causal body, are indeed the various types of functions. Since everyone is being helplessly driven to do some type of work in order to stay alive, one has to learn to do it in a detached manner. Detachment from the material world doesn't come all at once, just by talking about it. It is a disciplined process that penetrates in one's lifestyle with constant efforts and spiritual austerities. Self discipline is not just restraining of the physical organs of action and perception, it is much more than that. The physical restrain needs to be combined with spiritual purity. Self-control has to emerge from the deepest levels of awareness. The person who sits in meditation, and broods over the sensual pleasures of the world, he is indeed deluded about his realities. He is definitely not sure, what does he want and exactly what should be his goal in contemplation. Srī Kṛṣṇa calls this person of deluded understanding, a hypocrite. For example, some people who impulsively decide to renounce the comforts of family and take refuge in a monastery are escapists. Although they are physically at the monastery but their thoughts are still involved in the life they left behind. The act of renunciation has to proceed simultaneously at the three levels of consciousness—physical, psychological and spiritual. This totality is possible, only in step by step preparation which comes from performing all the duties of the world with an attitude of detachment. If the physical abstinence is not accompanied by emotional, mental and psychological withdrawal from the worldly enjoyments, the act of renunciation becomes hypocrisy.

Srī Kṛṣṇa condemns the person who claims himself to be a renunciate and the man of knowledge but still dwells upon the enjoyments of the senses. He can surely impress others for a short time; but because he has not disciplined himself well enough, his words don't carry much weight to impress others. This type of outward restraint is false and misleading. It is hypocrisy and self-cheating. The assimilation of any ethical discipline penetrates in one's lifestyle by living in the spirit of the Divine, and performing all the work in a detached state of mind. The process of controlling the senses of perception and action lies in the realm of the deepest awareness of the mind. In the words of Swami Satya Prakash Saraswati, "The escape from action is not easy. You may bind your feet and hands with iron chains and get them mutilated; you may cut your tongue and be dumb; try as you would to fetter your organs of action but that will not bring freedom from sensualities. It is initially the mind that initiates an activity; and therefore it is necessary to have an unattached mind." Srī Kṛṣṇa emphasizes the fact that the unity with the inner-self should be constantly maintained by the individual. The person who knows how to stay consciously connected with the Divine, he has the ability to control the organs of senses and he definitely excels in all respects.

Srī Kṛṣṇa declares the necessity of performing the prescribed duties for the sustenance and maintenance of the body. If a person resists in performing these duties he creates a serious problem for himself and for others. It is very difficult for human beings to exist on earth without performing any action at all. In words of Srī Ramanuja, "This statement on the superiority of activity *(Karma Yoga)* over *Jñana Yoga* is valid even when there is competency for one to adopt *Jñana Yoga*. For, if you abandon all activities to qualify yourself for *Jñana Yoga*, then, for you, who is thus inactive while following *Jñana Yoga*, even the nourishment of the body, which is necessary even for *Jñana-nishta*, will not be achieved". *Nityakarma* means the duties of day-to-day life regarding the personal hygiene and the duties towards the family, business and society. Since each individual is connected with others in some or the other way, so even being conscious of the personal hygiene is *swadharma* (one's duty). The personal cleanliness of an individual influences the well-being of other people. So it is the responsibility of each individual to understand the nature of his personal duty. In the words of Swami Chinmayananda, "Not to act at all is to disobey the laws of nature which shall, as we all know, bring about a cultural deterioration in ourselves".

यज्ञार्थात्कर्मणोऽन्यत्र लोकोऽयं कर्मबन्धनः।
तदर्थं कर्म कौन्तेय मुक्तसङ्गः समाचर॥ ९॥

yajñārthāt karmaṇo'nyatra loko'yaṁ karmabandhanaḥ
tadarthaṁ karma kaunteya muktasaṅgaḥ samācara

(9) The world is bound by actions, other than those performed for the sake of sacrifice (selflessly). Therefore, O'Arjuna, perform your work for that sake alone, being free from attachment.

सहयज्ञाः प्रजाः सृष्ट्वा पुरोवाच प्रजापतिः।
अनेन प्रसविष्यध्वमेष वोऽस्त्विष्टकामधुक्॥ १०॥

sahayajñāḥ prajāḥ sṛṣṭvā puro'vāca prajāpatiḥ
anena prasaviṣyadhvameṣa vo'stitvaṣṭakāmadhuk

(10) At the beginning of creation the Lord of all beings created mankind along with the sacrifice and said "by this you may prosper"; let this be the milch-cow of your desires.

देवान्भावयतानेन ते देवा भावयन्तु वः।
परस्परं भावयन्तः श्रेयः परमवाप्स्यथ॥ ११॥

devān bhāvayatānena te devā bhāvayantu vaḥ
parasparaṁ bhāvayantaḥ śreyaḥ paramavāpsyatha

(11) With this, you foster the gods and may those gods foster you; thus fostering each other, you will attain to the highest good.

इष्टान्भोगान्हि वो देवा दास्यन्ते यज्ञभाविताः।
तैर्दत्तानप्रदायैभ्यो यो भुङ्क्ते स्तेन एव सः॥ १२॥

iṣṭān bhogān hi vo devā dāsyante yajñabhāvitāḥ
tairdattānapradāyai'bhyo yo bhuṅkte stena eva saḥ

(12) The gods pleased (nourished) by the sacrifice will surely bestow upon you the desired enjoyments. He, who enjoys the bounties of the gods without offering them anything in return, is verily a thief.

यज्ञशिष्टाशिनः सन्तो मुच्यन्ते सर्वकिल्बिषैः।
भुञ्जते ते त्वघं पापा ये पचन्त्यात्मकारणात्॥ १३॥

yajñaśiṣṭāśinaḥ santo mucyante sarvakilbiṣaiḥ
bhuñjate te tvaghaṁ pāpā ye pacantyātmakāraṇāt

(13) The virtuous, who eat the remnants of the sacrifice (*yajña*) are released from all sins; but the wicked, who cook food only for their own sake, verily eat sin.

Commentary—After explaining the nature of transcendental-Self in the second chapter, here in these verses, Srī Kṛṣṇa explains the methods of self-realization and God-realization through the doctrine of Karmayoga. He also declares that this method of self-realization has been brought to the attention of mankind; at the very beginning of creation by the Lord Himself. "Live a life with the spirit of yajña". The spirit of yajña helps the individual to live in harmony with the inner-Self with others and with nature. Yajña, a well known religious term of the vedic tradition literally means the act which helps the individual to live in harmony with everybody and everything. The performance of yajña makes the inner world blend peacefully into the physical world. Srī Kṛṣṇa has used the term Yajña with its expanded meaning and contents. He presents the subtle meaning of yajña with reference to mutual harmony. In the words of Mahatma Gandhi, "Yajña means an act directed to the welfare of others, done without receiving or desiring a return for it, whether of a temporal or spiritual nature. Act must be taken in its widest sense, and must include thought, word and deed. It embraces not only humanity but all life." The performance of yajña is to perform all the activities as a worship and as an offering to the Supreme. Yajña transforms all work into yoga. The word Yajña (sacrifice) indicates the mutual dependence which exists between the created beings and the cosmic powers. The spirit of yajña conveys the idea of interdependence, continuity and the survival of the creation. It is the network of the services, performed selflessly by human beings, gods and the mother nature. Srī Kṛṣṇa presents the process of God-realization through the work performed as yajña (sacrifice).

The ancient vedic tradition has described the five types of yajñas: the Brahm-yajña, Deva-yajña, Pitri-yajña, Atithi-yajña and Balivaisvadeva-yajña. Brahm-yajña is to live a life which is totally surrendered to the Supreme divinity. It is to be firmly established in the realm of unbounded pure awareness out of which the universe emerges and by which it is sustained. Brahm-yajña is to perceive the presence of the Lord in the entire creation. It is to live in the awareness of the Supreme and to share that experience with others. It is to become enlightened and then enlighten the lives of others. Those who are blessed with Brahma vidya (the knowledge of the self), they look upon the entire universe as a spark of the Supreme spirit, and their service to humanity becomes the goal of their life. The universality of outlook and service to mankind eventually brings salvation to them. The second type of yajña is Deva-yajña. It is the performance of duties in harmony with others and with the cosmic powers of nature. Devata literally means the one who gives. The cosmic powers have appeared with creation in order to maintain and to sustain life in the universe. The cosmic powers are the sun god, wind god, fire god and water god. In order to live in harmony with these powers it is the duty of every individual to be familiar with their functions and be appreciative of their contributions. For example, the sun fills the earth with energy and light (electromagnetic field), the air carries vapours and then the rain water helps the food to grow. Food helps the sustenance of life on earth. All these cosmic powers are working in a co-operation with each other to help life on earth.

All these cosmic powers *(devatas)* are constantly giving to others with the spirit of sacrifice. For example, water, air, energy and sunlight—everything is free of charge and originally pure. Every person must understand and realize to make the appropriate use of these blessings. Any type of negligence on the part of the individual results in all types of catastrophes on earth. The calamities such as famine, earthquake, drought, epidemics and storms are the results of disharmony in nature. In the words of Swami Satya Prakash Saraswati, "Man and his civilization have contributed much more to the environmental pollution than the total animal kingdom. Our thick forests with millions of creatures of wild life are much less polluted than our big cities like London, New York, New Delhi and Tokyo." The basic reason for all the present ecological problems is that people have forgotten their duties toward nature and toward others. Using pesticides and other poisonous mixtures in the fields is another way of polluting the air and earth. The poison sceps into the ground and contaminates the underground water. The blowing wind disperses the toxins and rain transports it from one place to another. In order to live in harmony with nature and in order to get the full support of nature, the individual has to realize his duty at the personal as well as at the community level. It is the duty of every person to respect the bounties of nature and use the natural resources with respect and appreciation for the Lord.

All the various efforts for keeping the environment clean and healthy are regarded as the Deva-yajña. This is what Srī Kṛṣṇa has been emphasizing in the verse *"parasparam bhavayantah sreyah param avaesyath"* which means that fostering each other disinterestedly you will attain the highest good. If man performs his duty as yajña (Selflessly) it sincerely benefits him and the world at large. The third type of yajña is the 'Pitri-yajña'. Pitra is a Sanskrit word which means the ancestors of the human race. Pitri-yajña is performed in respect of the parents who have given us this beautiful life. This yajña involves the importance of peace, harmony and integrity in family for the proper growth of community and civilization. The advancement in human life both at physical, psychological and spiritual level depends upon the solidarity of the family. Human life is a great gift of God, a vehicle of self-realization. Human beings are uniquely privileged on this planet. Human potential are enormous. A human being can rise to the Divine status and can work in a copartnership with God. Humans are blessed with subjective awareness and so can experience the presence of the Divine in relation to others. As a part of the society it is indeed the duty of every man to give good progeny to the family, community and nation. Every individual is very unique, and to manifest his individual uniqueness is the personal duty of every individual. A family unit contributes a lot to the peace, happiness and the integrity of a community and country.

The fourth is Atithi yajña. In the words of Swami Satya Prakash Saraswati, "The word Atithi means the ever traveller in the service of mankind. The respectable priests, sannyasin and all those who have decided to dedicate their lives for the welfare of mankind, should be respected by the householders. These ever dedicated people serve the society, and help people to uphold the moral values. They go from town to town in order to enlighten the lives of other people. Such individuals should be respected and supported for their work." Atithi is also the person who knocks at our door without any prior information. Anybody who approaches for help should be treated with respect. The fifth one is Balivaisvadeva yajña. In some books it has been also called Bhuta yajña. The word bhuta stands for all living beings. Bhuta yajña describes the ideal of living in harmony with other creatures on earth. Vedic literature asserts very strongly that each and every individual should develop a sense of responsibility towards the well-being of other species on earth. Everything in the nature is meant to be shared with animals, birds and the plant kingdoms.

Srī Kṛṣṇa suggests that every activity becomes a cause of bondage, unless it is performed with the spirit of yajña, means the ideology of *swadharma*. The word saha-yajña means the work which is performed in co-operation with one another, without expecting anything in return. As the cosmic forces are working in co-operation with each other to sustain life on earth, similarly the human beings are expected to work selflessly in co-operation with each other to support life on earth. In the words of Srī Jaydayal Goyandka, "The commandment of the creator as quoted in the verse viz 'you shall prosper by this; may this yield the enjoyment you seek' represents the benediction pronounced by the creator on the humanity at large. The creator thereby assured man that it was for his sake that He had evolved the institution of sacrifice in the form of *swadharma*." Srī Kṛṣṇa makes it more clear in the verse eleven by declaring 'fostering each other disinterestedly and by supporting each other with the spirit of yajña, and by respecting each other, one can attain the highest good in life. It is indeed the performance of every activity with the spirit of yajña which helps the individual to accomplish the highest goal of attaining unity in yoga. The spirit of mutual give and take has been passed on to the entire creation since antiquity. For example the trees, the plants, the vegetation helps to clean the air and give rain showers, they give shelter, food, wood and fuel to all the species on earth. Similarly every man has a duty to save the forests and to save the fruit trees and also to plant more trees. Each generation is indebted to the previous generation in the sustenance and maintenance of life on earth. In order to keep the cycle of life going one must plant some trees for the use of future generations. While explaining the concept of *swadharma*, Srī Kṛṣṇa suggests very strongly, that each and everybody must realize the call of *swadharma*. Anybody who fails to realize his duty in relation to his rights, he deserves to be called a traitor. The human beings have been blessed with higher intelligence, that is why every individual bears the highest responsibility in maintaining the work order. *Swadharma* demands from man to live a life on earth by keeping Dharma upfront *(Dharma, Artha, Kama* and *Moksha)*. In the words of Swami Chidbhavanananda, "The grabbing man pays the penalty in the form of misery; the giver reaps the reward in the form of undiluted joy. The means to give somehow increases in the man who has a mind to give. The resources, the bodily effort and the mental disposition becomes multiplied in the man of yajña."

Srī Kṛṣṇa tells Arjuna that it is the duty of every individual to respect the spirit of sacrifice (yajña) which makes the life prosperous, auspicious, harmonious and peaceful. He says that the person who lives only for himself and holds his own selfish interests upfront, who accumulates wealth only for his sensual enjoyments, depriving others of their due share, he lives a sinful life. In the words of Swami Ramsukhdas, "We have to perform our duty of fostering others and doing good to them to the best of our resources such as intellect, power, time and material etc." In these verses Srī Kṛṣṇa declares that until and unless the human being understands the definition of his rights and duties, in a clear-cut perspective, there can be no peace on earth. A peaceful way of life is indeed characterized by the spirit of caring, sharing and giving and partaking of the due share only. The work which is performed with respect, dignity and devotion, that brings people together. The duties performed as yajña (sacrifice) bring equilibrium, peace, happiness, freedom and prosperity in society. It generates the attitude of service and sacrifice. Yajña is an expression of virtue, purity, kindness, giving and sharing. Yajña is the sharing of the material wealth, physical strength, knowledge, wisdom, learning, love and affection with others. In order to understand the meaning of ethical harmonious living, it is very important to understand the definition of yajña. In the words of B.G. Tilak, "The message of Geeta, that the individual's whole life should be turned into yajña, contains the essence of the entire Vedic religion".

अन्नाद्भवन्ति भूतानि पर्जन्यादन्नसम्भवः ।
यज्ञाद्भवति पर्जन्यो यज्ञः कर्मसमुद्भवः ॥ १४ ॥

annād bhavanti bhūtāni parjanyādannasambhavaḥ
yajñād bhavati parjanyo yajñaḥ karmasamudbhavaḥ

(14) All beings have evolved from food. The food is produced from rain, the rain ensues from sacrifice, and sacrifice is rooted in action.

कर्म ब्रह्मोद्भवं विद्धि ब्रह्माक्षरसमुद्भवम् ।
तस्मात्सर्वगतं ब्रह्म नित्यं यज्ञे प्रतिष्ठितम् ॥ १५ ॥

karma brahmodbhavaṁ viddhi brahmākṣarasamudbhavam
tasmāt sarvagataṁ brahma nityaṁ yajñe pratiṣṭhitam

(15) Know, that action has its origin in Brahma, and Brahma proceeds from the imperishable. Therefore, the all-pervading infinite (God) is always present in the sacrifice (yajña).

एवं प्रवर्तितं चक्रं नानुवर्तयतीह यः ।
अघायुरिन्द्रियारामो मोघं पार्थ स जीवति ॥ १६ ॥

evaṁ pravartitaṁ cakraṁ nānuvartayatīha yaḥ
aghāyurindriyārāmo moghaṁ pārtha sa jīvati

(16) He who does not follow the wheel of creation thus set in motion here; leads a sinful life; rejoicing in the senses. He surely lives in vain, O'Arjuna.

यस्त्वात्मरतिरेव स्यादात्मतृप्तश्च मानवः ।
आत्मन्येव च सन्तुष्टस्तस्य कार्यं न विद्यते ॥ १७ ॥

yastvātmaratireva syādātmatṛptaśca mānavaḥ
ātmanyeva ca santuṣṭastasya kāryaṁ na vidyate

(17) But the person who delights only in the Self, who remains satisfied in the consciousness of the Self and is contented in the Self alone; for him there is nothing to be done.

नैव तस्य कृतेनार्थो नाकृतेनेह कश्चन।
न चास्य सर्वभूतेषु कश्चिदर्थव्यपाश्रयः ॥ १८ ॥

naiva tasya kṛtenārtho nākṛteneha kaścana
na cāsya sarvabhūteṣu kaścidarthavyapāśrayaḥ

(18) For him there is no interest whatsoever in the performance of an action or its non-performance; nor does he depend on any creature for any object.

Commentary—In these verses Srī Kṛṣṇa tells Arjuna that the entire universe is mutually connected. The entire work-order in nature is very closely related to the activities of the human being. The cosmic powers work in perfect co-operation. For example, the sun with its heat evaporates water from the oceans, the rivers and reservoirs; the evaporated water comes back to earth in the form of rain to nourish the earth in order to grow food. Food helps the sustenance of life on earth. But some time there is the scarcity of rain which results in famine. These catastrophes on earth are usually caused by the negligence of man in performing the assigned duties. For example, if the man keeps chopping down the trees because he needs wood for fuel and housing, the forests become denuded of trees and eventually that results in the shortage of wood, food and rain. One should take from earth only as much as is needed to support the life. Earth reservoirs should be used wisely. The mother earth can definitely satisfy the basic needs of everyone but not the blind greed of the people. The trees save us from storms and also bring rain showers. The green forests and trees increase the volume of water and the volume of water increases the volume of food. In the words of Tolstoy, "Work produces food, the food produces work, that is the unending circle; the one is the consequence and cause of the other".

The modern science also believes in the same ideology. The fundamental concept of physics is that when an electron vibrates, the universe shakes, because everything in the universe is connected with one another which includes nature, humans, beasts, plants, rocks etc. It is the combined effort of everyone that keeps the wheel of creation in motion. It is indeed a participatory world where everything and everybody contributes in some way or the other. Srī Kṛṣṇa enlightens Arjuna about the personal responsibility of every individual in order to live in harmony with nature and with other people. The spirit of yajña creates harmony in the entire universe. The performance of work in the spirit of yajña helps people to understand the ideals of selfless action. He tells Arjuna that all the actions have their origin in Brahma, and Brahma springs from the imperishable. Therefore, the all pervading infinite God is ever present in yajña. By giving the similarities of macrocosm and microcosm, Srī Kṛṣṇa explains Arjuna that all our activities must correspond to the world order. Each and everybody should develop a sense of responsibility towards one's own duty. Human beings with their subjective awareness have the ability to make contact with the inner voice and receive the needed guidance from God. The indwelling voice guides everyone to perform his assigned duties by keeping in mind the global welfare. He declares that every individual, who is a member of family, society and country, should understand his duty at the personal level as well as the universal. He should perform every type of work very selflessly keeping in mind the maintenance of the world order. Anyone who fails to realize his duty, he lives a degraded, shameful and harmful life at the individual and also at the universal level. In the verse seventeen, Srī Kṛṣṇa makes it very clear that the one who is merged in the joy of the self and who is satisfied in the serenity of the Supreme-Self, he has indeed no obligatory duty to perform. The God-realized saint lives totally absorbed in the nature of God alone, for him the material world is only like a passing dream. Such a holy person contributes through his radiance and learning. A saint who has accomplished the goal of his life, he doesn't have any obligatory work to do. Such Brahma Jñani has been described in these words by the sage Yagvalkya—"It is that state in which one transcends joy and sorrow, the fears of old age and death. The knower of the Self overcomes all the desires for wealth, for progeny and cherished dreams. The Brahma-jñani devotes himself completely to the contemplation of the Self and regards all other thoughts as mere distractions."

तस्मादसक्तः सततं कार्यं कर्म समाचर।
असक्तो ह्याचरन्कर्म परमाप्नोति पुरुषः॥ १९॥

tasmādasaktaḥ sattaṁ kāryaṁ karma samācara
asakto hyācaran karma paramāpnoti pūruṣaḥ

(19) Therefore, always perform your work, without attachment, which has to be done; for a man who works without attachment he attains the Supreme.

कर्मणैव हि संसिद्धिमास्थिता जनकादयः।
लोकसङ्ग्रहमेवापि सम्पश्यन्कर्तुमर्हसि॥ २०॥

karmaṇaiva hi saṅsiddhimāsthitā janakādayaḥ
lokasaṁgrahamevāpi sampaśyan kartumarhasi

(20) It is through action, that King Janaka and others attained perfection. Even with a view to the maintenance of the world-order, you must perform action.

यद्यदाचरति श्रेष्ठस्तत्तदेवेतरो जनः।
स यत्प्रमाणं कुरुते लोकस्तदनुवर्तते॥ २१॥

yadyadācarati śreṣṭhas tattadevetaro janaḥ
sa yatpramāṇaṁ kurute lokastadanuvartate

(21) Whatever a great man does, the others also do the same; whatever standard he sets, the people follow.

Commentary—In these verses once again Srī Kṛṣṇa glorifies the magnificence of the Karmayoga which allows the purity of the Self, to become manifested in all respects. The power of Karma Yoga protects the individual from the harmful effects of attachment to the fruits of action and it also initiates the individual into the higher degrees of self-control and transcendence. Man is a social being and as a part of the family, society and nation, he has to play various roles. The success and happiness of the individual lies in playing each role efficiently, skilfully and successfully. The goal of life is to manifest the divinity from within and to live in peace with others. Srī Kṛṣṇa suggests to Arjuna that this task can be well accomplished by performing the assigned duties with an attitude of detachment and devotion.

Srī Kṛṣṇa asserts that a person can live a full and prosperous life in the world with his heart anchored to the Divine. All the work which is performed should be centred in the awareness of the Self. It is indeed a fact that by performing actions without attachment, just for the sake of Ishwara, a man attains *Moksha*. A Karmayogi performs all his work as a worship to the Divine. His duty itself becomes his penance and it is performed in meditating upon the Lord. In the words of Srī Vinobaji, "the result of the Karmayogi's action is that while his life goes on smoothly, his body and mind are radiant; and society too prospers. Besides these two benefits he also receives the great gift of *chitta-suddhi,* purity of mind." Vinobaji has given a beautiful illustration from the *Mahabharata*. He tells the story of the merchant Tuladhar (the balance-holder). A brahmin called Jajali goes to him to find true knowledge. Tuladhar says to him, "Brother, it is necessary to keep the beam of this balance always even". By constantly doing this external action, Tuladhar's mind too had become straight and sensitive. Whether a child comes into the shop or a grown up, his beam remains levelled for all, leaning neither this way nor that. One's action transforms one's mind. The Karmayogi's work itself becomes his worship. His mind is purified by it, and the clear mind receives the image of jñana, true knowledge. Gandhiji has also written very beautifully about the strength and splendour of Karmayoga. "The yoga of selfless action appears to me, to be the excellent way of attaining self-realization. This is the unmistakable teaching of the Geeta, that one who gives up action, he falls, but he who gives up only the reward, he rises. But renunciation of the fruits of action, in no way means indifference to the result. In regard to every action, one must know the result which is expected to follow, the means thereto, and the capacity for it. He who being thus equipped, is without desire for the result and is yet wholly engrossed in the due fulfilment of the task before him, he is said to have renounced the fruits of his actions." Srī Kṛṣṇa tells Arjuna that a person must perform the obligatory duties in relation to the family, society and country to the very best of his ability.

In the verse twenty, the Lord gives the example of the great Karma yogies who have been the great kshtriya kings and at the same time God-realized souls. Rajarishi King Janaka has been a great philosopher and a very enlightened man. He ruled the great empire of Mithila. He has been known as a *'Vedehi'* which means his sense of 'I and Mine' has been totally extinguished. He lived a life totally soaked in the nature of God. He has been a great saint and at the same time a very efficient administrator of a huge empire. King Janaka has been known as Acharya in *yoga vidhi*—an embodiment of the gospel of selfless action. Similarly Asvapti has been described in *Chhandogyopanishad* as an example of the one who had performed all his duties very efficiently, diligently and selflessly. These kings ruled their empires as the embodiment of the Supreme Divinity. In this verse, the others, besides King Janaka, means the great seers like Vivasvan, Vaivasvata, Manu and the King Iksvaku, those who have attained the state of perfection through the performance of their assigned duties. Performing the assigned work, as a worship to the Lord, purifies the individual and makes him receptive to the attainment of the higher goals. God realization is indeed easy if, only, the individual could learn to be at ease—to be in *sahaja-avastha*, as our scriptures describe *"uttama sahajavastha dwitiya dhyana dharana"* which means constantly being at ease within, is much more rewarding than the practice of contemplation and Meditation. An overall ease comes to the attitude of a person, who lives in the enhanced awareness, and performs all his work with the guidance of the Supreme-self. There is a miraculous power which benefits the individual as well as the family where he lives and in the society where he works. His outlook stretches itself to the welfare of the whole society. As Swami Vivekananda writes, "there are some in every country who are really the salt of the earth, who work for work's sake, who don't care for name or fame or even to go to heaven. They work, just because good will come out of it. Love, truth, unselfishness are not merely moral figures of speech. They form our highest ideals, because in them lies such a manifestation of Divine power." The word *Lokasangraha* means the mode of work which is performed with an attitude of sacrifice. It is that work which is done selflessly for the maintenance of the world order. It is the realization of mutual dependence between one another and the attitude of service towards the entire creation.

Srī Kṛṣṇa enlightens Arjuna about his duty as a warrior and also as a responsible member of the society. He tells that whatever a respectable person does in the community, usually the other people follow his example. The revered people are followed because of their sacrifices and high ideals. Such people become adorable because of their purity of character and the selflessness of their attitude. Every pure venerable individual embodies a little spark of the Divine and this light radiates in his activities. Srī Kṛṣṇa reminds Arjuna about the latter's great valour and heroism and how the entire community has always looked upon him as a model of bravery and valour. The entire country has always looked upon Arjuna as a great archer. Born as a prince, well-versed in vedic education, a great hero of many wars, the killer of extremely powerful demons like Nivatakavacas and others, Arjuna has always been worshipped by thousands of his fans throughout the country. Because of his most outstanding qualities as a hero, he has been addressed by various adorable names such as Partha, Gudakesha, Dhananjaya, Paramtapa, Kaunteya, Mahabaho, Bharata and many more. Srī Kṛṣṇa reminds Arjuna that it is only respectable for him to live up to the estimation and expectation of his people. His fall from the noble standards will cause a fall of the noble values in the entire society. He tells Arjuna that it is definitely from the inspiration and dedication of the virtuous men of heroism, that the entire society seeks guidance and leadership. The ordinary men tune themselves to the ideals of their duties, by following the path of the respectable ones. In the words of Swami Chidbhavannananda, "in public interest a person of eminence has therefore to put forth his best. Slighting or allowing godly gifts go to waste, amounts to slighting God Himself."

न मे पार्थास्ति कर्तव्यं त्रिषु लोकेषु किञ्चन।
नानवाप्तमवाप्तव्यं वर्त एव च कर्मणि॥ २२॥

na me pārthāsti kartavyaṁ triṣu lokeṣu kiñcana
nānavāptamavāptavyaṁ varta eva ca karmaṇi

(22) There is nothing in all the three worlds, O'Arjuna, that has to be done by Me, nor is there anything unattained that ought to be attained; yet, I engage Myself in action.

यदि ह्यहं न वर्तेयं जातु कर्मण्यतन्द्रितः ।
मम वर्त्मानुवर्तन्ते मनुष्याः पार्थ सर्वशः ॥ २३ ॥

yadi hyahaṁ na varteyaṁ jātu karmaṇyatandritaḥ
mama vartmānuvartante manuṣyaḥ pārtha sarvaśaḥ

उत्सीदेयुरिमे लोका न कुर्यां कर्म चेदहम् ।
सङ्करस्य च कर्ता स्यामुपहन्यामिमाः प्रजाः ॥ २४ ॥

utsīdeyurime lokā na kuryāṁ karma cedaham
saṅkarasya ca kartā syāmupahanyāmimāḥ prajāḥ

(23, 24) For, should I not engage Myself in action unwearied, men would follow My path in all respects, O'Arjuna. These worlds would perish, if I did not perform action; and I would be the cause of confusion, disorder and the destruction of the people.

Commentary—In these two verses, Srī Kṛṣṇa emphasizes the importance of performing one's duties by giving His own personal example. The Supreme Lord incarnates in the mortal world in order to set an example for others. When the God-incarnate appears as a human being in the course of life, He goes through all those rituals which have been prescribed for the welfare, human beings in the world. For example, Shri Rama and Srī Kṛṣṇa both went through all the necessary vedic *samskaras* which are performed at the different stages of life (*Jatakarma, Namakarma, Upaneana, Vedarambha,* the marriage and coronation etc.). They were sent to Gurukulum to be educated in various fields of knowledge. They performed all the duties which are expected of ordinary human beings, in order to set an example for others and to live a harmonized life on earth. Srī Kṛṣṇa has gone to Gurukulum and there he lived a very simple life of a student with his friend Sudama in order to set an example of an ideal student life. The life of Srī Kṛṣṇa illustrates the philosophy of *Karma Yoga.* At every step, there is a message, to educate people into the reality, that every individual is potentially Divine and the aim of life is to manifest the inner Divinity through the path of action. Srī Kṛṣṇa's entire life exhibits His glorious character and His sincere effort to uphold the greatness of Dharma in all respects. In the words of Swami Ramsukhdas, "When the Lord accepts to be the chariot driver of Arjuna, He performs His duty very carefully and efficiently so that other people may follow his example." Srī Kṛṣṇa tells Arjuna that even the God-incarnate lives an ordinary life on earth as ordained by the scriptural code, for the guidance of the community.

The life of a God-incarnate functions from the deepest levels of pure consciousness. Although on the surface His life appears to be like that of ordinary people, but the God-incarnate always remains firmly rooted in His essential nature as immutable and imperishable. So there is nothing in the three worlds which remains to be done, nor there is anything which needs to be acquired by Him; but still a God-incarnate works like ordinary human beings in order to guide the lives of the people in proper channels. Although the personal needs of a God-incarnate are met very easily, still He works diligently, skilfully and selflessly in order to guide the lives of others. He becomes a symbol of spiritual, moral and ethical guidance. Srī Kṛṣṇa intimates Arjuna of His own real nature and the nature of the God-realized soul. He tells that even if some one has transcended all the three stages of consciousness and has achieved the purpose of life, still the great one keeps himself busy in the welfare of others. The graciousness of human life is to perform the assigned duties with an attitude of service and humility. The self-realized individual, who is ever intent on desireless work, performs his obligatory duties as husband, wife, mother, father, teacher and son just as a service to others. Performing the assigned duties with full enthusiasm and in the spirit of detachment is like working through God and as an embodiment of the Lord Himself. Such a person is the walking manifestation of the unmanifested Supreme.

सक्ताः कर्मण्यविद्वांसो यथा कुर्वन्ति भारत।
कुर्याद्विद्वांस्तथासक्तश्चिकीर्षुर्लोकसङ्ग्रहम् ॥२५॥

saktāḥ karmaṇyavidvānso yathā kurvanti bhārata
kuryād vidvāns tathā'saktaś cikīrṣur lokasangraham

(25) As the ignorant man acts with attachment to action, O'Arjuna, so should the wise man act without attachment, desiring the welfare of the world.

न बुद्धिभेदं जनयेदज्ञानां कर्मसङ्गिनाम्।
जोषयेत्सर्वकर्माणि विद्वान्युक्तः समाचरन्॥ २६॥

na buddhibhedaṁ janayedajñānāṁ karmasaṅgināṁ
joṣayet sarvakarmāṇi vidvān yuktaḥ samācaran

(26) The wise man who is established in the Self should not unsettle the mind of the ignorant people who are attached to action; he should get them to perform all their duties, by performing action himself with devotion.

Commentary—These two verses are the continuation of the previous one, wherein Srī Krṣna is emphasizing the importance of performing the assigned duties in life time, with an attitude of detachment to the results. Srī Krṣna is using the term unwise and ignorant for those who act with attachment to the fruit. These people work like a drudge and act like beggars. They live their lives in the whirlpool of anxieties, and die with self-created bondage. He tells Arjuna that the man of inner-integrity and wisdom performs all his work without any attachment, and without any expectation of name and fame. He does his work diligently and enthusiastically with the ideal of sharing and giving. His work is performed as yajña and as an offering to the Divine. Such an individual helps in the continuation of the world order and also gets enlightened while doing his duties. In the words of Swami Vivekananda, "When you are doing any work, don't think of anything beyond. Do it as a worship and devote your whole self to it. For the time being let's work on, doing whatever happens to be our duty, and be ever ready to put our shoulders to the wheel. Then surely we will see light." He gives a very good example of a Karmayogi through this parable. Once a young sannyasin went to the forest with the goal of self-realization. After long meditation and yoga practices, one day while he was sitting under a tree, some dry leaves fell upon his head. He felt very angry. On the tree he saw two birds fighting with each other. As he looked up angrily, a flash of fire went out and reduced both the birds to ashes. He felt very proud and overjoyed at the advancement of his yogic powers. After a few days he had to go to a nearby town to beg for some food. He stopped at one door and called out for food—"Some food please". As he called, a voice came from inside the house, please wait. The young sannyasin became very angry and cried out once again in anger, 'food'. A voice came again from inside "Please don't think too much about your yogic powers; I'm neither the birds nor the leaves". The young sannyasin felt much astonished at the sharp insight of the woman. Finally when the lady of the house appeared at the door he politely enquired as to how did she find out all about his great adventure. She answered humbly and very politely, "I'm a simple housewife. I've made my work a worship of the Lord. I requested you to wait, because I've been serving my bedridden husband. Since childhood I've learnt to perform all my work very devotedly, lovingly and as a service to the Divine. My devoted service has illuminated my life. I feel consciously settled in God, even when I'm doing my household chores. I perform all my work as a worship to God. With the practice of Karmayoga, my intuition has been sharpened, so I could perceive your egocentric feelings and your adventure in the forest."

In the verse twenty-six, Srī Kṛṣṇa alerts the man of steadfast wisdom about something very subtle, which usually goes unnoticed by many. He declares that a wise person should not abruptly start instructing others into the gospel of selfless action and renunciation. He should take particular precaution in using the right words at the most appropriate moments. It is indeed difficult for ordinary folks to understand the philosophy of selfless actions. Sometime people under the false concept of detachment from actions actually stop doing even the work which has been recommended for the maintenance of the world order. Instead of making any progress, such people become easy victims of laziness, ignorance and total negligence. They overlook even their obligatory duties, while staying attached to the fruits of their work. In this verse Srī Kṛṣṇa tells that the man of wisdom should become very patient and methodical in introducing the high ideals to the public in general. The enlightened man should not confuse the mind of the ignorant, those are passionately attached to the worldly actions. Sometime the ignorant people become bewildered and confused when they are persuaded with high philosophies of selfless action. The man of integral wisdom and dedication should himself perform his work very diligently, devotedly and selflessly and thus encourage others into the high ideals of humility, purity, honesty and selfless service. The enlightened one has to come down to the level of those who need instruction. The dedicated image of the God-realized person inspires the work and the active participation of other people.

The word *Budhi-bhedam* stands for people from all walks of life. The people who say that the desire for the fruit of action is very natural, the detached attitude means to them the total abandonment of all work. Individuals of such shallow understanding are usually very unsettled and disoriented. It is very difficult for them to accept the profound ideals of selfless action just by listening about it; but when the man of integral wisdom works with them, he becomes their role-model, people do follow his cherished ideals and the style of his work. For example, if a person is preaching about faith in God, his each and every activity of life must manifest his own strong faith in the first place. His lifestyle should manifest the Divinity from within. Someone who preaches about the ideal of speaking truth, his every word must carry some weight to influence others. His lifestyle should manifest the value of speaking truth and all other spiritual ethics. The man of wisdom should endeavour to keep others engaged in the performance of their duties, while performing his own selflessly. An enlightened sage should hold a great responsibility towards his own character and activities because the common people follow in his footsteps. He should persuade others very slowly, gently, and very patiently by setting the unique example of his own personal life. The well-known maxim "Show me what you want me to do" works in all spheres of life.

प्रकृतेः क्रियमाणानि गुणैः कर्माणि सर्वशः।
अहङ्कारविमूढात्मा कर्ताहमिति मन्यते ॥ २७ ॥

prakṛteḥ kriyamāṇāni guṇaiḥ karmāṇi sarvaśaḥ
ahaṅkāravimūḍhātmā kartāham iti manyate

(27) All actions are performed—in all respects, by the modes of nature. The one whose mind is deluded by egoism, he thinks 'I am the doer'.

तत्त्ववित्तु महाबाहो गुणकर्मविभागयोः।
गुणा गुणेषु वर्तन्त इति मत्वा न सज्जते॥ २८॥

tattvavittu mahābāho guṇakarmavibhāgayoḥ
guṇā guṇeṣu vartant iti matvā na sajjate

(28) But he who knows the truth about the respective spheres of modes (Gunas) and their functions O'Arjuna, he clearly understands that the Gunas-as-senses move among the Gunas-as-objects; and he does not become attached.

प्रकृतेर्गुणसम्मूढाः सज्जन्ते गुणकर्मसु।
तानकृत्स्नविदो मन्दान्कृत्स्नविन्न विचालयेत्॥ २९॥

prakṛter guṇasammūḍhāḥ sajjante guṇakarmasu
tānakṛtsanavido mandān kṛtsanavinna vicālayet

(29) Those who are deluded by the qualities (gunas) of nature they remain attached to the functions of the gunas. The man of wisdom should not unsettle the minds of the ignorant, who do not know the whole truth.

Commentary—In the process of explaining the ideals which can liberate the mind from the feeling of I and Mine, so that the mind can function with the guidance of the Self alone, Srī Kṛṣṇa suggests Arjuna to examine the natural course of action. He enlightens Arjuna about the process, which leads to the activity from the outer world to the inner world, from the known to the unknown and from the body to the mind. The nature of all actions and the results which follow with the attachment to the rewards; everything originates from the preconceived opinion at the subconscious level of the mind. Even if someone intellectually accepts the ideal of detachment; it is still very difficult to practice. In general, the human behaviour is conditioned and quite unknown to individual himself. The soul is immortal and immutable while the body is mortal and mutable. The five material elements of nature constitute the physical body. Srī Kṛṣṇa calls the mother nature *prikriti—pri* means before and *kriti* means creation; also *pri* means forth and *kri* means to make. So the word *prikriti* means which brings forth the existence with various combinations. Motion in the *prikriti* is because of the propinquity of the Supreme-self. When the soul identifies with the Supreme-soul it remains luminous, untouched and pure. When the soul identifies with the body, it gets entangled in the intrigues of mind, intellect and ego. A very good description has been given in the *Kathaupanishad,* "Know the body to be a chariot and the soul to be the one sitting in the chariot, know the intellect as the charioteer and mind the reins. The senses are called the horses and the objects of the senses as the paths. When the Supreme-soul assumes affinity with the body, the senses and the mind, the man of wisdom call him the enjoyer."

The body, the senses, mind and intellect are the products of mother Nature and the qualities of human behaviour are also the product of Nature. All the activities of human life revolve around these characteristics *Sattva, Rajas* and *Tamas. Sattva,* as the term is self-explanatory, means clear and luminous like *Sat*—the truth. The thoughts, and the actions that are pure, virtuous lucid like *Sat* are considered to be Sattvic. *Tama* literally means darkness. The thoughts and actions which are enveloped by ignorance and darkness are of the *tamasic* nature.

The thoughts and activities characterized by *Rajas* are unsteady, fast and scattered. *Sattva, Rajas* and *Tamas* are the important components of human nature as well as everything else in the universe. All actions are performed due to the initiation from either one of these or the three together. When the embodied-Soul assumes the affinity with the mind, thoughts and these gunas, he thinks he is the doer of actions and expects rewards and fruits. But when the embodied-Soul remains seated in the chariot only as a rider, he just observes each activity of the body as a silent witness. In the words of Swami Ramsukhdas, "When the soul identifies itself with the body, it has attraction for nature and then it performs actions and has to reap their fruit in the form of pleasure and pain. As a matter of fact the attraction of the embodied-soul for the worldly objects is really attraction of

Nature in Nature. The feeling of 'I am the doer' and 'I am the enjoyer' are in Nature, not in the pure Self."

As a matter of fact the attachment to the fruit of actions is because of one's ignorance. The ignorance of identifying with the body, with ego, impulses and desires. It is because of this spiritual blindness, the concept of duality and rope of bondage exists. For example, it is the person's strong identification with his body, mind and ego which gives rise to the feeling of 'I and Mine'—it deludes his vision and thinking faculty. Ego yearns to win name and fame and it creates bondage for the individual. In order to overcome the pressure of egocentric thoughts one has to make some changes in the pattern of thoughts at the conscious level. All activities originate from thoughts and thoughts originate in the mind. When the mind is trained to work with the guidance of the Supreme-self, its identification with the ego starts fading. As long as the mind remains deluded and confused about its identity, it always associates itself with ego and creates bondage but when the mind learns to remain associated with the Supreme-self, it starts identifying itself with God, and realizes the Supreme God working through everything. As one progresses in the spiritual relationship with the Overself, one watches the play of life as a spectator. When 'I and Mine' is replaced by 'Thou and Thine', the sense of doership automatically perishes. Srī Kṛṣṇa suggests to Arjuna that the man of wisdom who is constantly settled in the serenity of the indwelling-Self, he perceives the truth about the spirit, matter and body. He also experiences the real nature of the mind, ego and the three qualities of the human nature. He has the ability to recognize the distinctions and also to make valid comparisons. He accomplishes all his work with his consciousness centred in the Overself. With his constant practice and awareness he can successfully erase the traces of his conditional behaviour and can also liberate himself from the limitations of mind, body and ego. The shift in identification from the egocentric self to the pure-self comes slowly with earnest practise and self-discipline. The devoted attitude in the performance of work purifies the inner instruments, the mind automatically starts identifying more with the Supreme-self. The embodied-Soul becomes aware of his true identity and functions very spontaneously and effortlessly.

मयि सर्वाणि कर्माणि सन्न्यस्याध्यात्मचेतसा।
निराशीर्निर्ममो भूत्वा युध्यस्व विगतज्वरः॥ ३०॥

mayi sarvāṇi karmāṇi sannyasyādhyātmacetsā
nirāśīrnirmamo bhūtvā yudhyasva vigatajvaraḥ

(30) Therefore, dedicating all actions to Me, with your mind focused on the Self, being free from desire, egoism and mental stress, fight the battle.

ये मे मतमिदं नित्यमनुतिष्ठन्ति मानवाः।
श्रद्धावन्तोऽनसूयन्तो मुच्यन्ते तेऽपि कर्मभिः॥ ३१॥

ye me matamidaṁ nityamanutiṣṭhanti mānavāḥ
śraddhāvanto'nasūyanto mucyante te'pi karmabhiḥ

(31) Those men who constantly follow this teaching of Mine with faith and without cavilling, they are also liberated from the bondage of actions.

ये त्वेतदभ्यसूयन्तो नानुतिष्ठन्ति मे मतम्।
सर्वज्ञानविमूढांस्तान्विद्धि नष्टानचेतसः॥ ३२॥

ye tvetadabhyasūyanto nānutiṣṭhanti me matam
sarvajñānavimūḍhāṅstān viddhi naṣṭānacetsaḥ

(32) But those who cavil at My teaching and do not follow it, know them to be absolutely ignorant, devoid of all knowledge and lost.

Commentary—In the verse thirty, Srī Kṛṣṇa suggests for a total surrender to the Supreme-soul. It is a commitment of selfless service to the Lord and the constant practice of living in the remembrance of the Divine. As a matter of fact all our actions are performed by the Lord Himself, but it is our assumed affinity to the body and mind that makes us to believe 'I am the doer'. So surrender means the giving up of the assumed identity with the ego and forming a new one with the Supreme-self. Srī Kṛṣṇa is emphasizing the word *sradha* (loving devotion) with surrender. Any type of devotion or worship is incomplete without *sradha.* In the words of Srī Ramakrishna, "The humble and the meek, who are ever dependent on the Lord, get over their defects, if any, very soon. The gracious Lord sees to it, that his erring devotees come around soon." Complete faith is indeed complete surrender. In partial surrender when a person is withholding a little bit of his egoistic nature, that itself becomes an obstacle on the path of selfless action. Total surrender from the individual with love, faith and devotion is what leads to the total acceptance from the Divine. It is a bridge that helps the individual to sail across the ocean of the ego-enveloped thoughts and the assumed identities. One may read all the scriptures in the world, and be well versed in philosophies but the inner awakening comes to the individual, only when he surrenders himself to the will of the God. The goal of spirituality is to enable the person to realize the presence of God within and learn to depend upon it. The spiritual experience can't be demonstrated or taught by words and prescribed in certain formulas; it begins only with faith in God and grows with dedication to God. It blossoms by offering all the work as a service to God.

Every honest and earnest effort contributes a lot to the goal of self-realization and freedom from the bondage of karma. Srī Kṛṣṇa asserts very strongly that it is indeed essential to supplement the knowledge of the self with love and devotion for God. With a surrender to the Divine, the person's attachment to the indwelling-Self blossoms in all respects. Attachment to the Divine leads towards detachment from the external world. Since every activity is performed as an offering to the Divine, the desire for name and fame vanishes in due time and all the insecurities and fears are washed away. Srī Kṛṣṇa concludes the message that the people who surrender to God are blessed with wisdom and the experiential knowledge of the Self. Their spiritual journey becomes easy, joyous, effortless, and very rewarding. Their life becomes an ever-renewing stream of spontaneous spiritual experiences. The honesty of their faith and practise helps them to be transported into the most cherished realms of Self-realization and God-realization. On the other hand, those who are always suspicious about the spiritual teachings and feel hesitant to surrender in God, they remain deluded and devoid of true knowledge.

सदृशं चेष्टते स्वस्याः प्रकृतेर्ज्ञानवानपि।
प्रकृतिं यान्ति भूतानि निग्रहः किं करिष्यति॥ ३३॥

sadṛśaṁ ceṣṭate svasyāḥ prakṛterjñānavānapi
prakṛtiṁ yānti bhūtāni nigrahaḥ kiṁ kariṣyati

(33) Even the man of wisdom acts in accordance with his own nature; all beings follow their nature, what can restrain accomplish?

इन्द्रियस्येन्द्रियस्यार्थे रागद्वेषौ व्यवस्थितौ।
तयोर्न वशमागच्छेत्तौ ह्यस्य परिपन्थिनौ ॥ ३४ ॥

indriyasyendriyasyārthe rāgadveṣau vyavasthitau
tayorna vaśamāgacchettau hyasya paripanthinau

(34) Attachment and aversion for the objects of senses abide in the senses; one should not come under their sway, because they are his enemies.

श्रेयान्स्वधर्मो विगुणः परधर्मात्स्वनुष्ठितात्।
स्वधर्मे निधनं श्रेयः परधर्मो भयावहः ॥ ३५ ॥

śreyān svadharmo viguṇaḥ paradharmāt svanuṣṭhitāt
svadharme nidhanaṁ śreyaḥ paradharmo bhayāvahaḥ

(35) Better is one's own duty, though devoid of merit, than the duty of another well performed. Even the death becomes blessed (gracious) in the performance of one's own duty; the duty of another is fraught with fear.

Commentary—In these verses Srī Krṣna indicates that the accomplishment in the goal of self-transformation is not achieved through suppression and repression. The process that helps the individual to sublimate and transmute the negative tendency is to make a surrender to the Supreme Lord. A total surrender results in the removal of all the destructive drives and prepares the individual for a constructive spiritual progress. The practice of self-transformation becomes very easy, enjoyable and spontaneous, when the mind is tuned to the serenity of the Divine. He suggests that a person does not have to withdraw from the world in order to make the spiritual advancement; because the performance of duties with detachment itself purifies the individual. The performance of duties with a detached attitude definitely and surely educates the person in all respects. When the individual progresses in yogic surrender, the procedure itself modifies the behaviour and actually the process itself becomes both the training and the teacher. So it is indeed very important for every individual to accelerate his day-to-day emotions to the height of inner consciousness, in order to overcome the stress, which is caused by the attachment and aversion for the objects of the senses. A person can control these two currents only if his mind corresponds to the state of transcendental consciousness. The moment a person is able to rise above the sway of opposites; the magnificence of *swadharma* unfolds itself and he becomes able to understand the real concept of his duties. The law of *swadharma* prevails over the entire universe; and in its absolute obedience lies peace, happiness and freedom of mankind. Srī Kṛṣṇa suggests that it is the unity in yoga and living a life in close relationship with the Divine which helps the individual to listen to the voice of the Self, and respect his own innate nature. He further suggests that every individual must train himself to choose and perform the work which is motivated by his own *svabhava*—the inner intuition. Human potential are enormous but unfortunately a major part of it remains unexplored in life.

Swadharma demands from every individual to explore his unique talents and manifest them by keeping in mind the global welfare. It is indeed the duty of every individual to get in touch with one's own speciality and enhance it, in order to achieve perfection in it. The moment one starts working on it, the power of Providence and inner intelligence provides the needed help for further advancement. Through self-discipline and determination, the hidden treasures unfold themselves to the surface of the conscious mind and the knowledge of the Self becomes revealed from within. Srī Kṛṣṇa tells Arjuna that following *swadharma* is indeed mandatory for every type of progress, advancement and contentment in life. One must learn to live by *swadharma*. Even the modern psychology believes that if an individual doesn't live his life in accordance with his own innate nature and specific traits of personality, the life becomes an utter failure for him. Following *swadharma* is like opening the door of the inner temple for the Lord to come and join in every work. Any work which is performed with the conscious assistance with God, brings out the very best of one's abilities and benefits the entire mankind. In the words of Carl Jung, the great German psychologist, "A certain kind of behaviour brings corresponding results, and the subjective understanding of these results gives rise to the experience which in turn influences the behaviour." A similar concept of behaviour pattern has been observed by the ancient sages. They believed very strongly that although on the surface all men look alike, yet they differ in their intellectual, spiritual and psychological levels. They said, people are indeed guided by some inner power to show inclinations for different types of work according to their abilities, capabilities and capacities.

In every society the work order is maintained by the people with the guidance of their own inner instinctive nature. In general, people divide themselves by their own choice. In past when the society had been more integrated than at present, and people were more religious and confident, they had been definitely more capable of making their own choices. In past the natural division in society functioned very well. At present in spite of the well organized education system, the modern universities have not been able to meet the cherished goals of education. Most of the college graduates look very confused and frustrated. Although they think they are equipped with all kinds of technical skills and education, they still don't know how to make the best use of them. The reason for this worldwide mass hysteria and hopelessness is the lack of self-confidence and self-respect, which happens due to the individual's conscious separation from the inner resources. Every individual can make a comfortable adjustment in society and in every field of life only if he corresponds to *swadharma* (the voice of the inner-self). Srī Kṛṣṇa reminds Arjuna that the performance of one's own duty, though unpleasant, is preferable to the duty of another well performed; another man's duty can be degrading, shameful and even fatal sometime. Every individual must try to understand his psycho-physical make-up and function in accordance with it. It is indeed the Dharma of every individual to explore from within his luminous, untainted and pure personality which is free from the sway of opposites; and which is unperturbed, peaceful, unconditioned and very impartial. In the words of Dr. Radhakrishnan, "We have not all the same gifts, but what is vital is not whether we are endowed with five talents or only one but how faithfully we have employed the trust committed to us."

अर्जुन उवाच

अथ केन प्रयुक्तोऽयं पापं चरति पुरुषः।
अनिच्छन्नपि वार्ष्णेय बलादिव नियोजितः ॥ ३६ ॥

atha kena prayukto'yaṁ pāpaṁ carati pūruṣaḥ
anicchannapi vārṣṇeya balādiva niyojitaḥ

Arjuna said :

(36) But impelled by what, O'Kṛṣṇa, does a man commit sin, even against his will, as though driven by force?

Commentary—In this verse Arjuna brings forth a question, why a man becomes involved in committing sin even though he doesn't want to? Why a person is forcibly dragged, against his will and judgment, towards the commission of a sinful act? What compels the individual to create problems for himself and for others? Arjuna says, O'Kṛṣṇa, what is that which compels a person to do which is prohibited by dharma and should not be done at all? Arjuna wants to know the force which disconnects a person from his *swadharma* and robs him of the reality of his discrimination and intuition. He addresses Srī Kṛṣṇa as Varshneya—means from the lineage of Vrishnis.

श्रीभगवानुवाच

काम एष क्रोध एष रजोगुणसमुद्भवः।
महाशनो महापाप्मा विद्धयेनमिह वैरिणम् ॥ ३७ ॥

kāma eṣa krodha eṣa rajoguṇasamudbhavaḥ
mahāśano mahāpāpmā vidhayenamiha vairiṇam

The Blessed Lord said :

(37) It is desire, it is anger born of the mode of passion; which is insatiable and most sinful. Know this to be the enemy in this respect.

धूमेनाव्रियते वह्निर्यथादर्शो मलेन च।
यथोल्बेनावृतो गर्भस्तथा तेनेदमावृतम् ॥ ३८ ॥

dhūmenāvriyate vahnir yathādarśo malena ca
yatholbenāvṛto garbhastathā tenedamāvṛtam

(38) As the flame is enveloped by the smoke, as a mirror by the dust and as an embryo by the amnion, so is this (knowledge) covered by that (desire).

आवृतं ज्ञानमेतेन ज्ञानिनो नित्यवैरिणा।
कामरूपेण कौन्तेय दुष्पूरेणानलेन च॥ ३९॥

āvṛtaṁ jñānametena jñānino nityavairiṇā
kāmarūpeṇa kaunteya duṣpūreṇānalena ca

(39) O'Arjuna, the wisdom stands enveloped by this constant enemy of the wise in the form of desire, which is insatiable like fire.

इन्द्रियाणि मनो बुद्धिरस्याधिष्ठानमुच्यते।
एतैर्विमोहयत्येष ज्ञानमावृत्य देहिनम्॥ ४०॥

indriyāṇi mano buddhiraśyādhiṣṭhānamucyate
etair vimohayatyeṣa jñānamāvṛtya dehinam

(40) The senses, the mind and the intellect are said to be its seat; through these it deludes the embodied-self by enveloping his wisdom.

तस्मात्त्वमिन्द्रियाण्यादौ नियम्य भरतर्षभ।
पाप्मानं प्रजहि ह्येनं ज्ञानविज्ञाननाशनम्॥ ४१॥

tasmāttvamindriyāṇyādau niyamya bharatarṣabha
pāpmānaṁ prajahi hyenaṁ jñānavijñānanāśanam

(41) Therefore, O'Arjuna, control thy senses from the very beginning and kill this sinful destroyer of knowledge and experiential wisdom.

इन्द्रियाणि पराण्याहुरिन्द्रियेभ्यः परं मनः।
मनसस्तु परा बुद्धिर्यो बुद्धेः परतस्तु सः॥ ४२॥

indriyāṇi parāṇyāhur indriyebhyaḥ paraṁ manaḥ
manasastu parā buddhiryo buddheḥ paratastu saḥ

(42) Senses are said to be superior (to the body), superior to senses is the mind; but higher than mind is the intellect and higher than the

intellect is indeed the indwelling-Self.

एवं बुद्धेः परं बुद्ध्वा संस्तभ्यात्मानमात्मना।
जहि शत्रुं महाबाहो कामरूपं दुरासदम्॥ ४३ ॥

evaṁ buddheḥ paraṁ buddhvā saṅstabhyātmānamātmanā
jahi śatrum mahābāho kāmarūpaṁ durāsadam

(43) Thus, knowing the indwelling-Self to be higher than the intellect and controlling the mind by the Self, O' Arjuna kill this enemy in the form of desire, which is very difficult to conquer.

Commentary—Srī Kṛṣṇa gives a very precise and decisive answer. He starts his answer with the word *kama*—the desire prompted by passion. The desire is indeed the cause of all infatuations, anger, delusion, confusion and the loss of discrimination. A passionate desire veils the insight of a person. It obscures the clarity of vision and the person loses his ability to judge things in their clear perspective. The word *kamarupena* in the verse thirty-nine indicates the desires arising for enjoyments of worldly objects. In reference to this, there is a story told by Swami Chinmayananda, "Once a young man was travelling in a train. At one platform a beautiful young lady dressed in fine silks, jewellery and perfume, boarded in his compartment. In speechless wonder, the man looked at her, and gave her a friendly smile. She was followed by a porter carrying a huge box of quite unusual dimensions. The lady with her alluring and flaunting smile looked at the young man and said, "Sir, if you don't mind, can I keep this box here". The porter then carefully lowered the box on the floor of the compartment and left. The lady sat next to the young man for a while and then at the next station she got up from the seat and went somewhere. As the train left the station, the man amused again himself with pleasant thoughts of the beautiful lady, coming back to the seat opposite to his. He looked at the huge box. Though the box was occupying a lot of space but because of the idea of enjoying the company of the beautiful lady, he decided to bear the inconvenience. The box set him musing. He thought perhaps the lady had gone to the bathroom and expected her to be back any minute. He kept wondering, what was in that box ? Perhaps jewellery, money, her beautiful clothes. The sweet perfume, which emanated from the box, tickled his nostrils. His mind kept imagining the wonderful journey ahead in the sweet company of the lady. At the next station two other men boarded the compartment. While looking at the big box, they asked the young man, "Sir, why don't you transfer this box to the luggage van?" The young man replied, "What does it matter if it is here?" The answer clearly declared that the box belonged to the young man. The more he looked at the box, the more his attachment for the box became stronger. The lady had not come back. The box was causing lot of inconvenience for the other passengers but the young man because of his infatuation for the beautiful lady didn't feel any inconvenience at all. After a little while the ticket checker entered the compartment and enquired about the box. All the other passengers pointed towards the young man. The ticket checker asked the young man politely to show the extra luggage ticket. When the young man said that he didn't buy that one, the ticket collector suggested him to buy extra ticket. He made a receipt, collected the required money and went by. The young man who was totally lost in his thoughts for the beautiful lady, quietly received the receipt of the extra luggage and dropped in his pocket.

After a few hours the young man's station of destination arrived. He was still engrossed in the thoughts of the lady, and hoped to see her at the railway station. He decided to take the box with him. He called two porters for help and ordered them to carry the huge box towards the exit. As he walked through the exit, a railway officer saw that unusual box and asked him to declare the contents of that box. When the young man gave some confused looks to the officer, he asked him if the box really belonged to him. The young man presented the luggage receipt. The officer asked for the key to open the box. When he refused to open, the officer became very suspicious and asked the young man to follow him to the police station. At the police station they opened the box, there laid inside the box a dead body heavily scented. The young man became very frustrated and refused to accept the box. He told the whole story to the officer but nobody was ready to believe him. The young man was handcuffed, arrested and sent to prison. After seven months of hard struggle with his law suits, he was released. He lost a part of his business, good name and lot of money also. He felt very ashamed for his stupid weakness and infatuation. This is exactly what Srī Kṛṣṇa means the wisdom, the discrimination gets enveloped by the all-devouring power of a passionate desire. It is indeed the perennial enemy of man. As a matter of fact, if a passionate desire is not checked at the right moment, it can cause much more pain than one can ever imagine. The desire, when satisfied, becomes greed and if it is not satisfied, it causes insecurity and anger. Desire originates from the mode of *Rajas* (passion). It compels the person for the possession of that particular desired object; and anybody who stands as an obstacle in his path becomes his enemy. Desire is indeed *nitya varina*—a perpetual enemy in all respects. As the *Manusmriti* describes, *"na jatu kameh kamanam upabhogena samyati, havisa Kṛṣṇavartmeva bhuya evabhivardhata"* which means the desire can never be satisfied by enjoying the objects of desire, it rather grows more and more as the flame grows more and more to which the fuel is given. There is a famous saying of Benjamin Franklin, "if a man could have even half of his wishes fulfilled, he would definitely double his troubles". Srī Kṛṣṇa suggests to Arjuna to recognize desire to be the perennial enemy of mankind. It is the fundamental cause of all the emotional conflicts, psychological and spiritual maladjustments. He suggests to Arjuna that in order to live in peace and happiness, the individual should learn to put a ceiling on desires.

In the verse forty-two, Srī Kṛṣṇa gives a hierarchy of the various levels of consciousness. He tells Arjuna that subtler than the senses is the mind and subtler than the mind is the intellect and subtler than the intellect is the supreme-Self. So through senses and mind one should make contact with the thinking faculty and let the thinking faculty act under the total awareness of the Supreme-Self. By living in direct consciousness of the indwelling-Self the individual can watch and control the cravings of the sense objects. It enables the person to monitor the flow of his thoughts and to accept which is good and to discard which is not good. The constant denial to worldly enjoyments, reduces the number of desires and gradually and slowly reduces them to nothing. In the words of Swami Ramsukhdas, "Desires appear and disappear, they have a beginning and an end. They are constantly decaying, if we don't have the new desire, the old desire whether it is satisfied or not, disappears itself." The more one learns to live in spiritual awareness, the more one feels satisfied in one's own inner-self. The individual needs to integrate the senses, mind and intellect and let them work under the full control of the inner awareness. In the last verse of this chapter, Srī Kṛṣṇa asserts that it is indeed with the realization of the Supreme-self only, when the inherent strength is released and the waves of the turbulent mind are brought under the conscious control of the individual. When the Divine consciousness is awakened, it illuminates the thinking faculty and one develops increased intuition. The real transitory nature of the mundane world, becomes clear and the life becomes very peaceful. As the individual feels settled in the Self, he does not yearn and crave for the material pleasures.

ॐ तत्सदिति श्रीमद्भगवद्गीतासूपनिषत्सु ब्रह्मविद्यायां
योगशास्त्रे श्रीकृष्णार्जुनसंवादे कर्मयोगो
नाम तृतीयोऽध्यायः ॥ ३ ॥

'Aum' tatsaditi Śrīmadbhagawadgeetā sūpaniṣatsu
brahmavidyāyām yogaśāstre Śrīkṛṣṇārjunasamvāde
Karmayogo nāma trtityodhyāyaḥ

'AUM TAT SAT'—Thus, in the Upanishad of the glorious Bhagawad Geeta, the science of the Brahman (Absolute) the scripture of yoga, the dialogue between Srī Kṛṣṇa and Arjuna—thus, ends the chapter three entitled *"Karmayoga"*.

इति श्रीमद्भगवद्गीतासु तृतीयोऽध्यायः ॥ ३ ॥

Chapter Four

JÑĀNA-KARMAYOGA

THE YOGA OF ACTION AND KNOWLEDGE

श्रीभगवानुवाच

इमं विवस्वते योगं प्रोक्तवानहमव्ययम्।
विवस्वान्मनवे प्राह मनुरिक्ष्वाकवेऽब्रवीत्॥ १॥

imaṁ vivasvate yogaṁ proktavānahamavyayam
vivasvānmanave prāha manurikṣvākave'bravīt

The Blessed Lord said :

(1) I taught this imperishable Yoga to Vivasvan (sun-god). Vivasvan taught it to Manu; and Manu taught to Ikshvaku.

एवं परम्पराप्राप्तमिमं राजर्षयो विदुः।
स कालेनेह महता योगो नष्टः परन्तप॥ २॥

evaṁ paramparāprāptamimaṁ rājarṣayo viduḥ
sa kāleneha mahatā yogo naṣṭaḥ parantapa

(2) Thus, handed down in regular succession, the royal sages knew this. But, through the long lapse of time, this yoga became lost to the world, O'Arjuna.

स एवायं मया तेऽद्य योगः प्रोक्तः पुरातनः।
भक्तोऽसि मे सखा चेति रहस्यं ह्येतदुत्तमम्॥ ३॥

sa evāyaṁ mayā te'dya yogaḥ proktaḥ purātanaḥ
bhakto'si me sakhā ceti rahasyaṁ hyetaduttamam

(3) This same ancient Yoga has been declared to you by Me today; for you are My devotee and My friend. This is the Supreme secret.

Commentary—Chapter four is the continuation of the philosophy of Karmayoga as propounded by Srī Kṛṣṇa in chapter three. Srī Kṛṣṇa tells Arjuna that the Yoga of selfless action is not a new concept. This discipline of action came into being with the creation and it has always existed since the times immemorial. It is the perennial wisdom which has assisted the existence of life in this universe in all respects. Although as old as the creation itself, it is ever fresh and ever renewing. Srī Kṛṣṇa calls this Yoga of selfless action to be primordial. The whole creation functions through the spirit of mutual interdependence. It is a network of services performed selflessly. Srī Kṛṣṇa declares that he has imparted the yoga of selfless action to the sun-god at the beginning of the creation. Sun is indeed the source of life and the symbol of light. It is the first created object. The sun radiates its energy for everything and everybody on earth. It is a huge electro-magnetic field. It has been serving the life on planet as a yogi. The sun is the embodiment of selfless action.

In the beginning of creation, there were only two luminary bodies, sun and moon known to man. That's why there were only two races: the solar race and the lunar race. In solar dynasty the knowledge of the integral discipline has been passed on from one to another. From the sun-god to Manu, from the sage Manu to Ikshvaku the ancestor of the solar dynasty. In the solar dynasty the other well-known kings were the great King Sagar, Anshuman, Daleep, Bhagiratha, Raghu, Aaj, Dashrath and Srī Rama and later his sons and the sons of his brothers onward. All these kings were very enlightened and ruled their kingdoms as embodiments of the Divine; especially Srī Rama, Himself being the God incarnate (Lord Vishnu). Srī Kṛṣṇa points out that the royal sages have been very well acquainted with the Yoga of selfless action. The royal teachers imparted the knowledge to kings and princes and to the other deserving candidates for self-realization and God-realization. The royal sages knew very well that if the king is enlightened with the knowledge of the Self, he will act as an embodiment of the Divine. If the ruler of the country is virtuous and upholds Dharma, he influences the life style of his people. If the king is well versed in the knowledge of selfless action, the people are automatically inspired to follow the lead. The royal sages propagated these ideals through the examples of their own self-disciplined lives. The kings also lived an austere, religious and disciplined lives without being attached to the royal pleasures. They ruled their kingdoms with an attitude of detachment and service. History has given us the wonderful examples of King Harishchandra and Srī Rama from solar dynasty. Srī Rama's whole life was a perfect example of *"Jñana-Karma-Sannyas Yoga"*. He performed all his duties as a king, as a husband and as a brother and as a father with the integral wisdom of *swadharma.* Kalidasa has written about the kings of the solar dynasty in these words, "Those kings received their taxes from their subject in the same way as the sun draws water from earth in order to give it back to the earth in the form of rain-shower." This means the money collected from the people was used for the welfare and the prosperity of the people appropriately. The kings served their public, rising above personal motives. The gospel of selfless action (yajña) has been practised as a spiritual discipline and as a necessity for living in perfect harmony. With the lapse of time as the people became more involved in the enjoyments of the material world, they slowly lost touch with ethical values. As a result, people became selfish and self-centred. Gradually with every generation as the practice of ethical values went down, and there came a decline in the practice of the yoga of action. Arjuna represents the human soul seeking help and guidance.

In the third verse, Srī Kṛṣṇa discloses His Supreme secret and tells Arjuna that the primordial concept of the yoga is being shared with him because he is a deserving candidate and a very dear devotee. He also discloses His real identity as the God-incarnate; which has remained so far a great secret to Arjuna and everybody else. The integral wisdom of yoga, which is of free access to the entire mankind, is perceived and practised by only a few because not everybody is able to perceive its magnificence. This knowledge becomes a *prasad* and comes as a grace to those only, who make connections with the Higher-self and are receptive to the voice of the Self. The wisdom of yoga remains unexplored, because of the personal ignorance of the individual; and when the majority of the society ignores the need for inner wisdom; it becomes distant for a while.

अर्जुन उवाच

अपरं भवतो जन्म परं जन्म विवस्वतः।
कथमेतद्विजानीयां त्वमादौ प्रोक्तवानिति॥ ४॥

aparaṁ bhavato janma paraṁ janma vivasvataḥ
kathametad vijānīyāṁ tvamādau proktāvaniti

Arjuna said :

(4) Later on, was Thy birth and earlier to it was the birth of Vivasvan (sun-god). How can I understand this; that You ever taught this yoga in the beginning?

Commentary—Arjuna brings forth this question because he has ignored the last word spoken by Srī Kṛṣṇa in the third verse, *rahasyam hyetaduttamam*—meaning this is indeed a great secret about My true identity which I have disclosed to you. Arjuna is still preoccupied in his own thoughts, and he listens only that, whatever he wants to hear. He has not been able to comprehend the truth of Srī Kṛṣṇa's real identity as God-incarnate (Lord Vishnu). As a matter of fact, earlier in the conversation Srī Kṛṣṇa has casually mentioned to Arjuna a part of his secret identity, *na tvevaham jatu nasam na tvam neme janadhipah*—there never was a time when I or you or these kings were not present. Also in the second chapter verse twenty the Lord has said, *na jaayate na mriyate va kadaacit.* Arjuna's mind rambles in confusion, and he brings forth this question, "your birth is very recent O' Kṛṣṇa while the birth of Vivasvan has been in antiquity, how can I believe that you taught this yoga to the preceptors of sun dynasty in the beginning". Arjuna wonders at the intriguing words of Srī Kṛṣṇa and so requests Him for clarification.

श्रीभगवानुवाच

बहूनि मे व्यतीतानि जन्मानि तव चार्जुन।
तान्यहं वेद सर्वाणि न त्वं वेत्थ परन्तप॥ ५॥

bahūni me vyatītāni janmāni tava cā'rjuna
tānyahaṁ veda sarvāṇi na tvaṁ vettha parantapa

The Blessed Lord said :

(5) Many births of Mine have passed as well as of yours,

O'Arjuna. I know them all, but you do not know them. O'Scorcher of the foes.

अजोऽपि सन्नव्ययात्मा भूतानामीश्वरोऽपि सन्।
प्रकृतिं स्वामधिष्ठाय सम्भवाम्यात्ममायया॥ ६॥

ajo'pi sannavyayātmā bhūtānāmīśvaro'pi san
prakṛtiṁ svāmadhiṣṭhāya saṁbhavāmyātmamāyayā

(6) Though I am unborn, of imperishable nature and the Lord of all beings, yet, governing My own Nature, I come into being through My power. (Yoga Maya).

यदा यदा हि धर्मस्य ग्लानिर्भवति भारत।
अभ्युत्थानमधर्मस्य तदात्मानं सृजाम्यहम्॥ ७॥

yadā yadā hi dharmasya glānir bhavati bhārata
abhyutthānamadharmasya tadātmānaṁ sṛjāmyaham

(7) Whenever there is decline of righteousness, (Dharma) and rise of unrighteousness, O'Arjuna, then I manifest Myself.

परित्राणाय साधूनां विनाशाय च दुष्कृताम्।
धर्मसंस्थापनार्थाय सम्भवामि युगे युगे॥ ८॥

paritrāṇāya sādhūnāṁ vināśāya ca duṣkṛtām
dharmasaṅsthāpanārthāya saṁbhavāmi yuge-yuge

(8) For the protection of the virtuous, for the destruction of the wicked, and for the establishment of righteousness (Dharma) I come into being from age to age.

Commentary—Srī Kṛṣṇa opens the conversation with specific words, "Both 'you and I' have passed through many births, you don't remember while I do remember all of them". Srī Kṛṣṇa asserts, I know them all because I hold a perfect control over My Nature (prakrti). The Lord is not bound by the modes of nature and by the strands of karma. He is ever pure, self-governed free and omniscient. The Lord is pure, lucid *Atman,* constantly present everywhere and in everything but still transcends all of them. He has full knowledge of the past, present and future. On the other hand, Arjuna is *jivatman,* bound by the modes of the nature and the rope of karma. When pure *atma* assumes its affinity to the body and to the material world, it gets trapped into the modes of nature and the status of *atman* comes to be known as a *jivatman.* While living under the slavery of nature, *jiva* starts losing its conscious connections with the Divine. The individual's conscious separation from the indweller results in disintegration, delusion and misery. On the other hand, the holy sages, those who remain perpetually connected with the Supreme-soul, their bond becomes much stronger to the higher-self in comparison to the material world. Their latencies of previous births are gradually washed out and they live consciously in the ever luminous nature of the Divine. The inner enlightenment gives them the ability to develop a special vision. They inculcate the strength to control their innate nature and the conditioned behaviour. They become very intuitive and can recall their previous experiences. They can also trace some of their previous lives. They develop the vision to predict their future also. Srī Kṛṣṇa the master of Yoga declares that although He is unborn and imperishable, yet resorting to His essential transcendental Nature, He manifests through His divine potency. Remaining unmanifested He appears to the manifested. Remaining settled in the infinitude of His essentiality; he appears to be finite.

In verse seven Srī Kṛṣṇa announces that whenever there is a decline of Dharma and the rise of Adharma, I manifest myself in order to re-establish the values of righteousness and to protect the virtuous people. The word Dharma, which derives its root from the word *dhar*—to uphold and maintain. Dharma means the code of conduct which is supported by the voice of the inner-self. Srī Kṛṣṇa is declaring in these verses that whenever there is a decline of righteousness and moral values, I manifest Myself as God-incarnate in order to uphold righteousness and to restore orderliness on earth. Dharma is a unique system of values which is determined by the inner-self; those guide the individual to perform his duty by keeping in mind the welfare of others. Dharma is the golden message of God, "treat others as you would like to be treated by them". It is a guidance from the Higher-self; devoid of all the external pressures from society. It is an inner awakening that enlightens the person to differentiate between the desirable and undesirable acts. *Swadharma* is the experiential realization of the Supreme-soul. Any activity which is carried on with the awareness of the indwelling light, becomes a source of peace for everybody, because in that lies the manifestation of God Himself. Any duty performed in this manner protects the rights of others and implies the general well-being.

It is generally noticed that most of the daily activities of the people are directly and indirectly related to others—the family members, friends, relatives, neighbours, etc. For example, a person's responsibility towards cleanliness is not just limited to the cleaning of his own house; the code of Dharma stretches it towards the whole neighbourhood and to the entire country and the world at large. The personal hygiene and cleanliness is expected from everyone because it interacts with the health of other people. So any type of dealing one undertakes and the advancement one proposes it should be in consideration to the well-being of others. In any society where people become very materialistic, the existential fear increases in all respects. When each individual is led single-mindedly, in the pursuit of wealth, the spirituality is usually pushed to the very far end. With the negligence of spiritual values usually people become selfish, self-centred and ignore *swadharma.* As E.F. Schumacher writes, "If human vices such as greed and envy are systematically cultivated, the inevitable result is nothing less than a collapse of intelligence." When the feeling of jealousy, greed, envy and peer pressure of every kind increases in the society, there comes the distortion of moral values, restlessness of mind and decline in ethics everywhere. Any type of material progress and happiness which is preferred over ethics, it becomes another form of misery. *Swadharma* teaches people to live in harmony with one another. It is the consciousness of the Divine which guides the person to live by the code of conduct upheld by Dharma. As the Upanishads declare, "Not by the means of wealth only can a man fulfil himself. He requires other dimensions which he has to develop, and that is spiritual self."

Accepting the presence of the Divine and performing every bit of work with the guidance of the Divine is Dharma; on the other hand conscious, separation from the Divine and living a life against the voice of the Supreme-soul is Adharma. Dharma brings people together while Adharma disintegrates. The decline of Dharma (righteousness) starts at the individual level and gradually spreads throughout the community and nation—causing a downfall of the entire human race. Decline of Dharma is the decline of morality, virtuosity and spiritual values everywhere. The decline of spiritual and moral standards generally happens due to the loss of self-respect and due to the loss of respect for God. The lack of faith in one's own self is also due to the lack of faith in God. When people lose their conscious touch with God, they lose touch with themselves and with everybody and everything around. People become very insensitive, selfish, corrupt and self-centred. This is what Srī Kṛṣṇa means to say in verse seven—Whenever there is the decline of righteousness and the rise of unrighteousness, O' Bharata, then I incarnate Myself; for the protection of the virtuous, for the destruction of the wicked and for the re-establishment of righteousness.

In these verses Srī Kṛṣṇa is speaking to Arjuna as the inner dweller of each and everyone of us. The Lord incarnates to enlighten people and to persuade them to recognize their own divinity by their own efforts. The Supreme Lord incarnates to make people realize that each and every human being is an eligible candidate for attaining the Supreme goal. When the God-incarnate comes in contact with people as an ordinary human being, He enlightens, awakens and guides everyone by the example of His own personal life. In the words of Srī Ramakrishna, "All the little brooks and ditches become full to the brim without any effort or consciousness on their own part; so when an incarnation comes, a tidal wave of spirituality breaks upon the world, and people feel spirituality in the air." The God-incarnate comes down to the level of humans, in order to educate people into graciousness of the human life. He strengthens their faith in God and also their reverence for the scriptures. He shows His personal compassion for people and inspires others into godliness. He encourages others by His own idealistic life and advocates that godliness can be attained through manliness. The God-incarnate helps people in restoring the values of Dharma. Although the Lord-incarnate can accomplish His work without manifesting Himself but in order to purify and inspire the human beings, He works with man. The God-incarnate likes His work to be accomplished through man in order to teach him about his greatness in human life. As Srī Rama says in the Ramayana, *"sab mumpriya, sab mumupajaye, sab te adhik jeev mohe bhaye"*—I like and love all the beings but the human beings are especially dear to Me.

The words *"paritranaya sadhunam vinasaya ca duskrtam"*—meaning for the deliverance and protection of the virtuous and for the destruction of the wicked. Proper respect and the protection of the spiritual sages is indeed very important for the maintenance of spirituality, morality and orderliness in society. These enlightened saints serve as the beacon lights for others. They guide the deluded people into the path of righteousness. Spiritual sages are the embodiment of truth, non-violence, continence and Dharma. As the *Ramayana* describes *"satav mai mohe mai jag dekha, mote adhik sant kar lekha"*. Every holy saint carries with him the graciousness and the integral wisdom of the Supreme which radiates from his speech and work. His spiritual nature acts as an eternal flame, which enlightens the lives of others. People find inspiration from him into living a virtuous, pure, honest and steadfast life. The society where the holy sages and the learned scholars are not respected and not supported for their work, the decline of Dharma becomes inevitable. That society goes to self-annihilation in course of time. So in order to maintain harmony and orderliness in the society, it is indeed very important to respect the learned scholars and the sages of the society, for their assistance and guidance. *"Santo bhumin tapasya dharianti"* means the saints by their austerities, chastity and purity sustain the earth. They should be definitely given due respect and reverence under all circumstances.

जन्म कर्म च मे दिव्यमेवं यो वेत्ति तत्त्वतः।
त्यक्त्वा देहं पुनर्जन्म नैति मामेति सोऽर्जुन॥ ९॥

janma karma ca me divyamevaṁ yo vetti tattvataḥ
tyaktvā dehaṁ punarjanma naiti māmeti so'rjuna

(9) He who thus understands My divine birth and actions in

essence; having abandoned the body, he is not born again. He comes to Me, O'Arjuna.

वीतरागभयक्रोधा मन्मया मामुपाश्रिताः।
बहवो ज्ञानतपसा पूता मद्भावमागताः ॥ १० ॥

vītarāgabhayakrodhā manmayā mām upāśritāḥ
bahavo jñānatapasā pūtā madbhāvamāgatāḥ

(10) Liberated from desire, fear and anger with the mind absorbed in Me, taking refuge in Me, purified by the austerity of wisdom, many have attained to My state of being.

ये यथा मां प्रपद्यन्ते तांस्तथैव भजाम्यहम्।
मम वर्त्मानुवर्तन्ते मनुष्याः पार्थ सर्वशः ॥ ११ ॥

ye yathā māṁ prapadyante tāṅstathaiva bhajāmyaham
mama vartmānuvartante manuṣyāḥ pārtha sarvaśaḥ

(11) In whatever way, men approach Me, so do I accept them; for all men follow My path in every way, O'Arjuna.

Commentary—*Divyam evam yo vetti tattvatah* means he who knows thus in essentiality. The individual who has realized the infinite behind the veil of finite; he moves forward step by step from less awareness to increased awareness. He recognizes the reality of every situation in life and rises above the baseless optimism and also the groundless despair. Srī Kṛṣṇa asserts that the topmost quality which characterizes an authentically enlightened individual is that he lives in God and enjoys freedom from all kinds of fears and attachments. A genuine devotion and attachment to God brings detachment from the material world and makes the person very detached, renounced, fearless and peaceful. Such a person feels at peace within himself and enjoys freedom in the form of Moksha while living his life. As Tagore has written in Gitanjali, "By all means they try to hold me secure, who love me in this world. But it is otherwise with thy love which is greater than theirs, and Thou keepest me free". A faithful and genuine devotion to God enables the individual to get acquainted with his own inherent potential. It is the association with the Divine which gives him the clarity of understanding and the purity of thoughts. It is the closeness of the Supreme-self which supplements the intellectual learning with the calmness of purified wisdom and spiritual composure. In the words of Swami Rama, "Essentially and qualitatively, a single drop of ocean has all the qualities of the ocean. When a drop meets the ocean it becomes the ocean."

Living a life in transcendental consciousness rewards the individual with sanctity, austerity and an attitude of detached service. In these verses Srī Kṛṣṇa is using the pronoun 'I' and 'Me' not just as God-incarnate but for the cosmic and universal Supreme-soul. The eternal reality, the transcendent Brahman, the inner witness of all which transcends cause, space and time. The innermost being of each and every one. In the verse eleven, Srī Kṛṣṇa Himself brings the clarification to Arjuna by telling "O' Partha as the aspirants approach Me, so do I accept and bless them. Human beings follow my path in so many different ways everywhere." Srī Kṛṣṇa asserts that an individual should try to penetrate behind the various shadows and pursue the one prime truth, which is the essence of all life. The entire universe is resting in God and seeks comfort and peace through Him only. Srī Kṛṣṇa assures Arjuna that He reciprocates with the same feelings and sentiments, with which the devotee approaches Him. For example Srī Kṛṣṇa has taken the role of a most wonderful charioteer for Arjuna, a most adorable husband of Rukmani, a sincere guide for the Pandavas. He has taken up the role of a most loving son for Nand and Yasoda and a sincere friend for the cowherd boys and Gopis. Lord lives in the heart of His devotees, those keep Him enclosed in their hearts.

The famous story of Jatila and Madusudana relates this truth. Once there was a boy named Jatila. He used to go to school alone through the jungle; often he felt very lonely and scared. He talked to his mother about his fear in the jungle. The mother who was a devotee of the Lord simply told her son that whenever he felt frightened he should call upon Madusudana. When the boy inquired about Madusudana, the Mother answered, "Madusudana is your brother." Afterwards whenever Jatila felt frightened while passing through the jungle, he called for his brother Madusudana. No one appeared at the first call, but the boy kept calling repeatedly and Madusudana (Lord Kṛṣṇa) appeared in the form of a young boy and escorted Jatila through the woods. It is indeed very true that Lord manifests Himself before His devotees, in the same form upon which the aspirant meditates. He helps the individual to awaken his own inner powers and guides him to rely upon that. The Lord approaches people in so many different ways to awaken their faith, to restore their faith, self-confidence and self-respect. Srī Kṛṣṇa tells Arjuna that everybody should have a clear perception of the highest truth and also a faithful acceptance of it.

काङ्क्षन्तः कर्मणां सिद्धिं यजन्त इह देवताः।
क्षिप्रं हि मानुषे लोके सिद्धिर्भवति कर्मजा॥ १२॥

kāṅkṣantaḥ karmaṇāṁ siddhiṁ yajanta iha devatāḥ
kṣipraṁ hi mānuṣe loke siddhir bhavati karmajā

(12) Those who desire the fruits of their actions, worship the gods in this world, because the success is quickly attained by men, through action.

चातुर्वर्ण्यं मया सृष्टं गुणकर्मविभागशः।
तस्य कर्तारमपि मां विद्ध्यकर्तारमव्ययम्॥ १३॥

cāturvarṇyaṁ mayā sṛṣṭaṁ guṇakarmavibhāgaśaḥ
tasya kartāramapi māṁ viddhyakartāramavyayam

(13) The fourfold work order has been created by Me according to the differentiation of Guna and Karma. Though I am the creator, know Me as non-doer and immutable.

न मां कर्माणि लिम्पन्ति न मे कर्मफले स्पृहा।
इति मां योऽभिजानाति कर्मभिर्न स बध्यते॥ १४॥

na māṁ karmāṇi limpanti na me karmaphale spṛhā
iti māṁ yo'bhijānāti karmabhirna sa badhyate

(14) Actions do not contaminate Me, because I have no desire for the fruit of actions. He who understands Me thus (in essence) is not bound by actions.

एवं ज्ञात्वा कृतं कर्म पूर्वैरपि मुमुक्षुभिः।
कुरु कर्मैव तस्मात्त्वं पूर्वैः पूर्वतरं कृतम्॥ १५॥

evaṁ jñātvā kṛtaṁ karma pūrvairapi mumukṣubhiḥ
kuru karmaiva tasmāttvaṁ pūrvaiḥ pūrvataraṁ kṛtam

(15) Having known this, the seekers of liberation from ancient times have also performed their actions. Therefore, do thou also perform action as the ancients did in their times.

Commentary—In verse twelve Srī Kṛṣṇa brings forth the mystery about the eternal law of Karma (cause and effect). He gives examples of the gods and goddesses described in the Vedas and Puranas. The four Vedas such as *Rig Veda, Yajur Veda, Sama Veda* and *Atharva Veda* have been revealed to the four rishies—*Agni, Vayu, Aditya* and *Angira* at the beginning of creation. Vedas are considered to be Divine Revelation which has been handed down to the humanity as a necessary guidance in order to live in peace and harmony. Although fully equipped with inner knowledge and wisdom, the human beings still need guidance from the sacred books in order to enhance their own abilities, both physically and spiritually. In the words of Professor Max Mueller, who translated the *Rig Veda* and also edited the well-known volume of *The Sacred Books of the East,* "The vedic literature opens to us a doorway in the education of human races, to which we can't find anything else parallel". The hymns of the Vedas describe the glories of the Supreme Lord and the perennial interdependence which exists between God, nature and the other created beings. The Vedic-hymns illustrate the close relationship of man and nature, and the realization of God through an intimate relationship with nature. Power and glory of God has been represented by the traditional Vedic personification of gods and goddesses. For example, a passage in the Veda describes the Devas like Virat, Purusha, Deva, Akasa, Vayu, Agni, Jala, Bhumi, etc. Virat signifies the god who illumines the world. The word Agni is derived from the root *'ancu'* and *'aga'*—the fire god. The word 'Visva' is derived from the root *visa,* to reside. The god is called Visva because in Him resides the entire creation. The word 'Vayu' is derived from the root *va,* meaning motion. 'Vayu' is the wind-god. The word 'Indra' comes from the root word *idi,* the god of rain. *Brahaspati*—the master of learning, the giver of knowledge. Varuna, *"varuno nama varah* *srethah"*. Aryma is another name of god (the god of justice). The word 'Jala' comes from the root word *Jal,* the water god. 'Prithvi' comes from the root word *prithu* means the earth. 'Kubera' the root word *kubi.* The *kubi* means that covers. The 'Candra' from the root word *cadi* means to delight. 'Mangala' comes from *magi* meaning motion. The word 'Sukra' comes from root word *isucir* which means that purifies. 'Rahu' from root word *raha* meaning who abandons and punishes the wicked ones. 'Ketu' come from *kita* means to heal. The word 'Yajña' comes from the root *yaja* means to harmonize and give. Dharamraja who shines in Dharma. As a matter of fact, every aspect of the Divine energy that gives support to sustain life on earth and also in the human body has been named Devata. There is a description of so many Devas in Vedas and Puranas and *Satapathe Brahmana.* For example, in macrocosm, the eight Vasus are Earth, Air, Water, Agni, Ether, Sun, Moon and stars are the abode of creation. In microcosm, the eleven Rudras are the different names of Pranas— Prana, Apana, Vyana, Samana, Udana, Naga, Kurma, Krikala, Devadatta, Dhananjaya. The twelve Adityas are the twelve months— and the twelve birth signs correspond to these twelve months of the year. Each birth sign also has a presiding deity.

Srī Kṛṣṇa tells Arjuna that the people, who desire the fruits of their actions, worship many different kinds of gods and goddesses in this world. Any specific type of worship, which is done with love and devotion, in that, the success follows quickly; because of the eternal law of karma. The worshippers of gods and goddesses are rewarded with wealth, progeny and other comforts of life. These worshippers think that the particular god or goddess is the giver of the bounties, and they don't understand that it is indeed the result of their own virtuous actions, which have been initiated by their connectedness with the Supreme-self. It is the performance of their own virtuous actions that gives them the desired fruit, which comes as a grace of the Divine. It is just like the echo of our own voice. It is indeed the power of Supreme which works in the performance of all the religious deeds through the media of gods and goddess. Srī Kṛṣṇa says that the Lord makes sure that everyone receives the appropriate fruit of his own actions performed with faith and devotion.

Srī Kṛṣṇa also enlightens Arjuna that the world is a vast field of mixed actions. People driven by their innate nature choose the kind of work that suits their liking and aspirations. These innate inclinations of people have brought into existence the fourfold work-order in society. The word caste is self-explanatory—means the role one has been assigned to play in his lifetime. Although all men look alike on the surface, yet their intellectual and physical abilities do differ from one another in so many different ways. People have always divided themselves into four different classes. The people in each class have always performed their duties, guided by their *swabhava* (innate nature). Even today we can observe this division of work in almost all the developed cultures of the world. For example, the teachers, philosophers, scholars form the first, the second one is administrators, managers, leaders, soldiers, and the third class is businessmen, industrialists and the fourth is workers, servants and the labourers. The caste system has been based on the *svabhava,* the inborn nature which is expressed in the type of work one chooses to perform. The self-imposed classification of people in society has always helped the community in the proper distribution of work according to the innate choice of every man. Srī Kṛṣṇa is emphasizing that each and every individual is very special and it is the responsibility of each individual to explore his speciality and try to enhance it. The society should also provide the opportunity and means for the full expression of one's *svabhava,* which eventually becomes one's own *swadharma.* People everywhere follow the fourfold law of their own instinctive behaviour and perform the work accordingly. Srī Kṛṣṇa says although it looks on the surface that 'I' created the fourfold division, but as a matter of fact it becomes created by itself—by the people, of the people, and for the people. Each and every individual is indeed the creator of the role he has chosen for himself to play in life.

Srī Kṛṣṇa is making it very clear to Arjuna that people perform all kinds of work, being initiated and motivated by their inborn nature. It is the *swabhava,* which seeks its expression and satisfaction into the performance of various activities. He asserts that "actions don't touch Me, nor do I aspire for the fruit of the actions—the one who understands Me to be so, he is not bound by any action." When the individual is able to develop a union with the transcendental-Self, he experiences that the work is actually being performed by the Self alone. This attitude brings freedom, liberation and peace to the individual. Srī Kṛṣṇa emphasizes that the people should work with the spirit of non-attachment. He also gives the example of ancient seers and sages who had constantly lived in the consciousness of the Divine, and performed their work, for work's sake. These great men of wisdom knew the complexities of Karma, and that is why they never became entangled with the fruit of their actions. Srī Kṛṣṇa is advising Arjuna to follow in the footsteps of his predecessors and perform his duty with an attitude of detachment, as ordained by the tradition. Srī Kṛṣṇa asserts the necessity of action and the performance of one's respective duty with due regard to the responsibility in society.

किं कर्म किमकर्मेति कवयोऽप्यत्र मोहिताः।
तत्ते कर्म प्रवक्ष्यामि यज्ज्ञात्वा मोक्ष्यसेऽशुभात्॥ १६॥

kiṁ karma kimakarmeti kavayo'pyatra mohitāḥ
tatte karma pravakṣyāmi yajjñātvā mokṣyase'śubhāt

(16) What is action? What is inaction?—Even men of wisdom are confused about it. Therefore, I must explain to you about action; by knowing which, you will be liberated from its evil effect.

कर्मणो ह्यपि बोद्धव्यं बोद्धव्यं च विकर्मणः।
अकर्मणश्च बोद्धव्यं गहना कर्मणो गतिः॥ १७॥

karmaṇo hyapi boddhavyaṁ boddhavyaṁ ca vikarmaṇaḥ
akarmaṇaśca boddhavyaṁ gahanā karmaṇo gatiḥ

(17) One must understand the truth about action, and the truth about the prohibited action. Likewise, the truth about inaction should also be known; for, mysterious is the nature of action.

कर्मण्यकर्म यः पश्येदकर्मणि च कर्म यः।
स बुद्धिमान्मनुष्येषु स युक्तः कृत्स्नकर्मकृत्॥ १८॥

karmaṇyakarma yaḥ paśyedakarmaṇi ca karma yaḥ
sa buddhimān manuṣyeṣu sa yuktaḥ kṛtsnakarmakṛt

(18) He, who sees inaction in action, and also action in inaction,

he is wise among men. He is a yogi, and a true performer of all actions.

Commentary—In these verses Srī Kṛṣṇa explains to Arjuna the triple classification about the nature of action. He emphasizes that life is indeed a vast field of actions. In order to assess the implications of action, it is important to understand what is action, prohibited action, and what is inaction.

He uses the term *karma, vikarma* and *akarma*. The common belief is that in order to become a renunciate the individual has to renounce all actions. A person can't become spiritual while performing worldly duties. The detachment is considered to be the cessation of worldly life. Here in these verses, Srī Kṛṣṇa extends and elaborates the meaning of the terms *karma, vikarm* and *akarm*; by understanding which the person becomes enlightened and attains freedom in his lifetime. He tells Arjuna that self-awareness is very important while doing any type of work. With self-observation one can understand clearly the nature of action and can function simultaneously at the physical, psychological and spiritual level in perfect unison. People suffer in life because most of the work is performed in a semiconscious state of mind. Most of the people generally work under a lot of pressure and frustration. In general, the human behaviour more or less is like an automated machine where the emotions, the memories, and the feelings find their expression like a preprogrammed floppy-disk. There are only a few in millions who are fully acquainted with the nature of their work and actually like and enjoy their assigned duties.

About *vikarma* Srī Kṛṣṇa means the activity which is performed in a deluded state of mind and also the activity about which the performer is not even aware. For example, people shake their leg unknowingly while sitting on a desk and others make some sounds out of nervousness while doing any type of work etc. These activities have been termed as *vikarma* which mean these are done unconsciously. The actions which are undertaken in a deluded state of mind, are considered to be *vikarma.* The forbidden actions are also called *vikarma.* Srī Kṛṣṇa tells Arjuna that it is very important to know about both, the nature of an action and the nature of prohibited action. The actions which are against the voice of the inner self are surely the prohibited actions. The nature of action is very intriguing; some time even the learned and the great leaders become confused in deciding between action and non-action; the right action and the forbidden action. There is a very thin line which separates action from non-action, and the right action from the prohibited action. Srī Kṛṣṇa says that one must understand the truth about performing right action. He makes it very clear that inaction doesn't mean the cessation of all activity, it is the renunciation of the desire of the fruits of action. Inaction as the term itself explains, inaction, means while doing action, the mind totally rests in that action, which manifests itself as Divine. In that case the work itself appears to be the manifestation of God and the devoted accomplishment of that work becomes the worship of God. In other words, we can say living in the Divine while performing all actions is inaction. It is the understanding of the truth that every activity proceeds from the indwelling light, and every bit of work is performed by the indwelling Self. Such actions become selfless and benefit the individual as well as others. One lives a life in a copartnership with God and performs all the work in complete copartnership with the Divine. In the words of Srī Shankaracharya, "This supreme position is recognized as inaction in action. Only they, who have attained self-knowledge and those who are on the path of self-knowledge, can be in this benign state."

The individual in his ignorance considers himself to be the doer. But when he establishes his connectedness with the Supreme-Self he learns to live in the blissful state of unity with the Divine and realizes that in truth everything is being done by the Lord Himself. This is the state of inaction in action. Perceiving inaction in action is to change the nature of bondage into freedom. In the words of Swami Vivekananda, "Mind requires to be cultured both in an active social life and in the silence of solitude. If the mind can maintain peace and calmness while being engaged in fighting a battle, it is seeing inaction in action." The actions which are performed with the consciousness of the indwelling light are always the right type of actions; contrary to the actions those are undertaken in a confused and deluded state of mind. The person has to train himself into a disciplined state of mind which seeks guidance from the indweller.

Srī Kṛṣṇa suggests that the yogi is not only that person who has renounced the world and sits in a cave to meditate, but also the one who lives a full worldly life with his mind anchored in God. Such an individual lives normal life in the world and still enjoys the blissful state of yoga. Srī Ramakrishna has given a very good example of this, "Perform all work in the world bearing God in mind constantly. He gives the example of some village girls in India, who carry four or five pitchers of water on their heads—stacked one over the other. As they walk home from the village well, they talk with their friends and sing songs. While walking and talking, a part of their attention always remains centred upon the proper hold of their pitchers. Similarly one should live in the world, perform all the assigned duties at the various stations of life, with the mind centred in the Supreme-self. Srī Ramakrishna also gives the example of a magnetic needle that always points towards the North, so that the sailing ship doesn't lose its direction. Similarly as long as the mind is directed towards God one can never get lost in the world. With this type of subtle training the mind becomes peaceful and every activity of the individual becomes inaction, in action. The union with the Divine helps one to inculcate the spirit and insight of *akarma* in life. The person performs all his work with a deep tranquillity of mind and always remains free from the bondage of action. Srī Satvalekar has given a beautiful illustration, "Man seated in a moving cart moves along with the carriage, but it is only the cart which is in motion. Similarly, a man of wisdom performs all his work in union with the Supreme-self sitting peacefully in the vehicle of his body, which moves while he remains still."

यस्य सर्वे समारम्भाः कामसङ्कल्पवर्जिताः ।
ज्ञानाग्निदग्धकर्माणं तमाहुः पण्डितं बुधाः ॥ १९ ॥

yasya sarve samārambhāḥ kāmasaṅkalpavarjitāḥ
jñānāgnidagdhakarmāṇaṁ tamāhuḥ paṇḍitaṁ budhāḥ

(19) He whose undertakings are all free from self-centred personal desires, whose actions have been purified in the fire of wisdom—him, the wise call a sage.

त्यक्त्वा कर्मफलासङ्गं नित्यतृप्तो निराश्रयः ।
कर्मण्यभिप्रवृत्तोऽपि नैव किञ्चित्करोति सः ॥ २० ॥

tyaktvā karmaphalāsaṅgaṁ nityatṛpto nirāśrayaḥ
karmaṇyabhipravṛtto'pi naiva kiñcit karoti saḥ

(20) Renouncing attachment to the fruits of action, ever contented and free from all kinds of dependence, he does not do anything, though fully engaged in action.

निराशीर्यतचित्तात्मा त्यक्तसर्वपरिग्रहः।
शारीरं केवलं कर्म कुर्वन्नाप्नोति किल्बिषम्॥ २१॥

nirāśīryatacittātmā tyaktasarvaparigrahaḥ
śārīraṁ kevalaṁ karma kurvannāpnoti kilbiṣam

(21) Having no desires, with his mind and body fully controlled, who has given up the desire for all sorts of possessions and performs only the necessary actions for the body; he is not tainted by sin (he is not subject to evil).

यदृच्छालाभसन्तुष्टो द्वन्द्वातीतो विमत्सरः।
समः सिद्धावसिद्धौ च कृत्वापि न निबध्यते॥ २२॥

yadṛcchālābhasantuṣṭo dvandvātīto vimatsaraḥ
samaḥ siddhāvasiddhau ca kṛtvāpi na nibadhyate

(22) Fully contented with whatever comes along, who is free from the pairs of opposites and envy, balanced in success and failure, even though he acts, he is not bound.

Commentary—These verses are the continuation of the previous verse where Srī Kṛṣṇa emphasizes upon the clear understanding and precise nature of action and inaction. In these verses He elaborates the same concept by enlightening Arjuna about some of the characteristics of the self-realized yogi. An individual who is eternally settled in the consciousness of the Divine, he becomes very independent, fearless, truthful and strong—both physically and emotionally. The individual starts realizing the transitory nature of the world around; and he understands that the perishable pleasures can not give fulfillment to the imperishable-Self. Gradually he loses interest in acquiring and accumulating them, and feels withdrawn from the sensory enjoyments. As a matter of fact, every being has a natural inclination for the conscious intimacy with the Divine; it is only because of his over-involvement in the material world that he loses his connection temporarily. In the unconscious mind his unity with the Divine always remains fresh and awake. So, even a little bit of effort on the part of the individual helps him to go back into the flow of the main stream of Bliss. When he realizes the unity with God, his love for God blossoms once again and every other desire becomes immaterial and insignificant. The person feels liberated from all the feelings of jealousy, greed, sense of possession and the desire for the fruits and rewards of his actions. It is indeed so true that the real wisdom lies within and can be experienced, whenever all the cravings and desires are gradually controlled. Describing the words *tamahuh panditam budhah,* Shri Ramsukhdas writes, "Those who have renounced the world, and enlighten the lives of others, everyone knows them; but a household saint is rarely known". Detachment from the fruit of action is definitely very difficult but not impossible. It can be nurtured slowly and steadily by living in the awareness of God; by cherishing the affinity with God. Detachment is not a passive reverie, it is to live in discipline and to work in discipline. It is a self-mastery which a person attains by means of self-awareness and self-knowledge. Srī Kṛṣṇa assures mankind that it is indeed possible for each and everyone to live a normal worldly life and still be balanced, detached, peaceful and settled in unity like a yogi. In the words of Swami Vivekananda, "He who is one with the Lord through yoga, performs all his actions by becoming immersed in concentration, and doesn't seek any personal benefit; such performance of work brings only good to the world, no evil can ever come out of it".

In the verse twenty-one and twenty-two, Srī Kṛṣṇa educates Arjuna about the characteristics of the Self-enlightened yogi. A self-realized person learns to rely upon his own resources, and his faith in God strengthens which helps him to face the ups and downs of life very courageously and peacefully. The spark of faith, which a person perceives in his association with the Divine, enlightens his own life and the life of all the others who come in contact. His steadfast faith inspires even the most sceptical ones. He awakens the faith of others by providing examples from his own life style. There is an incident from the life story of Srī Ramakrishana. He had throat cancer and suffered a lot in the last few months of his life. The doctors treated him with everything they could but nothing helped. Finally a well-known doctor who was well-acquainted with the spiritual powers of Srī Ramakrishna advised him and requested him to pray to the Holy Mother for his own recovery. Srī Ramakrishna who could hardly talk at that time said, "Shall I make such a request to the Mother. Doesn't Mother herself know what is good for me, She does whatever She thinks is best for me." He had strong faith in God and accepted whatever came along. A God-realized soul definitely develops an extraordinary strength to face the dualities of life. It is indeed the inner unison which distinguishes a God-realized soul from the others. This enlightened attitude keeps the individual detached and free, even though he is perpetually engaged in action.

गतसङ्गस्य मुक्तस्य ज्ञानावस्थितचेतसः ।
यज्ञायाचरतः कर्म समग्रं प्रविलीयते ॥ २३ ॥

gatasaṅgasya muktasya jñānāvasthitacetasaḥ
yajñāyācarataḥ karma samagraṁ pravilīyate

(23) He, who is totally unattached and liberated, whose mind is established in transcendental knowledge, who performs all his work in the spirit of yajña (selflessly)—his actions are entirely dissolved.

ब्रह्मार्पणं ब्रह्म हविर्ब्रह्माग्नौ ब्रह्मणा हुतम् ।
ब्रह्मैव तेन गन्तव्यं ब्रह्मकर्मसमाधिना ॥ २४ ॥

brahmārpaṇaṁ brahma havir brahmāgnau brahmaṇā hutam
brahmaiva tena gantavyaṁ brahmakarmasamādhinā

(24) For him, the act of offering is Brahman (God), the melted butter and oblation is Brahman. The oblation is offered by Brahman into the fire, which is Brahman. Thus, Brahman alone is to be reached by him, who meditates on Brahman in his work.

Commentary—The person who remains focussed upon his goal of attaining unity with the Supreme, he looks at everything and everybody from the deepest level of his being. His soul-awareness expresses itself in each and every field of his activity. As the words of an ancient saint describe, "The happy life is to rejoice to thee, of thee, and for thee. To perceive God in every work and everything is to accept the presence of the Divine and remain united with it." The individual who is firmly grounded in the self, he experiences the reality of the spiritual self in every aspect of life. He feels more like an instrument in the hands of God, for the yajña which needs to be performed in order to maintain the work-order of the universe. The person perceives the truth—that it is one and the only power which manifests through everything and works its way out through everything.

There is an illustration in Chhandogya Upanishad where the teacher asks his disciple to bring a fruit of the nyagrodha tree. The student brings it and hands it over to the teacher. The teacher gives it back to the student and instructs him to break it. When the student breaks it open, the teacher inquires from the disciple, "What do you see there". The disciple answers, "A little seed, my revered teacher." The teacher further instructs now break the seed and tell me what is inside the seed. The student answers "There is nothing inside the seed, Sir." Then the teacher explains that although there is nothing visible inside the seed, still the seed does have all the information to become a tree. That hidden energy which has no name and form is the 'Pure Being', the essence of life. That 'Pure Being' is indeed the Supreme-self. The man of wisdom, who is ever established in the knowledge of the self, does recognize it instantly. He remains firmly grounded in the field of pure awareness, and beholds Brahman in everything, in everyone and in every activity. He is the *Brahma-Karma-Samadhinam*—means he contemplates on Brahman and beholds the Brahman as the essence of all actions. In fact, everything in reality is Brahman, so when an individual realizes it and performs yajña he remains established in Brahman. He becomes free from all personal desires, aspirations, and the fruits of his work. His actions do not contaminate his *Antahkaran* (mind). In the words of Madhusudhana Saraswathi, "In a sacrifice, there are five constituents, the *karta* (doer), the *karma* (act), the instrument (karana), *sampradhana* the deity addressed as Adhikarani, the receptacle that is fire in which the oblation is poured. One who considers the sacrificial action in the light of Samadhi (consciousness in Brahman) has karma samadhi". This illustration, from the verse twenty-four, tells about the work style of a person who has realized oneness of existence in every sphere of action. Everything is Brahman for the enlightened person who remains grounded in the cosmic consciousness. It is an elevated and inspired level of consciousness which envelops in itself both the relative and the absolute fields of life. The life of a karmayogi becomes a nonstop yajña, wherein every work is performed as an oblation.

दैवमेवापरे यज्ञं योगिनः पर्युपासते।
ब्रह्माग्नावपरे यज्ञं यज्ञेनैवोपजुह्वति॥ २५॥

daivamevāpare yajñaṁ yoginaḥ paryupāsate
brahmāgnāvapare yajñaṁ yajñenaivopajuhvati

(25) Some yogis perform sacrifice (yajña) to the gods alone; while others offer sacrifice (selfless action) by the sacrifice itself, into the fire of Brahman.

श्रोत्रादीनीन्द्रियाण्यन्ये संयमाग्निषु जुह्वति।
शब्दादीन्विषयानन्य इन्द्रियाग्निषु जुह्वति॥ २६॥

śrotrādīnīndriyāṇyanye saṅyamāgniṣu juhvati
śabdādīn viṣayānanya indriyāgniṣu juhvati

(26) Some offer hearing and other senses as sacrifice into the fire of self-restraint. Others offer sound and the object of senses as sacrifice into the fire of the senses.

सर्वाणीन्द्रियकर्माणि प्राणकर्माणि चापरे।
आत्मसंयमयोगाग्नौ जुह्वति ज्ञानदीपिते॥ २७॥

sarvāṇīndriyakarmāṇi prāṇakarmāṇi cāpare
ātmasaṁyamayogāgnau juhvati jñānadīpite

(27) Some others offer the functions of the senses and the activity of the vital force (prana) into the fire of the yoga of self-control, lighted by the flame of knowledge.

द्रव्ययज्ञास्तपोयज्ञा योगयज्ञास्तथापरे।
स्वाध्यायज्ञानयज्ञाश्च यतयः संशितव्रताः॥ २८॥

dravyayajñāstapoyajñā yogayajñāstathāpare
svādhyāyajñānayajñāś ca yatayaḥ saṅśitavratāḥ

(28) Some others offer their material possessions (wealth), austerity and yoga as sacrifice; while others of self-restraint and rigid vows offer the scriptural studies and knowledge as sacrifice.

अपाने जुह्वति प्राणं प्राणेऽपानं तथापरे।
प्राणापानगती रुद्ध्वा प्राणायामपरायणाः॥ २९॥

apāne juhvati prāṇaṁ prāṇe'pānaṁ tathāpare
prāṇāpānagatī ruddhvā prāṇāyāmaparāyaṇāḥ

(29) Yet others, who are devoted to the breath control, sacrifice the outgoing breath into incoming and the incoming into outgoing, by restraining the movement of both.

अपरे नियताहाराः प्राणान्प्राणेषु जुह्वति।
सर्वेऽप्येते यज्ञविदो यज्ञक्षपितकल्मषाः॥ ३०॥

apare niyatāhārāḥ prāṇān prāṇeṣu juhvati
sarve'pyete yajñavido yajñakṣapitakalmaṣāḥ

(30) Others, who regulate their diet, they pour as sacrifice their life breaths into the life-breaths. All these are the knowers of sacrifice, whose sins have been destroyed by sacrifice.

यज्ञशिष्टामृतभुजो यान्ति ब्रह्म सनातनम्।
नायं लोकोऽस्त्ययज्ञस्य कुतोऽन्यः कुरुसत्तम॥ ३१॥

yajñaśiṣṭāmṛtabhujo yānti brahma sanātanam
nā'yaṁ loko'styayajñasya kuto'nyaḥ kurusattama

(31) Those who eat the sacred remnants of the sacrifice, which is like nectar, they attain to the eternal Absolute. Even this world is not for him, who does not perform sacrifice (selfless action)—how then the other, O'Arjuna?

एवं बहुविधा यज्ञा वितता ब्रह्मणो मुखे।
कर्मजान्विद्धि तान्सर्वानेवं ज्ञात्वा विमोक्ष्यसे॥ ३२॥

evaṁ bahuvidhā yajñā vitatā brahmaṇo mukhe
karmajānviddhi tānsarvānevaṁ jñātvā vimokṣyase

(32) Many forms of sacrifices are spread out before the Brahman (set forth as means of attaining Brahman in Vedas). Know them all as born of action; knowing thus, you will be liberated.

Commentary—After describing at length the nature of action and inaction, Srī Kṛṣṇa proceeds to enumerate the other techniques wherein one experiences inaction in action. In these eight verses, Srī Kṛṣṇa explains the various types of yajña in order to give an overall idea of the sacrificial acts and their importance towards the attainment of perfection in yoga. In the previous chapter the concept of yajña has been introduced. Yajña is a very significant act of worship and a wonderful method of forming a relationship with God, with nature, with other people and with other species at the same time. This is a mode of worship to God which was started at the beginning of creation. It has been handed down from one generation to another and it is still a valid technique of developing unity consciousness. Yajña literally means to offer a service to the Divine very selflessly. According to the ancient vedic tradition, there are five types of Mahayajñas, those have been ordained in the Vedas: the Brahma Yajña, Deva Yajña, Pitri Yajña, Atithi Yajña and Balivishvadeva Yajña. A householder has been always expected to perform yajña everyday, and also all the important religious ceremonies in vedic tradition are performed with yajña. The verse twenty-five explains that some people perform yajña as a worship to the gods and goddesses, while others who have been able to form an identity with the absolute, experience their individual-self being offered in service of the Supreme-self. They perform their every activity as a yajña with universal unity in mind. He proceeds further and explains that yajña is not just limited to the activity of igniting the fire in *Havankunda* and giving some oblations in the names of gods; yajña is indeed much more than this. Performing yajña is the initiation into the unity of yogic communion. Each vedic mantra is repeated with *idam na mama*, this is not mine, this is not for me. Srī Kṛṣṇa expounds upon the meaning and suggests that the life should be lived in the spirit of yajña (selfless) like an offering to the service of the Divine. He brings forth the hidden significance of yajña from various points of view. He gives various examples saying some people make offerings to the gods in yajña while others offer their individual self as an offering to thę Brahman. Some people offer their sense of hearing and other senses in the austerity of self-control; others offer the objects of senses into the fire of self-discipline. Some others offer the actions of senses and the activity of Pranas into the yogic-fire of self control lighted by the flame of wisdom. All these are various types of austerities, those are practised by the individual for self-purification and self-realization. The sensory organs are the gates and windows of our body, those come in contact with the objects of the material world. The senses catch the information and pass it over to the mind. The eyes are like a camera, that quickly catches and takes the picture of whatever comes within its reach. So any kind of program one watches on the television or anything in the surrounding, it is recorded by the eyes and printed into the ever renewing portfolio of the thought process. Whatever one hears, smells and perceives by the senses is definitely recorded, saved and brought back to the awareness of the individual in relation to the specific idea and action. A genuine aspirant maintains his positive control over the sensory organs and considers his austerity to be an oblation into the yajña of self-purification. This is indeed an act of sacrifice.

The proper regulation of prana, the vital force is also a form of yajña. The aspirant offers every little function of his prana into the contemplation on god. The functions of the vital forces are Prana, Apana, Vyana, Samana, Udana, Naga, Kurma, Krikala, Devadatta and Dhananjaya. The activity of breathing is Prana, the downward movement of the breath and out of the body is Apana. The contraction and expansion of the breath in the heart is called Vyana; when it helps in assimilation of food in the stomach area, it is called Samana. When the life force is pulled upward from the base of the spine it is called Udana. The eructation is called Naga, and Kurma helps in the opening of the eyelids. The Krikala is known as producing hunger and the Devadutta the yawning. The Dhananjaya permeates into the entire body and leaves the physical body only after death and cremation. When the life breath is offered into the life breath the rhythm of Prana becomes harmonized and it stabilizes the activities of mind. It helps concentration and contemplation on the Supreme-self. The impurities of mind are also checked and destroyed and the yogi feels settled in the indweller.

The verse twenty-eight indicates many other types of sacrifices performed by the aspirants. Some people offer material goods, wealth, austerities and their virtuous deeds as sacrifice; while others offer their scriptural studies and knowledge for the benefit of others. An enlightened person can clearly see the yajña which has pervaded in the entire nature since time immemorial. The sun rises at its own predetermined hour and starts serving the creation, the moon, the rain, the rivers and trees everything is working in harmony with one another, in order to serve life on the planet. The awakened one perceives the meaning *"paropkarayarth phalanti vrikshsa, paropkarayarth dohanti gavah, paropkarayarth vahanti nadia, paropkarayarth midam shariram"*—the trees bear the fruits for the welfare of others, the cows give milk for the welfare of others, the rivers are flowing constantly for the welfare of others, my body is intended to exist only for the welfare of others. The awakened one knows that the law of providence expects from the individual to understand the nature of *swadharma.* It is expected from human beings to earn the money by appropriate means and share a part of the earnings with the community for the proper work order. The Dravya-yajña is performed by donating a part of one's earnings for the construction of hospitals, schools, orphanages, the shrines, the free lodging places along the highways, libraries and the water tanks etc. In this type of yajña the fund-raising dinners are organized in order to collect money for the welfare of the community. The orphanages are supported in order to provide quality life and quality education to the orphans. The saints and other learned scholars are helped, those are trying to awaken the society with spiritual performances. Such type of services help the individual to maintain a balance in society. It gives self-satisfaction and enhances the spirit of sharing. This is indeed an austerity which purifies the individual and helps him in God-realization.

The word *swadhyaya* is a combination of two words. *Swa* means the indwelling light and *adhya* means to study. *Swadhyaya* means the study of the self. Srī Kṛṣṇa asserts that the study of the self becomes possible through various types of services performed for self-purification. *Swadhyaya* also means the study of scriptures and enlightening the lives of others with scriptural knowledge. Each one of these sacrifices plays a very significant role in its own way. Srī Kṛṣṇa proceeds to describe another mode of yajña in the verse twenty-nine. It is the offering of Prana into the disciplined mode of Prana in order to maintain a perfect control on Prana for yogic communion. Pranayama is the art of breathing that helps in concentration and yogic communion. It deals with the systematic functioning of the breath for yogic union. It is the subtle, invisible thread which helps the individual to move gently from the gross to the subtle levels of consciousness. Pranayama is performed with proper control of puruka, kumbhaka and rechaka. The puruka is the inhalation of fresh breath that brings the vital energy into the body and stimulates the system. The activity of exhalation, which is rechaka throws out the toxins and polluted breath from the digestion of food etc. The kumbhaka is the retention of Prana which vitalizes the body with energy. The activity of Pranayama is to maintain a positive control over the three modes of inhalation, retention and exhalation in a rhythmic manner without jerks. This rhythmic flow of Pranayama helps to regulate the thoughts. It helps one to develop a conscious control over the quality, quantity and direction of thoughts. The practice of Pranayama helps in exercising self-discipline. It helps in relaxation of muscles and the concentration of mind. Inner tranquillity, orderly thinking, improved memory, control over the worldly desires and an overall relaxed attitude are some of the rewards of Pranayama practised on regular basis. As a matter of fact it is an essential requirement for everybody. The process of inhalation and exhalation has been described as the pouring of one into the other and watching the entire process as a silent witness; this is inaction in action.

After describing the techniques of Pranayama and its benefits for yogic communion, Srī Kṛṣṇa proceeds to describe the other types of yajñas. Some individuals perform yajña in the form of regulating their diet. They monitor the quality, the quantity and the frequency of their food intake. Food is very essential for sustaining the body. If the quality and the quantity of food intake is neglected, it definitely becomes a treacherous ally. Discipline in eating habits gives strength, vitality and lot of self-respect. Disciplinary food habits are indeed the gateway towards union with God. In the words of Mahatma Gandhi, "Fasting and prayer give in the requisite discipline, spirit of self-sacrifice, humanity and resoluteness of will, without which there can be no progress." Srī Kṛṣṇa concludes that all these yajñas are various forms of worships. He makes it very clear to Arjuna that these are the means towards the attainment of knowledge which liberates the individual from the bondage of action.

श्रेयान्द्रव्यमयाद्यज्ञाज्ज्ञानयज्ञः परन्तप।
सर्वं कर्माखिलं पार्थ ज्ञाने परिसमाप्यते ॥ ३३ ॥

śreyān dravyāmayādyajñājjñānayajñaḥ parantapa
sarvaṁ karmākhilaṁ pārtha jñāne parisamāpyate

(33) Superior is sacrifice of wisdom to the sacrifice of material objects, O'Arjuna. All actions in their entirety culminate in wisdom.

तद्विद्धि प्रणिपातेन परिप्रश्नेन सेवया।
उपदेक्ष्यन्ति ते ज्ञानं ज्ञानिनस्तत्त्वदर्शिनः ॥ ३४ ॥

tadviddhi praṇipātena paripraśnena sevayā
upadekṣyanti te jñānaṁ jñāninastattvadarśinaḥ

(34) Attain this knowledge by prostration (humble reverence) by asking questions and by service. The men of wisdom, who have realized the truth, will instruct you in knowledge.

Commentary—In these verses Srī Kṛṣṇa suggests that the offering which is made in the form of pursuit for knowledge of the Supreme-self is indeed superior, because all activities culminate in knowledge. Jñana yajña here stands for the kind of wisdom which connects the individual to the Supreme-self. It is the experiential knowledge of the Self which enriches the quality of actions and transforms them into the yoga of action. When actions are performed with proper insight and inner calmness, the performance of actions becomes upgraded from karma to Karmayoga. Srī Kṛṣṇa tells that the initiation and guidance in the knowledge of the absolute truth is imparted by the learned seers. They are well versed in the study of

Vedas, Upanishads and other scriptures. Their wisdom and knowledge is always combined with their own experiential knowledge of the self. They should be approached with reverence, humility and with an attitude of service. The bookish knowledge is fragmentary and incomplete. The knowledge that comes as guidance from the teacher is from his own treasure of scriptural knowledge and personal experience. Since Vedic times the holy sages have emphasized upon the necessity of a teacher for spiritual guidance. *Shruti Bhagwati* supports it in these words *"parikshya lokan karma, chitan brahmano nirved Maya nasyah kritah kriten. Tad vigyanartham sa Gurumeva bhigachhat samita pani, shrotryam brahma nishtam."* In order to attain knowledge of the Eternal, one should approach the spiritual teacher who is well versed in Vedas and is established in Brahman. *Maundukya Upanishad* describes the same concept in these words: "When taught by a teacher who has realized himself as one with Brahman, a person attains the goal and becomes liberated from the rounds of birth, death and rebirth. Spiritual guidance is indeed the key to self-realization. In order to attain any type of spiritual progress one has to go through these four stages of spiritual advancement. The first one is *Atma-kripa* meaning the grace of the embodied self, in other words the personal effort and the decision of the individual. The second *Guru-kripa* means the grace of the Guru. The third, the *Shastra-kripa* means the understanding of the scriptures and the fourth one is the *Prabhu-kripa* meaning the grace of the Supreme Divinity. The proper understanding of the ancient scriptures, and the knowledge of the Self is possible with the grace and guidance of a learned teacher.

There is an incident from the life story of Swami Dayanand Saraswati. Swami Dayananda had read hundreds of books in search of truth. He went from one school to another in pursuit of knowledge but still felt hollow and restless, until he finally knocked at the door of his revered Guru. He approached Swami Virjananda with utmost humility and surrender. When Swami Dayanand, the aspirant, knocked at the door of his Guru, a voice spoke from inside of the hut and said, "Who is at the door?" Swami Dayanand's humble answer was *"yahi to janene aaya hun ke main kaun hun"*—I have come to your door to know "Who am I? and whom do I belong"? Swami Virjanandaji heard this answer, his heart was overwhelmed with love and joy for the earnest disciple. Swami Dayanandji prostrated himself at the feet of his Guru and pleaded him for his admittance. The single most important factor in initiation is the total surrender to Guru—approaching him with openness and humility, and without any sparks of a egocentric thoughts. A total surrender from the disciple leaves a great responsibility on the Master. In this respect there is another good example given by Srī Ramakrishna. He used to say, "As the fabled pearl-oyster leaves its bed at the bottom of the sea and comes up to the surface to catch rain water when the star Swati is in the ascendant. It floats about on the surface of the sea with its shell wide open until it succeeds in catching a drop of the marvellous Swati rain. Then it dives down to the sea-bed and there rests until it has succeeded in fashioning a beautiful pearl out of that raindrop. Similarly, there are some true and eager aspirants who travel from place to place in search of the mantra, the saving word, from a godly and perfect preceptor (Sadguru) which can open for them the gate of eternal bliss; and in the diligent search, if a man is fortunate enough to meet such a Guru and get from him the much-longed-for Mantra, that has the power to break all fetters, he leaves society at once and retires into the deep recesses of his own heart and strives their till he has succeed in gaining eternal peace." So it is not knowledge gathered and absorbed from the books only which brings awakening in the life. The wisdom comes from the words of the other enlightened soul and from one's own efforts. The words of the saints do purify us. It is indeed very important to find a blessed soul and accept him for guidance into spiritual knowledge.

यज्ज्ञात्वा न पुनर्मोहमेवं यास्यसि पाण्डव।
येन भूतान्यशेषेण द्रक्ष्यस्यात्मन्यथो मयि॥ ३५॥

yajjñātvā na punarmohamevaṁ yāsyasi pāṇḍava
yena bhūtānyaśeṣeṇa drakṣyasyātmanyatho mayi

(35) Knowing that, O'Arjuna, you will not again get deluded like this—by that knowledge you will see all beings without exception within yourself and then in Me.

अपि चेदसि पापेभ्यः सर्वेभ्यः पापकृत्तमः ।
सर्वं ज्ञानप्लवेनैव वृजिनं सन्तरिष्यसि ॥ ३६ ॥

api cedasi pāpebhyaḥ sarvebhyaḥ pāpakṛttamaḥ
sarvaṁ jñānaplavenaiva vṛjinaṁ santariṣyasi

(36) Even if you are the most sinful of all sinners, you will surely cross all the sins by the boat of knowledge alone.

यथैधांसि समिद्धोऽग्निर्भस्मसात्कुरुतेऽर्जुन ।
ज्ञानाग्निः सर्वकर्माणि भस्मसात्कुरुते तथा ॥ ३७ ॥

yathaidhāṁsi samiddho'gnir bhasmasāt kurute'rjuna
jñānāgniḥ sarvakarmāṇi bhasmasāt kurute tathā

(37) Just as the blazing fire reduces the fuel to ashes, O'Arjuna, similarly the fire of knowledge reduces all actions to ashes.

Commentary—These verses are a continuation of the previous ones, where Srī Kṛṣṇa has emphasized upon the importance of inner awakening. It is indeed the integral knowledge of the steadfast wisdom which enlightens thinking faculty and renders the power of eliminating attachments. The knowledge of the self is a blessing. It is with the guidance of the holy saints that an individual educates himself and becomes receptive to the indwelling grace and the transcendental experience. The reliance upon the steadfast knowledge strengthens the relationship with the inner Self and also works as a tool to know more about others. The spiritual growth brings transformation at various levels of consciousness and helps one to develop a unity consciousness. The individual perceives the world through the consciousness of the Divine, and visualizes the spark of the Divinity shining through each and every human being. He develops the universality of outlook and his every little bit of work becomes a service to mankind. In the words of Buddha "The man of wisdom has beauty in his countenance, satisfaction in his demeanour and enthusiasm in his work. He knows how to perform actions in a detached manner at the same time making them meritorious too." The proper knowledge of doing duties renders freedom and peace in all respects. The man of integral wisdom knows that all his acts of donations, and the performance of yajña etc. help him in self-purification. He knows that in the process of helping others he helps himself. He looks at human life as an opportunity to help others and an opportunity for increased self-purification. He feels grateful indeed that he has been blessed to share his life with others. He involves himself in raising funds for the poor students, serving people in the earthquake and flood afflicted areas, organizing religious activities for spiritual growth of others. Since all the actions of an enlightened person are performed with proper discriminating ability and integral wisdom, his entire life becomes an offering to the Divine. The knowledge of the Self is indeed an eye-opener and the eternal redeemer of the individual. The knowledge of the Divine has been compared to the flame of fire, which can disperse and dispel all the darkness no matter for how long it may have existed. It purifies the individual from the sins of the past and works as a beacon light for the present and future. It brings clarity and orderliness in life. The knowledge of the Self gives peace and happiness. It transforms all the intellectually realized ethics into the practical experiences of life. It helps one to use the God-blessed abilities for righteousness.

Srī Kṛṣṇa emphasizes that all types of spiritual services and the yajñas become beneficial only if performed with proper insight. These purificatory actions become the means of liberation, if co-ordinated with the knowledge of the Self. Therefore each and everyone who seeks emancipation and peace in the present life, must make appropriate efforts to illuminate the understanding which can enlighten the process of performing actions. As *Shruti Bhagwati* describes," Knowing which everything else becomes known", only that knowledge can transform all actions into the yoga of action, only such knowledge can remove the veil of duality, only such knowledge can kindle the flame of unity-consciousness and universal identity, only such knowledge can bless the individual with liberation and God-realization.

न हि ज्ञानेन सदृशं पवित्रमिह विद्यते।
तत्स्वयं योगसंसिद्धः कालेनात्मनि विन्दति॥ ३८॥

na hi jñānena sadṛśaṁ pavitramiha vidyate

tatsvayaṁ yogasaṅsiddhaḥ kālenātmani vindati

(38) Certainly, there is no purifier in this world like the 'transcendental knowledge'. He who becomes perfected in yoga, he experiences this, in his own-self, in due course of time.

श्रद्धावाँल्लभते ज्ञानं तत्परः संयतेन्द्रियः ।

ज्ञानं लब्ध्वा परां शान्तिमचिरेणाधिगच्छति ॥ ३९ ॥

śraddhāvānllabhate jñānaṁ tatparaḥ saṅyatendriyaḥ

jñānaṁ labdhvā parāṁ śāntim acireṇādhigacchati

(39) He, who is endowed with faith and who is devoted to it, who has disciplined his senses, he obtains knowledge. Having attained knowledge, he immediately attains Supreme-peace.

अज्ञश्चाश्रद्दधानश्च संशयात्मा विनश्यति ।

नायं लोकोऽस्ति न परो न सुखं संशयात्मनः ॥ ४० ॥

ajñaścāśraddadhānaśca saṅśayātmā vinaśyati

nāyaṁ loko'sti na paro na sukhaṁ saṁśayātmanaḥ

(40) The man who is ignorant, who has no faith, who is sceptical, he goes to destruction. For the suspicious man there is neither this world, nor the world beyond, nor any happiness.

योगसन्न्यस्तकर्माणं ज्ञानसञ्छिन्नसंशयम् ।

आत्मवन्तं न कर्माणि निबध्नन्ति धनञ्जय ॥ ४१ ॥

yogasannyastakarmāṇaṁ jñānasañchinnasaṅśayam

ātmavantaṁ na karmāṇi nibadhnanti dhanañjaya

(41) He who has renounced actions by unity in yoga, whose doubts have been destroyed by knowledge, and who is settled in the Self—actions do not bind him, O'Arjuna.

तस्मादज्ञानसम्भूतं हृत्स्थं ज्ञानासिनात्मनः ।

छित्त्वैनं संशयं योगमातिष्ठोत्तिष्ठ भारत ॥ ४२ ॥

tasmādajñānasambhūtaṁ hṛtsthaṁ jñānāsinātmanaḥ

chittvainaṁ saṅśayaṁ yogamātiṣṭhottiṣṭha bhārata

(42) Therefore, with the sword of knowledge, cut asunder the doubt in your heart, which is born of ignorance. Take refuge in Yoga and stand up, O'Arjuna.

Commentary—Starting with verse thirty-eight, Srī Kṛṣṇa declares that there is nothing else in the world which can equal the purifying power of the transcendental wisdom. The individual who is settled in yogic communion experiences it in due time. Srī Kṛṣṇa adds in the verse thirty-nine that the transcendental wisdom becomes revealed to the individual who holds firm faith, ardent devotion and determination. As a matter of fact, the person's relationship with the Divine is primordial and perennial, but one experiences the grace only in proportion to the degree of one's faith, reverence and devotion. Strong faith and loving devotion can make even the impossible to be possible. The word *sradha* has been pronounced in many ways by Srī Kṛṣṇa. *Sradha* is indeed the basis of spiritual life. Revelation of the Supreme is really difficult without the ardent faith, love and reverence. In the words of Swami Prabhupada, "This knowledge is the mature fruit of devotional service, and when one is situated in transcendental knowledge, he needs not to search for peace elsewhere, for he enjoys peace within himself." Living in the essential nature of the self is indeed living in perfect peace. *Sradha* is the ardent aspiration of the embodied soul for the grace and blessing of the Supreme-soul. It is the most sincere form of reverence arising from the deepest levels of the being. *Sradha* is an unwavering, most sincere and ardent form of faith which enables all the inner beauties of the Supreme-self to be revealed to the individual. It is like going into the most intimate and honest relationship with the Supreme-Soul, which gives strength and inner integrity. *Sradha* originates at the heart-centre by consciously living in the awareness of the Divine and gradually takes hold of the entire being. *Sradha* is indeed the dynamic force that nourishes the spiritual ideals. It illuminates the understanding of the scriptural knowledge and changes it into integral wisdom. *Sradha* strengthens the love and devotion, purifies the thoughts, unfolds the inner capacities and sanctifies—the entire attitude towards life.

In the verse forty, Srī Kṛṣṇa points out that the people those are devoid of ardent faith and are very suspicious by nature, definitely live a very empty and restless life. Being sceptical by nature, they are unable to develop any faith into anything. Since they don't have any firm faith in God, they lack faith in themselves also. They become very suspicious about others and find it very difficult to trust anybody. Due to lack of self-confidence and confidence in other people they live a very frustrated and unhappy life. They lack proper discrimination and make mistakes one after the other. For them there is no contentment and peace, neither in the present life nor in the life hereafter. As it is noticed in the modern educated societies, most of the people live a very fearful and stressful life. They are constantly haunted by the ghosts of distrust, doubt and suspicion. The question may arise, why these people can't trust others? The answer to this is—they don't trust their ownselves. Lack of faith and trust in their ownselves is due to lack of faith in God. In general, people are constantly knitting a web of self-doubt, self-rejection, guilt and fear around themselves. As the web of self-doubt grows bigger and bigger the individual becomes trapped in one's own self-created prison. He loses the ability and freedom of self-expression and self-confidence. In order to reinstate self-esteem, self-reliance, self-confidence, the person has to bring about a synthesis of the embodied self with the Supreme-self. The individual needs to integrate the various aspects of his nature and connect them with the Divine. Living in the nature of the Higher-Self does bring transformation in the attitude towards work and the overall personality of a person. Faith and respect for the self nourishes and promotes the spirit of Karmayoga. Towards the end of this chapter Srī Kṛṣṇa exhorts Arjuna to wake up, arise and come out of the ignorance which has been clouding his mind. He says, O'Arjuna, cut asunder with the sword of knowledge, all the doubts of your heart and take refuge in Yoga. He wants Arjuna to awake, arise and experience the dawn of wisdom, which has flashed forth from the distant horizon. He reminds Arjuna about the methods of fusing the steadfast wisdom with the performance of his actions. He encourages him to stand up to the occasion and act as the greatest warrior.

ॐ तत्सदिति श्रीमद्भगवद्गीतासूपनिषत्सु ब्रह्मविद्यायां
योगशास्त्रे श्रीकृष्णार्जुनसंवादे ज्ञानकर्मसंन्यासयोगो
नाम चतुर्थोऽध्यायः ॥ ४ ॥

'Aum' tatsaditi Śrīmadbhagawadgeetā sūpaniṣatsu
brahmavidyāyām yogaśāstre Śrīkṛṣṇārjunasamvāde
jñānakarmasannyāsayogo nāma caturtho'dhyāyaḥ

'AUM TAT SAT'—Thus, in the Upanishad of the glorious Bhagawad Geeta, the science of the Brahman (Absolute) the scripture of yoga, the dialogue between Srī Kṛṣṇa and Arjuna—thus, ends the chapter four entitled *"Jñānakarmayoga"*.

इति श्रीमद्भगवद्गीतासु चतुर्थोऽध्यायः ॥ ४ ॥

Chapter Five

KARMA-SANNYĀSAYOGA

THE YOGA OF ACTION AND RENUNCIATION

अर्जुन उवाच

संन्यासं कर्मणां कृष्ण पुनर्योगं च शंससि।
यच्छ्रेय एतयोरेकं तन्मे ब्रूहि सुनिश्चितम्॥ १॥

sannyāsaṁ karmaṇāṁ kṛṣṇa punaryogaṁ ca śaṁsasi
yacchreya etayorekaṁ tan me brūhi suniścitam

Arjuna said :

(1) O' Kṛṣṇa, you praise the renunciation of actions and then again the practice of Yoga; (the performance of selfless action)—tell me for certain, which one of these two is decidedly better.

Commentary—Here, Arjuna brings forth the similar type of question as before. The human mind has the habit to program its own portfolio, in respect of hearing, speaking and ignoring etc. The individual forms judgments and listens only to whatever suits him. Arjuna repeats the same type of question over and over again, because he pays attention to that only whatever he likes to hear. In the moments of selective hearing, the inner wisdom of the individual is usually lost temporarily and his concentration becomes very disintegrated. Arjuna is still so absorbed in his initial patterns of thoughts; he is constantly missing the very valid points of Śrī Kṛṣṇa's conversation. Besides, Arjuna has been trained as a warrior and an expert archer, he definitely doesn't have the inclination to absorb the spiritual philosophy. He feels confused about the conflicting statements-such as the renunciation and at the same time the performance of action in yoga. He requests Śrī Kṛṣṇa for detailed explanation and His decisive opinion; about the 'one' which is better. Śrī Kṛṣṇa knows the intricacies of the yoga philosophy and the process of its progressive realization step by step.

He is being very patient with Arjuna. He presents many options with the variety of interpretations for maximum comprehension.

श्रीभगवानुवाच

संन्यासः कर्मयोगश्च निःश्रेयसकरावुभौ।
तयोस्तु कर्मसंन्यासात्कर्मयोगो विशिष्यते॥ २॥

sannyāsaḥ karmayogaśca niḥśreyasakarāvubhau
tayostu karmasannyāsāt karmayogo viśiṣyate

The Blessed Lord said :

(2) Renunciation and the yoga of action both lead to the highest Bliss; but of the two, yoga of action is superior to the renunciation of action.

ज्ञेयः स नित्यसंन्यासी यो न द्वेष्टि न काङ्क्षति।
निर्द्वन्द्वो हि महाबाहो सुखं बन्धात्प्रमुच्यते॥ ३॥

jñeyaḥ sa nityasannyāsī yo na dveṣthi nā kāṅkṣati
nirdvandvo hi mahābāho sukham bandhāt pramucyate

(3) He should be known as a perpetual renouncer, who neither hates nor desires and who is free from all dualities. O'Arjuna, he is indeed easily liberated from bondage.

Commentary—In these verses Śrī Kṛṣṇa expounds on the meaning of Sannyasa (renunciation). He tells that renunciation and the performance of actions in Yoga, both lead to the highest good; but of the two, the yoga of action is indeed superior. In general the word Sannyasa is related to complete renunciation of the world. Renunciation is indeed an act of self-purification. It usually takes place either due to the painful experiences of life or because of the loving attachment with the Divine. The real renunciation is an awakened state of mind, wherein one comprehends the prime truth, and abandons the worldly enjoyments out of dispassion. Śrī Kṛṣṇa presents the most luminous gospel of selfless action in the surest, clearest and most approachable manner. He recommends to Arjuna to perform all duties while staying firm in steadfast wisdom. It is indeed important for everybody to learn to live in the consciousness of the Divine and chart out all activities in accordance with the guidance of the Higher Self. Work which is performed by keeping in mind the presence of God is actually non-reactive; because it is above the shadow of the ego-centric notions. It is performed in the purity and equanimity of the sublime. This has been described earlier, as inaction in action. Performance of actions with an attitude of detachment yields the rewards of Karma-sannyasa. Śrī Kṛṣṇa calls that individual a perpetual sannyasi, who has risen above the dualities of life. He works with the meditative serenity of inner peace and develops the capability to make purposeful, useful and harmonious choices. He knows how to direct his disciplined thoughts, ideas, wishes and moods. Such an individual is subjectively aware, alert, contented, peaceful and balanced. He performs all his activities in the meditative tranquillity and equipoise. He accepts life as it comes with all its aspects of honour and dishonour, loss and gain, pleasure and pain. Sruti Bhagwati also describes the state of renouncer in these words, "although engaged in the performance of duties, the one who maintains his balance and has no attachment to anything; whose work is characterized by the attitude of service and devotion to God, he is surely a Sannyasin, even before (renouncing the world) following the path of Sannyasa-yoga."

साङ्ख्ययोगौ पृथग्बालाः प्रवदन्ति न पण्डिताः।
एकमप्यास्थितः सम्यगुभयोर्विन्दते फलम्॥ ४॥

sāṅkhyayogau prathag bālāḥ pravadaṅti na paṅditāḥ
ekamapyāsthitaḥ samyagubhayorvindate phalam

(4) Children, not the learned, speak of knowledge (Samkhya) and the Yoga of action as distinct. He who is truly established in either, attains the fruits of both.

यत्साङ्ख्यैः प्राप्यते स्थानं तद्योगैरपि गम्यते।
एकं साङ्ख्यं च योगं च यः पश्यति स पश्यति॥ ५॥

yatsāṅkhyaiḥ prāpyate sthānaṁ tad yagairapi gamyate
ekaṁ sāṅkhyaṁ ca yogaṁ ca yaḥ paśyati sa paśyati

(5) The spiritual status which is obtained with the yoga of knowledge is also achieved with the yoga of action. He truly sees,

who sees the knowledge and the yoga of action as one.

संन्यासस्तु महाबाहो दुःखमाप्तुमयोगतः ।
योगयुक्तो मुनिर्ब्रह्म नचिरेणाधिगच्छति ॥ ६ ॥

sannyāsastu māhabāho duḥkhamāptumayogataḥ
yogayukto munirbrahma ṇacireṇādhigacchati

(6) O'Arjuna, renunciation is indeed difficult to attain without yoga. The sage who is established in yoga, he definitely reaches the Brahman very quickly.

Commentary—Samkhya-yoga literally means the method of making communion with the inner-self, with scriptural and experiential knowledge. This philosophy has been explained and discussed in almost all the ancient scriptures of India. The expounders of Samkhya-Yoga have been sages Kapila and Patanjali. In these verses Śrī Kṛṣṇa is using the word Samkhya in relation to the yoga of Divine knowledge. He tells that the individual of childish and immature understanding considers the yoga of knowledge and the yoga of action to be distinct and separate. A man of wisdom fully understands the subtlety of the concept and does not see any distinction between them. Śrī Kṛṣṇa tells that there is indeed a very important link between both. He asserts that the supreme state which is achieved by the Yoga of knowledge can be perfectly attained by the Yoga of action. A genuine aspirant synthesizes the essence of both. The essential knowledge of both is indeed complimentary to one another and makes the pursuit of the blissful state very easy and enjoyable.

The knowledge and proper performance of all actions purifies the individual and renders the attitude of selflessness. It does bless the individual with purity, clarity and purposefulness in performance. It is the integral wisdom which gives guidance, strength and transforms every action into the yoga of action. The yoga of knowledge and the yoga of action are indeed inseparable; following either brings the reward of both. Śrī Kṛṣṇa indicates that following the path of renunciation of the world, without proper knowledge of Karam-yoga can be dangerous and harmful in certain respects. A person cannot become a renunciate by merely giving up the family life or by running away from his duties out of frustration and failures. This type of renouncer loses self-respect and becomes a ridicule for himself and for everybody else. Karamyoga is definitely much more rewarding than Karam-sannyasa (renunciation of actions). It is the performance of action in yoga that prepares the individual for renunciation. It purifies the life at various levels. It renders the spirit of sacrifice, kindness, charity and compassion. It brings clarity of vision and sanctity of thoughts and action. The person who is devoted to selfless action, he becomes pure-minded and attains the status of a sannyasin in due time.

Śrī Kṛṣṇa uses the word *Yogyukta* which means performing all the work in yoga. The sage who has trained himself to perform all work while being established in the consciousness of the Divine, he definitely attains Brahman in due time. The word *Yogyukta* explains the subtle connectedness with the Divine during the performance of all work. In the words of Ved Vyasa as he describes in the *Mahabharata* 'the real and genuine renouncer is not he who has renounced all work, but the one who performs all work with an attitude of detachment'. Genuine renunciation is an attitude of mind, it is the inward understanding of performing all work for work's sake, with the positive spirit and proper insight. Working in Yoga renders inner peace, tranquillity and detachment from the external forces. It disperses delusion, confusion and frustration while making the path of renunciation enjoyable and interesting. Karmayoga is a means for attaining the state of renunciation. This is the essence of the spiritual pursuit in all respects. Speaking of Karma-sannyasa yoga, the great sage Yajnavalkya has declared that even a family member, who has devoted himself to the attainment of the knowledge of the Self, who remains detached to the fruits of actions, who is celebate and truthful— he should be considered a Sannyasi who attains liberation in due course of time.

योगयुक्तो विशुद्धात्मा विजितात्मा जितेन्द्रियः ।
सर्वभूतात्मभूतात्मा कुर्वन्नपि न लिप्यते ॥ ७ ॥

yogayukto viśuddhātmā vijitātmā jitendriyaḥ
sarvabhūtātmabhūtātmā kurvannapi na lipyate

(7) He, who is united with the Self in yoga, who is pure at heart, whose body and senses are under his control, who realizes his own Self, as the Self in all beings, he is not tainted by actions, while he performs.

नैव किञ्चित्करोमीति युक्तो मन्येत तत्त्ववित्।
पश्यञ्शृण्वन्स्पृशञ्जिघ्रन्नश्नन्गच्छन्स्वपञ्श्वसन् ॥८॥

naiva kiñcitkaromīti yukto manyeta tattvavit
paśyaṇ śṛṇvan spṛsañ jighrannaśnan gacchan śvapañ śvasan

प्रलपन्विसृजन्गृह्णन्नुन्मिषन्निमिषन्नपि ।
इन्द्रियाणीन्द्रियार्थेषु वर्तन्त इति धारयन् ॥९॥

pralapan visṛjan gṛhṇannunmiṣan nimiṣannapi
indriyāṇīndriyārtheṣu vartanta iti dhārayan

(8, 9) The knower of truth, who is united within, he believes 'I am not doing anything' even while—seeing, hearing, touching, smelling, eating, walking, sleeping, breathing, speaking, excreting, grasping, opening and closing the eyelids. He always remains convinced that the senses operate among the sense objects.

Commentary—These verses are the continuation of the term *Yogyukta* used in the previous verse by Śrī Krsna. Here He presents a detailed picture of the one who is genuinely settled in the yoga of action. The individual who remains constantly immersed in the nature of the Divine, he works with the Divine. As the absorption in the Supreme-self strengthens he feels, that the Lord Himself is working through his entire body. A *Yogyukta* manifests a firm unity of the individual-self with the Supreme-self. He perceives that he sees, hears, smells and touches and talks through God. All his sensory organs function under the guidance of the Supreme-soul in regard to the objects of the senses. Although his senses are engaged in all activities of the world; but he consciously remains connected with the Indweller that presides over the three worlds. He experiences the sweet will of the Lord in everything that takes place in everyday life. At this stage of awareness, the individual becomes blessed with the vision of unity consciousness and realizes the presence of God everywhere. He feels himself reflected in each and every being. In that case he enjoys sharing everything he possesses with other fellow beings. The individual-self feels a part of the cosmic self, and the universal-Self. In the words of Swami Chinmayananda, "*Yuktah* means, 'centred in the Self'. This Self-centredness can be in two grades of intensity: one, indicating the self-centredness of a seeker who, through study, reflection and meditation, tries to remain intellectually centred in the Self; and another, the self-absorption of one who, after the final realization of the Self in himself, comes to live vitally, at every moment, the experience of the Self (Atmavit)."

Harmonized by the Yoga of action a person enjoys the universality of God-consciousness and lives a life with the spirit of caring, giving and sharing, he helps others merely out of inner joy and contentment, The individual feels the Divine power working through him for the sustenance of the body and for the help of others. One becomes a co-agent in the activities of the Lord. In the words of Śrī Ramanuja, "a Karma Yogin remains engaged in the performance of pure actions prescribed by the *Sastras,* which are of the nature of propitiation of the Supreme person. By this, he becomes purified in mind. He thus subdues his self, i.e. subdues his mind easily, because his mind is engaged in the virtuous actions he has been performing before. Therefore his senses are subdued. His self is said to have become the Self of all beings."

ब्रह्मण्याधाय कर्माणि सङ्गं त्यक्त्वा करोति यः।
लिप्यते न स पापेन पद्मपत्रमिवाम्भसा ॥ १० ॥

brahmaṇyādhāya karmāṇi saṅgaṁ tyaktvā karoti yaḥ
lipyate na sa pāpena padmapatramivāmbhasā

(10) He who performs all his actions, offering them to the Divine and abandons all attachment, he is not touched by sin, just as the lotus leaf is not tainted by water.

कायेन मनसा बुद्ध्या केवलैरिन्द्रियैरपि।
योगिनः कर्म कुर्वन्ति सङ्गं त्यक्त्वात्मशुद्धये ॥ ११ ॥

kāyena manasā buddhyā kevalairindriyairapi
yoginaḥ karma kurvanti saṅgaṁ tyaktvātmaśuddhaye

(11) The yogins perform their actions merely with the body, the mind, the intellect and the senses, without any attachment—for the purification of the self (heart).

युक्तः कर्मफलं त्यक्त्वा शान्तिमाप्नोति नैष्ठिकीम्।
अयुक्तः कामकारेण फले सक्तो निबध्यते॥ १२॥

yuktaḥ karmaphalaṁ tyaktvā śāntimāpnoti naiṣṭhikīm
ayuktaḥ kāmakāreṇa phale sakto nibadhyate

(12) He who is united within, having renounced the fruits of actions, attains the highest peace; but the disintegrated man being impelled by desire, remains attached to the fruits and becomes bound.

सर्वकर्माणि मनसा संन्यस्यास्ते सुखं वशी।
नवद्वारे पुरे देही नैव कुर्वन्न कारयन्॥ १३॥

sarvakarmāṇi manasā sannyasyāste sukhaṁ vaśī
navadvāre pure dehī naiva kurvanna kārayan

(13) Mentally, renouncing the doership of all actions, the self-controlled embodied-self (Jivatma), rests peacefully in the city of nine gates, neither acting nor causing others to act.

Commentary—In these verses Srī Kṛṣṇa glorifies the magnificence of unity with the Supreme-soul which forms the basis of genuine renunciation. He explains to Arjuna that by living in constant awareness of the Supreme, one develops an intimate relationship with the Divine. The individual learns to live in the ardent love of the Divine and takes pride in offering all his work as a service to the Divine. As the bond of love and reverence grows stronger, the detachment and renunciation from the world dawns automatically and naturally.

Srī Kṛṣṇa gives the analogy of the lotus flower which blossoms beautifully above the surface of the water, with its roots settled in the stagnant pool. The lotus flower manifests the majesty and grace of the Divine. It is always smiling and looks very fresh because it keeps itself connected with the light of the sun. Similarly, a *Yogyukta* lives a peaceful, happy and contented life while he lives in the world and performs all the assigned duties of life. When a person performs all the assigned duties in the world with love, devotion and as an offering to the Divine, then he lives like the lotus flower which remains unsmeared by the swamp in which it blossoms. The sustenance of unity in yoga does not demand renunciation from the person; it only requires his perpetual unity with the Lord. With the practice of living in meditated unity, the person upgrades himself to the level of Divine consciousness and then, he is helped from within to maintain his spiritual status in all respects. In the words of Maharshi Mahesh Yogi, "a man of renunciation, a sannyasi, takes life easily as it comes, creating no tensions. This freedom from bondage can be reached either through wisdom or the practice of Yoga."

The attitude of offering all work as a service to the Divine brings freedom and also improves the person's relationship with his fellow beings. In the words of Dr. Radhakrishnan, "Man can't be satisfied by wealth, by learning, but by developing the quality of detachment, and renunciation; by making himself the instrument of a higher purpose, it is there, that the realization of the fulfilment of man abides, and it should be our endeavour to develop it." The purpose of devotion for God is to infuse a sense of giving and offering. Devotion is born out of intense love for God, which is reflected in almost all the activities of the individual. It mirrors the inner peace and the spirit of love for others. It is indeed a fact that the devotion for God can redeem the life of a person in all respects. In the verse twelve, Srī Kṛṣṇa states very clearly that the person who is integrated in the Self, he attains everlasting peace, by renouncing attachment to the fruits of actions; whereas the disintegrated person, who acts with attachment to the fruits of actions, he remains bound. Here the word *yuktah* has been used for the one who lives saturated in the awareness of the Higher-self and feels himself only an instrument in the hands of the Divine. On the other hand the one who lives attached to his mind, senses and intellect, he considers himself to be the doer; and always remains bound. The person who expects rewards, name and honour, he suffers emotional confusion, and always depends upon others for his peace and happiness. If the result of his work goes his desired way, his ego enlarges and expands; on the other hand, if the desired results are not there, he blames others for his failures and unhappiness. He definitely remains bound in both ways. So, in order to live a peaceful life, the individual has to integrate himself by regaining the original status of *yogyuktah.* One has to make special efforts for total surrender to the sublimity of the God-consciousness.

The verse eleven makes it clear : *yoginah karma kurvanti sangam tyaktvatmasuddhaya.* Those who are connected with God in yoga, they perform all the work merely for the purification of the mind. Working with the consciousness of God helps one to renounce the sense of 'I and Mine'. This attitude purifies the individual and also makes him efficient, competent and self-confident. As Tagore writes, "It shall be my endeavour to reveal Thee in my actions, knowing it is Thy power that gives me the strength to act." Any person with such a renounced attitude rests happily in the body, known as the city of nine gates. The nine gates of the body are the two eyes, two nostrils, two ears, the mouth and the two organs of excretion. It is a very famous analogy used in the Vedic literature for the physical body of the individual. The self-realized man who remains settled in the perennial presence of the master of the body (indwelling Supreme-Soul), he becomes detached and enjoys perfect peace under all circumstances.

न कर्तृत्वं न कर्माणि लोकस्य सृजति प्रभुः।
न कर्मफलसंयोगं स्वभावस्तु प्रवर्तते॥ १४॥

na kartṛtvaṁ na karmāṇi lokasya sṛjati prabhuḥ
na karmaphalasaṅyogaṁ svabhāvastu pravartate

(14) The Lord does not create the agency nor the actions for the world; nor does he connect actions with their fruits. It is only the innate nature that operates.

नादत्ते कस्यचित्पापं न चैव सुकृतं विभुः।
अज्ञानेनावृतं ज्ञानं तेन मुह्यन्ति जन्तवः॥ १५॥

nādatte kasyacitpāpaṁ na caiva sukṛtaṁ vibhuḥ
ajñānenāvṛtaṁ jñānaṁ tena muhyanti jantavaḥ

(15) The Omnipresent Lord takes neither the sin nor the virtue of any; the knowledge is enveloped by ignorance, therefore creatures

are bewildered.

Commentary—In these verses Srī Kṛṣṇa presents the deepest and the subtlest truth about the nature of actions. He makes it very clear that the life itself, and everything else around, is indeed a manifestation of all types of mixed actions. Human beings are very privileged species on earth. They are independent in the performance of their actions. People motivated by their inborn nature and circumstances perform good and bad deeds; and they are punished and rewarded accordingly. As a matter of fact, between God and destiny, there is something on which each and every person has his personal control; and that is the mode of performing his actions. In the words of Swami Vivekananda, "Karma is the eternal assertion of human freedom—the thoughts, words and deeds are the strings of the web, which we weave around ourselves". In a way, every individual himself is the creator of his own destiny. The present life is indeed the expression of one's own deeds. The Supreme Lord doesn't partake in the virtue and vice of anyone. It is because of the individual's strong identification with the body, that this great secret remains unknown to him. When the person becomes settled in the Supremacy of the Self, he learns to understand the impressions of the samskaras; those motivate the conditioned behaviour of his present life. He learns to watch and witness the hidden tendencies behind each action and attains his conscious control over the process. All the hidden latencies of many previous births are brought to the conscious mind and then extinguished in the flame of inner knowledge. The association with the inner intelligence purifies all the actions of the individual and helps him to reap the fruits of his deeds with peace and serenity. He becomes a quiet, alert witness to his mind and lives a peaceful, happy and contented life.

In general, it has been noticed that people blame God and others for their misfortunes. They fail to realize how anybody else can ever be responsible for their own sins and mistakes. Most of the sins are committed in life, because of person's own conditioned behaviour and due to the lack of self-knowledge. It is because of the individual's ego-centric nature, that he loses his conscious connections with the Higher Self and falls prey to the dictation of the lower-self. As described in the Vedas *"Esa uhy eva sadhu karna karayanti tam yam ebhyo lokebhya unninisate. Esa u evasadhu karma karayanti yam adho ninsate"*, the individual performs the virtuous deeds in order to be uplifted and the individual performs vicious deeds and falls in hell. So, as a matter of fact each and every person is the maker of his own destiny and is indeed responsible for his own fortunes and misfortunes. There are also some beautiful lines by Omar Khayyam, "Be careful, for the stock-in-trade of this world's market, it is the life you purchase for yourself."

ज्ञानेन तु तदज्ञानं येषां नाशितमात्मनः ।
तेषामादित्यवज्ज्ञानं प्रकाशयति तत्परम् ॥ १६ ॥

jñānena tu tadajñānaṁ yeṣāṁ nāśitamātmanaḥ
teṣāmādityavajjñānaṁ prakāśayati tat param

(16) To those, whose ignorance has been dispelled by the knowledge of the Self, for them, the knowledge reveals the Supreme Brahman like the Sun.

तद्बुद्धयस्तदात्मानस्तन्निष्ठास्तत्परायणाः ।
गच्छन्त्यपुनरावृत्तिं ज्ञाननिर्धूतकल्मषाः ॥ १७ ॥

tadbuddhayastadātmānas tanniṣṭhās tatparāyaṇāḥ
gacchantyapunarāvṛttiṁ jñānanirdhūtakalmaṣāḥ

(17) Those, whose mind and intellect are totally merged in God, who remain established in unity, and consider that as their Supreme goal they reach the state from which there is no return—their sins being dispelled by knowledge.

विद्याविनयसम्पन्ने ब्राह्मणे गवि हस्तिनि ।
शुनि चैव श्वपाके च पण्डिताः समदर्शिनः ॥ १८ ॥

vidyāvinayasaṁpanne brāhmaṇe gavi hastini
śuni caiva śvapāke ca paṇḍitāḥ samadarśinaḥ

(18) The man of wisdom looks with equanimity upon the Brahmin endowed with learning and humility, a cow, an elephant, and even a dog and a pariah.

इहैव तैर्जितः सर्गो येषां साम्ये स्थितं मनः ।
निर्दोषं हि समं ब्रह्म तस्माद् ब्रह्मणि ते स्थिताः ॥ १९ ॥

ihaiva tairjitaḥ sargo yeṣāṁ sāmye sthitaṁ manaḥ
nirdoṣaṁ hi samaṁ brahma tasmād brahmaṇi te sthitāḥ

(19) Even here the world is conquered by those, whose mind is established in equality. Brahman is indeed flawless and the same everywhere, therefore, they are established in Brahman.

Commentary—These verses are the continuation of the previous ones wherein Srī Kṛṣṇa explains to Arjuna that it is indeed the knowledge of Supreme-Self which enlightens the thinking faculty of the individual, it is the knowledge of the self which sharpens the discriminating ability, and helps the embodied-self to realize its identity with the Supreme-Self. When intuition is heightened, the individual occasionally gets in touch with his previous dormant *samskaras* of past lives. One develops the ability to understand one's dormant conditioned nature. The latencies are gradually brought to the surface of the conscious mind. The individual starts understanding the hidden motivations behind each thought and each activity. The constant vigilance in thought and actions renders ample awareness in all respects. The reward of living in self-awareness slowly brings freedom from the conditioned behaviour of past *samskaras.* When the accumulated negativity is eliminated from the mind, it becomes pure and clean. Since all this purification takes place with the association and help of the integral wisdom the individual learns to rely more upon one's own resources. The faith in the Supreme-Self strengthens and he feels confident and integrated in all respects. At that stage of enlightenment the individual can very well distinguish between right act and the wrong ones, between vice and virtue. When a person becomes united in yoga, his identification with the body starts fading; and his concept of duality also start vanishing. One feels oneself reflected in the Supreme-Soul and also in the hearts of other beings.

Srī Kṛṣṇa gives the example that a learned man endowed with the vision of equanimity looks upon a Brahmin, a cow, an elephant, a dog and even in outcast with the same attitude of respect and reverence. He perceives God shining through all of them. The knower of truth cognizes only the supreme Lord everywhere. He rises above the assumed disparities which are created because of nescience.

Cosmic unity is therefore the first step towards God-realization. It is indeed the beginning of genuine worship and intimacy with the Divine. In this verse Srī Kṛṣṇa indicates that living a life in the consciousness of the Infinite spirit everywhere is like conquering the entire creation. When the mind is settled in perfect equanimity, it tears the veil of the personal ego and enters into the realm of the universal self. One begins to feel the presence of the Lord within, and in everything and everybody else also. The Divine grace radiates from such an individual. He becomes the embodiment of peace, kindness, friendliness and compassion. He guides and illuminates the lives of other people. He moves around like a lighted candle which gives light to others and also lights up the lives of others, without any loss of his own.

न प्रहृष्येत्प्रियं प्राप्य नोद्विजेत्प्राप्य चाप्रियम्।
स्थिरबुद्धिरसम्मूढो ब्रह्मविद् ब्रह्मणि स्थितः॥ २०॥

na prahṛṣyet priyaṁ prāpya nodvijet prāpya cāpriyam
sthirabuddhirasaṁmūḍho brahmavid brahmaṇi sthitaḥ

(20) He who neither rejoices on receiving what is pleasant nor grieves on receiving the unpleasant; who is firm of understanding and undeluded; such a knower of Brahman is established in Brahman.

बाह्यस्पर्शेष्वसक्तात्मा विन्दत्यात्मनि यत्सुखम्।
स ब्रह्मयोगयुक्तात्मा सुखमक्षयमश्नुते॥ २१॥

bāhyasparśeṣvasaktātmā vindatyātmani yat sukham
sa brahmayogayuktātmā sukham akṣayam aśnute

(21) When the embodied-self is not attached to the external objects of the senses, and finds happiness within the Self—he becomes united with Brahman in yoga and enjoys the eternal Bliss.

ये हि संस्पर्शजा भोगा दुःखयोनय एव ते।
आद्यन्तवन्तः कौन्तेय न तेषु रमते बुधः॥ २२॥

ye hi saṅsparaśajā bhoga duḥkhayonaya eva te
ādyantavantaḥ Kaunteya na teṣu ramate budhaḥ

(22) The enjoyments that are born of contacts with the sense

objects are the source of pain; they have a beginning and an end, O'Arjuna. The wise man does not rejoice in them.

Commentary—Srī Kṛṣṇa indicates in these verses that when the embodied-self re-assumes his forgotten affinity with the Supreme-Self, the desire for the external enjoyments starts fading. The term *'Braham Yoga-yuktatma'* describes the state of transcendence. As the egoistic individuality fades, one starts enjoying the transcendental peace of unified field, which has been described as eternal Bliss in spiritual language. One perceives the relationship renewed every minute and every second of life. There is a feeling of novelty in his attitude of everyday life. The subtlety of his devotional love for the Divine become obvious in each and everyone of his expression. The feeling of contentment and inner fulfilment emanates from his gestures and demeanour. The person realizes the truth that the pleasure born of the contacts with the sensory objects are very transitory. The satisfaction is limited and it vanishes soon. They have a beginning and an end. Everything in the material world is hanging between the two dots—the Beginning and the End, the life and death. As Omar Khayyam has said, "Of all the threats of hell and the hopes of paradise, one thing is certain, that life flies, only one thing is certain, everything else is a big lie, the flower that has blown today must die." People suffer in this world because of their over attachment to the ever changing worldly enjoyments. They live in the ignorance of false values. Nobody wants to accept any change in life. It is because of the ignorance of the reality, people live their lives, enclosed within the boundaries of false values. They expect to enjoy the sensory pleasures till the last minute of their lives. *'bhoga na bhukta vayammave bhukta'*. The body becomes old with time but the desire for the enjoyments of the body remains young. Everything in the material world goes through the threefold stages of nature—birth, sustenance and death. It includes the human body, all the species, trees, plants, rocks, stars, rivers, planets, mountains and kingdoms etc. The maintenance of world order has been symbolized as *Trimurti,* in the form of *Brahma, Vishnu* and *Mahesh.* Everything in the world goes through birth, growth and death—creation, sustenance and dissolution are the three fundamental aspects of the creative evolution. Everything perceptible to the senses is indeed changeable. Anyone who does not want to accept the change and tries to go against the laws of nature he suffers in the long run. In the words of Srīdhara, "Things that are touched by the senses are called *samsparsa,* that is sense objects; enjoyments and pleasures born of sense objects are indeed the source of misery even at the time of enjoyment, involving competition, jealousy, etc. and they have a beginning and an end. Therefore, the discriminating person does not rejoice in them". The man of wisdom who perceives the subtle truth about the unchanging reality behind the curtain of changing materialistic world, he knows how to live in perfect harmony. He understands that the perishable sensory pleasures can't give everlasting happiness to the imperishable Self. He knows how to withdraw himself from the gross and fix his attention into the subtle. To him pleasure and pain are only the passing waves, impermanent and kaleidoscopic in nature; while the soul is permanent. The satisfaction which he draws from the inner resources becomes a way of life for him. It helps the person to live with the attitude of marvellous calmness, under all circumstances of life, and attain the Blissful state of yogic unity. The famous gospel of John : Know the truth and the truth shall make you free.

शक्नोतीहैव यः सोढुं प्राक्शरीरविमोक्षणात्।
कामक्रोधोद्भवं वेगं स युक्तः स सुखी नरः॥ २३॥

śaknotīhaiva yaḥ soḍhuṁ prākśarīravimokṣaṇāt
kāmakrodhodbhavaṁ vegaṁ sa yuktaḥ sa sukhī naraḥ

(23) He who in this world is able to resist the impulse, born out of desire and anger, before he gives up his body—he is indeed a yogi, he is a happy man.

योऽन्तःसुखोऽन्तरारामस्तथान्तर्ज्योतिरेव यः।
स योगी ब्रह्मनिर्वाणं ब्रह्मभूतोऽधिगच्छति॥ २४॥

yo'ntaḥsukho'ntarārāmas tathāntarjyotireva yaḥ
sa yogī brahmanirvāṇaṁ brahmabhūto'dhigacchati

(24) He who finds his happiness within, who rejoices within himself, who is illumined from within—that yogi attains absolute

liberation (Brahman Nirvana); because of his firm identification with Brahman.

लभन्ते ब्रह्मनिर्वाणमृषयः क्षीणकल्मषाः।
छिन्नद्वैधा यतात्मानः सर्वभूतहिते रताः॥ २५॥

labhante brahmanirvāṇam ṛṣayaḥ kṣīṇakalmaṣāḥ
chinnadvaidhā yatātmānaḥ sarvabhūtahite ratāḥ

(25) The Rishis obtain absolute freedom—whose sins have been destroyed and whose dualities are torn asunder. Who are self-controlled and always devoted to the welfare of all beings.

कामक्रोधवियुक्तानां यतीनां यतचेतसाम्।
अभितो ब्रह्मनिर्वाणं वर्तते विदितात्मनाम्॥ २६॥

kāmakrodhaviyuktānaṁ yatīnāṁ yatacetasām
abhito brahmanirvāṇaṁ vartate viditātmanām

(26) The ascetics those are free from desire and anger, who have controlled their mind and have realized the Self; for them the eternal Bliss (Brahmic Bliss) exists on all sides.

Commentary—In these verses Srī Kṛṣṇa tells Arjuna the real meaning of liberation or *moksha*. He makes it very clear that liberation or moksha is not something to be achieved only upon the departure from the world. Liberation and absolute Bliss can be achieved in one's present life-time and also in the life hereafter. Freedom is living in the awareness of the Divine, freedom is the acceptance of the self, freedom is living a life free from worldly desires, freedom is living in the nature of the Supreme-Soul.

At every step in life, the person's own hidden desires and impulses indicate to him very clearly that he is being a slave of his own desires. Overwhelmed by various cravings and yearnings every individual feels trapped and helpless. There is a famous saying, *"chaha churhi chaandari atha neechan ki neech, yun to puran brahman thaa jo chaaha na hoti beech"*—"Every person is essentially Divine, but because of his slavery to the worldly desires, he loses his conscious relationship with the inner Divinity". His multiple desires are the cause of his slavery and bondage during the life-time. It is the pursuit of false values, which imprisons the individual soul.

There is an illustration given by Rabindranath Tagore where he writes about the embodied-soul, who feels imprisoned and bound: "Prisoner, tell me, who was it, that bound you?" "Prisoner, tell me who was it that wrought this unbreakable chain?" "It was I", said the prisoner, "who forged this chain very carefully. I thought my invincible power would hold the world captive leaving me in freedom, undisturbed. Thus, night and day, I worked at the chain with huge fires and cruel hard strokes. When at last the work was done and the links were complete and unbreakable, I found that it held me in its grip." This is what happens to most of the people in the world. The desires of the worldly enjoyments are indeed the cause of imprisonment, bondage and slavery. People consider their luxuries to be their necessities and that is why they become trapped. In this context Frittj of Capra has written these words in his famous book, *The Tao Of Physics,* "The Second Noble Truth that deals with the cause of all suffering—trishna, the clinging, or grasping. It is the futile grasping of life based on a wrong point of view, which is called avidya, or ignorance, in Buddhist philosophy."

Worldly desires are indeed the major cause of human unhappiness and bondage. Srī Kṛṣṇa has given a beautiful example in this context in the earlier chapter. The verses sixty-two and sixty-three in chapter two describe the step by step calculated fall of man—The person infatuated by some worldly desires develops an attachment for them and the desire which remains unfulfilled ensues infatuation and anger. The anger creates confusion of memory and the loss of reason; from the loss of reason one perishes. This is the ladder of man's downfall as presented by Srī Kṛṣṇa to Arjuna. The desire, when unfulfilled, surely becomes the cause of anger and violence. It is the desire of accumulating more than others, it is the greed and envy that sets people against one another. As E.F. Schumacher writes, "A life which is devoted primarily to the pursuit of material ends, and to the neglect of the spiritual, sets man against man, and nation against nation. Man's needs are infinite and infinitude can be achieved only in the spiritual realm, never in the material. Man assuredly needs to rise above this humdrum 'world', the inner wisdom shows him the way to do it." The test of universal love is indeed the absence of greed and jealousy. Anybody who is able to resist the urges arising from the material world, he becomes liberated even in his life-time. Control over desires blesses the individual with inner purity and stability. The inner integrity helps him to put a strong ceiling on the unnecessary desires and the oneness with God occurs in due time. When a person becomes firmly established in his essential nature of the Supreme-self, he becomes very contented and peaceful. The joy of the Self is definitely free from all the external contacts. It is the consciousness of living in that bliss which withdraws the mind from worldly desires. When the individual trains himself into the unity with the Indweller, he starts coming out of the self-created web of selfish desires, and becomes enthusiastic in sharing and caring for others. The joyful, peaceful and contented attitude begins to emerge and the individual becomes very friendly and adorable. As the worldly desires begin to wane and vanish, the former fears and frustrations also starts fading. The individual already feels liberated in his present life. He becomes blessed with the right intuition and perception which brings liberation instantly. He lives in liberation and carries it along wherever he goes. Srī Kṛṣṇa concludes that any work, which is performed with complete devotion and dedication, leads the individual towards emancipation and moksha. First of all, it purifies the mind and transforms the day-to-day selfish emotions into devotion leading to satisfaction, universal brotherhood and contentment. The yogic unity helps the individual to develop detachment from worldly desires and the fruits of his actions. The inner purification, renunciation and liberation—this is a process of step by step progress towards self-realization and the attainment of Brahman-Nirvana, moksha or the absolute liberation.

स्पर्शान्कृत्वा बहिर्बाह्यांश्चक्षुश्चैवान्तरे भ्रुवोः ।
प्राणापानौ समौ कृत्वा नासाभ्यन्तरचारिणौ ॥ २७ ॥

sparśān kṛtvā bahir bāhyāñś cakṣuś caivāntare bhruvoḥ
prāṇāpānau samau kṛtvā nāsābhyantaracāriṇau

यतेन्द्रियमनोबुद्धिर्मुनिर्मोक्षपरायणः
विगतेच्छाभयक्रोधो यः सदा मुक्त एव सः ॥ २८ ॥

yateṅdriyamanobuddhir munir mokṣaparāyaṇaḥ
vigatecchābhayakrodho yaḥ sadā mukta eva saḥ

(27, 28) Shutting out the external sensory contacts, fixing the vision between the two eyebrows, controlling the outgoing and incoming breath flow, with the senses, mind and intellect fully restrained, and free from desire, fear and anger—the sage who aims at liberation, as his highest goal, he is verily liberated for ever.

भोक्तारं यज्ञतपसां सर्वलोकमहेश्वरम्।
सुहृदं सर्वभूतानां ज्ञात्वा मां शान्तिमृच्छति ॥ २९ ॥

bhoktāraṁ yajñatapasāṁ sarvalokamaheśvaram
suhṛdaṁ sarvabhūtānāṁ jñātvā māṁ śāntimṛcchati

(29) Knowing Me as the enjoyer of all sacrifices and austerities, the great Lord of all the worlds and the well-wisher (friend) of all beings, one attains peace.

Commentary—After giving an elaborate description about the yoga of action and the yoga of knowledge, Srī Kṛṣṇa explains that every human being has the unique ability to blend both for God-realization. Fusing both the path into one brings about unique results in the form of inner tranquillity and worldly fulfilment. Peace and success in present life and in the life hereafter depends upon understanding the nature of action. Actions performed with proper knowledge and sincere devotion definitely help the individual to achieve the final goal of life. In verses twenty-seven and twenty-eight, Srī Kṛṣṇa gives some glimpses of the yogi who practises meditation and enjoys the bliss of meditative experiences. By introducing one of the techniques of meditation towards the end of this chapter Srī Kṛṣṇa has emphasized the need of meditation in everyday life. Meditation means consciously attending to the thought pattern. It helps the assimilation of spiritual learning and its use in the practice of Karamyoga. It renews every aspect of every day life and makes the life very productive, constructive and fulfilling in all respects. These verses describe the systematic procedure of sitting posture which prepares the individual for a relaxed session of meditation. It helps one to withdraw the senses from the sense objects and focus them into the centre of consciousness which renders peace eventually.

The specific posture in which the attention is directed between the two eyebrows, opens the subtlest layers of mind and renders spiritual awakening. Between the two eyebrows is located the very important psychic station, the *Ajña Chakra*. It is also known as the third eye or the eye of intuition. Concentration at the *Ajña Chakra* gives the aspirant an inner integration. Systematic inhalation and exhalation of breath in meditation directs the mind and intellect to the indwelling spirit. The incoming of the breath is the absorption of the cosmic energy. It connects the Cosmic-Self to the embodied-self. The systematic inhalation and exhalation, which is followed by retention of the breath, guides the individual into peaceful meditation. The concentration of mind in yoga is to move inward to the doorway of self-discovery. The human mind once anchored to the Super Soul forms the habit of dwelling there. The peace and calmness it withdraws from within, manifests itself in the work which is performed by the person in day-to-day life. Experience of oneness in meditation blesses the individual with the taste of liberation and freedom in life. The liberated man dedicates all his work as an adoration to the God almighty. A dynamic peace and calmness radiates from him. His life becomes a total dedication and an embodiment of service. In the words of Jaydayal Goyandka, "As a result of this adoration, the grace of God begins to descend on him, and through Divine grace he speedily realizes His nature, glory, reality and virtues, and attains perfect peace." Srī Kṛṣṇa indicates the importance of synchronizing the performance of actions with proper knowledge and proper attitude. Appropriate understanding of the nature of work with devoted and meditative attitude is indeed the key to liberation in life and the life hereafter. In the last verse Srī Kṛṣṇa suggests to Arjuna for total surrender into the Supreme indweller who is the witness of all sacrifices, the well-wisher and the most reliable friend of every one. Resorting into His sovereignty with love and devotion—is indeed liberation, emancipation and moksha.

ॐ तत्सदिति श्रीमद्भगवद्गीतासूपनिषत्सु ब्रह्मविद्यायां
योगशास्त्रे श्रीकृष्णार्जुनसंवादे कर्मसंन्यासयोगो
नाम पञ्चमोऽध्यायः ॥ ५ ॥

'Aum' tatsaditi Śrīmadbhagawadgeetā sūpaniṣatsu
brahmavidyāyām yogaśāstre Śrīkṛṣṇārjunasamvāde
Karmasannyāsayogo nāma pañcamo'dhyāyaḥ

'AUM TAT SAT'—Thus, in the Upanishad of the glorious Bhagawad Geeta, the science of the Brahman (Absolute) the scripture of yoga, the dialogue between Srī Kṛṣṇa and Arjuna—thus, ends the chapter five entitled *"Karma-sannyāsa-Yoga"*.

इति श्रीमद्भगवद्गीतासु पञ्चमोऽध्यायः ॥ ५ ॥

Chapter Six

DHYĀNAYOGA

THE YOGA OF MEDITATION

श्रीभगवानुवाच

अनाश्रितः कर्मफलं कार्यं कर्म करोति यः।
स संन्यासी च योगी च न निरग्निर्न चाक्रियः॥ १॥

anāśritaḥ karmaphalaṁ kāryaṁ karma karoti yaḥ
sa sannyāsī ca yogī ca na niragnirna cākriyaḥ

The Blessed Lord said :

(1) He who performs obligatory duties without depending upon the fruits of actions—he is a true renunciate (Sannyasi) and a yogi; not the one who has renounced the sacred fire and the performance of action.

यं संन्यासमिति प्राहुर्योगं तं विद्धि पाण्डव।
न ह्यसंन्यस्तसङ्कल्पो योगी भवति कश्चन॥ २॥

yaṁ sannyāsamiti prāhur yogaṁ taṁ viddhi pāṇḍava
na hy asannyastasaṅkalpo yogī bhavati kaścana

(2) That which is called renunciation know that to be the yoga, O' Arjuna; for no one can become a yogi, without renouncing the selfish desires of the world.

आरुरुक्षोर्मुनेर्योगं कर्म कारणमुच्यते।
योगरूढस्य तस्यैव शमः कारणमुच्यते॥ ३॥

ārurukṣor muner yogaṁ karma kāraṇamucyate
yogārūḍhasya tasyaiva śamaḥ kāraṇamucyate

(3) Action is considered to be the means for the sage who aspires to ascend in yoga; when he is established in yoga, tranquillity of mind

is said to be the means.

यदा हि नेन्द्रियार्थेषु न कर्मस्वनुषज्जते।
सर्वसङ्कल्पसंन्यासी योगारूढस्तदोच्यते ॥ ४ ॥

yadā hi nendriyārtheṣu na karmasvanuṣajjate
sarvasaṅkalpasannyāsī yogārūḍhasta docyate

(4) When one becomes detached from the objects of senses and from actions, and has renounced all personal desires, then he is said to have ascended in Yoga.

Commentary—In continuation of the philosophy about the yoga of action, in these verses Srī Kṛṣṇa asserts very strongly that renunciation and the yoga of action are essentially the same. Perfection in one automatically renders the fruit of both. As explained earlier, the yoga of action literally means the type of actions which help the individual to develop a union or communion or communication with the Supreme-self. Yoga of action is the performance of work without the desire of seeking any fruit or reward. In these verses Srī Kṛṣṇa glorifies the nature of Karmayoga and asserts that a true sannyasi is one who renounces desires for the fruits of actions, and not the one who abandons all actions. A true renunciate performs all the obligatory actions and other rituals such as Agnihotra etc., merely out of his appreciation and devotion for the Lord.

The discipline of self-less action purifies the individual. It helps the person to rise above the dualities of life, it renders peace and inner tranquillity. Gradual contact with the Divine makes the individual more confident, and successful in all respects. The inner connectedness with the Supreme-self becomes manifested in his everyday life and detachment is also noticed in his every activity. So working in yoga is indeed the yoga of action and renunciation at the same time. The genuine renunciate is the one who works in unity with the Divine and not only the one, who puts on the attire of a renunciate and renounces the world. In the words of Adi Sankara, "He who has not discarded wishful resolve and attachment to the fruits of action, can't be a yogi with abstract contemplation. It never happens, for the thoughts of the result produces unsteadiness of mind. Mental clinging to the fruits of work distracts. Therefore, any doer, who has given up mental clinging to the fruits of actions is a yogi". The attitude of selfless action is indeed a very valuable means for self-purification and for total renunciation. Self-control and detachment in all respect is indeed a pre-requisite for yoga of action and renunciation. It is the attitude of selfless action which strengthens the yogic communion and the spirit of renunciation. A man of selfless action, who lives his life in constant association with God, performs all his assigned duties, with peace and tranquillity like a renunciate. His communion and union with the inner-self becomes second nature for him. A Karamyogi lives in the consciousness of God and performs all his work through the consciousness of God.

Srī Krṣṇa glorifies the attitude of detachment to the fruit of action, above the total renunciation from all actions. He makes it very clear that the attitude of selfless action is considered to be a means for the sage who aspires to ascend in yoga; when perfected in Karamyoga, the inner tranquillity becomes his means. The quietude of mind definitely forms the most important aspect of meditation and contemplation on God. A quiet mind enjoys resting in God. The profound message of these verses is that detachment to the fruit of action lies hidden in the inner peace and integrity. The inner peace lies hidden in the depth of person's connectedness with the Supreme spirit. Living in the awareness of the Supreme spirit is living in yoga and working in yoga and enjoying the bliss of renunciation in all respects. It is at this subtle level, the grace of inner tranquillity and the yoga of action is experienced. Learning to work with the guidance of the Indwelling light is indeed Karmayoga and renunciation in essence. Srī Krṣṇa asserts that renunciation is almost impossible until and unless the individual has trained himself to renounce all personal desires (Sankalpa).

उद्धरेदात्मनात्मानं नात्मानमवसादयेत्।
आत्मैव ह्यात्मनो बन्धुरात्मैव रिपुरात्मनः ॥५॥

uddharedātmanātmānaṁ nātmānamavasādayet
ātmai'va hyātmano bandhurātmaiva ripurātmanaḥ

(5) Let a man lift himself by his Self, Let him not degrade himself; for he himself is his own friend and he himself is his own enemy.

बन्धुरात्मात्मनस्तस्य येनात्मैवात्मना जितः ।
अनात्मनस्तु शत्रुत्वे वर्तेतात्मैव शत्रुवत् ॥ ६ ॥

bandhurātmatmanastasya yenātmaivātmanā jitaḥ
anātmanastu śatrutve vartetātmaiva śatruvat

(6) To him who has conquered his lower-self by the Higher-Self, his Self becomes a friend; but for him who has not conquered his lower-self his own Self-acts as an enemy.

Commentary—In the previous verses Srī Kṛṣṇa mentions that the individual, who is firmly established in the tranquillity of the Supreme-self, naturally becomes liberated from all worldly desires. The inner peace and satisfaction, which he draws from the inner unity, becomes incomparable to all the sensual enjoyments of the worldly objects. The person who is perpetually engaged in transcendental peace, he ascends in yoga and lives like a renunciate amidst worldly life. In these two verses, five and six, Srī Kṛṣṇa is emphasizing the fact that human potential are indeed enormous. The rise and fall of every individual is indeed within his own control. Everyone is born with two impulses constantly conflicting with each other. The conditioned nature invites the person to the enjoyment of the sensory pleasures of the material world; but while enjoying these sensual enjoyments, some voice from within keeps reminding the individual—"Go back where you belong". The moment one realizes the fundamental hollowness of worldly enjoyments one turns inward for comfort and is usually amazed by the silence of the inner realms. Slowly as one evolves into more co-ordinated thinking, one forms the habit of living in touch with the Divine. The scattered passions and desires are brought under control, the baser passions are checked and the individual lifts himself to the glorious status of self-realization and inner Bliss.

The individual soul being a fragment of the Cosmic Soul can rise to the status of the Supreme Self, and can actually work in a copartnership with God. As Swami Vivekananda has said, "Each soul is potentially divine." Srī Kṛṣṇa says, "let a man lift himself by his own self; let him not degrade himself; for he himself is his friend and he himself is his enemy". During the span of one's lifetime every person can rise to the height of a genius and can become the glory of the world, but if he ignores the voice of the inner-self and drifts away from *swadharma,* he can fall into the ditches of degradation. A man can be the splendour and majesty of the world but also the ridicule of it. In the words of Dr. Paul Brunton, "The divinity within us, the overself is always there, even when we disbelieve in it, and its presence is the secret, why sooner or later there must be a reaction in human life towards spiritual values. Only after we realize vividly our human insufficiency and our human inadequacy, we are likely to turn towards it for help." Connection with the inner Divinity is established slowly through constant and repeated practice of detachment and dispassion. When the individual cultivates his attachment for the Indwelling Divinity, he naturally becomes detached from the sensual pleasures of the world.

When a person becomes settled in the Self, he cultivates a sharp sense of discrimination and mastery over the mind. In this respect, he definitely acts like a friend of his own self and is elevated to the heights of perfection and God-realisation. On the other hand, when the individual acts recklessly under the slavery of his mind and senses he becomes his own enemy. The embodied-self that acts under the guidance of the Supreme-Self is elevated to the glorious destiny of God-realization, but the embodied-self that deviates from the voice of the Supreme-Self, falls into ditches of agony and shame. Every sincere, dedicated, disciplined and earnest act can draw the individual closer to Divine and help him to manifest the Divinity from within. Each and everybody has the ability and capacity to become whatever one chooses to be. Every person is indeed his own dear and reliable friend and also his own most dangerous enemy. It is said that once an illiterate washer woman was seen regularly attending the lectures of Emerson. When approached and asked as to how could she follow the most philosophical lecture of Emerson about transcendence, she answered innocently: "whatever else it might be, that I cannot comprehend, but he definitely convinces me of one thing, that I'm not a God-forsaken sinner and that I can really be a virtuous and self-realized woman. He has made me feel that I too am worth something in the sight of God and not a despised creature as they say."

The choice is personal and the efforts are also personal. It is the light from within that guides one at every step and helps one to adjust at every step. Evaluating spiritual awareness is indeed the necessity of human life. Being spiritual is becoming conscious of the inherent abilities and how to make the best use of them in respect to material and spiritual progress in life.

जितात्मनः प्रशान्तस्य परमात्मा समाहितः ।
शीतोष्णसुखदुःखेषु तथा मानापमानयोः ॥ ७ ॥

jitātmanaḥ praśāntasya paramātmā samāhitaḥ
śītoṣṇasukhaduḥkheṣu tathā mānāpamānayoḥ

(7) The self-controlled man, whose mind is perfectly serene and settled in the Supreme-Self, becomes balanced in cold and heat, in pleasure and pain, in honour and dishonour.

ज्ञानविज्ञानतृप्तात्मा कूटस्थो विजितेन्द्रियः ।
युक्त इत्युच्यते योगी समलोष्टाश्मकाञ्चनः ॥ ८ ॥

jñānavijñānatṛptātmā kūtastho vijitendriyaḥ
yukta ityucyate yogī samaloṣṭāśmakāñcanaḥ

(8) Who is satisfied with the knowledge and the experiential wisdom of the Self, who is steadfast and self-controlled, who considers a clod, a stone and a piece of gold alike; he is said to be established in yoga.

सुहृन्मित्रार्युदासीनमध्यस्थद्वेष्यबन्धुषु ।
साधुष्वपि च पापेषु समबुद्धिर्विशिष्यते ॥ ९ ॥

suhṛnmitrāryudāsīnamadhyasthadveṣyabandhuṣu
sādhuṣvapi ca pāpeṣu samabuddhirviśiṣyate

(9) He who regards the well-wishers, friends, enemies, indifferent, neutral, hateful, relatives, saint and the sinner alike, is indeed balanced and stands distinguished.

Commentary—In the previous verses Srī Kṛṣṇa glorifies the strength, the beauty, and the magnitude of the hidden resources of the human beings, and asserts, "Let a man elevate himself by his own self, let him not degrade himself, for the self alone is the friend of the self and the self alone is the enemy. An enlightened person becomes very self-disciplined and free from most of the restless desires. He enjoys inner peace and tranquillity without relying upon the luxuries and other means of material comforts. The unity in transcendence and the quietude of the Supreme-soul, makes the individual totally satisfied, contented and harmonized under all circumstances. For such a contented person if everything goes his way he enjoys it, but if it does not he never loses his peace of mind. Usually people suffer because of their own instability of mind, which is caused by the lack of faith and self-confidence. The ignorant and irresponsible people blame others for their failures and misfortunes, while in reality every individual is indeed responsible for his adversities and calamities. It is due to the spiritual ignorance, the person submits himself to the slavery of his conditioned lower nature and makes all kinds of mistakes and gets involved in undesirable deeds. On the other hand, a self-controlled individual who lives in spiritual awareness, rises above the conditioned slavery of nature and lives in perpetual tranquillity, happiness and contentment.

The individual who is settled in unity with Self, he lives in perpetual peace and carries inner peace in every sphere of his day-to-day life. Living at home with the family or working in the office, in the war and or in peace, it helps the individual to maintain a poised state of mind. He lives in permanent and unlimited joy of the self, beyond the kaleidoscopic influences of name and fame, honour and ignominy, pleasure and pain. He treats a friend and a foe, a criminal and a sage, a partial and impartial, alike, and holds equal love for them. He prays for the well-being of everyone and assures everybody that each individual is essentially a spiritual being and has the ability to enjoy the ecstasies of the ultimate bliss and fulfilment. He rises above all diversities and abides in the depth of silence, emerging from his own transcendence. He maintains his inner serenity even when involved in worldly activities. Nothing in the material world can divert his attention from spiritual serenity and calmness. All his decisions come from the depth of his inner guidancc and spiritual insight. As the adoption to superconsciousness becomes stronger, the individual becomes confident, self-reliant and his uniqueness is seen in every form of work he performs. His meditative attitude of mind manifests itself in every little gesture he makes and every bit of work he performs. His life become rhythmic, harmonious, effortless, peaceful and enjoyable in all respects.

योगी युञ्जीत सततमात्मानं रहसि स्थितः।
एकाकी यतचित्तात्मा निराशीरपरिग्रहः॥ १०॥

yogī yuñjīta satatamātmānaṁ rahasi sthitaḥ
ekākī yatacittātmā nirāśīraparigrahaḥ

(10) The yogi should constantly engage his mind in meditation, while living alone in solitude. Having controlled his mind and body and being free from the sense of possession and desire.

शुचौ देशे प्रतिष्ठाप्य स्थिरमासनमात्मनः।
नात्युच्छ्रितं नातिनीचं चैलाजिनकुशोत्तरम्॥ ११॥

śucau deśe pratiṣṭhāpya sthiramāsanamātmanaḥ
nātyucchritaṁ nātinīcaṁ cailājinakuśottaram

(11) On a clean spot, having established for himself a firm seat which is neither too high nor too low, and covered with a cloth, deer skin, and kusha-grass, one over the other.

तत्रैकाग्रं मनः कृत्वा यतचित्तेन्द्रियक्रियः।
उपविश्यासने युञ्ज्याद्योगमात्मविशुद्धये॥ १२॥

tatraikāgraṁ manaḥ kṛtvā yatacittendriyakriyaḥ
upaviśyāsane yuñjyād yogamātmaviśuddhaye

(12) Sitting there, on his seat with one-pointed mind; controlling the functions of mind and senses; he should practise yoga for the purification of the self.

समं कायशिरोग्रीवं धारयन्नचलं स्थिरः।
सम्प्रेक्ष्य नासिकाग्रं स्वं दिशश्चानवलोकयन्॥ १३॥

samaṁ kāyaśirogrīvaṁ dhārayannacalaṁ sthiraḥ

samprekṣya nāsikāgraṁ svaṁ diśaścānavalokayan

(13) Holding the trunk, head and neck straight, steady and still; he should fix the gaze on the tip of his nose, without looking in any other direction.

प्रशान्तात्मा विगतभीर्ब्रह्मचारिव्रते स्थितः।

मनः संयम्य मच्चित्तो युक्त आसीत मत्परः॥ १४॥

praśāntātmā vigatabhīr brahmacārivrate sthitaḥ

manaḥ saṅyamya maccitto yukta āsīta matparaḥ

(14) Peaceful and fearless, steadfast in the vow of celibacy, with mind fully disciplined and concentrated on Me; he should sit in yogic meditation—having Me as the Supreme goal.

युञ्जन्नेवं सदात्मानं योगी नियतमानसः।

शान्तिं निर्वाणपरमां मत्संस्थामधिगच्छति॥ १५॥

yuñjannevaṁ sadā'tamānaṁ yogī niyatamānasaḥ

śāntiṁ nirvāṇaparamāṁ matsaṅsthāmadhigacchati

(15) Thus constantly uniting his mind with Me, the yogi of disciplined mind, attains peace; the Supreme Nirvana, which abides in Me.

Commentary—In continuation of the previous verses, here Srī Kṛṣṇa is emphasizing that the yogi, who has trained himself to live in constant awareness of the Divine and has risen above dualities, should aspire for the ultimate goal of blissful freedom. It is indeed through regular practice of meditation, one gets the strength to maintain the state of transcendence and explore the Supreme state of permanent bliss (The Nirvana). It is only at the subtlest state of meditation where the knowledge of the Supreme-self is revealed to the individual and the total self-purification take place. The previous samskaras and latencies of many births are extinguished in the fire of self-knowledge and one enters into the realms of 'nirvikalpa' meditation. This state of awareness is beyond all desires, dreams and aspirations. This is the realm of unconditional love, the realm of ultimate peace, tranquillity and freedom.

In these verses Srī Kṛṣṇa explains step by step the procedure of going into the state of deep meditation. It is indeed very important to get acquainted with correct meditative postures. It helps the individual to achieve full benefits of meditation and also makes the meditation session relaxed and enjoyable. It is only when the body is fully relaxed that the thinking faculty can be brought under conscious control and deep meditation can take place. The purport of these few verses is to guide the aspirant towards a meditative state of mind. Srī Kṛṣṇa expounds the techniques for an inward vision of the Supreme spirit. It is a step by step explanation of the preliminaries needed in yoga for the enlightenment, and the ultimate union. First, it is indeed important to find a quiet place for meditation. It is advisable to practise meditation in fresh air, under the canopy of the open sky. It helps in self-expression by extending the vision into the vastness, near and far. It helps the inner thoughts and feelings to blend with the serenity of nature and creates harmony with nature. When the inner and outer nature start blending, meditation takes place naturally and easily. Quiet place has been highly recommended because during the meditation period, when the nerves are being trained to go into peace, even the slightest disturbance can create imbalance and harm the sensitive nerves. The cross-currents can create jerks and discomfort. If the individual meditates inside a room, it should be properly ventilated and detached from all strong smells. Even the incense burners should not be used; because any strong smell can disturb the flow of energy and easily distract the mind. The secluded places like the forest or a mountain peak are indeed ideal, but that doesn't mean that a householder can never practise meditation. Meditation practice is indeed possible while living at home and with the family. Any quiet and solitary corner of the house can be definitely appropriate for the practice. Before sitting for a meditation session it is good to close the door in order to avoid disturbance from things and people around. The meditation session becomes very rewarding if it is uninterrupted by external sounds. So a quiet and convenient corner in the house is good enough for meditation.

Second requirement is cleanliness. The external cleanliness definitely influences the inner state of thoughts, directly or indirectly. Cleanliness is for sure godliness, it sharpens and purifies the thinking faculty. Quiet and clean places do help in meditation and render inner peace and tranquillity. The external cleanliness promotes inner cleanliness and helps the individual to maintain self-purification. It is also important to choose a specific spot in the house and try to practise everyday at the same spot. It renders quick progress. The reason is that particular spot of meditation becomes energized with positive vibrations. In regular practice, when the person occupies to that particular spot and takes his seat making a certain posture, the flow of thoughts automatically begins to flow in an unbroken current towards the goal in meditation. In order to make the meditation session relaxed and enjoyable, a comfortable cushion has been recommended. It should be placed above the ground. The reason for it is to be above the ground; so that the body can be protected from the heat and dampness of the floor. Occasionally, sitting at a damp place for a long time can cause pain in the joints. Some meditators use a wooden seat covered with a blanket. Srī Kṛṣṇa has suggested in these verses the *Kusha* which is a grass cushion, that protects the individual from dampness and also keeps the platform warm in winter. Over the grass base of Kusha, a four-fold blanket has been suggested with the deer skin on the top. The deer skin (Mrigchala) has been recommended especially for the meditators in the forest because it protects the person from harmful bugs and insects. The deer skin has the quality to keep away the harmful crawling insects on the ground. A person planning to practise meditation in the house doesn't require a deer skin cushion. It is not one of the essentials. Although there are some other reasons for using the deer skin, according to Swami Sivananda, "It generates electricity in the body quickly and doesn't allow leakage of electric current from the body. It is full of magnetism." All these suggestions are for making the posture comfortable. A four-fold blanket provides enough padding in order to support the hips and buttocks. Actually if one elevates the buttocks with a low cushion, that helps in keeping the spine straight and relieves unnecessary pressure on the lower back. This position locks the spine immediately and aligns the neck and head automatically.

The ideal recommended posture is indeed the *padmasana.* The *padmasana* is the full lotus position. *Padmasanas* is stretching the right foot and placing over the left thigh and the left foot over the right thigh, with the soles of the feet pointing upward, and heels touching the pelvic bone. For a beginner in meditation, this posture is slightly difficult, so it is appropriate to start with the simple posture, the crossed legs position with a cushion supporting the buttocks area. This simple posture is called *sukhasana. Sukhasana* is an ideal posture for the beginners, wherein the right foot is placed under the left thigh and the left foot under the right thigh. Hands are placed over the knees with head, neck and back properly aligned. Another well recommended posture is *sidhasana* which helps the spine to remain straight and makes the meditation session very productive for a long time. This posture helps the person to develop an extra control over sensual desires. This posture has a remarkable calming effect over the entire nervous system. With gradual and regular practice one learns to move from *sukhasana* to *sidhasana* and from *sidhasana* to *padmasana,* the full lotus posture.

The recommended posture for meditation definitely requires the proper alignment of lower back, neck, shoulder, trunk and head. The vertical column should be erect and at ninety degree from the ground. Perpendicular position of the vertebral column helps the proper functioning of the nervous system. It helps in relaxation of the muscles and withdrawal from the physical body. It harmonizes the breathing rhythm and calms down the mind in all respects. When the head, neck and the spinal cord become vertical, the gaze can be easily concentrated on the tip of the nose, between the two eyebrows. After sitting in the meditative posture, one should close the eyes and start breathing gently. After a few minutes the individual should set his index finger in the middle of the two eyebrows and put a little bit of pressure upon the eyelids and eyeballs, gently moving them from the outer corners to the inner corners towards the central point between the two eyebrows. Try to maintain an equal distance from both the eyes to the bridge of the nose. It helps the facial muscles to relax and maintain control over the sensory organs of the face area. This spot between the two eyebrows is called *bhrumadhya.* Directing the vision inward towards the bridge of the nose helps in concentration. It is at this spot between the two eyes from where the breath control starts and one experiences the light between the two eyebrows. By meditating at this point the individual can clearly visualize the white rays emanating from the centre. One feels the entire body being revitalized from this centre, giving a conscious control over all the muscles of the body and the breathing system.

This is a very traditional posture of meditation as described by the ancient sages since the Vedic times. This position describes the vertical and horizontal alignment. It helps the energy to flow uninterrupted from the base of the spine and enables the mind to experience illumination and silence. It creates balance at various psychic stations and helps the body to relax and enjoy the inner peace. By keeping the body straight and steady, the breathing pattern can be monitored very easily. The maximum amount of oxygen can be inhaled in and also the thought process can be controlled. This alignment helps the pranic energy to flow through the spinal column uniformly, rhythmically and properly. It energizes the body and at the same time makes the person feel very relaxed and serene. Tranquillity in breathing is followed by tranquillity of thoughts, senses, mind and body. The undisturbed position of head and neck with lower back cleans the subtle passages of pranic energy and releases the tension from all over the body. When the brain feels relaxed, the body energy is saved.

There are many other reasons why the upright position is recommended in meditation. This posture helps in the general well-being of the individual. It creates balance in various organs of the body. The purpose of this posture is to awaken the primal force so that it can move upward and give relaxation. We generally notice that whenever someone feels depressed, overburdened with worries and stress, he is guided by the innate nature to straighten up. The moment one straightens up with a jerk, the head, neck and back become aligned and one feels a little revitalized and relaxed. It is like a built-in feature of human nature to overcome the stress in physical body. It is a natural response of the physical body to bring a change in the stressed mental make-up. This activity is motivated by the primal force stored at the base of the spine. The goal of meditation is to get acquainted with this reservoir of golden light and use it for physical well-being, self-realization and God-realization. The proper âlignment of spine prepares the individual for the awakening of the *kundalini.* The Sanskrit word *'kundala'* means coiled. The primal force coiled up at the base of the spinal cord, perineum, is *kundalini.* According to Patañjali Yoga Sutra, it is at the base of the spine from where the seventy two thousands nadis (energy canals) arise and connect the entire body with the primal source of energy. With the proper alignment of neck, head and the lower back, the *sushumna nadi* is awakened. Along the route of *sushumna nadi* there are many psychic stations. The aspirant is required to focus awareness at these various psychic stations in order to experience the flow of energy. The first one is *mooladhara* at the base of the spine. On the disc at this point, there is a triangle emanating white and golden light. One perceives the luminous white rays going in all directions but specifically pointed upward. This station had the elemental qualities of the earth. While meditating at this root centre, one feels charged with the primal energy and also the elemental (symbolic) qualities of earth, which is firmness, steadiness and patience. The energy at this point is perceived and visualized as the deep red lotus with four petals. The Sanskrit letters written on this petals are *Sam, Sham, Vam* and *Sham.* The Beeja mantra of *mooladhara chakra* is *lam* and in the centre of this lotus is a *Shivalingam.* A golden colour serpent with three and a half coils, encircles the Shivalingam, with its tail tucked in the mouth. *Mooladhara* psychic station is presided by the creator of the universe, the Brahma Himself, the presiding goddess at this centre is Dakini, who controls the element of skin in the body. In meditation with the proper alignment of the spine, the primal energy is aroused from the base and directed to travel upward through all the other stations along the *sushumna nadi.*

The second psychic station along the *sushumna* is the *swadhisthana chakra. 'Swa-dhisthana'* literally means 'one's own abode'. This station is perceived and visualized in meditation as lotus with six petals around a disc and with the symbol of crescent in the centre. The Sanskrit mantras on these petals are *Bam, Bham, Mam, Yam, Ram* and *Lam.* The Beeja mantra of this psychic station is *Vam.* The presiding Lord of the centre is Vishnu and the presiding deity is *Rakini* who controls the element of blood. The colour is deep orange and it is related with the survival of the race. The elemental quality of swadhisthana is water. This station is connected with the conscious and unconscious thoughts of the present and also with the latencies of the many previous lives. It is possessed with the present and remote memories. It is indeed the storehouse of the most primitive and instinctive behaviour which relates to the survival of the species. This psychic station is related to sexual urge and to the organs of reproduction and excretion. The exact location of this *chakra* is at the level of the pubic bone or we can say coccyx at the distance of about four inches in the front part of the body from the *mooladhara.*

The third psychic station along the *sushumna* is the *manipura chakra. Manipura* combines two words. *Mani* literally means the jewel and *pura* means the city, combined together it means the city of jewels. Fire (heat) is the element for this *chakra* and the colour is bright yellow. The Lord of *Manipura* is *Rudra* and the deity is *Lakini* who controls flesh in body. It is perceived and visualized as the bright deep yellow colour lotus with ten petals. The Sanskrit words written on these petals are *dam, dham, nam, tam, tham, dam, dham, nam, pam;* and *pham*, the Beeja mantra of this psychic station is *Ram.* It is situated at the level of the navel in the front of the body, corresponding to a centre on the spine. Meditating at this point enables the individual to enhance the elemental qualities of fire such as purity and vitality.

The next one is the *Anahata chakra. Anahata* means the unstruck. This is the root spot of all sounds. It is located between the two breasts known as the heart centre. This psychic centre divides the body in Northern and Southern hemispheres. It is at this centre that the person is remade spiritually, emotionally and ethically. It is the focal point of emotional and psychological maturity. It is perceived and visualized by the meditator as dark green lotus with twelve petals. The Sanskrit mantras inscribed on these petals are *kam, kham, gam, gham, nam, cham, chham, jam, jham, nam, tam* and *tham*. The Beej mantra for meditation at this specific centre is *yam*. The Lord of the centre is *Isha* and the deity is *Kakini*. It is felt to be located within the spine corresponding to the point located behind the two breast bones. It is perceived and visualized in front of the chest and also inside the spine along the route of *sushumna*. This *chakra* can be noticed as the star of David, shooting forth its rays all around. The air is the element of this psychic station.

The fifth *chakra* is the *Visuddhi Chakra*. As the term explains it is the centre of purification. In meditation it is perceived and visualized as a blue lotus with sixteen petals. These are inscribed with the Sanskrit mantras such as *am, am, im, im, um, um, rim, rim, lrim, lrim, em, aim, om, aum, am* and *ah*. The Beej mantra of this *chakra* is *ham*. *Shiva* and *Parvathi* combined together preside over the centre and the deity is *Sakini*. It is located in the region of the throat, along the route of *sushumna*. At this psychic station one experiences drops of nectar dripping from the *sahasrara*. Some yogis do taste the nectar very consciously by rolling the tongue backward to the very far end of the throat. When the tip of tongue is turned backward into the throat, it tastes the blissful elixir of life (amritam) and feels exhilarated, and in some cases also a bit intoxicated. Some meditators who sit in meditation for a long time at stretch, they receive their full nutrition from this blissful Divine elixir. The taste of this blissful elixir can't be described in words and also cannot be compared with any other taste in the world. It supersedes all other tastes of the material world. It renders peace and contentment. The nectar originates in the *Sahasrara*, cascades through Bindu and drips from *Lalana Chakra* at the point located in the upper palate, right at the base of the tonsils. Ether is the element of *Vishudhi chakra*.

The sixth psychic station located between the two eyebrows is known as *Ajña chakra*. It is also known as the command centre. In general it is called the eye of intuition. There are two famous methods of receiving knowledge. One source of knowledge is tuition, which is received from the teachers and also accumulated from books. The other source of knowledge is intuition, through which the individual is awakened from within. In the words of Swami Abhedananda, "Intuition is that power by which the subjective mind can perceive the result without reasoning and without questioning". Meditation at this centre enables the individual to observe and experience almost all the events simultaneously, at the physical and as well as at spiritual levels of consciousness. This psychic station is experienced and visualized as silver-Indigo lotus with two petals. The Sanskrit mantras written on these petals are *ham* and *ksham.* The Beeja mantra of this centre is the Holy syllable *'Aum'*. Shiva is the Lord of the centre and the presiding deity is *Hakini* who controls the subtle mind. At the centre of this *chakra* is visualized Indigo lotus with white tiny crescent moon. The element for this *chakra* is mind. It is at this point that the psychic currents *ida* and *pingala* are integrated and the breath flow is regulated to bring the mind under conscious control. The three red lines running from top to bottom indicate the triads of Nature. The Holy syllable AUM can be seen in the middle of these lines. This centre connects one with the remote and present memories and also enables the individual to see in future. This is considered to be the most important centre of spontaneous meditation. Concentration at this point helps the person to understand the depth, beauty and the joy of the spiritual unfoldment. Awakening at this centre acquaints the individual to his own inherent potential. Meditation at this point between the eyebrows, known as *bhrumadhya,* awakens the desire for liberation, salvation and *mohksha.*

The seventh centre along the *sushumna* is known as *Sahasrara.* It is the seat of consciousness which holds all the other *chakras* within itself. It is like a radiant dome at the crown of the head. It is at this point the Vedic sages used to grow a long tuft of hair. The ancient Rishis used to comb the hair upward and role at the top of the head, to protect this special soft spot, where the spiritual energy is stored. Starting from *mooladhara* to this seventh *chakra*, *'Sahasrara'* is the psychic passage which can be perceived and visualized during meditation. Only a spark of the dormant energy from the *mooladhara* can open up this entire passage along the *sushumna. Sahasrara* as the name denotes is a lotus of thousand petals extending in almost all directions; on these petals, there are the Sanskrit alphabets. The element of this *chakra* is pure consciousness and the colour is shining violet-white. A *Shivalingam* can also be visualized in the centre as the seat.

Srī Kṛṣṇa suggests that while sitting in an upright position, when the psychic current flows along the *sushumna nadi,* self-purification takes place at various levels of consciousness. As the primal energy moves, the impurities are washed away and the feeling of peace and tranquillity takes place. One feels relaxed and concentrated. The mind calms down and rests into the blissful realm of pure consciousness. Observance of celibacy in thoughts, words and deeds comes easily and naturally. The individual doesn't have to struggle for complete abstinence from sexual life; the gratification comes with inner contentment. In the words of Swami Prabhupada, "Whereas others are forced to restrain themselves from sense-gratification, a devotee of the Lord automatically refrains because of superior taste".

When a person learns to live in the transcendence of the Divine nature, he becomes eligible for *nirvana,* the ultimate peace and tranquillity, in the form of emancipation.

नात्यश्नतस्तु योगोऽस्ति न चैकान्तमनश्नतः ।
न चातिस्वप्नशीलस्य जाग्रतो नैव चार्जुन ॥ १६ ॥

nātyaśnatastu yogo'sti na caikāntamanaśnataḥ
na cātisvapnaśīlasya jāgrato naiva cārjuna

(16) Yoga is not for him who eats too much, nor for him who does not eat at all; it is not for him who sleeps too much, nor for him who is ever awake, O' Arjuna.

युक्ताहारविहारस्य युक्तचेष्टस्य कर्मसु ।
युक्तस्वप्नावबोधस्य योगो भवति दुःखहा ॥ १७ ॥

yuktāhāravihārasya yuktaceṣṭasya karmasu
yuktasvapnāvabodhasya yogo bhavati duḥkhahā

(17) The man who is regulated in diet and recreation, disciplined in the performance of work, who is regulated in sleep and wakefulness,

for him the Yoga becomes the destroyer of pain.

Commentary—In continuation of the previous verses, Srī Kṛṣṇa declares that for any type of accomplishment in yogic meditation, it is indeed very important to avoid the extremes in all respects. It has been indicated very clearly in these verses that the union and communion in meditation is indeed very difficult, for the one who eats too much, or the one who fasts too often and for too long. It is also not for him who sleeps for long hours and also not for him who keeps himself ceaselessly awake. Success in meditation and Yoga is achieved by maintaining a regular balance in everyday life. Regulated diet and recreation promotes longevity and happiness in life. It enhances purity, stability and integrity. A disciplined life is indeed a key to success in Yoga and meditation. Also the performance of assigned duties at various stages of life are indeed important and one must perform them diligently, lovingly and skilfully. Proper performance of work renders peace and self respect. Yoga meditation should never be taken as a punishment. It should come to the individual's day to day life very naturally and spontaneously.

In general, the over-indulgence of any type creates imbalance in life and makes the yogic meditation difficult. Over-indulgence creates stress and affects the immune system creativity, productivity and the quality of work. It is indeed very important to adopt a balanced course of action in all respects. For example, Lord Buddha adopted a very difficult mode of austerity in the beginning of his pursuit. He went to the extremes of fasting for too long and actually tortured his physical body. The penance should not become a punishment to the point that instead of giving redemption it becomes a bondage. One should definitely avoid excess and extremes in all types of activities. Srī Kṛṣṇa indicates the necessity of maintaining an intelligent moderation in everything for the cultivation of yogic communion. A disciplined and regulated pursuit helps the individual to maintain a proper balance at the physical, mental and spiritual levels. It is a fact that the person who is regulated in diet, recreation and work, he becomes very harmonized in his daily life and for him the yogic meditation becomes a source of God-realization.

यदा विनियतं चित्तमात्मन्येवावतिष्ठते।
निःस्पृहः सर्वकामेभ्यो युक्त इत्युच्यते तदा॥ १८॥

yadā viniyataṁ cittām atmanyevāvatiṣṭhate
niḥspṛhaḥ sarvakāmebhyo yukta ityucyate tadā

(18) When the perfectly disciplined mind rests in the Self alone, and is free from the yearning for the objects of desires, one is said to be united in Yoga.

यथा दीपो निवातस्थो नेङ्गते सोपमा स्मृता।
योगिनो यतचित्तस्य युञ्जतो योगमात्मनः॥ १९॥

yathā dīpo nivātastho neṅgate sopamā smṛtā
yogino yatacittasya yuñjato yogāmatmanaḥ

(19) As a lamp placed in a windless spot does not flicker, is the simile used for a yogi of subdued mind, who is practising to unite in Yoga with the Self.

यत्रोपरमते चित्तं निरुद्धं योगसेवया।
यत्र चैवात्मनात्मानं पश्यन्नात्मनि तुष्यति॥ २०॥

yatroparamate cittaṁ niruddhaṁ yogasevayā
yatra caivātmanātmānaṁ paśyannātmani tuṣyati

(20) Where the mind becomes peaceful and restrained by the practice of Yoga, wherein one beholds the Self within the self, one rejoices in the Self alone.

सुखमात्यन्तिकं यत्तद्बुद्धिग्राह्यमतीन्द्रियम्।
वेत्ति यत्र न चैवायं स्थितश्चलति तत्त्वतः॥ २१॥

sukhamātyantikaṁ yat tad buddhigrāhymatīndriyam
vetti yatra na caivāyaṁ sthitaś calati tattvataḥ

(21) Where one experiences transcendental bliss, which is perceived only by the subtle intellect, and which is beyond the grasp of the senses, established in that state, one never moves from the essential truth.

Commentary—In these verses Srī Kṛṣṇa brings to Arjuna's

attention some glimpses of the individual established in the unity with the Divine through concentration of mind. A disciplined mind sails easily into the deeper realms of meditation and the supreme bliss. Concentrated attention is indeed a pre-requisite for success in meditation. It prepares the mind and body for the delicate path to tread in the deeper layers of consciousness. Concentration helps the individual to form a positive control over thinking faculty and to direct thoughts towards the desired goal. Although it is difficult to pinpoint when the conscious concentration becomes settled in meditation session; but definitely concentration leads towards the higher realms of transcendence.

A concentrated mind is very stable. Srī Kṛṣṇa has compared a concentrated mind to a lamp that doesn't flicker at a spot which is sheltered from the wind. The simile of a steady flame is indeed the most appropriate illustration for a concentrated and steadfast mind. In deep concentration, the mind starts losing its contacts with things and ideas which usually crowd upon the mind. When the scattered attention is brought under conscious control, it can really perform miracles of all kinds. On an average people don't utilize their inherent potential of a concentrated mind, as Emerson used to say: "One prudence in life is concentration and one evil is dissipation". Any individual with a concentrated mind performs work with great efficiency and accuracy. He performs work much faster than an average person. Concentration improves the learning ability and apprehension in all respects. It purifies the emotions, strengthens the self-confidence and brings clarity of ideas. It is also important to know that a concentrated mind is the highly relaxed mind. The relaxed mind is for sure very peaceful and tranquil and also capable of experiencing the superconscious state of transcendence.

There are many different ways to learn concentration. Concentration on a sound helps the individual to get tuned to the sound of internal *nada* which vibrates from the *anahat chakra.* When the mind learns to enjoy the melody of the internal *nada,* it settles quickly into the subtle layers of consciousness leading into deep meditation. Every person in the world is born with the sound of celestial *nada* which vibrates uninterruptedly from the *anahat chakra* at the heart centre. The little infants know instinctively as how to listen and enjoy the blissful sound. In general it is noticed that the little infants smile and exhilarate in their deep sleep. It is indeed the sound of *nada* which amuses them in their state of inner unity with the Self. An infant knows and recognizes the primordial sound very easily; but as the person grows old, the external sounds of the materialistic world do overcrowd his mind. When the mind of the individual becomes more and more involved in the external sounds, it almost forgets about the inner *nada.* The person loses his touch with the inner sound and inner serenity. The concentration on the sound brings back the memory of the primordial sound to the individual and helps him to recognize and experience its true nature.

Trataka or fixing gaze on some external or internal object is also a powerful method of concentration. *Trataka* means steady one-pointed gazing. One starts the *trataka* practice with open eyes which is slowly followed by visualization. This practice makes the thoughts one-pointed and harmonious. When all the thoughts are directed towards one specific subject, slowly the flow becomes spontaneous and natural like the continuous flow of oil as poured from one vessel into another. The concentration encloses the thoughts into small circle, and the scattered attention into collectiveness. It helps the individual to develop tremendous psychic power and intensity in meditation. Such concentration is quickly followed by a state of peaceful meditation.

Some yoga teachers highly recommend the use of mantra for concentration in meditation. The word mantra is a combination of two words *mana* and *tra*—*mana* means the mind and *tra* means to emancipate. Our scriptures describe it as *"manae trayati iti mantra"*, a word which emancipates the mind is mantra. According to some scholars mantra is a word or a group of words that expresses the concept of God and the universe. Instinctively the senses and mind are accustomed to the habit of chasing sense objects. Mantra jaap brings a change in one's thought pattern. It helps in concentration. Mantra jaap literally means the storing and restoring of a spiritual idea.

It is like printing impressions of certain spiritual words and vibrations into the deepest layers of the consciousness.

It is a well-known fact that the infinite Divinity can't be perceived by the finite sense organs. In order to transcend the finite, the individual has to train himself to be constantly connected with the Infinite. With constant mantra jaap, slowly but surely the mind gets into the habit of transcending the finite boundaries and rests into the infinite Divinity. The habit of living in constant touch with the Supreme-Self makes the practice of concentration and meditation very easy. Persistent repetition of mantra helps in purifying, cleansing and emptying the mind. Concentration on mantra jaap has the power to awaken within the mind the corresponding awareness of the Supreme-Self and efficiently guide the mind into meditation.

The breathing rhythm also influences the concentration of mind. There is a very subtle and powerful relationship between the breath and the thinking faculty. The stability of mind is closely related to the breathing pattern and the other functions of the body. That is why it is indeed essential to observe the breathing rhythm and bring it under conscious control. The irregular and the fast breathing pattern indicates stress and tension in mind and body, while a deep rhythmical breathing pattern signifies tranquillity and a peaceful state of mind. Breath awareness helps in maintaining emotional tranquillity and equanimity in all respects. It is indeed an essential aspect of concentration and also for developing a conscious control over mind and body. After sitting in a comfortable position with proper alignment of spine, the individual should pay attention to the inhalation and exhalation of breath in order to avoid the unnecessary jerks. The systematic flow of breath helps concentration and meditation. In this context, there is a very good example in Chhandogya Upanishad as translated by Dr. Radhakrishnan, "Just as a bird tied by a string after flying in different directions, when doesn't find a resting place anywhere else, it settles down at last to the place where it is bound, exactly like that, the mind after running in various directions without finding silence and peace anywhere else, settles down in breath. The breath is the manifestation of the Supreme-Self, *Atman.* The word *Atman* has been derived from

An, which means to breathe. As described in the *Rigveda, "Atma te vatah"—Atman* is the breath of life. So when the mind settles down into the breath, it nestles in the Supreme-Self." Concentration with breath control is the most well-known type of meditation practice. Meditation session takes the mind to a state where it does not oscillate and becomes pure and enlightened. With the regular and continued practice, the mind starts retiring from the pleasures of the sensual enjoyments and becomes very steadfast and resolute.

Meditation in any form helps the individual to transcend the conscious level of awareness and experience the ultimate truth. Serenity and peace are characteristics of the Supreme-Self. Once the mind is purified, it grasps the reality and likes to dwell there perpetually. As the mind starts identifying itself with the Supreme-Self, it enjoys and rejoices in the Self. The more the mind dives into the joyous state the more contented one feels. In the words of Maharishi Mahesh Yogi, "When merging into the being, it cognizes being as its own Self and gains bliss consciousness, the yogi finds contentment in the Self. The bliss of this state eliminates any sorrow great or small. This state of self-sufficiency leaves one steadfast in oneself and fulfilled in eternal contentment". The joy of transcendence is indeed boundless and quite incomparable to anything else in the world. As the individual elevates himself into the higher states of transcendence—the state of completeness with the Self is experienced, which liberates the individual from all kinds of *sankalpa* and *vikalpa.*

यं लब्ध्वा चापरं लाभं मन्यते नाधिकं ततः।
यस्मिन्स्थितो न दुःखेन गुरुणापि विचाल्यते॥ २२॥

yaṁ labdhvā cāparaṁ lābhaṁ manyate nādhikaṁ tataḥ
yasminsthito na duḥkhena guruṇāpi vicālyate

(22) Having obtained that which one considers nothing else superior to it; wherein established, the individual is not shaken even by the deepest sorrow.

तं विद्याद्दुःखसंयोगवियोगं योगसंज्ञितम्।
स निश्चयेन योक्तव्यो योगोऽनिर्विण्णचेतसा॥ २३॥

taṁ vidyād duḥkhasaṅyogaviyogaṁ yogasamjñitam
sa niścayena yoktavyo yogo'nirvinnacetasā

(23) This state is known by the name of Yoga which is free from the contacts of sorrow. This Yoga should be practised with determination and concentration of mind.

Commentary—Here in these verses the state of yogic unity and the joyful experience of transcendence has been described. The infinite joy of connectedness with the Supreme-Self is indeed phenomenal, sublime and very difficult to express in words. Srī Kṛṣṇa tells that each and every individual must make efforts to tread the noble path of meditation and self-unfoldment. In the words of Swami Chidabhavanananda, "In truth man's nature is happiness. Due to ignorance he binds himself to pain, if the pain is removed his natural state is revealed."

The freedom from pain and sorrow is surely possible only by going back into the main stream of Bliss, and by diving deep into the Blissful state of transcendence. *Sruti Bhagvati* declares, "nothing in the world is superior to the unity experienced with the Self; it is the attainment of what ought to be achieved and the accomplishment of everything for whatever one desires". It is like falling in love with one's own essential nature, one's own essential divinity, one's own glamour and greatness, one's own peace and tranquillity. In yoga meditation when the mind is totally emptied from all types of thoughts, the psychological void is achieved. The catching up of this silence between the two thoughts, and just being there, is going into the unity with the Supreme-Self. Although in the beginning, the individual can stay in the silence, only for few seconds but with gradual practice as the silence extends longer and longer, the meditation period becomes long, effortless and very enjoyable. This is the state of pure awareness and pure transcendence. After reaching there, no one wants to return to the hustle and bustle of the mundane world; and when one returns, he is revitalized with tremendous positive energy to work very successfully in his day-to-day life.

Srī Kṛṣṇa asserts strongly that there is a place into the realm of the supreme Divinity for each and everyone; all one needs is determination and ceaseless practice. It is indeed achieved by one's own personal decision, attitude and efforts. None of the spiritual teachers and prophets or a Guru can really help anybody completely. They can help for sure to some extent in guiding the person towards the path of perfection but the ultimate goal is to be achieved by the individual's own efforts. Every person has to tread the path all by himself and has to overcome the obstacles all alone. The yoga of concentration has to be practised with firm resolution, determination and loving devotion. Srī Kṛṣṇa suggests that the first and foremost duty of every individual is to become re-established in a communion with the indwelling Divinity, and then live the worldly life with the guidance of that Divinity. Resorting to the quietude of the Self is Yoga, and then the practice of that yoga in everyday life is *sannyasa.*

सङ्कल्पप्रभवान्कामांस्त्यक्त्वा सर्वानशेषतः।
मनसैवेन्द्रियग्रामं विनियम्य समन्ततः॥ २४॥

saṅkalpaprabhavān kāmāṅs tyaktvā sarvānaśeṣataḥ
manasaivendriyagrāmaṁ viniyamya samantataḥ

शनैः शनैरुपरमेद् बुद्ध्या धृतिगृहीतया।
आत्मसंस्थं मनः कृत्वा न किंचिदपि चिन्तयेत्॥ २५॥

śanaiḥ śanairuparamed bhuddahyā dhṛtigṛhītayā
ātmasaṁsthaṁ manaḥ kṛtvā na kiñcidapi cintayet

(24, 25) Abandoning all desires which arise from the thoughts of the world and fully controlling the mind from the entire group of senses, let him gradually attain tranquillity, with the intellect held in firmness; having made the mind established in the Self, let him not think about anything else.

यतो यतो निश्चरति मनश्चञ्चलमस्थिरम्।
ततस्ततो नियम्यैतदात्मन्येव वशं नयेत्॥ २६॥

yato-yato niścarati manaścañcalam asthiram
tatas-tato niyamyaitad ātmanyeva vaśaṁ nayet

(26) For whatever reason, when the restless mind wanders away, he should restrain it and bring it under the control of Self alone.

प्रशान्तमनसं ह्येनं योगिनं सुखमुत्तमम्।
उपैति शान्तरजसं ब्रह्मभूतमकल्मषम् ॥ २७ ॥

praśāntamanasaṁ hyenaṁ yoginaṁ sukhamuttamam
upaiti śāntarajasaṁ brahmabhūtamakalmaṣam

(27) The Supreme Bliss comes to the yogi whose mind is at peace, whose passion (rajas) has been subdued, who is sinless and has become identified with the Brahman.

युञ्जन्नेवं सदात्मानं योगी विगतकल्मषः।
सुखेन ब्रह्मसंस्पर्शमत्यन्तं सुखमश्नुते ॥ २८ ॥

yuñjannevaṁ sadātmānaṁ yogī vigatakalmaṣaḥ
sukhena brahmasaṅsparśam atyantaṁ sukhamaśnute

(28) Thus constantly uniting the mind with the Self, the yogi becomes free from sins and easily attains the infinite Bliss of oneness with Brahman.

Commentary—In these verses Srī Kṛṣṇa once again insists upon the necessity of concentration on the Supreme Self. Each and every minute of life should pass with the consciousness of the indwelling light. The person needs to monitor the quality of each thought that passes through the mind, and must form a habit of having a conscious control over it. It is indeed the one-pointedness of mind on the Supreme-Self that guides one to the regions of transcendence. The person has to be very patient and move forward just one step at a time. Slow and steady practice brings firm and steady results. Steadfastness is indeed the most important characteristic of an aspirant who is seeking unity with the Self. The entire process of yogic communion should be very natural, enjoyable and easy. The Supreme-self is not just a fantasy or a vague aspiration. God is indeed a reality that can be experienced and enjoyed. It is as real as the air we breathe, feel and touch. *Yunjann-evam* literally means getting in touch with that and feeling the close association with that. It is the experience of touch, unity and connectedness that guides one into identifying himself with Brahman. It is the *samasparsa*—the touch of the Supreme Divinity—which is expressed as the deep ecstasy which arises from the depths of the inner tranquillity. *Samasparsa* is being in the ecstatic unity in transcendence. Srī Sankara interprets *Brahma Samasparsa* as unity with the Brahman, Srī Ramanuja interprets it as the experience of the Brahman, and Srīnivasan as contact with the Brahman. All the highly recognized joys of the material world do not fall into any category of the joy that arises from one's connectedness with God. It is the most incomprehensible, incomparable and inexhaustible bliss. The joy of the oneness with pure being is untainted, and unconditional. Although it involves tremendous courage and determination to start the inward journey towards the exploration of the Supreme soul; but as the individual moves ahead it really becomes the most enjoyable adventure. The silence of bliss, which is experienced at the innermost levels of consciousness, manifests itself in the individual's behaviour and daily activities. In general, the transformation takes place in behaviour very slowly. Occasionally it is not as noticeable to the individual himself as it is noticed by others. The spiritual progress reflects the purification of mind and body.

सर्वभूतस्थमात्मानं सर्वभूतानि चात्मनि।
ईक्षते योगयुक्तात्मा सर्वत्र समदर्शनः॥ २९॥

sarvabhūtasthamātmānaṁ sarvabhūtāni cātmani
īkṣate yogayuktātmā sarvatra samadarśanaḥ

(29) He whose self is established in Yoga, he beholds the self abiding in all beings and all beings in the Self. He sees equality everywhere.

यो मां पश्यति सर्वत्र सर्वं च मयि पश्यति।
तस्याहं न प्रणश्यामि स च मे न प्रणश्यति॥ ३०॥

yo māṁ paśyati sarvatra sarvaṁ ca mayi paśyati
tasyā'haṁ na praṇaśyāmi sa ca me na praṇaśyati

(30) He who sees Me everywhere and sees everything existing in Me, I am never out of sight for him, nor is he ever out of My sight.

सर्वभूतस्थितं यो मां भजत्येकत्वमास्थितः।
सर्वथा वर्तमानोऽपि स योगी मयि वर्तते॥ ३१॥

sarvabhūtasthitaṁ yo māṁ bhajatyekatvamāsthitaḥ

sarvathā vartamānopi sa yogī mayi vartate

(31) He who, being established in oneness, worships Me dwelling in all beings, that yogi ever resides in Me, though engaged in all forms of activities.

आत्मौपम्येन सर्वत्र समं पश्यति योऽर्जुन।

सुखं वा यदि वा दुःखं स योगी परमो मतः॥ ३२॥

ātmaupamyena sarvatra samaṁ paśyati yo'rjuna

sukhaṁ vā yadi vā duḥkhaṁ sa yogī parmo mataḥ

(32) He who, through the reflections of his own-self, sees equality everywhere, be it pleasure or pain, he is considered a perfect yogi, O'Arjuna.

Commentary—In these verses Srī Kṛṣṇa makes it very clear that the unity with the Supreme Lord in meditation does manifest itself in the daily activities of the individual and in his relationship with others. The spiritual intimacy with the Self is the key, that opens the doorway to an intimate relationship with others. Once an individual recollects his Divine inheritance, he is bound to act from the depth of his spiritual nature, which is pure, original and unconditional. The Divine nature holds no duality. It springs forth from the purity, honesty, and the universality of oneness. A God-realized person beholds nothing else but a reflection of the Supreme-self alone, in everybody and everything. *Ishavasam idam sarvam*—the entire universe is pervaded by God alone.

These verses explain some of the progressive steps of God-realization and Self-realization. It is indeed a fact that when the boundaries of ego are dissolved and the unification with the indweller is established, the individual-self feels reflected in the Higher-self and gradually into the self of the others. Srī Kṛṣṇa tells that such an individual resides in Me, works through Me, talks and acts through Me. He becomes a conscious participant in experiencing the pains and pleasures of other people.

There is an incident from the life story of Srī Ramakrishna as described by Christopher Isherwood. Once Mathur a great devotee of Srī Ramakrishna took him for a pilgrimage to some of the holy places of north western India. Their first stay was made at the shrine of Shiva at Deoghar. In that village Srī Ramakrishna was overcome with compassion for the poverty of the villagers. He said to Mathur, "you are a steward of Mother's estate. Give each one of these people in the village, at least one piece of cloth and one good meal. When Mathur hesitated, Ramakrishna refused, even to discuss the problem, and started shedding tears over the plight of the villagers. "You wretch!" he cried, "I'm not going to Banaras of yours! I'm staying here with these poor people." Finally Mathur yielded and they went on towards Banaras.

This is what Srī Kṛṣṇa means to say in the verse thirty-two: *'atmaupamyena sarvatra samam pasyati yo rjuna sukham va yadi va duhkham'*—seeing the self reflected in the entire creation and sensing the pleasure and pain of others as for himself. Unity in yoga with the Supreme-self reorients the perspective of the individual and the duality disappears. The reason why a yogi can experience such subtlety of cosmic oneness is because of his strong bond with the indwelling-Self. When the love and devotion for God moves in the consciousness of the individual, there are many psychological transformations which are noticed in the behaviour of the person. The individual-self and the universal-Self are indeed one in essence. In meditation when the embodied-self recognizes his essentiality with the Supreme-self; he merges into the oneness and the separation disappears. When the person feels himself consciously being a part of the Omniscient and Omnipresent, he surely beholds himself reflected in others. Cosmic unity takes place automatically. *Atma-aupamya* is indeed the experiential knowledge which initiates the individual to experience equality in everything and everywhere. He perceives his happiness in the happiness of others and embraces the entire creation with the equality of vision in all respects. Srī Kṛṣṇa tells Arjuna that such an individual is never lost to Me; and neither am I lost to him. I live in him and he lives in Me, whatever be the style of his living. This verse reveals the experiential unity in which the individual becomes one with the Supreme and also with the entire current of life. This is the experience of one's own completeness.

अर्जुन उवाच

योऽयं योगस्त्वया प्रोक्तः साम्येन मधुसूदन।
एतस्याहं न पश्यामि चञ्चलत्वात्स्थितिं स्थिराम्॥ ३३॥

yo'yaṁ yogastvayā proktaḥ sāmyena madhūsudana
etasyāhaṁ na paśyāmi cañcalatvātsthitiṁ sthirām

Arjuna said :

(33) This Yoga of equanimity, which has been declared by you, O' Krsna, I don't see that it can be steady and lasting because of the instability of the mind.

चञ्चलं हि मनः कृष्ण प्रमाथि बलवद् दृढम्।
तस्याहं निग्रहं मन्ये वायोरिव सुदुष्करम्॥ ३४॥

cañcalaṁ hi manaḥ kṛṣṇa pramāthi balavad dṛḍham
tasyāhaṁ nigrahaṁ manye vāyoriva suduṣkaram

(34) Mind is very restless O'Kṛṣṇa,—turbulent, powerful and very stubborn. I believe that it is as difficult to control as the wind.

Commentary—Here Arjuna brings forward a natural question. He feels doubtful about the steady continuance of the yoga of equanimity. Arjuna wonders at the possibility of attaining a total control on mind which runs faster than the speed of sound. The power of human mind is enormous. Mind is directly or indirectly attached to every thought and every activity of life. It accepts and rejects the ideas and brings forth various suggestions at every point. In the words of Swami Shivananda, "Mind is compared to a quicksilver because its rays are scattered over various objects. It is compared to a monkey because it jumps from one object to another. It is compared to moving air because it is *chanchala.* It is compared to a rutting furious elephant because of its passionate impetuosity." Arjuna wants to hear from Srī Kṛṣṇa some techniques for culturing the waves of mind. He wants to know more about the means of restraining the restless thoughts.

श्रीभगवानुवाच

असंशयं महाबाहो मनो दुर्निग्रहं चलम्।
अभ्यासेन तु कौन्तेय वैराग्येण च गृह्यते॥ ३५॥

asaṅśayaṁ mahābāho mano durnigrahaṁ calam
abhyāsena tu kaunteya vairāgyeṇa ca gṛhyate

The Blessed Lord said :

(35) Without doubt, O' mighty-armed (Arjuna), the mind is restless, very hard to control; but by practice and by dispassion O' son of Kunti, it can be controlled.

असंयतात्मना योगो दुष्प्राप इति मे मतिः।
वश्यात्मना तु यतता शक्योऽवाप्तुमुपायतः॥ ३६॥

asaṅyatātmanā yogo duṣprāpa iti me matiḥ
vaśyātmanā tu yatatā śakyo'vāptumupāyataḥ

(36) The yoga is indeed very difficult to attain for a person of unrestrained mind—this is My opinion. But for the self-controlled one, who strives ceaselessly, it becomes possible through proper practice.

Commentary—In reply to Arjuna's question, Srī Kṛṣṇa starts the conversation with very pleasant words—sure it is a very difficult task to control the mind but definitely not impossible; the turbulent waves of mind can be controlled with proper practice. The conditioned habits can be brought to awareness and slowly eliminated. The violent, turbulent and stubborn mind can be controlled by repeated and conscious resolute efforts. Gradual practice is for sure the most recommendable means for the achievement of the goal. The mind bound by its inherent nature dwells in those ideas and objects to which it has been attached for some reason. Due to the over-attachment, the mind forms the habit of thinking about the same ideas, over and over again. It is because of these conditioned habits that an individual usually dwells in repeated patterns of worrying over the same thing. With proper analysis the individual can clearly observe that most of the thoughts which are being repeated today are from yesterday or somewhere in past. So at some point the individual has to learn to become aware of the thoughts and actually come out of the self-created web. The key to freedom is to monitor the quality, quantity and the direction of thoughts. Srī Kṛṣṇa agrees with Arjuna that the weaning away of mind from its preoccupied ideas is indeed like enclosing the wind into some boundaries from its natural sway; but slow and steady practice definitely makes everything possible. Consistent practice, sincere efforts and determination can always make even the impossible to be possible. Human potential are enormous and the Supreme-self is indeed more powerful than the human mind. While admitting the difficulty of controlling the mind Srī Kṛṣṇa presents the suggestions of subduing the mind with *abhyasa* and *vairagya*—means practice and dispassion. With repeated contemplation on the Higher-self, as the mind settles in the serenity of the Supreme, it naturally starts withdrawing from the pressure of sensual attractions. When the bonds with the Supreme-self are strengthened, the person's bonds with the sensory pleasure become weak and the *vairagya* (dispassion) takes place automatically. Srī Kṛṣṇa assures Arjuna that controlling of the mind is indeed possible with firm resolution and concentrated practice. Repeated persuasion is the key that locks the mind to the Blissful state of inner unity and unlocks its associations with the material world.

There is a mantra in *Athravaveda* that beautifully describes the powers of determination and resolution. "Gather your abilities O' embodied-self, discard vigilantly the characteristics of the malignant forces and move ahead with resolution, in order to enter into the realms of the absolute glory; only the resolute and steadfast person is the one who wins the battle." By repeated guidance and gradual practice the mind can be brought under conscious control and directed to the desired goal of life. In the process of contemplation, if the mind is not consciously attended, it slips here and there and gets involved into a lot of unnecessary gossip. The individual should train the mind to stay concentrated on the desired words of a mantra or any other form and shape. With constant and regulated practice on the particular words and shape, the mind slowly goes into the gap which lies between the shape and the meditator. It happens slowly and naturally, without the meditator himself being aware of it. As the mind glides into the self-luminous realms of the pure intelligence, it enjoys dwelling in that light and silence. The concentrated mind draws the joy of the Self, learns to enjoy the inner peace and slowly becomes dissipated from the outer world. The joy of the self brings *vairagya, tyaga* and renunciation automatically.

अर्जुन उवाच

अयतिः श्रद्धयोपेतो योगाच्चलितमानसः ।
अप्राप्य योगसंसिद्धिं कां गतिं कृष्ण गच्छति ॥ ३७ ॥

ayatiḥ śraddhayopeto yogāccalitamānsaḥ
aprāpya yogasaṅsiddhiṁ kāṁ gatiṁ kṛṣṇa gacchati

Arjuna said :

(37) He who is endowed with full faith, but is undisciplined and whose mind slips away from yogic communion, having failed to attain perfection in yoga, where does he go? O' Kṛṣṇa.

कच्चिन्नोभयविभ्रष्टश्छिन्नाभ्रमिव नश्यति।
अप्रतिष्ठो महाबाहो विमूढो ब्रह्मणः पथि॥ ३८॥

kaccinnobhayavibhraṣṭaś chinnābhramiva naśyati
apratiṣṭho māhābāho vimūḍho brahmaṇaḥ pathi

(38) Thus, fallen from both, doesn't he perish like a dissipated cloud, O' Kṛṣṇa; lacking firm support and bewildered in the path that leads to the Brahman.

एतन्मे संशयं कृष्ण छेत्तुमर्हस्यशेषतः।
त्वदन्यः संशयस्यास्य छेत्ता न ह्युपपद्यते॥ ३९॥

etanme saṅśayaṁ kṛṣṇa chetturmahasyaśeṣataḥ
tvadanyaḥ saṅśayasyāsya chettā na hyupapadyate

(39) This doubt of mine, O' Kṛṣṇa, Thou shouldst dispel completely; for no one else except You can clear this doubt.

Commentary—In these verses Arjuna brings forth a general question which is usually asked by the aspirants. The path of God realization and liberation is indeed very difficult. Even when the person is endowed with full faith and believes in the validity of truth, still he can slip and stagger while heading towards the accomplishment of his goal. The realization of God which is indeed free of access to everyone, is still attained only by very few in millions. In some cases, in spite of the faithful efforts when the individual doesn't make any worthwhile progress, he becomes very frustrated and withdraws himself from the pursuit. He feels very discouraged, lost and deluded. Arjuna requests for an answer for all this confusion. He wants to know more about the destiny of such an aspirant, whose mind is not properly controlled and due to inadequate efforts who fails to achieve perfection in yoga.

श्रीभगवानुवाच

पार्थ नैवेह नामुत्र विनाशस्तस्य विद्यते।
न हि कल्याणकृत्कश्चिद्दुर्गतिं तात गच्छति॥४०॥

pārtha nāiveha nāmutra vināśastasya vidyate
na hi kalyāṇakṛtkaścid durgatiṁ tāta gacchati

The Blessed Lord said :

(40) O'Arjuna, neither in this world nor hereafter there is any chance of destruction for him; for no one, who does the virtuous deeds ever comes to grief.

प्राप्य पुण्यकृतां लोकानुषित्वा शाश्वतीः समाः।
शुचीनां श्रीमतां गेहे योगभ्रष्टोऽभिजायते॥४१॥

prāpya punyakṛtāṁ lokānuṣitvā śāśvatīḥ samaḥ
śucīnāṁ śrīmatāṁ gehe yogabhraṣṭo'bhijāyate

(41) Having attained to the world of the righteous, and having lived there for countless years; he who has fallen from yoga, is reborn in the family of the virtuous and prosperous.

अथवा योगिनामेव कुले भवति धीमताम्।
एतद्धि दुर्लभतरं लोके जन्म यदीदृशम्॥४२॥

athavā yogināmeva kule bhavati dhīmatām
etaddhi durlabhataraṁ loke janma yadīdṛśam

(42) Or he is born in a family of the enlightened yogins, although this type of birth is very difficult to obtain in this world.

तत्र तं बुद्धिसंयोगं लभते पौर्वदेहिकम्।
यतते च ततो भूयः संसिद्धौ कुरुनन्दन॥४३॥

tatra taṁ buddhisaṅyogaṁ labhate paurvadehikam
yatate ca tato bhūyaḥ saṅsiddhau kurunandana

(43) There, he regains with increased intuition, the knowledge of his previous birth and strives much more than before for perfection, O' Arjuna.

पूर्वाभ्यासेन तेनैव ह्रियते ह्यवशोऽपि सः।
जिज्ञासुरपि योगस्य शब्दब्रह्मातिवर्तते ॥ ४४ ॥

pūrvābhyāsena tenaiva hriyate hyavaśo'pi saḥ
jijñāsurapi yogasya śabdabrahmātivartate

(44) Initiated by the force of his former practice, he is carried on irresistibly. Even if he merely strives to know about yoga, he transcends the Sabad Brahman.

प्रयत्नाद्यतमानस्तु योगी संशुद्धकिल्बिषः।
अनेकजन्मसंसिद्धस्ततो याति परां गतिम् ॥ ४५ ॥

prayatnādyatamānastu yogī sanśuddhakilbiṣaḥ
anekajanmasanśiddhastato yāti parām gatim

(45) The yogi who strives earnestly, he becomes purified from all sins, perfected gradually through many births, he reaches the supreme state.

Commentary—In these verses Srī Kṛṣṇa assures and comforts Arjuna—that the virtue of good work is never lost. The doer of blessed work is always rewarded both in the present life and in the life hereafter. Srī Kṛṣṇa assures with firm conviction about the law of karma—the cause and effect. Any one who fails to achieve perfection in Yoga, still remains destined to reach the state of perfection in the life hereafter. There is no fall for one who slips from yoga because the immediate and the distant future both are the products of the moment in hand. He tells Arjuna that people live under the false impression, that the present life is a complete life and there is nothing beyond this. They forget that the present life has its strings attached with past and to the life hereafter. The present life is not complete in itself; it is just one pause in the eternal continuity of past and future. The present day is an extension of yesterday and it is also stretching its boundaries into the next day onward. Death is not the end of life. It is only a transition; not an absolute annihilation.

According to the law of karma the embodied-self keeps evolving around the *sanskaras* until it finally rests in the Supreme-soul. He assures Arjuna that the efforts made by an individual for self-realization and God-realization can never be wasted. The pursuit of an individual is carried on to his next life. He is reborn in the family of the learned people where he resumes his practice for further progress towards the attainment of the final goal. He is born in a pious and prosperous family that gives him an opportunity for suitable completion of the task which remained incomplete in the previous life. Although living in the midst of all luxuries, he feels irresistibly drawn to the yoga of inner communion, guided by some unknown powers. Such an individual, whether born in a royal family or in the house of a businessman, is intuitively persuaded towards the path of self-realization and God-realization. The intuition compels him to pursue the path of yoga. He regains all knowledge of previous births and makes use of that for the yogic unity in transcendence. If for some reason, he deviates from the path; some unknown power from within keeps reminding him of his goal. The doer of the virtuous deeds is blessed with all the conducive conditions for the completion of his goal. The favourable religious environment in the family helps him in re-establishing which was acquired earlier. The enlightened aspirant does not have to start the yogic practice from the required preliminaries, he continues from the specific status which was reached by him in the previous births. The progressive realization of the Supreme-self is indeed a very difficult task, if not impossible it is surely very difficult to accomplish in the short span of a single life time. The spiritual advancement, which a person makes in one life, definitely accompanies him to the next life and becomes helpful to him for further spiritual progress.

History is full of such illustrations. The spiritual achievement of the great sages like Srī Shankaracharya, Swami Ramakrishna Paramahansa and Swami Vivekananda were not the work of their present life, they were definitely born with unmatched calibre of spiritual inheritance. They were born with spiritual achievements of their many previous lives which inspired them for further spiritual growth in their present lives. Swami Vivekananda was born in a very rich, virtuous, educated and prosperous family. His grandfather was a highly enlightened person. As Ramakrishna used to mention in his conversation, there are eighteen characteristics of Divine power which manifest through human beings at one or the other stage of their life. Out of eighteen, even if two or three are nurtured properly, that can enable the person to become enlightened and earn great name and fame in the field of spirituality. Ramakrishna used to assure Naren (Vivekananda) that he had been blessed with all the eighteen. Vivekananda was indeed born as an enlightened one with heightened awareness. That's why Ramakrishna with his keen spiritual insight could see through the *samskaras* of Naren that the young man was definitely special and stood above the ordinary.

Srī Kṛṣṇa emphasizes the fact that nobody should ever renounce the performance of good deeds. The virtue of good work and yogic practice is never wasted. Whenever it is earned by the individual, it goes into his spiritual treasury and always remains under his custody. Sometimes it may stay dormant for a while, but sooner or later the yogic unity manifests itself on the conscious levels of awareness and guides the individual for the attainment of the goal. The words of Srī Kṛṣṇa are full of assurance, optimism and relief. He gives a message of hope peace and happiness for the frustrated, bewildered, puny mortals. He tells the frustrated human beings that they should not give up their ethics and righteousness under the pressure of unpleasant circumstances. The individual should always respect and uphold Dharma under all situations of life. Virtue of good work is definitely rewarding and always helpful in yogic communication eventually.

The word Sabad-brahman has been used for yogic communication in the verse forty-four. Sabad-brahman stands for the primordial sound AUM, the eternal nada. Its meaning is purely metaphysical and relates directly with the very core of one's existence. In Sabad-brahman lies the essence of the Supreme being, the eternal principle, which has expressed itself in the world around us. The entire creation has originated from the primordial word and from the primordial sound. Transcending the Sabad-brahman means the transcending the bonds of Prakriti. Srī Kṛṣṇa assures that any one who has been inspired by his previous latencies and strives for yogic communion he eventually goes beyond the realm of Sabad-brahman into the unified field of transcendence. He emphasizes that the freedom of the embodied-soul is a journey from less awareness to heightened awareness, from unreal to real, from grosser truth to subtle truth and from bondage to freedom. It is an evolution in which the Supreme-self becomes revealed to the individual step by step slowly and gradually. Whatever spiritual progress is attained at one point, it is carefully watched, recorded and preserved all along. Every individual keeps picking up the scattered pieces wherever they were left in the previous life and puts them together once again in each and every life quite diligently and carefully. The previous efforts definitely motivate and guide the individual for further achievements.

तपस्विभ्योऽधिको योगी ज्ञानिभ्योऽपि मतोऽधिकः।
कर्मिभ्यश्चाधिको योगी तस्माद्योगी भवार्जुन ॥ ४६ ॥

tapasvibhyo'dhiko yogī jñānibhyo'pi mato'dhikaḥ
karmibhyaścādhiko yogī tasmādyogī bhavā'rjuna

(46) The yogi is thought to be more revered than the ascetic, he is considered to be greater than the man of knowledge; yogi is indeed superior to those who perform ritualistic actions. Therefore, Arjuna you be a yogi.

योगिनामपि सर्वेषां मद्गतेनान्तरात्मना।
श्रद्धावान्भजते यो मां स मे युक्ततमो मतः ॥ ४७ ॥

yogināmapi sarveṣāṁ madgatenāntarātmanā
śraddhāvānbhajate yo māṁ sa me yuktatamo mataḥ

(47) Among all the yogis, he who worships Me with full faith and devotion, with his mind focused on Me, I consider him to be the most devout yogi.

Commentary—In these two verses Srī Kṛṣṇa concludes the conversation with special emphasis on the supremacy of Yoga. He exhorts Arjuna to become a devoted yogi. The word Yoga, as described earlier, has been derived from the Sanskrit word 'yuj', which literally means union, communion and communication with the Supreme. Yoga is living in the consciousness of the inner self. It is like living a life totally soaked in the nature of the Divine. Srī Kṛṣṇa considers this state of perpetual connectedness with the indweller, to be far better than all the austerities, the scriptural knowledge and the performance of all the rituals. The word *Tapasvi* stands for the one who is practising severe penances and austerities. The penances are generally done for the purification of the body and mind. The austerities make the mind very receptive to the voice of the inner self. Sometime people get involved in the rigidity of penances, and the austerity itself becomes a cause of bondage, instead of being a source of liberation. The ascetic becomes involved in obtaining the supernatural powers and gets caught in the bonds of mere show-off. The man who pursues the scriptural knowledge only, he has an unfortunate chance of becoming a victim to egoism and braggery. Scriptures are indeed a great source of information, inspiration and intellectual growth but for the real spiritual growth the person has to form the habit of living in yoga more than anything else. In the words of Swami Ramakrishna, "What is the good of mere book learning? The learned may at best be adapt in aptly and accurately quoting from scriptures. One's lifelong repeating them verbatim affects no change in one's life. But what is told in the scriptures has to be applied to life and improvement brought on it".

Ritualism and asceticism both are indeed good for the pursuit of spiritual growth, and are surely good for maintaining self-discipline and self-purification. The prescribed rituals in scriptures have been written by the sages who were guided by the light of Self. The reason why Srī Kṛṣṇa is announcing the supremacy of Yoga over everything else is because until and unless one learns to live in the consciousness of the Divine, it is natural for anyone to slip from the path of spiritual growth. The performance of rituals, the disciplined dietary habits, the moral observances, the charitable deeds, the severe penances, yajñas and other ceremonial worships, each one of these do play a very significant role in the process of self purification; only if practised with unity in Yoga. In the last verse of this chapter Srī Kṛṣṇa makes it very clear that the yogi who worships Me with his mind totally focused on Me, is definitely considered to be the best in Yoga. The Yoga of devotion transcends all the other methods and it is superior to all penances, scriptural knowledge and performance of rituals.

Srī Kṛṣṇa is constantly glorifying the devotee who worships the Lord with loving devotion. The words *sraddhavan bhajate yo mam*— who worships Me with reverence, love and faith. *Sraddha* is not blind faith, it is the spirit of honest appreciation and loving devotion for the Supreme. *Sraddha* is the upholding of truth with revered appreciation for it. The word *Sraddha* is the combination of two words—*shrat* and *dha. Shrat* means root or truth and *dha* means to uphold, maintain or support. So *sraddha* means to uphold and support the truth as understood by the individual. It is cherished at the heart centre and upheld by firm devotion. The reason why Srī Kṛṣṇa is emphasizing upon the word *sraddha* is because it promotes the stability of loving devotion for God and it enhances the love and heartfelt appreciation for God. It helps the individual to develop spiritual intimacy and strengthens his bond with the Supreme-self. When the mind develops spiritual love, the individual lives in Yoga, works through Yoga, and communicates with others through the serenity of Yoga. All his activities are guided from the purity of the Self. A yogi achieves a state of heightened consciousness. The practice of yoga makes the person very alert, active, diligent and intuitive. Yoga helps the individual to manifest the very best of his abilities. The person attains better understanding of his own self and of other people. He develops a harmonious interaction with others. Yoga which is attained through loving devotion and contemplation has been upheld in great reverence by Srī Kṛṣṇa. A yogi's life is gracious, glorious and becomes an example for others. Srī Kṛṣṇa exhorts Arjuna to become a yogi in order to achieve the very best in human life and in the life hereafter.

ॐ तत्सदिति श्रीमद्भगवद्गीतासूपनिषत्सु ब्रह्मविद्यायां
योगशास्त्रे श्रीकृष्णार्जुनसंवादे ध्यानयोगो
नाम षष्ठोऽध्यायः ॥ ६ ॥

'Aum' tatsaditi Śrīmadbhagawadgeetā sūpaniṣatsu
brahmavidyāyām yogaśāstre Śrīkṛṣṇārjunasamvāde
dhyānayogo nāma ṣaṣṭho'dhyāyaḥ

'AUM TAT SAT'—Thus, in the Upanishad of the glorious Bhagawad Geeta, the science of the Brahman (Absolute) the scripture of yoga, the dialogue between Srī Kṛṣṇa and Arjuna—thus, ends the chapter six entitled *"Dhyānayoga"*.

इति श्रीमद्भगवद्गीतासु षष्ठोऽध्यायः ॥ ६ ॥

Chapter Seven

JÑĀNAVIJÑĀNAYOGA

THE YOGA OF WISDOM AND KNOWLEDGE

श्रीभगवानुवाच

मय्यासक्तमनाः पार्थ योगं युञ्जन्मदाश्रयः।
असंशयं समग्रं मां यथा ज्ञास्यसि तच्छृणु॥ १॥

mayyāsaktamanāḥ pārtha yogaṁ yuñjan madāsrayaḥ
asaṅśayaṁ samagraṁ māṁ yathā jñasyasi tacchṛṇu

The Blessed Lord said :

(1) With your mind focused on Me, O' Arjuna, and taking refuge in Me through the practice of yoga—listen, how you can know Me, for sure in My entirety.

ज्ञानं तेऽहं सविज्ञानमिदं वक्ष्याम्यशेषतः।
यज्ज्ञात्वा नेह भूयोऽन्यज्ज्ञातव्यमवशिष्यते॥ २॥

jñānaṁ te'haṁ savijñānamidaṁ vakṣyāmyaśeṣataḥ
yajjñātvā ne'ha bhūyo'nyajjñātavyam avaśiṣyate

(2) I shall teach you in detail the wisdom alongwith the experiential knowledge which makes it distinguished; having known which nothing else remains to be known.

मनुष्याणां सहस्रेषु कश्चिद्यतति सिद्धये।
यततामपि सिद्धानां कश्चिन्मां वेत्ति तत्त्वतः॥ ३॥

manuṣyānāṁ sahasreṣu kaścid yatati siddhaye
yatatāmapi siddhānāṁ kaścinmāṁ vetti tattvataḥ

(3) Among thousands of men, scarcely one strives for perfection; and those who strive and attain perfection, scarcely there is one, who knows Me in essence.

Commentary—This chapter is a continuation of the concept of Yoga where Srī Kṛṣṇa uses the terms such as *yogam yunjanmadasrayah. Yogam* is living in the awareness of the Divine and *yunjan* is the conscious acceptance of that fact. In the case of *yunjanmadasrayah*, the aspirant takes refuge in yogic unity and actually develops an affinity, a liking and love for the association with the Divine, and in the process of his developing attachment to the Supreme, the detachment from the world takes place automatically. As the intimacy with the indweller strengthens, a unique relationship is established and the grace of Divine springs forth from the hidden resources. *Shruti Bhagwati* declares, "when the mind is purified and the resolve is firm, then all the knots of conflicting emotions are released and the knowledge of the Supreme becomes revealed to the individual".

In these verses Srī Kṛṣṇa unfolds to Arjuna the knowledge of the Self alongwith the knowledge of the manifested Divinity. He emphasizes upon the fact that the Divine and the manifestation of the Divine are not separate from one another. Both are very intimately connected. It is the knowledge of the Supreme-self which unfolds the mysteries about other branches of knowledge; such as the physical self, the psychological self and the spiritual self. It is through the art of developing a communion with the Supreme-self, the embodied self becomes enlightened in due time. It is the intimacy with the indwelling Supreme-soul, which marks the fundamental basis for the acquaintance with everything that exists within and without. A similar kind of statement has been made by Rishi Udalaka to his son Savetaketu 'Know, by knowing which everything else is known'. The similar type of words do occur in 'Mandukya Upanishad' *"kasmin bhagavo vijnate sarvam idam vijantam bhavati"*. Srī Kṛṣṇa uses the terms jñana and vijñana—jñana is the spiritual knowledge which is attained through the study of the sacred books and also through the lessons imparted by an accomplished teacher. This is called *paroksha jñana.* The vijñaa is visesha jñana which means the experiential knowledge obtained through inner intuitional wisdom and self-realization. Vijñana is also called the *aparoksha jñana*. Srī Kṛṣṇa declares that when an aspirant takes refuge in the Supreme-soul, the individual is blessed with the knowledge of real and unreal; also the nature of unmanifest and manifest Divinity. So, in order to understand the Supreme-self as the manifested Divinity, one needs to start from within, the spiritual-self. In general, people start their inquiry from the gross to the subtle, from matter to the spirit. In that process of scientific inquiry, it is very hard to comprehend the truth, because after some solutions, the answers themselves become the questions. On the other hand when the aspirant moves from the subtle to the gross, the exploration of the manifested Divinity becomes very easy. Srī Kṛṣṇa emphasizes the necessity of understanding both aspects in order to realize the unique oneness that prevails in the universe. The inner and the outer must blend in order to understand the underlying Absolute-truth.

In the third verse Srī Kṛṣṇa tells Arjuna that the knowledge of the indwelling Divinity, although free of access to the entire mankind, is only pursued by the few. Out of millions and many millions, scarcely a few strive for God realization; and out of those real aspirants hardly there is only one, who perceives some glimpses of Me and only one out of those, who knows Me in reality. There is a saying in *Kathoupanishad, "...Uthishthat jagrat prapya varaninbodhataa, kshurasya dhara nishita duratya, durgam pathastat kavyo vadanti...",* Arise, awake and achieve which is yours, with the help of those who have experienced the truth; the wise proclaim that the path for God-realization is sharp like an edge of a razor and hard to step on.

भूमिरापोऽनलो वायुः खं मनो बुद्धिरेव च।
अहङ्कार इतीयं मे भिन्ना प्रकृतिरष्टधा॥ ४॥
bhūmirāpo'nalo vāyuḥ khaṁ mano buddhireva ca
ahaṅkāra itīyaṁ me bhinnā prakṛtiraṣṭadhā
अपरेयमितस्त्वन्यां प्रकृतिं विद्धि मे पराम्।
जीवभूतां महाबाहो ययेदं धार्यते जगत्॥ ५॥
apareyam itastvanyāṁ prakṛtiṁ viddhi me parām
jīvabhūtāṁ mahābāho yayedaṁ dhāryate jagat

(4, 5) Earth, Water, Fire, Air, Ether, Mind, Intellect and Ego, this is the division of My eight-fold Prakrti (Nature). This is My lower

Nature, and other than this is My transcendental Nature. It is the life-element, O'Arjuna, by which this universe is sustained.

एतद्योनीनि भूतानि सर्वाणीत्युपधारय।
अहं कृत्स्नस्य जगतः प्रभवः प्रलयस्तथा ॥ ६ ॥

etad yonīni bhūtāni sarvāṇītyupadhāraya
ahaṁ kṛtsnasya jagataḥ prabhavaḥ pralayastathā

(6) Know, that all the created beings have evolved from this two-fold nature. I am the origin of the whole universe, as well as the dissolution.

मत्तः परतरं नान्यत्किञ्चिदस्ति धनञ्जय।
मयि सर्वमिदं प्रोतं सूत्रे मणिगणा इव ॥ ७ ॥

mattaḥ parataraṁ nānyat kiñcid asti dhanañjaya
mayi sarvamidaṁ protaṁ sūtre maṇigaṇā iva

(7) There is nothing else besides Me, O'Arjuna. Everything is strung on Me, like the clusters of gems on a string.

Commentary—In these verses Srī Kṛṣṇa is introducing to Arjuna various aspects of manifest and unmanifest Divinity. He knows that in order to understand the subtle nature of the indwelling Divinity, it is very important to understand the difference between the twofold aspects of the divine nature. He explains the separate characteristic of the apparent aspects of Divine nature and how it relates to the unmanifested. Srī Kṛṣṇa starts with the manifest Divinity which is eight-fold, such as earth, water, fire, air, ether, mind, intellect, and egoism. This eight-fold nature constitute the human body and the bodies of the other creatures. This is known as the *apara prakriti;* also in other words the gross manifestation. Beyond the gross is the subtle nature of the Divine known as *para prakriti,* which forms the essence of everything. He further adds that the entire universe has its origin into two prakritis, which have their origination in Me; I am Myself the origin and the dissolution of the entire universe. Shridhara Swami explains the verse in these words, "The inert prakriti evolves the body. The Sentient Prakriti, which is a part of Me, enters into all bodies as the experiencer and sustains them through its work. These two prakrities of Mine are born of Me." *Shruti Bhagwati* has also declared that this two-fold nature, the matter and the self form the aggregate of all beings, having the Supreme-soul as their source. In reference to this Swami Tapasyananda has described this concept in these words, 'The *para* and *apara prakritis* of the Lord are eternally expressing as the cyclic process of time consisting in kalpa or a period of manifestation, and pralaya or a period of dissolution. They come into being through a process of evolution, and dissolve into the original state through a process of involution. This alternation goes on eternally'.

The Supreme-self, the essence of all life, is indeed the creator, the sustainer and the annihilator of the entire creation. Srī Kṛṣṇa declares that O'Arjuna there is nothing beyond Me, and besides Me. The entire creation is threaded in Me, on Me and around Me like the rows of beads. He declares Himself to be the thread running through the entire creation. The life principle of animate and inanimate, the gross and subtle, the apparent and hidden, the material and non-material, the real and unreal. In other words, everything manifest or unmanifest is essentially the nature of the Divine. The entire universe is held together by the supreme Lord Himself. As the thread running through the cluster of beads, remains unseen, so is the Supreme Lord, while holding and sustaining everything, remains unseen to the mortal eyes. In order to comprehend the omniscience of the Lord, the individual has to understand the nature of both the material and the spiritual-self. It is only with the proper understanding of both, that the individual can understand the distinction between them and learn to identify himself with the real. The pure consciousness is the power behind all the apparent powers, life behind all apparent life forms, the beauty behind everything which appears to be beautiful and peace whatever appears to be peaceful. Forming an acquaintance with that reality which is at the root of the entire manifestation, is like becoming acquainted with everything else within and without. The omniscience of the Supreme-Lord is the only truth that prevails at the heart of the entire creation.

रसोऽहमप्सु कौन्तेय प्रभाऽस्मि शशिसूर्ययोः ।
प्रणवः सर्ववेदेषु शब्दः खे पौरुषं नृषु ॥ ८ ॥

raso'hamapsu kaunteya prabhā'smi śaśisūryayoḥ
praṇavaḥ sarvavedeṣu śabdaḥ khe pauruṣaṁ nṛṣu

(8) I am the taste in water, O'Arjuna. I am the radiance in the moon and in the sun. I am the sacred syllable 'AUM' in all the Vedas; sound in the ether and virility in men.

पुण्यो गन्धः पृथिव्यां च तेजश्चास्मि विभावसौ।
जीवनं सर्वभूतेषु तपश्चास्मि तपस्विषु॥ ९॥

puṇyo gandhaḥ pṛthivyāṁ ca tejaścāsmi vibhāvasau
jīvanaṁ sarvabhūteṣu tapasca'śmi tapasviṣu

(9) I am the pure fragrance in the earth and the brilliance in the fire. I am the life in all beings, and austerity in ascetics.

बीजं मां सर्वभूतानां विद्धि पार्थ सनातनम्।
बुद्धिर्बुद्धिमतामस्मि तेजस्तेजस्विनामहम्॥ १०॥

bījaṁ māṁ sarvabhūtānāṁ viddhi pārtha sanātanam
buddhir buddhimatāmasmi tejas tejasvināmaham

(10) Know Me, to be the eternal seed of all beings, O'Arjuna. I am the intelligence of the intelligent and the brilliance of the brilliant.

बलं बलवतां चाहं कामरागविवर्जितम्।
धर्माविरुद्धो भूतेषु कामोऽस्मि भरतर्षभ॥ ११॥

balaṁ balavatāṁ cāhaṁ kāmarāgavivarjitam
dharmāviruddho bhūteṣu kāmo'smi bhartarṣabha

(11) Of the strong, I am the strength, which is devoid of passion and attachment; in all beings I am that desire, which is not opposed by Dharma (righteousness) O'Arjuna.

Commentary—Going from gross to subtle, Srī Kṛṣṇa explains to Arjuna that everything in the universe is endowed with some unique characteristics. It is that uniqueness which makes it special and separates it from the rest. This particular quality of that object, which differentiates it from the rest and makes it very special, is indeed the splendour of the Divine which forms the source of the universe and remains veiled from the vision of the human beings. Srī Kṛṣṇa explains to Arjuna the various levels of manifestations from the grossest to the subtlest. He wants his disciple to become aware that all the specific qualities are various attributes of the one and the only Supreme-soul.

He starts with the five components such as earth, water, ether, fire and air. He tells Arjuna that the sapidity in water, the radiance in the moon and sun, the sacred syllable AUM in the *Vedic mantras,* sound in ether, virility in men, the sweet fragrance in earth, the brilliance in fire, the life force in all beings, the austerity which distinguishes the ascetics from the rest—everything manifests itself as the special attribute of the Lord. In order to make the point more clear Srī Kṛṣṇa declares that He is the eternal seed of all beings, the essence of life. He continues that He is the intelligence of the intelligents, the glory of the glorious and the splendour of the splendid, and He is the integrity that protects one from over-attachment and going against the Sanatan Dharma. In these verses the emphasized fact is that any unique characteristic of anything is only the expression of the Divine power inherent in that. Ultimate power manifests itself in various forms and shapes. *Ekodevah sarvabhutesu gudhah sarvavyapi sarvabhutan tantaratma,* one Supreme Lord, all pervading the inner self of all. There is another saying in Upanishad *"eak eva hi bhutama, bhute bhute vavasthita, ekdha buhuda chavie drishayate jal chander vat",* one Supreme Lord manifesting in various forms and shapes appears to be different as the reflection of moon appears different in separate water bodies. Just as the reality of reflection is moon so the reality of this manifestation is God. Srī Kṛṣṇa also mentions *pranavah sarvavedesu* I am the sacred syllable AUM in the Vedas. It is known as the Beej mantra; it is the primordial sound that envelops the entire creation. Taittreya Upnishad describes, *"AUM Iti Brahman, AUM Iti Idam Sarvam"*—AUM is the essence of everything around and everything is the manifestation of AUM. According to Bhartrihari, a great scholar of India, "The mantra AUM is identified as the root mantra. Out of which all mantras arise. The sacred syllable is held to have flashed forth into the heart of Brahma while absorbed in deep meditation and to have given birth to Vedas that contain all knowledge."

The same concept has been supported by *Mandukya Upanishad: "omityetadksharmind sarv tasyopavyakhyan bootam bhavbhavishya-diti sarvamonkar ave".* "The holy syllable AUM is indeed the imperishable Brahman and the universe is the exposition of His glory. AUM is all what existed in the past, whatever exists now and whatever will exist in the future." AUM represents the sound energy of the universe. As pronounced, it starts from the back of the throat, fills the mouth and closes the lips with M. The fourth element is the silence. Silence out of which the sound emerges, which underlies it and into which it goes. Concentration on the sound of AUM opens the secret doorway in the heart centre and connects one to the indwelling supreme-self. Also at the same time it connects one with the throbbing being that pervades in the entire universe. The philologists believe that all the vowels have originated from AUM, and have asserted very strongly that if one concentrates and repeats the vowels for a few minutes, like A E I O U, the sound of AUM can be heard resonating very clearly. The consonants are considered to be the images and reflections of the primordial sound. AUM is considered to be the source of all the alphabets in Sanskrit and the source of all the languages. In the words of Srī Aurobindo, "AUM is the universal formulation of the energy of sound and speech, that which contains and sums up, synthesizes and releases, all the spiritual power and all the potentiality of Vak and Shabda". According to *Mandukya Upanishad* AUM symbolizes the triads in time and space. The three syllables of AUM symbolizes the three stages everybody goes through everyday. 'A' symbolizes the waking stage (conscious level), 'U' describes the sleeping stage and 'M' stands for dream stage. When written in Sanskrit, there is a curved line on the top which stands for dreamless sleep—deep sleep; when the individual-soul merges into the universal-soul. The dot on the curved line represents the Supreme Divinity in us. This stage is known as *turiya* in meditation which is beyond the three levels of consciousness. Three syllables also personify the three stages of evolution in the universe. A stands for *adimata* (beginning), U stands for *utkarsha* (sustenance) and M stands for *mitti* (annhilation). It also describes *akara, ukara* and *makra*—combine together *omkara*. This means that everything we see in the universe is going through an evolution. It comes into existence, it is sustained for a while and then it is annihilated. Everything is enclosed within the grasp of the swift moving time. Meditation on the holy syllable AUM, enables one to get in touch with the various stages of consciousness and experience the reality of the world. The primordial sound of AUM is called the *nada*. It is the sound which can be heard and contemplated upon with concentration in the heart centre. Srī Kṛṣṇa glorifies the sacred syllable pranava while giving a description of His specific manifestations. He makes it very clear to Arjuna that all these entities with their specific characteristics have originated from Me alone. The entire universe exists in Me. He winds up the topic by declaring "I am indeed the primeval seed of the entire creation."

ये चैव सात्त्विका भावा राजसास्तामसाश्च ये।
मत्त एवेति तान्विद्धि न त्वहं तेषु ते मयि॥ १२॥

ye cai'va sātvikā bhāvā rājasāstāmasāśca ye
matta eve'ti tān viddhi na tvahaṁ teṣu te mayi

(12) Know that all those states of *sattva, rajas* and *tamas* originate from Me alone. I am not in them yet, they are in Me.

त्रिभिर्गुणमयैर्भावैरेभिः सर्वमिदं जगत्।
मोहितं नाभिजानाति मामेभ्यः परमव्ययम्॥ १३॥

tribhir guṇamayair bhāvairebhiḥ sarvamidaṁ jagat
mohitaṁ nābhijānāti māmebhyaḥ paramavyayam

(13) The whole world is deluded by these three qualities originating from the Prakirti (Nature), and fails to recognize Me; who is beyond them and imperishable.

दैवी ह्येषा गुणमयी मम माया दुरत्यया।
मामेव ये प्रपद्यन्ते मायामेतां तरन्ति ते॥ १४॥

daivī hyeṣā guṇamayī mama māyā duratyayā
māmeva ye prapadyante māyāmetāṁ taranti te

(14) The Divine illusion (Maya) of Mine consisting of three qualities *(gunas)* of nature is very difficult to transcend. However, those who take refuge in Me alone, cross over this illusion (Maya).

न मां दुष्कृतिनो मूढाः प्रपद्यन्ते नराधमाः।
माययापहृतज्ञाना आसुरं भावमाश्रिताः॥ १५॥

na māṁ duṣkṛtino mūḍhāḥ prapadyante narādhamāḥ
māyayāphṛtajñānā āsuraṁ bhāvamāsritāḥ

(15) The evil-doers, deluded and the lowest among men do not seek refuge in Me; being deluded by the illusive nature (Maya), they lack proper knowledge and follow the ways of the demons.

Commentary—These verses are the continuation of the declaration made by Srī Kṛṣṇa in the previous verses; there is nothing as such that exists besides Me and beyond Me, the entire creation is threaded on Me as the clusters of yarn beads formed by knots on a thread. As in the necklace of the yarn beads there is nothing besides the thread, so in the universe there is nothing besides the Supreme Lord Himself. Srī Kṛṣṇa is using the word Maya for His Divine manifestation, which originates from the triads of mother nature. The three aspects of nature evolve around the variety of thoughts known as *sattvic, rajsik* and *tamsik.* The three gunas act as instruments for the expression of the thinking faculty. Human behaviour revolves around the expression of these three gunas. In the words of Srī Ramanuja, "When nature comes into the fullness of actualization, its sway on the Purusha, the Jivas still under the bondage to matter, is established in full swing. Prakriti deludes them into self forgetfulness and they look upon Prakriti as all in all. Their consciousness is suppressed into a materialistic mould and the Supreme power of which, Prakriti itself is a lower mode is concealed effectively. In matter the bound Jiva perceives the whole of reality and the whole of value. Nature traps the soul in many forms, as the object of enjoyment, as the body, as the senses and the subtle forces operative in less cognizable ways. The principle consequence of this enslavement is the loss of the vision of God."

The trifold Nature has its origin in the Supreme and is sustained by the Supreme. Human behaviour, impulses, liking and disliking are controlled by the triads of nature. People under the slavery of the gunas (trifold nature) create false values for themselves, those conceal the Supreme truth that lies beyond the perception of senses. In the words of Fichte, "Our seeing itself hides the object we see; our eye itself impedes our eye." Srī Kṛṣṇa has used the word Maya for the illusive expression of the Divine potency. The word has also been used in Upanishads, "the primordial nature is known as Maya and the controller is the Supreme Lord Himself." In the *Ramayana* also it is described as *"go gocher jaha lagi man jai yo sab Maya janeo bhai"*— as far as the eyes can see, it is indeed the expression of the primordial nature. In the words of Swami Sivananda, "Maya is the upadhi of Iswara. It is the material cause of the universe. It is constituted of the three gunas". People all over the world are living their lives, conditioned with the illusive power of Maya. It controls the human mind, senses and intellect. Maya attracts the individual with various temptations and deludes his faculty of discrimination. The person becomes its victim quite unknowingly and unconsciously. Subordination of the individual-self, to the play of the gunas such as *satvic, rajas* and *tamas* is Maya. For example, over-attachment to the worldly objects and hoping them to remain permanent is living under the illusive play of Maya. In reference to this there is an illustration in the *Mahabharata,* where Yaksha asks a question to Yudhishtra "What is the greatest surprise in the world?" Yudhishtra answered, "Every moment people are dying and departing from the world and yet those who are alive think as they will never die." Everyone knows the truth of life and death but still clings to everything he possesses. People usually forget that their sojourn in the world is very limited, and each and everyone has to depart, still nobody likes to talk about death. They want to escape from the truth and avoid the topic. This is Maya—the spell of Maya. Over-attachment and the feeling of possessiveness is surely due to the spell of Maya. Srī Kṛṣṇa is emphasizing this truth with the phrase: *"Mam mayadureataya"*. It is the snare of Maya that conditions the unconditioned pure self into his limited identity, the infinite into the boundaries of finite.

The play of Maya is all round us and the people are falling into its trap, one after the other. Srī Kṛṣṇa suggests a solution which can help the individual to escape its snare. The solution is total surrender to the Divine. *"Mam eva ye prapdyante mayam etam taranti te"*— those who seek refuge in Me alone they get the strength and insight to cross the traps of all illusions. Love and adoration for the inner Divinity helps them to develop detachment from the material world.

Those who are firmly established in the joy of the Supreme-self, for them the enjoyments of the material world surely become immaterial. They can see beyond the veil of Maya and perceive the permanent joy, which originates in their association with the Supreme Bliss. Their undivided devotion brings spontaneous help from the Lord and they are liberated from the traps of conditioned life ruled by Maya. The moment when the person stops following the shadow of Maya, it vanishes for him and he becomes emancipated from its tricks and treats.

In verse fifteen, Srī Kṛṣṇa gives some glimpses of the people who remain strongly enslaved by the snare of the illusive nature. They become emotionally disturbed and fragmented. These people may appear wealthy and prosperous on surface but they become spiritually poor. These deluded men of meagre understanding follow the ways of demons. Due to the lack of proper insight they fall into the traps of immoral activities and illegal decisions. Srī Kṛṣṇa calls them *'mudhah'* and *'duskrtino'*. Mudhahs are the foolish people, those who don't care for themselves and for others. These deluded ones take enjoyment in falsehood, deceit, robbery and other atrocious deeds. Their ethics are low and they live a very selfish life. Such individuals talk about their disbelief in God, out of their false vanity and egoism. They prefer sensual happiness over ethics. Srī Kṛṣṇa tells that these foolish and vile men of evil thoughts do not adore Me and live a life dominated by the demoniac nature.

चतुर्विधा भजन्ते मां जनाः सुकृतिनोऽर्जुन।
आर्तो जिज्ञासुरर्थार्थी ज्ञानी च भरतर्षभ॥ १६॥

caturvidhā bhajante māṁ janāḥ sukṛtino'rjuna
ārto jijñāsurarthārthī jñānī ca bharatarṣabha

(16) Four kinds of virtuous men worship Me, O'Arjuna. These are the distressed, the seeker of knowledge, the seeker of wealth, and the man of wisdom O'Bharata.

तेषां ज्ञानी नित्ययुक्त एकभक्तिर्विशिष्यते।
प्रियो हि ज्ञानिनोऽत्यर्थमहं स च मम प्रियः॥ १७॥

teṣāṁ jñānī nityayukta ekabhaktir viśiṣyate
priyo hi jñānino'tyarthamahaṁ sa ca mama priyaḥ

(17) Of these, the man of wisdom, who is ever united with Me in yoga, through single minded-devotion, is the foremost. I am extremely dear to the man of wisdom and he too is very dear to Me.

उदाराः सर्व एवैते ज्ञानी त्वात्मैव मे मतम्।
आस्थितः स हि युक्तात्मा मामेवानुत्तमां गतिम्॥ १८॥

udārāḥ sarva evaite jñānī tvātmaiva me matam
āsthitaḥ sa hi yuktātmā māmevānuttamāṁ gatim

(18) All these are noble indeed, but the man of wisdom I regard to be My very Self; for he is steadfast, ever united in the Self, and has resorted to Me alone as the Supreme goal.

बहूनां जन्मनामन्ते ज्ञानवान्मां प्रपद्यते।
वासुदेवः सर्वमिति स महात्मा सुदुर्लभः॥ १९॥

bahūnāṁ janmanām ante jñānavān māṁ prapadyate
vāsudevaḥ sarvamiti sa mahātmā sudurlabhaḥ

(19) At the end of many births, the man of wisdom seeks refuge in Me alone, realizing that 'Vasudeva is all.' It is indeed very difficult to find such a great soul (Mahatma).

Commentary—In these verses, Srī Kṛṣna tells Arjuna that there are four kinds of virtuous people who worship Me. By using the word *sukrtino,* he qualifies, upholds and appreciates all of them. He appreciates every one of them, whatever may be the motive or the mode of their worship. He starts with the distressed one, who becomes afflicted and suffers from some physical and emotional agony. Even in distress, when a man approaches the Divine with a genuine appeal for recovery and inner strength, the help definitely comes. An honest prayer is bound to bring recovery with special blessings. It blesses the individual with an experience of love and compassion, humility and gratitude. A person has two choices in the time of adversity, one is to complain, blame, fret and fume, and run into an argument with God. The other is to take refuge in the Divine with faith and humility.

When the person takes refuge in God, it opens a doorway for him, that leads to the source of peace and endurance. The positive energy is withdrawn from the inner resources and it enlightens the person in all respects. The inner strength helps the individual to develop respect for suffering, instead of complaining and blaming others. The person learns to deal with the problems with a positive attitude and courage. Instead of demanding attention and pity from others, he learns to educate himself with the help of God. His brief contact with the source of strength gives him such an insight, which is incomparable to any external treatment. The positive strength which comes in short flashes, eventually helps him in self-realization. The second category of God worshippers is the person who worships in order to get his desires fulfilled. This person is the seeker of wealth and worldly enjoyments. His aim in life is to amass wealth from all sources, his love and devotion for God is indeed also very conditional and selfish. Although his desires are very personal but still he is helped by the Lord because he takes refuge in Him for help. God blesses him with insight to make more money and be successful in business. Such type of devotion to God, although conditional, is also good. Such a devotee is not spiritually enlightened, but still better than those egoists who out of their vanity don't pray to God at all and also never feel thankful for the Divine's blessings.

The third type of devotees are the seekers of knowledge. Such aspirants are totally dedicated to the desire to acquire knowledge of various branches of education. Such a person is always insatiate for more and more knowledge. He has a keen desire to get enlightened about physical, material, psychological and spiritual realms of knowledge. He is very inquisitive, very hard working and very knowledgeable. Such a devotee is also appreciated and helped by the Divine because the Lord knows very well that in the process of intellectual inquiry his devotee is actually pursuing the path of self-discovery. In due course of time, he is blessed with heightened intuition and can separate the spiritual world from the material, the real from the unreal, the perishable from the imperishable.

The fourth type of devotee is the man of wisdom, who loves and adores the Supreme Lord out of his affinity and friendship. The man of wisdom is highly enlightened and can well differentiate real from the unreal. Such an aspirant enjoys the association of the Divine and his devotion is very firm and undivided. He seeks refuge in God because he finds spontaneous satisfaction only in the association of God. The man of wisdom seeks an intimate relationship with God through Yoga and constant awareness. His devotion is one-pointed and undivided and far above any selfish motives. He calls upon God out of his love and adoration and just because he likes to work as an instrument of God. Srī Kṛṣṇa declares all of them to be noble and virtuous, but the man of wisdom to be his very favourite friend, because the aspirant loves Him for His sake only. Srī Kṛṣṇa goes to the extent of saying that the man of wisdom is very dear to Me and I am dear to Him; he is verily My own self because he has resorted in the supreme-Self as his highest goal of life. Seeking the supreme-Self as the highest goal is indeed rare and very difficult, resorting to God out of pleasure and enjoyment is also very rare. Loving the self for the self's sake is also very rare. Human history has some examples of such devotees. The great devotees Dhruva, Prahalada, Tulsidass, Surdass and Meerabai sacrificed all royal comforts in the loving pursuit of the Supreme God. Their love and devotion has been indeed one-pointed, determined and very steadfast.

The embodied-soul's journey from one birth to another is evolutionary. Srī Kṛṣṇa has assured Arjuna in the previous chapter that the virtue of good work is never lost. It is saved, preserved and it appears in the following births where the individual is again guided by the *samskaras* of his previous birth. The soul's journey is a constant progression, moving from less awareness to increased awareness, from less intuitive wisdom to heightened intuition. In the words of Swami Vivekananda, "In plants the obstacle to the soul's manifestation is very high; in animals a little less; and in men still less; in cultured, spiritual men still less and in the men of perfection the obstacle vanishes all together." He further adds, "The pleasures of the Self is what the world calls religion."

The insignia of evolution, which distinguishes the human from the animals, is the increased awareness of the Self. Human life is considered to be a great gift of the Divine because in human life the individual is born fully equipped with subjective awareness. He can perceive and experience his essential nature. The relationship formed with inner-self in one life-time is like one step towards the goal of realization. Each step in life contributes towards the evolutionary journey. The previous good *samskaras* become very helpful towards the performance of virtuous deeds in the present life. As the association with the Lord strengthens, the goal of self-realization comes closer and closer; and at the end of many births the individual is blessed with God realization; and perceives *"Vasudeva sarvam iti"*—Vasudeva is all. Here Vasudeva stands for the Supreme consciousness which presides over the cause, space and time; and also transcends all. The God-realized individual comprehends the fundamental essentiality; that the omniscience of the Lord is the only truth, which lies at the heart of the entire creation. He seeks refuge in Vasudeva—persues Him as the highest goal and also the means to attain his goal. He rises above the limitations of the limited embodied-self and perceives himself to be a part of the Cosmic-self. His mind works in unity with the universal mind and his heart expands its horizon in all directions. He feels himself a fragment of the entire universe and helps others as if they are a fragment of his ownself. Srī Kṛṣṇa calls such an individual a Mahatma which literally means a noble and virtuous soul; who stands above the rest of the crowd, and who becomes an embodiment of the Divine. The consciousness of the Cosmic-self *(Vasudeva sarvam iti)* is an experience, crystalized by the individual in two distinct ways. In one, he reduces his individual-self to zero and merges into the oneness of the universal-self; and in the other, he encloses within himself the entire universe.

कामैस्तैस्तैर्हृतज्ञानाः प्रपद्यन्तेऽन्यदेवताः ।
तं तं नियममास्थाय प्रकृत्या नियताः स्वया ॥ २० ॥

kāmais tais-tair hṛtajñānāḥ prapadyante'nyadevatāḥ
taṁ-taṁ niyamamāsthāya prakṛtyā niyatāḥ svayā

(20) Those whose wisdom has been distorted by desires, resort to other gods, observing this or that rite; swayed by their own inherent nature.

यो यो यां यां तनुं भक्तः श्रद्धयार्चितुमिच्छति।
तस्य तस्याचलां श्रद्धां तामेव विदधाम्यहम्॥ २१॥

yo-yo yāṁ-yāṁ tanuṁ bhaktaḥ śraddhayārcitumicchati
tasya-tasyācalāṁ śraddhāṁ tāmeva vidadhāmyaham

(21) Whatever form a devotee seeks to worship with faith—I make his faith in that firm and unflinching.

स तया श्रद्धया युक्तस्तस्याराधनमीहते।
लभते च ततः कामान्मयैव विहितान्हि तान्॥ २२॥

sa tayā śraddhayā yuktas tasyā'rādhanamīhate
labhate ca tataḥ kāmān mayaiva vihitānhi tān

(22) Endowed with steadfast faith, he engages in the worship of that form and obtains the objects of his desire, verily granted in reality by Me alone.

अन्तवत्तु फलं तेषां तद्भवत्यल्पमेधसाम्।
देवान्देवयजो यान्ति मद्भक्ता यान्ति मामपि॥ २३॥

antavattu phalaṁ teṣāṁ tad bhavaty alpamedhasām
devān devāyajo yānti madbhaktā yānti māmapi

(23) The rewards attained by these people of limited understanding are temporary. The worshippers of gods go to gods, but My devotees come to Me.

Commentary—In the previous verses, Srī Kṛṣṇa has expressed his deep appreciation for the man of wisdom who seeks the Supreme Divinity as his ultimate goal in life. Such an individual loves the Supreme God and adores the Lord out of his sincere love and reverence. He understands that the real happiness lies only in worshipping God for God's sake. The words of his prayers are full of adoration and appreciation for the Divine's gifts and bounties. In verse twenty, Srī Kṛṣṇa gives some glimpses of the people who are led by multiple desires. Srī Kṛṣṇa calls such folks *hrtajnanah* meaning deprived of discriminating ability.

Srī Kṛṣṇa tells Arjuna that people of shallow understanding, those who pray for the fulfilment of their material desires, eventually lose their contact from the indwelling Supreme Soul. In the state of greed and utter frustration, they pursue very short-termed goals. They approach various forms of gods and goddesses for the fulfilment of their desires. In order to please the personal gods and goddesses they take several vows and follow several methods of worship. Some people keep fasts on certain days and observe other penances, charities, and yajñas in order to be blessed with the desired fortunes. The method of worship also differs from one goddess to another depending upon the nature of the desire. They switch their faith from one deity to another in order to be blessed with various boons and bounties. These people of shallow insight worship these gods and goddesses as separate entities from the Supreme Divinity. They fail to perceive the power of the absolute working through their adorable deities. It is indeed one God that takes different roles to play. As Brahma the creator, as Vishnu the sustainer, and as Shiva the destroyer. The Supreme Divinity is called Varuna as the god of water, He is Vayu in the external world and Prana or breath in the body. He is Agni in the form of fire.

Srī Kṛṣṇa has described to Arjuna in previous verses, that as people approach Me, so do I seek them; people from every faith are trying to perceive the inner Divinity. It is indeed so immaterial—the kind of method one adopts in worship or the rituals one chooses to perform—each one of them attains Me. Srī Kṛṣṇa expresses His pity and concern for such people of meagre understanding, who worship gods and goddesses for the attainment of worldly desires. He tells Arjuna that the rewards earned by these people are indeed short-termed and perishable. The worshippers of the deities become trapped in the bondage of multiple desires; those follow them from one life to another. Srī Kṛṣṇa appeals the people to recognize reality behind the transitory world and try to make connections with the absolute reality which forms the essence of life and is indeed unchanging and immutable. When the individual realizes that there is only one Supreme Divinity, who resides in the heart of all, One God who is above all the gods and goddesses, he makes genuine efforts to contact that Supreme reality. The indwelling light supersedes all the forms and shapes of the Divine. Srī Kṛṣṇa tells mankind not to be deluded by the names, forms, shapes and glamour of the gods and goddesses. Accept the entire creation as the manifestation of the Supreme Divinity and know for sure that every activity is rooted in the Supreme and is sustained by the Supreme Divinity Himself.

अव्यक्तं व्यक्तिमापन्नं मन्यन्ते मामबुद्धयः।
परं भावमजानन्तो ममाव्ययमनुत्तमम्॥ २४॥

avyaktaṁ vyaktimāpannaṁ manyante māmabuddhayaḥ
param bhavamajānanto mamāvyayamanuttamam

(24) The ignorant regard Me, the unmanifest, as having manifestation, they do not know My Supreme Nature, which is unchanging and unsurpassed.

नाहं प्रकाशः सर्वस्य योगमायासमावृतः।
मूढोऽयं नाभिजानाति लोको मामजमव्ययम्॥ २५॥

nāhaṁ prakāśaḥ sarvasya yogamāyāsamāvṛtaḥ
mūḍho'yaṁ nābhijānāti loko mām ajamavyayam

(25) I am not revealed to all, veiled by My Yoga-Maya (divine potency). The deluded ones in this world, do not recognize Me as the unborn and the imperishable Supreme spirit.

वेदाहं समतीतानि वर्तमानानि चार्जुन।
भविष्याणि च भूतानि मां तु वेद न कश्चन॥ २६॥

vedāhaṁ samatītāni vartamānāni cā'rjuna
bhaviṣyāṇi ca bhūtāni māṁ tu veda na kaścana

(26) I know all the beings of the past, the present, O'Arjuna and even the future, but no one knows Me.

Commentary—These verses are the continuation of the previous ones where Srī Kṛṣṇa states very clearly that endowed with personal faith, when an individual worships a particular god or goddess, he is indeed blessed with that desired object, which is in reality granted by Me alone. The gods and goddesses are only instrumental. People worship other deities considering them as separate from the supreme absolute reality. The gods and goddesses are the various attributes of one God. People usually worship these gods and goddesses being motivated by various worldly desires. When some one's desire is fulfilled, that particular goddess becomes famous and other people also start worshipping that deity for the fulfilment of their desires and dreams. Srī Kṛṣṇa is declaring in these verses that these folks of limited understanding do not have the insight into the real nature of the absolute Reality.

Similarly, when the absolute Lord, who is unborn and imperishable manifests Himself as God incarnate, the ordinary people can't perceive His Divinity. The transcendental nature of the Divine can be perceived only by those who have transcended themselves and have made connections with their own inner-self. The folks identifying themselves with material bodies can never perceive the Divinity of the Absolute; they can not experience the unmanifest beyond the veil of manifested. Those who are not introduced to the inner Divinity in transcendence they definitely fail to recognize the Supreme Lord, when He incarnates Himself for the welfare of mankind. God reveals His identity to those only who identify themselves with the Supreme Soul and live in the perpetual remembrance of the Divine. In the words of Swami Tapasyananda, "The Divine incarnate making Him specially significant is His being rooted in the Supreme Divinity. He is the *anugraha sakti*, the redeeming power of God, manifesting as an embodied being for a cosmic purpose. Men at large are not able to plumb the depths of the personality of God incarnate and grasp His transcendental significance." For example, Srī Kṛṣṇa, the Divine incarnate, has been recognized as unborn, immutable, imperishable and the embodiment of the absolute truth only by a few. The kuru grandsire Bhisma, who always lived in the awareness of the indwelling light, could surely recognize Srī Kṛṣṇa as God incarnate. He announced the truth about Lord Kṛṣṇa in the royal assembly of the King Yudhisthra. Similarly Kunti and her sons always took refuge in Srī Kṛṣṇa because they recognized in Him some heavenly power. It was their faith in Srī Kṛṣṇa which kept them united and confident. Similarly, Draupadi also held very strong faith in Srī Kṛṣṇa and the Lord always helped her, because she visualized some unknown Supreme power working through Srī Kṛṣṇa. The Lord reveals Himself only to His devotees, who hold undivided faith in Him and seek refuge in Him under all circumstances. In *Kathoupanishad* it has been described very clearly, "The Supreme Self can be perceived only by him, whom the self chooses to be". In the words of Swami Ramakrishna, "It is possible for the swan to separate milk from water and partake of the former only. The other birds are unable to do this. Ishwara is mingled with Maya; He is non-dual with it. The ordinary people can't distinguish Him from Maya but the Paramahansas—the men of perfection—are always able to cognize Ishawara to the exclusion of Maya."

In verse twenty-six, Srī Kṛṣṇa enlightens Arjuna about the nature of God incarnate. Although the Lord manifests Himself as an ordinary individual, He still maintains His transcendental nature and remains rooted in His essentiality. He lives like an ordinary person, but in constant awareness of His real nature. He remains beyond the limitations of time, cause and space. Srī Kṛṣṇa tells Arjuna that He knows everything which has happened in the past and which is happening in the present; He is also aware of the future of all beings. He knows the destiny of everyone, but they are not aware of it. People themselves are the creators of their past, present and future without being aware of it. Although at the deeper level of the self, the embodied-soul has the knowledge of past and future but the conscious mind which constantly identifies with the physical body remains totally ignorant about the truth. Since the God incarnate is completely aware of His Divine essence, He lives in the world as totally free from all bondages and snares of the trifold Nature. The God-incarnate although appears to be an embodied-self, but He lives in the body as transcendental self. The mind of the God-incarnate is the Cosmic mind, that's why He knows about everything and about everybody. In the words of Srī Aurobindo, "Divine in his Supreme transcendental being, unborn, immutable and superior to all these partial manifestations can't be easily known to any living creature. He is self-enveloped in this immense clock of Maya. That is His Yoga Maya by which He is one with the world and yet beyond it, immanent but hidden, seated in the hearts of all but not revealed to every being."

इच्छाद्वेषसमुत्थेन द्वन्द्वमोहेन भारत।
सर्वभूतानि सम्मोहं सर्गे यान्ति परन्तप॥ २७॥

icchādveṣasamutthena dvandvamohena bhārata
sarvabhūtāni sammohaṁ sarge yānti parantapa

(27) Through the delusion of the pairs of opposites, arising from desire and aversion, O'Arjuna, all the creatures become subject to delusion at birth, O' Parantapa.

येषां त्वन्तगतं पापं जनानां पुण्यकर्मणाम्।
ते द्वन्द्वमोहनिर्मुक्ता भजन्ते मां दृढव्रताः॥ २८॥

yeṣāṁ tvantagataṁ pāpaṁ jnānāṁ puṇyakarmaṇām
te dvandvamohanirmuktā bhajante māṁ dṛḍhavratāḥ

(28) But the men of virtuous deeds, whose sins have come to an end, those are liberated from the delusion of the pairs of opposites, they worship Me, with firm resolve.

जरामरणमोक्षाय मामाश्रित्य यतन्ति ये।
ते ब्रह्म तद्विदुः कृत्स्नमध्यात्मं कर्म चाखिलम्॥ २९॥

jarāmaraṇamokṣāya māmāśritya yatanti ye
te brahma tadviduḥ kṛtsnamadhyātmaṁ karma cākhilam

(29) Those who take refuge in Me and strive for deliverance from old age and death, they know all about the absolute Brahman, the Self and the entire field of actions.

साधिभूताधिदैवं मां साधियज्ञं च ये विदुः।
प्रयाणकालेऽपि च मां ते विदुर्युक्तचेतसः॥ ३०॥

sādhibhūtādhidaivaṁ māṁ sadhiyajnaṁ ca ye viduḥ
prayāṇakāle'pi ca māṁ te vidur yuktacetasaḥ

(30) Those who realize Me within the Adhibuta, in the Adhidaiva and in the Adhiyajña, also realize Me at the time of death with their minds united in Yoga.

Commentary—As described in the previous verses, the lord is the knower of all beings and also 'the Trikal Darshi'—the knower of past, present and future. Although the God-incarnate acts like an ordinary human being but He always remains rooted in His essential transcendental nature. The God-incarnate exists as the universal-self and the Cosmic-self. His mind is universal mind, that's why he knows everything about everybody while others don't. In these verses Srī Kṛṣṇa gives the reason, why ordinary people get entangled in the net of Maya and live in duality. He tells Arjuna that it happens right at the time of birth when the person comes into the world of mortals. As identification with the body becomes stronger the identification with the Supreme Self starts becoming weaker and weaker. Identification with the mind, body and ego, gives rise to a lot of conflicted emotions. People waste a major part of their life-time in making judgments about themselves being worthy or unworthy. This experience of separate identity grows stronger and gives rise to the emotions of attraction and aversion, pleasure and pain, the feelings of fear, jealousy, anxiety and greed. The pairs of opposites exist as long as duality exists. Every experience of happiness and unhappiness, attraction and aversion that takes place, directly corresponds to the degree of one's spiritual awareness. People those are spiritually enlightened can generally rise above the pairs of opposites and live a balanced life. So in order to bring any changes in the attitude, the individual has to bring some changes in the degree of self-awareness. This is what Srī Kṛṣṇa explains in the next verse, "People settled in the integrity of the Self are constantly habituated in the performance of virtuous deeds. The loving dedication inspires them to establish some close bonds of mutual friendship with the Self which helps them to rise above the selfish limitation of the individual-self. Once the unity with the Cosmic-self is established, the individual feels blessed with heightened insight. He learns to educate himself in the habit of living in the consciousness of the indwelling Lord. Living a life in the awareness of the Supreme-Self is like living in eternity, where duality does not exist and the opposites carry no meaning at all.

The fear of old age and death haunts each and everyone because of the self-assumed separate identity. When the embodied-self merges into the Cosmic-self, the limited identity of the individual-self starts vanishing, and with that vanishes the fear of death. Srī Kṛṣṇa declares that those virtuous ones, whose sins have been washed away by the habituated virtuous deeds, they rise above the dualities and all fears. Their habit of living in God grows stronger with age. For them even the old age becomes enjoyable, pleasant and free from all the fears of death. A devotee of the Lord spends his time in singing the glories of the Divine and feels free and fearless in all respect. He lives in contentment, freedom and dies in contentment and freedom.

The last verse concludes that God and his Divine manifestation are not two separate entities. *'Avyakt'* is the supreme Lord unmanifested and *'Vyakti'* is His individual manifestation. The supreme Lord Himself becomes everything which is manifested. God is the source of all life, the animate and inanimate. Appropriate perception of the God's manifestation is indeed the greatest achievement of spiritual life. The entire creation rests upon Him. It is His Divine potency which is expressing itself everywhere. The existence of fruit rests upon the flower, the existence of flower rests upon the leaf, the leaf upon the trunk of the tree, the tree upon the root and the root upon the seed. If one opens the seed there is nothing visible to the naked eye but still the seed has complete information of becoming a tree. The Lord Himself is the determining factor in everything which occurs in the material, psychological and even in the spiritual realms. Although perennially established in transcendence, Lord is Adhibuta, Adhidaiva and Adhiyajña dwelling in the bodies of all beings.

ॐ तत्सदिति श्रीमद्भगवद्गीतासूपनिषत्सु ब्रह्मविद्यायां
योगशास्त्रे श्रीकृष्णार्जुनसंवादे ज्ञानविज्ञानयोगो
नाम सप्तमोऽध्यायः ॥ ७ ॥

'Aum' tatsaditi Śrīmadbhagawadgeetā sūpaniṣatsu
brahmavidyāyām yogaśāstre Śrīkṛṣṇārjunasamvāde
jñānavijñānayogo nāma saptamo'dhyāyaḥ

'AUM TAT SAT'—Thus, in the Upanishad of the glorious Bhagawad Geeta, the science of the Brahman (Absolute) the scripture of yoga, the dialogue between Srī Kṛṣṇa and Arjuna—thus, ends the chapter seven entitled *"Jñānavijñānayoga"*.

इति श्रीमद्भगवद्गीतासु सप्तमोऽध्यायः ॥ ७ ॥

Chapter Eight

AKṢARABRAHMAYOGA

THE YOGA OF THE IMPERISHABLE BRAHMAN

अर्जुन उवाच

किं तद् ब्रह्म किमध्यात्मं किं कर्म पुरुषोत्तम।
अधिभूतं च किं प्रोक्तमधिदैवं किमुच्यते॥ १॥

kiṁ tad brahma kim adhyātmaṁ kiṁ karma puroṣottama
adhibhūtaṁ ca kiṁ proktam adhidaivaṁ kim ucyate

Arjuna said :

(1) What is Brahman? What is *adhyatma*? What is action? O' Supreme person. What is called *adhibuta*? And what is said to be *adhidaiva*?

अधियज्ञः कथं कोऽत्र देहेऽस्मिन्मधुसूदन।
प्रयाणकाले च कथं ज्ञेयोऽसि नियतात्मभिः॥ २॥

adhiyajñaḥ kathaṁ ko'tra dehe'smin madhusūdana
prayāṇakāle ca kathaṁ jñeyo'si niyatātmabhiḥ

(2) Who and how is Adhiyajña here in this body, O'Kṛṣṇa? And how You are to be realized at the time of death by the self-controlled?

Commentary—The dialogue opens again with a bundle of questions from Arjuna. He requests for detailed explanation on the philosophical terms such as *Brahman, adhyatma, adhibhuta, adhidaiva* and *adhiyajña*. Arjuna also requests for detailed information in relation to the realization of God at the time of death. He says, "O' Kṛṣṇa, how are you to be known at the time of death by the self-controlled?" Arjuna seeks to know how the self-controlled aspirants can meditate and contemplate on God at the final hour of their departure from the world.

श्रीभगवानुवाच

अक्षरं ब्रह्म परमं स्वभावोऽध्यात्ममुच्यते।
भूतभावोद्भवकरो विसर्गः कर्मसंज्ञितः॥ ३॥

akṣaraṁ brahma paramaṁ svabhāvo'dhyātmam ucyate
bhūtabhāvodbhavakaro visargaḥ karmasaṁjñitaḥ

The Blessed Lord said :

(3) The Supreme imperishable is Brahman; Its essential nature is known as *adhyatma.* The creative force which brings forth the existence of beings is called Karma (action).

अधिभूतं क्षरो भावः पुरुषश्चाधिदैवतम्।
अधियज्ञोऽहमेवात्र देहे देहभृतां वर॥ ४॥

adhibhūtaṁ kṣaro bhāvaḥ puruṣaś cādhidaivatam
adhiyajño'ham evātra dehe dehabhṛtāṁ vara

(4) *Adhibuta* pertains to My perishable nature; and the conscious principle Purusha is the *adhidaiva.* I am the *adhiyajña* here in this body, O' Arjuna.

अन्तकाले च मामेव स्मरन्मुक्त्वा कलेवरम्।
यः प्रयाति स मद्भावं याति नास्त्यत्र संशयः॥ ५॥

antakāle ca māmeva smaran muktvā kalevaram
yaḥ prayāti sa madbhāvaṁ yāti nāstyatra saṁśayaḥ

(5) At the time of death, he who departs from the body thinking of Me alone, he attains to My essential nature, there is no doubt of this.

यं यं वापि स्मरन्भावं त्यजत्यन्ते कलेवरम्।
तं तमेवैति कौन्तेय सदा तद्भावभावितः॥ ६॥

yaṁ-yaṁ vāpi smaran bhāvaṁ tyajaty ante kalevaram
taṁ-tamevaiti kaunteya sadā tadbhāvabhāvitaḥ

(6) Whatever a person thinks at the time of his death while leaving his body, to that only he goes, O' Kaunteya, because of his being constantly absorbed in that thought.

तस्मात्सर्वेषु कालेषु मामनुस्मर युध्य च।
मय्यर्पितमनोबुद्धिर्मामेवैष्यस्यसंशयम् ॥७॥

tasmāt sarveṣu kāleṣu mām anusmara yudhya ca
mayy arpitamanobuddhir mām evaiṣyasy asaṁśayam

(7) Therefore at all times, think of Me alone and fight the battle. With your mind and intellect thus fixed on Me, Thou shall surely come to Me alone.

अभ्यासयोगयुक्तेन चेतसा नान्यगामिना।
परमं पुरुषं दिव्यं याति पार्थानुचिन्तयन् ॥८॥

abhyāsayogayuktena cetasā nānyagāminā
paramaṁ puruṣaṁ divyaṁ yāti pārthānucintayan

(8) He who is established in the yogic meditation through constant practice, and does not let his mind wander after anything else, he surely attains the Supreme resplendent Divine Purusha, O'Arjuna.

Commentary—These verses are answers to Arjuna's questions, in regard to the scriptural terms such as what is Brahman? What is *adhyatma*? and what is Karma? What is *adhibhuta* and who is called to be Adhidaiva? Who is *adhiyajña*, and how that relates here in the body? Arjuna also wants to know the techniques of experiencing God-realization at the time of death. Srī Kṛṣṇa answers each question in the order of Arjuna's interrogation. In order to enlighten upon the profundity of each philosophical term, Srī Kṛṣṇa explains one by one. He starts with word *aksharam* means the imperishable, immutable, indestructible and eternal is the Supreme Brahman. The entire world is rooted in Brahman. Everything in the world is experienced, grasped and perceived through Brahman. The multiplicity of the world is revealed through the medium of one imperishable reality. Brahman is the *sanatan* principle of all existence. In *Taittriya Upanishad* Bhrigu, the son of the Varuna, requests his father to enlighten him about the nature of Brahman. The father replied: O' dear son, that from which everything emanates, by which everything is sustained and into which everything enters eventually is Brahman. The Rishi explains that Brahman is the substratum of the universe and can be perceived only with penances and disciplinary observances—*Brahma-Vijñana-Sadhana.* During the process of tough penances, as the aspirant moves from one perceptual experience to another, he determines for himself that there is only one eternal principle of consciousness which exists at the heart of the entire universe. The Supreme Brahman is the power behind matter and life, mind and intelligence that controls each one of them. The nature of Brahman is indeed inexplicable. The son of the Rishi finally experiences for himself the spiritual ecstasy of the infinite principle. The final vision satisfies all the inquiries of the aspirant. After the experience of the ultimate reality everything becomes self-evident, nothing remains to be known any more. *Anando Brahmeti vyajanti*—means "Bliss is Brahman." All the beings are born from the Bliss, they are sustained by the Bliss and into the Bliss they enter at the departure upon attaining salvation.

Describing the magnitude of the Akshara Brahman, the Rishi Yagvalakya, a great scholar of the Vedic time, tells Gargi—O' Gargi, it is indeed at the orders and signals of the 'Akshara Brahman' (The imperishable supreme Divinity) that the heaven and earth are held together. He is called *paramam* because he is beyond the reach of senses, mind and intellect. O' Gargi, the knowers of Brahman describe 'That' as the Absolute. The unmodified, pure, consciousness is 'Akshara Brahman' which continues to exist in its own permanent (Infinite) state. The essential nature of Brahman is called *adhyatma.* According to Srī Ramsukhdas, One's own nature or self is called *adhyatma,* the path of spirituality is also called *adhyatma,* the science of the soul is also called *adhyatma,* but here in this verse it has been used for one's self."

The next part of the verse *bhutabhavodbhavakaro bhuta* stands for all living beings. The creative act which brings forth the existence of both sentient and insentient, which promotes and fosters their cause, is designated as Karma. In the creative force abides the Supreme Brahman. In the words of Srī Shankracharya, "The origin of all creatures is known by the term Karma for it forms the seed, as it were, of all beings; it is in virtue of this act that beings animate and inanimate come into existence after passing through rain and other regions of life. It is constant birth of things in time, *udbhava,* of which the creative energy of Karma is the principle. All this mutable becoming, emerges by a combination of the powers and energies of nature, *adhibhuta,* which constitutes the world and is the object of the soul's consciousness."

After giving the details on the imperishable aspect, Srī Kṛṣṇa draws Arjuna's attention towards the *'kshara bhava'*—the perishable; which comes forth due to the creative force known as Karma. The manifestation of the Supreme in nature is the *'kshara bhava'*.

The entire creation comes into existence from one *bhava* or one thought only, that forms the seed of the primal will *"ek se anek'*—which means "Let me be many." This one thought *"bhava"* becomes the creative force, when energized by the Supreme Brahman. The thought, *ek se anek*, started at the beginning of the creation and is still powerful. It can be still observed very clearly that everything in nature is spreading out, forming various roots, seeds and eggs. Every seed brings forth millions of similarities. It is hard to count and determine the number of their resemblances. Every seed has the inherent desire to become a tree, then again the tree has the inherent desire—"Let me be many" so the cycle goes on. It applies to all beings and everything in macrocosm as well as in microcosm. In human body the cells are constantly splitting and giving birth to new cells. The old cells are dying and being replaced by the new ones. The Vedas have explained this principle in these words : *Yatha purav macal payasch*—everything being replaced by the identical ones. So it is indeed the inherent desire "Let me be many," which is primordial yet still ever fresh all around in creation. This is what Srī Kṛṣṇa means by *"bhuta-bhavodebhava-karo"* in the third verse of this chapter.

In the entire creation, the potential dynamism, the splendour, the glory and the charisma of the Supreme Lord can be observed very vividly and very clearly. The entire creation is indeed the expression of the Supreme Divinity. *Adhibhuta* has been called the *'kshara bhava'* because the material structure is made up of five elements such as ether, air, water, fire and earth. All these elements integrate and disintegrate with time. This constant change is called *'kshara bhava'* means the perishable nature of the substance. Srī Kṛṣṇa has explained the embodied-soul as Purusha, the indweller, and has designated the purusha as *adhidaiva,* means the presiding Lord. According to Swami Chidbhavananada, the word Purusha comes from the root word *pri* which means to fill. The Pura or Puri means a city or fortress. He who resides in a 'puri' is the 'Purusha'. He is designated as *adhidaiva.*

According to ancient scriptures, there are many prayers addressed to a large number of gods and goddesses. These deities have been recognized and acknowledged in the cosmos and as well as in the body. There is a mantra in *Rigveda, "napaesho vidtheshu prajata abhim yagam vi charant purvi"* meaning there are many powers in the forms of gods, those move around taking part in sacrifice. "There is a very popular morning prayer recited by people the moment they wake up from sleep—*prithvi sagandha sarasastathaph sparshi vayurjwalanam satejah nabhah sasabdam maheta sahaite kurvantu sarve mama suprabhatam*—means let the fragrance of the earth, the various tastes of water, the pleasing touch of wind, the lustre of the sun and the words of the vast horizon fill the early hours of morning with pleasure and peace." All the five chief elements those constitute the body had been considered gods and goddesses. The earth has been always addressed as mother, being symbolic of fertility. The water as Varun the water-god, the wind-god as Maruta or vayu, fire-god as energy, ether as the Akasha, the god of sound and word, the sun-god and the moon-god, and the other cosmic powers became manifested with the manifestation of creation. The worship of these deities is performed out of appreciation. These powers are working in co-operation with each other in order to support life on the planet. The worship of nature has been highly recommended in the holy books of almost all religions, so that human beings can learn from the sacrifice and co-operative efforts of these cosmic powers. According to Vedas the creative aspect of the Supreme Divinity is called Brahma, Vishnu the sustainer and Shiva the annihilator. Devraj Indra has been designated as the head of the five elemental powers. All the three aspects of 'Trimurti' are the representations of the different attributes of the Supreme-Brahman; and all of these draw their power from one original source. Similarly, there are deities and gods in the human body who help the different organs to work in perfect co-operation with one another. For example the presiding *daiva* of eyes are the Sun and Moon, the speech is Agni (fire) and the hearing is ether (aksha) (shbad). The *daiva* of the organs of defecation is Yama, of the reproductive organs is the Prajapati, and the controller of hands and arms is the Indra. Indra is also known as "Daivraja Indra". The presiding *daiva* of the forehead is the Shiva and of digestion is the Vaishvanara.

As a matter of fact our hands and five fingers are also the five *daivas;* those act as the switch-board for the entire body. The thumb is Agni (fire), the index finger is Vayu (air), the middle finger is Ether, the ring finger is earth and the little finger is Indra (electricity). So in the macrocosm as well as in the microcosm all these gods and goddesses are controlled by the Supreme-Lord. The controller of these *daivas* in the body has been called *adhidaiva.* All these *daivas* in the body work under the direct control of the Supreme Divinity and also with the power of the Supreme-Divinity. None of these have any independent existence of their own. Purushotam, the Supreme indweller presides over each and every function of the body. All organs in the body work in perfect unison. There is one vital force that presides over the inner cosmos and guides the entire functioning of the body. This work order of perfect co-operation for the sustenance of the body is called *Yajña. Yajña* literally means sacrifice (selfless activity). The perfect work order is maintained by the indweller, the Supreme-Lord. Srī Kṛṣṇa tells Arjuna, *"adhiyagno ham eva tra dehe"* which means I alone am the *Adhiyajña* here in the body. Every little activity in the body takes place with the power of the indwelling Purusha. The entire body is sustained and held in order, with the power of the Supreme-Self. In the words of Jaydyal Goyandka, "The Lord speaks of that unmanifest subtle and all-pervasive aspect of His as *Adhiyajña* in this verse and in order to show His identity with it, he openly declares 'I Myself *Adhiyajña.*"

In these verses Srī Kṛṣṇa is presenting a suggestive view-point, in order to convince Arjuna that the Supreme-Self is indeed the essence of the entire manifestation, whether it concerns the individual body or the cosmic body. All the voluntary and involuntary activities of the body are only the various manifestation of the transcendental consciousness. All the external worships in the form of rituals and prayers are directed towards one and the only focal point, which is Brahman. There is only one, Supreme Power that shines through each activity one performs, each word one speaks etc. In the words of Srī Aurobindo, "Possessing at once the calm of the immutable existence and the enjoyment of the mutable action, there dwells in man the Purushottama. He is not only remote from us in some supreme status beyond but he is here too, in the body of every being, in the heart of every man and in nature."

After giving answers to six questions of Arjuna in the verse five and six, Srī Kṛṣṇa proceeds to answer the last question relating to the realization of the Lord at the time of death. Srī Kṛṣṇa tells very emphatically that whichever thought one recollects at the time of death, to that thought only one goes O' Kaunteya; because of one's perpetual absorption in that thought. The thought that occupies the mind at the last hour of death really determines the nature of rebirth. As a matter of fact, the life-style and personality of every individual is determined by the quality of his thoughts. The entire life of a person revolves within the cycle of past, present and future. The thoughts and feeling which a person is experiencing today is the product of yesterday and all that one thinks today automatically determines the life of tomorrow. So the thoughts, the ideas and the notions one cherishes during his life-time definitely become the dominant ideas of the last hour of death and determine the destiny in future. The journey of the physical body ends at death, but the journey of the soul goes on, for further expression of the cherished thoughts and latencies. Death is like a long sleep, it is a transition. As observed in our daily life, our dreams are usually the manifestation of some thoughts those flashed through the mind during that day or somewhere in the past. Just one thought becomes one dream, exactly like that, one dominant thought takes its expression in the form of another life. So whatever object one remembers while leaving the body, that is what one becomes because of one's constant involvement in that particular thought.

There is a true incident as narrated by a saint. This saint actually met the family where the incident took place. There is a family in Zambia in which a little girl Reena went through some very traumatic experiences. This little girl, at the age of six, suddenly started showing an unusual behaviour. She insisted upon visiting a family that lived in the nearby town. The parents felt very difficult to deal with the situation; they didn't know anything about that particular family. When the little girl became very hysteric about it, they consulted their family doctor who suggested to fulfil the wish of their daughter. When they were driving, the little girl of six gave them directions and the address of the particular home where she wanted to go. When they reached there, she quickly jumped out of the car and dashed into the house as if she knew everything about that place. First of all she went into a room and looked at everything around as if she was searching for something very specific in mind. While she was looking at the photographs on the walls around, suddenly a seven years old boy entered that room. The moment she saw that little boy, tears rolled down her eyes. She touched him, hugged him and immediately forgot everything as to why she was even there. For her it was like coming out of a deep sleep. Both the parents of the little boy and the little girl felt very strange about the whole incident. When Reena's parents inquired about the mother of that seven-year old boy, they were told that his mother had died at the time of his birth. During the conversation between both the parents, it became evident that in her previous life, somehow, the girl Reena had been the wife of their oldest son who died in childbirth seven years ago. Most probably at the time of her death she was pre-occupied and worried about her newly born. Although the desire to see her newly-born baby remained dormant in the deepest layers of her mind till the age of six, it slowly started appearing in the conscious mind and ultimately became the most dominant and crucial desire. After meeting her baby boy, the desire and anxiety was satisfied and the remote memory disappeared. The well-being of her newly born was indeed one of the dominant thoughts that determined her present life. So when Arjuna brings forward the question for Srī Kṛṣṇa as to how the Supreme-Lord can be realized at the time of death Srī Kṛṣṇa answers "He who departs thinking of Me alone at the time of death, he attains My Supreme-State because of his perpetual absorption in Me."

According to Swami Tapasyananda, "The force of the word *ca* translated here as even is that it is only if the thought of God is dominant idea of one's life, and has been occupying one's mind all through one's life, the thought of Him will come to one's mind at the last moment. Man should not think hypocritically that he can live an unholy life all through, and achieve his spiritual welfare by thinking of Him at the last moment. One will find it impossible to do so." This is indeed a fact that one can't meditate on God at the last minute of departure unless the individual has trained himself for it during his lifetime. The love and devotion of the Divine educates the individual to experience the presence of the Divine at the time of death. If a person lives a life in the awareness of the Supreme-Self while working in office, while eating, while talking or doing other activities of daily life, the contemplation on God comes very effortlessly at the time of death. Srī Kṛṣṇa enlightens Arjuna about the mysteries of the thinking faculty and how an individual can make the very best use of it. He presents the most revolutionary statement *'tasmat sarvesu kaleshu mam anusmara yudhya ca'*—Arjuna keep Me in your thoughts at every minute and fight the battle. With mind and reason totally absorbed in Me, you will come to Me. Living a life in perpetual awareness of the Lord should become a state of mind—a style of life. The inner Divinity must become the individual's perpetual companion, consciously present in each and every thought, word and deed. Living in spiritual awareness is indeed the closest approach to the God-realization during the life-time and at the time of death. Srī Kṛṣṇa suggests to Arjuna to practice the Yoga of living in the consciousness of the Divine and work with the awareness of the Divine. It is through the yogic practice that the individual can remain grounded in the essentiality of the Self and operate in the physical world through the guidance of the indwelling Supreme-Self. It is through the practice of Yoga, the dissipated and fragmented individual-self pulls itself together to become an essential part of the universal Self. The yogic discipline helps the person to experience the inner vision, that guides him for a single-minded meditation on the Supreme-Puruhsa.

कविं पुराणमनुशासितार-
मणोरणीयांसमनुस्मरेद्यः ।
सर्वस्य धातारमचिन्त्यरूप-
मादित्यवर्णं तमसः परस्तात् ॥ ९ ॥

kavim̐ purāṇam anuśāsitāra

manor aṇīyānsam anusmared yaḥ

sarvasya dhātāram acintyarūpa

mādityavarṇam̐ tamasaḥ parastāt

(9) He, who contemplates on the Omniscient, the Primordial, the Ruler, subtler than an atom, the sustainer of all, the inconceivable, effulgent like the sun and beyond the darkness of ignorance.

प्रयाणकाले मनसाऽ चलेन,

भक्त्या युक्तो योगबलेन चैव।

भ्रुवोर्मध्ये प्राणमावेश्य सम्यक्,

स तं परं पुरुषमुपैति दिव्यम्॥ १०॥

prayāṇkāle manasā'calena

bhaktyā yukto yogabalena caiva

bhruvormadhye prāṇam āveśya samyak

sa taṁ paraṁ puruṣam upaiti divyam

(10) At the time of death with a steadfast mind, endowed with devotion and the power of Yoga, who can firmly hold the life-breath in the middle of the two eyebrows, he surely reaches that resplendent supreme purusha.

यदक्षरं वेदविदो वदन्ति,

विशन्ति यद्यतयो वीतरागाः।

यदिच्छन्तो ब्रह्मचर्यं चरन्ति,

तत्ते पदं संग्रहेण प्रवक्ष्ये॥ ११॥

yad akṣaraṁ vedavido vadanti

viśanti yad yatayo vītarāgaḥ

yad icchanto brahmacaryaṁ caranti

tatte padaṁ saṁgraheṇa pravakṣye

(11) That state which the knowers of Vedas call eternal, where in the ascetics enter, being free from attachment and desiring which they practise continence—that goal I must declare to you briefly.

सर्वद्वाराणि संयम्य मनो हृदि निरुध्य च।
मूर्ध्न्याधायात्मनः प्राणमास्थितो योगधारणाम्॥ १२॥

sarvadvārāṇi saṁyamya mano hṛdi nirudhya ca
mūrdhanyādhāyātmanaḥ prāṇamāsthito yogadhāraṇām.

ओमित्येकाक्षरं ब्रह्म व्याहरन्मामनुस्मरन्।
यः प्रयाति त्यजन् देहं स याति परमां गतिम्॥ १३॥

omityekākṣaraṁ brahma vyāharan mām anusmaran
yaḥ prayāti tyajan dehaṁ sa yāti paramāṁ gatim.

(12, 13) Having closed all the doors of senses and firmly restoring the mind in the heart and the life-breath in the crown of the head; established in the yogic concentration he who utters the single syllable AUM the Supreme Brahman and remembers Me while departing from his body, he certainly attains the Supreme Goal.

Commentary—The conversation opens with some melodious words in adoration of the Supreme, full of ardent love and devotion. Srī Kṛṣṇa suggests to meditate upon the Supreme-Purusha, who is omniscient, primordial, sustainer, the Lord of the universe. He is subtler than the subtlest, inconceivable ever-luminous like the sun and far beyond the darkness of ignorance. The Lord though inconceivable for an ordinary person can be experienced and contacted through Yoga. In order to experience the inconceivable, one must practise meditation regularly which helps the individual to rise above the finite boundaries of the body, mind and intellect. Srī Kṛṣṇa assures that yogic communion with the Supreme is indeed possible for each and every individual, provided the person is ready to go through the essentials in the form of self-discipline and immovable devotion for the Lord. In order to experience the transcendental state of Supreme Divinity at the time of death, the individual has to practise meditation regularly. At the time of parting the person usually recollects the past memories. His entire life runs like a video tape in the mind. In every religious tradition, the relatives and friends of the person make all kinds of efforts to make his departure peaceful. They read the prayers and hymns from the holy books. That does help some but the real effort has to be made by the person himself. He has to make special efforts for concentration on the Divine at special focal points of concentration in the body. Concentration on the incoming and outgoing breath with contemplation at the special psychic stations in body makes the last minute very easy and pleasant. The thought process can be brought under control only with the rhythmic flow of breathing. As the thoughts start calming down, the mind settles in the breath and the breath rests in the heat and the heat in the Supreme-Self. This way the departure of the soul from the body becomes effortless and peaceful. Srī Kṛṣṇa suggests that the individual should try to withdraw the senses from the sense object and direct the attention at the heart centre *anahat chakra. Anahat chakra* is the focal point of mergence into the ever vibrating primordial sound of the holy syllable AUM. When the life force becomes integrated, it enters into the cavity of the heart centre, and immediately recognizes the sound of AUM and instantly joins the Nada. From this station the person should direct the infused breath with the vibrating sound of AUM upward at the *Aajña chakra* at the space between the two eyebrows. When the life force withdraws itself from all the other nine gates of the body (two eyes, two ears, mouth, two nasal passages, organs of defecation and reproduction) and moves upward, it gradually settles between the two eyebrows, and enables the person to infuse the diffused movement into the Supreme Soul. Slowly the body consciousness starts failing and the person becomes more conscious of the indwelling Supreme spirit. Finally the inner intelligence guides and directs all the life force towards the crown of the head from where it departs from the tenth gate of the body. This is considered to be the yogic way of departing from the body and merging into the Supreme Soul.

An illustration like this has been described in *Kathoupanishad,* "Purusha the Supreme-Self, perpetually abides in the cavity of the heart, almost about the size of a *angustha* (thumb). With concentration on the rhythm of the breath and vibrations of the holy syllable AUM, the person directs with firmness the life force from the heart as the wind is forced out from a flute. Out of all the hundred and one arteries of the heart *(shatam caikaca hridayaya nadias)*, there is one which goes towards the crown of the head. The Matri Upanishad has described it as the *sushumna* artery which connects the heart to the soft spot at the top of the head. This soft spot at centre of the skull is called *brahma randhra*. This is the tenth gate in the body used by the yogins at the time of departure from the mortal body. This is a doorway to Brahman. When the individual mounts up and leaves from this gate, he merges into the rays of the sun and becomes a part of the Supreme-Self. *Tayordhvamaann amrtatvam et* means departing upward from there one attains immortality. When the mind is withdrawn from the senses, and concentrated on the sound of AUM, the embodied-soul breaks up the ties of bondage effortlessly and the departing moment becomes very peaceful. While giving an elaborate description of the technicalities, Srī Kṛṣṇa has been constantly emphasizing upon the word *mamanusmran* which means repeated remembrance of Me with the recitation of the holy syllable AUM is indeed very important.

Srī Kṛṣṇa has highly glorified the power and importance of the holy syllable AUM in the verse eleven and thirteen. He explains the secret of contemplation on the sound of AUM and clarifies that concentration on AUM comprises the worship of both Nirguna and Saguna aspects of the absolute Brahman. The most magnificent syllable AUM has been considered the closest to the 'word' in Divine consciousness. *Akara-Ukara-Makara* the three combined together is OMKARA. *Akara* stands for Iswara, *Ukara* stands for Moolprakriti and *Makara* stands for Mayasakti. AUM has been highly exalted in the Vedas, the Upanishads, Geeta as well as in other religious scriptures. AUM has also been called Pranava. There is an illustration in *Atharva Veda* in which Indra defeats the demons with concentration on AUM. The illustration signifies that man can conquer his demonic nature with meditation on the sound of AUM. *Kathopanishad* describes AUM as Para Brahman itself. *Yajur Veda* portrays the glory of AUM for the realization of Brahman. AUM represents the absolute Brahman. It is believed that AUM symbolizes all the triad in space and time—'A' stands for *Adimata* (beginning), 'U' stands for *Utkrsha* (progress) and 'M' for *Miti* (dissolution). Yet another theory states 'A' to be symbolic of *vac* (word), 'U' represents *mana* (mind), 'M' for *prana* (breath). According to *Mandukya Upanishad,* 'A' stands for the conscious level, 'U' stands for dream stage and 'M' stands for deep sleep. The scriptures also describe that after uttering these three letters in one rhythm there is a half syllable that leads the individual into silence. That silence is the fourth stage of consciousness known as *turyia.* This is the stage of union with the indwelling supreme-self. Concentration on the sound of AUM connects one with the throbbing being of the universe. All the vowels have originated from the sound of AUM and the consonants are the images and fragments of AUM. In the words of Sanjukta Gupta, 'Meditation on AUM should lead the *sadhaka* to a state of consciousness in which the mind merges in the mantra until it stops being aware of the sound of resonance; it reaches the end of the resonance, this indicates the state of primal unity and ineffability."

In these verses Srī Kṛṣṇa, while glorifying the greatness of AUM, emphasizes the necessity of concentration on the sound of AUM at the heart centre. Meditation on this mystic syllable AUM is the most beneficial austerity practised during the life time which makes the hour of death a blessed experience. The reason why Srī Kṛṣṇa suggests to concentrate on the sound at the heart-centre because the sound of the holy syllable can be experienced originating from the *Anahat Nada.* It perpetually resounds from there. As described in the previous chapter, there are seven well known psychic stations in human body called the seven chakras. These psychic stations are located along the *sushumna nadi.* In yoga meditation the awareness is guided through these stations with full consciousness to the *Anahat chakra* and later to the *Ajña chakra* located between the two eyebrows. The heart *chakra* can be felt to be located between the two breasts almost at the level of the physical heart. In meditation it is experienced, inside the spine and also behind the breast bone. 'Anahat', as the word itself explains, means unstruck sound. At this centre vibrates a celestial sound which can be heard in deep meditation. When the meditator withdraws his attention from all other external sounds of the sensory organs, this celestial sound can be heard automatically. At the grossest level the sound of *nada* is more or less like the sound of humming bees—a little deeper, it can be heard more like the melody of a flute. The third sound is more like the far off ringing bells, and as the meditator dives deeper into the subtle layers of consciousness the *nada* is heard like the sound of the celestial conch. Further, at the deeper levels of consciousness one hears the sound of *Vina* and at the subtle level one can hear the sound of drums which slowly changes into some kind of thunder as heard in the sky before lightning. At the most subtle level of this *chakra*, the individual hears the vibrating melody, which resonates like the sound of AUM. These various levels of sound have been described in Vedas and also how the basic seven sounds of music have originated from the primordial nada the AUM. The seven basic sounds or the swara as described in the Sama Veda are—*sa re ga ma pa dha ni sa* (do re me fa so la ti da). The sound of AUM is difficult to capture, but the person who practises regular meditation on it captures the sound effortlessly. The individuals who have trained themselves in *nada yoga,* for them a quick absorption in the sound of the holy syllable becomes very easy; they also know how to channelize the life force with the sound of AUM at the time of death. Srī Kṛṣṇa intends to enlighten Arjuna that both the sound of AUM and rays of the Supreme-Self can be vividly contacted in meditation at the heart centre. The primordial sound that resonates from the *Anahat chakra* is a part of the universal *nada* which encompasses the entire universe.

अनन्यचेताः सततं यो मां स्मरति नित्यशः।
तस्याहं सुलभः पार्थ नित्ययुक्तस्य योगिनः ॥ १४ ॥

ananyacetāḥ satataṁ yo māṁ smarati nityaśaḥ
tasyā'haṁ sulabhaḥ pārtha nityayuktasya yoginaḥ

(14) He who constantly remembers Me with undivided attention, to him I am easily attainable, O' Partha, since he is ever united in Yoga.

मामुपेत्य पुनर्जन्म दुःखालयमशाश्वतम्।
नाप्नुवन्ति महात्मानः संसिद्धिं परमां गताः ॥ १५ ॥

mām upetya punarjanma duḥkhālayam aśāśvatam
nā'pnuvanti mahātmānaḥ saṁsiddhiāṁ paramāṁ gatāḥ

(15) Having come to Me, these great souls are not born again (here) which is the abode of sorrow and is transitory, for they have

reached the highest perfection.

आब्रह्मभुवनाल्लोकाः पुनरावर्तिनोऽर्जुन ।
मामुपेत्य तु कौन्तेय पुनर्जन्म न विद्यते ॥ १६ ॥

ābrahmabhuvanāllokāḥ punarāvartino'rjuna
mām upetya tu kaunteya punarjanma na vidyate

(16) From the realm of the Supreme creator, all the worlds are subject to return again and again, O' Arjuna. But having attained Me, O' son of Kunti, there is no rebirth.

Commentary—After giving some glimpses of the techniques which help the individual in God-realization at the time of departure, Srī Kṛṣṇa draws Arjuna's attention back to the concept of *ananyabhakti* meaning undivided devotion for the Divine. Although it is important to learn and practice the various techniques of yoga meditation but these techniques become more rewarding if supported by *ananya-cetah satatam yo mam* i.e. living in the awareness of the Self. The person who lives a life in constant adoration of the Divine and offers all his work as a service to the Divine, he is liberated from the bondage of karma while living in the world. Salvation, emancipation after death, does not mean anything special to him because he lives in freedom and departs from the world in freedom. For such a person who holds an undivided adoration for the Divine, his absorption in the sound of AUM at the time of death comes as a second nature to him. He lives his life in harmony with the primordial *nada* and so he departs in perfect peace with the primordial Self. When the association with the Supreme-self becomes the joy of life and the richness of every moment, the life becomes an eternal reservoir of peace and happiness. Srī Kṛṣṇa declares in clear words that anyone who thinks of Me without deviation, who offers himself in My service with undivided attention, surely attains Me and all My love. Such a person lives under the blessings of My blissful umbrella—always in My protection and always within My reach. In the words of Srī Ramakrishna, "A real devotee of the Lord, instead of indulging in various thoughts, he enters into the most intimate relationship with the Lord and makes Him of his own, teases Him with importunities and takes pride in Him. He further used to say, if once a man gains love of God, if once the chanting of His holy name brings thrill to the devotee with joy, what effort is needed for the control of passions afterwards, the control comes of itself." The word *satatam* and *nityash* exactly means perpetually and constantly all the time. Another important message which Srī Kṛṣṇa brings forward in the verse fifteen and sixteen is—That the one who is totally devoted to the Lord, incessantly lives in God. For him the highest aspiration of life is closeness with the Divine and the service to the Divine. In perpetual unity with the Supreme Lord, the individual is blessed with the rich experience of one's own immortality. The moment one experiences one's own Divinity the transitory nature of the mundane world becomes more and more explicit. The clarity of vision and the understanding is in itself liberation and emancipation in all respects. Srī Kṛṣṇa calls him mahatma—means the great soul who consciously becomes a part of the Supreme-Soul; such a special one is not born again after reaching the state of perfection.

Srī Kṛṣṇa mentions that in all the three worlds—right from the realm of Brahma to the mundane world—creatures are rolling in the cycle of birth-death and rebirth. The cycle goes on, until one realizes one's own Divine essence. The person who becomes connected with the Supreme-Self in Yoga and devotes himself to the Lord with undivided devotion is indeed blessed with salvation.

सहस्त्रयुगपर्यन्तमहर्यद् ब्रह्मणो विदुः ।
रात्रिं युगसहस्त्रान्तां तेऽहोरात्रविदो जनाः ॥ १७ ॥

sahasrayugaparyantam aharyad brahmaṇo viduḥ
rātriṁ yugasahasrāntāṁ te'horātravido janāḥ

(17) Those who know that the day of Brahma extends to a thousand epochs (yugas) and also the night extends to a thousand epochs, they are the knowers of the day and night (reality about time).

अव्यक्ताद्व्यक्तयः सर्वाः प्रभवन्त्यहरागमे ।
रात्र्यागमे प्रलीयन्ते तत्रैवाव्यक्तसंज्ञके ॥ १८ ॥

avyaktād vyaktayaḥ sarvāḥ prabhavanty aharāgame
rātryāgame pralīyante tatrai'vāvyaktasaṁjñake

(18) From the unmanifested, all the manifestations emerge at the commencement of the Brahma's day; at the coming of the night, they merge verily into that alone, which is called unmanifested.

भूतग्रामः स एवायं भूत्वा भूत्वा प्रलीयते।
रात्र्यागमेऽवशः पार्थ प्रभवत्यहरागमे ॥ १९ ॥

bhūtagrāmaḥ sa evāyaṁ bhūtvā-bhūtvā pralīyate
rātryāgame'vaśaḥ pārtha prabhavaty aharāgame

(19) The multitude of beings, being born again and again, are dissolved helplessly at the coming of the night, O' Partha. It comes forth again at the beginning of the day.

Commentary—In these verses Srī Kṛṣṇa presents some cosmological concepts in relation to the cycle of time as described in the ancient scriptures. He acquaints Arjuna with the duration of the period of cosmic manifestation and annihilation. Human comprehension staggers in comprehending the time span of Brahma's day and night which expands into infinity. These units of time have been called the day and the night of Brahma, from whence it manifests and into which it dissolves. Time is endless; it has no beginning and no end. The experience of the duration of time is relative; its division and distribution is something for us to experience. Regarding the duration of the day and the night of Brahma (the creator), the calculations have been made in a certain order, which is known as the wheel of time (Kala chakra). Freedom from the cosmic wheel of time and the rounds of birth, death and rebirth has been called salvation (Nirvana). The entire emergence of the creation, its sustenance and dissolution—everything is controlled by the absolute creator (Brahma).

The time duration, which includes the manifestation of the world, its sustenance and annihilation is called 'Kalpa'. The duration of one day of Brahma is called 'Kalpa', and the night is called 'Pralaya'. Thirty rounds of such days and nights is called one month of Brahma and twelve such months put together make one year of Brahma; and one hundred such years constitute the span of Brahma's life. The word *'yuga'* in the verse stands for the four *yugas* described in ancient scriptures of cosmology. The four *'yugas'* are 'Satyuga', 'Treta yuga',

'Dwapara' and 'Kali yuga'. These four 'yugas' together form one 'Mahayuga' or 'Caturyugi'; which is equal to 12,000 x 360 or 43,20,000 human years. One thousand 'Mahayuga' form one 'Kalpa'. According to the figures available in cosmological calculations the 'Satyuga' started on the ninth day of the Lunar calendar in 'Kartika month' on Wednesday morning. The duration has been approximately 17,28,000 years. Next has been the 'Treta yuga'. It started on the third day of the ascending moon in month 'Vishakha' on Monday morning. The duration of 'Treta' has been 12,96,000 years. Next to 'Treta' has been the 'Dvapara'. It started in 'Magha month', on 15th of lunar calendar on Friday morning. The duration has been 8,64,000 years. The 'Kaliyuga' started on the Lunar date, the 13th in 'Bhadra month' at the middle of night on Sunday.

In verse eighteen, Srī Kṛṣṇa tells Arjuna about repeated emanation of the embodied beings from the unmanifest Brahma; and their annihilation at the advent of the night of Brahma. The embodied beings keep revolving into the rounds of birth, death and rebirth until they realize the bondage for themselves, and make efforts for their liberation. Multitude of beings come into existence out of compulsion, bound by the law of karma. This has been going on since time immemorial and does not stop even when everything gets annihilated into the primordial prakriti at the fall of Brahma's night. The word *'avash'*, used by Srī Kṛṣṇa, is in itself self-explanatory; all beings appearing into existence and merging back into the unmanifest are indeed tied very strongly with the rope of their own respective karmas. Everyone in the world is moving around, as if programmed in his self-created software of latencies, memories, karmas and samskaras. This software is called the subtle body. Each individual's subtle body is the subtlest spark of Brahma. It is indeed the Brahma (the creator) who brings forth the creation.

The question may arise who is *Brahma*? The word *Brahma* is different from the word *Brahman*. The word *Brahman* denotes the Supreme Soul, 'The Absolute.' And the word *Brahma* means one of the aspects of the *Trimurti*—the *Brahma, Vishnu,* and *Mahesh*. *Brahma* is the creator of the universe. The word *Brahma* has been derived from the root word *brh,* meaning to grow and expand. *Brahma* is the cosmic subtle body. The subtle body is constituted of mind, intellect and ego *(mana, budhi, ahankara).* All the thoughts, Karmas and samkaras are indeed the creation of mind intellect and ego. It is under the slavery of mind, intellect and ego, the embodied soul becomes helplessly bound. The individual-self by his own ignorance creates this trap for himself; and becomes bound. *Brahma* the creator is the sum-total of all the subtle bodies and so is called the universal subtle body. *Brahma* symbolizes the embodied-self with its inner instruments, such as mind, intellect and ego. The inner instruments are the store house of thoughts, memories and latencies of the past and present. The present is the manifestation of yesterday and also fore-runner of tomorrow. It is the individual himself, who brings forth every new birth for himself in accordance with the respective data programmed in his own software. Just as the seed is subjected to recurrence, so are the thoughts of an individual. The entire creation dissolves at the night of *Brahma* which is *Pralaya* and comes back into manifestation bound by the previous karmas, at the beginning of each new *Kalpa.* It is exactly as the siblings off shoot from the seeds. The Vedic sages has described this process in these words: *yatha purva makalpayas*—as contemplated and created earlier. According to Swami Ramsukhdas, "The multitude of beings is ever the same. But because of their nature, full of attachment and aversion, they are born again and again under compulsion, at the time of the cosmic day, and are dissolved in Him at the approach of the cosmic night." By using the word 'same multitude of beings', Srī Kṛṣṇa means the same expression of the conditioned behaviour of beings. The thoughts, which stay dormant in the deepest layers of the consciousness, appear on the surface of the conscious level and find their expression in different lives. The old desires pursue their fulfilment in a life-time and give new birth to many more new desires. People check-in in this world with a baggage of old desires to be fulfilled; and also check-out with some baggage of new desires because of their additional shopping in every new life. Most of this behaviour is very unconscious and quite, unknown to the individual himself. It happens compulsively and helplessly. Man is indeed a helpless creature, bound by his own emotions, and remains helpless until he surrenders himself totally to the Divine and becomes enlightened about the real and unreal.

परस्तस्मात्तु भावोऽन्योऽव्यक्तोऽव्यक्तात्सनातनः ।
यः स सर्वेषु भूतेषु नश्यत्सु न विनश्यति ॥ २० ॥

parastasmāttu bhāvo'nyo'vyakto'vyaktāt sanātanaḥ
yaḥ sa sarveṣu bhūteṣu naśyatsu na vinaśyati

(20) Beyond this unmanifested, verily there is another unmanifested, Eternal, which does not perish even when all existence perish.

अव्यक्तोऽक्षर इत्युक्तस्तमाहुः परमां गतिम् ।
यं प्राप्य न निवर्तन्ते तद्धाम परमं मम ॥ २१ ॥

avyakto'kṣara ityuktastam āhuḥ paramāṁ gatim
yaṁ prāpya na nivartante taddhāma paramaṁ mama

(21) This Unmanifested and Imperishable is said to be the highest goal, upon attaining which, there is no return. That is My Supreme Abode.

पुरुषः स परः पार्थ भक्त्या लभ्यस्त्वनन्यया ।
यस्यान्तःस्थानि भूतानि येन सर्वमिदं ततम् ॥ २२ ॥

puruṣaḥ sa paraḥ pārtha bhaktyā labhyastvananyayā
yasyāntaḥ sthāni bhūtāni yena sarvam idaṁ tatam

(22) That Supreme transcendent Purusha, O'Arjuna, is attainable by undivided devotion; within whom all the beings reside and by whom all this is pervaded.

Commentary—In these verses, Srī Kṛṣṇa draws Arjuna's attention towards his own essential nature (his own *swaroopa*). Beyond the Divine manifestation is the unmanifested *Brahma* but beyond that is another unmanifested which does not undergo any change. That immutable unmanifested forms the substratum of the entire universe. The supreme state of transcendence is unchangeable, imperishable and ever blissful. The individual who attains the Supreme-state of transcendence do not return to the world of mortals. He rests in his own *swaroopa* (the essential nature). The pursuit for peace and the highest abode of tranquillity must start early in lifetime. It starts with a shift in awareness when the individual questions himself, "Why my life is so conditioned, why every event takes place so helplessly, why I feel bound and enslaved to all the circumstances?" The pursuit and inquiry into all these questions gives him the clue of bondage and then he makes efforts for liberation.

Srī Kṛṣṇa suggests that those who start this pursuit definitely march through it eventually into the highest abode from where they don't return to the world of mortals. The person who has experienced the presence of the unmanifested, he moves effortlessly towards the attainment of the goal. The transcendental experience is a blessing of the Divine, but is surely attained by one's own efforts and insight. In the first line of the verse twenty-two, Srī Kṛṣṇa suggests very casually *Purushah sa parah partha bhaktya labhyas tv ananyaya.* The supreme transcendental personality can be experienced and contacted with undeviated devotion. Single minded devotion is indeed one method which has been highly advocated by Srī Kṛṣṇa. History is full of examples from the life stories of the great devotees who attained perfection and liberation through undeviated devotion. The devotional songs of Meerabai are saturated with unconditional devotion to the Lord. Each word of her couplets is full of her love for Srī Kṛṣṇa. Meera, as inspired by her previous latencies of earlier births, developed deep devotion for the Divine in her early childhood. Once a sage visited the palace of her father and gave Meera an idol of Lord Kṛṣṇa. She loved Lord Kṛṣṇa in that image and gradually the image became settled in the shrine of her heart. She lived her entire life in the consciousness of the supreme. Her undivided devotion has been so beautifully expressed in her songs.

Meera's happiness is with Shyama only.

Please allow me to serve you O' Kṛṣṇa

I have been waiting to be in your kind service.

You are the companion of my many lives,

My master, and my Lord.

Take a permanent seat

In the groves of my heart.

Only your love is true,

Only your friendship is eternal.

While going through the devotional songs of Meera one can really perceive her single-minded devotion for the Lord. Her words clearly indicate the spirit of living in the transcendence. Although some of her words describe the separation from the Lord but she does not feel herself to be lost in separation. She indicates the consciousness of constantly living in the presence of her Lord. Her identification with the Supreme-Self is very subtle, powerful, positive and full of self-assurance. The songs of Meera echo the integral wisdom, where in the individual-self enters into the unity with the absolute-Self. Srī Kṛṣṇa suggests that the individual becomes blessed with undivided devotion for the Lord, only when he understands his eternal relationship with the Supreme personality. He perceives that the embodied-self and the Supreme-Self are inter-related as the water and the dew or as the water vapour and snow balls. When identity with the Supreme-Soul is recognized and established, it grows stronger and the undivided devotion and adoration for the Lord is strengthened. The individual elevates himself to the purity of the unconditional love and perceives the omniscience of the Lord by whom the entire world is pervaded.

यत्र काले त्वनावृत्तिमावृत्तिं चैव योगिनः ।

प्रयाता यान्ति तं कालं वक्ष्यामि भरतर्षभ ॥ २३ ॥

yatra kāle tvanāvṛttim āvṛttiṁ caiva yoginaḥ

prayātā yānti taṁ kālaṁ vakṣyāmi bharatarṣabha

(23) The time in which the yogis do not return after they depart and also the time when they do return again, of that, I shall tell you, O' best of the Bharatas (Arjuna).

अग्निर्ज्योतिरहः शुक्लः षण्मासा उत्तरायणम् ।

तत्र प्रयाता गच्छन्ति ब्रह्म ब्रह्मविदो जनाः ॥ २४ ॥

agnir jyotir ahaḥ śuklaḥ ṣaṇmāsā uttrāyaṇam

tatra prayātā gacchanti brahma brahmavido janāḥ

(24) Fire, light, the day time, the moonlit fortnight, the six months of the sun's northern course—departing in that time; the men who know Brahman go to Brahman.

धूमो रात्रिस्तथा कृष्णः षण्मासा दक्षिणायनम्।

तत्र चान्द्रमसं ज्योतिर्योगी प्राप्य निवर्तते ॥ २५ ॥

dhūmo rātristathā kṛṣṇaḥ ṣaṇmāsā dakṣiṇāyanam

tatra cāndramasaṁ jyotir yogī prāpya nivartate

(25) Smoke, the night time, the dark lunar fortnight, the six months of the sun's southern course—having obtained the lunar light, the yogi returns (to the world of mortals).

शुक्लकृष्णे गती ह्येते जगतः शाश्वते मते।

एकया यात्यनावृत्तिमन्ययावर्तते पुनः ॥ २६ ॥

śuklakṛṣṇe gatī hy ete jagataḥ śāśvate mate

ekayā yāty anāvṛttimanyayā'vartate punaḥ

(26) The bright and the dark paths of the world are verily thought to be perennial. By the one a person leaves not to return, while by the other he returns again.

नैते सृती पार्थ जानन्योगी मुह्यति कश्चन।

तस्मात्सर्वेषु कालेषु योगयुक्तो भवार्जुन ॥ २७ ॥

naite sṛtī pārtha jānan yogī muhyati kaścana

tasmāt sarveṣu kāleṣu yogayukto bhavārjuna

(27) Knowing these two paths, O'Arjuna, the yogi is not deluded. Therefore, at all times, stay united in Yoga, O'Arjuna.

वेदेषु यज्ञेषु तपःसु चैव

दानेषु यत्पुण्यफलं प्रदिष्टम्।

अत्येति तत्सर्वमिदं विदित्वा

योगी परं स्थानमुपैति चाद्यम् ॥ २८ ॥

veduṣu yajñeṣu tapaḥsu caiva

dāneṣu yat puṇyaphalaṁ pradiṣṭam

atyeti tat sarvam idaṁ viditvā
yogī paraṁ sthānam upaiti cādyam

(28) The yogi, who realizes this profound truth, he transcends all the rewards of the meritorious deeds attached to the study of the Vedas, performance of sacrifices, austerities, and charities—he attains the Supreme primal status.

Commentary—These verses are in continuation of Srī Kṛṣṇa's answer to Arjuna's question about the journey of the soul hereafter. He draws Arjuna's attention to the fact that human mind remains connected with the changes in nature right from the day when the person is born until the time of his departure from the world. As in birth signs, the position of the sun and moon is considered the most important so is the position of sun and moon at the time of death. The equatorial line which forms the centre divides the earth in two hemispheres—the northern and southern. The equator is at the zero degree and receives the sun rays at exact ninety degree throughout the year. There are two Equinoxes in a year, the spring Equinox on March 21st and the autumn Equinox on Sept. 23rd. From zero degree northward at the 23.5 degree is the tropic of Cancer and at 23.5 degree southward is the tropic of Capricorn. As the earth goes around the sun in 365 days, on Dec. 22nd the sun's rays occupy the tropic of Capricorn at 90 degree and that marks the winter solstice. It is at this time, the Northern course of the sun starts and it is called *Uttarayana* in Sanskrit. At that time the sun is considered to be in the birth sign of Capricorn. From this point (the tropic of Capricorn) starts the Northern course known as *Uttarayana* which ends on June 21st at 23.5 degree Northward from the equator at the tropic of Cancer. This is called the summer solstice from where the sun's southern course starts which is known as *Daksinayana.* 'Daksin' means the South and *'ayana'* means to dwell. Human nature is very closely connected to mother nature. As the inborn nature of the person is determined in natal chart, by the position of the Sun and Moon at the time of birth, similarly the position of the Sun and Moon does influence the journey, hereafter at the time of death. It is for this reason Srī Kṛṣṇa introduces Arjuna to some of these terms of the mystic philosophy, religion and astrology. The Lord wants Arjuna to understand the very strong bond of human mind with nature, right from the moment of birth to death.

Srī Kṛṣṇa starts the conversation in verse twenty-four with the words such as fire and light which stands for the heat in body, day time, the ascending phase of the Moon and the Northern course of the Sun known as Uttarayana. Srī Kṛṣṇa is emphasizing the word 'light' (jyoti) which helps the departing person to leave through the path of Light. This path of light and fire has been called *aarchira path* in the ancient religious scriptures. At the time of death, it is surely the heat in the body which guides the life force to make an easy departure from the body. It is the heat that keeps the breath and phlegm in balance, the awareness and the remembrance of the Lord's name clear and precise. The mind stays alert and easily glides into the inner cave of the heart. When the mind and intellect are fully awake the yogi can direct the life-force in the desired direction. As mentioned earlier in this chapter, out of the hundred and one arteries of the heart, there is one which goes to the crown of the head. This special spot in the centre of the skull in spiritual language is called Brahmarandhra. The life force going upward through this soft spot in the centre of the skull goes to Brahman. So the fiery light in the body, the day time, the waxing phase of the Moon and the Sun in the northern course, all of these together harmonize the light and heat in the body and the cosmos. The harmony between the macrocosm and microcosm keeps the mental make up of the individual in perfect balance. The individual feels at total peace within and concentrates at the goal while departing from the body. He knows how to withdraw the senses from the sense object into the mind and how to fuse the mind into the breath, and breath into the light, and light into the sun and into the Absolute. This is called the *Archira Path* or the path of light.

The other one mentioned here is the path of darkness. Smoke is symbolic of darkness, ignorance and confusion. The word *dhumah* stands for the presiding deity of the smoke which symbolizes darkness. The word *Ratrih* also symbolizes the deity presiding darkness. The waning phase of Moon is the dark fortnight and the six months of the Sun's southern course (Daksinayana) also symbolizes darkness. Smoke in the body stands for the imbalance state of the breath, which makes the movement of the phlegm and air in the body very difficult. When the breathing rhythm is severely interrupted, the person's breath makes loud noise. This causes a great loss of heat in the body, and the person feels very uncomfortable. The difficulty in breathing causes confusion of mind and the embodied-self becomes deluded. When the person feels unable to direct the breath in the desired direction, he feels totally surrounded by the cloud of thick smoke, in the form of helplessness. When the mind is confused, it creates emotional conflict because it is uncertain about the upcoming moment. The thought process becomes scattered and the clarity of goal is lost. Moon represents the world of emotions and essentially matter. When yogi goes to the region of the Moon he returns to the world of mortals. Srī Kṛṣṇa explains Arjuna the two paths; from the path of fire and light one attains salvation and from the path of darkness the person comes back to the world of mortals. The path of light is travelled by the man of inner integrity. The yogi who is ever connected with the Lord in yoga, who acts in yoga, thinks and moves in yoga, he leaves his body in the light of yoga. The inner integrity helps his mind to be one pointed towards the goal and enables him to leave his mortal body with a clarity of vision. The yogi who lives in unity with Brahman he is naturally directed towards oneness with *Brahman* at death. He doesn't have to make any special effort for proper alignment. The person who knows the art of living, he definitely knows the art of dying. Srī Kṛṣṇa wants Arjuna to understand the importance of yogic unity in life. He emphasizes that the individual should learn to live in the awareness of the Divine under all circumstances. All the religious practices, all austerities, penances, study of religious scriptures, yajnas and charities are indeed very helpful for self-purification; but once the yogic unity is established with the Divine, the devotee transcends all these religious disciplines. He identifies himself with the Divine and educates himself to live in the consciousness of the Divine from minute to minute of his life. Srī Kṛṣṇa suggests Arjuna to live in the consciousness of the Supreme Lord and fight the battle. Face the life with courage, self-reliance, self-confidence, inner strength and dignity.

ॐ तत्सदिति श्रीमद्भगवद्गीतासूपनिषत्सु ब्रह्मविद्यायां
योगशास्त्रे श्रीकृष्णार्जुनसंवादे अक्षरब्रह्मयोगो
नाम अष्टमोऽध्यायः ॥ ८ ॥

'Aum' tatsaditi Śrīmadbhagawadgeetā sūpaniṣatsu brahmavidyāyām yogaśāstre Śrīkṛṣṇārjunasamvāde akṣarabrahmayogo nāma aṣṭmo'dhyāyaḥ

'AUM TAT SAT'—Thus, in the Upanishad of the glorious Bhagawad Geeta, the science of the Brahman (Absolute) the scripture of yoga, the dialogue between Srī Kṛṣṇa and Arjuna—thus, ends the chapter eight entitled *"Akṣarabrahmayoga"*.

इति श्रीमद्भगवद्गीतासु अष्टमोऽध्यायः ॥ ८ ॥

Chapter Nine

RAJAVIDYARAJAGUHYAYOGA

THE YOGA OF THE SOVEREIGN SCIENCE AND SOVEREIGN SECRET

श्रीभगवानुवाच

इदं तु ते गुह्यतमं प्रवक्ष्याम्यनसूयवे।
ज्ञानं विज्ञानसहितं यज्ज्ञात्वा मोक्ष्यसेऽशुभात्॥ १॥

idaṁ tu te guhyatamaṁ pravakṣyāmy anasūyave
jñānaṁ vijñānasahitaṁ yaj jñātvā mokṣyase'śubhāt

The Blessed Lord said :

(1) To thee, who does not cavil, I shall now unfold the most profound secret of wisdom combined with the experiential knowledge, by knowing which you will be released from evil.

राजविद्या राजगुह्यं पवित्रमिदमुत्तमम्।
प्रत्यक्षावगमं धर्म्यं सुसुखं कर्तुमव्ययम्॥ २॥

rājavidyā rājaguhyaṁ pavitram idam uttamam
pratyakṣāvagamaṁ dharmyaṁ susukhaṁ kartum avyayam

(2) This is the sovereign wisdom, the sovereign mystery, the most purifying excellent and easy to comprehend by direct experience. It is in accordance with the Dharma (righteousness) and renders happiness. It is easy to accomplish and imperishable.

अश्रद्दधानाः पुरुषा धर्मस्यास्य परन्तप।
अप्राप्य मां निवर्तन्ते मृत्युसंसारवर्त्मनि॥ ३॥

aśraddadhānāḥ puruṣā dharmasyā'sya parantapa
aprāpya māṁ nivartante mṛtyusaṁsārvartmani

(3) Persons lacking faith and reverence in the sacred doctrine

(Dharma) O' Arjuna, fail to attain Me. They revolve in the path of the world of death.

Commentary—Srī Kṛṣṇa opens the conversation with encouraging words of strong faith and reverence. The word *anasuyave* explains all this. Arjuna's faith, reverence and the inquisitiveness of mind has been self-evident to Srī Kṛṣṇa. Recognizing Arjuna to be the most desirable candidate, Srī Kṛṣṇa opens the conversation very straightforwardly. To be uncritical is one of the most admirable characteristics of a genuine aspirant. In the words of Saint Matthew, "Ask and it shall be given to you; seek and you shall find; knock, and it shall be opened unto you, for everyone that asketh receiveth; and he that asketh findeth; and to him that knocketh it shall be opened." For comprehending the mysteries of spiritual knowledge, one really doesn't have to have much pre-requisite in philosophy and religion. The knowledge of the Supreme Divinity is inherently present in all of us; it becomes revealed, when the individual takes refuge in God and pursues spirituality with undeviated devotion. Srī Kṛṣṇa is emphasizing on the doctrine of enlightenment and God-realization through loving faith and devotion. He considers it to be the noblest and the most rewarding method. The expression *pratyaksavagamam* means to be experienced and realized by direct communion and communication. It has been called the Supreme purifier because it is the fulfilment in itself and at the same time also a means for increased fulfilment. It removes all blemishes from the heart of the individual in the process itself. It is pleasurable to practise and its enjoyment renews every minute. It is surely imperishable. People who lack the insight of comprehending its sovereignty, purity and supremacy, they generally become involved in the intellectual discussion and difficult penances. Srī Kṛṣṇa declares that those who overlook the subtle power of devotional services to the Divine, and remain involved in the structural explanations of the tough and dry reason, they are generally deprived of the true experiential knowledge of the Self, and are bound to the repeated returns in the world of mortals.

मया ततमिदं सर्वं जगदव्यक्तमूर्तिना ।
मत्स्थानि सर्वभूतानि न चाहं तेष्ववस्थितः ॥ ४ ॥

mayā tatam idaṁ sarvaṁ jagad avyaktamūrtinā
matshāni sarvabhūtāni na cāhaṁ teṣvavasthitaḥ

(4) This whole universe is pervaded by Me, in My unmanifest aspect. All the beings exist in Me, but I do not dwell in them.

न च मत्स्थानि भूतानि पश्य मे योगमैश्वरम्।
भूतभृन्न च भूतस्थो ममात्मा भूतभावनः॥ ५ ॥

na ca matsthāni bhūtāni paśya me yogam aiśvaram
bhutabhṛan na ca bhūtastho mamātmā bhūtabhāvanaḥ

(5) Nor do the beings exist in Me; behold My divine Yoga! I Myself am the creator and sustainer of all beings, yet I do not dwell in them.

यथाकाशस्थितो नित्यं वायुः सर्वत्रगो महान्।
तथा सर्वाणि भूतानि मत्स्थानीत्युपधारय॥ ६ ॥

yathākāśasthito niyam vāyuḥ sarvatrago mahān
tathā sarvāni bhūtāni matsthānītyupadhāraya

(6) As the mighty wind, always rests in the ether, while it moves everywhere; likewise know thou, that all created beings rest in Me.

Commentary—Srī Kṛṣṇa has been repeatedly trying to enlighten Arjuna about his own divine potential, for him to act effortlessly and skilfully. It is indeed important for Arjuna to realize and experience the power of his own inner resources. Arjuna has to experience that he exists in God and all his activities are being carried on with the help of the power from within. He has to overcome his egocentric individuality and work in an alignment with the Supreme soul. Arjuna has to understand the indwelling God as the true essence of life and act consciously from the source within. God is beyond cause, space and time. God neither influences any activity nor is influenced by any emotion, feeling or action. The Absolute is pure luminous and imperishable. It is only a fragment of the Supreme Soul who is trapped into its own limited individuality and claims himself to be the embodied-self. This individual-self, under the tyranny of personal ego, likes to form its own separate identity and wants to stay aloof and secluded. All these beings are fragments of the Super-soul. They draw their energy from one and the only source. All beings are created in accordance with their own *swabhava* (innate nature) and are indeed supported and sustained by the Lord Himself. This is what Srī Kṛṣṇa says, they dwell in Me but I don't dwell in them. The Supreme Lord nourishes the entire creation, yet is not bound by anything. Man is created, nourished and sustained by the Supreme-self but unfortunately still remains unaware of the Lord's presence within. Man lives in his own limited identity, created from his own limited egocentric point of view.

The soul's identification with the body is very deep-rooted and is very difficult to overcome. This separate identification of the embodied-self is the cause of all fears and insecurities in life. Srī Kṛṣṇa knows that Arjuna will co-operate enthusiastically, skilfully, peacefully, and harmoniously only when he is blessed with the experiential knowledge of his own essentiality and perceives his individual-self to be a perennial fragment of the Universal-self. Arjuna has to clearly understand and experience the truth that he is indeed a fragment of the Supreme-power; and a very unique manifestation of the Lord Himself. By giving the example of the immeasurable space and as the air rests in that, Srī Kṛṣṇa wants Arjuna to comprehend the infinitude of Brahman, and experience its connectedness. It is only after the personal experience of his connectedness with the cosmic Self, Arjuna will intelligently cooperate in all respects. It is only after the perceptual knowledge of his own immortality that he will feel more like an instrument in the hands of the Divine power.

The moment a person consciously experiences the inner Divinity, and feels himself a part of the ever renewing current, his lifestyle changes instantly. His insecurities and fears are washed away with inner enlightenment. The individual becomes awakened in all respects and learns to live in the renewed concept of reality. His capacity to work becomes enormous and he works in perfect harmony with *swadharma.* His vision becomes one-pointed and his purpose of life becomes very clear to him.

सर्वभूतानि कौन्तेय प्रकृतिं यान्ति मामिकाम्।
कल्पक्षये पुनस्तानि कल्पादौ विसृजाम्यहम्॥७॥

sarvabhūtāni kaunya prakṛtiṁ yānti māmikām
kalpakṣaye punas tāni kalpādau visṛjāmyaham

(7) All beings, O' Kaunteya (Arjuna), go into My Nature, at the end of each *kalpa* and again at the beginning of the next *kalpa*, I send them forth again.

प्रकृतिं स्वामवष्टभ्य विसृजामि पुनः पुनः।
भूतग्राममिमं कृत्स्नमवशं प्रकृतेर्वशात्॥८॥

prakṛtiṁ svam avaṣṭabhya visṛjāmi punaḥ-punaḥ
bhūtagrāmam imaṁ kṛtsnam avaśaṁ prakṛter vaśāt

(8) Having hold on My nature, I send forth again and again the multitude of beings, subject to the helplessness of their own nature.

न च मां तानि कर्माणि निबध्नन्ति धनञ्जय।
उदासीनवदासीनमसक्तं तेषु कर्मसु॥९॥

na ca māṁ tāni karmāṇi nibadhnanti dhanañjaya
udāsīnavadāsīnam asaktaṁ teṣu karmasu

(9) These actions do not bind Me, O'Dhananjaya (Arjuna), for I remain seated like the one unconcerned and unattached in those actions.

मयाध्यक्षेण प्रकृतिः सूयते सचराचरम्।
हेतुनानेन कौन्तेय जगद्विपरिवर्तते॥१०॥

mayādhyakṣeṇa prakṛtiḥ sūyate sacarācaram
hetunānena kaunteya jagad viparivartate

(10) Under My supervision, Nature gives birth to all, the moving and the unmoving—by this means O' Kaunteya (Arjuna) the world revolves.

Commentary—As described in the previous chapter, the duration of one day of Brahma is known as *kalpa* and the night is called *praylaya.* The three hundred and sixty five *kalpa* together form a year of Brahma and hundred such years forms the span of Brahma's life. The four yugas together form one *mahayuga* or *caturyugi* which is equal to 43,20,000 human years. One thousand *mahayuga* form one *kalpa*. The end of one *kalpa* and beginning of the next one is the time-span from the beginning of the new creation and to the final annihilation. At the onset of each *kalpa,* Brahma emanates from the Supreme Divinity, with the mass collection of the *samskaras* and the latencies bringing each being into existence. At the end of each *kalpa* all embodied-souls merge into the Cosmic-soul, bonded by their own individual latencies. It is the individual's slavery to thoughts, desires and dreams that helplessly brings him back to the rounds of birth-death and rebirth over and over again. Srī Kṛṣṇa declares clearly that the people, who live and die under the slavery of the triads of nature, become trapped into the delusion of 'I and Mine'. They keep rolling back and forth into many lives. The indirect message is that for liberation and emancipation, one must change the inherited habits of the conditioned behaviour and the false identifications. The false identities are the cause of slavery to nature and bondage to thoughts and actions. A complete understanding with proper insight of the real and unreal is very important for freedom during the life and hereafter. The entire creation obviously moves bonded by the conditions and limitations imposed upon the beings by themselves. To make it clear Srī Kṛṣṇa uses the word *Avasam* which means moving helplessly. There are some lines by Omer Khayyam which also explain the same truth quite vividly : "And that inverted Bowl we call the sky, where under, crawling coop't, we live and die, Lift not thy hands to it for help, for it rolls, impotently on as, You and I." Bonded by the slavery of their own conditioned nature, woven in latencies and thoughts, the beings move helplessly in the rounds of many births. All the beings move spontaneously, helplessly, unknowingly as conditioned by their own habits. In the words of Swami Ramsukhdas, "How surprising it is that a man is bound by having affinity with those actions and their fruits, things and men etc. that perish. The mundane objects are all perishable but affinity with them persists. The men die but affinity with them still remains, how foolish really." Each new *kalpa* brings an opportunity for the beings to elevate themselves to the transcendental awareness and realize their forgotten identity with the Divine. Those who make efforts, regain their lost empire, but others those who don't realize their slavery, remain revolving into the cycle of *samsara* which goes on and on.

After presenting some glimpses of the conditioned nature of beings, Srī Kṛṣṇa draws Arjuna's attention again towards the liberated nature of the Supreme-soul. The Absolute Divinity brings forth the entire creation, nourishes and sustains but still remains unconcerned and unattached. The Lord acts as the witnessing director of the mighty universe. He uses the *prakriti* (Nature) as an instrument for bringing forth creation. Mother nature works under the direct guidance of the pure-Self. Shri Janeshwariji has given a very good example: "Just as the subject ruled by a king go about their business, so is the God's relation with Prakriti, it is the Nature that acts. The full moon produces great tides in the sea, it does not have to exert itself for that purpose. The piece of iron though heavy moves towards the magnet, which is close by, but the magnet does not become exhausted thereby." This is indeed a great mystery of the Lord's work. The nature works under the direct superintendence of the Lord, it is the Divine potency manifesting in each and everything but the absolute Lord is not in them. Nature goes through some changes and modifications but the Supreme-soul remains uncontaminated, unchangeable and imperishable.

अवजानन्ति मां मूढा मानुषीं तनुमाश्रितम्।
परं भावमजानन्तो मम भूतमहेश्वरम्॥ ११ ॥

avajānanti māṁ mūḍhā mānuṣīṁ tanum āśritam
paraṁ bhāvam ajānanto mama bhūtamaheśvaram

मोघाशा मोघकर्माणो मोघज्ञाना विचेतसः।
राक्षसीमासुरीं चैव प्रकृतिं मोहिनीं श्रिताः॥ १२ ॥

moghāśā moghakarmāṇo moghajñānā vicetasaḥ
rākṣasīṁ āsurīṁ caiva prakṛtiṁ mohinīṁ śritāḥ

(11,12) The fools disregard Me, dwelling in human form. They do not know My transcendental nature, as the great Lord of all beings.

With vain hopes, vain actions and with vain knowledge, they senselessly become possessed of the deceitful nature of demons and monsters.

Commentary—In continuation of the previous verse Srī Kṛṣṇa enlightens Arjuna about the truth, why beings are caught in the meshes of delusion and perpetual rounds of birth-death and rebirth. The invisible Supreme power permeates the entire creation and is very subtle to comprehend without earnest efforts. The power exists and dwells in every being from the subtlest to the grossest, from the littlest to the biggest. Srī Kṛṣṇa says that the fools disregard and ignore the presence of the Divine in the body and get trapped in the coils of Maya. They are deluded, that is why they fail to realize the power of the Divine that manifests through everything. Trapped in their own conditioned behaviour they fail to develop any relationship with the Supreme-soul. They overlook the supremacy of the Divine which transcends the perishable matter and also the imperishable embodied-self. In their delusion they ignore the presence of the Divine within and get trapped into the snare of the lower nature which is demoniacal and fiendish. These people are constantly involved in the pursuit of selfish motives and unconsciously get involved in the activities which are against Dharma (moral code). Because of their ignorance of the presence of the Divine within themselves, their life becomes consciously disconnected from the Supreme-soul within, and also from the indwelling-self in others. They become very insensitive and selfish. They enjoy in creating troubles for others and in harming others. Such people like to become an obstacle in the progress of others, both materially and spiritually. Srī Kṛṣṇa is emphasizing upon the need for experiencing the Supreme-self residing in the human body. Without accepting the consciousness of the presence of Divine in body, one lives a life, which is helplessly ruled by conditioned nature. He condemns those fools who remain unaware of the transcendental nature of the Self. They become possessed of deceitful nature of demons and monsters. Since they remain devoid of the rich experience of the Higher-self within, their life becomes a total waste. Srī Kṛṣṇa also tells Arjuna that these people of limited understanding can never recognize the Lord when He incarnates in human form. It is beyond their comprehension to believe that the Lord Himself can ever assume the human form and can appear as the God-Incarnate; who lives among others as an ordinary human beings. The Supreme Lord incarnates on earth, in order to teach human beings that the Divine status is a prerogative of every embodied-soul. The God-incarnate guides other people into accepting the laws of Dharma. Srī Kṛṣṇa says that the people of meagre understanding fail to experience the Divinity within, they remain deprived of such an enriching experience.

महात्मानस्तु मां पार्थ दैवीं प्रकृतिमाश्रिताः।
भजन्त्यनन्यमनसो ज्ञात्वा भूतादिमव्ययम्॥ १३॥

mahātmānastu māṁ pārtha daivīṁ prakṛtim āśritāḥ
bhajanty nanyamanaso jñātvā bhūtādim avyayam

(13) But the great souls, O' Partha (Arjuna), resorting to the divine nature, devote themselves to Me, with undistracted mind; knowing Me as the source of entire creation and imperishable.

सततं कीर्तयन्तो मां यतन्तश्च दृढव्रताः।
नमस्यन्तश्च मां भक्त्या नित्ययुक्ता उपासते॥ १४॥

satataṁ kīrtayanto māṁ yatantaś ca dṛḍhavratāḥ
namasyantaś ca māṁ haktyā nityayuktā upāsate

(14) Always singing My glories and endeavouring with determined vows, prostrating before Me with love and humility, they worship Me with steadfast devotion.

ज्ञानयज्ञेन चाप्यन्ये यजन्तो मामुपासते।
एकत्वेन पृथक्त्वेन बहुधा विश्वतोमुखम्॥ १५॥

jñānayajñena cāpyanye yajanto mām upāsate
ekatvena pṛthaktvena bahudhā viśvatomukham

(15) Others worship Me through their offerings of integral knowledge, as the One, as distinct and as manifold, facing in all directions.

Commentary—The individuals who are ever united in constant identity with the Supreme-Self, they gradually rise above the limitations of the egocentric self; from *jivatma* they rise to the heights of Mahatma which means a great soul. The purity, virtuosity and piety of the Divine shines through them. They become the embodiment of the Supreme-Self. They are always living in God, walking with God and working with God. Their each word comes from the depths of their love and devotion for God. The chanting of the Lord's holy name is always on their lips, and the contentment of inner fulfilment reflects through their gestures. They are steadfast in their vows, and are perpetually striving for self-realization and God-realization. The absorption into the appreciation of the Lord, becomes their favourite past time, their entertainment and enjoyment. The word *yatantah* stands for constant endeavour i.e. always making conscious efforts for unity consciousness. *Narad Bhakti Sutra* gives some glimpses of such Divine love in these words: *Tasmin ananyata tad virodhisu udasinata ca*—the unification with the Lord in every way. For a true devotee of the Lord, renunciation means the merging of the individual soul into the universal soul. Glorifying the greatness of God's love—*Narad Bhakti Sutra* describes *phalarupatvat* devotion for God is in itself the fruit. Srī Kṛṣṇa explains to Arjuna that some devotees maintain their unity with the Divine by singing His glories, chanting His name and offering all their work as a service; while others serve the Supreme-Soul by identifying themselves with 'Sat-chit-anand'—truth, awareness and bliss. For these men of wisdom the duality of form and shape disappears and they live in constant unity with the Lord. They remain deeply grounded in the awareness of the Divine and also experience the Lord reflected through others. They worship the Absolute Lord as 'One', undivided and pure consciousness.

'Jñana-yajña' encompasses in it the study of the scriptures, the knowledge of the Supreme Lord and also the proper sharing of that knowledge with others. 'Jñana-yajña' is an endeavour on the part of the devotee to observe the expression of eternal principle manifesting through every little molecule and through each and every being. It is also the devotion to the Lord with proper insight combined with scriptural knowledge. It strengthens the faith and promotes the spiritual understanding. A Jñana Yogi lives in constant remembrance of the Divine and beholds the auspicious vision of the Supreme everywhere.

He moves around in the world beholding his own self being reflected through everyone and everything.

अहं क्रतुरहं यज्ञः स्वधाहमहमौषधम्।
मन्त्रोऽहमहमेवाज्यमहमग्निरहं हुतम्॥ १६॥

ahaṁ kratur ahaṁ yajñaḥ svadhāham aham auṣadham
mantro'ham aham evājyam aham agnir ahaṁ hutam

(16) I am the Vaidika ritual and also the yajña, I am the offering given to ancestors, I am the medicinal herb of oblation. I am the sacred hymn, I am the clarified butter, I am the fire, I am the act of offering the oblation.

पिताहमस्य जगतो माता धाता पितामहः।
वेद्यं पवित्रमोङ्कार ऋक्साम यजुरेव च॥ १७॥

pitāham asya jagato mātā dhātā pitāmahaḥ
vedyaṁ pavitram oṅkāra ṛksāma yajureva ca.

गतिर्भर्ता प्रभुः साक्षी निवासः शरणं सुहृत्।
प्रभवः प्रलयः स्थानं निधानं बीजमव्ययम्॥ १८॥

gatir bhartā prabhuḥ sākṣī nivāsaḥ śaraṇaṁ suhṛt
prabhavaḥ pralayaḥ sthānaṁ nidhānaṁ bījam avyayam.

(17,18) I am the Father of this world and also the Mother, the sustainer and the Grandfather. I am the object of sacred knowledge, I am the purifier and the sacred syllable AUM. I am *Rigveda, Samveda* and also the *Yajurveda.* I am the goal, the supporter, the Lord, the witness, the abode, the refuge, and the well-wisher. I am the origin and the dissolution, the resting place, the store-house and the imperishable seed of the universe.

तपाम्यहमहं वर्षं निगृह्णाम्युत्सृजामि च।
अमृतं चैव मृत्युश्च सदसच्चाहमर्जुन॥ १९॥

tapāmy aham ahaṁ varṣaṁ nigṛhṇāmy utsṛjāmi ca
amṛtaṁ caiva mṛtyuś ca sadasaccāhmarjuna

(19) I radiate heat, I withhold and send forth the rain, I am immortality as well as death, I am being as well as non-being,

O'Arjuna (existence and non-existence).

Commentary—The expression *visvatomukham* used in the verse fifteen means the universal form, facing everywhere. Lord is the essence of the universe and sustains creation. The world *Visva* is derived from the root word *Visa* which means to reside. God is called 'Visva' because in Him resides the entire world. Although different things and beings seem to be different, in forms, shapes and characteristics, but everybody and everything is rooted in the essentiality of the Supreme Soul.

'That Thou art' is the eternal truth of all existence. The diversity of the universe, the multiplicity which exists in the ever renewing stream of life, there is only one reality. In the words of Shri Ramanuja, "Everything originates from the primordial state itself, embedded in God and goes back to it when it loses its gross existence. God projects the aggregate of manifold beings into manifestation through the power of subtle nature lodged in Him and they are governed by the laws of nature sustained by Him." This verse echoes the fact, explained in the verse twenty-fourth of the fourth chapter, that there is nothing beside the one Supreme-being, shining through the entire existence. The Lord says I am the one who performs the *yajña,* I am the *samagri,* the mixtures of herbs and the medicinal root and leaves used for offering with the purified butter. The *agnihotra*, which every individual is expected to perform everyday for self purification and for the purification of the air, is basically performed with the clarified butter *(ghee)* and with the mixtures of leaves and roots of medicinal plants. The clarified butter, when offered as an oblation in the fire, sends forth its wonderful fragrance for miles and miles and also acts as a cleansing agent. The herbal plants used for offerings are fumigating substances (herbs) and highly beneficial in purifying environment.

Amba *(Magifera Indica Linn)*	Amra *(Spondias Magifera)*
Babul *(Acacia)*	Bargad *(Ficus Benga Lensis)*
Neem *(Mellia Azadirachta)*	Gular *(Ficus Glomerata)*
Peepal *(Ficus Religiosa)*	Palash *(Butea Frondosa-Roxb)*
Ashoka *(Saraca Indica)*	Chandan *(Sandalwood Powder)*
Kapur kachri *(Hedychillim, Spicatum)*	Gugal *(Boswellia Serrate Roxb)*

Nar-kachura *(Curcuma Coesia Roxb)* Sugandh bala *(Pavinica Odorata)*
Illayachi green *(Cardamom green)* Laung *(Cloves)*
Dalchini *(Cinnamon)* Kesar *(Saffron)*
Curcuma Zedoria Roxb—

In the verse sixteen, the word *Mantras* stands for the sacred hymns of the Vedas used in *Agnihotra* while making oblations. A *mantra* may consist of a syllable, a single word or a group of words; it is a concise prayer. Regarding the source of *mantras,* it is said that at the beginning of creation some privileged souls were blessed with inner vision. In their deep contemplation they heard some sounds and words which have been called *mantras.* The Rishis have declared that when the mind gets in tune with the inner *Nada* (primordial sound), it can recognize the voice of the universal-self. The sounds which are heard in state of inner unity are universal. Mantras of the *Vedas* are indeed the voice of the Supreme-self and belong to the entire mankind. *Vedas* itself mean the knowledge of the Self to be used and meditated upon by everyone. They present the essence of one supreme being the Supreme Lord who is the Father, Mother, the creator and sustainer of the universe. Srī Kṛṣṇa tells Arjuna that I am the sacred syllable AUM and the entire knowledge of the *Vedas.* AUM is known as the sacred mantra. *Omkar* stands for *Akara, Ukara, Makara*—in short AUM. *Maundukya Upanishad* describes—*Omityetadaksharamidam sarvam tasyopavyaakhyaanam bhootam bhavad bhavishyaditi sarvamomkaara eva*—means the holy syllable AUM is indeed the imperishable Brahman, and the universe is the exposition of His glory, AUM is whatever existed in the past, whatever exists now and will exist in the future. The entire creation has originated from the primordial word, and the primordial sound AUM. As about the *Vedas,* Srī Kṛṣṇa says I am the knowledge of the *Vedas.* The term *veda* signifies the knowledge and wisdom of the Divine. The word *veda* has originated from the root word *vid* mean to know. *Veda* is the wisdom of the supreme given to mankind for the harmonious development and guidance on earth and other planets. According to the holy sages, *Vedas* have been revealed by the omniscient supreme Lord in the beginning of creation. There are four *Vedas.* The names are *Rigveda, Yajurveda, Samaveda* and *Atharvaveda;* each of these have one *upangveda.* The *Rigveda*, which comprises 10,589 hymns, is divided into ten volumes. It is called *Rigveda* because it consists *mantras* called *riks* which exactly means that it describes the nature of all things. *(richastuto).* The ten volumes of *Rigveda* are called the ten *mandalas.* In the first *mandala* there are 1976 *mantras* comprising 191 *suktas.* In the second *mandala* there are 40 *suktas* and 429 *mantras.* The third *mandala* has 62 *suktas* and 617 *mantras.* The fourth *mandala* comprises 87 *suktas* and total 729 *mantras.* In the fifth *mandala*, there are total 727 *mantras* only. In the sixth *mandala* there are 57 *suktas* and 565 *mantras.* In the seventh *mandala* there are 104 *suktas* and 851 *mantras.* In the eighth *mandala* there are 105 *suktas* and 1726 *mantra;* in the ninth *mandala* 114 *suktas* and 1097 *mantras.* The tenth *mandala* has 190 *suktas* and 1754 *mantra.* All the ten *mandalas* comprises together the 1018 *suktas* and 10,589 *mantras.* The *Upaveda* of *Rigveda* is *Ayurveda* and as the word explains itself, it is the science of life. *Ayurveda* describes anatomy, herbs, astronomy, astrology and many other kinds of tantras and yantras etc. It also describes *Patanjali Yogasutra, Charakashastra* and the description of surgical instruments as illustrated in Shusruta. *Rigveda* is full of prayers and poems, explaining the glories of the Divine such as how the heavenly elixir becomes ready to be offered with adoration and dedication to the Divine. It protects and dispels all ignorance and makes the individual blessed.

The second one is *Yajurveda.* The *Upaveda* of this *Veda* is *Dhanurveda. Yajurveda* gives a large description of military science. Treatise written on weapons arms and ammunitions etc. It also deals with rituals performed at various stages of life and also at various occasions in life. The total *mantras* of the *Yajurveda* are 2086. The third one is *Samveda* and its *Upaveda* is *Gandharvaveda. Samveda* refers to melodies, music, art, drama, creative writing etc. It includes the knowledge of sound and beats in music. It illustrates the composition of music notes etc. In *Samaveda* there are 1875 *mantras.* The fourth one is the *Atharvaveda* which comprises the total of 5,977 *mantras.* The *Upaveda* of *Atharvaveda* is *Arthveda;* which is a scripture of various branches of education. For example, the metallurgical, mechanical, technical engineering, aircrafts, finances, economics, telegraph, sociology and statistics. A part of *Arthveda* deals with the various branches of physics, psychology and natural sciences and arithmetic. The digits are numbered from the unit to billions and trillions. Although in verse sixteen the Rishi Vyasa has mentioned only three *Vedas* of the early vedic time, the recognition of the fourth, the *Atharvaveda*, came to be known to mankind long after the evolutionary awakening of various fields in sciences.

The word *ca* ending in the verse sixteen synthesizes the idea of one Supreme Lord manifesting through various media of manifold creation. One Supreme-Self splashing in millions of streaks, forms, thoughts, ideas, words and phases. Millions and trillions of reflections of one absolute reality.

In verse eighteen, Srī Kṛṣṇa declares I am the goal, the supporter, the Lord, the witness, the abode, the shelter, the most sincere friend and the imperishable seed of creation. The Lord is indeed the Supreme-state of absolute tranquillity, peace, and happiness. He is supporter, protector and of course the witness of both what has been done in the past and what is going to be done by individual in the future. The witness self has been beautifully described in the Upanishads, "The Brahman becomes the witness of the thoughts and activities when the Absolute is faced by the concept of objectivity. The one reality becomes involved into the subject-object associationship. Although it does not influence a bit the purity of Brahaman's innate nature, which always remains rooted in the pure essentiality but also act as a witness." Srī Kṛṣṇa asserts that I am indeed the most reliable, honest and sincere friend of beings. I am the origin, dissolution and the last resort at the time of total annihilation.

Srī Kṛṣṇa says I am the storehouse of thoughts, desires, latencies, in the form of primeval urge that manifests at the onset of every new creation. In brief, I am both the manifest and unmanifest and also the being and non-being. As about the explanation of *sat* and *asat* the imperishable Supreme is *sat* which means immutable and non-changing. The term *asat* stands for all which is the transient and perishable manifestation of the Divine. According to Shri Ramanuja, *sat* has been called as present existence and *asat* as past and future existence. Tibaut, another great scholar, says *sat* is the spirit and *asat* is the matter.

Srī Kṛṣṇa is emphasizing the fact that, in the middle of manifested diversity in the world, a person should always remain conscious of the Absolute Reality as the substratum of creation. Living a life in the consciousness of that one illuminator, who is reflecting through everything and everybody is really knowing and experiencing God. Being aware of the underlying unity in diversity is God-realization. As Tagore has written in *Gitanjali*, "Through birth and death, in this world or in others, wherever Thou leadest Me, it is Thou, the same one companion of my endless life; who ever linkest my heart with bonds of joy to the unfamiliar. When one knows Thee, then alien there is none, then no door is shut, Oh grant me, my prayer that I may never lose the bliss of Thy touch, of the One in the play of many."

त्रैविद्या मां सोमपाः पूतपापा,
यज्ञैरिष्ट्वा स्वर्गतिं प्रार्थयन्ते।
ते पुण्यमासाद्य सुरेन्द्रलोक-
मश्नन्ति दिव्यान्दिवि देवभोगान्॥ २०॥

traividyā māṁ somapāḥ pūtapāpā
yajñair iṣṭvā svargatiṁ prārthayante
te puṇyām āsādyā surendrālokam
aśnanti divyān divi devabhogān

(20) The knowers of the three *Vedas,* who partake *soma* and are purified of all sins, who perform yajña seeking to reach the heaven; they surely obtain the holy world of the Lord of gods, and enjoy the celestial pleasures of the gods.

ते तं भुक्त्वा स्वर्गलोकं विशालं,
क्षीणे पुण्ये मर्त्यलोकं विशन्ति।
एवं त्रयीधर्ममनुप्रपन्ना,
गतागतं कामकामा लभन्ते॥ २१॥

te taṁ bhuktvā svargalokaṁ viśālaṁ
kṣīṇe puṇye martyalokaṁ viśanti

evaṁ trayīdharmam anuprapannā
gatāgatṁ kāma kāmā labhante

(21) Having enjoyed the extensive heavenly world, they enter again into the world of mortals upon the exhaustion of their virtuous deeds. Thus confirming to the doctrine enjoined in the three *Vedas* and desirous of worldly enjoyments, they repeatedly come and go.

Commentary—In these verses Srī Krsṇa is drawing Arjuna's attention to the various types of rituals described in the *Vedas.* The vedic rituals are meant to be performed for self-purification and at the same time for self-realization and God-realization also. Vedic rituals are designed for mankind to live a balanced, prosperous and blissful life on earth and attain salvation in due time. For example, the 'Trikal Sandhya', as described in *Samaveda,* explains various specific rewards for the performer of the offerings made at different times of the day.

The offering made early morning is offered to 'Vasus', The individual sings prayers in appreciation of the 'Vasus' and asks for their blessings. The three fires symbolize the heaven, sky and earth. The eight Vasus are the abodes of the whole creation : earth, water, fire, air, ether, moon and sun and the stars. The midday offerings are made to the *Rudras. Vedas* describe eleven Rudras. These are ten vital airs—Prana, Apana, Vyana, Samana, Udana, Naga, Kurma, Krkala Devadatta and Dhanajaya—with the consciousness as the eleventh. The offering in the evening is made to Adityas and Agni. It is in the adoration to the Adityas who reside in heaven. These are twelve months of the year. The Adityas are worshipped to have victory over fast running time (Kala).

The term *trividhya* stands for the proper knowledge of the conception of 'Trimurti' as described in *Veda. Rigveda* is full of many hymns written in the glory of Brahma, Visnu and Rudra. The Trimurti is the three-fold manifestation of the Supreme. There are many rituals connected with the worship of these three aspects of Supreme Divinity. There are many hymns those give explanations of the three worlds. Some hymns which with *"bhur bhavah svah"—bhur* symbolizes the physical body composed of five components : earth, water, air, ether and energy. In prayer the individual seeks for full harmony with nature and its forces. *Bhuvah* is a prayer to the God as a controller of astral body. The five senses of perception and five sensory organs of action, mind and intellect. It also includes the five pranas : Pran, Apan, Udan, Vyam and Saman. *Svah* indicates the indwelling light, Supreme Self. *Bhur* stands for material self—*Bhavah* stands psychological self and *Svah* for the Spiritual self. It is 'being', 'becoming' and 'Bliss'.

The *Satapatha Brahmana* enumerates many deities and devas. There are many gods and goddesses who are addressed during the Vedic rituals. All the rituals are basically performed in the appreciation of the cosmic powers. These prayers and offerings can also be directed towards the achievement of certain material gains. That definitely depends upon the thoughts (bhava) and attitude of the individual. The rituals do purify the individual as the Srī Kṛṣṇa say *putapapa* which means purified from sins, but at the same time all these rituals can be performed in order to fulfil worldly desires.

Tri-Vidyah also refers to the knowledge of the three Vedas: *Rig, Yajur* and *Sam.* A scholar well-versed in the study of the *Vedas* is generally called a *Trivedi.* This is one of the family names used among the Brahmins. A scholar of *Tri-Vidyah* is expected to be highly learned and the knower of the Divine. But unfortunately even the great scholars of the *Vedas* are occasionally left deprived of the knowledge of the Supreme. Bookish knowledge is not enough for the first hand experience of the inner Divinity. Even the knowers of the *Vedas*, the great scholars, have to learn to live in the consciousness of the divine in order to experience the presence of the Divine. They have to engage themselves in loving service of the Divine in order to experience the closeness of the Divine.

The word *Somapah* stands for the enjoyer of *Soma. Soma* is another name of Moon. According to *Charaka Shastra*, soma is a medicinal plant. This small plant grows into only fifteen leaves. During the bright half of the lunar month, with the ascending face of Moon, the leaves of this plant appear one each day; and with the descending phase of Moon, the plant sheds all the leaves again exactly in the original pattern of one each day. On the full moon day it is in full blossom. The leaves of this plant are used to make a drink which purifies and stabilizes the emotions. It helps in maintaining the inner integrity. It helps in Yoga meditation by filling the mind with ecstasy, joy and loving devotion for the Supreme Soul. *Soma* also stands for Moon which symbolizes peace, tranquillity and coolness. Moon rays are very pleasing, soothing and cool. There is a *vedamantra* in *Rigveda* *"Om svastaye va yumupab ravamahei soman svasti bhuvanasya yaspathih brhasptim sarvaganam svastaye svastaya aditya so bhuvantu nah"* which means, may we transform our mind as pure as *soma,* in order to live a life of grace and humility. The persons who has been blessed with the grace of *Soma* tranquillity, is called *Saumya* meaning graceful. There is a vedic hymn which is used for describing the peaceful state of a person—*Saumya, Saumyo guno petham.* These vedic rituals promote the respect for nature and are performed to live in closeness with nature. The human nature is surely notorious. People have used the performance of these rituals all along the history of mankind to secure various types of merits. In some respects the performance of rituals have made the people ego-centric also. Srī Krṣna indicates that these rituals when performed with desires and rewards in mind are helpful in attaining the worlds of the celestial. Such *upasanas* are known as *'sakama upasana'*. These worships are performed with deep devotion, reverence and genuine efforts in order to secure certain rewards, and increase enjoyments of life. The rewards of such worships are indeed great in the present life and in lives hereafter. When the worship is done with sincerity of feelings and honesty of heart in order to secure heavenly joys, the individual is definitely rewarded; but the malady is that with the fulfilment of worldly desires, people usually become greedy and are trapped in the fulfilment of one after the other. The vedic rituals should be performed merely out of love and appreciation for the Supreme Divinity and also for self-purification at all levels.

अनन्याश्चिन्तयन्तो मां ये जनाः पर्युपासते।
तेषां नित्याभियुक्तानां योगक्षेमं वहाम्यहम्॥ २२॥

anayāścintayanto māṁ ye janaḥ paryupāsate
teṣāṁ nityābhiyuktānāṁ yogakṣemaṁ vahāmy aham

(22) The men who worship Me alone with undivided devotion, to those ever united in thought with Me, I bring full security and personally attend to their needs.

Commentary—These words of assurance from Srī Kṛṣṇa have moved the hearts of millions around the world. The language is simple, precise and heart-touching. Here is a powerful message reflecting the profound assurance from the Divine. Srī Kṛṣṇa has declared in these words to the entire mankind "Have faith in Me, I will always take care of you". The word *ananya* has been mentioned earlier also but here it means more than just undivided devotion; here it means perpetual unification. *Ananya-bhava* literally means the total identification with the object of devotion. Lord being the ruler of all situations glorifies the work of his devotees by providing for all their needs and taking care of whatever is already in the possession of the devotees. Faith with profound reverence is what explains *nityabhiyuktanam*.

As a matter of fact, living in Yoga has its own measure, the ceremonial worship, prayers and rituals can't tip its scale. It is like living in the transcendental consciousness and working through it. In this case, the individual resorts completely to the gracious unity with the Supreme Self. He works through the Lord—living a life in the perpetual consciousness of the Lord. History is full of many miracles which have come across the lives of ardent devotees. In the words of Howard Thurman: "Whence comes this power which seems to be the point of referral for all experiences and the essence of all meanings? No created thing, no single unit of life can be the source of such fullness and completeness. For in the experience itself, a man is caught and held by something so much more than he can ever think or be that, there is but one word by which its meaning can be encompassed—God."

The story 'Footprints' is an example which elucidates the truth. One night a man had a dream. He dreamt he was walking along the beach with the Lord. Across the sky flashed scenes from his life. For each scene, he noticed two sets of footprints in the sand; one belonging to him, and other to the Lord. When the last scene of his life flashed before him, he looked back at the footprints in the sand. He noticed that many times along the path of his life there was only one set of footprints. He also noticed that it happened at the very lowest and the saddest time in his life. This really bothered him and he questioned the Lord about it. "Lord, you said, that once I decided to follow you, you would walk with me all the way. But I have noticed that during the most troublesome time in my life, there is only one set of footprints. I don't understand, why, when I needed you most, you would leave me." The Lord replied, "My child, My precious child, I love you and I would never leave you. During your times of trial and sufferings, when you see only one set of footprints, it was then that I carried you." Almost each step in life is a process leading towards a new level of inner awakening. Once one learns to live in the awareness, each step, each activity and each thought enhances the faith and strengthens the inner relationship. The unconscious relationship with the Supreme-self becomes more and more conscious, real and alive. The conceptual reality becomes experiential and subjective.

Srī Kṛṣṇa suggests to the entire mankind to inculcate a strong faith in God and purify the heart with faith and devotional service. A purified heart becomes receptive to the voice of the innerself and can distinguish between the real and unreal, the transitory and permanent, the embodied-self and the transcendental self. He assures that the devotee may forget sometime to take care of what he has, but the Lord Himself looks through his interest and makes sure that everything of His devotee is secure and in perfect order.

येऽप्यन्यदेवताभक्ता यजन्ते श्रद्धयान्विताः।
तेऽपि मामेव कौन्तेय यजन्त्यविधिपूर्वकम्॥ २३॥

ye'pyanyadevatābhaktā yajante śraddhāyanvitāḥ
te'pi māmeva kaunteya yajanty avidhipūrvakam

(23) Even those who are the devotees of other gods and worship them with faithful reverence, even they, O'Kaunteya, worship Me alone in essence, though not in accordance with the right approach.

अहं हि सर्वयज्ञानां भोक्ता च प्रभुरेव च।
न तु मामभिजानन्ति तत्त्वेनातश्च्यवन्ति ते॥ २४॥

ahaṁ hi sarvayajñānāṁ bhoktā ca prabhureva ca
na tu mām abhijānanti tattvenātaścyavanti te

(24) I alone am the receiver of all offerings and I alone am the Lord; but they do not know Me in essence, hence they fall.

यान्ति देवव्रता देवान्पितॄन्यान्ति पितृव्रताः।
भूतानि यान्ति भूतेज्या यान्ति मद्याजिनोऽपि माम्॥ २५॥

yānti devavratā devān pitṝn yānti pitṛvratāḥ
bhūtāni yānti bhūtejyā yānti madyājino'pi mām

(25) The worshippers of gods go to the gods, the worshippers of manes reach the manes and of the evil spirits (Bhuta) go to the evil spirits. Those who worship Me alone, they surely come to Me.

Commentary—In these verses Srī Kṛṣṇa is bringing to Arjuna's attention the fact that although people worship many different forms of gods and goddesses but in reality, their offering is made to the one and the only Supreme Power manifested through different forms and names. Srī Kṛṣṇa tells Arjuna with assurance *te pi mameva kaunteyayajantyavidhi-purvakam*—they are surely worshipping Me alone, but not in accordance with proper method. He exhorts mankind to understand the truth about the offerings made to different minor gods and goddesses and to the Absolute, unchangeable. Although the access to the power and blessings of gods and goddess, the manes and the Bhutas is very easy and the rewards are indeed very glamorous, but all these boons are surely the sources of further bondage. These people worship the Supreme Power without recognizing Him in essence, so they get caught in the transitory boons and eventually do fall from the real purpose of human life which is God-realization and Self-realization. The word *cyavanti te* indicates that the people who worship the Lord without proper insight they live in ignorance and die in ignorance, their fall is indeed inevitable.

In the verse twenty-five, Srī Kṛṣṇa makes it very clear that an individual is essentially whatever he or she thinks and meditates upon. If a person concentrates upon the monster all day long, the individual ends up becoming a monster sooner or later. This is an indisputable fact about human psychology because the worshipper draws upon himself the identification of the one being worshipped. For example, any spirit when it appears to the person, either in a dream or in worship, it generally communicates in the language of the worshipper. To some extent it clearly shows that the communication with the spirit is nothing else but a personal dialogue unconsciously made by the person himself to his ownself. It is a psychological fact that a person likes his own language and always likes to communicate in that only. These people get lost in the mixed notions of worship and make it very difficult for themselves to find their connection back to the supreme Divinity. These verses are intended to give people clear insight into the truth that can enlighten and guide them into Self-realization and God-realization. Supreme-self is the origin, the source and shelter of all the other manifestations worshipped as gods and goddesses. It is a psychological fact that the reward for any work or any activity is generally wrapped around the thoughts with which the worship has been performed. A person gets what he meditates upon, a person becomes whatever he thinks and contemplates upon. The worshipper of gods and goddesses reach the realms of gods and goddesses; the worshipper of evil spirits go to the realm of the evil spirits but the devotees of the Lord, those meditate upon indwelling-Self only, surely go into unity with the Supreme-Self.

पत्रं पुष्पं फलं तोयं यो मे भक्त्या प्रयच्छति।
तदहं भक्त्युपहृतमश्नामि प्रयतात्मनः॥ २६॥

patraṁ puṣpaṁ phalaṁ toyaṁ yo me bhaktyā prayacchati
tad ahaṁ bhaktyupahṛtam aśnāmi prayatātmanaḥ

(26) A leaf, flower, fruit, water; whoever offers Me with loving devotion, I accept the pious offering of the pure minded with great joy.

यत्करोषि यदश्नासि यज्जुहोषि ददासि यत्।
यत्तपस्यसि कौन्तेय तत्कुरुष्व मदर्पणम्॥ २७॥

yatkaroṣi yad aśnāsi yaj juhoṣi dadāsi yat
yat tapasyasi kaunteya tat kuruṣva madarpaṇam

(27) Whatever you do, whatever you eat, whatever you offer in

sacrifice (yajña), whatever you give as charity, whatever austerity you practice O'Kaunteya—perform that as an offering to Me.

शुभाशुभफलैरेवं मोक्ष्यसे कर्मबन्धनैः ।
संन्यासयोगयुक्तात्मा विमुक्तो मामुपैष्यसि ॥ २८ ॥

śubhāśubhaphalair evaṁ mokṣyase karmabandhanaiḥ
sannyāsayogayuktātmā vimukto māmupaiṣyasi

(28) Thus, you will remain free from the bonds of actions, yielding auspicious and inauspicious results. With the mind ever united in the Self with the Yoga of renunciation, you will be liberated and come to Me.

Commentary—In these verses Srī Kṛṣṇa draws Arjuna's attention to the truth that the real goal in worship is accomplished by the honesty of faith and loving devotion for the Lord. A person does not have to be rich or learned or very well-known to become a devotee of the Divine. Supreme Lord cares more for the *bhavana* (thought) and the loving devotion than anything else. Srī Kṛṣṇa says: "Devotees who offers a leaf, flower, fruit or even water I accept it with great joy." He assures that the one who offers the most expensive bouquet of flower is dear to Me, but the one who offers merely some leaves and water is also dear to Me. The one who offers a piece of bread is dear to Me and also the one who offers the pudding is dear to Me; as long as it is offered with genuine love and devotion. It is indeed the feeling the thought which counts the most in genuine worship.

Srī Kṛṣṇa tells Arjuna that the most important and valuable offering which He wants from His devotees is their perpetual conscious connectedness with Him. He wants everyone to stay united with Him. Every activity of life should be performed as a worship. When every act is centred around consciousness of the Divine, the entire life is transformed into a continuous adoration of the Supreme. When the devoted love of the Lord settles in the heart, the person's love for life blossoms in all respects. The presence of the Supreme is felt and perceived perpetually. Speaking about closeness to the Divine, there are some beautiful words of undivided devotion written by Tukaram: "Divine joy is seething through my entire being, and all my emotions are unified in the Lord, as the rivers meet in the ocean. The

Lord Himself is the caretaker of my *sanchit, prarabdh* and *kriyaman karmas.* They are not bondage to me any more. I am freed from the effects of age and death. I rejoice in my soul pervading all."

Srī Krṣṇa tells Arjuna in verse twenty-six that with total surrender to the Divine one becomes free from the results of auspicious and inauspicious actions. An individual, who is connected in Yoga with the Supreme Self, performs all his work with the guidance of the inner-self, and if by mistake any forbidden action takes place, the person is immediately checked by the voice of the indwelling Lord, and he is saved promptly from bondage in future. In the words of Swami Chidbhavananda, "The good and bad results of karma contribute for the continuity of the cycle of births. But when they are all offered to the Lord, they become as ineffective as the burnt up seeds, which are unable to sprout any further. In this way the yogi becomes free from bondage". Such an individual lives his life like a *sanyasi* totally detached from the mundane world and completely attached to the spiritual realm of the Divine. The attitude of offering every thing, every thought and every action to the Divine is what constitutes the Yoga of renunciation. The genuine spirit of loving devotion for God is not the abandonment of worldly activities, it is the performance of each and every activity with the spirit of detachment and as an offering to the Divine.

समोऽहं सर्वभूतेषु न मे द्वेष्योऽस्ति न प्रियः।
ये भजन्ति तु मां भक्त्या मयि ते तेषु चाप्यहम्॥ २९॥

samo'haṁ sarvabhūteṣu na me dveṣyo'sti na priyaḥ
ye bhajanti tu māṁ bhaktyā mayi te teṣu cāpyaham

(29) I am alike to all beings; to Me there is none hateful or dear, but those who worship Me with devotion are in Me and I am also in them.

अपि चेत्सुदुराचारो भजते मामनन्यभाक्।
साधुरेव स मन्तव्यः सम्यग्व्यवसितो हि सः॥ ३०॥

api cetsu durācāro bhajate mām ananyabhāk
sādhureva sa mantavyaḥ samyag vyavasito hi saḥ

(30) Even if the most wicked person worships Me with undivided devotion, he too should be regarded a saint, for he has taken a right resolve.

क्षिप्रं भवति धर्मात्मा शश्वच्छान्तिं निगच्छति।
कौन्तेय प्रति जानीहि न मे भक्तः प्रणश्यति॥ ३१॥

kṣipraṁ bhavati dharmātmā śaśvacchāntiṁ nigacchati
kaunteya pratijānīhi na me bhaktaḥ praṇaśyati

(31) Soon he becomes virtuous (righteous) and secures lasting peace, O' Kaunteya, know for sure, My devotee does not perish.

मां हि पार्थ व्यपाश्रित्य येऽपि स्युः पापयोनयः।
स्त्रियो वैश्यास्तथा शूद्रास्तेऽपि यान्ति परां गतिम्॥ ३२॥

māṁ hi pārtha vyapāśritya ye'pi syuḥ pāpayonayaḥ
striyo vaiśyās tathā śāūdraste'pi yānti parām gatim

(32) Seeking refuge in Me O' Partha, even those who are born of the wombs of sin—as well as the women, merchants and *sudras,* they all attain the Supreme state.

किं पुनर्ब्राह्मणाः पुण्या भक्ता राजर्षयस्तथा।
अनित्यमसुखं लोकमिमं प्राप्य भजस्व माम्॥ ३३॥

kiṁ punarbrāhmaṇāḥ puṇyā bhaktā rājarṣayas tathā
anityam asukhaṁ lokam imaṁ prāpya bhajasva mām

(33) How much more then the holy Brahmins and the devoted royal sages; therefore, having come to this transitory, sorrowful world, devote yourself in worship to Me.

मन्मना भव मद्भक्तो मद्याजी मां नमस्कुरु।
मामेवैष्यसि युक्त्वैवमात्मानं मत्परायणः॥ ३४॥

manmanā bhava madbhakto madyājī māṁ namaskuru
mām evaiṣyasi yuktvaivam ātmānaṁ matparāyaṇaḥ

(34) Fix your mind on Me, be devoted to Me, adore Me, salute Me in reverence; thus being united in Yoga with Me and taking Me as your ultimate goal, surely you will come to Me.

Commentary—Srī Kṛṣṇa opens the conversation with the declaration, I am alike to all beings, there is none hateful or dear to Me; but the one who is devoted to Me, that individual lives in Me and I live in that individual. He further adds that even if a criminal, or a sinner, worships Me with undivided loving reverence, he should be considered a saint, because he has taken a right resolve and has resorted to My essentiality. Srī Kṛṣṇa assures that anybody who takes refuge in Me, and has taken the resolve to live in the consciousness of the Supreme, that person eventually becomes virtuous, righteous and attains lasting peace. The emphasis is on words *Pratijanhi na me bhaktah pranasyati*—which means, 'know this for sure that My devotee never perishes'. These words of assurance echo the eternal truth that with a genuine surrender from an aspirant, the God's grace penetrates into the individual's life in more than thousand different ways. Once the faith is strengthened the entire life moves under the compassionate umbrella of the Supreme. Shri Ramakrishna used to say: "If a devotee takes one step towards the Supreme, the Lord takes ten steps towards the devotee".

The spontaneous change, that takes place in any person's thinking faculty and over-all personality, is directly related to the inner enlightenment. It is inner wisdom that guides one in the right direction, it is inner wisdom that makes one receptive to the voice of inner-self, it is the inner wisdom that initiates one into surrender. It is through intuition that one comes into contact with someone who is already on the path of enlightenment, and the person is initiated for surrender in the Divine. There is a true incident from the life story of a great saint Pandit Lekhramji. One time he was giving a lecture on the philosophy of Karma, 'The way we sow the way we reap'. He was emphasizing that nobody can escape from it. Among the audience, there was also sitting a well known ferocious robber named Moghla with his gang. The robber was deeply touched by the words of Shri Lekhramji. At the end of the lecture the robber approached Swamiji and said, "is it really true that no one can escape the fruits of his actions. Swamiji responded sure "It is indeed one hundred percent true". The robber Moghla requested Swamiji for self-purification from all the bad deeds and crimes he had committed in several previous years. Swami Lekhram consoled the robber and said take refuge in God. It is never too late. Give up all your hideous sinful thoughts and work with purity from today. Live in the awareness of the Divine and righteousness will penetrate into your life step by step. He explained to the robber that inspite of all the unfavourable situations in life, and inspite of all the sins and shame, each and everyone is a perfectly eligible candidate for making full surrender to the Divine any time of his life.

This is what Srī Kṛṣṇa is telling Arjuna in verse thirty that even if the very wicked person worships Me, he should be considered virtuous because of his enlightened resolve, and total surrender to the Divine. In the words of Srī Ramakrishna, "The more a man approaches the universal being, the newer and the closer becomes the revelation of the Lord's infinite nature, and in the end he merges in Him through the consummation of knowledge. The Lord's grace lights on him alone who offers Him love and devotion."

After going over various methods of loving devotion to God, Srī Kṛṣṇa assures Arjuna that the undistracted devotion and contemplation upon the Supreme-Self trains the individual to live in constant awareness of the Divine, and purifies the person in all respects. In the words of Shri Vinobaji, "The essence of the matter is that if we give over to the Lord all our actions, the life acquires strength and skill from this, and the attainment of *moksha* comes within our grasp. With action on one side and devotion on the other, combining both *karma* and *bhakti* makes the life more and more beautiful."

In the last verse, Srī Kṛṣṇa emphasizes upon the loving devotion once again because that is something within the reach and access to everyone. To love is a natural instinct. When the feelings are saturated with the love of the Divine, the loving contemplation comes very easily and naturally without any special efforts. The love for God initiates the individual into a close friendship with God which develops into intimate relationship with God. When the bond with the Self strengthens in close intimacy the individual becomes fully dedicated to the Lord in his thoughts, words and deeds. He lives in the thoughts of the Divine and works through the consciousness of the Divine. The goal of his life becomes the attainment of the Supreme Lord. The process is easy and within the reach of everyone. There is nothing new to learn, because every individual is born with this natural instinct of 'Love'. Just a shift in awareness brings marvellous results.

ॐ तत्सदिति श्रीमद्भगवद्गीतासूपनिषत्सु ब्रह्मविद्यायां
योगशास्त्रे श्रीकृष्णार्जुनसंवादे राजविद्याराजगुह्य-
योगो नाम नवमोऽध्यायः ॥ ९ ॥

'Aum' tatsaditi Śrīmadbhagawadgeetā sūpaniṣatsu
brahmavidyāyām yogaśāstre Śrīkṛṣṇārjunasamvāde
Rājavidyārājaguhyayogo nāma navamo'dhyāyaḥ

'AUM TAT SAT'—Thus, in the Upanishad of the glorious Bhagawad Geeta, the science of the Brahman (Absolute) the scripture of yoga, the dialogue between Srī Kṛṣṇa and Arjuna—thus, ends the chapter nine entitled *"Rājavidyārājaguhyayoga"*.

इति श्रीमद्भगवद्गीतासु नवमोऽध्यायः ॥ ९ ॥

<u>Chapter Ten</u>

VIBHUTIYOGA

THE YOGA OF THE DIVINE MANIFESTATIONS

श्रीभगवानुवाच

भूय एव महाबाहो शृणु मे परमं वचः।
यत्तेऽहं प्रीयमाणाय वक्ष्यामि हितकाम्यया॥ १॥

bhūya eva mahābāho śṛṇu me paramaṁ vacah
yatte'haṁ prīyamāṇāya vakṣyāmi hitakāmyayā

The Blessed Lord said :

(1) Once again, O' mighty armed, listen to My Supreme word, since you are very dear to Me, I will speak to you for your welfare.

न मे विदुः सुरगणाः प्रभवं न महर्षयः।
अहमादिर्हि देवानां महर्षीणां च सर्वशः॥ २॥

na me viduḥ suragaṇāḥ prabhavaṁ na maharṣayaḥ
aham ādir hi devānaṁ maharṣīṇāṁ ca sarvaśaḥ

(2) Neither the gods, nor the great seers, know about My origin. I am the prime cause of all the gods as well as of the great seers in every way (in all respects).

यो मामजमनादिं च वेत्ति लोकमहेश्वरम्।
असम्मूढः स मर्त्येषु सर्वपापैः प्रमुच्यते॥ ३॥

yo mām ajam anādiṁ ca vetti lokamaheśvaram
asammūḍhaḥ sa martyeṣu sarvapāpaiḥ pramucyate

(3) He who knows Me as unborn, beginningless and as the Supreme Lord of the universe; he is undeluded among the mortals and is liberated from all sins.

Commentary—In these verses Srī Kṛṣṇa opens the conversation with the most intimate words of special concern for Arjuna so that he can perceive the omniscience of the Lord everywhere and also become aware of his participation in the work of the Divine. Srī Kṛṣṇa tells Arjuna that neither the celestials nor many of the seers and sages can completely comprehend the secret origin of the Supreme; and anybody who understands the truth that God is unborn and beginningless, is indeed pure and definitely undeluded among men. Srī Kṛṣṇa knows that in order to enhance Arjuna's devotion, it is necessary for him to understand the Lord's attributes and magnificence of His manifestation. The loving devotion leads towards the understanding of the mysteries of the Divine attributes and also to the knowledge of the Supreme Self. The Yoga of devotion enhances the spirit of the Yoga of action and eventually guides the person to the realization of the Supreme.

The true devotion guides the individual into the proper understanding of the self and from the understanding of the Divine arises deep devotion again. Devotion becomes meditation and meditation becomes the most enriching experience of unity with the Divine, enriched with love and surrender. Srī Kṛṣṇa assures Arjuna that whoever knows the Lord in essence and lives a life totally connected with the Supreme-Self, he is eventually purged of all sins. The transcendental experience of the Supreme-Self washes of all the sins, all the guilt and shame, those appear as obstructions for the spiritual life. Here the word 'sin' stands for all those actions which are done against the voice of the inner-self, sin is contaminated by selfishness. The individual becomes selfish when he ignores the voice of the Supreme indwelling Divinity. So liberation from sins is indeed possible only with the connectedness to the Divine. In order to make all ideas and activities virtuous, one must learn to live in the awareness of the Divine and work under His direct guidance. The moment when the individual re-establishes the lost connection with the indwelling Divinity and becomes introduced once again to the purity of the self, the transformation takes place slowly and the individual is purged of sins.

बुद्धिर्ज्ञानमसम्मोहः क्षमा सत्यं दमः शमः।
सुखं दुःखं भवोऽभावो भयं चाभयमेव च॥४॥

buddhi jñānam asammohaḥ kṣamā satyaṁ damaḥ śamaḥ
sukhaṁ duḥkhaṁ bhavo'bhāvo bhayaṁ cābhayameva ca

अहिंसा समता तुष्टिस्तपो दानं यशोऽयशः।
भवन्ति भावा भूतानां मत्त एव पृथग्विधाः॥५॥

ahinsā samatā tuṣṭistapo dānaṁ yaśo'yaśaḥ
bhavanti bhāvā bhūtānāṁ matta eva pṛthagvidhāḥ

(4, 5) Intellect, wisdom, undeludedness, forgiveness, truthfulness, self-restraint, self-control, pleasure and pain, being and non-being, fear and fearlessness, non-violence, equanimity, contentment, austerity, charity, honour and ignominy—all these various qualities of the beings originate from Me alone.

Commentary—In continuation of the central theme of this chapter that everything in the world originates from the Lord alone, Srī Kṛṣṇa speaks about the feelings, activities and ideas which originate from various levels of existence—both physical and psychological in relation to life. It is a step by step approach to the mysterious ladder taking towards the realization of the Lord's magnificent expressions. *Buddhi* refers to the faculty of reason, wisdom and discriminating ability. The discrimination between right and wrong, real and unreal, spirit and matter. The word non-delusion refers to the clarity of the vision and the clarity of understanding. The ability that gives freedom from doubt and ignorance. Forgiveness is a virtue highly exalted for spiritual growth. Truthfulness is the presentation of facts in clear-cut honesty of heart. Speaking truth is an austerity and it purifies thoughts. There is a Mantra in *Vedas* "*Om adhbhirgaatrani shudhyanti manaasatyen shudhyante*" as for the cleanliness of the physical body, the person is required to take shower with soap and water, similarly for the purification of (thoughts) *mana* (mind) one must learn to speak the truth. Speaking the truth purifies thoughts because it keeps one connected with the supreme truth, the God in us. Speaking truth is a great principle of life. The *samah* and *damah* stand for self control at all the three levels of thought, word and deed. *Samah* is the conscious control over thinking faculty and *Damah* stands for the control over the senses of actions. So together it is the conscious control over the senses of perception and actions.

Sukham-dukham is pleasure and pain, and *bhavo-abhava* stands for existence and non-existence. *Bhayam ca-bhayameva ca*—fear and fearlessness. Ahimsa is non-violence. Non-violence means not to violate the laws of the inner-self. Non-violence also stands for "*manasa vachya karmana*"—Do not hurt anyone by thought, word and deed. In words of Gandhiji, "the religion of non-violence is not meant merely for the rishis and saints. It is meant for the common people as well. Non-violence is the law of our species as violence is the law of the brute. The spirit lies dormant in the brute and he knows no law but that of physical might. The dignity of man requires obedience to a higher law—to the strength of the spirit." *Samata* stands for equanimity, the maintenance of balance under all circumstances, and the attitude of equality towards all beings.

The other word in this verse is *tusti*—contentment. In the words of Srī Sarada Deviji, "There is no treasure equal to contentment and no virtue equal to fortitude". *Tapah* means austerity. There are many types of austerities recommended for self-purification. The word *tapa* itself is self-explanatory meaning the process that cleanses and purifies. *Danam* is charity. Being charitable is really a great blessing of the Supreme. The virtue of charity blossoms in life from the individual's proximity to the Supreme-Self. It is only when the presence of the self is perceived in others, the spirit of caring and sharing takes place. The holy scriptures recommend that one should donate at least ten per cent of one's earnings to the good cause in community. The reservoir of Divine energy is all around the individual. Each and every person makes use of this energy by one's own choice and inclination. Srī Kṛṣṇa is drawing Arjuna's attention towards the diversity as seen in the universe. Everything is the Divine's manifestation. Nothing can manifest itself without the Divine potency. Everything is flowing from one source, although appearing in multitude of diversity.

महर्षयः सप्त पूर्वे चत्वारो मनवस्तथा।
मद्भावा मानसा जाता येषां लोक इमाः प्रजाः॥ ६॥

maharṣayaḥ sapta pūrve catvāro manāvas tathā
madbhāvā mānasā jātā yeṣāṁ loka imāḥ prajāḥ

(6) The seven great sages, and the more ancient Sanaka etc., and the Manus are possessed of powers like Me and born of My mind; all these creatures in the world have descended from them.

एतां विभूतिं योगं च मम यो वेत्ति तत्त्वतः।
सोऽविकम्पेन योगेन युज्यते नात्र संशयः॥ ७॥

etāṁ vibhūtiṁ yogaṁ ca mama yo vetti tattvataḥ
so'vikampena yogena yujyate nātra saṁśayaḥ

(7) He who knows this divine glory and the yogic power of Mine in essence, becomes established in unshakable yogic communion, there is no doubt about it.

अहं सर्वस्य प्रभवो मत्तः सर्वं प्रवर्तते।
इति मत्वा भजन्ते मां बुधा भावसमन्विताः॥ ८॥

ahaṁ sarvasya prabhavo mattaḥ sarvaṁ pravartate
iti matvā bhajante māṁ budhā bhāvasamanvitāḥ

(8) I am the source of all, from Me everything proceeds; understanding thus, the men of wisdom worship Me, endowed with devotion.

मच्चित्ता मद्गतप्राणा बोधयन्तः परस्परम्।
कथयन्तश्च मां नित्यं तुष्यन्ति च रमन्ति च॥ ९॥

maccittā madgataprāṇā bodhayantaḥ parasparam
kathayantaśca māṁ nityaṁ tuṣyanti ca ramanti ca

(9) With their mind absorbed in Me, and their life centred on Me, enlightening each other, always speaking of Me, they ever remain contented and delighted.

तेषां सततयुक्तानां भजतां प्रीतिपूर्वकम्।
ददामि बुद्धियोगं तं येन मामुपयान्ति ते॥ १०॥

teṣāṁ satatayuktānāṁ bhajatāṁ prītipūrvakam
dadāmi buddhiyogaṁ taṁ yena māmupayānti te

(10) To those who are ever united in devotion, and worship Me with love, I grant that Yoga of integral wisdom by which they attain Me.

तेषामेवानुकम्पार्थमहमज्ञानजं तमः ।
नाशयाम्यात्मभावस्थो ज्ञानदीपेन भास्वता ॥ ११ ॥

teṣām evānukampārtham ahaṁ ajñānajaṁ tamaḥ
nāśayāmyātmabhāvastho jñānadīpena bhāsvatā

(11) For them, out of mere compassion I dwell in their hearts (self) and destroy the ignorance-born darkness by the luminous lamp of wisdom.

Commentary—In these verses, Srī Kṛṣṇa is introducing Arjuna to the mystery of Divine manifestations, from the view point of *samashti* and *vyashti*. The word *samashti* encompasses the cause for entire creation the cosmic mind and *vyashti* stands for the basic urge which becomes fulfilled through mind, intellect and ego. The seven revered sages are also called the *Saptarishis*. They are primordial and do possess the divine powers and transcendent vision. The names of these revered sages are *Marci, Angira, Atri, Pulastya, Pulaha, Kartu* and *Vasishta*. The more ancients are the *Kumaras, Sanaka, Sanatana, Sanandana* and the *Sanatakumaras*. The word *Manavastatha* stands for the fourteen Manus. They are *Svayambhuva, Savavocisa, Vaivasvata, Savarni, Daksasavarni, Brahmasavarni, Dharmasavarni, Rudrasavarni, Devasavarni* and *Indrasavarni* etc. Srī Kṛṣṇa tells Arjuna that all of these are born of My mind and the entire world of various creatures have emanated from them. Srī Kṛṣṇa is emphasizing the word *Manasa Jatah*—born of My mind. There are two types of creatures in the world—The *binduja* and the *nadaja*. The *binduja* are born from the male and female relationship. The *nadaja* come into existence out of Divine will, in other words, they are the expression of a mere thought. The revered seven sages, the four *Kumaras* and the *Manus* are the *Nadajas.* All the other creatures in the world, those have come into existence are called the *bindujas.* There is a detailed description of these seven revered seers, the ancient Kumaras and the Manus in the ancient *Puranas* and the *Mahabharat's Santi Parva*. The *Vayu Purana* describes at length the splendid characteristics of the ancient seven seers. The *Prajapati* and the seven revered seers and the four Kumaras and Manus are the thoughts which have originated from the will of the Supreme Lord, as described by Srī Kṛṣṇa, "born of My mind". These expressions of the God's will, possessed of powers exactly like Him, are seven seers known to each and every individual in the form of five senses of perception with intellect and the I in the form of ego. The same supreme-self expressed in the name of four Kumaras the more ancients ones are the *mana, buddhi, chit* and *ahankar*. These are the eleven reflections which have come forth from the will of the Supreme before the creation of the universe. From the Supreme came (*Brahma*) creative power of the mind, from *Brahma* the four Kumaras and the later the seven sages, and from them came forth the innumerable universes with innumerable varieties of manifestations.

Srī Kṛṣṇa enlightens Arjuna of the prime truth that the innumerable universes are indeed the manifestations of one thought that emanated from the Supreme. The opulence of the Divine manifestation is just phenomenal. The primordial power of the Supreme can be observed evolving itself into innumerable varieties. The word 'Vibhuti' stands for magnificence in several different ways. *Vi* stands for *vishesha* means special and *'bhut'* means beings. Another illustration of the word is majestic appearance or special Divine expression. *Vi* + *bhu* means appear, expand, and manifest. The entire universe is an expression of the power and the majesty of the creator. Srī Kṛṣṇa the knower of human psychology understands the difficulty of Arjuna in comprehending the depth, the width and expansion of the Supreme. Besides, Srī Kṛṣṇa knows that just the factual knowledge is not enough for proper absorption of truth, the individual has to experience it personally. Using the word *tattvatah* makes it very clear. One must understand in essence and make it a personal experience for the revelation of the Supreme-self. Srī Kṛṣṇa has indicated many times in so many previous verses that He is the source of the entire universe, He is the origin of the entire creation. He is the substratum of the entire Divine manifestation, but still Arjuna has not been able to comprehend the gist of the matter. Srī Kṛṣṇa knows that there is a process that can enlighten the individual and eliminate the circular pattern of old thinking. There is a method that can help one to re-group one's thinking faculty into a newer and purer image. That's why

He intends to arouse Arjuna's devotion for the Supreme-Self. Loving devotion for God and surrender to the majesty of the Divine helps the person to form a new identity that guides him to the exalted spiritual experience. With loving devotion the aspirant moves step by step into the newer dimensions of self-awareness and personal comprehension of the ultimate truth. The undivided devotion actually brings the aspirant in contact with the most intimate experiences of the Supreme-Self.

Once devotion is aroused with a convinced understanding, the aspirant remains constantly aware of the eternal truth in the midst of everything else that goes in life. The word *bodhayantah parasparam* indicates the mutual enlightenment that goes on between two enlightened devotees. A genuine devotee who always lives soaked in the consciousness of the Divine, he likes to share his personal experiences with others. Endowed with ardent love for God and the passionate quest for self-realization, these individuals openly exchange the experience of their loving devotion. The two spiritually enlightened individuals are the two streams of ardent devotion, overflowing into one another, enjoying the ecstasies of the Divine love and strengthening the faith of each other. They live in the rapturous joy and contentment of the Supreme-Self. In the tenth verse Srī Kṛṣṇa has used the compound word *Anukampartham* which means out of My compassion and special love I eliminate the ignorance of My devotees and enlighten them with inner knowledge. This illustrates the intimacy of the Lord with his devotees. He tells Arjuna that these devotees of the undivided devotion are very dear to Him. He helps them to grow in their spiritual love and inner wisdom. When these devotees are coming closer to Him, He helps them to grow in the Yoga of wisdom, and the Supreme Bliss of self knowledge. He strengthens their faith by taking care of their personal needs and by providing them personal security.

In the verse eleven, Srī Kṛṣṇa declares the great secret, "I help them to light the luminous lamp of wisdom from their own indwelling light." The expression *atmabhavastho* explains the great secret of Srī Kṛṣṇa's message about the revelation of the presence of Divine from the innermost levels of the consciousness. This revelation comes as a grace of the Divine and opens the new vistas of self-understanding and God-realization. It is like the emergence of a new power from within in the form of increased intuition. *Atmabodhasta* is the inner awakening. When the mind becomes one-pointed and intuitive, the light of knowledge flashes forth from within. It illuminates everything and gives utmost clarity to the thoughts. This wisdom is the perceptual knowledge of the indwelling soul. It comes in the form of divine grace and blessing. It is the heightened capacity of self-understanding which opens the hidden horizons of the Supreme's domain, in the microcosm as well as in the macrocosm. Accepting the presence of the Divine is the initial step, which is strengthened by accepting the consciousness of the presence of the Lord through the experiential knowledge of the Self. It is the perceptual experience that brings transformation in the attitude of acceptance. The Supreme-self, who is the substratum of the entire existence, becomes revealed only when sufficient efforts are made for the revelation. Once the mind opens to the inner-guidance, the indwelling Supreme-self automatically reveals its magnificence. The most important requisite in the process of God-realization is to wait with willingness, faith and confidence, and to synchronize thoughts, feelings and actions in the appropriate direction. As one learns to live in the ecstasy of the ardent love and devotion for the Supreme, one experiences that the eye of intuition is being activated, which slowly guides the person towards the possibility of new subjective perception and experiences. There are some beautiful lines written by a Sufi poet—

Harmei dil mein makin thaa, mujhe maaloom na thaa.
rage jaan say bhi karin thaa, mujhe maaloom na thaa.
Main kahin hoon, woh kahin hai, aisa guman thaa mujhako.
main jahaan thaa, woh vahin thaa, mujhe maaloom na tha.
dil se paradaa jo uthaa, ho gaee roshana aankhen.
isa dil men hee paradaa nasheen thaa, mujhe maaloom na thaa.

हरमे दिल में मकीं था, मुझे मालूम न था।
रगें जाँ से भी करीं था, मुझे मालूम न था।

मैं कहीं हूँ, वो कहीं है, ऐसा गुमां था मुझको।
मैं जहाँ था, वो वहीं था, मुझे मालूम न था।
दिल से परदा जो उठा, हो गई रोशन आँखें।
इस दिल में ही परदा नशीं था, मुझे मालूम न था।

अर्जुन उवाच

परं ब्रह्म परं धाम पवित्रं परमं भवान्।
पुरुषं शाश्वतं दिव्यमादिदेवमजं विभुम्॥ १२॥

paraṁ brahma paraṁ dhāma pavitraṁ paramaṁ bhavān
puruṣaṁ śāśvataṁ divyam ādidevam ajaṁ vibhum

Arjuna said :

(12) Thou are the Supreme Brahman, the Supreme abode, the Supreme purifier, the primordial Divine Purusha, the Primal God, unborn and the omnipresent.

आहुस्त्वामृषयः सर्वे देवर्षिर्नारदस्तथा।
असितो देवलो व्यासः स्वयं चैव ब्रवीषि मे॥ १३॥

āhus tvām ṛṣayaḥ sarve devarṣi nāradastathā
asito devalo vyāsaḥ svayam caiva bravīṣi me

(13) All the sages have thus declared of You, as also the celestial sage Narada, so also Asita, Devala and Vyasa, and even You—Yourself are telling this to me.

सर्वमेतदृतं मन्ये यन्मां वदसि केशव।
न हि ते भगवन्व्यक्तिं विदुर्देवा न दानवाः॥ १४॥

sarvametad ṛtaṁ manye yanmāṁ vadasi keśava
na hi te bhagavanvyaktiṁ vidur devā na dānavāḥ

(14) I believe all this to be true which You are telling me O' Kesava, neither the gods nor the demons O' Blessed Lord, know your manifestation.

स्वयमेवात्मनात्मानं वेत्थ त्वं पुरुषोत्तम।
भूतभावन भूतेश देवदेव जगत्पते॥ १५॥

svayam evātmanātmanaṁ vettha tvaṁ puruṣottama
bhūtabhāvana bhūteśa devadeva jagatpate

(15) You alone know Yourself, by Yourself, O' Supreme person, O' source and Lord of beings, O' God of gods, O' master of the universe.

वक्तुमर्हस्यशेषेण दिव्या ह्यात्मविभूतयः।
याभिर्विभूतिभिर्लोकानिमांस्त्वं व्याप्य तिष्ठसि ॥ १६ ॥

vaktum arhasy aśeṣeṇa divyā hyātmavibhūtayaḥ
yābhir vibhūtibhir lokān imāns tvaṁ vyāpya tiṣṭhasi

(16) Therefore, You alone without reserve, can describe in full Your Divine manifestations, by which attributes and glories, You remain pervading in these worlds.

कथं विद्यामहं योगिंस्त्वां सदा परिचिन्तयन्।
केषु केषु च भावेषु चिन्त्योऽसि भगवन्मया ॥ १७ ॥

kathaṁ vidyāmahaṁ yoginstvāṁ sadā paricintayan
keṣu-keṣu ca bhāveṣu cintyo'si bhagavan mayā

(17) How may I know You, O' Master of Yoga, while constantly meditating upon You; in what particular form, O' blessed Lord, You are to be meditated upon by me?

विस्तरेणात्मनो योगं विभूतिं च जनार्दन।
भूयः कथय तृप्तिर्हि शृण्वतो नास्ति मेऽमृतम् ॥ १८ ॥

vistareṇātmano yagaṁ bibhūtiṁ ca janārdana
bhūyaḥ kathaya tṛptirhi śṛṇvato nāsti me'mṛtam

(18) Tell me again in full detail, Your power of yoga and Your divine manifestations O' Janardana (O'Kṛṣṇa); for I am not yet satisfied by hearing Your nectar-like words.

Commentary—In these verses, Arjuna praises the profound teachings of Srī Kṛṣṇa and expresses his desire to know more about the attributes of the Lord. Arjuna's inquiry about the various manifestation of the Divine has been aroused because of his deep devotion and love for the Supreme. He gathers his courage, and he requests Srī Kṛṣṇa to speak in further detail about the magnificence of the divine glories. He wants to know how to recognize the Lord in brilliance, beauty, valour, prosperity, power, austerity and penance. He expresses his undeviated faith and says O' Kṛṣṇa, I believe with respect in everything which You are telling me, but it is only You who knows the truth about Yourself. You alone know about your infinite powers. How can I recognize you with your various divine manifestations. Please tell me your specific manifestations in order to contemplate upon you and to make conscious connections with You in Yoga. He brings up the names of great sages and devotees like *Narada, Asita, Devala, Vyasa*, and others those have acclaimed Srī Kṛṣṇa as the divine person, the primordial god, and the Supreme Lord. Although he understands the omniscience of the Lord, but still he wants to know more about the mystery of unity in diversity. Arjuna makes an appeal for a vivid, detailed explanation of the various significant manifestations. He feels the necessity to get acquainted with the attributes which can spontaneously help him to maintain his unity with the Lord. In order to cognize the presence of the Supreme, to live a life totally absorbed in the devotion of the Supreme, in constant remembrance of the Lord, it is indeed necessary to know more in full details about the magnificence of the Supreme.

श्रीभगवानुवाच

हन्त ते कथयिष्यामि दिव्या ह्यात्मविभूतयः ।
प्राधान्यतः कुरुश्रेष्ठ नास्त्यन्तो विस्तरस्य मे ॥ १९ ॥

hanta te kathayiṣyāmi divyā hyātmavibhūtayaḥ
prādhānyataḥ kuruśreṣṭha nāstyanto vistarasya me

The Blessed Lord said :

(19) Yes, I must tell you My Divine manifestations but only the specific ones, O' best of the Kurus, for there is no limit to My magnitude.

अहमात्मा गुडाकेश सर्वभूताशयस्थितः ।
अहमादिश्च मध्यं च भूतानामन्त एव च ॥ २० ॥

aham ātmā guḍākeśa sarvabhūtāśayasthitaḥ
aham ādiśca madhyaṁ ca bhūtānāmanta eva ca

(20) I am the indwelling-soul, O' Gudakesha (Arjuna), seated in the hearts of all beings, I am the beginning, the middle, as well as the end of all beings.

आदित्यानामहं विष्णुर्ज्योतिषां रविरंशुमान्।
मरीचिर्मरुतामस्मि नक्षत्राणामहं शशी ॥ २१ ॥

ādityānaṁ ahaṁ viṣṇur jyotiṣāṁ ravir aṁśumān
marīcir marutām asmi nakṣatrāṇām ahaṁ śaśī

(21) Among the Adityas, I am Vishnu, among the luminaries, the radiant Sun, I am Marichi among the Maruts, and the Moon among the stars.

वेदानां सामवेदोऽस्मि देवानामस्मि वासवः।
इन्द्रियाणां मनश्चास्मि भूतानामस्मि चेतना ॥ २२ ॥

vedānāṁ sāmavedo'smi devānām asmi vasavaḥ
indriyāṇāṁ manaś cāsmi bhūtānām asmi cetanā

(22) Of the *Vedas,* I am the *Samaveda;* I am Vasva (Indra) among the gods; among the senses I am the mind; and of the living beings, I am the consciousness.

रुद्राणां शंकरश्चास्मि वित्तेशो यक्षरक्षसाम्।
वसूनां पावकश्चास्मि मेरुः शिखरिणामहम् ॥ २३ ॥

rudrāṇāṁ śaṅkaraś cā'smi vitteśo yakṣarakṣasām
vasūnāṁ pāvakaś cā'smi meruḥ śikhariṇām aham

(23) Among the Rudras, I am Sankara, among the Yakshas and Rakshasa (demons), I am Kubera. Among the Vasus I am the god of fire and of the mountains, I am the Meru.

Commentary—At the genuine request of Arjuna, Srī Kṛṣṇa gives the description of various divine manifestations. This is the description of only some prominent ones, because it is not possible to explain the magnificence in its entirety. *"Prabhu ananta, prabhu ki lila ananta"*—the Supreme Lord is boundless, inexplicable and so are His glories, attributes and manifestations. Srī Kṛṣṇa opens the conversation by saying, I am the essence of life and seated in the hearts of all beings. He wants to awaken Arjuna's inner potentials so that the later can understand his own essentiality. The Supreme Lord is the beginning, the middle and also the end of all beings. The entire creation emanates from the Lord, is sustained by the Supreme Lord and goes into the Lord at the end. It is indeed one and the same power working as the substratum of the universe. From the beginning to the end, there is nothing besides the manifestation of the Supreme-self. The Upanisads declare the immanence of God in these words, "Know Him, who is the origin and the dissolution of the universe—the source of all virtues, the destroyer of all sins, the master of all good qualities, the immortal and the abode of the universe—as seated in your own heart. He is perceived in different forms and shapes, in the tree of *samsara.* May we realize Him—the transcendent and adorable master of the universe."

Srī Kṛṣṇa proceeds further by telling, "I am the *Vishnu* among the *Adityas*. According to the ancient scriptures there are twelve Adityas, the twelve months of the year. Their names are *Amusu, Dhata, Indra, Aryama, Vivasva, Bhaga, Parjanya, Dvashta, Mitra, Vishnu, Varna* and *Pusha*. The names of these *Adityas* start from the month of April ending in March. Among all the *Adityas* the most revered is the *Vishnu*, the month of January, which announces the beginning of *Uttarayana,* the northern course of the Sun. It announces the beginning of the time of enlightenment and spiritual progress. Among the luminaries I am the radiant Sun, the great electro-magnetic field, the source of all energy. The Sun has been always viewed with respect and reverence as the most venerable representative of the Divine. The Sun has been called the *Yogi-Raaj* by Srī Kṛṣṇa Himself in the earlier verses. Sun worship has been a part of the religious worship in many parts of the world. There are many hymns in the *Vedas* which describe the glory of the Sun god such as *"Aadidev namastubyam, praseeda mam Bhaskara, Divakara namastubyam—prabhakara namastetu*. In the next part of this verse Srī Kṛṣṇa declares that among the forty-nine wind-gods "I am the glow of the *Marichi."* The names of forty-nine wind-gods are *Sattvajyoti, Aditya, Satyajyoti, Tiryagjoyti, Sajyoti, Jyotisman, Harita, Rtajit, Susena, Senajit, Satyamitra, Abhimitra, Harimitra, Krta, Satya, Dhruva, Dharta, Vidharta, Vidharaya, Dhvanta, Dhuni, Ugra, Bhima, Abhiyu, Saksipa,*

Idrk, Anyadrk, Yadrk, Pratikrt, Samiti, RK, Samrambha, Idrksa, Purusha, Amyadrksa, Cetasa, Samita, Samidrksa, Pratidrksa, Maruti, Sarata, Deva, Disa, Yajus, Anuḍrk, Sama, Manusa, Vis, Marichi has been considered to be the glow of all the *Maruts*. Next is, among the Nakshatras I am the Moon. According to Vedic astrology and astronomy, there are twenty-seven *Nakshatras* or the group of constellations. The names are *Ashvini, Bharani, Kirtika, Rohini, Mrugshirsh, Ardra, Punarvasu, Pushya, Ashlesha, Magha Purva Phalguni, Uttra Phalguni Hasta, Chitra, Swati, Vishakha Anuradha, Jyeshtha, Mool Purva Shadha, Uttara Shadha, Sharvan, Dhanisshtha, Shattara, Purva Bhadrapada, Uttra Bhaḍrapada, Revati.* Although the name of the heavenly body moon is not one of these constellations but the positions of all these are used in relation to the movements of the Moon. All the constellations draw their importance, splendour and glory from the luminous star Moon. The Vedic calendar is still calculated according to the ascending and descending phases of the Moon. Moon is the most important star in the Vedic astrology, any birth sign and constellation, in effect at any particular time are the ones which the moon has conjoined. The sun signs are important to some extent but the preparation of any natal chart is made with the position of the Moon in relation to one of the other twenty-seven constellation at the time of birth. Birth sign means the Moon sign.

In the verse twenty-two, Srī Kṛṣṇa says: "I am *Samaveda* among the *Vedas.*" There are four *Vedas—Rigveda, Yajurveda, Samaveda* and *Atharvaveda.* As the main theme of *Rigveda* is knowledge in all respects, similarly that of *Samaveda* is ardent devotion for God, in other words *Upasana.* The significance and glory of *Samaveda* has been also explained in Brahmanas and in other spiritual literature of Vedic religion. *Shatapath* describes "*Sarvesa va esha vedanam raso yatsam*". *Samaveda* is the quintessence of all the *Vedas. Gopatha* describes *Samaveda eva yasha—Samaveda* is glorious, splendid and illustrious. *Samaveda* is full of the sweetest hymns written in the glory and magnificence of the Supreme Lord. The word *Sama* has been derived from *Sama-santvene*—means which renders inner peace and tranquillity. The hymns of *Samaveda* are used in devotional music and also for proper knowledge of *Swara.* In the words of Swami

Dayananda Saraswati: "*Sayanti Khandyanti dukhani yena tava atra sarvedhatubhie manin eti karan karti manin*". The contemplation on the hymns of *Samaveda* can put an end to all the miseries. Everyone should meditate and recite the hymns of *Samaveda* with love and devotion. The very first hymn of *Samaveda* is: O' God come to us in the form of knowledge and loving devotion, make your seat in the temple of the heart. There is another very famous hymn of *Samaveda—"Ekam sadvipra bahuda vadanti"*. The Supreme Lord is one, but He is called by various names.

In the next part of the verse, Srī Kṛṣṇa declares, "Among the gods I am Indra." Indra has been usually called as Devraj Indra meaning the chief one, the Lord of gods. There are many cosmic bodies called as gods, such as Moon-god, Sun-god, Wind-god, Fire-god etc. Devraj Indra is the chief, the foremost one. Srī Kṛṣṇa declares Indra to be His own self, for Arjuna to specify His glory as an attribute.

After mentioning the Vasava the Lord of gods (Indra)—Srī Kṛṣṇa immediately shifts Arjuna's attention towards the *Indriyas* (sensory organs) in the body and the director of *Indriyas,* the mind—as in the macrocosm so in microcosm. In the body it is indeed the mind acting as Indra—the chief of the *Indriyas.* So among the gods in the body, Mind is the chief that illuminates, energizes, regulates and directs the sensory organs. The senses of perception and actions such as sight, smell, taste, touch, hearing, speech, hands, feet, organs of generation and defecation, the eleventh one is the mind—the ruler and the director of all the *Indriyas* (sensory organs). Srī Kṛṣṇa declares the mind in human body to be His Divine glory because it occupies the foremost place among the sensory organs. Mind has been called the receptacle. The entire world is perceived through the mind. The master of senses is indeed the mind, and senses obey the orders of the mind as their administrator. In the next part of the verse Srī Kṛṣṇa says, "I am the consciousness in the living beings."

God is the life-force or the life-energy that sustains the entire creation. *Cetana* is a sanskrit word that stands for life-force, it sustains and maintains the body. The moment when the consciousness leaves the living being, the body is declared as dead and ready to be cremated or buried. The consciousness in the body is known as the *Shiva*. When *Shiva* leaves the body, it is declared as *shava* means dead. The *shava* is a Sanskrit word that stands for the dead body. So the consciousness in the body indeed represents the Divine glory, and splendour.

In the verse twenty-third, Srī Kṛṣṇa declares—Among the eleven *Rudras* "I am *Shankra*." The scriptures describe eleven *Rudras* such as *Hara, Bahurupa, Tryambaka, Aparajita, Vrsakapi, Sambhu, Kapardi, Raivata, Mrgavyadha, Sarva* and *Kapali*. These *Rudras* are the bestower of supreme blessedness, exalted joy and bliss, or can bc described as the bestowers of personal desires and dreams. Among these, *Shankara* is considered to be the Lord of the rest, *Sh + kar* – means who bestows auspiciousness and goodness. Srī Kṛṣṇa declares Himself to be the *Shankara*. Kubera is the Lord of genies, *Yaksas* and *Raksasas*. Kubera is also the Lord of wealth. According to *Bhagvatam Purana,* "Kubera is the grandson of the ancient (seer) Rishi Pulastya. He performed long penances and was blessed with the position as the custodian of the riches in the universe. The word Vasu stands for abode. The eight Vasus are *Dhara, Dhruva, Soma, Ahah, Anila, Anala, Pratyusa* and *Prabhasa*. In other words these are the abodes of the creation and also known as earth, water, fire, air, ether, moon, sun and the stars. Srī Kṛṣṇa declares *Pavaka* or the fire-god to be His Divine attribute. Fire is the purifier and considered to be the most venerable in all respects. As the first hymn of *Rigveda* describes *"agni mide purohitam yajnasya devam ritvijam hotaram ratnadhatamam"* meaning Agni, the object of adoration, the most bounteous, the bestower of wealth both in physical and spiritual. Among the high-peaked mountains I am the Meru. The Meru mountain peak is known for its golden glamour and splendour in the ancient *Puranas.* It is believed to be the axis around which all the heavenly bodies rotate. It is considered to be the centre of the universe, the great reservoir of gold and jewels. The *Puranas* declare that on the top of the golden mountain is the seat of the Supreme Lord.

This mythological mountain peak is an allegorical description of the spinal cord in the human body, the golden peak representing the full lotus; the *Brahmaranda* is the seat of the Divine. Along the spinal cord are the various psychic stations through which the life-force moves. In yogic meditation when this energy is consciously controlled and directed upward, it opens and awakens many levels of the subconscious mind and brings purification at the various levels of consciousness. Moving towards the peak of the mountain at the top of the head, is usually the goal in yogic contemplation. This peak of the mountain is considered to be a reservoir of great jewels and gold in the form of God-realization and self-realization. Therefore Srī Kṛṣṇa speaks of the mount Meru as to be one of His attributes.

पुरोधसां च मुख्यं मां विद्धि पार्थ बृहस्पतिम्।
सेनानीनामहं स्कन्दः सरसामस्मि सागरः ॥ २४ ॥

purodhasāṁ ca mukhyaṁ māṁ viddhi pārtha bṛhaspatim
senānīnām ahaṁ skandaḥ sarasām asmi sāgar

(24) Among the priests, know Me to be their chief, the Brihaspati, O' Partha. Among the army generals, I am Skanda (Kartikeya) and of the reservoirs of water, I am the ocean.

महर्षीणां भृगुरहं गिरामस्म्येकमक्षरम्।
यज्ञानां जपयज्ञोऽस्मि स्थावराणां हिमालयः ॥ २५ ॥

maharṣiṇāṁ bhṛgur ahaṁ girām asmyekam akṣaram
yajñānāṁ japayajño'smi sthāvarāṇāṁ himālayaḥ

(25) Among the great seers, I am Bhṛgu; of the words, I am the monosyllable "AUM"; of yajñas, I am the Jaap-yajña (silent repetition of the Lord's name) and among the immovables, the Himalaya.

अश्वत्थः सर्ववृक्षाणां देवर्षीणां च नारदः।
गन्धर्वाणां चित्ररथः सिद्धानां कपिलो मुनिः ॥ २६ ॥

aśvatthaḥ sarvavṛkṣāṇāṁ devarṣīṇāṁ ca nāradaḥ
gandharvāṇāṁ citrarathaḥ siddhānāṁ kapilo muniḥ

(26) Among all the trees, I am the Asvattha, among the celestial sages I am Narada, Chitraratha among the gandharvas and among the perfected sages, I am the sage Kapila.

उच्चैःश्रवसमश्वानां विद्धि माममृतोद्भवम्।
ऐरावतं गजेन्द्राणां नराणां च नराधिपम् ॥ २७ ॥

uccaiḥśravasam aśvānāṁ viddhi māmamṛtodbhavam

airāvataṁ gajendrāṇāṁ narāṇāṁ ca narādhipam

(27) Among the horses know Me to be the nectar-born celestial horse Ucchaisrava, The Airavata among the lordly elephants and among men the King.

Commentary—In continuation of the description of well-known attributes Srī Kṛṣṇa tells Arjuna that among the priests, know Me to be their chief the Brihaspati, the most revered son of the great sage Angira. Brihaspati has been called the chief even by the celestials. He has been a well known scholar of the *Vedas,* the six systems of philosophy, the *Smriti* and *Puranas.* There are many hymns in *Vedas,* written in the glory of Brihaspati. The one in *Rigveda* is: *"Brihaspatirustraia havysood kanikdradwadashvatirudajata"* which means the priest Brihaspati guides the people upward and speeds their offerings. He chants with affirmation as he leads them. His rhythmical chants illuminate the macrocosm and the microcosm. The hymns become charged with the spiritual power, as the great priest Brihaspati chants them. The great priest Brihaspati, the well-known repository of learning and wisdom, has been always known for his penances and yajñas. The great sage Brihaspati represents the Jupiter among the nine heavenly bodies. The Jupiter travels around the sun in eleven years. During this time there are four very special combinations in cosmic bodies when the special prayers are held at four holy pilgrimages in India. These well known spiritual celebrations are held in reverence of the great priest Brihaspati. When the sun is in the Aries and the Jupiter in Aries, it is held at Allahabad; when sun is in the Aries and the Jupiter is in Cancer, it is held at Nasik, when Sun in Aries the Jupiter in the Libra, it is at held Ujjain and when Sun in the Aries and Jupiter in the Aquarius, it is held at Haridwar. The pilgrimage Haridwar has been very famous for penances and other acts of purification. Haridwar, as the word explains itself, means the doorway to the God. Haridwar is one of the four places where Brihaspati has performed hard penances in the past. All these four places are very holy and well known for pilgrimage. There are many hymns which have been written in the adoration and appreciation of this great priest;

who has been known for his learning, wisdom, kindness and compassion. The great teachings of the sage have been imparted to the celestials from time to time. These teachings are described at great lengths in the sacred *Puranas* and also in *Santi Parva* and *Anusasana Parvas* of *Mahabharata.* Skanda, the son of Lord Shiva, is also known by the name of Kartikeya. He is very strong, active and endowed with most wonderful qualities of an army general. He has led many battles on behalf of the Lord against the demons. He killed the most ferocious demons Tarakasur. He is also known as Subramaniam in Southern India. People worship him as the embodiment of valour, bravery and as an ideal general. Srī Kṛṣṇa declares Kartikeya to be His Divine glory and His very self.

In the next part of the verse, Srī Kṛṣṇa speaks about the glory of the great ocean. He declares that among the reservoirs of water I am the ocean. Ocean is the chief source of water on earth and also it represents the infinitude of the Supreme-Lord. Ocean is indeed the magnificence of the Divine. Among the seven celestial seers, the great sage Bhṛgu has always held a very prominent position, a great scholar and the revealer of many sacred hymns and mantras. From his lineage have appeared many great sages who have contributed a whole lot to literature, poetry, music, art and power of sacred mantras. He holds a very respectable position in the field of music and the knowledge of *shabda.* He is worshipped as an embodiment of the Supreme and the bestower of great musical and literary talents. In the words of Jaydayal Goyandka, "Bhṛgu is the chief of all the great seers. He is a great devotee of God, highly enlightened and full of spiritual glow: "Hence the Lord declares him to be His own self."

As described earlier in chapter seven, Srī Kṛṣṇa has declared AUM to be His own Self and also in chapter eight He tells that the person who leaves his physical body while dwelling in the sound of the sacred syllable AUM, he attains the supreme state of liberation. AUM which is the supreme holy syllable represents the *sabda-brahman.* Describing the development of the world in *Rigveda,* it is written that "*Vac* is Brahman". It is the *Vac* that envelops the entire creation. It is the *Vac* the *shabd* that holds the world; which is manifested in everything around, it is the *vac* that sustains all the three worlds. The *Mandukya Upanishad : "Omityetadksharmind sarv tasyopavyakhyan bootam bhavbhavishyaditi sarvamonkar eva"*—the holy syllable AUM is indeed imperishable Brahman and the universe is the exposition of His glory. AUM is whatever has existed in the past, whatever exists now and whatever will exist in future.

The holy syllable AUM is indeed the symbol of the Supreme. The *Chandogya Upanishad* opens with the declaration for concentration on AUM for meditation and contemplation. *"AUM ity etad aksaram udgitam, upasita, AUM iti hrdgaynti tasyopavyakyanam"*— The loud chanting which begins with AUM, helps in contemplation and meditation. It connects the outer world to the inner world forming a unity for the macrocosm to blend into the microcosm. It connects the aspirant to the primordial sound, the *nada.* AUM is the pure sound resonance that emanates at the heart centre from the *anahat nada.* The sound of the holy syllable AUM helps the aspirant to glide through the three important stages in meditation. The first one that stands for 'A' is *Aniruddha,* which means passing over the boundaries of the gross body and slowly gliding into the subtle. 'U' stands for going into the subtle which is called *Pradyumna.* As the aspirant loses the consciousness of the gross body and moves into subtle body, the increased awareness guides him into the third stage that stands for 'M' the *Samkarsana.* At this point the aspirant is automatically pulled towards the eternal *nada* and goes into unity with primordial sound. AUM represents the supreme Divine power. With the concentration and contemplation on the sound of AUM, the aspirant identifies himself with the Divine power, which directs him to a state of superconsciousness where the mind goes into complete unity with the transcendental being. As described earlier in chapter seven and eight, the holy syllable AUM describes all the cosmic stages of creation from the most mystical to the very distinct. The one syllable AUM represents the entire Divine potency manifesting in the entire world that exists around. According to Shri Ramsukhdas, "At first the monosyllable AUM was revealed. Then Gayatri was revealed from AUM. The *Vedas* were revealed from Gayatri and on the basis of *Vedas* have been written the other scriptures and *Puranas* etc. Lord has declared AUM to be his divine glory.

In the next part of the verse twenty-five, Srī Kṛṣṇa declares that among the different forms of worship "I am the *Jaap-yajña*". The word *jaap* stands for silent repetition of the Divine name. The *mantra jaap* is indeed a vehicle of spiritual illumination in the form of God-realization and self-realization. The silent recitation of the Divine name uplifts the person from the lower-levels of the egocentric-self to the loftier heights of the universal-self. It helps one to live in the light of pure awareness, which guides one to self-unfoldment and God-realization. It provides a new direction to the individual's thoughts and channelizes them into a more blissful and productive thinking. *Jaap* strengthens the person's unity with the Supreme-Self. It helps one to regulate and harmonize the entire thinking faculty into a certain order. It gives one the ability to grasp the mysteries of the Divine, through a very simple and effortless method. Srī Kṛṣṇa declares silent *mantra jaap* as the most appropriate method of worship. It strengthens the relationship with the inner-self very effortlessly and naturally. Silent *Jaap* is like being in constant communion with God and working in a copartnership with God. It brings inner peace and tranquillity. The habit of the silent inward *jaap* sets the whole life in tune. The silent *mantra jaap* (recitation) helps one to experience the essence of something which is real and yet waiting to be revealed to us; something so close to our heart yet seems so far off. Although one can start the spiritual quest according to the mode of choice, such as verbal prayer, worship, chanting etc.; but slowly one need something short, concise and brief but comprehensive in expression, which can envelop the entire thinking faculty.

Silent mantra recitation keeps one in harmony with the pure spiritual nature. In the beginning the aspirant has to consciously develop the habit but subsequently it just becomes a second nature to him. The recitation of *jaap* is felt at all times. It keeps one in touch with the inner-self and checks all kinds of astray thoughts. Quiet *mantra* recitation is indeed a complete austerity in itself. It keeps polishing the inner instruments and as it joins the rhythm of breath, it ultimately joins the rhythmic sound of the primordial *nada.* In words of the great sage Vashista, *"japastu sarva dharme bha parmo dharm uchate"*.

Silent *jaap* is the most highly recommended techniquc of practising dharma *"Jap nishto divaj shretha sarve yajan phalam labhate"*—means a spiritual aspirant intent on quiet *mantra jaap* gets reward of all types of yajñas. The silent recitation of the Divine name can be practised by the entire mankind irrespective of their age, sex, caste, country and nationality. *"Sarve te japa yajnasya narhatah shodashim kalam"*—means all the other rituals and external offerings that one performs would not constitute even one-sixteenth part of the ritual of inward worship which is quiet and silent *mantra jaap*. Quiet *jaap* leads towards the quietness of mind. It is a very powerful method of calming the thoughts. In quiet *jaap* there is no loss of physical energy, and it strengthens the spirit of surrender. It is a very appropriate method of worship and establishing inner unity with the Divine. Further in the same verse Srī Kṛṣṇa declares that among the immovable "I am the Himalayas". The Himalayan peaks are the highest in the world and also famous for the natural beauty and bounties of the Divine. The Himalaya is said to be the abode of Lord Shiva.

In the verse twenty-six, Srī Kṛṣṇa says that among all the trees I am the 'Asvattha'. Asvattha is the Pipal tree also known as Ficus Religiosa. This tree is frequently planted for worship, it purifies the air. Almost every part of this tree is used for medicinal purposes. The bark of this tree has been found very useful in *Ayurveda.* The bark contains 3.8 per cent tannin and the dry leaves are used in many different remedies. This tree is very sacred and usually its wood is not used for fuel. The leaves of this tree are beautiful and strong enough to be used for painting with water colour. Pipal tree stays green almost throughout the year and its life span usually extends to many centuries. It is worshipped as the embodiment of Lord Vishnu. The leaves and bark of the tree are used for the cure of many ailments such as the congestion of chest with excessive phlegm, remittent fever, hiccough, upset stomach, vomiting, worms in stomach, even leprosy and psoriasis.

Srī Kṛṣṇa declares the Divine rishi Narada as his attribute. The sage Narada has been recognized as the highly enlightened devotee of the Lord and also an expert revealer of the devotional *mantras.* The *Narada Bhakti Sutras* have been translated by various scholars. Narada's way of singing the divine's love is just remarkable. He tells in his Aphorism that the path of devotion is the most natural way to God-realization. He describes God's loving devotion as an unparalleled joy of life. *Narada Bhakti Sutra* asserts that it is not only the scholarly knowledge that makes one spiritual, it is the personal experiential love for God which unfolds the glory of the Divine and arouses devotional love for the Supreme.

The sage Narada has emphasized upon the company of holy men, and the practice of silent *mantra jaap.* There are many illustrations in sacred scriptures where Narada is continuously enlightening the lives of people, about the sublimity of Lord's devotion. It is believed that when a sincere aspirant of the Lord cries in devotional love, Narada appears as a spiritual teacher and gives his blessings with a sacred mantra; so Narada is indeed the glory of God.

Srī Kṛṣṇa says that among the Gandharvas, "I am the Chitraratha". *Gandharva Veda* is the upaveda of the *Samaveda.* It describes the knowledge of sound, composition of musical notes, and the compositions of the beat and rhythm. In ancient scriptures the celestial musicians have been called *gandharvas.* Chitraratha has been the most talented and well known *gandharva,* an expert dancer and well-versed in various branches of music. He has been considered the most proficient music master. Arjuna learnt music and dancing from Chitraratha. *Siddhas* means the perfected ones, who have achieved the highest goal in the form of God-realization. Srī Kṛṣṇa says among the seers of perfection "I am the Kapila Muni". The Sanskrit word Muni stands for the one who has achieved perfection in the art and science of *manan,* concentration, reflection and meditation.

The sage Kapila was the son of Devahuti and sage Kardama. The sage Kapila has been the most revered among the sages of *Samkhya* philosophy. He was born as a very enlightened one. He has been highly respected by the teachers of *Samkhya* system. In continuation of His attributes Srī Kṛṣṇa tells Arjuna that among the horses know

Me the celestial horse Ucchaisravas which came from the churning of ocean with the celestial nectar; and also among the elephants, the mighty Airavata which came with other precious blessings.

The word *Naradhipa* stands for the king or the ruler. Srī Kṛṣṇa declares the king among men to be His Divine glory. The king is regarded as the embodiment of God because he takes care of people in all respects. He protects, fosters and also guides his subjects to righteousness. A king is considered to be the best among men and so he has been also called the Lord's magnificence.

आयुधानामहं वज्रं धेनूनामस्मि कामधुक्।

प्रजनश्चास्मि कन्दर्पः सर्पाणामस्मि वासुकिः॥ २८॥

āyudhānām ahaṁ vajraṁ dhenūnām asmi kāmadhuk

prajanaścāsmi kandarpaḥ sarpāṇām asmi vāsukiḥ

(28) Of weapons I am the thunderbolt; among cows, I am the celestial wish-yielding cow (Kamadhenu); of the progenitors, I am the God of Love; and of the Serpents, I am Vasuki.

अनन्तश्चास्मि नागानां वरुणो यादसामहम्।

पितृणामर्यमा चास्मि यमः संयमतामहम्॥ २९॥

anaśt aścāsmi nāgānāṁ varuṇo yādasām aham

pitṝṇām aryamā cāsmi yamaḥ saṁyamatām aham

(29) I am Ananta among the snakes and among the aquatic creatures and water gods, I am the Varuna. Among the ancestors, I am the Aryaman and I am Yama among the governors.

प्रह्लादश्चास्मि दैत्यानां कालः कलयतामहम्।

मृगाणां च मृगेन्द्रोऽहं वैनतेयश्च पक्षिणाम्॥ ३०॥

prahlādaścāsmi daityānaṁ kālaḥ kalayatām aham

mrgāṇāṁ ca mrgendro'haṁ vainateyaśca pakṣiṇām

(30) I am Prahlada among the demons; among the reckoners I am Time, among the beasts I am the Lion, and Garuda among the birds.

पवनः पवतामस्मि रामः शस्त्रभृतामहम्।
झषाणां मकरश्चास्मि स्त्रोतसामस्मि जाह्नवी॥ ३१॥

pavanaḥ pavatām asmi rāmaḥ śastrabhṛtām aham
jhaṣāṇāṁ makaraścāsmi srotasām asmi jāhnavī

(31) I am the wind among the purifiers (the speeders), among the wielders of weapons, I am Rama; among the fishes I am alligator and among the rivers I am the holy Gaṇga.

Commentary—The word Vajra in the verse twenty-eight stands for the thunderbolt. It is a most powerful weapon that can't be shattered. About this weapon there is a story in our *Puranas.* Once there was a very ferocious demon Vritrasur who always caused troubles to the celestials. One time all the gods met together and decided to attack Vritrasur. The gods approached Brahma for help. He suggested to the gods that killing Vritrasur could be very difficult with any ordinary weapon. He told them to contact the great sage Dadhichi. The sage Dadhichi who had done very tough penances became possessed with some special powers. He knew that even after he left his mortal body, his bones would still retain specific power of his long penances. So Brahma suggested to the gods to contact the great sage and request him to allow the use of his bones, after he dies in order to make a special weapon that would kill Vritrasur. Devaraj Indra approached the rishi and related the problem created by Vritrasur. The great Rishi Dadhichi told Devaraj Indra that he would be more than happy to sacrifice his life for the welfare of righteousness. He immediately prepared himself to go into deep meditation and breathed his last. Indra quickly ordered Vishvakarma to prepare a powerful weapon with the bones of the sage's body in order to kill the demon. That weapon has been called 'Vajra'.

The word Kamadhuk stands for the wish granting cow of the sage Vasishta that yields all the desired objects. Srī Kṛṣṇa declares Kamadhenu to be His Divine glory. The other word Kandarpa in this verse has been used for the progenitor, the god of the progenitive urge that leads to procreation. Srī Kṛṣṇa expresses His respect for the progenitive instinct when it is followed in accordance with the laws of Dharma. It becomes a Divine glory when applied with scriptural injunction. Vasuki, the yellow coloured Naga, has been considered the most revered among the serpents. In the words of Swami Chidbhavanananda, "Vasuki is the symbol of Sakti, the cosmic energy. In man the dormant power is called the *Kundalini Sakti* or the coiled up energy symbolized as serpent power." As a matter of fact Vasuki stands for the coiled up *Kundilini* in human body which helps the aspirant for God-realization.

In continuation of the previous verse, in verse twenty-nine, Srī Kṛṣṇa mentions the word Naga for serpent. The Nagas are a special class of serpents. The word Ananta signifies the serpent-god 'Sesha Naga' of thousands heads. The serpent-god Ananta is the seat of Lord Vishnu. As a matter of fact, the Lord Vishnu is the Supreme-Self, the consciousness in the body. The Sesha Naga symbolizes His Divine potency which is indeed Ananta, means immeasurable, which is upholding the entire creation on its many thousand hooded head. Sesha Naga is the mightiest power, so Srī Kṛṣṇa speaks of it, as His magnificence. Varuna is the Lord of water and has always held a very revered place among the Vedic gods and goddesses. The word Varuna comes from two root words—*vara* means desire and *vrn* means to accept. Life comes out of water, is sustained through the medium of water and goes into the water. So worship of water-god Varuna has been an ancient Vedic tradition. There are many hymns in the *Vedas* written in the glory of Varuna. Worship of Varuna has been considered the worship of Lord Himself—*"Varuno nama varah sresthah."*

The Aryaman stands for the presiding deity of the ancestors. The yajñas performed especially on the fourteenth day of the descending moon, known as *Amavasya,* when it is dark all around, the offerings are made in the name of Aryaman. Yama is the Lord of death, the deity endowed with supreme wisdom and the virtue of treating the beings with total impartiality. The laws of *Yama* are inexorable. In *Kathoupanisad*, there are elaborate teachings of Yama imparted to Nachiketa. Among the demons "I am the great devotee Prahlada". Prahlada was a very pious soul, a faithful loving devotee of the Lord and also a very successful king. Prahlada, the son of Hiranayakashipu, has been a great devotee of Lord Vishnu. Inspite of repeated threats of his father, Prahlada regularly prayed to the God. One time the demon Hiranayakashipu pushed Prahlada down from the top of the mountain but the boy was not injured. Another time, the child Prahlada was thrown into the sea but he was not drowned. He was also poisoned one time and was forced to be bitten by snakes, but nothing could harm him. He kept chanting the holy name of Lord Vishnu under all adversities. Once the king Hiranyakashipu compelled his son Prahlada to stand in front of a mad elephant to be killed; but the elephant lifted the little boy carefully to sit on the back. At last Hiranyakashipu decided to burn Prahlada alive with the help of his sister Holika. Holika was burnt to ashes but Prahlada kept chanting the Divine name and came out alive. In this verse Srī Kṛṣṇa, while glorifying the undivided and honest devotion of Prahlada, has called him as one of his attributes. Srī Kṛṣṇa speaks of Prahlada as His very Self.

The word Kala stands for time. The entire creation functions under the concept of time. Time is indeed the ultimate of everything which is apparent in the world. It is the measure in the world of relativity. All appearances and disappearances of things animate and inanimate are controlled by time. Srī Kṛṣṇa declares time to be His glory identical with His magnificence. Among the beasts, Srī Kṛṣṇa declares Himself to be the lion. Lion has been recognized to be very powerful and king of the beasts. The lion is courageous, strongest and holds very dignified bearing. Among the birds, I am the Garuda. Garuda has been regarded as the king of the birds, and also the vehicle of Lord Vishnu. Among the purifying agents Srī Kṛṣṇa declares Himself to be the 'wind'. The word Rama in the verse signifies the great incarnation of Lord Vishnu Bhagavan Srī Ramchandra. The greatness of Srī Rama, as described in the great epic *Ramayana* is unparalleled. Srī Rama as an incarnation has been represented as an ideal son, an ideal king, a faithful husband, faithful friend, a revered brother, a great warrior of extraordinary valour, a wonderful teacher and a loving father.

The sage Valmiki has also described Srī Rama as ever equipped with bow and arrow at all times. The wielding of arrows and the bow definitely symbolizes Srī Rama at all times and under all circumstances. Among the fishes Alligator is the most powerful, the largest fish in the ocean. Being the largest and the most powerful is its distinction. Srī Kṛṣṇa declares this distinction to be His Divine magnificence. Of the rivers I am the Ganga. Ganga is the holy river of India. It has its origin in the Himalayan mountains of North India. The origin is known as Gangotri situated at the height of 3024 M from the sea level. At Haridwar, the very famous pilgrimage of India, the mighty Ganga hurries down from the hills to the luxuriant plains and ridges. The Ganga is worshipped as the holy mother. Thousands of pilgrims from all over the country go to the holy Ganga for a sacred bath, which purifies the individual physically as well as psychologically. It is believed that the water of Ganga contains some special healing components. This water can be stored in a bottle for years. It is used for many skin diseases. The bank of the holy river in Haridwar has been named after the footprints of Srī Hari (The Lord Vishnu). Srī Kṛṣṇa designates Ganga as one of His attribute.

सर्गाणामादिरन्तश्च मध्यं चैवाहमर्जुन।
अध्यात्मविद्या विद्यानां वादः प्रवदतामहम्॥ ३२॥

sargāṇām ādir antaś ca madhyaṁ caivā'ham arjuna
adhyātmavidyā vidyānāṁ vādaḥ pravadatām aham

(32) Among creations, I am the beginning, the middle, and the end O' Arjuna. Among sciences, I am the science of the Self and the *Vadah* (logic) of those who debate.

अक्षराणामकारोऽस्मि द्वन्द्वः सामासिकस्य च।
अहमेवाक्षयः कालो धाताहं विश्वतोमुखः॥ ३३॥

akṣarāṇām akāro'smi dvandvaḥ sāmāsikasya ca
aham evākṣayaḥ kālo dhātāhaṁ viśvatomukhaḥ

(33) Of letters I am 'A', of word-compounds, I am the dual, I am verily the imperishable Time; I am the sustainer, facing in all directions.

मृत्युः सर्वहरश्चाहमुद्भवश्च भविष्यताम्।
कीर्तिः श्रीर्वाक्च नारीणां स्मृतिर्मेधा धृतिः क्षमा॥ ३४॥

mṛtyuḥ sarvaharaś cāham udbhavaś ca bhaviṣyatām

kīrtiḥ śrīr vāk ca nārīṇāṁ smṛtir medhā dhṛtiḥ kṣamā

(34) I am the all devouring death and the source of things yet to come. Among the feminine virtues I am glory, fortune, speech, memory, wisdom, steadfastness, firmness and forgiveness.

बृहत्साम तथा साम्नां गायत्री छन्दसामहम्।

मासानां मार्गशीर्षोऽहमृतूनां कुसुमाकरः॥ ३५॥

bṛhatsāma tathā sāmnāṁ gāyatrī chandasām aham

māsānāṁ mārgaśīrṣo'ham ṛtūnāṁ kusumākaraḥ

(35) Of the hymns, I am the *Brihatsaman,* among the Vedic metres I am the *Gayatri.* Among the months I am Margashirsha, and of seasons the spring.

द्यूतं छलयतामस्मि तेजस्तेजस्विनामहम्।

जयोऽस्मि व्यवसायोऽस्मि सत्त्वं सत्त्ववतामहम्॥ ३६॥

dyūtaṁ chalayatām asmi tejastejasvināmaham

jayo'smi vyavasāyo'smi sattvaṁ sattvavatām aham

(36) Of the deceitful, I am the gambling; I am the glory of the glorious and the victory of the victorious. I am determination and the goodness of the good.

Commentary—Srī Kṛṣṇa declares Himself to be the beginning, the middle and also the end. Everything in the universe comes in existence with the power of the Supreme. It is sustained by the power of the Supreme and also annihilated with the power of the Divine. So it is indeed one power that works as the substratum of the entire manifested world. Lord is the essence of creation. It is only one and the same entity that works as Brahma the creator, Vishnu as the sustainer and also the Shiva or Rudra as the annihilator. All the names and forms are only the various manifestations of the ultimate Reality. Srī Kṛṣṇa has called the knowledge of the Self to be one of His attributes. All other branches of knowledge are incomplete, because after reaching certain point, the answers themselves become questions. *Upanishads* describe the greatness of the knowledge of Self in these words, "By knowing which nothing else remains to be known", it renders total fulfillment and contentment in all respects.

In verse thirty-two, Srī Kṛṣṇa declares *Vada* to be His glory. *Vada-samvad* has been given due importance and reverence in the exchange of ideas. *Vada* stands for the method where the individual presents some facts with the pure motive of arriving at the right conclusion. Here one brushes aside all personal prejudices and follows the facts very faithfully. It is a very direct and genuine approach of being enlightened and also of enlightening others. *Vada-samvad* is very useful and important but *vivada*, which is a form of discussion where the individuals enter into an argument and start criticizing each other with arrogance and ignorance, is not beneficial. One should stay away from *vivad* and *vikhyad.*

Word 'Aksara', here in the verse thirty-three, signifies the first letter of the holy syllable AUM. As described earlier that the origin of the AUM is the *Brahma nada* the primordial sound. The letter 'A' is the most important among the five 'vowels'. The linguists claim that none of the consonants can be pronounced correctly without this letter. In almost all the languages of the world 'A' is the first letter. The *Upanishad* describes *"Akaro vai sarva vak"*—means Aksara with prominent sound of 'A' makes the essence of all spoken words. Srī Kṛṣṇa speaks of 'A' as one of His attributes. Of the compound words 'I am the *dvandwa'*. *Dvandwa* is the word-compound in which both the words are relatively important. In order to comprehend the meaning of one, the relative word has to be there. Each word maintains its own individuality and also relativity. For example, pleasure and pain, loss and gain, day and night, honour and ignominy etc. Time as mentioned earlier in this chapter is beginningless and endless. The concept of time has existed ever since the beginning of creation. Time is considered to be primordial as is the manifested Divinity. The Lord is the sustainer of creation, watching everything in all direction. His grandeur can be felt, touched, and experienced in everything at all places.

In the verse thirty-four, Srī Kṛṣṇa declares, 'I am the all devouring death and the source of things yet to come.' Death is indeed all-devouring, all-consuming and the most powerful annihilator. Nothing in the world can escape death. It levels down the entire creation in due time. The Lord Himself is the all consuming death and also the source of new life yet to appear. These lines from *Gitanjali* definitely explain this truth—"Thou hast made me endless, such is thy pleasure. This frail vessel thou emptiest again and again and fillest it ever with fresh life."

The next part of the verse describes the most well-known feminine qualities such as glory, prosperity, speech, memory, wisdom, steadfastness and forgiveness. These qualities are indeed the manifestation of Divinity in a woman. These are the expression of the excellencies of Divine glory. Srī Kṛṣṇa calls these virtues to be His Divine magnificence. As described earlier, there are four *Vedas,* but *Samaveda* has been designated as the Lord's glory. The Samaveda is full of devotional hymns. Out of all these hymns the most unique ones are the *Brihatsama.* These are usually dedicated towards the end of the prayer known as *Atiratra.* These hymns are highly devotional in nature. These psalms have been sung by many artists on various auspicious occasions. Srī Kṛṣṇa speaks of these most melodious hymns as to be His attribute.

Gayatri mantra has been always known as the *maha-mantra* in the *Vedas.* In the words of *Gayatri* lies the whole universe. Meditation with the chants of *Gayatri* connects one to the throbbing Being who is the essençe of life. It is believed that *Gayatri* came out of the primordial sound AUM and all the four *Vedas* emanated from *Gayatri.* In the *Vedas, Gayatri* has been given the name as *Vedmata* meaning the mother of knowledge and wisdom. The glory of *Gayatri* has been described throughout the vedic literature. The great *Gayatri mantra "AUM bhoor bhuah svah tat savitur varenyam bhargo devasya dheemahi dhiyo yo nah prachodayat."* According to the *Vedic* tradition, *Gayatri mantra* should be taught as the first lesson to each child of the family. It should be introduced as the first prayer to the youngster. The importance of learning *Gayatri mantra* has been highly emphasised at the time of *upanayan samskar.* The recitation of the first three words, *Bhur, Bhuvah* and *Swah*, connects the individual to all the three levels of consciousness. The three levels are physical, psychological and spiritual. *Bhur* symbolizes the physical body composed of five components such as earth, water, air, ether and energy. With prayer one asks for full harmony and support with the cosmic forces. The word *Bhava* stands for the thought process as a controller of the astral body or the inner nature. *Swa* stands for the indwelling light, the Supreme-self. The *Gayatri jaap* brings harmony at all the three levels of consciousness. It keeps electrifying the thoughts with spiritual power. It purifies the thoughts speech and action.

There are about 24,000 hymns in the four *Vedas.* The essence of all those have been combined into twenty-four syllables called *Gayatri.* Atri *rishi* has been the great seer who sang it for the first time in the most melodious tune, since then it has been known as *Gayatri. Gayatri* is also known as *Savitri,* a *mantra* which is used for the worship of sun-god. The holy scriptures describe that anybody who worships the rising sun with the recitation of *Gayatri,* receives special blessings from the Divine. The worshippers of sun usually live a very long life. *Maitri upanisad* describes the glory of *Gayatri* in these words "*Gayatri* is the splendour, the beauty and glamour of *Savitri.* Let us meditate on *Savitri* with the chanting of its holy words". There are thousands of translations of *Gayatri mantra.* In the words of Swami Shivananda, "Let us meditate on God Almighty and His glory Who has created the universe, who is remover of all sins and ignorance. May He enlighten our intellect". The ancient scriptures describe "*Gayatri chandasam mateti*" which means *Gayatri* is the mother of all the hymns in *Vedas.* Similarly in the *Devi Bagavatham,* the glory of *Gayatri* has been described in these words. "*Sarva Ved sar bhutha Gayatriastu samarchana Brahmadyopi sandyayam Tha dhyayanthi japanti cha*" means the worship of *Gayatri* constitutes the entire essence of all the *Vedas.* Even Brahma himself meditates on *Gayatri.* Swami Dayananda Saraswati, a great commentator on *Vedas,* has given the meaning of *Gayatri* in these words "O' omnipotent Lord Thou are the dearest life breath. Keep us away from evil intentions and physical sufferings. May we have the pure vision in our mind. O' God lead us from darkness to light. May Thy kindness direct our thoughts towards the righteous path. May we surrender all our work to you and attain ultimate emancipation and liberation."

Anand Swamiji has written a book on *Gayatri* and gave it the name as *'Gayatri Maha Mantra'*. He writes the meaning of *Gayatri* in these words "O Divine power, you are the creator and sustainer of the universe, may we meditate on thy glorious splendour, and offer all our activities to your humble service. Bless us with mental, spiritual and intellectual strength. Give us the ability of total surrender. Please illuminate our mind with thy grace and inspire our spiritual perception". The great *Gayatri mantra* is easy to recite. It can be used by everybody everywhere in the entire creation. There is no restriction. It is a compact prayer and in most cases it does prepare the individual for all kinds of advanced spiritual awareness. Our scriptures describe *Gayatri upasana nitya sarveveda samreeta. yahya vina tavadhpato Brahmanasyasti sarvatha* which means that all the *Vedas* declare, the meditation on *Gayatri* as an obligatory worship for each individual. The negligence of this brings about the downfall of the person in every way. Srī Kṛṣṇa speaks of *Gayatri* as one of His attributes.

In the next part of the same verse, Srī Kṛṣṇa says "Of all the months I am the Margasirsha" and of seasons the beautiful spring 'Kusumakarah'. Since ancient times the month of Margasirsha (Nov-Dec) has been considered very sacred and very auspicious for religious worship. Both the "Ekadashies" in this month which is the eleventh day of the ascending moon and eleventh lunar day of the descending phase of moon are observed as a spiritual discipline. Some people observe fasting for the entire month of Margishrisha and spend the whole time in meditation and religious disciplines. Charities made in this month are especially auspicious and rewarding. It is believed that the fruit of charity comes back to the person, ten times in return. Margasirshsa as the name itself is self-explanatory—means the topmost route for liberation and Salvation. Fasting and meditation observed on *Mokshda Ekadeshi* promotes the increased understanding, intelligence and intuitive ability. Some people stay absorbed in meditation on the *Mokshda Ekadashi*, for almost the entire night for perfection in *mantra jaap,* peace and tranquillity.

Of seasons, the spring season has been always celebrated as the king of seasons *(Rituraaja).* Spring is the beginning of new life in all respects. From extreme cold to extreme heat this is the time of the year which is pleasant, brisk and full of fragrances. People all over the world celebrate spring. In Japan the doll festival, in Thailand the spring is celebrated with the exchange of fragrant coloured water. In England people dance in the meadows and green fields. In India people wear yellow and saffron outfits and celebrate the spring with the worship of the goddess Saraswati. The saffron colour signifies warmth and enlightenment, auspiciousness, maturity and spirituality. The goddess Saraswati is the deity of learning, fine arts, music, sciences and languages. In this season the music gatherings are held in parks and green meadows. In verse thirty-six Srī Kṛṣṇa declares I am gambling of the deceitful plays, I am glory of the glorious and the victory of the victorious. The word *tejah* used by Srī Kṛṣṇa stands for the purity and spiritual glory. *Tejah* has been derived from the root word *tija* which means to shine. Srī Kṛṣṇa declares *tejah* to be His attribute.

वृष्णीनां वासुदेवोऽस्मि पाण्डवानां धनञ्जयः।
मुनीनामप्यहं व्यासः कवीनामुशना कविः॥ ३७॥

vṛṣnīnām vāsudevo'smi pāṇḍavānāṁ dhanañjayaḥ
munīnām apyahaṁ vyāsaḥ kavīnām uśanā kaviḥ

(37) Among the Vrishnis I am Vasudeva; among the Pandavas I am Dhananjaya (Arjuna), I am Vyasa among the sages and among the poets I am Shukracharya.

दण्डो दमयतामस्मि नीतिरस्मि जिगीषताम्।
मौनं चैवास्मि गुह्यानां ज्ञानं ज्ञानवतामहम्॥ ३८॥

daṇḍo damayatām asmi nītir asmi jigīṣatām
maunaṁ caivāsmi guhyānāṁ jñānaṁ jñānavatām aham

(38) I am the principle of punishment, of those who punish. I am statesmanship of those who seek victory. Among the secrets I am silence and wisdom of the wise.

यच्चापि सर्वभूतानां बीजं तदहमर्जुन।
न तदस्ति विना यत्स्यान्मया भूतं चराचरम्॥ ३९॥

yaccāpi sarvabhūtānāṁ bījaṁ tadahamarjuna
na tadasti vinā yat syān mayā bhūtaṁ carācaram

(39) I am seed of all living beings O' Arjuna. There is no being animate or inanimate that can exist without Me.

नान्तोऽस्ति मम दिव्यानां विभूतीनां परन्तप।
एष तूद्देशतः प्रोक्तो विभूतेर्विस्तरो मया ॥ ४० ॥

nānto'sti mama divyānāṁ vibhūtīnāṁ parantapa
eṣa tū'ddeśataḥ prokto vibhūter vistaro mayā

(40) There is no end of My Divine attributes O' Arjuna. This is only a brief description given by Me of the particulars of My infinite glories.

यद्यद्विभूतिमत्सत्त्वं श्रीमदूर्जितमेव वा।
तत्तदेवावगच्छ त्वं मम तेजोंऽशसम्भवम् ॥ ४१ ॥

yad-yadvibhūtimat sattvaṁ śrīmad ūrjitameva vā
tat-tad evāvagaccha tvaṁ mama tejoṁśasambhavam

(41) Every such thing as is glorious, prosperous, powerful, know that to be a manifestation of the fragment of My divine splendour.

अथवा बहुनैतेन किं ज्ञातेन तवार्जुन।
विष्टभ्याहमिदं कृत्स्नमेकांशेन स्थितो जगत् ॥ ४२ ॥

athavā bahunaitena kiṁ jñātena tavārjuna
viṣṭabhyāham idaṁ kṛtsnam ekāṁśena sthito jagat

(42) What is the need of your knowing all these in detail O' Arjuna. I exist supporting the whole universe, with the single fragment of Myself.

Commentary—Srī Kṛṣṇa tells in the verse thirty-seven that 'among the Vrishnis, I am the Vasudeva'. In the *Yadava* dynasty, the great *Satvata* had seven sons—Bhajamana, Bhaji, Divya, Devavrata, Andhaka, Mahabhoja and Vrishni. The Vrishni had two sons, Sini and Anamitra. From the *Yadava* line, the son of Sini carried on the name of his family as Vrishnis. Vasudeva the son of Shursen had been married to Devaki. Vasudeva had been known for his ethics, righteousness and truthfulness. When he was born, the celestial conches blared out-loud to announce the birth of a child who would become in future the father of the Divine incarnation. The son of Vasudeva Srī Kṛṣṇa Himself is also known as Vasudeva. Among the sons of Pandu, Srī Kṛṣṇa says I am Dhananjaya. As described in the first chapter, Dhananjaya is one of Arjuna's names. Arjuna, a great warrior, has been also a great devotee of the Lord. His valour and bravery has been known all over the world. Srī Kṛṣṇa tells Arjuna that "among the Pandavas I am Arjuna"; by telling Arjuna to be one of His magnificence, Srī Kṛṣṇa reminds Arjuna of his real identity. He reminds Arjuna that he is not just a son of Kunti, he is the magnificence of the Divine glory. The valour and outstanding archery of Arjuna is indeed the Lord's attribute. Arjuna's brilliance and splendour is manifestation of the Lord's potency, so he should rise above the limited individuality to the oneness with the supreme-self. In the *Mahabharata*, it is described very vividly that Srī Kṛṣṇa tells Arjuna, O' great Arjuna you are indeed the divine *nara* and 'I' the God *Narayana.* "In the past when I appeared on earth as the sage Narayana you came with me in the form of *nara.* So Arjuna you are indeed the embodiment of My Divinity."

The word *muni* represents the very enlightened sage who knows how to direct the mind completely into the silence of the Supreme-self. When a *muni* comes out of deep contemplation, he brings to the world, a bouquet of inner wisdom and knowledge. He brings out from the depths of his subconscious mind the jewels of the inner stability, peace and wisdom. The contribution of the sage Vyasa has been totally unparalleled and outstanding in the field of religious literature and philosophy of ancient Vedic religion. As a God-realised soul, he compiled the Vedic hymns into four sections and wrote the *Brahma Sutras.* Later on realizing the inability of people in general to comprehend the philosophy of the Vedas, he wrote *Puranas. Bhagwatam* is the most magnificent masterpiece written by the great sage Vyasa. He wrote the greatest epic of the world, the *Mahabharata.* In words of Jaydayal Goyandka, "The sage Vyasa is a part manifestation of God, and a repository of all the noble virtues. Being thus the foremost of all sages, Vyasa has been declared by the Lord as the same as Himself."

The word *kavi* in the next part of the same verse means the poet. Among the poets Srī Kṛṣṇa says "I am Sukracharya". The son of the great sage Bhrigu, Sukracharya has been a very revered teacher in the field of poetry, music, astrology, astronomy, *tantra* and *mantra siddhi.* The aspirant who are in pursuit of *mantra siddhi* (perfection), they seek refuge in the guidance of Sukracharya. The poets and musicians worship the sage Sukracharya for enlightenment with persistent penances and austerities. Sukracharya has been blessed with special knowledge of reviving the dead with *sanjeevani mantra.* He is also known as *kavi* and *Usanas*. *Sukraneeti* is one of his monumental works on statesmanship. It is the outstanding work of Sukracharya. He has been a well-known guide in politics, statesmanship, and in the sciences of secret and rare *mantras.*

In the verse thirty-eight, Srī Kṛṣṇa says, "I am the punishment of those who punish." The sceptre for the culprits, wicked and unrighteous is indeed the attribute of the Divine because it helps to maintain law and order in society. The authority of punishment which is exercised by the gods, goddesses, kings and rulers is indeed the glory of the Supreme. The other word 'Niti' stands for righteousness. Srī Kṛṣṇa says that for people who seek victory and virtuous name "I am the righteousness." Srī Kṛṣṇa is emphasising the fact that the victory that is combined with righteousness is in fact the glory of the Lord. The conquest with the law of Dharma and morality is the real victory that lasts longer and brings peace and prosperity. A king, a ruler, and a leader becomes adorable to his people and the embodiment of the Divine when he conquers with Dharma. Conquering others with material force only in the form of military power or money is definitely incomplete and it does not last very long. The victory becomes complete and brings peace and prosperity when the ruler adopts the means of ruling with righteousness, and helps people to maintain their freedom through self-identification and self-respect. Srī Kṛṣṇa declares righteousness to be one of his attributes. In the next part Srī Kṛṣṇa says, "I am silence, among the great secrets." Silence is indeed a great virtue and a great blessing of the Divine. *Mauna Vrata* is one of the austerities performed by the sages. *Mauna Vrata* literally means a resolve to stay silent. It trains the individual to perceive inner silence and peace and tranquillity of the indwelling Self. Quietness of speech leads to the quietness of thoughts and control over the activities of mind. The *Kathoupnisad* declares *"Ychadhang manasi prajndt-chchajjan aanmani jnanmatmani mahati niyechchtdyachchacdyant aatmani"*—means let the wise man restrain his speech in his mind, the mind in his intellect or knowledge, the knowledge or intellect in his great self and his self in his ever peaceful Supreme-Self. Silence is indeed the opulence, the glory and the grandeur of the Divine.

In the next part of the verse, Srī Kṛṣṇa declares, "I am the knowledge of the men of knowledge." Being knowledgable is a magnificence of the Supreme. It is the manifestation of the Lord's opulence. The wise man is respected in the world because of his wisdom, heightened intuition and integrity which is indeed the reflection of the Lord through him. Every distinction of a wise man manifests the glory of Lord. In the next four verses, Srī Kṛṣṇa concludes his long explanation with the words "O' Arjuna I am indeed the seed of all beings. The animate or inanimate nothing can exist without Me". It is one and the only divine energy which is manifesting through the entire creation. Lord is the essence of everything in the universe. God is the seed and the ultimate source of origin for beings and non-beings. The omnipresence of God can be experienced and perceived everywhere and in everything. The glories of the Divine are being reflected through the specific opulence of everything and every activity. The attributes of the Lord are surely infinite and very difficult to comprehend. Srī Kṛṣṇa says, "I have described to you only a small fraction of My infinite magnitude. Everything that is glorious, splendid, prosperous and outstanding; and everybody who is brilliant, powerful, prosperous, peaceful, well known, victorious and wise—Know thou that to be my magnificence". Any particular quality should be regarded as the Lord's attribute.

The word *athva* in the verse forty-two brings out an alternative suggestion. It conveys the ultimate declaration that one must understand the fact that the entire universe is being held together by a small fraction of the Lord's yogic power. The Divine potency is indeed holding everything together and also reflecting through everything. In the words of Swami Chidbhavanananda, "Lord is expressing Himself. Whatever catches our imagination, draws our attention, sends us into raptures and infuses bliss into us, that is none but the glory of the God." It is indeed so difficult to comprehend the infinitude of the supreme; the human understanding can catch only a small fraction of it, so it is just enough to know and remember that the Lord is everything. By giving a little glimpse of the eighty-two attributes and majesties (Majestic manifestations), Srī Kṛṣṇa intimates Arjuna that any type of particular glory, achievement, name or fame that comes to the individual should be considered to be the manifestation of the Supreme. One should not get deluded by the masks and should learn to appreciate and see the splendour of the Divine behind all masks. One should try to pierce through the personal egoistic identity into the prime truth that works behind the whole phenomenal achievement. This attitude of seeing the lord's opulence and majesty in everything keeps one perpetually connected with the inner-self and strengthens his identification with the Supreme-Self. It helps the person to tear down the curtain of egocentric-self and enter into the realm of the Supreme-self. It initiates the individual into recognizing the expression of Divine grace in every bit of activity that is special and particular. It helps one to feel the omnipresence of the Omnipresent; within and without, from the minutest to the grossest. It arouses the respectful devotion for the greatest power and strengthens the devotion of those who are making efforts for God-realization. In the entire creation whatever is expressed as unique and special in the form of learning, austerity, virtue, beauty, valour and victory, splendour and glory, mighty and meritorious, knowledge and intelligence, wisdom and intuition etc. presents itself as the attribute of Supreme Lord.

A mere thought of perceiving every uniqueness as the majesty of the Divine, fills the heart with loving devotion for the Lord. It intensifies the love for Lord and helps in single-minded contemplation on the Lord. This is the truth that needs to be accepted, recognized and practised in order to prepare the mind for contemplation and yogic communication.

ॐ तत्सदिति श्रीमद्भगवद्गीतासूपनिषत्सु ब्रह्मविद्यायां योगशास्त्रे श्रीकृष्णार्जुनसंवादे विभूतियोगो नाम दशमोऽध्यायः ॥ १० ॥

'Aum' tatsaditi Śrīmadbhagawadgeetā sūpaniṣatsu brahmavidyāyām yogaśāstre Śrīkṛṣṇārjunasamvāde vibhūtiyogo nāma daśamo'dhyāyaḥ

'AUM TAT SAT'—Thus, in the Upanishad of the glorious Bhagawad Geeta, the science of the Brahman (Absolute) the scripture of yoga, the dialogue between Srī Kṛṣṇa and Arjuna—thus, ends the chapter ten entitled *"Vibhūtiyoga"*.

इति श्रीमद्भगवद्गीतासु दशमोऽध्यायः ॥ १० ॥

Chapter Eleven

VISVARUPADARSANAYOGA

THE YOGA OF THE VISION OF THE UNIVERSAL FORM

अर्जुन उवाच

मदनुग्रहाय परमं गुह्यमध्यात्मसञ्ज्ञितम्।
यत्त्वयोक्तं वचस्तेन मोहोऽयं विगतो मम॥ १॥

madanugrahāya paramaṁ guhyamadhyātmasañjñitam
yattvayo'ktaṁ vacastena moho'yaṁ vigato mama

Arjuna said :

(1) By the most profound words of spiritual wisdom which You have spoken out of Your compassion for me, my delusion has been dispelled.

भवाप्ययौ हि भूतानां श्रुतौ विस्तरशो मया।
त्वत्तः कमलपत्राक्ष माहात्म्यमपि चाव्ययम्॥ २॥

bhavāpyayau hi bhūtānāṁ śrutau vistaraśo mayā
tvattaḥ kamalapatrākṣa māhātmyamapi cāvyayam

(2) The origin and dissolution of beings have been heard by me in full detail from Thee, O' Lotus-eyed Lord, and also your immortal glory O'Supreme Lord.

एवमेतद् यथात्थ त्वमात्मानं परमेश्वर।
द्रष्टुमिच्छामि ते रूपमैश्वरं पुरुषोत्तम॥ ३॥

evametad yathāttha tvamātmānaṁ parameśvara
draṣṭumicchāmi te rūpam aiśvaraṁ puruṣottama

(3) You are precisely what you have declared Yourself to be

O'Supreme Lord, but I have a desire to see Your Divine form, O'Purushottama (Supreme Purusha).

मन्यसे यदि तच्छक्यं मया द्रष्टुमिति प्रभो।
योगेश्वर ततो मे त्वं दर्शयात्मानमव्ययम्॥४॥

manyase yadi tacchakyam mayā draṣṭumiti prabho
yogeśvara tato me tvaṁ darśayātmānamavyayam

(4) O'Lord, if you think that it can be seen by me, then, O'Lord of the Yoga, reveal to me Your imperishable form.

Commentary—This chapter opens with an expression of Arjuna's gratitude, appreciation and contentment. The word *madanugrahaya* reveals Arjuna's inner satisfaction, joy and fulfilment to some extent. He says O' Kṛṣṇa out of your compassion and grace you have imparted to me, your profound words of wisdom in relation to your magnificence and majesty. I am indeed deeply impressed, enlightened and thrilled. My ignorance born of delusion has been dispelled. I surely believe every word you have spoken about the evolution and dissolution of the universe. I am enlightened about your great immanence and feel very blessed indeed. I understand and believe that you are exactly as you declare yourself to be, but, I want to see your cosmic form O' Lord of Yoga. So if you consider me worthy of beholding your universal form, please be kind and reveal to me your eternal immutable Self.

Revelation of the cosmic vision comes to the aspirant with a special grace of the Supreme-Self. It comes to the earnest devotee who is possessed with undivided genuine devotion for God. Although each and everyone has an access to the Divine grace and revelation but only one in many millions becomes blessed with it; because only one in million pays the price for it. Spiritual vision is indeed an act of grace, from the Supreme-Self. In the previous chapter, verse eleven, Srī Kṛṣṇa declares that those who take refuge in the Supreme-Self, to them I reveal Myself out of my compassion and kindness. I help them to realize and recognise the Supreme indwelling Lord who resides in the depth of their own hearts. I help them to experience and realize their own divinity with their own help.

This chapter is a great blessing to the aspirants which guides the individual from the formless to the One with form and shape, from the abstract to a concrete realization of the Absolute. In the process of enlightenment, Arjuna has realized that in order to experience the embodied-self as an eternal part of the cosmic-self, the experience of revelation is indeed important. He perceives the necessity of a personal and first hand experience. So he expresses his humble desire in the most beseeching words *Manyase yadi tac chakyam* if you consider me worthy of this, please show me your eternal majestic self.

श्रीभगवानुवाच

पश्य मे पार्थ रूपाणि शतशोऽथ सहस्रशः।
नानाविधानि दिव्यानि नानावर्णाकृतीनि च॥५॥

paśye me pārtha rūpāṇi śataśo'tha sahasraśaḥ
nānāvidhāni divyāni nānāvarṇākṛtīni ca

The Blessed Lord said :

(5) Behold My forms O'Partha by hundreds and thousands, multifarious and divine, of many colours and shapes.

पश्यादित्यान्वसून्रुद्रानश्विनौ मरुतस्तथा।
बहून्यदृष्टपूर्वाणि पश्याश्चर्याणि भारत॥६॥

paśyādityān vasūn rudrān aśvinau marutastathā
bahūny adṛṣṭapūrvāṇi paśyāścāryāṇi bhārata

(6) Behold the Adityas, the Vasus, the Rudras, the Asvins, and also the Maruts. Behold many more wonders, never seen before, O'Bharta (Arjuna).

इहैकस्थं जगत्कृत्स्नं पश्याद्य सचराचरम्।
मम देहे गुडाकेश यच्चान्यद् द्रष्टुमिच्छसि॥७॥

ihaikasthaṁ jagat kṛtsnaṁ paśyādya sacarācaram
mama dehe guḍākeśa yaccānyad draṣṭumicchasi

(7) Now behold within this body of Mine, the whole universe centred in One—the moving and the unmoving, O'Arjuna, and whatever else you desire to see.

न तु मां शक्यसे द्रष्टुमनेनैव स्वचक्षुषा।
दिव्यं ददामि ते चक्षुः पश्य मे योगमैश्वरम्॥ ८॥

na tu māṁ śakyase draṣṭumanenaiva svacakṣuṣā
divyaṁ dadāmi te cakṣuḥ paśya me yogamaiśvaram

(8) But surely, you cannot see Me with these eyes of yours; therefore, I must bless you with divine vision. Behold My divine power of yoga.

Commentary—Srī Kṛṣṇa opens the conversation with the words, O' Partha, I can reveal to you the multitude of My Divinity with hundreds and thousands of multifarious forms, shapes and colours. You will see the Adityas, the Vasus, the Rudras, the two Aswins, the Maruts all centered in My body and many more other wonders which are beyond the comprehension of human intellect. Srī Kṛṣṇa wants Arjuna to see how the world of diversity with beings and non-beings, animate and inanimate is centred and settled in 'One' unity of the Supreme Ishwara.

In the verse eight, Srī Kṛṣṇa enlightens Arjuna about his limited identity with the physical body. He tells Arjuna that the latter cannot behold the cosmic form with his normal physical eyes; he has to be blessed with special eye of intuition in order to experience the revelation. Srī Kṛṣṇa wants Arjuna to realize that the vision of the cosmic-self is beyond the comprehension of the ordinary intellect. The experience of the transcendental-Self becomes possible only with the grace of the Supreme-Self. The Lord showers the grace when the aspirant makes genuine efforts with a complete surrender to the Lord. It is like going into the field of yogic unity and catch the first hand experience of the Lord's magnificence and infinity.

The divine vision is the expansion of the individual-self, from the individual identity into the cosmic identity, from the boundaries of time, space and cause into the timeless infinity. Being blessed with Divine vision is to be awakened into the field of pure consciousness. It is like piercing through the veil of egocentric-self into the pure, unconditioned natural-self and to experience the timeless field of consciousness.

संजय उवाच

एवमुक्त्वा ततो राजन्महायोगेश्वरो हरिः।
दर्शयामास पार्थाय परमं रूपमैश्वरम्॥ ९ ॥

evamuktvā tato rājan mahāyogeśvaro hariḥ
darśayāmāsa pārthāya paramaṁ rūpamaiśvaram

Sanjaya said :

(9) After saying this, O' King, the great Lord of Yoga, Hari (Srī Kṛṣṇa) revealed to Arjuna His supreme Divine form.

अनेकवक्त्रनयनमनेकाद्भुतदर्शनम् ।
अनेकदिव्याभरणं दिव्यानेकोद्यतायुधम्॥ १० ॥

anekavaktranayanamanekādbhutadarśanam
anekadivyābharaṇaṁ divyānekodyatāyudham

दिव्यमाल्याम्बरधरं दिव्यगन्धानुलेपनम्।
सर्वाश्चर्यमयं देवमनन्तं विश्वतोमुखम्॥ ११ ॥

divyamālyāmbaradharaṁ divyagandhānulepanam
sarvāścaryamayaṁ devamanantaṁ viśvatomukham

(10,11) Possessing many mouths and eyes, presenting many wonderful sights, with numerous celestial ornaments and with numerous divine uplifted weapons. Wearing heavenly garlands and garments, anointed all over with divine sandal-pastes; totally marvellous, resplendent, boundless and facing in all directions.

दिवि सूर्यसहस्रस्य भवेद्युगपदुत्थिता।
यदि भाः सदृशी सा स्याद्भासस्तस्य महात्मनः॥ १२ ॥

divi sūryasahasrasya bhaved yugapadutthitā
yadi bhāḥ sadṛśī sā syad bhāsas tasya mahātmanaḥ

(12) If the effulgence of a thousand suns were to blaze forth all at once in the sky, that might resemble the effulgence of that mighty Being.

तत्रैकस्थं जगत्कृत्स्नं प्रविभक्तमनेकधा।
अपश्यद्देवदेवस्य शरीरे पाण्डवस्तदा॥ १३ ॥

tatraikasthaṁ jagatkṛtsnaṁ pravibhaktamanekadhā
apaśyad devadevasya śarīre pāṇḍavas tadā

(13) There, resting at one place in the body of the God of gods, Arjuna then saw the whole universe with its manifold divisions.

ततः स विस्मयाविष्टो हृष्टरोमा धनञ्जयः।
प्रणम्य शिरसा देवं कृताञ्जलिरभाषत ॥ १४ ॥

tataḥ sa vismayāviṣṭo hṛṣṭaromā dhanañjayaḥ
praṇamya śirasā devaṁ kṛtāñjlirabhāṣata

(14) Then Arjuna overwhelmed with amazement, his hair standing on end, reverentially bowed down his head before the Lord and spoke with folded hands.

Commentary—These six verses from nine to fourteen illustrate some glimpses of the cosmic form of the Lord, as seen by Sanjaya. Sanjaya has been blessed with a special vision from sage Vyasa, in order to relate a live commentary of the war in Kurukshetra. In these verses Sanjaya relates to the blind king in Hastinapur the glimpses of the cosmic body of the Lord. This chapter has been called the 'Vishvarupa Darshan Yoga' means the union with Lord through His universal vision. In the verse nine Sanjaya opens the conversation with words 'Maha Yogeshvarah and Hari' for Srī Kṛṣṇa in order to acquaint the blind king with the unparalleled yogic power of the Lord. He tries to bring to the attention of the king that Srī Kṛṣṇa is indeed the Supreme Lord, the Hari and the great master of the yogic powers. Sanjaya feels overwhelmed with amazement and relates the magnificence and glory of the universal form to Dhritarastra in these words. "O' king, Arjuna has been privileged to see the Supreme Lord of the universe possessing many mouths and many eyes, with innumerable and wondrous sights. The majestic deity adorned with many celestial ornaments, holding various kinds of weapons, with His face looking in all directions.

The luminosity from the face is radiating everywhere and His splendour cannot be equated with the light of a thousand suns bursting forth simultaneously. He looks at the universe extending and expanding in all directions from the body of the Lord. Arjuna beholds from the cosmic body of the Lord the entire world emanating and then being re-absorbed again. The entire universe with thousands of galaxies seems to be resting in one supreme being. The very first word of verse thirteen '*Ekastham*' stands for the fact—centred in the cosmic body. Arjuna looks at the universal body as 'One' unified field into which are centred all the diversities. He beholds the cosmic body as encompassing the whole world of multitude diversities into one unity.

Overwhelmed with amazement and exhilaration he gathers himself together and bows to the cosmic person with both hands folded in profound reverence. Arjuna salutes with both hands in a gesture of respect, reverence and submission. The expression *Pranamya sirasa devam* literally means that I bow and pay respect to the Supreme Divinity in You. In the words of Swami Chidbhavanananda, "When a yogi is blessed with the vision of God, its exuberance reveals itself through spiritual charge it induces in his body and mind. Being struck with blissful amazement is the effect it brings to his mind. The hair standing on end, the head bowing down in reverence and the palms joining in spontaneous adoration are the marks of ecstasy visible on his body."

Arjuna feels overwhelmed with amazement and thrilled with joy at the most blessed sight of the Supreme. His relationship with Srī Kṛṣṇa becomes transformed into a loving communion with the cosmic-Self. He feels blessed, elated and grateful indeed and also feels inspired to sing the glories of Srī Kṛṣṇa. He speaks in profound reverence, love, devotion and from the intensity of his innermost feelings.

अर्जुन उवाच

पश्यामि देवांस्तव देव देहे,
सर्वांस्तथा भूतविशेषसंघान्।
ब्रह्माणमीशं कमलासनस्थ-
मृषींश्च सर्वानुरगांश्च दिव्यान्॥ १५ ॥

paśyāmi devāns tava deva dehe
sarvāns tathā bhūtaviśeṣasaṅghān

brahmāṇamīśaṁ kamalāsanastha-

mṛṣīṅś ca sarvān uragānś ca divyān

(15) O'Lord, I see all the gods in Your body, and also the various multitude of beings; Brahma the Lord seated on His lotus-throne, Shiva and all the other sages and the celestial serpents.

अनेकबाहूदरवक्त्रनेत्रम्,

पश्यामि त्वां सर्वतोऽनन्तरूपम्।

नान्तं न मध्यं न पुनस्तवादिं,

पश्यामि विश्वेश्वर विश्वरूप ॥ १६ ॥

anekabāhūdaravaktranetraṁ

paśyāmi tvāṁ sarvato'nantarūpam

nāntaṁ na madhyaṁ na punastavādiṁ

paśyāmi viśveśvara viśvarūpa

(16) I see Your infinite form on all sides with numerous arms, stomachs, mouths and eyes. I see neither Your end, nor the middle nor the beginning. O' Lord of the universe, O'cosmic form.

किरीटिनं गदिनं चक्रिणं च,

तेजोराशिं सर्वतो दीप्तिमन्तम्।

पश्यामि त्वां दुर्निरीक्ष्यं समन्ताद्-

दीप्तानलार्कद्युतिमप्रमेयम् ॥ १७ ॥

kirīṭinaṁ gadinaṁ cakriṇaṁ ca

tejorāśiṁ sarvato dīptimantam

paśyāmi tvāṁ durnirīksyaṁ samantād

dīptānalārkadyutimaprameyam

(17) I see You with the crown, mace and discus—a mass of radiance shining everywhere; having a brilliance like that of a blazing fire and sun; dazzling and immeasurable on all sides.

त्वमक्षरं परमं वेदितव्यं,

त्वमस्य विश्वस्य परं निधानम्।

त्वमव्ययः शाश्वतधर्मगोप्ता,

सनातनस्त्वं पुरुषो मतो मे ॥ १८ ॥

tvamakṣaraṁ paramaṁ veditavyaṁ

tvamaśya viśvasya paraṁ nidhānam

tvamavyayaḥ śāśvatadharmagoptā

sanātanas tvaṁ puruṣo mato me

(18) You are the imperishable, the Supreme being, worthy to be known. You are the ultimate resort of the universe, you are the eternal guardian of the primeval Dharma (Righteousness). You are indeed the primeval Purusha, so I believe.

अनादिमध्यान्तमनन्तवीर्य-

मनन्तबाहुं शशिसूर्यनेत्रम्।

पश्यामि त्वां दीप्तहुताशवक्त्रम्,

स्वतेजसा विश्वमिदं तपन्तम् ॥ १९ ॥

anādimadhyāntamanantavīrya-

manantabāhuṁ śaśisūryanetram

paśyāmi tvāṁ dīptahutāśavaktram

śvatejasā viśvamidaṁ tapantam

(19) I see You without beginning, middle or end, of infinite power—with innumerable arms and with the moon and the sun as your eyes. The blazing fire, Your mouth—scorching the universe with your radiance.

द्यावापृथिव्योरिदमन्तरं हि,

व्याप्तं त्वयैकेन दिशश्च सर्वाः।

दृष्ट्वाद्भुतं रूपमुग्रं तवेदं,

लोकत्रयं प्रव्यथितं महात्मन् ॥ २० ॥

dyāvāpṛthivyoridamantaraṁ hi

vyāptaṁ tvayaikena diśaśca sarvāḥ

dṛṣṭvādbhutaṁ rūpamugraṁ tavedaṁ

lokatrayaṁ pravyathitaṁ mahātman

(20) The space between heaven and earth and in all the quarters is indeed pervaded by You alone. Seeing this most miraculous and dreadful form of Yours, the three worlds are trembling with fear, O' Supreme-soul.

अमी हि त्वां सुरसंघा विशन्ति,
केचिद्भीताः प्राञ्जलयो गृणन्ति।
स्वस्तीत्युक्त्वा महर्षिसिद्धसंघाः,
स्तुवन्ति त्वां स्तुतिभिः पुष्कलाभिः ॥ २१ ॥

amī hi tvāṁ surasaṁghā viśanti
kecid bhītaḥ prāñjalayo gṛṇanti
svastītyuktvā maharṣisiddhasaṅghāḥ
stuvanti tvāṁ stutibhiḥ puṣkalābhiḥ

(21) The hosts of gods are entering in You; some in fear with palms joined together are chanting your glories. The multitudes of sages and perfected ones are saying "May it be well," and adore Thee with special hymns of devotional praises.

रुद्रादित्या वसवो ये च साध्या,
विश्वेऽश्विनौ मरुतश्चोष्मपाश्च।
गन्धर्वयक्षासुरसिद्धसंघा,
वीक्षन्ते त्वां विस्मिताश्चैव सर्वे॥ २२ ॥

rudrādityā vasavo ye ca sādhyā
viśve'śvinau marutaś coṣmapāś ca
gandharvayakṣāsursiddhasaṅghā
vīkṣante tvāṁ vismitāś caiva sarve

(22) The Rudras, Adityas, Vasus, the Sadhyas, Viswas, the Aswins, the Maruts, the manes, the host of Gandharvas, Yakshas, Asuras, and the perfected ones, they are all looking at You in deep amazement.

रूपं महत्ते बहुवक्त्रनेत्रं,
महाबाहो बहुबाहूरुपादम्।

बहूदरं बहुदंष्ट्राकरालं,

दृष्ट्वा लोकाः प्रव्यथितास्तथाहम् ॥ २३ ॥

rūpaṁ mahatte bahuvaktranetraṁ

mahābāho bahubāhūrupādam

bahūdaraṁ bahudaṅṣṭrākarālaṁ

dṛṣṭvā lokāḥ pravyathitāstathāham

(23) Having seen Thy immeasurable form with numerous mouths, and eyes, O'Kṛṣṇa, with myriad arms and thighs, feet, bellies and fearful teeth, the entire world is in panic, and so am I.

नभःस्पृशं दीप्तमनेकवर्णं,

व्यात्ताननं दीप्तविशालनेत्रम्।

दृष्ट्वा हि त्वां प्रव्यथितान्तरात्मा,

धृतिं न विन्दामि शमं च विष्णो ॥ २४ ॥

nabhaḥspṛśaṁ dīptamanekavarṇaṁ

vyāttānanaṁ dīptaviśālanetram

dṛṣṭvā hi tvāṁ pravyathitāntarātmā

dhṛtiṁ na vindāmi śamaṁ ca viṣṇo

(24) When I see Thee touching the sky, blazing with numerous colours, with your mouth wide open and the large shining eyes, my heart trembles with fear and I find neither courage nor peace, O' Lord Vishnu.

दंष्ट्राकरालानि च ते मुखानि,

दृष्ट्वैव कालानलसन्निभानि।

दिशो न जाने न लभे च शर्म,

प्रसीद देवेश जगन्निवास ॥ २५ ॥

daṅṣṭrākarālāni ca te mukhāni

dṛṣṭvaiva kālānalasannibhāni

diśo na jāne na labhe ca śarma

prasīda deveśa jagannivāsa

(25) Having seen your mouth with fearful teeth, resembling the blazing fire of the cosmic dissolution, I have lost the sense of direction and inner peace. Be gracious O' Lord of the gods and the abode of the universe.

अमी च त्वां धृतराष्ट्रस्य पुत्राः,
सर्वे सहैवावनिपालसंघैः ।
भीष्मो द्रोणः सूतपुत्रस्तथासौ,
सहास्मदीयैरपि योधमुख्यैः ॥ २६ ॥

amī ca tvāṁ dhṛtarāṣṭrasya putrāḥ
sarve sahaivāvanipālasaṅghaiḥ
bhīṣmo droṇaḥ sūtaputrastathāsau
sahāsmadīyairapi yodhamukhyaiḥ

वक्त्राणि ते त्वरमाणा विशन्ति,
दंष्ट्राकरालानि भयानकानि ।
केचिद्विलग्ना दशनान्तरेषु,
संदृश्यन्ते चूर्णितैरुत्तमाङ्गैः ॥ २७ ॥

vaktrāṇi te tvaramāṇā viśanti
daṅṣṭrākarālāni bhayānakāni
kecidvilagnā daśanāntareṣu
saṁdṛśyante cūrṇitairuttamāṅgaiḥ

(26, 27) All the sons of Dhritarastra with the crowds of other kings, Bhishma, Drona, Karna and with the chief warriors of our side as well, are rushing into your mouths, which is so fearful to look at. Some can be seen sticking in the gaps between the teeth with their heads crushed completely.

यथा नदीनां बहवोऽम्बुवेगाः,
समुद्रमेवाभिमुखा द्रवन्ति ।
तथा तवामी नरलोकवीरा,
विशन्ति वक्त्राण्यभिविज्वलन्ति ॥ २८ ॥

yathā nadīnāṁ bahavo'mbuvegāḥ
samudramevā'bhimukhā dravanti

tathā tavāmī naralokavīrā

viśanti vaktrāṇyabhivijvalanti

(28) As the diverse torrents of rivers rush towards the ocean, similarly these warriors of the mortal world are rushing into Your blazing mouths.

यथा प्रदीप्तं ज्वलनं पतङ्गा,

विशन्ति नाशाय समृद्धवेगाः।

तथैव नाशाय विशन्ति लोकास्–

तवापि वक्त्राणि समृद्धवेगाः ॥ २९ ॥

yathā pradīptaṁ jvalanaṁ pataṅgā

viśanti nāśāya samṛaddhavegāḥ

tathaiva nāśāya viśanti lokās

tavāpi vaktrāṇi samṛddhavegāḥ

(29) As the moths rush into the blazing fire for their own destruction, so also these creatures are hurriedly rushing into Your mouth for their destruction.

लेलिह्यसे ग्रसमानः समन्ताल्–

लोकान्समग्रान्वदनैर्ज्वलद्भिः।

तेजोभिरापूर्य जगत्समग्रं,

भासस्तवोग्राः प्रतपन्ति विष्णो ॥ ३० ॥

lelihyase grasamānaḥ samantāl-

lokān samagrān vadanair jvaladbhiḥ

tejobhirāpūrya jagat samagraṁ

bhāsasta vogrāḥ pratapanti viṣṇo

(30) Devouring all the worlds on every side with Thy flaming mouths, Your fiery rays are filling the whole world with your effulgence O' Lord Vishnu.

आख्याहि मे को भवानुग्ररूपो,

नमोऽस्तु ते देववर प्रसीद।

विज्ञातुमिच्छामि भवन्तमाद्यं,

न हि प्रजानामि तव प्रवृत्तिम् ॥ ३१ ॥

ākhyāhi me ko bhavānugrarūpo

namo'stu te devavara prasīda

vijñātumicchāmi bhavantamādyaṁ

na hi prajānāmi tava pravṛttim

(31) Tell me who You are in this dreadful form? I bow down to You, O' Supreme Divinity. Be gracious—I want to know You, O'Primal one in reality, for I fail to comprehend Your purpose (intent).

Commentary—These verses from fifteen to thirty-one have been significantly upheld in reverence. In order to realize one's own immortality and comprehend the concept of one's own essentiality, the individual has to move into the subtlest levels of consciousness, where all the diversities merge into one unity. The experience of the Divine vision is going into increased awareness of the mind, wherein the individual feels like a part of the universal mind and looks at everything through the eyes of the cosmic mind.

Srī Kṛṣṇa gives Arjuna enough time and liberty to see and admire the majesty of the Supreme Divinity. He gives enough time to Arjuna to comprehend the immanence, the grandeur, the splendour of the Divine glory. He gives him the guidance to understand the relativity of time and feel the magnificence of that which lies beyond the concept of space, time, and cause. He intends for Arjuna to see the vision of the transitory, everchanging and mortal world through the windows of universal mind where the concept of time and space vanishes. Arjuna sees the entire creation as one single unit in the cosmic body of the Lord.

With the vision of the *Visvarupa,* Arjuna becomes privileged to see the Lord Vishnu with His celestial crown, mace conch and discus. Lord Vishnu is one aspect of the trinity, such as Brahma, Vishnu and Mahesh. Brahma the creator, Lord Vishnu the sustainer and Mahesha the annihilator. Lord Vishnu is always shown with crown which signifies His sovereignty over the creation. He is shown with four hands. In one hand is the lotus and in other, the celestial conch. The conch stands for maintaining harmony in the three worlds of consciousness—the physical, psychological and spiritual. The conch stands for the call to live in harmony with inner-self with other creatures and nature. If the individual can learn to live in harmony, his life becomes a blessing and he lives like a lotus flower. Lord Vishnu is shown as carrying His mace in one hand and the disc in other. The individual who does not live by voice of the inner-self and disrespects *swadharma,* he is knocked down occasionally with the mace of the Divine. The knocking by mace comes to the person in the form of failures, fears, disappointments and physical miseries. If the person does not learn the lesson of living a pure life with repeated punishments then Lord uses the discus. Also if entire society becomes corrupt and people start losing their moral and ethical values, the Lord uses the annihilating discus to eliminate the immoral, unethical and wicked people in order to bring peace and harmony in society. The Supreme-Lord is the protector of Dharma. He Himself is the primordial righteousness that sustains life on earth.

In *Kritanjali,* Arjuna sings the glories of the Lord. The appearance of the cosmic form enlightens him about the prime truth, that the entire creation exists in the body of the Supreme Lord. He is awakened to the truth that behind the veil of entire activity, it is the will of God which prevails and keeps every thing in motion. Every activity revolves around the will of the Divine, every change which occurs in the form of life and death is an expression of the Lord's will. The appearance of the cosmic form enlightens Arjuna of his own reality in relation to the Supreme-Self and to the world. Arjuna becomes enlightened about the reality of God incarnation, whom he has considered merely his dear friend, cousin and the king of Dwaraka. He looks at his friend Kṛṣṇa the charioteer in deep veneration, reverence, submission and fear. The sight of the cosmic form can be indeed overwhelming. Fear, astonishment, wonder and amazement are the feelings which can arise naturally in the mind of the person who goes through that unusual experience.

There is a similar story about Jesus Christ when he was blessed with the Divine revelation. He also felt fearfully amazed, deeply exhilarated and surprised, and later heard the voice from inside "Do not be afraid, it is only Me." There is a similar kind of incident in which Srī Ramakrishna was blessed with Divine vision. He has described his experience in these words, "I had a marvellous vision of the Mother, and fell down unconscious. It was as if houses, doors, temples and everything else vanished altogether, as if there was nothing anywhere! And what I saw was infinite, shoreless sea of light; a sea that was consciousness. However far and in whatever direction I looked, I saw shining waves, one after another, coming towards me. They were raging and storming upon me with great speed. Very soon they were upon me; they made me sink down into unknown depths. I panted and struggled and lost consciousness".

The experience of the Divine vision enlightens Arjuna about the power of the Supreme Lord as the creator, the sustainer and the annihilator, all in 'One'. A similar kind of experience has been recorded from the life story of Swami Ramakrishna in which he had the experience of the trinity all in one. The revelation transported him into the realm beyond time and space. "One day he saw a woman of exquisite beauty coming up from the Ganga near the Panchavati. As she came nearer, she seemed to become more and more obviously pregnant. Her womb swelled visibly until she gave birth to a beautiful child which she held in her lap with the greatest tenderness. Suddenly her expression changed. She became ferocious and terrible. She began to eat the child, grinding its flesh and bones between her teeth and swallowing them. Then she turned back and went back into the Ganga".

Arjuna is also awakened to the marvellous unity which exists in the multitude of plurality around. He salutes to the Lord in deep reverence, submission, veneration and in terror at the same time. He still finds it difficult to comprehend the magnitude of the all powerful Lord. Arjuna, who is not fully awakened, does not understand the motive of Lord's revelation and requests for further explanation. He says, I desire to know You, O' primordial One in essence and also your purpose of revealing this cosmic form to me in various aspects.

श्रीभगवानुवाच

कालोऽस्मि लोकक्षयकृत् प्रवृद्धो,
लोकान्समाहर्तुमिह प्रवृत्तः।
ऋतेऽपि त्वां न भविष्यन्ति सर्वे,
येऽवस्थिताः प्रत्यनीकेषु योधाः॥ ३२॥

kālo'smi lokakṣayakṛt pravṛddho
lokān samāhartumiha pravṛttaḥ
ṛte'pi tvāṁ na bhaviṣyanti sarve
ye'vasthitāḥ pratyanīkeṣu yodhāḥ

The Blessed Lord said :

(32) I am the Time, the mighty world-destroyer; here engaged in the extermination of the worlds. Even without you all these warriors arrayed in hostile battle will cease to be.

तस्मात्त्वमुत्तिष्ठ यशो लभस्व,
जित्वा शत्रून् भुङ्क्ष्व राज्यं समृद्धम्।
मयैवैते निहताः पूर्वमेव,
निमित्तमात्रं भव सव्यसाचिन्॥ ३३॥

tasmāt tvamuttiṣṭha yaśo labhasva
jitvā śatrūn bhuṅkṣva rājyaṁ samṛddham
mayaivaite nihatāḥ pūrvameva
nimittamātraṁ bhava savyasācin

(33) Therefore, you stand up, and win the glory. Conquer the enemies and enjoy the unrivalled empire. They have been already killed by Me; you be merely an instrument O' Arjuna.

द्रोणं च भीष्मं च जयद्रथं च,
कर्णं तथान्यानपि योधवीरान्।
मया हतांस्त्वं जहि मा व्यथिष्ठा,
युध्यस्व जेतासि रणे सपत्नान्॥ ३४॥

droṇaṁ ca bhīṣmaṁ ca jayadrathaṁ ca
karṇaṁ tathānyānapi yodhavīrān
mayā hatāṅstvaṁ jahi mā vyathiṣṭhā
yudhyasva jetāsi raṇe sapatnān

(34) Drona, Bhishma, Jayadrath, Karna and other brave warriors—these have been already killed by Me. Do not be distressed with fear. Fight, you will surely conquer the enemies in the battle.

Commentary—Srī Kṛṣṇa declares to Arjuna, I am the all-devouring time. The 'Time' as '*Kala'* has been described in our scriptures. 'Mahakala' is one of the names of the Lord Shiva. The trinity that describes the three aspects of the Supreme Lord is Brahma the creator, Vishnu the sustainer and Shiva the annihilator. The time is constantly destroying and swallowing everything. Everything we see around comes into existence, is sustained for a while and is consumed over a period of time. The entire past is buried in the various layers of time and all the present and future will be eventually. It is the measure of all events and incidents. Annihilation of things, objects and people is continuously going on. Srī Kṛṣṇa assures Arjuna about his victory and reminds him of the declaration made earlier in chapter four verse seven, "Whenever there is decline of righteousness, the (primordial Dharma), then I manifest Myself", He assures Arjuna that the destruction and extermination of all these warriors arrayed in the battle is indeed within His time plan. The re-establishment of Dharma must take place in order to maintain peace, harmony and orderliness in society. He awakens Arjuna to the reality that Time the mighty destroyer, does not need Arjuna's help for annihilation, everything has been designed within the plan of the Lord. So he should stand up and earn the credit that has been made available to him. Srī Kṛṣṇa consoles the hero and encourages him.

In the previous conversation Srī Kṛṣṇa has declared 'The Time' to be His magnificence. Time is the majesty of the Divine, the power that works invisibly behind everything, it modifies, transforms, deteriorates and slowly brings to the final destruction. Srī Kṛṣṇa knows that in order to gain mastery over time, individual has to contact the ultimate reality which is beyond the limitations of all devouring time. The person has to learn to live in present in order to see the flow of time and actually be there. When the individual goes in unity with the present moment he can actually control the flow of time, and direct the waves in the desired directions. Srī Kṛṣṇa wants Arjuna to realize and understand the subtle power of time, get hold of it and be the master, the ruler and the controller.

Divine vision is the eye of intuition, the eye of increased sensitivity and awareness. It is an ability to freeze time in present and perceive the past, present and future all together. It is to enter into the unity of universal mind that creates all events. Divine vision is to be awakened to the height of awareness from where one can perceive the present, the past as well as the future. It is a threefold experience all at once. It is similar to the type of experience wherein a person stands high on the top of the mountain from where he beholds everything on the top of the mountain, in front of it and also what lies behind, which has remained hidden earlier. Experiencing the three in one is what the scriptures describe as *Trikal Darshan.* Srī Kṛṣṇa has been initiating Arjuna to see into the distant future and calculate the proper strategy of the situation at hand. He wants Arjuna to understand the truth that it is the Divine potency which manifests through everything. So the magnificence and opulence of everything should be considered to be the majesty of the Divine, the attribute of the Supreme spirit. There is nothing separate from the supreme source. God is the reservoir of energy and the God's attributes are the manifestations of Divine potency. So the Lord and his attributes are not separate from one another. It is one substance appearing in many forms and shapes.

Srī Kṛṣṇa wants Arjuna to realize that he is a co-worker with God in the mammoth work of eliminating the negativity and destroying the wicked and vicious people. Establishment of morality and Dharma is a co-operative enterprise of God and man. In reality the great war has been a Divine plan executed for the destruction of the evildoers and harmful agents in society and also for the re-establishment of Dharma.

संजय उवाच

एतच्छ्रुत्वा वचनं केशवस्य,
कृताञ्जलिर्वेपमानः किरीटी।
नमस्कृत्वा भूय एवाह कृष्णं,
सगद्गदं भीतभीतः प्रणम्य ॥ ३५ ॥

etacchrutvā vacanaṁ keśavasya
kṛtāñjalir vepamānaḥ kirīṭī
namaskṛtvā bhūya evāha kṛṣṇaṁ
sagadgadaṁ bhītabhītaḥ praṇamya

Sanjaya said :

(35) Having heard these words of Srī Kṛṣṇa, Arjuna with his both hands joined together in respect, trembling and prostrating, once again addressed to Lord Kṛṣṇa in a chocked voice overwhelmed with fear and reverence.

Commentary—In this verse the word '*kirti*' has been used for the special crown of Arjuna. This celestial crown has been given to Arjuna by the Devraj Indra. Arjuna, a great warrior, had helped Indra in killing the demons *Kala* and *Khanja*, and some others. Through this verse Sanjaya reveals to Dhritrashtra the glimpses of the Lord's cosmic form and Arjuna's reaction to the Lord's words spoken in verses thirty-two to thirty-four. The words of consolation and encouragement.

अर्जुन उवाच

स्थाने हृषीकेश तव प्रकीर्त्या,
जगत् प्रहृष्यत्यनुरज्यते च।
रक्षांसि भीतानि दिशो द्रवन्ति,
सर्वे नमस्यन्ति च सिद्धसंघाः ॥ ३६ ॥

sthāne hṛṣīkeśa tava prakīrtyā
jagat prahṛṣyaty anurajyate ca
rakṣāṅsi bhītāni diśo dravanti
sarve namasyanti ca siddhasaṅghāḥ

Arjuna said :

(36) O'Kṛṣṇa, right it is that the universe rejoices and is filled with love while glorifying Thee. The terrified demons flee in all directions and all the perfected ones bow to you.

कस्माच्च ते न नमेरन्महात्मन्,
गरीयसे ब्रह्मणोऽप्यादिकर्त्रे।
अनन्त देवेश जगन्निवास,
त्वमक्षरं सदसत्तत्परं यत्॥ ३७॥

kasmācca te na nameran mahātman
garīyase brahmaṇo'pyādikartre
ananta deveśa jagannivāsa
tvam akṣaraṁ sadasat tat paraṁ yat

(37) And why should they not salute you O' great Supreme-soul. Thou are the greatest, even greater than Brahma, the original creator. O' Infinite Being, O' God of the gods. Thou are the imperishable, the being, the non-being and that which is beyond both.

त्वमादिदेवः पुरुषः पुराणस्-
त्वमस्य विश्वस्य परं निधानम्।
वेत्तासि वेद्यं च परं च धाम
त्वया ततं विश्वमनन्तरूप॥ ३८॥

tvamādidevaḥ puruṣaḥ purāṇas-
tvamasya viśvasya paraṁ nidhānam
vettā'si vedyaṁ ca paraṁ ca dhāma
tvayā tataṁ viśvam anantarūpa

(38) You are the Primal God, the most ancient Purusha and the ultimate resort of the universe. You are the knower, the knowable and the Supreme abode. The universe is pervaded by you, O'Lord of infinite forms.

वायुर्यमोऽग्निर्वरुणः शशाङ्कः,
प्रजापतिस्त्वं प्रपितामहश्च।

नमो नमस्तेऽस्तु सहस्रकृत्वः,

पुनश्च भूयोऽपि नमो नमस्ते ॥ ३९ ॥

vāyur yamo'gnir varuṇaḥ śaśāṅkaḥ

prajāpatis tvaṁ prapitāmahaśca

namo namaste'stu sahasrakṛtvaḥ

punaśca bhūyo'pi namo namaste

(39) You are the windgod, he god of death, the god of fire and the god of water, the moongod. You are the creator, the Father of Brahma and the great-grandsire of all. Salutations to You a thousand times; salutations, repeated salutations to You once again.

नमः पुरस्तादथ पृष्ठतस्ते,

नमोऽस्तु ते सर्वत एव सर्व।

अनन्तवीर्यामितविक्रमस्त्वं,

सर्वं समाप्नोषि ततोऽसि सर्वः ॥ ४० ॥

namaḥ purastād atha pṛṣṭhtaste

namo'stu te sarvata eva sarva

anantavīryāmitvikramas tvaṁ

sarvaṁ samāpnoṣi tato'si sarvaḥ

(40) Salutation to Thee in front and from behind, I salute You from all sides, O'infinite in might and infinite in prowess You encompass all, therefore You are all.

सखेति मत्वा प्रसभं यदुक्तं,

हे कृष्ण हे यादव हे सखेति।

अजानता महिमानं तवेदं,

मया प्रमादात् प्रणयेन वापि ॥ ४१ ॥

sakheti matvā prasabhaṁ yaduktaṁ

he kṛṣṇa he yādava he sakheti

ajānatā mahimānaṁ tavedaṁ

mayā pramādāt praṇayena vāpi

यच्चावहासार्थमसत्कृतोऽसि,

विहारशय्यासनभोजनेषु।

एकोऽथवाप्यच्युत तत्समक्षं,

तत्क्षामये त्वामहमप्रमेयम्॥ ४२॥

yaccāvahāsārtham asatkṛto'si

vihārśayyāsanabhojaneṣu

eko'thavā'pyacyuta tatsamakṣaṁ

tatkṣāmaye tvāmahamaprameyam

(41, 42) Regarding Thee as a friend, I have carelessly addressed You, O'Kṛṣṇa, O'Yadava, O'friend and so on, not knowing Your greatness and magnificence. It has been merely out of my ignorance or affection that You have been slighted by me in jest, while playing, resting or at meal time, either alone or in the company of others, O'Kṛṣṇa, please forgive me, O'incomprehensible one.

पितासि लोकस्य चराचरस्य,

त्वमस्य पूज्यश्च गुरुर्गरीयान्।

न त्वत्समोऽस्त्यभ्यधिकः कुतोऽन्यो,

लोकत्रयेऽप्यप्रतिमप्रभाव॥ ४३॥

pitāsi lokasya carācarasya

tvamasya pūjyaś ca gururgarīyān

na tvatsamo'sty abhyadhikaḥ kuto'nyo

lokatraye'pyapratimaprabhāva

(43) You are the Father of the world, moving and unmoving. You are the most venerable teacher (Guru) and highly adorable. There is no one equal to You in all the three worlds; how can there be any one greater than You. O'Lord of unequalled power.

तस्मात् प्रणम्य प्रणिधाय कायं,

प्रसादये त्वामहमीशमीड्यम्।

पितेव पुत्रस्य सखेव सख्युः,

प्रियः प्रियायार्हसि देव सोढुम्॥ ४४॥

tasmāt praṇamya praṇidhāya kāyaṁ
prasādaye tvāmahamīśamīḍyam
piteva putrasya sakheva sakhyuḥ
priyaḥ priyāyārhasi deva soḍhum

(44) Therefore I prostrate before You and request for Your grace O'Lord. As a father forgives his son, a friend to his friend, a lover to his beloved; even so shouldst Thou forgive me, O'Lord.

अदृष्टपूर्वं हृषितोऽस्मि दृष्ट्वा,
भयेन च प्रव्यथितं मनो मे।
तदेव मे दर्शय देव रूपं,
प्रसीद देवेश जगन्निवास ॥ ४५ ॥

adṛṣṭapūrvaṁ hṛṣito'smi dṛṣṭvā
bhayena ca pravyathitaṁ mano me
tad eva me darśaya deva rūpaṁ
prasīda deveśa jagannivāsa

(45) Having seen what was never seen before—I am delighted, but my mind is distressed with fear. Reveal to me, O'God, that other form of Yours. Be gracious, O' Lord of the gods, and abode of the universe.

किरीटिनं गदिनं चक्रहस्त-
मिच्छामि त्वां द्रष्टुमहं तथैव।
तेनैव रूपेण चतुर्भुजेन,
सहस्त्रबाहो भव विश्वमूर्ते ॥ ४६ ॥

kirīṭinaṁ gadinaṁ cakrahastam
icchāmi tvāṁ draṣṭumahaṁ tathaiva
tenaiva rūpeṇa caturbhujena
sahasrabāho bhava viśvamūrte

(46) I desire to see You as before, with Your crown, holding a mace and a discus in your hand. Please resume again that four-armed form, O' thousand-armed, universal Being.

Commentary—These ten verses starting from thirty-six to forty-six are a bouquet of *Kritanjali* means adoration of the Lord in profound reverence and heartfelt devotional love. It is a very spontaneous gesture of the one who becomes enlightened. Arjuna feels exhilarated and starts singing the glories of the Lord, out of his love and devotion. He addresses the Lord as 'Ananta' which means the one who is beginningless, beyond the boundaries of time, space and cause. He is the God of gods, the abode of the entire universe. The Lord is imperishable and beyond the real and unreal.

There is only one reality that upholds everything together and acts as the casual force behind the change, yet there is another reality that watches all the changes but never gets involved in any activity. This is the transcendental reality, which is also known as '*Aksharateet*'—beyond and above the '*Kshar*' and '*Akshar*'. In deep exuberance and state of being overjoyed at the immanence of the Lord, Arjuna calls Srī Kṛṣṇa the Primal, Ancient prusha and the ultimate support of the universe. He is the sublime knower and ultimate object of knowledge also. He pays respectful salutation to the Lord from the depth of his heart. The words of Arjuna's melodious adoration form a unique part of this chapter. These verses are highly melodious, poetic and also deeply philosophical. Arjuna tells Srī Kṛṣṇa that he treated the Lord as an ordinary person while playing and eating meals etc. There were moments when he did not pay due respect to Him. Arjuna feels guilty and ashamed of himself and requests for forgiveness.

The intimacy, which has been expressed in the words of Arjuna, reflects the primordial relationship which exists between *Nara* and *Narayana*—the Supreme-soul and the Individual-soul. These verses express the purity of relationship which lies between the Lord and his genuine devotee. In these verses Arjuna expresses the honesty and the purity of his love with respect, reverence and innocence. He feels that the Lord has possessed him at every level of his consciousness. He realizes for the first time that his life is indeed meant to serve the Lord. He salutes in adoration like a most accomplished devotee and exuberantly sings the glories of Srī Kṛṣṇa. It is a very natural and spontaneous expression of heart soaked in love and intimacy of the divine. The aspirant feels like singing in deep ecstasy, saluting and prostrating in ardent love.

It is indeed natural that when personal relationship with God is invoked through prayers and adoration, a spontaneous transformation takes place in the attitude of the individual. Arjuna sings the glories of the Lord from the depth of his heart in transcendence. These verses are pure expression of genuine feelings, when the individual goes beyond the limitations of his personal individuality into the realm of yogic unity.

Towards the concluding words of *Kritanjali*, Arjuna expresses his innocent desire to see Srī Kṛṣṇa in His familiar form with the crown, mace and discus in hand. He requests Lord in these words, 'I am extremely blessed having seen what was never seen before, but I am a little distressed and confused. I surely long to see your form, the one very familiar to me. O' Lord of the universe, please be gracious and show me your gracious Divine form.

श्रीभगवानुवाच

मया प्रसन्नेन तवार्जुनेदं,
रूपं परं दर्शितमात्मयोगात्।
तेजोमयं विश्वमनन्तमाद्यं,
यन्मे त्वदन्येन न दृष्टपूर्वम्॥ ४७॥

mayā prasannena tavā'rjune'daṁ
rūpaṁ paraṁ darśitam ātmayogāt
tejomayaṁ viśvamanantamādyaṁ
yanme tvadanyena na dṛṣṭapūrvam

The Blessed Lord said :

(47) O'Arjuna, being pleased with you I have revealed to you through My power of Yoga, this Supreme, effulgent, infinite, primeval cosmic form of Mine; which no one else has seen before.

न वेदयज्ञाध्ययनैर्न दानैर्न च
क्रियाभिर्न तपोभिरुग्रैः।

एवंरूपः शक्य अहं नृलोके,

द्रष्टुं त्वदन्येन कुरुप्रवीर ॥ ४८ ॥

na vedayajñādhyayanairna dānairna ca

kriyābhir na tapobhirugraiḥ

evaṁrūpaḥ śakya ahaṁ nṛloke

draṣṭuṁ tvadanyena kurupravīra

(48) Neither by the study of *Vedas* and yajña, nor by charity, nor by rituals and neither by severe penances, can I be seen in this form in the world of men by any one else except you, O'hero of the Kurus.

मा ते व्यथा मा च विमूढभावो,

दृष्ट्वा रूपं घोरमीदृङ् ममेदम्।

व्यपेतभीः प्रीतमनाः पुनस्त्वं,

तदेव मे रूपमिदं प्रपश्य ॥ ४९ ॥

mā te vyathā mā ca vimūḍhabhāvo

dṛṣtvā rūpaṁ ghoramīdṛṅ mamedam

vyapetabhīḥ prītamanāḥ punas tvaṁ

tad eva me rūpamidaṁ prapaśya

(49) Do not be afraid, nor bewildered, on seeing such an awesome form of Mine. Shedding all your fears and with a gladdened heart, behold once again the other familiar form of Mine.

Commentary—In these three verses, Srī Kṛṣṇa explains the uniqueness of that special relationship which exists between the Lord and His ardent devotee. Srī Kṛṣṇa tells Arjuna that neither by the study of the *Vedas* or by the performance of yajña only, nor by the charities and performance of rituals and severe austerities only, the Lord can be visualized in the cosmic form. The vision of the Lord comes as a blessing to the person who is totally devoted to the Supreme Lord, who lives in God and works through the guidance of the Lord. These austerities are indeed great preparatory steps towards self-purification and self-realization but the ultimate goal is reached only with blessings of the Divine. The Divine vision and experience comes with a special grace to a totally integrated and devoted individual. These austerities should be performed as a service to the Divine and in the spirit of loving appreciation to the Divine. Srī Kṛṣṇa is emphasizing that the vision of His cosmic form is surely a rare blessing that comes to the individual who is purified with austerities and is totally surrendered to the Supreme-self in fervent devotion like Arjuna. The person who is dedicated to the Lord, who lives his life in the consciousness of the Lord, he becomes an eligible candidate to visualize the cosmic form. It is definitely considered to be a grace of the Supreme Lord.

In verse forty-nine, Srī Kṛṣṇa consoles Arjuna and tells him to behold His familiar form once again. Srī Kṛṣṇa, the knower of human mind, perceives very clearly that Arjuna is not yet fully prepared to hold on to the cosmic vision for too long. He realizes the restlessness, the fear and the confusion of His devotee. The Lord transports Arjuna back to the world of mortals and liberates him from his fears. Srī Kṛṣṇa resumes His familiar human form of the God-incarnate.

संजय उवाच

इत्यर्जुनं वासुदेवस्तथोक्त्वा,
स्वकं रूपं दर्शयामास भूयः।
आश्वासयामास च भीतमेनं,
भूत्वा पुनः सौम्यवपुर्महात्मा ॥५०॥

ityarjunaṁ vāsudevas tathoktvā
svakaṁ rūpaṁ darśayāmāsa bhūyaḥ
āśvāsayāmāsa ca bhītamenaṁ
bhūtvā punaḥ saumyavapur mahātmā

Sanjaya said :

(50) Having thus spoken to Arjuna, Lord Vasudeva showed to him again His own form. Assuming His gentle appearance, the exalted one (Srī Kṛṣṇa) comforted and consoled the terrified Arjuna.

Commentary—In this verse the word *svakam rupam* stands for Srī Kṛṣṇa's own familiar form. As mentioned earlier, Sanjaya has been also blessed with the Divine vision from sage Vyasa in order to relate the live commentary of the war in Kurukshetra. He has been equally astonished and terrified while looking at the cosmic form of the Lord. In previous verses he has given a detailed description to the blind king. Here in this verse, he announces that after consoling the terrified Arjuna, the Lord Vasudeva has re-assumed His very familiar form as known to everybody. Sanjaya is trying to remind Dhritrashtra about the sovereignty of Srī Kṛṣṇa as an incarnation of the Supreme Lord.

अर्जुन उवाच

दृष्ट्वेदं मानुषं रूपं तव सौम्यं जनार्दन।
इदानीमस्मि संवृत्तः सचेताः प्रकृतिं गतः॥५१॥

dṛṣṭvedaṁ mānuṣaṁ rūpaṁ tava saumyaṁ janārdana
idānīmasmi saṁvṛttaḥ sacetāḥ prakṛtiṁ gataḥ

Arjuna said :

(51) Having seen this human form of yours which is graciously peaceful O'Kṛṣṇa, now I have regained my composure and am restored to my own natural self again.

Commentary—This spiritual experience of communicating with the Supreme-Self can become a very fearful experience for the individual who remains attached to the physical body and is not fully prepared for the ultimate unity. In order to enjoy the benediction-showering form of the Lord, the individual has to transcend his physical consciousness and enter into the field of timeless mind. A similar experience has been traced from the life of Swami Vivekananda. Srī Ramakrishna, the great enlightened teacher of Vivekananda, wanted his most deserving disciple to experience his own self-expansion and to perceive the cosmic unity. The experience of expanded consciousness was not very pleasant for Vivekananda. He felt as if the entire creation was revolving and dissolving into one thing. He felt like losing his individual-self. He felt very confused, bewildered and frightened. The great master Ramakrishna could very well observe that Vivekananda was not yet ready for the Divine communication. So the great master immediately withdrew his disciple from the transcendental state of consciousness back in to the natural state of body consciousness.

श्रीभगवानुवाच

सुदुर्दर्शमिदं रूपं दृष्टवानसि यन्मम।
देवा अप्यस्य रूपस्य नित्यं दर्शनकांक्षिणः॥५२॥

sudurdarśamidaṁ rūpaṁ dṛṣtavānasi yanmama
devā apyasya rūpasya nityaṁ darśanakāṅkṣiṣaḥ

The Blessed Lord said :

(52) It is indeed very difficult to see this form of Mine which you have just seen. Even the gods are always desirous to behold this form.

नाहं वेदैर्न तपसा न दानेन न चेज्यया।
शक्य एवंविधो द्रष्टुं दृष्टवानसि मां यथा॥५३॥

nāhaṁ vedairna tapasā na dānena na cejyayā
śakya evaṁvidho draṣṭuṁ dṛaṣṭavān asi māṁ yathā

(53) Neither by the study of the *Vedas,* nor by penances and charities, nor by rituals, can I be seen in this form as you have seen Me.

भक्त्या त्वनन्यया शक्य अहमेवंविधोऽर्जुन।
ज्ञातुं द्रष्टुं च तत्त्वेन प्रवेष्टुं च परन्तप॥५४॥

bhaktyā tvananyayā śakya ahamevaṁvidho'rjuna
jñātuṁ draṣṭuṁ ca tattvena praveṣṭuṁ ca parantapa

(54) But only by undivided devotion, however, O' Arjuna, I can be seen in this form, be known in essence and also perceived and experienced.

मत्कर्मकृन्मत्परमो मद्भक्तः सङ्गवर्जितः।
निर्वैरः सर्वभूतेषु यः स मामेति पाण्डव॥५५॥

matkarmakṛn matparamo madbhaktaḥ saṅgavarjitaḥ
nirvairaḥ sarvabhūteṣu yaḥ sa māmeti pāṇḍava

(55) He who performs all his actions for Me, considers me as his Supreme goal, and is totally devoted to Me, who is non-attached and free from malice towards all beings, surely comes to Me, O' Arjuna.

Commentary—In these verses Srī Kṛṣṇa tells Arjuna that the experience of the Divine vision is indeed a very special blessing. It cannot be achieved merely by the study of *Vedas* or by the performance of austerities or by giving charities. Even the great sages keep longing for a blissful experience of the Divine vision. He declares in the verse fifty-four that it is only through the single-minded devotion and one-pointed contemplation, the Supreme Lord can be experienced, perceived and visualized. An undeviated devotion is indeed the truest measure of love for God. When the devotee forgets his individuality and surrenders himself to the Lord, he enters into the culmination of Divine love and grace. The study of *Vedas* is indeed very important for self-knowledge and self-purification. The Vedic rituals and austerities are very good but these are only the means for the final goal of Divine vision. These are some essentials for the spiritual growth. It is only the ardent devotion which educates the individual and cultures his mind to live in the consciousness of the Divine. It is through undivided devotion the person experiences the exclusive aspect of living in God and working for God. It is indeed faithful devotion which qualifies the person for the vision of the Divine. In the words of Shri Ramanuja, "The glorification of undivided Bhakti as the one pathway to the knowledge, vision and final attainment of God, puts an end to all the controversies with regard to the proximate means of release."

The intimacy that the individual develops in ardent devotion, it gradually blossoms into ineffable unity with the Lord. This is what Srī Kṛṣṇa expounds in verse fifty-four, *"jñatum drastum ca tattvena pravestum"*—with unswerving devotion one understands Me, perceives Me in essence and gradually enters into Me and becomes a part of Me. This is what the *Vedas* have declared as "Being-Becoming and Bliss." It is indeed through loving adoration and perpetual dedication that the individuality of the embodied-soul finally gets absorbed into the totality of the Supreme, and the individual enters into the blissful transcendence. That gives the individual an extraordinary sensory perception through which one feels as everything is being initiated and performed by the Supreme only. The individual is guided by one's own subconscious knowledge and lives a life guided completely by his own inner sources. It enriches the life and makes it very fascinating and adorable. One discovers, recognizes and enhances the inherent dormant powers, and makes the very best use of them. The ardent devotion literally transforms the personality and brings some significant changes to the life-style for the better.

A totally dedicated individual surrenders everything to the Lord. He works for God and does all his duties as service to God. When his entire life becomes an offering to the Supreme then he considers the God Himself as the doer, the master and the governor of all his actions. He surely becomes detached from the strings of mind, ego and body. Freedom from mind and body, immediately brings freedom from the feeling of 'I and Mine', and oneness with the Supreme takes place automatically. The spiritual transformation tears the thin veil of ignorance and one enters into the Divine consciousness. In the words of Swami Tapasyananda, "In these verses is given an uncompromising statement of the Self-sufficiency of Bhakti for the highest spiritual attainment. It is not a mere subordinate discipline for gaining what some call *chitta-suddhi* (purification of the mind) to be abandoned in preference to a more advanced discipline which is called *janana-nishta*, considered the direct establishment in non-dual understanding, and thus the immediate means of spiritual enlightenment. To a devotee with unswerving devotion, it is stated that the Lord bestows the awakening from the life of ignorance. He is then said to enter into Him, i.e., his ego is dissipated and he becomes an unobstructed part and parcel of the Divine Life".

In the verse fifty-five, Srī Kṛṣṇa declares the pre-requisites required of a devotee for the attainment of God-realization. He tells Arjuna that the individual should learn to offer all his work as a service to the Lord. He should consider God-realization as the prime goal of his life, developing an intimate relationship with the Divine through devotion. He should try to liberate himself from worldly attachments, and should become free from malice towards all other beings. These essentials can be effortlessly cultured by living in an intimate relationship with God. When the person is devoted to the Lord and loves the Supreme with single-minded devotion, he becomes transformed and gradually enters into unity with the Lord. To love and appreciate, adore and respect is a very natural instinct. It is inherent in each and everyone, it only needs to be transformed into love for God. It is a switch in awareness from the worldly desires to the desire for God-realization.

It is attachment for God which naturally brings detachment from the material world. It is with the awareness of spiritual intimacy, the person experiences the cosmic intimacy and unity with the Universal-self. It tears all the veils of enmity, and dissolves all the barriers of jealousy and separateness. The person, who is totally devoted to the Divine, becomes free from malice, jealousy and all other insecurities. This whole process of spiritual advancement is very natural, psychological and takes place very naturally and easily. Srī Kṛṣṇa is emphasizing that when the person starts the spiritual journey with an attitude of loving adoration to the Divine with total surrender, the realization of the Supreme-Self happens automatically in due time.

ॐ तत्सदिति श्रीमद्भगवद्गीतासूपनिषत्सु ब्रह्मविद्यायां
योगशास्त्रे श्रीकृष्णार्जुनसंवादे विश्वरूपदर्शनयोगो
नाम एकादशोऽध्याय: ॥ ११ ॥

'Aum' tatsaditi Śrīmadbhagawadgeetā sūpaniṣatsu
brahmavidyāyām yogaśāstre Śrīkṛṣṇārjunasamvāde
viśvarūpadarśanayogo nāma ekādaśo'dhyāyaḥ

'AUM TAT SAT'—Thus, in the Upanishad of the glorious Bhagawad Geeta, the science of the Brahman (Absolute) the scripture of yoga, the dialogue between Srī Kṛṣṇa and Arjuna—thus, ends the chapter eleven entitled *"Viśvarūpadarśanayoga"*.

इति श्रीमद्भगवद्गीतासु एकादशोऽध्याय: ॥ ११ ॥

Chapter Twelve

BHAKTIYOGA

THE YOGA OF DEVOTION

अर्जुन उवाच

एवं सततयुक्ता ये भक्तास्त्वां पर्युपासते।
ये चाप्यक्षरमव्यक्तं तेषां के योगवित्तमाः ॥ १ ॥

evaṁ satatayuktā ye bhaktāstvāṁ paryupāsate
ye cāpyakṣaramavyaktaṁ teṣāṁ ke yogavittamāḥ

Arjuna said :

(1) Those devotees who are ever steadfast and thus worship Thee, and those who worship the imperishable and unmanifested, which of these are better versed in Yoga?

Commentary—This chapter opens with a question from Arjuna in relation to the concept of ardent devotion, which has been genuinely and gloriously emphasized by Srī Kṛṣṇa towards the end of the previous chapter. Arjuna brings forth this question about the worship of the Supreme Lord with form and shape and without form and attributes. He wants to know the difference between the meditation upon the manifested form and contemplation upon the unmanifested, infinite, omniscient.

After having a vision of the cosmic form of Srī Kṛṣṇa, Arjuna is surely convinced that Srī Kṛṣṇa is Lord Vishnu's incarnation, but he still wants to know more about it. He has known Srī Kṛṣṇa since childhood as a most intimate friend, as a guide, and also as a cousin. Although he has always liked Him, loved Him and respected His opinion about everything, but after the cosmic vision of the Lord, his respect and adoration has intensified. He feels like worshipping Srī Kṛṣṇa as the Lord of the Universe but still feels a little bit confused.

He speaks about his doubt in these words—those devotees, who are ever steadfast in Yoga and thus worship Thee, and those who worship the imperishable and unmanifested, which of these are better versed in Yoga? Actually through the words of Arjuna, the great Sage Vyasa has voiced the most pertinent question usually expressed by many during their pursuit in spiritual evolution. The anxiety to explore the relative worth of the two types of worshippers has been a perennial quest of many. Arjuna wants to know the comparative relevance of devotional service offered to the personal God and contemplation upon the impersonal, indwelling. As a student of Vedic tradition, Arjuna has been always taught that the Supreme-Soul is attributeless, formless, omniscient and omnipresent; but after visualizing the God's cosmic form, his old concept has taken a new meaning. Although practically in every previous chapter Srī Kṛṣṇa has emphasized on the worship of the personal form of God but apparently Arjuna has not paid any attention. He is definitely convinced that devotion to personal God is indeed the best approach in spiritual pursuit but he still wants to confirm it from Srī Kṛṣṇa.

श्रीभगवानुवाच

मय्यावेश्य मनो ये मां नित्ययुक्ता उपासते।
श्रद्धया परयोपेतास्ते मे युक्ततमा मताः ॥ २ ॥

mayyāveśya mano ye māṁ nityayuktā upāsate
śraddhayā parayo'petās te me yuktatamā matāḥ

The Blessed Lord said :

(2) Those who concentrate their mind on Me, stay united with Me in contemplation; those are steadfast and worship Me with supreme faith—I consider them to be the best in Yoga.

ये त्वक्षरमनिर्देश्यमव्यक्तं पर्युपासते।
सर्वत्रगमचिन्त्यं च कूटस्थमचलं ध्रुवम् ॥ ३ ॥

ye tvakṣaram anirdeśyamavyaktaṁ paryupāsate
sarvatragamacintyaṁ ca kūṭasthamacalaṁ dhruvam

सन्नियम्येन्द्रियग्रामं सर्वत्र समबुद्धयः।
ते प्राप्नुवन्ति मामेव सर्वभूतहिते रताः ॥ ४ ॥

sanniyamyendriyagrāmaṁ sarvatra samabuddhayaḥ
te prāpnuvanti māmeva sarvabhūtahite ratāḥ

(3, 4) But those who are devoted to the imperishable, the indefinable, the unmanifest, the omnipresent, the unthinkable, the immovable and the eternal; having restrained all their senses in totality, with equanimity of mind, also reach Me, while intent on the welfare of all beings.

Commentary—Srī Kṛṣṇa opens the conversation with the words "*mayy aevesya mano ye mam*" which means concentrating their thoughts on Me. Living in the thoughts of the Supreme divinity is indeed living in Yoga. Throughout His dialogue Srī Kṛṣṇa has emphasized upon the word *"shradhaya"* meaning the spirit of ardent faith, as a prerequisite for having communion with God. In yogic unity with the indwelling-Self the individual lives in the consciousness of God, works in the awareness of God and feels the presence of Lord in everything and everywhere. In the words of Jaydayal Goyandka, "Accepting with reverence, as more than evident, the existence of God, His various descents, his utterances, power, virtues, glory, sports, and greatness etc. is what is known as supreme faith; and he who cultivates absolute dependence on God like the great devotee Prahlada is said to have been endowed with Supreme faith". Srī Kṛṣṇa emphasizes the importance of steadfast devotion with complete surrender as essential, for the goal in ultimate yogic communion. After speaking about his priority in relevance to the mode of concentration and worship, Srī Kṛṣṇa expresses his opinion about the contemplation on the unmanifest and says that those who worship the imperishable omnipresent, the undefinable, the immovable, and eternal with complete self-control and with equanimity of mind towards all beings, they also reach Me. As a matter of fact, in spiritual pursuit, as the worshipper advances in spiritual growth from less awareness to increased awareness, the 'One' being worshipped also changes, till the individual reaches the shrine within his ownself. It is indeed a fact that it is very difficult to draw a line between the worship of *saguna* and the meditation on *nirguna.* In the process of worshipping *saguna,* the person actually meditates upon *nirguna,* who hides behind the *saguna.* So by being devoted to either one is indeed worshipping the both at the same time. The Supreme Divinity and his manifestations cannot be separated. It is after performing the worship of *saguna* for many years, the individual educates himself to live in the consciousness of *nirguna* and rises to the 'ideal' behind the 'idol'. For example, in some states of India especially Maharashtra and Bengal—there is a *visarjana* ceremony which forms the culmination of worship. Around the Navaratra time people worship various forms of gods and goddesses made of clay. After the worship for nine days all the deities are taken in a procession to the Ganga or to the nearby sea coast for *visarjana.* The *visarjana* means giving away the concept of forms and names. It is like rising above the concept of *saguna* to *nirguna,* from idol to the ideal, from less awareness to the increased awareness. In the process of worship for ten days the individual is expected to understand the transitory nature of form and move into the reality of formless.

Swami Vivekananda has also given a very good example in this respect. "A man is journeying towards the sun and takes a photograph at each step. How different would be the first photograph from the second, and still more from the third or the last, when he reaches the real sun! But all these, though differing so widely from each other, are true, only they are made to appear different by the changing conditions of time and space. It is the recognition of this truth which has enabled the Hindus to perceive Universal truth of all religions, from the lowest to the highest. It has made of them the only people who never had religious prosecutions." Similarly, when the ardent devotee gets closer to the experiential knowledge of the indwelling-Self, he needs less and less help in the form of signs and symbols for concentration. The aspirant rises above personal God to the impersonal, immutable, omnipresent dwelling in the heart of his own self. He realizes the essential truth, behind the *saguna* and *nirguna.* There is a story in our *Puranas* which reconciles this. Once Lord Rama the God-incarnate asked his great devotee Hanuman, "O son tell me what type of relationship you hold for Me and how you meditate upon Me. Srī Hanuman replied O' Rama sometime I look upon You as 'Purna', the undivided 'One', at other moment I look upon You as undivided but at the same time reflecting through everything and everybody. Then I look upon myself as a fragment of You. At other times, I contemplate upon You as my Divine master and think of myself as Your humble servant. When however I am blessed with inner unity and the experiential knowledge of the Self then I perceive that 'I am Thou' and 'Thou art I'—*Tattvamasi*".

It is indeed a fact that in the course of spiritual progress, an inspired devotee is blessed with the first hand experience of holy communion. In the words of Dr. Radhakrishnan, "once you realize that the Reality is something to be felt, something to be experienced, you do not attach much importance to the method by which you attain it. They become subordinate and merely instrumental". People give different names to God in the process of their spiritual pursuit. The form of approach differs from one individual to another depending upon his own personal level of understanding. That's why Srī Ramakrishna used to say, it is just enough to have faith in God—many are the names of God and many are the methods through which one approaches the Divine. No one should argue on the issue that only my faith is correct and all others are wrong. The crescents, the crosses and symbols are only some visual aids for strengthening spiritual concepts. The ancient religious literature describes "*Saadhakaanam hitarthaaya Brahmano rupakalpana*"—means the Supreme Brahman is formless. An aspirant gives name and form according to his own imagination. The *Sruthi Bhagawati* declares "*Ekam Sadvipra Bahuda vadanti*", i.e. it is only one Truth manifesting in various forms and shape. "*Akaasat Patitam toyam yatha gacchati sagaram, Sarva deva namaskara Kesavam pratigacchati*" means worship the Lord in any form you like and address Him by any name which pleases you, it is indeed directed to one and the only Supreme Lord.

The Absolute Truth is indeed beyond the reach of sensory perception. It is formless, nameless, and inexplicable. So either the person has to transcend above the finite to experience the infinite or to bring the infinite to the level of finite perception in some form and shape. People definitely need some kind of expression of the inexplicable in order to concentrate in the beginning of their spiritual pursuit. The ancient religious literature explains that the sages who wrote the Vedic hymns have described the God as Omnipresent, Omniscient, indefinable, unthinkable, and all pervading. Later on the Sages like Vashist, Vyasa, Kashyap, Atri, Bharadwaj, Angirasa and Brighu believed in God as *saguna* and *nirguna* both. Tulsi Das has also written in the *Ramayana, Nirguna saguna dou brahamma swarupa akath anadhi anupa. Gin ke rahi bhavana jeysi prabhu murat tin dhekyoi tesi.* Srī Kṛṣṇa himself has spoken in the previous verses *"Ye yatha mam prapadyantae tamstathai va bhajamy aham"*. As people approach Me so do I seek them. The reason why Srī Kṛṣṇa expresses the concept of *saguna* and then immediately after that the concept of *nirguna* because he knows that in the process of spiritual growth it is a natural progression to move from one concept to another. The aspirant switches from one to another at various stages of his spiritual advancement. Although the *saguna* worship may take place at first, ultimately one slips into *nirguna* otherwise the goal is not achieved. For example, Uddhava a great devotee of Srī Kṛṣṇa, had worshipped his Lord in *saguna* and *nirguna,* both at the same time. In the third verse, Srī Kṛṣṇa tells Arjuna that when the aspirant transcends into unity with the Supreme-Soul, he goes into the experience of unity with the entire creation, because there is nothing else besides the omniscience of the Divine. He lives in the consciousness of the Lord and perceives His presence everywhere and in everyone. The experience of his Yogic communion reflects through his day-to-day activities. His service to the other fellow beings becomes a service to the Supreme Lord. In the process of concentration on the unmanifest, the aspirant moves from the subtle to the gross, from the indwelling-Self to the universal-Self, while in the other approach of personal worship of God, the individual moves from the gross to the subtle—and from the subtle to the gross again.

क्लेशोऽधिकतरस्तेषामव्यक्तासक्तचेतसाम् ।
अव्यक्ता हि गतिर्दुःखं देहवद्भिरवाप्यते ॥ ५ ॥

kleśo'dhikataras teṣāmavyaktāsaktacetasām
avyaktā hi gatir duḥkhaṁ dehavadbhiravāpyate

(5) There are greater obstacles for those whose minds are set on

the unmanifest; for the goal—the unmanifested is very difficult to attain by the embodied beings.

ये तु सर्वाणि कर्माणि मयि संन्यस्य मत्पराः।
अनन्येनैव योगेन मां ध्यायन्त उपासते॥ ६॥

ye tu sarvāṇi karmāṇi mayi sannyasya matparāḥ
ananyenaiva yogena māṁ dhyāyanta upāsate

तेषामहं समुद्धर्ता मृत्युसंसारसागरात्।
भवामि नचिरात् पार्थ मय्यावेशितचेतसाम्॥ ७॥

teṣāmahaṁ samuddhartā mṛtyusaṁsārasāgrāt
bhavāmi nacirāt pārtha mayyāveśitacetasām

(6, 7) But those who worship Me, surrendering all their actions to Me, regarding Me as their supreme goal, meditate on Me with undivided devotion; whose minds are totally absorbed in Me, I become their saviour and liberate them from the ocean of death-bound existence, Oh! Arjuna.

मय्येव मन आधत्स्व मयि बुद्धिं निवेशय।
निवसिष्यसि मय्येव अत ऊर्ध्वं न संशयः॥ ८॥

mayyeva mana ādhatsva mayi buddhiṁ niveśaya
nivasiṣyasi mayyeva ata ūrdhvaṁ na saṅśayaḥ

(8) Settle your mind in Me alone, let your intellect dwell in Me, then you will live in Me alone, there is no doubt about this.

Commentary—In continuation of the previous verses, Srī Kṛṣṇa expresses his concern for the devotees who are endeavouring for the subtlest experience of the unmanifest. By using the words "*Klesoadhikataras tesam avyaktasakta-cetasam*", Srī Kṛṣṇa alerts mankind that the transcendence into the realm of the unmanifest is very difficult as long as the individual holds his identification with the physical body. This identification starts right after birth and becomes stronger as the person grows older. Identification with the body is '*dehabhimana*'—the feeling of 'I and Mine'. The identification of the embodied-Self with the body, mind and ego expresses itself as a great obstacle in the process of communion with God. It becomes a curtain between the *Nara* and *Narayana,* between the embodied soul and the universal soul. The great Sufi poet Omarkhayyam has described this in these words, "There was a door to which I found no key, There was a veil past which I could not see. Some talk awhile of me and Thee, There seemed—and then no more of Thee and me. Thee in me who works behind, I lifted my veil to find a lantern—amid the darkness, And cried—it is Me in thee blind."

In essence every individual-Soul is a fragment of the Supreme Soul, pure, luminous and free—but its identification with ego corrupts the "Antahakarana" (Thinking faculty) and becomes the cause of dualities. When the individual identifies with ego, he becomes enslaved by its bewitching intrigues, and loses his conscious connections from the Supreme Self; which results in total disintegration. The individual starts acting against the voice of the indwelling God and ignores the ethical code of Dharma. The most appropriate example in this case can be the character of Ravana in the great Hindu epic *Ramayana.* Ravana was a learned person. It was due to his identification with ego and the sensual pleasures of the body which made him egocentric. He started thinking himself as the most powerful person on earth. His activities became unethical, immoral and harmful to others. In the words of Eugene Davis, "Almost all problems experienced by human beings are due to their delusions (false beliefs) and illusions (mistakes in perception) because of strong ego-identification. Unaware of their true spiritual nature, their powers of discernment are flawed and their ability to reason is diminished. Ego-fixation also results in self-centered behaviour that prevents soul awareness from expanding as it is inclined to do."

In consideration of the method of worship, Srī Kṛṣṇa makes it very clear to mankind that as long as there exists identification with the body, mind and ego—the experience of the indwelling Supreme Soul is very difficult. In order to experience the holy communion with the indwelling-soul, the feeling of 'I and Mine' has to be replaced with the feeling of 'Thou and Thine'. Srī Kṛṣṇa suggests a wonderful method in the verse eight for this transition from the feeling of 'I-ness' to 'Thy-ness' in these words *"mayy eva mana adhatsva mayi buddhiṁ nivesaya"*—just fix your mind on Me alone and let your intellect dwell in Me, and then you will live in Me, there is no doubt about it. As identification with God becomes stronger, individual's identification with the ego becomes week and gradually it fades away. It is a training of accepting the presence of Lord and also living in the consciousness of God at the same time. The bliss of living a life in the consciousness of the Divine is indeed very rewarding, but it does not take place all at-once. There is a process to it. It is a step by step spiritual progress. The individual has to learn to live in the presence of God every single minute of his life. Swami Chinmayananda gives a very good example: "a dancer never forgets the rhythm of the drum to which she keeps steps, a musician is ever conscious of the background hum. Similarly a devotee is advised not to take up religion as a part-time entertainment or as a temporary escapism, but to consider the Lord as the supreme goal to be achieved in and through life." It is the spontaneous love for the Divine, the spirit of service for the Divine which brings transformation in the attitude of the individual. Alignment with consciousness of the Divine, educates the mind to operate directly under the guidance of the Supreme Divinity. It is not the calculated devotion, it is indeed the ardent loving devotion that brings transformation and arouses the spirit of selfless action.

It is indeed the identification with body which gives meaning to many desires, and in order to fulfil those desires, the individual descends into the world of mortals from birth to birth. Srī Kṛṣṇa assures in verse seven that the devotees who are engaged in the perpetual adoration of Me and offer all their work as a service to Me, definitely become free from the bondage of actions. This is a very difficult task to accomplish but surely not impossible. Srī Kṛṣṇa assures that the one who takes refuge in Me, I personally take care of them. He promises to rescue his devotees from the ocean of death-bound existence. The assurance of Srī Kṛṣṇa in verse eight definitely helps the individual to reach the ultimate goal of self realization. It presents an encouraging insight into spiritual pursuit. Perfection in Yoga is definitely the perpetual absorption in the Lord. As a matter of fact mind, intellect and ego are not three separate entities. Mind represents the totality of sense perception which leads towards new ideas, desires and aspirations in the form of *sankulpa*. The same faculty when takes decision it is called intellect and further when this faculty considers itself as the doer it is called ego. So by living in thoughts of the Divine the mind becomes educated, cultured and trained in all respects. The word Me generally used by Srī Kṛṣṇa stands both for personal worship of Srī Kṛṣṇa as the supreme Lord and also for the indwelling Supreme-Self of every being.

अथ चित्तं समाधातुं न शक्नोषि मयि स्थिरम्।
अभ्यासयोगेन ततो मामिच्छाप्तुं धनञ्जय॥ ९॥

atha cittaṁ samādhātuṁ na śaknoṣi mayi sthiram
abhyāsayogena tato māmicchāptuṁ dhanañjaya

(9) If, however, you are not able to fix your mind steadily on Me, then through the Yoga of constant practice seek to attain Me, Oh! Arjuna.

अभ्यासेऽप्यसमर्थोऽसि मत्कर्मपरमो भव।
मदर्थमपि कर्माणि कुर्वन्सिद्धिमवाप्स्यसि॥ १०॥

abhyāse'pyasamartho'si matkarmaparamo bhava
madarthamapi karmāṇi kurvan siddhimavāpsyasi

(10) If you are not capable of such practice, be thou intent on doing work for My sake, even by performing actions for My sake you will attain perfection.

अथैतदप्यशक्तोऽसि कर्तुं मद्योगमाश्रितः।
सर्वकर्मफलत्यागं ततः कुरु यतात्मवान्॥ ११॥

athaitadapyaśakto'si kartuṁ madyogamāśritaḥ
sarvakarmaphalatyāgaṁ tataḥ kuru yatātmavān

(11) If you are unable to do even this, then take refuge in My yogic unity and renounce the fruit of all actions, being self-controlled.

श्रेयो हि ज्ञानमभ्यासाज्ज्ञानाद्ध्यानं विशिष्यते।
ध्यानात्कर्मफलत्यागस्त्यागाच्छान्तिरनन्तरम्॥ १२॥

śreyo hi jñānamabhyāsājjñānād dhyānaṁ viśiṣyate
dhyānāt karmaphalatyāgas tyāgācchāntiranantaram

(12) Better indeed is knowledge than practice, (without proper insight) better than knowledge is meditation, superior to meditation is renunciation of the fruits of actions—from renunciation one attains peace immediately.

Commentary—In these verses, starting from nine to twelve, Srī Kṛṣṇa presents the hierarchy of methods conducive to the training of yogic communion. Although there are many different names which have been given to yogic discipline, the goal is to learn to live in the consciousness of Supreme. People from all sections of the society adopt different methods according to their temperaments, spiritual progression, and personal taste. The first one suggested by Srī Kṛṣṇa is a *Abhyasayoga. Abhyasa* means constant practice with repeated effort of living in the transcendence of the Divine. Constant remembrance of the Lord purifies the mind from all material contamination and brings the individual in the most intimate relationship with the Divine. Men literate or illiterate, ignorant or enlightened, rich or poor, everyone can use this method with equal benefit. It may sound odd to many, but it is indeed a fact that the process of self-purification dawns simply by the most simplest method of remembering the Lord perpetually. Practise surely makes someone nearly perfect in due time. In the modern sustainable educated societies, sometimes it happens that the so-called intellectual, learned, and scholars fail to accept the spiritual power of something so simple. Their egocentric thoughts battle against it with the load of their obscurities. Constant practice of God's remembrance connects the individual to the essence of life and makes the yogic communion spontaneous and easy. Although in the initial stages it demands conscious efforts but gradually it just becomes second nature and the presence of consciousness of God is felt at all times. Srī Kṛṣṇa suggests to culture the thoughts with the rhythm of God's remembrance, and nurture the mind with the awareness of the Divine. By placing the yoga of practice upfront in the hierarchy, Srī Kṛṣṇa has presented a wonderful method of God worship for people from all sections of society. It is an unparalleled method for the householders, for students, and for others with their busy schedules.

Srī Kṛṣṇa indicates that the spirit of true devotion and yogic communion becomes possible with faith, willingness and acceptance. When the individual accepts to live in awareness of the consciousness of the Divine, he automatically dedicates all his work as a service to the Divine. The work offered as a service to the God is called *Madarpana karma, Madartha karma* and *Mata karma. Madarpana karma* are those which are started with some personal motive (*sankalpa)* but offered as a service to God during or after performance. For example, a person organizes a yajña with some motive in mind, but during and after the performance he offers the entire worship to the Lord as an appreciation. He takes it as a gesture of being thankful to the Lord for health, wealth and happiness. The other type of activities are called the *Madartha karma*—those are dedicated to the God from the very beginning. There are people in every community who are constantly involved in serving others. For them the opportunity to serve God becomes inclusive of the reward. For these people work itself becomes worship of God. The third type is the *Mata karma* which help the individual to maintain peace and harmony in society. The work performed with the attitude of *Mata karma* promotes the spirit of selfless action and enhances the spirit of service. Srī Kṛṣṇa enlightens Arjuna about the nature of actions and tells that just to accept the idea of presence God is not enough, let the idea possess the individual. The person should live a life which is completely attuned to the voice of the Supreme Self. As Dr. Radhakrishnan says, "Live soaked in the nature of the Divine. Do not have an instant of the life separated from the Divine. *Uttama sahja avastha, Dwitya dhyana dharna"*—living in the awareness of the divine is being at ease and at peace within one's own self. Srī Aurobindo has called this *Sayujya mukti*; it is all kinds of union at once. There is total unification with the Supreme. The practice of remembering Lord is the key that opens the door to the innermost shrine of the Lord. With totality of faith in God; the love and devotion blossoms in all respects and the performance of every activity becomes very rewarding and fulfilling. As Tagore writes, "when thou commandest me to sing, it seems that my heart would break with pride; I look at thy face and tears come to my eyes—All that is harsh and dissonant in my life melts into one sweet harmony—and my adoration spreads wings like a glad bird on its flight across the sea. It shall be my endeavour to reveal thee in my actions knowing it is thy power that gives me strength to act."

In verse twelve, Srī Kṛṣṇa gives His decisive opinion about the most appropriate method of worship. He expresses His genuine appreciation for the work which is performed as an offering to the Supreme Self. In verse twelve, Srī Kṛṣṇa tells Arjuna that knowledge is indeed better than practice carried on without proper insight, meditation is superior to knowledge but renouncing attachment to the fruits of actions is even better; with renunciation peace follows quickly. Here the emphasis has been given to the truth that all religious practices such as fasting, performance of rituals and charities should be carried on with proper insight and knowledge. For example, Patanjali Yoga Sutra describes, "*Tad japa tad artha Bhavanam*"—means the *mantra jaap* must be done by meditating upon the meaning of the *mantra.* It is indeed a fact that the mechanical repetition is one thing; and intelligent assimilation is quite another. In order to achieve proper assimilation, one must allow the truth to penetrate understanding. Human nature is a mixed melody of many aspects—body, mind, intellect, ego and consciousness. In order to bring all these faculties together and to let them work in perfect harmony, it is important to make any practice intelligible, enjoyable, useful and meaningful. Any religious practice, which is performed with proper insight, helps the intellectual faculty to be used for the service of the contemplative end. Proper understanding helps intellect to merge into the deepest layers of the consciousness and helps the mind to get settled in the transcendence of the Supreme-Self. The need of religious practice with proper insight has been emphasized by Yaska in Nirukta *stharunai bharhar kila bhudhitya ved na vijanate yotharm yothraga se, sankalam bhadrmashnute sa nakmeni jyana vidhutepamama*—menas he who repeats the *mantra* without understanding its meaning is like an ass carrying a load of sandalwood; it knows only the weight of the load, but it does not enjoy the fragrance. In order to achieve the full benefit of *Mantra-jaap* or any other religious practice, it is indeed important to understand the meaning of it. It should be sufficiently intelligible and performed with ardent faith, love and devotion. The next part of this verse explains that meditation is indeed better than knowledge. Meditation is combination of two words—medi and tation which means to attend the thoughts with attention and intention. It is one of the greatest art of life wherein the person becomes introduced to his own self in all respects. In meditation session the individual learns to attend, watch, observe and behold the movement of his thoughts, aspirations and dreams. It is one of the highest form of discipline which is cultivated with practice of living in constant awareness of the Self.

In verse twelve, the word knowledge stands for the study of scriptures. There are people who are well read but still not at peace with themselves. Accumulating the scriptural knowledge is very good but it is only a tool for self-realization and God-realization. Theoretical knowledge of some facts is one thing but practical assimilation of knowledge is quite another. It is the meditative experience that unfolds the hidden intricacies of scriptural knowledge to be used for personal experience. The subjective and independent contemplation is very important in order to transform bookish knowledge into intelligent understanding and assimilation. It is indeed through inward contemplation, meditation and assimilation that scriptural knowledge is transformed into wisdom. The goal in meditation is to attend to the quality, quantity and direction of thoughts and to hold a positive control over it. It is a state of peace and tranquillity. It is a blessing to be able to meditate peacefully but a great percentage of population find it very difficult. For most of people, meditation period passes in vain, with the mind behaving more like a monkey. A constant struggle seems to be required to accomplish something which should be absolutely effortless. The basic reason for this struggle is lack of preparation on the part of the meditator. The person who is trying to meditate, generally he has to struggle with the internal dialogue that goes on at various levels of mind. This internal dialogue originates from contacts with other people and from the day-to-day activities of life. It originates from the expectations and from attachment to the fruits of actions. Srī Kṛṣṇa, the knower of human psychology, understands the obstacles, which generally arise in the process of meditation session. That is why in the hierarchy of preferences He declares that renunciation of attachment to the fruits of actions is even better than meditation. It renders peace quickly.

Renunciation to the fruits of actions purifies the mind and eliminates all causes of disturbances appearing in spiritual progress. In reality, it is not the action that binds, it is the attachment to the fruit of action which binds the individual. The binding quality lies in the attachment to the desire of reward, recognition and appreciation. The thoughts of recognition and expectations from others are the ghosts which haunt people day and night. This chattering which is born out of expectations, it settles deep down in the thinking faculty and keeps coming to the surface of consciousness very frequently. It is this chattering that disturbs the mind in meditation and becomes an obstacle in the process of self-realization. All the scriptural knowledge and every method of meditation fails, until the individual educates himself to the attitude of selfless action. In order to be a successful meditator, the individual has to rise above the expectations and limitations of name, fame and rewards.

The attitude of performing actions without attachment to rewards does not come all at once. It doesn't take place just by talking about it. There is a process to its training and cultivation. The process involves the spirit of unconditional love and devotion to God. When life becomes totally devoted to the Supreme, the performance of every activity becomes a service to the Supreme. As consciousness of the presence of Divine blossoms, the entire lifestyle becomes a constant remembrance of the Divine. When the aspirant advances in unification with the Divine, the spirit of renunciation to the fruits of actions takes place naturally. The inner unity, peace and security helps the individual to rise above the futility of worldly name, fame and the desires of recognition. As a matter of fact, the Gospel of selfless action works as a remarkable tool in any method of worship whichever the person chooses for God-realization. Almost all other methods revolve around it and draw their completeness from it. Renunciation of the fruits of all actions, is indeed the touchstone of success in spiritual life.

अद्वेष्टा सर्वभूतानां मैत्रः करुण एव च।
निर्ममो निरहङ्कारः समदुःखसुखः क्षमी॥ १३॥

adveṣṭā sarvabhūtānāṁ maitraḥ karuṇa eva ca
nirmamo nirahaṅkāraḥ samduḥkhasukhaḥ kṣamī

सन्तुष्टः सततं योगी यतात्मा दृढनिश्चयः।
मय्यर्पितमनोबुद्धिर्यो मद्भक्तः स मे प्रियः॥ १४॥

santuṣṭaḥ satataṁ yogī yatātmā dṛḍhaniścayaḥ
mayyarpitamanobuddhir yo madbhaktaḥ sa me priyaḥ

(13, 14) He who is free from hatred towards all creatures, friendly and compassionate, who is free from the feeling of mineness and egoism, balanced in pain and pleasure, forgiving, always contented, steadfast in Yoga, self-controlled and very determined, with his mind and intellect dedicated to Me—that devotee of Mine is very dear to Me.

यस्मान्नोद्विजते लोको लोकान्नोद्विजते च यः।
हर्षामर्षभयोद्वेगैर्मुक्तो यः स च मे प्रियः॥ १५॥

yasmān nodvijate loko lokān nodvijate ca yaḥ
harṣāmarṣabhayodvegair mukto yaḥ sa ca me priyaḥ

(15) He by whom the world is not agitated and who cannot be agitated by the world; who is free from exhilaration, resentment, fear and anxiety—he is dear to Me.

अनपेक्षः शुचिर्दक्ष उदासीनो गतव्यथः।
सर्वारम्भपरित्यागी यो मद्भक्तः स मे प्रियः॥ १६॥

anapekṣaḥ śucir dakṣa udāsīno gatavyathaḥ
sarvārambhaparityāgī yo madbhaktaḥ sa me priyaḥ

(16) He who is free from desires, pure, dexterous, and mature, who is free from disappointments and totally detached from all commencements, that devotee of Mine is very dear to Me.

यो न हृष्यति न द्वेष्टि न शोचति न कांक्षति।
शुभाशुभपरित्यागी भक्तिमान्यः स मे प्रियः॥ १७॥

yo na hṛṣyati na dveṣṭi na śocati na kāṅkṣati
śubhāśubhaparityāgī bhaktimānyāḥ sa me priyaḥ

(17) He who neither exhilarates nor hates, neither grieves nor craves, who is the renouncer of both auspicious and inauspicious, and also endowed with devotion—he is dear to Me.

समः शत्रौ च मित्रे च तथा मानापमानयोः।
शीतोष्णसुखदुःखेषु समः सङ्गविवर्जितः॥ १८॥

samaḥ śatrau ca mitre ca tathā mānāpamānayoḥ
śītoṣṇasukhaduḥkheṣu samaḥ saṅgavivarjitaḥ

(18) Who is alike to a foe and a friend and also the same in honour and dishonour, cold and heat, pleasure and pain, who is poised and detached.

तुल्यनिन्दास्तुतिर्मौनी सन्तुष्टो येन केनचित्।
अनिकेतः स्थिरमतिर्भक्तिमान्मे प्रियो नरः॥ १९॥

tulyanindāstutir maunī santuṣṭo yena kenacit
aniketaḥ sthiramatir bhaktimān me priyo naraḥ

(19) Who remains balanced in criticism and praise and holds control over speech, who is contented with anything that comes and not attached to his place of dwelling; who is firm in mind and fully devoted—that man is dear to Me.

ये तु धर्म्यामृतमिदं यथोक्तं पर्युपासते।
श्रद्दधाना मत्परमा भक्तास्तेऽतीव मे प्रियाः॥ २०॥

ye tu dharmyāmṛtamidaṁ yathoktaṁ paryupāsate
śraddadhānā matparamā bhaktās te'tīva me priyāḥ

(20) Those who follow this immortal Dharma as declared above, endowed with faith, who regard Me as their supreme goal, those devotees are exceedingly dear to Me.

Commentary—Starting from verse thirteen, Srī Kṛṣṇa gives a detailed description of the hallmarks of a genuine devotee. He describes the equipoise of a true devotee and his relationship with others in day to day life. These are the characteristic features of a man of undeviated devotion and the guidelines for spiritual progress. He starts from the word *advesta* which literally means non-envious. A true devotee of the Lord bears no ill-will towards anybody because he understands the perennial pervasiveness of the Divine. He lives in awareness of the divine and looks upon everyone through the eyes of the Self. The individual who is settled in identity with God, he becomes automatically settled in identity with the entire creation. He looks upon the entire creation as a living organism united within the essentiality of the Lord. He understands clearly that ill-will towards others separates the individual from others and as well as from the Supreme Divinity. He is very friendly and compassionate. In the words of Jaydayal Goyandka, "God is full of boundless compassion and love so it is indeed natural that His devotee too who has attained perfection should possess these virtues". Kindness and compassion is a way of expressing the spiritual intimacy one holds with his own inner-Self. When the individual resorts into the magnificence of *prajñya* (increased awareness), his inner love and stability is reflected into *karuna* (compassion) towards its fellow beings. This kind of enlightened person develops cosmic unity. He feels at home wherever he goes and creates an aura of friendliness all around. He wins the confidence of others. He touches the heart of others with the magic of his inner purity and honesty. A genuine devotee of the Lord definitely differs from others in respect of his approach towards life. He always works in harmony with others. His each and every activity is prompted from the calmness of heart. A genuine devotee of the Lord acts, speaks and works directly from the centre of his being and remains liberated from the feeling of 'I and Mine'. The word *Nirmamo nirahankarah* literally means totally detached and free from the feeling of mineness. When someone lives totally saturated in the awareness of the Supreme, his detachment from the body and the material world takes place naturally. When the attachment to the centre of the being is strengthened, the feeling of 'I and Mine' is replaced by 'Thou and Thine'. It is a shift in attitude that takes place slowly and effortlessly.

The other characteristics of a true devotee which have been mentioned in this verse are *sama-duhkha-sukhah ksami* which literally means balanced in pleasure and pain and also very forgiving. A true devotee of the Lord who is established in the nature of the Divine, he definitely becomes very strong both psychologically and physically. Each new day brings something new to the life of an individual who lives in unity with God. As an ancient poet has written, "He who feels secured within, he can live in perfect peace, amid the ups and downs of life." The word *ksami* stands for the individual who is blessed with the virtue of forgiving others. Anybody who feels secure within his own self, he lives in peace and harmony with others. He is always caring, loving and forgiving. The reason why some people cannot forgive others because they are insecure and lack the strength of forgiving which comes from the bonding with the Self. On the other hand, for a true devotee of the Lord who is perennially united within, for him to forgive and forget comes very naturally. A forgiving soul is indeed a blessed and liberated soul, who enjoys constant unity with the Supreme.

In verse fourteen, Srī Kṛṣṇa has used the word *santustah* meaning contentment. There is no treasure equal to contentment in this world. The person who lives in the nature of the Supreme-Self, he becomes very appreciative and thankful. A thankful heart is indeed a contented heart. It is the inner connectedness with the indwelling-Self, which initiates the individual into the appreciation of what he possesses. As Tagore writes, "Day by day thou art making me worthy of the simple, great gifts that thou gavest to me unasked—this sky and the light, this body and the life and the mind—saving me from perils of over much desire". The next characteristic which has been mentioned in the same verse is *yatatma drdhaniscayah* meaning self control and firm determination. Anybody who is established in the Yoga of the Self, he lives his life controlled from within. He has full mastery over the senses of actions and perceptions. He is also very determined and very positive, because he feels very secure and confident. Any person who is firmly settled in the nature of the Supreme Divinity, he becomes very secure and positive. His entire life functions from the centre of his being and his activities are guided from the integrity of the inner-Self. Determination is a great virtue that forms the foundation of success, happiness and tranquillity in life. It manifests the depth of faith and also mirrors the steadfastness of integral wisdom.

The other well-known hallmark of a genuine devotee, which Srī Kṛṣṇa describes in the same verse is *mayyarpita-manobuddhir*—means with the mind and intellect totally dedicated to Me. The activities of a true devotee are centred around the consciousness of the Divine. He is always very sensitive towards the well being of the entire creation. He respects law and order in society and helps others to live in harmony with each other. As a matter of fact when the mind and intellect of the individual are anchored to the divine, he naturally works through the guidance of the Divine. His inclination towards a virtuous, spiritual and ethical living comes without much efforts and obedience to moral law comes instinctively. He does not have to wrestle to be ethical and spiritual, it happens very naturally. The term *harsamarsa-bhayodvegair mukto* describes the peaceful status of the devotee who feels liberated from the feelings of anger, fear, anxiety and jealousy. An individual who is settled in the tranquillity of the Self, he lives a very peaceful and balanced life. All his work conforms to the maintenance of spiritual law of the Divine. A serene joy emanates from his work, equanimity and tranquillity prevails in his overall personality. No one ever gets agitated by his words and deeds, also he himself is not agitated by others. He never injures any one in his thoughts, words and deeds. Since he feels himself reflected in others, he tries to give security and protection to other beings and also maintains his equilibrium under all circumstances. His integrity is rooted in the steadfastness of his faith and in the experiential knowledge of its realization. It is attachment to the inner Divinity that accounts for his detachment to the outward disturbances. He lives like a stalwart tree unperturbed by all kinds of storms and thunder.

The other characteristics mentioned in the verse sixteen are *anapeksah sucir daksaudasino gata-vyathah, sarvarambha-partiyagi*. The word *anapeksah* means free from all desires. A true devotee of the Lord who surrenders himself to the will of the Divine—surely becomes free from all sorts of worldly desires. He draws his happiness from the never-ending treasure within. He perfectly understands that the thirst for worldly possessions is never ending. Desires keep springing up one after the other and corrupt the thinking faculty. As *Manu Samriti* describes "*na jatu kamah kamanam upabhogna samyeti havisa Kṛṣṇavartmeva bhuya evabhivardhate"*—means desires can never be satisfied by the enjoyment of wordly objects; the desires grow more and more like the fire into which fuel is poured. A true devotee of the Lord who lives in the awareness of the Divine knows how to put a ceiling on his desires. As Tagore writes, "when desire blinds the mind with delusion and dust O thou holy one come with thy light and thunder and wake me up". The word *sucir* stands for internal and external purity. A devotee of the Lord is always pure in his thoughts, words and deeds. His lifestyle becomes a mirror into which the other people can perceive a clear reflection of the Divine. He imparts purity even to the places of his visits. The other word used here is *daksa* meaning very skilful and meticulous. The association with the Divine ensures faith, self-reliance and self-respect. It is indeed the depth of faith in the Self which is expressed in the excellency of the work. Excellency in work is a state of mind which blossoms with self-reliance and self-respect. Skill in every activity comes out naturally in a person who is settled in the Supreme-Self. It is an attitude which is inculcated and nurtured in yogic practice with devotion to one's own spiritual nature. A man of steadfast wisdom is intellectually sharp, diligent, very enthusiastic and very determined. His experience of unity with the Supreme-Self gives him satisfaction, skilfulness and perfection in each and every one of his activity. People who don't enjoy their work are surely those who have lost their conscious connections with the God in them. The separateness from inner resources results into lack of self-respect, self-reliance, self-confidence, enthusiasm and creativity in work. They become careless and sluggish in the performance of their work. They stop taking pride in their work and so the quality of their performance naturally goes down. So, in order to revive the system and to improve the quality of work, it is indeed very important to inculcate self-respect among the workers by arousing their faith in their ownself. Excellency in any performance is a clear reflection of the inner unity and connectedness to the source of life. A true devotee of the Lord knows how to explore his uniqueness and to make the best use of it. His intuitive ability helps him to search into the great order of things as they prevail in the universal mind. He understands his potentials and also knows what is expected of him at various stages of life.

The next characteristic is "*udasino*" which means mature. A man who is fully devoted to the supreme-Self is indeed dexterous, mature, impartial and very determined. He makes quick, wise and very mature decisions. Every word which he speaks comes from the steadfastness of his wisdom. Maturity is increased awareness and heightened intuition. Intuition as the word itself is self-explanatory, is education from within. It cannot be acquired from any external source, it has to be revealed from within by one's own personal effort. It is the grace of the Divine which becomes revealed in the form of inner knowledge, maturity and heightened awareness. People usually propagate that maturity comes with age, that is true to some extent; but there is a great majority of people who never become mature. Lack of maturity reflects lack of self-confidence, and lack of self-confidence reflects lack of faith in one's own self. An overall maturity in life takes place in direct proportion to the alignment with the Supreme-Self. It is not surprising to believe that maturity doesn't come with age only; it comes from inner security, when the individual is sufficiently tuned with the integral wisdom of the self. The other word which has been used by Srī Kṛṣṇa is *gata-vyathah.* A true devotee of God understands all the intrigues of life and also perfectly knows that he himself is the cause of every situation as it occurs. He does not blame others for his failures and misfortunes. He neither complains nor worries over the inevitable that hides in distant future. He rises above the trivial changes of day-to-day life. The experiential knowledge of his own immortality liberates him from all sorts of pains and fears.

The next characteristic in the same verse is *sarvarambha-parityagi.* There are many words in this compound concept. *Sarv* means all, *arambha* means which has to start, *parityaghi* means he renounces. A true devotee of the Lord is the renouncer of all the new commencements. This expression also means that he renounces the desire of starting any new project before he finishes the one in hand. He weighs every moment and every new plan in the scale of precision. He calculates very carefully the need of every project and also its benefits in all respects. He has the ability and strength to put a ceiling over all those desires and plans which are for only personal benefit. The expression *sarvarambha-parityagi* also means that a true devotee of the Lord is the one, who feels himself only an instrument in the performance of the Lord's work. He feels he is aiding his master's plan for the maintenance of the work-order. He has no personal desire for self-recognition and self-importance. He feels himself only a part of the mammoth plan which needs to be carried out during his lifetime. He considers himself only a participant in the continuation of that *yajña* which goes on in creation.

The other characteristic is *yo na hrishyati na dveshti*—he neither rejoices nor hates. A person who is firmly settled in the wisdom of the Self, becomes very enlightened and looks at every situation from an enlightened point of view. He does not get attached to the moments of high appreciation and also he is not disturbed in the moments of deep criticism. He always maintains his balance in the ups and downs of life. The other characteristic *na shochati na kankshati* means he neither grieves nor worries. Grieving over mistakes and worrying about the unknown are two very well known negative habits. A majority of people are trapped in the circular patterns of worrying. A French philosopher has written, "My life has been full of deadly misfortunes, but most of them did not happen." This clearly declares that a life becomes what one contemplates upon all day long. So, a devotee of the Lord who perpetually lives in the consciousness of the Self, becomes a controller of his mind and thinking faculty. He has the ability to check and monitor every single thought that passes through thinking faculty. He does not allow his thoughts to run riot. He understands that grieving and worrying has never helped anyone to solve any problem in life. He knows how to tap the thoughts and direct them into proper channels of useful thinking. His emotional life is guided by the awareness of the Supreme. He knows how to withdraw his attention from useless grieving, worrying, resentments and anxieties. His adjustment to the circumstances is quite spontaneous and natural. A true devotee of the Lord always moves with the flow of life. He lives in the state of perpetual fulfilment and satisfaction. His entire work span becomes an offering, dedicated to the service of the Divine and he feels himself only a humble servant of the Supreme.

He rises above all the dualities and enjoys the peaceful state of living in the unified field of perfect unity.

The other characteristic mentioned in this verse seventeen is *subhasubha-parityagi* which means the renunciation of both auspicious and inauspicious. In general, any situation becomes auspicious or inauspicious in direct proportion to the message sent out by one's own mind. A proper alignment with the Supreme-Self, makes every event in life very auspicious and the misalignment makes every event inauspicious. Every individual creates his own interpretation of the situation depending upon one's own state of mind. The individual who is firmly settled in the tranquillity of the Self, naturally becomes very peaceful and tranquil; he elevates himself from the limitations of auspicious and inauspicious. He considers nothing else sacred except what comes from the inner purity and inner wisdom. He is fully acquainted with his own abilities and perfectly knows how to work through various situations of life. He is very firm, positive, and confident in his relationship with others.

The other hallmark of a true devotee, as enumerated by Srī Kṛṣṇa, is *samah satrau ca mitre ca*—means the one who is equal to friend and foe. In general, love for one person and hatred for the other comes up when a person calculates everything from his own limited point of view. A man of steadfast wisdom, who perennially lives in the Divine consciousness, naturally looks at everybody from a totally different point of view. He feels the love and majesty of the Lord, kindness and friendliness of the Lord reflected through everyone. This is indeed very true that to like or dislike someone is a totally personal conditioned behaviour which can be completely de-conditioned by living in the awareness of the Higher-self. In the realm of deepest awareness everybody is pure and totally uncontaminated. A devotee who lives in the awareness of the Lord, he naturally becomes non-envious and perfectly secure. In the realm of the Higher-Self, wherein everything illuminates in the light of the Self, in that state of inner unity, the concept of friend and foe does not exist.

The other characteristic is indeed *tatha manapamanayoh* which means the one who is equipoised in honour and ignominy, praise and blame. A person feels honoured or dishonoured when he identifies with his body and it is his identification with ego that makes him feel happy in honour and unhappy in dishonour. Anchorage with the indwelling-Self dissolves all the boundaries of personal-self and promotes the joy of living in eternity. There is an incident from the life story of an enlightened saint, who lived in a small hut outside the town. One day someone stole his cooking pots, pans and other belongings. He went to the nearby police station to report the theft and get some help. The police-clerk was very rude to him and also wanted some bribe for writing the report. The holy man did not have any money and refused to pay. The police-clerk did not treat the holy man with any respect and also ordered him to leave. It was only after a few months, that the clerk's son became very ill. After all kinds of treatment when the child's health was deteriorating somebody suggested him to approach the holy saint who lived outside the town. The clerk who was very concerned about his son's health naturally agreed to see the holy man. As he reached the cottage of the saint, he was shocked to see that the holy saint was the same person, who had come earlier to the police station for some help. When he approached closer he felt very humiliated. He begged and requested the saint for forgiveness. On the other hand the holy man had forgotten all about it. As a matter of fact, he himself came forward to bless the police-clerk and his son for speedy recovery. The enlightened saints who are perpetually in anchorage with the Divine consciousness, they are usually very forgiving and non envious. The kindness and generosity of the Lord reflects through their words and deeds. Their interpretation of each event is very different from the ordinary, even when someone takes advantage of them or does not treat them with respect they don't take it as a personal insult. An enlightened person always interprets everything and every situation in the light of the indweller and never hangs on to the unpleasant experience of the past. He has the strength to forget and forgive. This is the unique characteristic which distinguishes him as a man of true devotion.

The other quality of the enlightened devotee is *sitosna-sukha-duhkhesu samah sanga-vivarjitah* meaning who is equipoised in heat and cold, happiness and distress, and pleasure and pain. An enlightened devotee holds equanimity in situations which arise from the pairs of opposites. It is indeed one of the most valuable blessings of the Divine. Generally people lose their balance of mind, both in success as well as in the failures. The man of wisdom understands clearly that the life flows between the opposites (pleasure and pain), touching both at the same time, that's why he maintains his balance under all circumstances. He accepts the life as it comes along. He admits and believes in the truth that there is a purpose behind each and every situation whether it is favourable or unfavourable. As the Viktor E. Frankl writes, "if there is a meaning in life at all, then there must be a meaning in suffering. Suffering is an incredible part of life even as fate and death. Without suffering and death life cannot be complete." He further writes, "no one should think that these considerations are unworldly and too far removed from real life. It is true that only a few people are capable of reaching such high moral standards." This equipoise of the enlightened devotee is called the inner awakening and inner strength that comes with the grace of the Divine. Living in the remembrance of the supreme Lord brings the experience of living in eternity, which is far above the changing phases of the material world. When the structure of inner life is transformed it naturally brings transformation in the entire outlook of the person. It gives a totally new meaning to life. The inner tranquillity of mind helps the individual to remain undisturbed in all situations and under all circumstances.

The other characteristic enumerated by Srī Kṛṣṇa in the verse nineteen is *tulya ninda stutir mauni*—means always remains balanced in blame and praise and also keeps his mind and speech under control. Maintaining quietness in honour and ignominy is indeed the most praiseworthy characteristic. As a matter of fact human mind evaluates and equates a situation as honourable or dishonourable in direct proportion to the self-created gauge of conditioned thinking. A simple remark about someone's car or house can be considered as an appreciation and also a cynical criticism at the same time. A person who is settled in the fulfilment of the Supreme-Self, he is not disturbed by the variety of remarks made by other people. As Fitzgerald has written, "the true test of a first-rate mind is the ability to hold two contradictory ideas at the same time". The quietness of speech is an austerity which is prompted by the quietness of the mind. A person who remains grounded in the quietness of transcendence, naturally stays undisturbed in all types of situations. *Mauna* literally means silence. It is not only the silence of speech; it also refers to the silence of mind. It refers to the direct control over thoughts in quantity, quality and direction. *Mauna* is an attunement with the metaphysical reality from where the flow of life receives its guidance and direction in all respects. This attunement with the source of life reflects itself in a very miraculous way, into the day-to-day activities of the individual. It manifests the beauty and the equipoise of those silent levels of consciousness, where the disturbances are far less than what one experiences at the grosser levels of awareness. About silence Gandhiji has written, "Experience has taught me that silence is a part of spiritual discipline of a votary of truth. Proneness to exaggerate, to suppress or modify the truth wittingly or unwittingly is a natural weakness of man, and silence is necessary in order to surmount it. Silence is both a physical and a spiritual necessity." He further writes, "I have observed the spiritual value of silence. The time when I could hold best communion with God, has been indeed during the time of silence (*Mauna vrata*)". *Mauna vrata* heightens the awareness and makes one receptive to the inner knowledge of the Self. *Mauni* is the one who observes silence, it stands for the enlightened devotee who has a total control over his speech and mind.

The other characteristics is *santusto yena kenacit* "means contented in all respects. Contentment is indeed a blessing of the Divine. Contentment makes life richer, broader, larger and lovable. It promotes inner wisdom, faith, courage and also longevity. Anyone who is truly contented will not develop tensions, anxieties, insecurities, fears and worries. Contentment is promoted from inner security and tranquillity. There is a famous saying "a contented person is not necessarily the one who has the best of everything; he just makes the best of whatever he has". Contentment can be recognized as inner enlightenment. In the *Mahabharta* a contented individual has been described in these honourable words—"he who is contented with what he wears, and satisfied with food he eats, and satisfied with the place where he lives, is called a *Brahmana*. Appreciating the spirit of contentment Gandhiji has written "a man falls from the pursuit of an ideal of plain living and high thinking, the moment he plans to multiply his daily wants. History gives an ample proof of this. Man's happiness really lies in contentment and also whatever is true for the individual is true for the society." A contented society is a prosperous and healthy society. When the people are at peace within themselves, they remain at peace with others also.

The next quality of an enlightened devotee is "*sthira-matir*" meaning integrated and steady. A devotee is for sure a man of steadfast wisdom. He is very determined, confident and sure of his each and every activity. Steadfastness of mind is a reward of faith in God and faith in one's own resources. For example, all the great teachers of the world like Socrates, Plato, Jesus Christ and Mahatma Gandhi have been the believers in their own thoughts. It has been the self-faith and self-reliance that gave them steadfastness of mind and power of determination. Gandhiji believed in himself and was always sure that every word, which he spoke, came from the honesty of his heart. He always believed that he worked in a copartnership with God; and whatever has been true for him must be true for others also. He always remained positive, firm and determined about his ideas because he felt that God has been working through him. A man of steadfastness becomes very familiar with the power of providence and knows how to express divine ideas through his words and deeds. His words are always very clear and influential. He is constantly aware of his goals and moves ahead with full confidence. Steadfastness, conformity and self-reliance is a great virtue and a great blessing of the Divine. In the words of Calvin Coolidge "Nothing in this world can take the place of persistence. He further adds the slogan 'press on' has solved and always will solve the problems of the human race."

Srī Kṛṣṇa concludes the characteristics in verse twenty. These thirty-nine hallmarks of a true devotee are indeed the codes of primordial Dharma. Srī Kṛṣṇa declares this to be the Dharma of mankind. Living a life in conformity to the voice of the Supreme Self is indeed living by the code of Dharma. Performing all duties with the guidance of the Supreme-Self is indeed the sustenance of Dharma. Srī Kṛṣṇa declares that anybody who is endowed with strong faith and understands the meaning of living a life which is constantly united with the consciousness of the Higher-self, he definitely knows his Dharma. Anybody who believes in this truth and has the experiential knowledge of this, has surely tasted the nectar of immortal wisdom, touching the height of *swadharma.* Srī Kṛṣṇa asserts that ardent devotion to the Supreme-Self is a highly recommended path for self-realization and God-realization. The devotional love is indeed the ultimate in spirituality. It helps the person to be initiated into a total surrender to the Divine; which brings an overall transformation in due time. Being in love with the Supreme-Self is indeed Being, Becoming and Bliss. The scriptural saying, "The Angels are lost in the perpetual contemplation of an infinite glory" is indeed the truth of devotional connectedness.

ॐ तत्सदिति श्रीमद्भगवद्गीतासूपनिषत्सु ब्रह्मविद्यायां
योगशास्त्रे श्रीकृष्णार्जुनसंवादे भक्तियोगो
नाम द्वादशोऽध्यायः ॥ १२ ॥

'Aum' tatsaditi Śrīmadbhagawadgeetā sūpaniṣatsu
brahmavidyāyām yogaśāstre Śrīkṛṣṇārjunasamvāde
bhaktiyogo nāma dvādaśo'dhyāyaḥ

'AUM TAT SAT'—Thus, in the Upanishad of the glorious Bhagawad Geeta, the science of the Brahman (Absolute) the scripture of yoga, the dialogue between Srī Kṛṣṇa and Arjuna—thus, ends the chapter twelve entitled *"Bhaktiyoga"*.

इति श्रीमद्भगवद्गीतासु द्वादशोऽध्यायः ॥ १२ ॥

Chapter Thirteen

KṢETRAKṢETRAJÑAVIBHĀGAYOGA

THE YOGA OF THE KNOWLEDGE OF THE FIELD AND THE KNOWER OF THE FIELD

श्रीभगवानुवाच

इदं शरीरं कौन्तेय क्षेत्रमित्यभिधीयते।

एतद्यो वेत्ति तं प्राहुः क्षेत्रज्ञ इति तद्विदः ॥ १ ॥

idaṁ śarīraṁ kaunteya kṣetramityabhidhīyate

etad yo vetti taṁ prāhuḥ kṣetrajña iti tadvidaḥ

The Blessed Lord said :

(1) This body O'Arjuna is called the field and he, who knows this, is called the knower of the field by the Sages.

क्षेत्रज्ञं चापि मां विद्धि सर्वक्षेत्रेषु भारत।

क्षेत्रक्षेत्रज्ञयोर्ज्ञानं यत्तज्ज्ञानं मतं मम ॥ २ ॥

kṣetrajñaṁ cāpi māṁ viddhi sarvakṣetreṣu bhārata

kṣetrakṣetrajñayor jñānaṁ yat tajjñānaṁ mataṁ mama

(2) Know Me as the knower of the field in all fields, O'Arjuna. The knowledge of the field and the knower of the field is considered to be the true knowledge by Me.

तत्क्षेत्रं यच्च यादृक्च यद्विकारि यतश्च यत्।

स च यो यत्प्रभावश्च तत्समासेन मे शृणु ॥ ३ ॥

tat kṣetraṁ yācca yādṛk ca yadvikāri yataśca yat

sa ca yo yatprabhāvaś ca tat samāsena me śṛṇu

(3) That field, what it is like, and what are its modifications and whence it is, also who is the knower of the field and what are his powers—hear all that from Me in brief.

ऋषिभिर्बहुधा गीतं छन्दोभिर्विविधैः पृथक्।
ब्रह्मसूत्रपदैश्चैव हेतुमद्भिर्विनिश्चितैः ॥४॥

ṛsibhirbahudhā gītaṁ chandobhir vividhaiḥ pṛthak
brahmasūtrapadaiś caiva hetumadbhir viniścitaiḥ

(4) The sages have sung about this very distinctively in Vedic hymns with multifold descriptions and also in the conclusive and reasoned text of the *Brahma-sutras.*

महाभूतान्यहङ्कारो बुद्धिरव्यक्तमेव च।
इन्द्रियाणि दशैकं च पञ्च चेन्द्रियगोचराः॥५॥

mahābhūtānyahaṅkāro buddhiravyaktameva ca
indriyāṇi daśaikaṁ ca pañca cendriyagocarāḥ

इच्छा द्वेषः सुखं दुःखं संघातश्चेतना धृतिः।
एतत्क्षेत्रं समासेन सविकारमुदाहृतम्॥६॥

icchā dveṣaḥ sukhaṁ duḥkhaṁ saṁghātaś cetanā dhṛtiḥ
etat kṣetraṁ samāsena savikāramudāhṛtam

(5, 6) The great elements, the ego, intellect, unmanifested primordial Nature, the ten senses, along with mind and five objects of senses. Desire, aversion, pleasure and pain, body, consciousness, fortitude—this is the field with its modifications described briefly.

Commentary—The dialogue opens with the pronoun. This body is a field, O' Arjuna. Anything which is pointed out as 'this or that' automatically separates itself from the one who is making the statement. The use of the demonstrative adjective such as *idam* in reference to the (body) *shariram* clearly indicates that the body is separate from the indwelling-soul. Srī Kṛṣṇa opens the conversation in a very dramatic style in order to draw Arjuna's attention towards the answer of the previous question which was brought forward in the beginning of chapter twelve—the question about the worship of God with attributes and without attributes. Srī Kṛṣṇa has answered it very precisely in the second and third verse of the previous chapter. He has also alerted mankind about the apparent difficulties in regard to the worship of the unmanifest, omniscient Lord. Srī Kṛṣṇa indicates that the experience of the formless, imperishable, unmanifest and all-pervading is indeed difficult as long as the embodied-self is centred in the identification of the body. The assumed affinity of 'I and Mine' blocks the channels for the subtle experience of the indwelling-self. The embodied-soul generally relates itself only to the physical body and hardly perceives any conscious connection with the unmanifest. The yogic unity with the Supreme-Soul which has been considered to be the goal of human life, is indeed very difficult to achieve until the embodied-soul consciously learns to separate itself from the physical body. The normal gestures in daily conversation such as 'my body is hurting' or I have a body-ache, or my memory is failing today, or my mind is confused, clearly indicate the separateness which exists between the 'I' and the body; but hardly anybody understands the subtle meaning of these statements. People live their entire life with the consciousness deeply rooted in the identification with the physical body.

Srī Kṛṣṇa asserts the importance of acquaintance with the Supreme-soul; which enlightens and integrates the individual in all respects. Realization and the experiential knowledge of the Supreme-soul helps the individual to separate himself from the body, mind and intellect. It is indeed the identification with the body that imprisons the embodied-self, and becomes the cause of all the painful experiences and the trivial problems of life. The studies in medical science have proved it all along that any kind of physical pain which the individual suffers, originates from the deeper layers of mind. If the patient learns to visualize his body and the indwelling-soul as the two separate fields, the treatment becomes very easy and cure becomes accessible. The medical science and research has expounded upon the truth that little children have more tolerance against deadly diseases than the adults. The recovery in case of children is usually very fast and almost sixty per cent more in comparison to the adults. The answer is very simple and straight—children, by nature, identify themselves more to the presence of the indwelling-soul than the adults. Generally children pay very little attention to a scratch, bruise, abrasion and even to a big wound, their recovery is very fast and quick.

Srī Kṛṣṇa wants Arjuna to understand and realize his identity as a fragment of the Supreme-soul, and experience the magnitude of his infinite nature. It is only human life in which a person can experience the presence of Divine within. He has subjective awareness of the Supreme-Self which makes human birth so meaningful and also a vehicle of self-realization and God-realization. It is only in human body the embodied-self can realize his infinite capacity and eligibility for salvation and liberation. A human being has the ability to make an analytical study of the material body, mind and the intellect separately. He can enhance the power of reasoning and experience for himself, the presence of God within the body as the controller, spectator, and also the Lord of the entire creation.

When a person trains himself to live as an observer of himself, he lives in a totally different world as compared to ordinary life. The moment when he separates himself from the body, he gets a chance to become acquainted with his own real nature. With this attitude the individual observes himself as a spectator, who stands apart from the play and marks most clearly its merits and demerits. As a witness of his ownself he gives himself a chance for self-analysis and self-improvement. He realizes the essential truth that I am separate from the body and I am the *Brahman*. The day when a person experiences this prime secret, his real education begins. He progresses both psychologically and spiritually, and an overall transformation takes place. His life becomes very easy and effortless and success follows him in every sphere of life. In the moments of self-unfoldment one wakes up to the totality of new reality and all his fears of being tyrannized by others or being enslaved and overpowered by others vanish instantly.

There is a story from ancient scriptures. Once a demon caught hold of a man and started tyrannizing him. The demon made the poor man work without giving any rest. Any moment when the man stopped working even for a minute the demon threatened him, "I will kill you and destroy you if you ever stopped working". The terrified man worked ceaselessly for months and finally could not stand the threat any more. He gathered his courage and said "O.K. you can kill me, and eat me if you like but I cannot work like this". The poor man who was frustrated and tired, finally realized the truth that the demon will not eat him because he needed a servant and if the servant is destroyed, who will do his work? So with his reply "O.K. destroy me," the tyrant power of the demon came to an end. With the revelation of essential truth that I am not this body, the individual starts living a life, which is consciously connected with the indweller. He lives in the awareness of the imperishable working in a co-partnership with His majesty. Socrates, the great philosopher of Greece, was well acquainted with this ultimate truth and did explain to his followers at the time of his death. The night before when he was to be sentenced to death, he explained to his followers "this body is very old and close to the time to be perished with age. What heroism and valour they are showing the others by trying to destroy it with poison. This body is indeed perishable and mortal. I am not this body. I am the one who is witnessing the entire play." He also added "know thyself and you are free, immortal and imperishable". Srī Kṛṣṇa emphasizes in the very first verse of this chapter that the one who understands and beholds the body as a separate entity from himself, he is called the man of wisdom and the knower of true knowledge. In order to awaken Arjuna to the meaning of *Tat tvam asi* (you are indeed the Self), Srī Kṛṣṇa opens the conversation with the words *idam sariram*—this body.

As noticed, the other significant word in the first verse is *ksetra* meaning a field. *Idam sariram kaunteya ksetram ity abhidhiyate*—means this body O'son of Kunti is a field. The modern physicist describes the field as an abstraction which expresses the influences of the forces of nature. According to a physicist everything in the universe expresses itself in some kind of field. There are many fields of forces such as the gravitational field, the electromagnetic field and the quantum field. Any type of force becomes manifested through a field only. So the field can be described as an abstraction which takes any form and shape in respect to cause, effect and time. The word field which the modern physicist is using to describe the most well known forces of nature has been used by Srī Kṛṣṇa in relation to the forces which express themselves through the bodies of all beings. Each body is an expression of the force of thoughts, memories and latencies.

The physical body is a field which is a manifestation of the forces of the mind, intellect and ego. When Einstein was trying to describe the unified field from where all other fields draw their power, he wrote, "My religion consists of a humble admiration of the illimitable, superior spirit who reveals Himself in the slightest detail we are able to perceive with our frail and feeble mind". While using the word field for the body, Srī Kṛṣṇa intends to enlighten Arjuna about the condition in nature which has the potential of producing a force which is called the field.

People generally wonder at the phenomenon of life as from where it emerges and into what it goes? What is destiny? Why there is so much disparity among human beings in relation to looks, intelligence, capabilities and potentialities? Why there are so many different species and from where do they come? The uniqueness of every individual is really mind boggling. Medical science has confirmed that the body of every individual is formed with a combination of forty-eight chromosomes one receives from both the parents. These forty-eight chromosomes from the mother and father practically comprise the heredity of an individual. Still although born from the same parents, all the brothers and sisters are very different from one another. A scientific fact which the science of genetics is bringing to the attention of modern scientists has been explained by Srī Kṛṣṇa. He illustrates very clearly why each individual is so unique and so different in his likings, dislikings, attitude and intelligence, and also what is destiny? Srī Kṛṣṇa gives answer to all these questions in verses five and six. He presents a detailed description of the field. Srī Kṛṣṇa explains that physical, psychological and causal bodies constitute the totality of the field. The great elements—such as ether, air, water, fire and earth—constitute the entire material world and the physical human body which is also called the gross body. The gross body is a field of expression of the invisible forces of the subtle body. The egoism, intellect, mind, the ten senses and the five objects of senses constitute the totality of the subtle body. When the embodied-self identifies with 'I and Mine' it is called ego, when it identifies with *sankalpa and vikalpa* it is called the mind, and when it identifies with the faculty of reason and discrimination it is called the intellect. The word

Avyakatam stands for the unmanifested primordial Nature which has been called the *Mahad Brahma.* "*Indriyani desaikam ca*" refers to the five senses of perception such as seeing, hearing, tasting, touching and smelling. The five senses of action are feet, hands, organs of reproduction and organs of defecation for eliminating waste from the body. The word "*panca Cendriyagocarah*" denotes the objects of the senses manifesting as matter on which the senses thrive. These are the fivefold pastures of the senses perceived through sight, touch, smell, hearing and tasting. This aggregate of twenty-three with the consciousness as the twenty-fourth constitutes the totality of the body both at the subtle and the gross levels. These are the famous twenty-four *tattavas* as described in the *Samkhya* philosophy. The subtle body is constituted of thoughts, memories latencies and *samskaras,* those find their expression into the field of gross body. The thoughts and memories are transformed into *samskaras* and the *samskaras* give shape to *karmas*; the *karmas* are expressed as destiny. Since the urges, desires and thoughts of people are very different from one another, that's why the destiny of each person is different. The body is only an expression of some thoughts and some memories, stored within the very core of the embodied-self.

Subtle body is a field of all kinds of information from the present and many previous lives. This information is stored in the form of memories and thoughts. Each individual is different because of his own personal data which he records and stores in the field of information and manifests through the physical body. Every single thought that flashes through the mind is duly recorded and stored in the field of information and expressed in so many different ways by the individual. Every type of discomfort or comfort, which the body expresses, comes from the reservoir of latencies and memories of the past and present. The recorded data in mind gives shape to all the activities of daily life. It fosters desires, fears and all kinds of dreams. It augments all passions, hopes, cravings, doubts, delusions and ignorance. The thoughts, ideas and memories can be perceived and experienced as vibrations in the informational field of the subtle body and actually seen manifested as anger, depression, heart attack, pain in the stomach, headache and other diseases of the physical body.

Every expression in physical body has its roots hidden in the data of the subtle body. Mind and body connection are indeed very strong. Most of our discomforts, conflicts and diseases are manifestations of our impious, bitter, jealous, insecure and unhealthy thoughts. People energize their bodies with virtuous thoughts and definitely contaminate their bodies with vicious thoughts. Any thought which is perceived to be conflicting and against the voice of the indweller, that is definitely harmful for the physical body.

From this, it becomes quite clear that the memories, latencies and *samskaras* are the cause of all that which becomes manifested in the physical body. The gross body is a field which expresses the influences of the subtle body (mind). It takes form and shape in respect of the cause and effect. For example, if one closely observes the entire span of life until today one can realize that the entire life is only a bundle of memories. Every single moment of life is transformed into a memory. Last year, last week, yesterday and till last few hours of even today, every moment has been transformed into some kind of memory and *samskara*. All those years of great joy, the most cherished moments of life, the most difficult sufferings, every minute has changed into some latencies which have been duly recorded and saved in the field of subtle body. The entire life is only a series of thoughts flashing, passing, and being constantly stored in the memory bank. In simple language it can be described "the way we sow the way we reap" just as the seed sown in a field yields the corresponding type of crop in due time, similarly the seeds planted in the form of thoughts take shape into actions and yield their fruits in due time. The entire life is a vast field of action and also revolves around the wheel of memories and *samskaras*. No one can escape the law of *karmas*. People reward and punish themselves because of their own *karmas*. The hidden latencies in the subtle body motivate the entire range of activities. The old pattern of thoughts direct and determine the direction for new patterns and thus the individual keeps revolving around the wheel of his own *karmas*. The hidden thoughts keep coming to the conscious surface of the mind and motivate actions of present life in all respects. Each and every person punishes or rewards himself because of the law of cause and effect.

There is a true incident that relates this truth. Once there lived a rich man who had two sons. After his death his entire estate was equally given to both the sons. After a few years the younger brother died leaving his young widow behind. One evening the older brother went to her house and killed his sister-in-law. At night he wrapped the body and dumped it in the nearby deserted well. Nobody suspected anything and naturally he escaped punishment. Later on, he decided to leave the village for some time and went to another place. There he started his own business. One day while he was driving back home he noticed a young lady crying for help on the road side. He parked his car and rushed to help her. As he approached her and gave her some water to drink, she opened her eyes for a few minutes but died instantly. Other people gathered around the dead body and called the police. After going through all investigations the police arrested the young man. After many trials the law declared death penalty for him. The day when authorities were going to put him in electric chair he was asked for the last wish. He cried and said I surely want to tell the entire world that nobody can ever escape punishment for his own vicious and criminal deeds. No matter where one goes, the guilt and crime accompanies the individual and punishment comes in due time. He further added, believe me, I have not killed this woman but this punishment indeed is justified because I had killed another woman, a few years ago and had escaped punishment at that time. The law of *karma* is indeed very powerful. The ultimate truth is, 'the way we sow the way we reap'. Every one is bound in the cycle of cause and effect. Each and every activity which the individual performs has its origin in the impressions of the past. In the words of Swami Sivananda, "If the individual does evil actions, he sows the seeds of sin, manures with evil and reaps a crop of sin. He undergoes the pain of *samsara* viz. birth, decay, old age, sickness and the three kinds of afflictions. If he does virtuous actions, he sows the good seeds of virtue and reaps the crop of happiness".

In vedic terminology, the subtle body is called the '*Manomayakosha*' meaning the store house of thoughts. It has the predominance of mind. The gross body is called the *Annamayakosha. Anna* means the grain and *kosha* means the storage. It has the predominance of food which sustains the physical body. These fields are also called the *sarira*. The word *sarira* comes from the root word *srīhimsayam* which means cover or sheath. These fields are the bodies, covers or the sheaths of the embodied self. There are two reasons why the body has been called a field or *ksetra*. The root word of *ksetra* is *ksi* which means decays and undergoes constant changes. In physical body the old cells are dying and being replaced by the new ones. In subtle body the thoughts and ideas are constantly flashing, splitting and giving shape to new ideas. Srī Kṛṣṇa enlightens Arjuna about the fact that the *ksetra* (the body) which undergoes constant change and modifications is quite separate from the *Ksetrajña* (the knower of the body). In the second verse of this chapter Srī Kṛṣṇa declares "Know me as *Ksetrajña* in all the *Ksetras*"—understand Me as the knower of the field in all the fields. He further adds that the one who understands this mystery is considered to be the man of true knowledge and wisdom. Whereas in chapter two, Srī Kṛṣṇa has explained to Arjuna about immortality of the soul, in this chapter the same truth has been repeated in these words—those who know the reality of this body as a field and the one who sustains this body as the knower of the field he is called a man of wisdom. The demonstrative pronoun *sah* in verse three refers to the *ksetrajña* and His glory. In the fourth verse Srī Kṛṣṇa expresses His deep appreciation for all those vedic scholars and the authors of *Brahmasutras* who have highly expounded upon the glory of *Ksetrajña*. The words of these hymns are highly convincing, decisive, alluring, fascinating and heart captivating. The precision of expression is totally remarkable. *Brahmasutras* have also been called *Sariraka Sutras* because a part of these scriptures deal with *sarira* the *ksetra* as a field. The real nature of the field and the knower of the field as described in these books is totally phenomenal. In the words of Swami Chidbhavanananda, "the knower of the field is the innermost Self in all beings. The individual-soul and the universe have no independent existence. Therefore Lord Himself is the *Ksetrajña* in all the *Ksetras*.

The supreme Lord is the proprietor of all fields. He pervades in all fields and sustains them. He is the inner dweller who shines through every atom of the field. His powers are infinite. It is indeed very important for every individual to understand the relationship between the field and the knower of the field. In the forthcoming verses Srī Kṛṣṇa unfolds many mysteries about the nature of various fields. He explains the inter-connectedness of the fields and how each one is sustained and energized by the knower of the field. The expression '*Yatasca yat*' conveys the intention of Srī Kṛṣṇa about his special emphasis upon the origin of all fields wherein lies the destiny of all beings. The emphasized idea in these verses is to know, to experience and to understand the magnificence of the knower of the field who dwells in all bodies. The most rewarding aspect of spiritual advancement is surely actualized when the individual is capable of separating the Self from the mind, body and the intellect. *Na mai deha, Na mai deha ke Dharma, na mai prana na indriyas karma, na mai mana budhi chitha ahankara, gunatita mai ina sai nayara*—which means I am not this body, nor its rituals. I am not the prana (the vital breath) nor the sensory organs. I am neither the mind nor the intellect and egoism. I am the One who witnesses the play of all.

अमानित्वमदम्भित्वमहिंसा क्षान्तिरार्जवम् ।
आचार्योपासनं शौचं स्थैर्यमात्मविनिग्रहः ॥ ७ ॥

amānitvamadambhitvamahiṁsā kṣāntirārjavam
ācāryopāsanaṁ śaucaṁ sthairyamātmavinigrahaḥ

इन्द्रियार्थेषु वैराग्यमनहङ्कार एव च ।
जन्ममृत्युजराव्याधिदुःखदोषानुदर्शनम् ॥ ८ ॥

indriyārtheṣu vairāgyamanahaṅkāra eva ca
janmamṛtyujarāvyadhiduḥkhadoṣānudarśanam

(7, 8) Absence of vanity, unpretentiousness, non-violence, forbearance, uprightness, service to the teacher, purity, steadfastness and self-control. Dispassion towards the objects of the senses, absence of egoism, perception of misery and evil, inherent in birth, death, old age and disease.

असक्तिरनभिष्वङ्गः पुत्रदारगृहादिषु ।
नित्यं च समचित्तत्वमिष्टानिष्टोपपत्तिषु ॥ ९ ॥

asaktiranabhiṣvaṅgaḥ putradāragṛhādiṣu
nityam ca samacittatvam iṣṭāniṣṭopapattiṣu

मयि चानन्ययोगेन भक्तिरव्यभिचारिणी ।
विविक्तदेशसेवित्वमरतिर्जनसंसदि ॥ १० ॥

mayi cānanyayogena bhaktiravyabhicāriṇī
viviktadeśasevitvamaratir janasaṅsadi

(9, 10) Non-attachment and the attitude of non-possessiveness towards son, wife, home and others. Perennial equal-mindedness on the attainment of all desirable and the undesirable. An undivided devotion for Me through Yoga of contemplation. Resort to solitary places and avoidance from the mass of people.

अध्यात्मज्ञाननित्यत्वं तत्त्वज्ञानार्थदर्शनम् ।
एतज्ज्ञानमिति प्रोक्तमज्ञानं यदतोऽन्यथा ॥ ११ ॥

adhyātmajñānanityatvaṁ tattvajñānārthadarśanam
etajjñānamiti proktamajñānaṁ yadato'nyathā

(11) Steadfastness in the knowledge of the Self, clear perception of the aim of true knowledge—All this is declared to be the knowledge and whatever opposed to this is called ignorance.

Commentary—In these verses, Srī Kṛṣṇa enlightens Arjuna about that knowledge which is conducive to self-realization and God-realization. This knowledge helps the individual to understand the difference between the field and the knower of the field. He presents an elaborate, systematic description of the moral practices those are helpful in spiritual awakening and also in living a harmonious peaceful life. These ascetic qualities are the characteristics of a person who becomes tuned to the integral wisdom of the Self. He opens the conversation with the words *amanitvam* and *adambhitvam* meaning the total absence of egoism and hypocrisy. It is also called the attitude of humility which is the negation of egocentric thoughts and vanity. True humility means being humble and receptive to the voice of the indwelling spirit. Humility combines veneration with receptivity. The attitude of humility does bless the individual with self-understanding, inner-growth and psychological and physical strength. It helps the individual to rise above the narrow boundaries of egocentric thoughts and actually experience the presence of the Divine within. It prepares the individual for a total surrender to the Supreme-Soul. When the person yields himself to the grace of the indwelling-God, he becomes a channel of the cosmic power for others. As Jesus has said, 'Blessed are the meek, for they shall inherit the earth'. The attitude of humility brings with it the total absence of the hypocrisy. A person who is humble and polite, who is totally surrendered to the Lord, he does not need to advertise anything about his penances and ascetic virtuous qualities because he considers all virtues to be the expressions of the nature of the Lord Himself. He is free from false vanities, show off and pedantry.

The other spiritual discipline which is mentioned in this verse is non-violence. The attitude of non-violence promotes love and honesty in thoughts, words and deeds. Non-violence literally means *manasa vachya karmana* i.e. do not hurt others by thought, word and deed. For example, harbouring harmful thoughts against others is surely violence, abusing others is violence, using harsh annoying and unpleasant words in conversation is violence and inflicting physical injury on others is indeed violence. The total absence of violence is definitely an ascetic discipline. It is a training which is inculcated by constant vigilance over the thinking faculty. It is an education that gradually disciplines the person for living in total harmony with the inner-self and with others. In the words of Gandhiji "I have applied the principle of non-violence in almost every walk of life—domestic, institutional, economic and political. I know of no single case in which it has failed. The rishis, who discovered the law of non-violence in the midst of violence, were greater geniuses than Newton. They were themselves greater warriors than Wellington. Having themselves known the use of arms, they realized their uselessness, and taught a weary world that its salvation lay not through violence but through non-violence." Attitude of non-violence initiates the person to obey the law of Higher-Self, and promotes his inner-strength. Non-violence is indeed the summit of conscious connectedness with the indweller.

The attitude of forgiveness, forbearance and tolerance gives the individual a deep spiritual insight. It gives one the opportunity to assess and judge every situation and every person in the light of the self. It marks the basis of self-understanding and at the same time understanding of others. The virtue of patience makes the person very strong, confident and determined. The man of forbearance puts up with everything. He never retaliates because he is very secure and tranquil himself. He understands the shortcomings of others and actually helps them to improve in all respects. The next virtue as mentioned in this verse is *arjavam* which means straightforwardness and honesty. Uprightness and honesty is very natural and spontaneous to a person who is centred in self-awareness. Proper respect and service to the teacher has been also emphasized earlier in the thirty-fourth verse of the fourth chapter. Proper respect to the preceptor is an act of spiritual discipline, which is necessary for the attainment of self-realization. Reverence for the teacher is inspired from the attitude of humility and total negation of ego. It is a well-known truth that the person who thinks he knows everything about the subject, he immediately closes all the doors of learning for himself. Without humility no one can make any progress towards the quest of self-realization. The aspirant who approaches the teacher with the simplicity of a child with guileless heart, he wins the attention of his teacher and becomes blessed.

The other austerity which Srī Kṛṣṇa brings to Arjuna's attention is the *saucam* i.e. the internal and external cleanliness and purity which is essential for spiritual advancement. Since every individual is connected with others at home, in community and in society, personal cleanliness and hygiene becomes almost mandatory for everyone. The personal hygiene of each individual interacts with the well-being of the other. The personal cleanliness at the individual level is an expression of self-respect and inner unity. The external purity surely reflects internal purity which takes place by constant connectedness with the source of life. The inner piety and purity of thought reflects itself in fair and clean dealings with others. The virtue of steadfastness has been mentioned next in the sequence of disciplinary practices. Steadfastness is an austerity that reflects the person's strong faith in the Self. It reflects self-confidence, self-respect and self-reliance.

Steadfastness means the consistency of all efforts to the realization of the goal.

The next ascetic practice recommended in the verse is *atmavinigrahah*—self-restraint practised at various levels of mind and body. Self-discipline is the key that opens the doorway to a respectable and dignified life-style; and also to the realization of the God within. In order to inculcate the values of orderliness in life the ancient sages of vedic times have suggested to divide the total life span of hundred years into four stages. First twenty-five years are expected to be devoted to learning and education. During this period the student is expected to stay *brahmachri* meaning to practice celibacy and live a very simple and truthful life. The second stage is the *Grhastha Ashrama*—this period starts from the age of twenty-five and goes on up to fifty. During these years the individual is expected to be married and raise a good family. He should follow the ethical means of making money and make the very best use of his abilities in all respects. The third stage is *Vanaprasta* which starts at the age of fifty, when the individual should gradually detach himself from worldly life and take time for the inward journey. The fourth stage is *Sanyasa* which tentatively starts at the age of seventy-five. This is the period of life when the individual is expected to get involved in some kind of volunteering work as a service to the Divine. During these years the maximum time is devoted to meditation, self-study, self-realization and God-realization. In these last twenty-five years of life the individual is expected to prepare himself for liberation in the present life time and in the life hereafter. In these verses Srī Kṛṣṇa enlightens Arjuna very systematically about the necessity of practising various disciplinary penances. These ethical values help the individual to live a peaceful and prosperous life and also prepares him for the attainment of spiritual knowledge. The person who practises self-control, celibacy, simplicity, honesty, straightforwardness, purity and humility in the early years of his life, definitely becomes very balanced and one-pointed towards the achievement of the final goal. He has the strength and wisdom to create a prosperous life style at a certain stage of life and also has the insight to retire from the servitude of the finite comforts. Such an awakened individual is surely led into the state of inner detachment from the grace within. He does not have to make any special effort for concentration and meditation on the Divine; it comes to him very naturally. When the heart finds its comfort within and rejoices in the unity with the indweller, the concentration on the Self takes place effortlessly.

Starting from the practice of living a life with total absence of egoism upto the point when the mind totally merges in the Supreme Self, Srī Kṛṣṇa outlines the essentials of true knowledge which gives the insight for self-analysis, self-scrutiny, self-realization and a desire for self-improvement. It brings orderliness in life and re-orients the individual to the clarity of the goal in life with inner poise and equanimity. The true knowledge as described in these verses is the means for bringing orderliness, discipline and asceticism in life. It educates the individual at the various levels of his personality. In verse eleven, Srī Kṛṣṇa makes it very clear in these words *adhyatma-jñanityatvam tattvajñarthadarsanam*—by living a life in accordance with true knowledge a person gets a chance to know more about himself, and in due time he becomes an eligible candidate for the experience of the Ultimate truth.

ज्ञेयं यत्तत् प्रवक्ष्यामि यज्ज्ञात्वामृतमश्नुते।
अनादिमत्परं ब्रह्म न सत्तन्नासदुच्यते॥ १२॥

jñeyaṁ yat tat pravakṣyāmi yaj jñātvāmṛtamaśnute
anādimat paraṁ brahma na sat tannāsad ucyate

(12) I shall tell you that which has to be known, and by knowing which one attains immortality; the beginningless Supreme Brahman, which is called neither existent *(sat)* nor non-existent *(asat).*

सर्वतः पाणिपादं तत्सर्वतोऽक्षिशिरोमुखम्।
सर्वतः श्रुतिमल्लोके सर्वमावृत्य तिष्ठति॥ १३॥

sarvataḥ pāṇipādaṁ tat sarvato'kṣiśiromukham
sarvataḥśrutimalloke sarvamāvṛtya tiṣṭhati

(13) With hands and feet everywhere, with eyes, heads and face on all sides, with ears everywhere He pervades in the worlds enveloping everything.

सर्वेन्द्रियगुणाभासं सर्वेन्द्रियविवर्जितम् ।
असक्तं सर्वभृच्चैव निर्गुणं गुणभोक्तृ च ॥ १४ ॥

sarvendriyaguṇābhāsaṁ sarvendriyavivarjitam
asaktaṁ sarvabhṛccaiva nirguṇaṁ guṇabhoktṛ ca

(14) Perceived through the functions of senses, yet devoid of all senses; unattached yet sustaining all; transcends the qualities of nature yet their experiencer.

बहिरन्तश्च भूतानामचरं चरमेव च ।
सूक्ष्मत्वात्तदविज्ञेयं दूरस्थं चान्तिके च तत् ॥ १५ ॥

bahirantaś ca bhūtānāmacaraṁ carameva ca
sūkṣmatvāt tad avijñeyaṁ dūrasthaṁ cāntike ca tat

(15) Exists without and within all beings, the unmoving and also the moving. Extremely subtle and incomprehensible; very far away and yet so near is That.

अविभक्तं च भूतेषु विभक्तमिव च स्थितम् ।
भूतभर्तृ च तज्ज्ञेयं ग्रसिष्णु प्रभविष्णु च ॥ १६ ॥

avibhaktaṁ ca bhūteṣu vibhaktamiva ca sthitam
bhūtabhartṛ ca tajjñeyaṁ grasiṣṇu prabhaviṣṇu ca

(16) The 'One' which is undivided yet exists as if divided in all beings; known as the sustainer of all beings, and also the devourer and the creator.

ज्योतिषामपि तज्ज्योतिस्तमसः परमुच्यते ।
ज्ञानं ज्ञेयं ज्ञानगम्यं हृदि सर्वस्य विष्ठितम् ॥ १७ ॥

jyotiṣāmapi tajjyotis tamasaḥ param ucyate
jñānaṁ jñeyaṁ jñānagamyaṁ hṛdi sarvasya viṣṭhitam

(17) That, the Light of all lights, is said to be beyond darkness: The knowledge, the object of knowledge, as well as the goal of knowledge is seated in the hearts of all.

इति क्षेत्रं तथा ज्ञानं ज्ञेयं चोक्तं समासतः ।
मद्भक्त एतद्विज्ञाय मद्भावायोपपद्यते ॥ १८ ॥

iti kṣetraṁ tathā jñānaṁ jñeyaṁ coktaṁ samāsataḥ
madbhakta etad vijñāya madbhāvāyopapadyate

(18) Thus the field, the knowledge and the knowable have been illustrated briefly. My devotee who understands all this, he enters into My being.

Commentary—In these verses, Srī Kṛṣṇa draws Arjuna's attention towards the knower of the fields and explains the importance of being consciously engaged in the awareness of that supreme soul. Srī Kṛṣṇa calls that power the Supreme *Brahman,* the absolute, the beginningless which is far above *sat* and *asat*—real and unreal, existent and nonexistent. In the words of Swami Ramsukhdas, "He cannot be called existent because something can be existent in relativity with something else which is non-existent. The term day is used only in relativity with the night, but if there is no night, the day cannot be called the day. The Lord cannot be called non-existent because He surely exists everywhere." Relativity is the law that fundamentally underlies everything in the physical world, the events and things become known in relation to something else. Every tentative explanation is an approach to the revelation of the relative truth and not the final conclusion. Everything in the universe is going through a constant reinterpretation. The concept of relativity declares for sure, that one should aim at looking into the truth for himself and not to accept everything based upon the inherited habits of perceptual thinking about the world. Srī Kṛṣṇa wants Arjuna to pursue the validity of the knower of the field and become introduced with that. He wants Arjuna to be awakened from the systematic self-deceptive logical explanation and engage into the subtlest adventure of experiencing the one beyond the boundaries of existent and non-existent. The *sat* and *asat* is determined by the intellect. The *para Brahman* is beyond and above the boundaries of mind, speech and intellect. That power is indeed inexplicable and far above the relative terms such as existent and non-existent, manifested and unmanifested. The Supreme consciousness transcends all the levels of personal experiences; words cannot describe that and the sense of perception cannot experience that. In the words of Swami Sivananda, "It is one without a second.

It is not the object of senses. It is beyond the reach of mind and the senses. It is actionless. It is the great transcendental and unmanifested absolute. It is always the witnessing subject in all objects".

The absolute Brahman pervades the entire creation. His hands and feet are everywhere, his eyes and faces are in all directions. He exists in the world enveloping everything. A hymn in *Rig Veda* gives the same type of description of the cosmic supreme soul. "*Vishvata caakshurta vishvato mukho, vishvato bahurat vishav taspata. Sa Bhabubhyam dhamti sampatre dhawabhumi jananya deva Eka*"—means all around are the eyes, mouths and feet of that Paramatma deva, the creator of the universe. *Shruti Bhagwati* has also given a similar description *Sahasra-sirsa Purushah Sahasraksah Sahasra-pat Sa bhumin, visvato vrtva aty atisthad dasangulam*—means thousand heads, thousand eyes, thousand feet envelopes the entire earth, surrounding the universe on all sides; stands only within the breadth of ten fingers. Srī Kṛṣṇa explains to Arjuna how the life force manifests through everything, which can be seen with eyes, touched, tasted and experienced through other senses. The knower of the field is indeed the energizer and the experiencer of all the sense objects, but still remains detached and aloof as a silent witness. The super power can be experienced by everyone through the functions of the sensory organs and still transcends everything. The world is created, maintained and sustained by that power still that acts only as a witness.

The Supreme power exists diffusing its abundance in everything, that which is within the boundaries of perception and in everything which is beyond that. In the words of Swami Prabhupada, there are unlimited heads, legs, hands and eyes and unlimited living entities. All are existing in and on the Supreme-Soul. Therefore the Supreme-Soul is all-pervading. *Kathopanisad* gives a beautiful description "*Asino duram vrajati sayano yati sarvatah*" resides in all directions far and wide, although apparently lying on a seat, goes everywhere. Although perpetually absorbed in transcendental bliss still engaged everywhere. Srī Kṛṣṇa describes the Supreme-Self as "*Suksmatvat tad avijneyam*"—extremely subtle and beyond the comprehension of senses. The subtlety of the Supreme-Soul is totally incomprehensible by human mind and intellect. Although that power appears to be divided among creatures, still it is undivided. The appropriate analogy which can be given in this respect is that of the hologram; in which any piece separated from the hologram carries with it the totality of the object. In the language of the modern era the super-soul can be described as an holographic entity. The cosmic-soul is the omnipotent substratum from where plurality of the world is projected. The Supreme power individualizes itself as individual manifestations wherever the mediums are made available. Everything in the world appears through the medium of the Lord, is sustained and maintained by the Lord and eventually goes back into the Lord. Everything rests in His omnipotent majesty and after the cosmic annihilation, it rests in Him again.

In the description of the glories of the Supreme-Soul Srī Kṛṣṇa says "light of all lights, He is said to be beyond darkness. He is knowledge, the object of knowledge and also the goal of all knowledge. Although the Lord is present everywhere, He can be perceived as seated in the hearts of everyone." Srī Kṛṣṇa regards the experiential knowledge of the Absolute Divinity, to be the goal of entire learning; because when the individual perceives the essentiality of that, there remains nothing else to be known. The same description occurs in dialogue between Rishi Udalaka and his son Savetaketu in *Chhandogyopanisad*—"Do you know, by knowing which everything else is known". The entire learning of the world is immaterial, unless one experiences the absolute truth of the transcendental Supreme Soul. Just as by analyzing the components of only one drop of water, the quality of the entire water reservoir becomes known, similarly by contacting the Supreme-Soul within one's ownself everything else in the universe becomes known. As noticed in everyday life, that practically all kinds of learning is initiated by the self, enhanced by the self, and also accomplished by the self. In the process of any inquiry, at first the individual becomes acquainted with one's own nature, then the nature of the Supreme-Self and eventually the nature of everything and everybody else around. Knowing God and knowing a friend or a son or daughter may appear different on surface but all of them are known only through the study of the Self. Self-realization which transcends the conditioned experiences gradually becomes the spiritual endeavour. It is only with the experiential knowledge of the Lord within, that all other experiences of life become meaningful; and all the staggering notions of the absolute truth become intelligible and vividly clear.

Srī Kṛṣṇa declares the heart to be the dwelling place of the Supreme-Self in body. *Vedas* and *Upanisads* have also indicated that the Supreme-Soul is seated in everyone's heart. The *Kathopanisad* says, "*Angustham atrah puruso ntaratma sada jananam hrdaye samnivistah"*—About the size of a thumb the omnipresent God ever dwells within the heart. The supreme power can be directly experienced in a very intimate relationship at the heart centre. In ancient scriptures of India as well as in other religious traditions of the world, concentration on the heart centre has been highly emphasized. The heart centre is also known as the *anahat chakra* in yogic terminology. A detailed description of the various *chakras* (the psychic stations) have been discussed in the previous chapters. It is from the *anahat chakra*, the primordial sound of *Aum* can be heard very clearly and vividly. In meditation session, as the individual concentrates deeply into the silent realms of the heart, the sound of *Aum* becomes very clear and alluring. It is in meditation on the sound of *Aum*, one experiences the presence of the Supreme-Soul. As awareness becomes settled into the sound of the eternal *nada,* the individual contacts the Supreme Divinity very vividly and positively. Jesus has also written, "discover the Lord in your heart and then in the heart of thy neighbour". It is at the heart centre, the act of purification starts and the spirit of surrender takes place. It is at the heart centre where the love for the Lord is awakened and the presence of the Divine is personally experienced. Concentration at heart between the two breasts at the focal point of *anahat chakra* enables the person to pierce through the mask of mind, intellect and body and awaken the indweller *(Antharyami)* who is lodged in the very centre of the being. The ancient scriptures describe (heart centre) *anahat chakra* as the twelve petalled lotus, with two inter-laced triangles. One triangle that points upward symbolizes higher awareness; the triangle pointing downward represents worldly awareness and involvement in the material world.

The contemplation and meditation at the heart centre is a very rewarding experience in spiritual pursuit. St. Marcus has described this in these words, "when grace possesses the ranges of the heart, it rules over all the members of the thoughts. For there in the heart, is the mind and all the thoughts—within the heart are unfathomable depths. The Lord dwells within it in His kingdom there." In *Upanisads* the heart centre has been called the *Guha (Hriday-guha)* which means the cave of the heart and also *Pundarika* meaning the lotus of the heart. *Hriday-akash* means the space in the heart where the indweller *(Antharayami)* resides. There is a description in *Kathopanisad*—difficult to perceive, hidden in the depth of the heart is the *atman*—the inner self of all, the only controller. There are several other hymns in *Vedas*, those describe the temple of the heart, the shrine in the form of lotus and the innermost cave of the heart. It is strongly believed in almost all religious traditions that it is at the heart centre where the man is remade. It is by meditating at the heart centre the individual is awakened to the Divinity within. When the person is awakened, the Supreme power radiates from him in the form of charismatic warmth, love and compassion. Such an individual becomes very sensitive to the needs of other people and the purity of Divine love emanates from his personality. The other people feel drawn to his awakened shrine and he becomes a channel of sharing divine love with others. The *Upanisads* have described *hridyantar jyothi* which means that the Lord is experienced as light at the heart centre. This light represents the Divine Self, radiant and magnificent. The light of life can be actually visualized and experienced vividly at the heart centre. This is indeed a very powerful psychic station for integrating the psychic energy. The experience of connectedness at the heart centre is considered to be the most valuable accomplishment in spiritual journey. In the beginning of the meditation session one starts the practice by concentration on the sound of *Aum* or any other mantra. The aspirant is suggested to concentrate at the *hridaya akasha*—the space between the two breasts. In meditation the individual perceives from within that the beat of his heart and the sound of *Aum* have started merging into one another. Gradually the mind also joins the sound and the individual feels settled in the cave of the heart.

There is a beautiful poem written by Rabindranath Tagore in relation to this rich experience of the Self within. "It is the most distant course that comes nearest to thyself, and that training is the most intricate which leads to the utter simplicity of a tune. The traveller has to knock at every alien door to come to his own, and one has to wander through all the outer worlds to reach the innermost shrine at the end. My eyes strayed far and wide before I shut them and said "Here art thou!" It is for sure a well known truth as proclaimed by the learned sages that the person who has trained himself to live a life in consciousness of the indweller for him God surely resides in the temple of the heart while for others he is very far away. The joy of the inner peace, the sublime ecstasy of the Divine love, the intensity of the self-absorption is known only to those who have experienced the presence of the Supreme in *hridaya kosha.* In verse eighteen, Srī Kṛṣṇa tells Arjuna that the person who understands the field and the knower of the field, as two separate entities, he definitely enters into My state of being. The aspirant who takes refuge in the Lord with intellectual apprehension of the truth, coupled with proper insight and devotion, he surely attains liberation. The person who can comprehend and visualize the light of the Supreme-Soul in his own heart and then the same light in all other fields of the universe, he definitely enters into the essentiality of the Supreme Lord. He transcends the material world and rises above the boundaries of cause, effect, space and time.

प्रकृतिं पुरुषं चैव विद्ध्यनादी उभावपि।
विकारांश्च गुणांश्चैव विद्धि प्रकृतिसम्भवान्॥ १९॥

prakṛtiṁ puruṣaṁ caiva viddhyanādī ubhāvapi
vikārānś ca guṇānś caiva viddhi prakṛtisambhavān

(19) Know that the Prakriti (Nature) and Purusha (Spirit) are both beginningless; and also understand that all modifications and the qualities are born of Nature.

कार्यकरणकर्तृत्वे हेतुः प्रकृतिरुच्यते।
पुरुषः सुखदुःखानां भोक्तृत्वे हेतुरुच्यते॥ २०॥

kārya karaṇa kartṛtve hetuḥ prakṛtirucyate
puruṣaḥ sukhaduḥkhānāṁ bhoktṛtve heturucyate

(20) The Primordial Nature is considered to be the cause of effect, instrument and agent; while the embodied-soul is said to be the cause in regard to the experience of pleasure and pain.

पुरुषः प्रकृतिस्थो हि भुंक्ते प्रकृतिजान्गुणान्।
कारणं गुणसङ्गोऽस्य सदसद्योनिजन्मसु॥ २१॥

puruṣaḥ prakṛtistho hi bhuṅkte prakṛtijān guṇān
kāraṇaṁ guṇasaṅgo'sya sadasad yonijanmasu

(21) The soul while settled in identification with Nature experiences the qualities born of nature; it is the attachment to these qualities that becomes the cause of birth in good and evil wombs.

उपद्रष्टानुमन्ता च भर्ता भोक्ता महेश्वरः।
परमात्मेति चाप्युक्तो देहेऽस्मिन्पुरुषः परः॥ २२॥

upadraṣṭānumantā ca bhartā bhoktā maheśvaraḥ
paramātmeti cāpyukto dehe'smin puruṣaḥ paraḥ

(22) The Supreme spirit while dwelling in this body is also called the spectator, the counsellor, the sustainer, the experiencer, the great Lord and the Supreme-Self.

य एवं वेत्ति पुरुषं प्रकृतिं च गुणैः सह।
सर्वथा वर्तमानोऽपि न स भूयोऽभिजायते॥ २३॥

ya evaṁ vetti puruṣaṁ prakṛtiṁ ca guṇaiḥ saha
sarvathā vartamāno'pi na sa bhūyo'bhijāyate

(23) He who thus knows the Purusha (soul) as well as the Prakriti (Nature) with the qualities (attributes); even though engaged in all respects, he is not born again.

Commentary—After giving a long description of the field and the knower of the field, Srī Kṛṣṇa proceeds to describe the relationship of the Purusha with the primordial Nature. In verse nineteen, Srī Kṛṣṇa declares "know the primordial Nature and the spirit both to be beginningless; and also know that all the modifications and qualities are born of Nature". Although the Matter and the Spirit both are beginningless but the matter undergoes all kind of modifications while the spirit is changeless, immutable and free from all modifications. The Nature (matter) is the cause of the universe while the Spirit is free from cause and effect. It is only because of soul's identification with the body that the embodied-soul appears to be the experiencer. In the production of body, mind, intellect and senses the mother nature is instrumental. The primordial Nature, which has been declared to be the cause of all activities, brings forth evolutes and instruments. The sages declare the embodied-soul to be the experiencer. The instrumental agency is the means by which the activities are performed, it has been declared as *karana.* In respect to the explanation in the verse twenty, the *karana* are the organs of perception, action, mind, intellect and ego. The word *ubhavapi* clearly expresses that the spirit and the primordial Nature are two different entities and also both beginningless. The Divine and the potency of the Divine (Divine manifestation) are inseparable from each other. Their association is indeed beginningless and there is a specific reason for this association also. Mother Nature cannot become a cause of anything by itself, neither the spirit, which is changeless, can become the experiencer. Srī Kṛṣṇa emphasizes that the primordial Nature is the basis of causation and the Spirit when identifies with the body, it becomes the experiencer of pleasure and pain. In the words of Dr. Radhakrishnan, "The blissful nature of Self is stained by joy and sorrow on account of its identification". The embodied-self superimposes the sensations of the physical body and becomes the experiencer of misery and comfort. It is the attachment to these which eventually becomes the cause of birth in virtuous and evil wombs. The sensations arising from various experiences of life are for sure the cause of bondage and also of good and bad destiny. In the words of Swami Chinmayananda, "As its desire, so is its will" is a scriptural declaration of an eternal truth. While living in the world, the "knower-of-the-Field" experiences the pleasures and joys interpreted by the world-of-Matter and gets attached to them and thereby develops residual impressions *(vasanas)* and takes to conducive fields where it can eke out its cherished satisfaction through vivid experiences." The embodied-self, the *jivatama, bhokta* the conditioned-self, the individual-soul, the *shariri* and *samsari* are all the synonymous terms.

The entire life-span is vast field of activities. The embodied-self enshrouded in ignorance considers himself the author thereof and identifies with the pleasure and pain. It is surely the misconception of his identifications which prolongs the cycle of his birth, death and rebirth. The pure-Self is indeed above all changes and modifications. The Supreme-Self is ever luminous, uniform, changeless and immutable. It is the soul's identification with the body and the attachment to the qualities of nature which becomes the cause of bondage and the rounds of births in good and evil wombs. The slavery of the embodied-soul to the modes of the material Nature goes on until the individual-soul realizes his true identity with the Supreme-Soul. In the words of Srī Ramanuja, "The cause for the Purusha's association with Prakirti may be described in the following way. The Purusha may happen to be embodied in a particular body. He gets interested in seeking certain pleasures and tries to avoid certain pains that are open to the body and are caused by Prakirti in the form of that body. Accordingly, he engages in actions for procuring those pleasures and for eliminating pains. The actions may be virtuous or vicious. In order to undergo the consequences of those actions he transmigrates in course of time into good or bad embodiments. Then again he initiates actions. As a result he is reborn again. Thus, as long as he does not develop the virtues which would enable him to realize his pure-Self, he keeps on moving in this world of transmigration."

In these verses, Srī Kṛṣṇa draws Arjuna's attention to the truth which enlightens the individual and persuades him into the rediscovery of the Supreme-Self within. It is a guidance into the progressive realization of the indwelling-self and an inner exploration at almost all the various levels of consciousness. In the verse twenty-two, Srī Kṛṣṇa tells Arjuna that an individual can perceive and experience the presence of the indwelling Lord who resides in the body and beholds everything as a witness. The expression *upadrasta* literally means the by-stander, the on-looker or the silent witness. When the *Purusha* simply observes all the thoughts going in and out of the mind, and beholds all the actions; he acts as a spectator and is called *upadrasta*. For example, a person takes the role of an on-looker of his own mind and body when he relates subtle events of his dream, where the thoughts turn magically into things and forms. The power that gives validity to both dreaming and waking experience is one and the same—the silent on-looker. It is the same awareness (consciousness) which functions in both the aspects. The silent on-looker describes even the dreamless sleep when the physical body and the subtle body both are at rest. Even in deep sleep there is someone who is witnessing the state of complete rest and the perfect unity with the Higher-self. Who is that witness? This is indeed the silent indweller who resides in the hearts of all.

The other role played by the indweller is that of *anumanta*—the one who suggests, guides and permits. The inner consciousness observes every single thought and acts as a guide to the individual in determining as what ought to be done and what ought not to be done. The role of the indweller is called *Bharta* when the same power is experienced as the sustainer and the controller of the body. It is indeed the vital force that sustains the body, by helping the food to be digested and by protecting and guarding the body from diseases and all kinds of other dangers. When the indwelling embodied-soul observes a *sankalpa* arising from the depth of the mind, he is called the observer but when the embodied-soul becomes a participant in the fulfilment of that *sankalpa,* he is called the enjoyer—the *bhokta* or the experiencer. At that level of consciousness the embodied indweller becomes the experiencer of pleasure and pain, loss and gain, honour and ignominy. As a controller of various functions in the body, the indweller is also called the *Mahesvarah.* The term *Mahesvarah* is self-explanatory. *Mah*—the great and *Esvarah* means the Lord. The indwelling Lord acts as the master of mind, intellect, ego, senses and all other subtle powers which work for the sustenance of the body. The expression *paramatmeti capyukto deheasmin Purushah parah* indicates clearly that the spirit dwelling in the body is called by different names in respect to the role assumed. When the indwelling-spirit assumes affinity with the Supreme-Soul, and rises above the limited identity of the *jivatama,* the individual experiences the transcendence into the higher state of *Paramatma.* It is the conscious connectedness of the *jivatama* with the *Para-atma*. The *Paramatma* and the *atma* are both the same super power that controls the substratum of everything and forms the essence of all life.

Every single entity in the universe is a part and parcel of the Supreme Lord and is very intimately associated with that power. The material energy as well as the spiritual energy both of these are the manifestations of the Supreme-Soul. In the verse twenty-three, Srī Kṛṣṇa says that the one who understands the truth concerning the material nature and the indwelling spirit together with the qualities, in whatever condition he may be at present, he surely attains liberation. Such a person lives an emancipated life, regardless of his present duties; and he attains freedom from the ever revolving cycle of birth, death and rebirth. Srī Kṛṣṇa is emphasizing that with proper knowledge of the Supreme Spirit and the primordial nature one attains the discriminating ability which helps him to separate the real from the unreal, the conditioned from the unconditioned, and mortal from the immortal. He performs his duties in the light of the knowledge of the Self and in a perfect copartnership with God. He lives his life as a witness and as an on-looker to his own mind and body. This enlightened individual lives his life which is totally centred to the core of his being and his identification with the body, mind and ego vanishes in due time. In the words of Swami Sivananda, "the action of the one who knows the spirit and matter, who has gained the knowledge of the Self are burnt by the fire of knowledge. Just as the seeds fried in the fire do not sprout again, so also the actions burnt in the fire of knowledge cannot produce new bodies or further births. In his case they are *karmabhasa* (mere semblance of *karma*). They are not effective causes and cannot produce further births." The individual who understands and perceives the Supreme-Soul and the manifested primordial nature separately, he definitely learns to live in the world with a heart anchored to the indwelling Lord.

ध्यानेनात्मनि पश्यन्ति केचिदात्मानमात्मना।
अन्ये सांख्येन योगेन कर्मयोगेन चापरे॥ २४॥

dhyānenātmani paśyanti kecid ātmānamātmanā
anye sāṅkhyena yogena karmayogena cāpare

(24) Some, by meditation, perceive the Self, in the self, by the self; others by the Yoga of knowledge, and still others by the Yoga of action.

अन्ये त्वेवमजानन्तः श्रुत्वान्येभ्य उपासते।
तेऽपि चातितरन्त्येव मृत्युं श्रुतिपरायणाः॥ २५॥

anye tvevamajānantaḥ śrutvānyebhya upāsate
te'pi cātitarantyeva mṛtyuṁ śrutiparāyaṇaḥ

(25) Others, not knowing thus; worship as they have heard from others; they too cross beyond death, by being devoted to whatever they hear respectfully.

Commentary—In these verses, Srī Kṛṣṇa explains different paths generally adopted by the seekers of knowledge for God-realization and self-realization. He tells Arjuna that some aspirants, through the practice of meditation, perceive the Self, by the Self, within the Self; others by the Yoga of knowledge and yet others by the Yoga of action. Also there are others who become devoted to the Lord upon hearing from others. They too attain the Supreme-goal just by being devoted to whatever they hear from others. Meditation as described earlier is a technique of contemplation, wherein the individual tries to attend to his thoughts. In meditation practice one tries to monitor the quality of thoughts, the quantity and the direction of thoughts. In the process of monitoring the thinking faculty, the person experiences for himself the majesty of the indweller. The techniques which are used by the yogis, saints, seers, mystics and the householders do vary to some extent but in general, everyone follows similar guidelines. All the prescribed techniques are generally meant to induce a contemplative mood that would assist the person for inner integration, peace and tranquillity. The key to success in meditation is the constant regular practice and the steadfastness in attitude. It is one of the greatest arts in life. In meditation session the individual learns to attend, watch, and behold the internal dialogue which goes on in mind incessantly. He educates himself in monitoring the movements of his thoughts and learns to direct them into the quietness of the Self. Success in meditation is indeed quite difficult because occasionally the waves of thoughts surge and subside in a very disgusting manner. Sometime people become very frustrated and discouraged in the beginning. The sages indicate that when the effort in meditation is purely linked with the religious pursuit, and the goal of self-realization then the assistance for the success comes from within. The grace of the indweller is revealed in the daily meditation session and the person is guided into the yogic unity in due time. The advanced meditators do experience the ecstatic trance and occasionally enter into the state of prime unity with the Lord. The yogins derive deep satisfaction from such an experience. The subtle joy and the exhilarating experience of this union can only be understood by those who have really experienced it in their own self. Meditation is not just a religious practice. It is for sure a necessity of life. It helps the individual to live in perfect harmony with his innerself and with others. Srī Kṛṣṇa tells Arjuna in the same verse that some other people explore into the subtlety of the Supreme-self with sequential and logical thinking. The term *Samkhya* has been described earlier in relation to the *Samkhya-yoga.* This is the analytical and philosophical reasoning, yoked with Yoga that guides the person towards the doorway of the ultimate reality.

The study of scriptures definitely strengthens the purity of reason, and the intellect becomes very discriminative which helps the person to differentiate the real from unreal. In the practice of *Samkhya-yoga* also, the aspirant has to drop all his sequential, logical and philosophical reasoning eventually in order to experience the light of his own self. In order to be awakened to one's own inherent essentiality the individual has to fuse his personal will and let the illusion of separateness disappear. This experience of unity comes to the individual in the form of a very unique gift of the Divine. The word *Karamyogenecapare* stands for the Yoga of action. As described earlier, the Yoga of action means the performance of all the actions in Yoga (connectedness with the God). A *Karam yogi* who perpetually lives in God and performs all his work with the consciousness of the God, he also perceives clearly the presence of God within his body. He knows how to live in the world with his heart constantly centred in the Supreme Lord. For this kind of aspirant, the life becomes an offering to the Divine and his work becomes the worship of the Divine.

By concluding the methods with the word "*sruti-parayanah*", Srī Kṛṣṇa has made the truth very clear that the longing for the yogic communion which is initiated from the purity of heart is indeed very powerful. It definitely brings transformation, self-realization and God-realization in due time. An honest attitude in prayer is the very essence of success to the goal of self-realization. There are people who are not acquainted with techniques of meditation at all and they do not understand much about philosophies of the scriptures but just by learning from the seers and saints devotedly, they attain God realization and become eligible for liberation. Srī Kṛṣṇa has mentioned in chapter ten verse eleven *anukampayartham*—out of compassion I enlighten them about their *atmabhavastha*—true nature of their own self. Each and every individual is for sure an eligible candidate for the experience of the ultimate reality. Everyone has inherent ability and capacity for inner awakening and enlightenment. The only thing which quickens the individual's spiritual growth is the genuine devotion and the purity of his heart. In the words of Jaydayal Goyandka, "The compound adjective *Srutiparayanah* refers to those who take with reverence and love to the diligent practice of what they have heard from others. Receiving instructions from others and carrying them out with extreme reverence is what is meant by worshipping even as they have heard."

यावत्सञ्जायते किंचित्सत्त्वं स्थावरजङ्गमम्।
क्षेत्रक्षेत्रज्ञसंयोगात्तद्विद्धि भरतर्षभ ॥ २६ ॥

yāvat sañjāyate kiñcit sattvaṁ sthāvarajaṅgamam
kṣetrakṣetrajñasaṁyogāt tad viddhi bharatarṣabha

(26) Whatever being is born, moving or unmoving, know that it is through the union of the field and the knower of the field, O' best of the Bharatas.

समं सर्वेषु भूतेषु तिष्ठन्तं परमेश्वरम्।
विनश्यत्स्वविनश्यन्तं यः पश्यति स पश्यति ॥ २७ ॥

samaṁ sarveṣu bhūteṣu tiṣṭhantaṁ parameśvaram
vinaśyatsvavinaśyantaṁ yaḥ paśyati sa pasyati

(27) He who beholds the Supreme Lord existing equally in all beings, as the imperishable within the perishable, he truly sees.

समं पश्यन् हि सर्वत्र समवस्थितमीश्वरम्।
न हिनस्त्यात्मनात्मानं ततो याति परां गतिम्॥ २८॥

samaṁ paśyan hi sarvatra samavasthitamīśvaram
na hinstyātmanātmānaṁ tato yāti parāṁ gatim

(28) Who sees the Supreme Lord present, equally everywhere, he does not destroy the Self by the self; therefore, he attains the Supreme goal.

Commentary—In these verses, once again, Srī Kṛṣṇa draws Arjuna's attention to the knower of the field; who is perceived being manifested in creation. Whatever comes into existence moving or unmoving, it emanates from the union of the field and the knower of the field. Although the field of matter is insentient but when the spirit plays through the field, it energizes the field. On the surface it may appear that the Supreme Spirit has become the field but in essence it maintains its essential separateness. The field and the knower of the field both exist in a very mystical union. Einstein, the well-known scientist, has written, "the observer enters into every observation. All the experiences of everything in creation are coupled with experiencing the Self because both are indeed inseparably fused in each and every perception". Srī Kṛṣṇa points out to the observer of all appearances and declares that he who sees the same Lord equally dwelling in the entire creation, he really knows how to perceive the imperishable within the perishable. The world of multiple existences originates from the 'One' and the only ultimate reality. There is a hidden unity which encloses all beings of the entire creation moving or unmoving, sentient or insentient like a large circle encloses several small concentric circles within. The primordial Nature may wear millions of masks such as a rock, a tree, a bird or a human being, but there is only one hidden actor behind everything. The Super-soul centered in the universe acts as an energizer to each and every little atom and molecule.

The expression *yah pasyati sa pasyati* literally means that he truly sees—who sees one Lord as the essence of entire creation. He is the man of wisdom, who perceives unity behind the diversity. In the words of Swami Rama, "All that comes into existence, whether sentient or insentient, arises from the union of *Purusha* and *Prakriti*, these two fundamental principles are the principles of the one Absolute without a second. *Purusha* controls *Prakriti* as the body is controlled by its knower." The expression *vinasyatsv avinasyantam yah pasyati sa pasyati* indicates that the one who perceives the One imperishable, hidden behind the perishable, the immutable behind the mutable, and the unchanging Reality behind the changeable, he is the knower of true knowledge. The man of integral wisdom is the one who is well acquainted with the mysteries of unmanifested appearing and disappearing in the universe.

In the words of Dr. Radhakrishnan, "This knowledge presupposes unity or oneness of thought and being, a unity that transcends the differentiation of the subject and the object. Such knowledge is revealed in man's very existence. It is unveiled rather than acquired. This knowledge is concealed in ignorance and when the latter is removed the former manifests itself. What we are that we behold, and what we behold that we are. Our thought, our life and our being are uplifted in simplicity and we are made one with the truth." The Supreme reality has to be apprehended personally and directly. The *Upanisads* have declared this truth "the Self is revealed to the individual by *adhyatma yoga* i.e. the study of the Self; and *jñana-prasadana* meaning the knowledge of the Self", which comes to the individual as a *prasada* (grace) of the Divine. When the individual is blessed with the grace of the Lord from within, the idea of real becomes a revelation of the real, the conceptual becomes perceptual, the impenetrable becomes easy to penetrate, the inaccessible comes within the access. The expression "*na hinasty atmanatmanam*" means he does not degrade himself. The person who perceives the Lord seated in his own heart he always lives in harmony with the voice of the Self. His every thought and every activity proceeds in perfect alliance with the voice of the indweller. He never violates the inner dictates and does everything from inner purity and honesty. He never gives himself a chance to be debased to the extremity of low self-respect. He is always alert and very conscious of his every thought, word and deed.

प्रकृत्यैव च कर्माणि क्रियमाणानि सर्वशः।
यः पश्यति तथात्मानमकर्तारं स पश्यति॥ २९॥

prakṛtyaiva ca karmāṇi kriyamāṇāni sarvaśaḥ
yaḥ paśyati tathātmānamakartāraṁ sa paśyati

(29) He who sees, that all the actions are being performed by *Prakriti* (Nature) and the Self is not the doer, he truly sees.

यदा भूतपृथग्भावमेकस्थमनुपश्यति।
तत एव च विस्तारं ब्रह्म सम्पद्यते तदा॥ ३०॥

yadā bhūtapṛthagbhāvamekasthamanupaśyati
tata eva ca vistāraṁ brahma saṁpadyate tadā

(30) When he sees, that the whole variety of beings are centred in 'One' and their expansion is from that 'One' alone, then he attains Brahman.

अनादित्वान्निर्गुणत्वात् परमात्मायमव्ययः।
शरीरस्थोऽपि कौन्तेय न करोति न लिप्यते॥ ३१॥

anāditvānnirguṇatvāt paramātmāyamavyayaḥ
śarīrastho'pi kaunteya na karoti na lipyate

(31) Beginningless, and beyond the qualities of Nature, the Supreme-Self is imperishable. Although existing in the body O'Arjuna, neither acts nor is attached.

यथा सर्वगतं सौक्ष्म्यादाकाशं नोपलिप्यते।
सर्वत्रावस्थितो देहे तथात्मा नोपलिप्यते॥ ३२॥

yathā sarvagataṁ saukṣmyād ākāśaṁ nopalipyate
sarvatrāvasthito dehe tathātmā nopalipyate

(32) As the all-pervading ether is not tainted, because of its subtlety, even so the Self, although dwelling everywhere in the body, is not tainted.

Commentary—In these verses, special emphasis has been placed upon the utmost importance of living a life, which is totally centred in the consciousness of the Supreme reality. It liberates the individual from the false identifications and initiates him for selfless action. Srī Kṛṣṇa tells Arjuna to get in touch with the silent observer and learn to live consciously in the awareness of that. Everything in the world is going through constant change of *adimatha, utkrsta* and *miti*—it comes into existence, it sustains for a while and then it dies. All activities in the body—such as eating, drinking, walking, sleeping and even meditation and trance—are performed by nature. The indwelling-Self witnesses and beholds every movement and every activity. For example, when the person sits in meditation, the Self watches the person trying to meditate. It observes all the efforts, all the struggles, the failures and the successes. Even in transcendental meditation the Self observes each and every movement of the person while entering into the trance. The indwelling-Self is eternal, pure, lucid and awakened; and devoid of all modifications. The ultimate success in God-realization is to be able to perceive the Self as the witness of all activities. A deep insight makes it very clear that the Self transcends all experiences and also the flow of time in which all the activities take place. The change can be perceived only by the one who is changeless, the mutation can be perceived only by one who is immutable. So it is essential to have a clear understanding of the distinction which exists between the thought and the one who is aware of that thought.

The expression *bhuta-prthag-bhavam* stands for the variety of creation that emanates from the union of the knower of the field and the field. The separateness and the individualism that exists among the beings is because of the varieties of thoughts that emerge from each individual mind. The entire world has come out in a self-determined fashion. Each and every atom, molecule and creature that has come into existence has been motivated by its own memorized latencies of the previous state of existence. Individual mind is indeed the cause of continuity which prevails in the universe. It is indeed through mutual interaction that the qualities of primordial Nature become manifested into existence. The universe is constantly rotating through many phases. Each stage follows the previous one which has become latent. The new comes into existence from the heritage of all that which has existed previously. The Supreme-Self, although seated everywhere in the macrocosm as well as in the microcosm, still remains aloof as a silent witness only. Srī Kṛṣṇa tells Arjuna in verse thirty that when a person perceives the diversified existence of all beings centered in the Supreme spirit then hc attains *Brahman.* A self-realized person experiences the ultimate truth about the Supreme indweller in the body, who neither acts and nor is involved in any respect. The Lord dwells in the body and beholds everything as a silent witness. There are some beautiful lines by the poet Rumi, "I am so close to you, I am distant. I am so mingled with you, I am apart. I am so open, I am hidden."

यथा प्रकाशयत्येकः कृत्स्नं लोकमिमं रविः ।
क्षेत्रं क्षेत्री तथा कृत्स्नं प्रकाशयति भारत ॥ ३३ ॥

yathā prakaśayatyekaḥ kṛtsnaṁ lokamimaṁ raviḥ
kṣetraṁ kṣetrī tathā kṛtsnaṁ prakāśayati bhārata

(33) As the one sun illuminates the whole universe, so also the Lord of the field illuminates the entire field, O'Arjuna.

क्षेत्रक्षेत्रज्ञयोरेवमन्तरं ज्ञानचक्षुषा ।
भूतप्रकृतिमोक्षं च ये विदुर्यान्ति ते परम् ॥ ३४ ॥

kṣetrakṣetrajñayorevamantaraṁ jñānacakṣuṣā
bhūtaprakṛtimokṣaṁ ca ye viduryānti te param

(34) Those who perceive the distinction between the field and the knower of the field with the eye of wisdom; and the deliverance of beings from *Prakriti* (Nature), they attain the Supreme.

Commentary—In continuation of the previous philosophy, Srī Kṛṣṇa tells Arjuna that as the sun illuminates the entire universe, so also the master of the field illuminates the entire field. The person who perceives this truth with the eye of wisdom and sufficient discrimination, he surely attains liberation from the evolutes of the primordial nature. Srī Kṛṣṇa has already declared in the very beginning of this chapter that true knowledge is indeed the knowledge of the Supreme-self; which is revealed to the individual by his own efforts from his own resources. The inner awakening unfolds the prime truth about the *ksetra* and the *ksetrajña* and emancipates the individual from the intrigues of his conditioned behaviour. It is through the experiential knowledge of the Supreme-Self that a person can attain liberation from the cruel clutches of *Maya* (primordial nature). Srī Kṛṣṇa assures in this verse that the one who contacts the indweller and understands the distinction between the body and the Master of the body, he becomes liberated in due time. In the words of Swami Tapasyananda, "There are two categories in the consciousness of man—the object and the subject, the 'seen' and the 'seer'. The 'seen' is in the field, the body; the 'seer' is the Spirit, the *jiva.* The body-mind is the 'field' because it is the environment in association with which the 'seer' the *jiva,* enjoys the fruits of his actions and also undergoes spiritual evolution. Thus the body-mind is its adjunct, the instrument through which the Spirit contacts objects. Still, it is only the 'seen' the 'object', because the 'seer', the *jiva,* is not part of it but distinct from it and master of it."

ॐ तत्सदिति श्रीमद्भगवद्गीतासूपनिषत्सु ब्रह्मविद्यायां
योगशास्त्रे श्रीकृष्णार्जुनसंवादे क्षेत्रक्षेत्रज्ञविभागयोगो
नाम त्रयोदशोऽध्यायः ॥ १३ ॥

'Aum' tatsaditi Śrīmadbhagawadgeetā sūpaniṣatsu
brahmavidyāyām yogaśāstre Śrīkṛṣṇārjunasamvāde
kṣetrakṣetrajñavibhāgayogo nāma trayodaśo'dhyāyaḥ

'AUM TAT SAT'—Thus, in the Upanishad of the glorious Bhagawad Geeta, the science of the Brahman (Absolute) the scripture of yoga, the dialogue between Srī Kṛṣṇa and Arjuna—thus, ends the chapter thirteen entitled *"Kṣetrakṣetrajñavibhāgayoga"*.

इति श्रीमद्भगवद्गीतासु त्रयोदशोऽध्यायः ॥ १३ ॥

Chapter Fourteen

GUṆATRIYAVIBHĀGAYOGA

THE YOGA OF THE DIVISION OF THE THREE GUNAS

श्रीभगवानुवाच

परं भूयः प्रवक्ष्यामि ज्ञानानां ज्ञानमुत्तमम्।

यज्ज्ञात्वा मुनयः सर्वे परां सिद्धिमितो गताः॥ १॥

paraṁ bhūyaḥ pravakṣyāmi jñānānāṁ jñānamuttamam

yajjñātvā munayaḥ sarve parāṁ siddhim ito gatāḥ

The Blessed Lord said :

(1) I shall teach you again the supreme knowledge, the highly reverend knowledge; by knowing which, all the sages have attained the supreme perfection, being liberated from the world.

इदं ज्ञानमुपाश्रित्य मम साधर्म्यमागताः।

सर्गेऽपि नोपजायन्ते प्रलये न व्यथन्ति च॥ २॥

idaṁ jñānamupāśritya mama sādharmyamāgatāḥ

sarge'pi nopajāyante pralaye na vyathanti ca

(2) Those who have taken refuge in this knowledge, have attained unity with Me. They are not born at the time of creation, nor are they disturbed at the time of dissolution.

मम योनिर्महद् ब्रह्म तस्मिन्गर्भं दधाम्यहम्।

सम्भवः सर्वभूतानां ततो भवति भारत॥ ३॥

mama yonir mahad brahma tasmin garbhaṁ dadhāmyaham

sambhavaḥ sarvabhūtānāṁ tato bhavati bhārata

(3) The great Brahma (primordial nature) is My womb; in that, I place the seed, from that, is the birth of all beings O'Arjuna.

सर्वयोनिषु कौन्तेय मूर्तयः सम्भवन्ति याः।
तासां ब्रह्म महद्योनिरहं बीजप्रदः पिता॥ ४॥

sarvayonişu kaunteya mūrtayaḥ sambhavanti yāḥ
tāsāṁ brahma mahad yoniraham̐ bījapradaḥ pitā

(4) Of all the bodies, those take birth from different wombs, O'Arjuna—the great Brahma (Mother nature) is their womb and I am the seed giving Father.

Commentary—Chapter fourteen is a continuation of the previous chapter where Srī Kṛṣṇa describes at length about the field and the knower of the field with respective characteristics. The *kshetra* and *kshetrajña* are two separate entities. It is through their union only that the entire creation comes into existence. It is due to interaction of the primordial nature and the Supreme spirit that the individualization of the Spirit takes place into endless varieties. The conversation opens with the declaration by Srī Kṛṣṇa with the words *Param bhuyah pravaksyami jñanam uttamam*—I must tell you a little more in detail about the transcendental knowledge and wisdom, having known which, all the sages have attained Supreme Bliss and liberation. As described earlier in chapter seven, everyone is born with the knowledge of the Self, and it is there within the access of every human being. It is not something to be acquired from some body, it actually needs to be revealed to the individual from within. This integral knowledge of the Supreme-self becomes foreign to the person because of his own negligence and ignorance. Srī Kṛṣṇa feels the urgent need for Arjuna to be awakened once again to the wisdom of the over-Self. He tells that He is going to enlighten him more about the inherent knowledge which will connect him once again to the source of his essential being. It is a progressive realization from the conscious state of mind to the superconscious state of mind, from the conditioned finite awareness to infinite awareness. In this conversation Srī Kṛṣṇa reveals the secret which obscures the true knowledge from the individual. Step by step Arjuna is being guided beyond the realms of matter into the mysteries of the subtle fields of consciousness. It is only after one transcends the gross body and enters into the subtle, the person can comprehend the tyranny of matter, and actually realize the bondage of the conditioned behaviour. He also becomes acquainted with infinite bliss of the Supreme Divinity. The liberation and emancipation mentioned in the second verse stands for the training of living a life in the awareness of the Divine. Srī Kṛṣṇa has mentioned the word *muni* in the first verse. The word *muni* comes from *mauni* which means the one who is totally absorbed in silence and quietude of the Supreme-Soul. When the mind of a person becomes silent and free from all types of *samkalpa-vikalpa* (desires and aspirations) the *mana* (mind) rests in *mauna* and he is called a *muni*. A Muni, who is perpetually absorbed in the nature of the Supreme, he is not disturbed even at the time of dissolution of the universe. For a *muni* the embodied-self becomes totally merged into the cosmic-Self. His personal individuality is totally dissolved in the universal-self that is why he attains freedom from the rounds of birth-death and rebirth. According to Srī Sankaracharya: "living a life in the bliss of the Supreme-Self, in the integral wisdom of the Supreme-Soul is like living in eternity". The expression *mamsadharmyam agatah* means have attained unity with Me. It is the supreme state of perfection wherein the individual-soul recognizes its origin and enjoys the tranquillity and peace of the infinite. In the words of Swami Sivananda, Srī Kṛṣṇa declares in this verse "having resorted to this knowledge, they are assimilated into My own nature. They have attained to My being. They have become identical with Me. They live in Me with no thought of 'Thou or I'. They go beyond birth and death."

In the third verse, the *Prakriti* (primordial nature) has been declared to be the *Mahat Brahma*. *Brahma* means which expands immeasurably. In ancient scriptures especially the *Vedas* it has been called the '*Hiranyagarbha*'—the cosmic womb of the beings. There is a hymn in *Atharva Veda*, "*Om hiranyagarbhah samavarta taagre bhootasya jaatah patireka aaseet, sa daadhaara prithiveem dyaa-mutemaam kasmai devaaya havishaa vidhema*"—means at the very dawn of creation has been the *hiranyagarbha* (golden womb). The seed of all the elemental composition, and the Lord of all existence, who upholds the heaven and earth together. Our humble salutation to that Supreme Lord. *Hiranyagarbha* the cosmic subtle body is the other name of *Brahma*. The individual subtle body is the mind, intellect and ego. It is also called the causal body which is responsible for the creation of the gross body. The mind, intellect and ego are the channels through which every little sensation is perceived, received, processed, assimilated, metabolized and manifested through thoughts, words and deeds. The sum of all the subtle bodies in the creation is the *hiranyagarbha*, or the *Mahat Brahma*. Srī Kṛṣṇa says my womb is the great *Brahma* where I place the seed which gives birth to all the creatures of the universe. The primordial nature is the womb which becomes impregnated by the Lord of the universe. Mother nature is the womb in which the Divine consciousness penetrates and becomes seated as the seed giving Father. It is the potency of the Divine which vitalizes the inert nature and makes it to grow and manifest itself as the most spectacular creation. It is indeed the potency of the Supreme spirit which is seen being expressed in each and everything of the universe. The Lord himself is the Father of the universe who vitalizes and energizes the primordial nature, which orchestrates the entire play in the universe. As described in chapters seven and thirteen, it is the One and the only One ultimate reality which manifests itself in the innumerable forms and shapes, within various grades of potentialities bound by their own latencies. The Matter is indeed the cosmic mother of the entire spectacular universe and the Ishwara is the cosmic Father. The multitude of beings comes into existence from the union of matter and the Supreme Spirit. It is the identification of the spirit with matter which actually vitalizes the matter and gives life to the inert matter.

As described earlier in the previous chapter, when the Supreme-soul identifies with the body, it is called the embodied-soul i.e. the individualized soul or the *jivatma*. Everyone in the creation is born from the union of Mother Nature and the Lord of the Universe as the Father. Just as a child inherits the characteristics of both the mother and father, exactly like that every being inherits the qualities of the material nature and also the qualities of the Supreme Divinity. When the embodied-soul takes upon the human body, it becomes very attached to the body; *jivatma* craves to enjoy everything in the world but being a fragment of the Divine, the embodied-spirit definitely feels comforted in the unity with the Super Spirit. The embodied-soul becomes confused because of multiple identities in life and that is why sometime in the midst of all worldly enjoyments, the individual feels very lonely, and occasionally seeks the forgotten identification. *Jivatma* being the fragment of the Supreme Lord can rise to the height of genius, but if he ignores the inner connection and drifts away from *swadharma* he can fall into the ditches of degradation. Every embodied-soul is potentially the Supreme-Soul. The goal of the human life is to experience the Divinity from within and to live a life which is consciously aligned to the Supreme-soul. Any misalignment from within results into conscious separation from the source of life and slavery to Matter. The Matter is a twisted rope of three gunas. The gunas are the attitude with which the mind interprets everything. The gunas are the primary constituents of Nature; and are surely responsible for the rise and the fall of *jivatma* in the world. These modes of nature definitely create confusion for *jivatma* and the later forgets its true identity. The involvement with these essential qualities of nature becomes the cause of slavery to material world and also the cause of birth, death and rebirth.

सत्त्वं रजस्तम इति गुणाः प्रकृतिसम्भवाः।
निबध्नन्ति महाबाहो देहे देहिनमव्ययम्॥ ५॥

sattvaṁ rajas tama iti guṇāḥ prakṛtisambhavāḥ
nibadhnanti mahābāho dehe dehinamavyayam

(5) *Sattva* (purity), *Rajas* (passion) and *Tamas* (dullness)—these qualities born of Nature O'Arjuna, bind the imperishable spirit to the body.

तत्र सत्त्वं निर्मलत्वात् प्रकाशकमनामयम्।
सुखसङ्गेन बध्नाति ज्ञानसङ्गेन चानघ॥ ६॥

tatra sattvaṁ nirmalatvāt prakāśakamanāmayam
sukhasaṅgena badhnāti jñānasaṅgena cānagha

(6) Of these *Sattva* (purity) being immaculate, luminous and healthy binds by attachment to happiness and by attachment to knowledge, O' Arjuna.

रजो रागात्मकं विद्धि तृष्णासङ्गसमुद्भवम्।
तन्निबध्नाति कौन्तेय कर्मसङ्गेन देहिनम्॥ ७॥

rajo rāgātmakaṁ viddhi tṛṣṇāsaṅgasamudbhavam

tannibadhnāti kaunteya karmasaṅgena dehinam

(7) Know thou, *Rajas* to be of the nature of passion, which is the source of thirst and attachment; it binds O'Kaunteya, the embodied-self through attachment to action.

तमस्त्वज्ञानजं विद्धि मोहनं सर्वदेहिनाम्।
प्रमादालस्यनिद्राभिस्तन्निबध्नाति भारत ॥८॥

tamastvajñānajaṁ viddhi mohanaṁ sarvadehinām

pramādālasyanidrābhis tannibadhnāti bhārata

(8) Know, *Tamas* to be born of ignorance, it deludes the embodied beings and binds through negligence, indolence and sleep O' Arjuna.

सत्त्वं सुखे सञ्जयति रजः कर्मणि भारत।
ज्ञानमावृत्य तु तमः प्रमादे सञ्जयत्युत ॥९॥

sattvaṁ sukhe sañjayati rajaḥ karmaṇi bhārata

jñānamāvṛtya tu tamaḥ pramāde sañjayatyuta

(9) The mode of *Sattva* binds one with attachment to happiness, *Rajas* attaches one with obsession to work O'Arjuna, while *Tamas* veiling the knowledge attaches one to heedlessness and laziness.

रजस्तमश्चाभिभूय सत्त्वं भवति भारत।
रजः सत्त्वं तमश्चैव तमः सत्त्वं रजस्तथा ॥१०॥

rajas tamaś cābhibhūya sattvaṁ bhavati bhārata

rajaḥ sattvaṁ tamaś caiva tamaḥ sattvaṁ rajastathā

(10) *Sattva* prevails having overpowered *Rajas* and *Tamas,* O'Arjuna. *Rajas* prevails having overpowered *Sattva* and *Tamas* and likewise *Tamas* manifests overpowering *Sattva* and *Rajas.*

Commentary—In these verses Srī Kṛṣṇa draws Arjuna's attention to the innate nature of man, and brings forth its examination and its melodies. As explained in the previous verse, every individual is a child of the Primordial nature and of the Supreme Lord; so he inherits the qualities of both. Every embodied-soul expresses himself through the inborn disposition which is ruled by the three types of tendencies of Nature. These three qualities inherent in the behaviour of every person are called the gunas in Sanskrit. Guna literally means the inherent property, quality or the motivating force. These gunas are the *Sattva, Rajas* and *Tamas.* All the thoughts, ideas, desires, notions and actions of the individual are fostered and motivated by these three gunas. As a matter of fact the entire human behaviour can be categorized into three types. These modes of nature are present in all human beings, though in different degrees. These qualities are very distinct and manifest themselves very clearly in the overall personality of every person. The entire creation of human beings is a drama, orchestrated by these three qualities inherent in the basic attitude of every embodied-soul. These qualities—the *Sattva, Rajas* and *Tamas*—bind the pure imperishable soul into the strings of conditioned behaviour and into the repeated rounds of birth, death and rebirth. The three gunas form a twisted rope of self-designed behaviour of the individual which enslaves the pure spirit into matter. The infinite spirit feels finite and bound in all respects. The free and unbounded soul feels trapped and imprisoned and sometime very helpless. The process in which the spirit becomes bound is going to be discussed in the forthcoming verses. Srī Kṛṣṇa asserts in these verses that the proper knowledge of these qualities of nature is very important to be understood by every human beings. The appropriate understanding of these qualities of matter, and the way a person becomes influenced by them; needs to be ascertained in order to live a harmonious life and also to make spiritual progress. These qualities, although quite distinct from one another, can be perceived in perfect co-operation with one another. Sometimes *Sattva* predominates the nature of the person and at other time the *Rajas* and *Tamas.* The *Sattvic* quality gives enlightenment, purity, serenity, luminosity and tranquillity; it is generally represented by the colour white. With the predominance of *Sattva*, the individual remains consciously connected with the purity of the Divine. This tendency illuminates the thinking faculty and elevates the intuitive ability which blesses the individual with positive attitude and faith in God. The *Sattvic* quality is very helpful for a balanced, happy, pure and healthy lifestyle. All actions performed with *Sattvic* attitude are harmonious, enlivening, elevating and redemptive.

The *Sattva* endowed actions promote the *Sattva-vriti* which guides the person towards a total fulfilment. The individual enjoys internal and external purity with emotional maturity and stability.

In the words of Swami Chidbavananda, "The *Sattva* guna may be compared to an evenly made clear glass. Light passes through it unobstructed and undiminished. Things seen through that glass are as vividly visible as to a normal naked eye. The *Sattva* is similarly transparent to the brilliance of Atman. Seeing the things objectively in their true perspective is the secular knowledge. Seeing the Atman as He is—is the sacred knowledge." Srī Kṛṣṇa tells Arjuna in the sixth verse that *Sattva* is pure, luminous, illuminating, serene and healthy but at the same time he alerts mankind with these words *sukhasangena badhnati jñanasangena ca nagha—Sattva* binds by attachment to happiness and by attachment to knowledge. Srī Kṛṣṇa tells Arjuna about the golden fetter that comes with the predominance of *Sattva.* The hunter *Sattva* begins to bind the individual by arousing his attachment to knowledge and happiness. A *Sattvic* person performs all types of virtuous and pious deeds. He performs austerities, the *yajñas* and other charitable activities. A *Sattvic* person becomes involved in building temples, and organizing spiritual workshops by saints and learned scholars. Such an individual sometime goes overboard and starts neglecting his assigned duties as a member of the family and the community. He becomes obsessed towards the *Sattvic* joy and the same golden fetter becomes the cause of his bondage. Sometime a man of knowledge becomes involved in his comparison with others and rejoices in his superiority of knowledge and excellence. He feels greatly pleased when honoured; and forgets that the name and fame given by the people are indeed very transitory and momentary.

The knowledge and happiness are really an illusion. The attitude of accumulating knowledge generates the attitude of possessiveness. Occasionally, the hankering for knowledge creates imbalance in life and becomes a cause of bondage. In the guise of subtle thrill and happiness it lays the trap of slavery for the individual to the extent that he forgets about his personal health and hygiene. The *Rajasic* attitude is marked by excessive activity. It is represented by the colour red. The *Rajasic* attitude of mind engenders and promotes greed and desire for the sensual enjoyments. The person runs after wealth as if forced by an insatiable demon. His greed increases like a flame which is fostered by the oil. A millionaire craves to be a multi-millionaire and a multi-millionaire desires to be a billionaire. When the individual becomes intoxicated with very high ambition, he falls into the traps of undesirable means of accumulating wealth. He feels very restless, dissipated, unregulated and becomes enslaved to the performance of some purposeless activities. The expression *trsna sanga-samudhbhavam* indicates that the *Rajasic* attitude enhances the cupidity and attachment. This promotes the desire for accumulating wealth, saving, protecting and yet dreaming for more. A *Rajasic* person is perpetually working day and night to possess, to procreate and to protect. He is always worried and fearful of losing what he possesses and continuously concerned about making more.

The *Tamasic* attitude of mind is characterised by laziness, indolence, forgetfulness, and it is symbolized by black colour and also the dark navy blue. The word *Tam* literally means darkness. The *Tamasic* attitude reflects inner darkness which expresses itself in heedlessness, sleepiness, indolence, negligence and lack of proper insight. The *Tamsic* individual misconceives the truth and misinterprets it. He lacks consistency towards accomplishments of any goal. He remains idle and sleeps more than the body requires. He postpones every little bit of work for tomorrow. Such a person feels confused and deluded and usually cannot make any sensible decision. He generally becomes very passive, depressed and lives a life which is only partially awake. He feels dependent, very helpless and degraded. The *Tamsic* attitude of mind enshrouds the inner light of self-awareness and the individual takes it for granted. He accepts carelessly his self-degrading habits and the non-performance of the necessary duties.

These three modes of nature although quite distinct in their expression, still manifest themselves in co-ordination and cooperation with one another. The predominance of one can be observed in relation to the other two. A person manifests the *Sattvic* qualities of his nature by consciously overpowering the *Rajas* and *Tamas*. When the *Rajasic* tendency is expressed in the behaviour of an individual, the other two are partially dormant. Similarly when the *Tamasic* attitude predominates the personality of an individual, the *Sattvic* and *Rajasic* qualities become enshrouded. Any tendency that overpowers by suppressing others, manifests its essentiality. In the words of Srī Aurobindo, "All men have in them in whatever degree the *Rajasic* impulse of desire and activity, the *Sattvic* boon of light and happiness and all have their share of *Tamasic* incapacity, ignorance or nescience. But these qualities are not constant in any man in the quantitative action of their force or in the combination of their elements; for they are variable and in a casual state of mutual impact, displacement and interaction".

सर्वद्वारेषु देहेऽस्मिन्प्रकाश उपजायते।
ज्ञानं यदा तदा विद्याद्विवृद्धं सत्त्वमित्युत॥ ११॥

sarvadvāreṣu dehe'smin prakāśa upajāyate
jñānaṁ yadā tadā vidyād vivṛddhaṁ sattvamityuta

(11) When through every gate of the body, the light of wisdom shines forth, then it may be understood that *Sattva* is predominant.

लोभः प्रवृत्तिरारम्भः कर्मणामशमः स्पृहा।
रजस्येतानि जायन्ते विवृद्धे भरतर्षभ॥ १२॥

lobhaḥ pravṛttirārambhaḥ karmaṇāmaśamaḥ spṛhā
rajasyetāni jāyante vivṛddhe bharatarṣabha

(12) Covetousness, activity, enterprise, restlessness and craving—these arise when *Rajas* is predominant, O'Arjuna.

अप्रकाशोऽप्रवृत्तिश्च प्रमादो मोह एव च।
तमस्येतानि जायन्ते विवृद्धे कुरुनन्दन॥ १३॥

aprakāśo'pravṛttiś ca pramādo moha eva ca
tamasyetāni jāyante vivṛddhe kurunandana

(13) Darkness, lack of effort, negligence and mere delusion—

these arise when *Tamas* is predominant, O'Arjuna.

यदा सत्त्वे प्रवृद्धे तु प्रलयं याति देहभृत्।
तदोत्तमविदां लोकानमलान्प्रतिपद्यते ॥ १४ ॥

yadā sattve pravṛddhe tu pralayaṁ yāti dehabhṛt
tadottamavidāṁ lokān amalān pratipdyate

(14) When the embodied-self meets death, while *Sattva* is predominant, then he attains to the pure world of the knowers of the highest.

रजसि प्रलयं गत्वा कर्मसङ्गिषु जायते।
तथा प्रलीनस्तमसि मूढयोनिषु जायते ॥ १५ ॥

rajasi pralayaṁ gatvā karmasaṅgiṣu jāyate
tathā pralīnas tamasi mūḍhayoniṣu jāyate

(15) When the individual dies with the predominance of *Rajas,* he is born among those who are attached to action. Meeting death in *Tamas,* he is born in the wombs of the deluded.

Commentary—In these verses Srī Kṛṣṇa gives a detailed description of the characteristics of each mode of nature, for more comprehensive understanding. Every tendency reveals its special and distinctive characteristics. It is indeed very important for every individual to introspect and monitor very carefully the pattern of his thoughts every single minute of his life. One must study intelligently the inter-locked mutual play of the three qualitative modes of nature. The proper understanding of each promotes the state of equilibrium, peace and happiness in the present life and into the life hereafter. Srī Kṛṣṇa tells Arjuna in verse eleven that at the dawn of *Sattvic* attitude the light of awareness shines through all the gates of the human body. The person's intellectual illumination and inner wisdom reflects itself through each and every one of his activity. The holy sages have given the simili of *Sattva* with the rising sun which eliminates darkness and the person can perceive things in the light of the Self. Just as the brilliance of the moon rushes in all directions on a full moon night, so the light of the Supreme Soul illuminates each and every level of the thinking faculty. A *Sattvic* person thinks clearly and can differentiate between the right and wrong, the good and bad, what should be done and what should be avoided. For example, he knows the type of food he should eat which is healthy for the body; and the type of books he should read for intellectual growth; and the type of friends he should associate with. In the words of Swami Sivananda, "The ears shun whatever is improper to be heard. The eyes abandon what they should not look at. The tongue avoids to speak anything that is not right to speak of. The mind is not attracted by the sensual objects. Purity thus increases gradually by *jaap,* meditation and self-restraint. If there is increase of *Sattva,* there is also the increase of knowledge." The *Sattvic* attitude promotes connectedness with the indwelling-self, which enhances the integral wisdom and knowledge. When the thoughts are perpetually settled in the light of the Self, the mind automatically recoils from sensory objects and starts enjoying the quietude of the Supreme-self. The *Sattva* people experience the grace of God in everything and their lives become the reflection of the inner purity and *swadharma.* By observing self-control, honesty, chastity and charity they become very peaceful within themselves and also the role model for others. In the words of Jaydayal Goyandka, "The height of illumination and the feeling of lightness in the body and the growth of perspicuity and keenness in the mind and senses— this is, what is meant by the dawn of light and the dawn of wisdom".

With the predominance of *Sattva,* the individual feels purified both internally and externally. His ability to discriminate is heightened and his dispassion replaces passion, quietude replaces restlessness and the spirit of sharing replaces the tendency of possessiveness. His day-to-day emotions are accelerated into the purity of love and compassion for others. He feels purified in thoughts, words and deeds. He experiences a special joy in sharing with others and working for the welfare of mankind. He feels a great satisfaction in running some free services for others such as water-huts, medical clinics for the poor, the free supply of food, clothing and books etc. At the dawn of *Sattva* the individual experiences a flood of light gushing forth, from each and every cell of his body as if all the doors and windows of a tightly closed house have been opened to the rosy sunshine once again.

The hallmarks of *Rajas* are characterized by activities, movements, restlessness, many-fold desires, dissatisfaction and dissipation. The symbolic colour of *Rajas* is red. When the *Rajas* tendency waxes strong, suppressing *Sattva,* the person's life becomes very passionate and restless. He allows the senses to indulge in all kinds of worldly enjoyments. A person with *Rajasic* attitude cannot remain at peace even for a few minutes; he is always thinking about the means to make more money. His mind runs riot seeking to usurp the wealth and prosperity, of even others. The greed of such a person increases so much that anything which lies beyond the reach of his grasp, only that escapes his attention. The expression *Lobah pravvittiraarambhah* explains the most outstanding characteristic of *Rajasic* person; whose greed of multiplying wealth has become totally uncontrollable. The mind of such a person wanders as if many demons have possessed him. His attitude reflects total restlessness and the absence of steadiness. He demands immediate results and also keeps changing his path quickly. In the words of Srī Ramanuja, "when niggardliness, restlessness, engagement in actions calculated to bring about advantageous results, uncontrolled indulgence in sense-propensities and the desire for sense-objects are found, we are to infer that *Rajas* is predominating in the individual at the time". The individual increases his activities unnecessarily and almost out of proportion. His desire for amassing wealth grows to the extent that his life becomes very unstable, anxious, worried and restless.

In verse thirteen, Srī Kṛṣṇa presents some glimpses of the *Tamasic* attitude of mind. With the predominance of *Tamas* the individual becomes very careless, lazy and negligent. *Tamas* is symbolized by the colour black and the navy blue. A *Tamasic* person lives in a deluded world of total ignorance which is far beyond the realities of life. When the *Tamasic* tendency waxes in the mind of an individual, he loses the ability to perceive things clearly and intelligently. He acts very whimsically without any clear purpose and goal in mind. The mist of delusion, laziness, negligence and forgetfulness hangs heavy over his thinking faculty. Even if he has the ability and the capacity to achieve something; he does not make appropriate efforts. He always blames others for his failures and misfortunes. He lacks initiative and the clarity of purpose in life. A *Tamasic* person lives in a state of pitifulness. He thinks nothing creative and useful for himself and for others.

In verse fourteen and fifteen, Srī Kṛṣṇa draws Arjuna's attention to the truth that all these tendencies of mind are nurtured under the specific influence of the Gunas and form an important part of one's personality. These tendencies become deeply rooted in the subtle levels of mind and accompany the individual as *samskaras* from one life to another. This accumulated data in the mind determines the type of life one lives in present life and also the type of life hereafter. As discussed earlier in the previous chapter, the entire life-span of the individual is controlled by the mind and intellect, which is a storehouse of thoughts, memories and latencies. The present life of the individual is an expression of past latencies and also the memories of the present. The human mind is a storehouse as well as the transmitter of all the memories. Each life is a bundle of accumulated memories, those are brought into play by the embodied-soul. The old memories are very strong and stubborn. The deep-rooted mental habits, the ingrained ideas and notions, the expectations and associations, all of these form the mental video film which accompanies the subtle body at the time of death. Almost all images of one life-time with the previous one supply information to the future mental images at the time of transition from one life to another. At the time of death, the mind unfolds the deepest layers of information to the individual, wherein every little experience has been recorded during the life time. The entire multitude of experiences right from the day one, when the child is conceived into the mother's womb, till the last minute of death, exist in the mind as a recorded information. At the time of death, the person beholds almost all the episodes of his life in flashback, especially those moments which were very intense and important. The entire past returns vividly in an unwinding web of deeply focussed incidents and memories. The individual feels as if he is walking backward, until the very early years of his life are reached. In that state of awareness, if the individual is able to detach himself from the mortal body, he looks at himself not only as others did during his lifetime but also as his own collection of memories. He confronts the consequences of all his acts and deeds which he egoistically and relentlessly ignored during the lifetime. He realizes the truth that every moment, happy or unhappy, good or bad, has been for sure self-earned.

Srī Kṛṣṇa tells Arjuna that life is not just locked in present, it is a continuity of thoughts and memories. The thoughts of today receive their continuation from those of yesterday and will express in the destiny of tomorrow. Every single thought of life is an extension of the past, seeking its expression into the actions of future. This continuity prevails throughout the lifetime and also continues even after death when the physical body perishes. In verse fourteen, it has been made very clear that when a person leaves his body with the predominance of *Sattva* (purity) he attains the realms of the enlightened ones. He goes to the worlds of those who have experienced the highest reality. It is indeed the clarity of his own pure thoughts that guides him into the regions of the knowers of the Highest. The expression *Uttamavidam* stands for the knowers of the truth, the learned sages and saints. When a person leaves his body with the preponderance of passionate thoughts and *Rajasic* tendencies, he is born among those who are attached to the worldly enjoyment, and the excessive activities. If the individual dies with the predominance of *Tamasic* thoughts, he is born in the womb of the deluded, ignorant, and also in the lowest grades of human beings and other species. The vast disparity which exists among all the species of the world, it clearly indicates the truth that every being comes to the world, wrapped all around with the memories of the previous lives. Everyone checks-in with some baggage of *samskaras,* and also checks-out with the luggage of memories, latencies and *samskaras* because of his added shopping in every life. The present life is indeed a preparation for the immediate next life and for many more to come in the distant future.

कर्मणः सुकृतस्याहुः सात्त्विकं निर्मलं फलम्।
रजसस्तु फलं दुःखमज्ञानं तमसः फलम्॥ १६॥

karmaṇaḥ sukṛtasyāhuḥ sāttvikaṁ nirmalaṁ phalam
rajasas tu phalaṁ duḥkhamajñānaṁ tamasaḥ phalam

(16) The fruit of good action is *Sattvic* and pure; while the fruit

of *Rajas* is pain and sorrow—ignorance is the fruit of *Tamas.*

सत्त्वात्सञ्जायते ज्ञानं रजसो लोभ एव च।
प्रमादमोहौ तमसो भवतोऽज्ञानमेव च॥ १७॥

sattvāt sañjāyate jñānaṁ rajaso lobha eva ca
pramādamohau tamaso bhavato'jñānameva ca

(17) *Sattva* promotes knowledge and *Rajas* promotes greed, while heedlessness and delusion arise from *Tamas* and also the ignorance.

ऊर्ध्वं गच्छन्ति सत्त्वस्था मध्ये तिष्ठन्ति राजसाः।
जघन्यगुणवृत्तिस्था अधो गच्छन्ति तामसाः॥ १८॥

ūrdhvaṁ gacchanti sattvasthā madhye tiṣṭhanti rājasāḥ
jaghanyaguṇavṛttisthā adho gacchanti tāmasāḥ

(18) Those who are settled in *Sattva* go upward. The *Rajasic* dwell in the middle and the *Tamasic* remaining under the influence of the lowest qualities go downward.

Commentary—Here in these verses, Srī Kṛṣṇa asserts the prime truth that every action has its reaction; this is a universal law and nobody can escape it. The reward of righteous acts is indeed pure and blessed, the result of the *Rajasic* activities is painful and that of *Tamasic* which is attempted in delusion is unhappiness and frustration. When the work is attempted with the purity of thoughts and with the clarity of vision, it results in self-realization and inner happiness. The result and fruit of the passionate actions, which are not properly organized and attempted in confusion, is definitely unsatisfactory and painful. The work performed in a deluded state of mind results in sorrow. The individual of *Sattvic* thoughts is pure and integrated. He always lives in the awareness of the indwelling-self and works in perfect harmony with others. He is very organized and his goals are very clear to him. The experiential knowledge of the Supreme-Self promotes the realization of God in his own self as well as in others. The expression *urdhvam gacchanti sattva-stha* means the person who is settled in the purity of *Sattvic* knowledge, he rises upward from the limited identifications and rests in the realization of Supreme consciousness. He surrenders to the Lord and accepts the guidance from within. He is always very positive, cheerful and at peace with himself. The higher state of increased awareness means emotional maturity and spiritual growth, when the person becomes acquainted with the purpose of life and meaning of his existence.

The fruit of *Rajas* is definitely pain and frustration. A *Rajasic* person increases the field of his activities unnecessarily and almost out of proportion. His desire for amassing wealth grows to the extent that his life becomes very restless and unstable. Desire for one thing leads to the desire for something else. His restlessness does not stop until death. He remains involved in his business plans till the last minute of his departure from the world. This type of individual lives a life which is enshrouded with deep anxieties and he dies with the thoughts of anxieties. Srī Kṛṣṇa tells in verse eighteen, *madhye tisthanti Rajasaḥ* means the *Rajasic* person dwells in the middle. He is born again and again as the one dedicated to excessive activities until he is awakened with the consciousness of the Lord and pursues the goal of self-realization and God-realization. A *Tamasic* person definitely goes downward because he lives in a deluded world of ignorance which is beyond the realities of life. He lacks discriminating ability and does not know how to make proper use of that which is in his possession. There is a true incident from the life of an old woman who kept saving the money underneath the kitchen stove. She had thousands of dollars in her possession but still lived in utter poverty. At the time of death when she lost her voice, she kept pointing towards the stove, in order to tell her family about the hidden treasure. Few days after her death, her family found several bundles of dollars underneath the stove, those were half burnt and destroyed. This is indeed the *Tamasic* attitude which suggests to the person to live a life in a semiconscious state; in which he cannot differentiate between the right and the wrong type of activity. A *Tamasic* person lives his life in ignorance and dies in pain and ignorance. He is born in the lowest grades of human beings and other species. The human birth, instead of being an opportunity for spiritual growth and liberation, proves to be a total waste for him and that constitutes the most tragic fall and failure of human life.

नान्यं गुणेभ्यः कर्तारं यदा द्रष्टानुपश्यति।
गुणेभ्यश्च परं वेत्ति मद्भावं सोऽधिगच्छति॥ १९॥

nānyaṁ guṇebhyaḥ kartāraṁ yadā draṣṭānupaśyati
guṇebhyaś ca paraṁ vetti madbhāvaṁ so'dhigacchati

(19) When the seer beholds no agent other than the qualities of nature, and perceives the transcendent beyond the qualities, he attains My being.

गुणानेतानतीत्य त्रीन्देही देहसमुद्भवान्।
जन्ममृत्युजरादुःखैर्विमुक्तोऽमृतमश्नुते ॥२०॥

guṇān etānatītya trīn dehī dehasamudbhavān
janmamṛtyujarāduḥkhair vimukto'mṛtamaśnute

(20) When the embodied-self transcends the three Gunas, out of which the body is evolved, then he is released from birth, death, old age and misery; he attains immortality.

Commentary—In these two verses, Srī Kṛṣṇa once again repeats the prime truth which enlightens the individual about the distinction between the spirit and matter. The expression *Drasta* refers to the word *idam* used in the very first verse of the chapter thirteen. These specific words have been used to remind Arjuna of his true identity as a fragment of the Supreme-Self. Srī Kṛṣṇa wants Arjuna to understand the distinct characteristic of both; the primordial nature and the Supreme-Soul. Although both of these are beginningless still they are quite different in certain aspects. Nature is endowed with attributes while the Supreme-Self is attributeless. Nature *(prakriti)* is bound by the three Gunas while the Supreme Lord is *Nirguna Brahman*—beyond and above the bondage of all Gunas. Nature undergoes modifications and changes while the Supreme-Soul is imperishable and unchanging. It is only when the soul identifies with the body and the modes of nature, embodied-soul becomes the doer and experiencer. The realization of the Supreme-Soul beyond the Gunas is realized when the individual soul re-establishes his conscious relationship with the indweller and identifies himself with the Divinity within. That is the state of self-realization and inner awakening. In the process of self-revelation the individual-soul is reminded of his Divinity and primordial relationship with the Supreme-Soul.

The realization of the one, who is centred in the consciousness of the Supreme-Self is expressed in these words—*I am neither ego nor reason, I am neither mind nor thought. I cannot be heard nor cast into words, nor by smell nor sight ever caught : No elements have moulded Me, no bodily sheath is my lair. I cast aside hatred and passion, I conquered delusion and greed. No touch of pride caressed Me, so envy never did breed. Virtue and vice or pleasure and pain are not my heritage. I have no misgivings of death, no chasms of race divide Me. I dwell within the senses but they are not my home, Consciousness and joy am I and Bliss is where I am found.* This is the song of the soul, identifying with the Supreme-Soul. This is the state of enlightenment when the individual-soul witnesses the play of the mind, intellect and ego merely as a silent witness; and keeps his identity settled in the Supreme-Soul. In the state of self-realization, the individual rises above the trap of the Gunas and the games of mind. He becomes free from the bondage of all sufferings, old age, death and rebirth. When the embodied-self learns to act as a witness with the help of undivided devotion and meditation he develops unity with the indweller. He observes everything very clearly and intelligently. He experiences the pure knowledge of the self and tastes the freedom of the unconditioned purity of the self. He is awakened to a higher reality and from there he makes the effort towards the attainment of the highest goal of life. Srī Kṛṣṇa asserts in verse nineteen that when the enlightened person perceives no agent of action other than the modes of nature, he perceives the transcendent beyond the qualities and attains My state of being. He rises above the triad of nature out of which the body originates. He elevates himself from the experiences of all physical and psychological pains. The identification with the indwelling light blesses the individual with the joy of positive, peaceful and tranquil living. This is indeed a very special and rare experience for the embodied-soul—the state of *Jivamukta.*

अर्जुन उवाच

कैर्लिङ्गैस्त्रीन्गुणानेतानतीतो भवति प्रभो।
किमाचारः कथं चैतांस्त्रीन्गुणानतिवर्तते ॥ २१ ॥

kair liṅgais trīn guṇānetān atīto bhavati prabho
kimācāraḥ kathaṁ caitāṅs trīn gunānativartate

Arjuna said :

(21) What are the hallmarks of the man, who has transcended the three Gunas, O'Lord? What is his conduct, and how does he transcend the three Gunas (qualities)?

श्रीभगवानुवाच

प्रकाशं च प्रवृत्तिं च मोहमेव च पाण्डव।
न द्वेष्टि सम्प्रवृत्तानि न निवृत्तानि कांक्षति॥ २२॥

prakāśaṁ ca pravṛttiṁ ca mohameva ca pāṇḍava
na dveṣṭi saṁpravṛttāni na nivṛttāni kāṅkṣati

The Blessed Lord said :

(22) When there is enlightenment, activity and delusion in life O'Arjuna, he does not dislike them; nor does he long for them when they are absent.

उदासीनवदासीनो गुणैर्यो न विचाल्यते।
गुणा वर्तन्त इत्येव योऽवतिष्ठति नेङ्गते॥ २३॥

udāsīnavadāsīno guṇair yo na vicālyate
guṇā vartanta ityeva yo'vatiṣṭhati neṅgate

(23) He, who remains unconcerned and does not feel disturbed by these qualities; he acts merely as a witness. He understands that only the Gunas are in operation, so he remains firm and established in the Self.

समदुःखसुखः स्वस्थः समलोष्टाश्मकाञ्चनः।
तुल्यप्रियाप्रियो धीरस्तुल्यनिन्दात्मसंस्तुतिः॥ २४॥

samaduḥkhasukhaḥ svasthaḥ samaloṣṭāśmakāñcanaḥ
tulyapriyāpriyo dhīras tulyanindātmasaṅstutiḥ

(24) He, who is balanced in pain and pleasure and remains centred in the Self; who looks upon a clod, a stone, and a piece of gold as of equal worth, who remains balanced amidst the pleasant and the

unpleasant, who is steadfast and regards both blame and praise of himself as equal.

मानापमानयोस्तुल्यस्तुल्यो मित्रारिपक्षयोः।
सर्वारम्भपरित्यागी गुणातीतः स उच्यते॥ २५॥

mānāpamānayostulyas tulyo mitrāripakṣayoḥ
sarvārambhaparityāgī guṇātītaḥ sa ucyate

(25) Who maintains his balance in honour and dishonour, who is equal to a friend and foe, who is detached in all undertakings—he is said to have transcended the Gunas (qualities).

मां च योऽव्यभिचारेण भक्तियोगेन सेवते।
स गुणान्समतीत्यैतान्ब्रह्मभूयाय कल्पते॥ २६॥

mām ca yo'vyabhicāreṇa bhaktiyogena sevate
sa guṇān samatītyaitān brahmabhūyāya kalpate

(26) Who serves Me with an undeviated Yoga of devotion, he rises above the Gunas and becomes fit, to be one with Brahman.

ब्रह्मणो हि प्रतिष्ठाहममृतस्याव्ययस्य च।
शाश्वतस्य च धर्मस्य सुखस्यैकान्तिकस्य च॥ २७॥

brahmaṇo hi pratiṣṭhāham amṛtasyāvyayasya ca
śāśvatasya ca dharmasya sukhasyaikāntikasya ca

(27) For, I am the abode of Brahman, the immortal and the imperishable, of the primordial eternal Dharma and of Absolute Bliss.

Commentary—In verse twenty-one, Arjuna requests Srī Kṛṣṇa to explain the hallmarks of the one who has transcended the three modes of nature; out of which the entire creation is evolved. He desires to know more about the lifestyle of that special individual who lives beyond the sway of the qualities of nature. Arjuna wants to comprehend the genuine meaning of liberation and spiritual fulfilment and also wants to know how does the man of realization behaves and acts in relation with others in the world. In the next four verses from twenty-two to twenty-five, Srī Kṛṣṇa enumerates the characteristics of the one who has transcended the three qualities of nature. He tells

Arjuna that the modes of nature are always present in everybody in various levels. An enlightened person, who is well acquainted with the modes of nature, can comprehend their appearances and disappearances quite intelligently. He lives as a master and controller of these modes and manipulates them according to his choice and need. A person, who is settled in the wisdom of the Higher-self, is very intuitive and knows how to deal with every situation as it occurs. He has a clear-cut perspective of everything as it exists. He does not get puffed up at his own state of being enlightened and learned, and also does not worry if actions bear no fruit at all. He knows his limitations, and understands exactly where lies the bondage and where lies the freedom. He is well acquainted with the nature of *Sattva* and monitors his behaviour when the *Sattvic* qualities predominates his thinking faculty. He is also well aware when the *Rajasic* tendencies lay their trap in the form of excessive activity and also when the heedlessness overtakes him.

An enlightened person, who has risen above the slavery of the Gunas, he is very intelligent, always very alert, very vigilant and perpetually centred in the awareness of the super-consciousness. For example, when *Sattva* shines through his nature, he does not become involved in vain discussions. He does not indulge in mere show off and does not brag about his inner enlightenment and special psychic powers. He always maintains his imperturbable, inner calm and quietude. Whenever some one showers praises upon him, he takes every word of appreciation as an appreciation of the Lord within. Any complement that comes from others, he takes that as the pure quality of *Sattva* being reflected from the words of the other person; '*Sattva* complementing the *Sattva*'—in other words, Gunas acting upon the Gunas. This is the illuminated state of mind, of a *Gunateeta,* who has risen above the play of the Gunas. He regards honour and dishonour, loss and gain, pleasure and pain, as only passing phases of life. He considers that a mere appearance and disappearance of the kaleidoscopic dispositions. A *Gunateeta* is not devoid of all the Gunas, he is above and beyond the slavery of the Gunas. For him the slavery of Guna has become *Atita.* The one who has experienced the reality about the qualities of nature; he understands very clearly, as what it is to be the slave of one's own nature and what it is to be the master and controller of one's own nature. When the impulse for action is awakened, he accepts it as a call from the Supreme Lord and works for the welfare of the humanity. He considers all his plans and projects as God-ordained work. He never lets his ego expand for the work well done and does not regret much for the mistakes either. He neither feels forced to start a new project nor painful at the failure of his attempt. He is very well acquainted with the nature of *Tamas* also. A *Gunatita* knows very well when the *Tamas* waxes strong suppressing *Sattva* and *Rajas*; he immediately becomes alert and does not let negligence, sloth and laziness make unnecessary advances. Popping up of the thoughts of greed and jealousy in human mind are very natural but the individual's involvement in those is very personal. A *Gunateeta* who has risen above the slavery of nature; he observes and monitors every little wisp of thought that passes through his mind. He beholds, perceives and acts only as a spectator. He knows how to remain free from the circular pattern of worrying and being involved in the old memories, mistakes and habits of past. He is always vigilant and never lets his mind become involved in unnecessary thinking about past and future. He knows how to educate his mind about living in the present, from moment to moment. The individual who has attained an appropriate mastery over the modes of nature, for him a clod of earth, a stone and a coin of gold or silver are alike. He is always very peaceful and maintains his neutral outlook towards everything that comes along.

There is a very interesting incident from the life story of Guru Gobind Singh as described by Rabindranath Tagore. The great Sikh teacher, sat on the rock reading scriptures, when Raghunath, his disciple, proud of his wealth, came and bowed to him and said, 'I have brought my poor present unworthy of your acceptance.' Thus saying he displayed before the teacher a pair of gold bangles wrought with costly stones. The master took up one of them, twirling it round his finger, and the diamonds darted shafts of light. Suddenly it slipped from his hand and rolled down the bank into the water. 'Alas', screamed Raghunath, and jumped into the stream. The teacher set his eyes upon his book, and the water held and hid what it stole and went its way. The daylight faded when Raghunath came back to the teacher tired and dripping. He panted and said, 'I can still get it back if you show me where it fell.' The teacher took up the remaining bangle and throwing it into the water said, "It is there."

In verse twenty-six Srī Kṛṣṇa tells Arjuna that the person who is perpetually engaged in unswerving devotion to Me, he definitely transcends the qualities of nature and becomes an eligible candidate for the Divine status. Any person who rests in the essential nature of the Divine and is constantly connected with the Lord in the Yoga of undivided devotion.; he surely attains a positive control over the triad of the Gunas. He serves the Lord through everyone of his activities by constant adoration and meditation. In verse twenty-seven Srī Kṛṣṇa declares that I am the highest spiritual experience, the abode of immortality, the primordial Dharma and the absolute Bliss. In the last two verses of this chapter Srī Kṛṣṇa has emphasized once again upon the necessity of unswerving devotion for the Supreme Lord; which can help each and every individual to be awakened to his own source of life. One should try to establish constant identity with God by devotional love, contemplation and a non-stop *jaap* of the holy *mantra.* As the oil poured from one vessel into another, falls in an unbroken stream, similarly when the mind learns to stay absorbed uninterruptedly in the awareness of the God, the individual moves from ignorance to light, from unreal to real and from bondage to freedom. God's grace and *kripa* comes to the one who requests for it with undeviated love, devotion and adoration. Buddha and Srī Sankaracharya have not been chosen for the Lord's grace just out of random; they achieved the grace, through a total surrender to the Supreme Lord. They earned the grace by their own penances, austerities, ardent devotion and unconditional love for the Divine. The grace of the Supreme Lord is not an exception to certain rules of caste, creed and nationality; the grace follows the eternal law of unswerving devotion, meditation and unconditional love for the God. Srī Kṛṣṇa indicates in His dialogue that, it is only the *Sattva* attitude of mind that opens the doorway for knowledge, wisdom, self-improvement and spiritual awakening. Both *Rajas* and *Tamas*, can lead towards the moral fall of the individual. Each and every little thought, which originates in the mind is transformed into action and every action is transformed into *samskara*. The *samskaras* are the dormant traces in the person's sub-conscious mind, those accompany the embodied-soul from one birth to another. It is very important to remember that human life is a great gift of God. Human beings are blessed with subjective awareness of the Supreme-soul. Every individual has the potential to experience the presence of God within his own self and receive sufficient guidance for self-realization and God-realization. It is only in human life that the individual-soul gets an opportunity for self-examination, transformation and liberation. It should be the endeavour of every individual to learn to live a life consciously connected with the Divine and with a total control over the qualities of nature. Human life should become a means of redemption. As mentioned earlier in chapter six verse five by Srī Kṛṣṇa "*uddhared atmana tmanam na tmanam avasadayet atmai va hy atmano bandhur atmai va ripur atmanah*"—let a man lift himself by his own Self; let him not degrade himself; for he himself is his own friend and he himself is his own enemy.

ॐ तत्सदिति श्रीमद्भगवद्गीतासूपनिषत्सु ब्रह्मविद्यायां योगशास्त्रे श्रीकृष्णार्जुनसंवादे गुणत्रयविभागयोगो नाम चतुर्दशोऽध्यायः ॥ १४ ॥

'Aum' tatsaditi Śrīmadbhagawadgeetā sūpaniṣatsu brahmavidyāyām yogaśāstre Śrīkṛṣṇārjunasamvāde guṇatrayavibhāgayogo nāma caturdaśo'dhyāyaḥ

'AUM TAT SAT'—Thus, in the Upanishad of the glorious Bhagawad Geeta, the science of the Brahman (Absolute) the scripture of yoga, the dialogue between Srī Kṛṣṇa and Arjuna—thus, ends the chapter fourteen entitled *Guṇatriyavibhāgayoga.*

इति श्रीमद्भगवद्गीतासु चतुर्दशोऽध्यायः ॥ १४ ॥

Chapter Fifteen

PURUSHOTTAMAYOGA

THE YOGA OF THE SUPREME PERSON

श्रीभगवानुवाच

ऊर्ध्वमूलमधःशाखमश्वत्थं प्राहुरव्ययम्।
छन्दांसि यस्य पर्णानि यस्तं वेद स वेदवित्॥ १॥

ūrdhvamūlamadhaḥśākham aśvatthaṁ prāhuravyayam
chandānsi yasya parṇāni yas taṁ veda sa vedavit

The Blessed Lord said :

(1) Having its roots above and branches below, the *asvattha*, tree is known to be indestructible. Its leaves are the Vedic hymns (metres); he who knows it, is the knower of the Vedas.

अधश्चोर्ध्वं प्रसृतास्तस्य शाखा,
गुणप्रवृद्धा विषयप्रवालाः।
अधश्च मूलान्यनुसन्ततानि,
कर्मानुबन्धीनि मनुष्यलोके॥ २॥

adhaścordhvaṁ prasṛtās tasya śākhā
guṇapravṛddhā viṣayapravālāḥ
adhaś ca mūlānyanusantatāni
karmānubandhīni manuṣyaloke

(2) Its branches extend below and above, nourished by the Gunas. The objects of the senses are the shoots and its rootings are stretched forth—below in the world of men, resulting in the bondage of actions.

न रूपमस्येह तथोपलभ्यते,
नान्तो न चादिर्न च सम्प्रतिष्ठा।

अश्वत्थमेनं सुविरूढमूल-
मसङ्गशस्त्रेण दृढेन छित्त्वा ॥ ३ ॥

na rūpamasyeha tathopalabhyate
nānto na cādirna ca sampratiṣṭhā
aśvatthamenaṁ suvirūḍhamūlam
asaṅgaśastreṇa dṛḍhena chittvā

(3) Its real form is not thus perceived here, neither its end, nor its origin, nor its foundation; having cut off this deep-rooted tree with the strong axe of non-attachment.

ततः पदं तत्परिमार्गितव्यं,
यस्मिन्गता न निवर्तन्ति भूयः।
तमेव चाद्यं पुरुषं प्रपद्ये,
यतः प्रवृत्तिः प्रसृता पुराणी ॥ ४ ॥

tataḥ padaṁ tat parimārgitavyaṁ
yasmin gatā na nivartanti bhūyaḥ
tameva cādyaṁ puruṣaṁ prapadye
yataḥ pravṛttiḥ prasṛtā purāṇī

(4) Then, that highest goal should be pursued, whither having reached no one returns again. Saying "I seek refuge in the primordial Purusha, from whom has streamed forth this ancient current of the world".

निर्मानमोहा जितसङ्गदोषा,
अध्यात्मनित्या विनिवृत्तकामाः।
द्वन्द्वैर्विमुक्ताः सुखदुःखसंज्ञैर्-
गच्छन्त्यमूढाः पदमव्ययं तत् ॥ ५ ॥

nirmānamohā jitasaṅgadoṣā
adhyātmanityā vinivṛttakāmāḥ
dvandvairvimuktāḥ sukhaduḥkhasañjñair
gacchantyamūḍhāḥ padamavyayaṁ tat

(5) Free from egoism and delusion, victorious over the evils of

attachment, perennially absorbed in the study of the Self; totally free from desires and the pairs of opposites such as pleasure and pain, the undeluded reach the eternal state.

न तद्भासयते सूर्यो न शशाङ्को न पावकः।
यद् गत्वा न निवर्तन्ते तद्धाम परमं मम ॥ ६ ॥

na tad bhāsayate sūryo na śaśāṅko na pāvakaḥ
yad gatvā na nivartante tad dhāma paramaṁ mama

(6) Neither the sun, nor the moon, nor the fire illuminates that; having reached there, they do not return that is My Supreme Abode.

Commentary—Here Srī Kṛṣṇa proceeds to reveal the true nature of the Supreme-self. The dialogue opens with the description of nature and form of the *samsara* (world). In chapter thirteen, Srī Kṛṣṇa has given an elaborate description of the field of experiences *(kshetra)* and also the knower of the field *(kshetrajña)* separately. Here in this chapter the field of experiences is being presented with the unique allegory of a Aswattha tree. Aswattha literally means "that which will not remain the same till tomorrow". It is perpetually changing, constantly growing and expanding in all directions. The roots of this tree are strongly entangled deep down in the world of men; nourished by actions and experiences. The roots represent the results of past actions, the branches, the buds and the drop down aerial roots—represents the cycle of birth, death and rebirth going on ceaselessly. The expression *nanto na cadihr* stands for no beginning and no end in space or time; it has been conceived as *avyayam* (eternal) by the seers of truth. The roots of the tree are deeply soaked in the primordial ancient principle of sempiternal urge to action as mentioned by the sages—*pravrtti.* Srī Kṛṣṇa mentions in the fourth verse *yatah pravrttih prasrta purani*—means the activity that has streamed forth from the ancient energy in the distant past. In the words of Srī Aurobindo, "its branches stretch down below and it extends and plunges into other roots, well-fixed and clinging roots of attachment and desire with their consequences of more and more desire and an endlessly developing action." There is a description of Asvattha tree in *Kathopanisad* also "The tree with roots above in Brahman and branches below."

According to Professor Ranade, there is a description of similar kind of tree in Scandinavian mythology as illustrated in Carlyle's picturesque "Its boughs with their buddings and disleafings—events, things, catastrophes—stretch through all lands and times. Its boughs are histories of nations. The rustle of it is the noise of human existence. It grows there, the breath of human passion rustling through it—It is Igdrasil, the Tree of Existence. It is the past, the present and future."

Asvattha also stands for the tree of banyan family, which throws the branches down into the ground those become the roots again. The tree of *samsara* which is mentioned in the first verse with its roots above in the Supreme consciousness, is the body. The seat of *Brahaman* is in the *Brahmarandra* (the crown of the head) from where the entire body is nourished and sustained. At the time when the baby is conceived, it is in the Brahmarandra, where the consciousness becomes seated. At that time the thoughts of the mother, the thoughts of the father and the thoughts of the incoming soul, enter together as one uniform thought into the consciousness of the mother. This triple combination of thoughts and *samskaras* expresses itself into a unique personality of the person. So it is quite clear that the root of life is just a bunch of memories those are nourished by the source of life. The tree of *samsara* is deeply rooted in the Supreme consciousness. As the *Matri Upanisad* describes—The world is the manifestation of just one thought. Each and every life is merely the expression of some thoughts. So the thoughts and *karmas* are indeed the roots of this *samsara.*

Srī Kṛṣṇa says roots upward means the life starts from the roots above those are settled in the *Brahmarandra* in the form of thoughts and latencies. The life is an expression of information fed by the software of memories in the *Brahmarandra*. The development of the human body in the mother's womb, starts with brain and the rest follows accordingly. The roots of life are in the *Brahmarandra* (crown of the head) from where the elixir of life is supplied to the rest of the body. *Brahmarandra* is the reservoir of the immortal elixir; which drips constantly in the back of the throat and then channelized to the rest of the body. The great yogins know very well how to make the best use of this elixir in meditation. They energize their bodies constantly with this nectar of immortality. In the words of Swami Chidbhavanananda, "The speciality of the Banyan tree is that it supplies sap from above and sends forth the branches down into the earth. In this respect the functioning of the *samsara* resembles that of the banyan tree. Both of them receive their sustenance from above and come down to earthly existence". The tree of life which has originated and grown from the primordial being Narayana is the reservoir of memories, latencies and *karmas.* The *karmas* of all kinds such as *sanchit, prarabdh* and *bija* are the roots of the tree of the *samsara.* Sanchit Karmas are the deeds performed in the past lives. These held impressions are stored in the subtle body. These are also called *samskaras*; those determine the quality of present life. The *prarabdha karmas* are the impressions and latencies those determine the conditioned behaviour of the person. These *samskaras* sometime force the individual into the performance of certain type of activities even against his will.

The power of *karma* presides over the entire course of life. Every single movement and activity in life have been pre-designed to some extent. All experiences of life such as happiness, unhappiness, sufferings, and blessings, appear and disappear in a certain order as if designed by someone in the past. Metaphysically analyzed it can be determined that the *sanchit* and the *prarabdha karma* are the ones, those manifest themselves in the form of destiny. The third type of *karmas* those have been described by the sages are the *bija karmas*; which a person performs out of his free will in the present life. The *bija karmas* originate from the past *samskaras* and new aspirations. Every person is born with a free will to exercise his thoughts and deeds; but he is surely bound to experience the result of each and every one of his action. *Karmas* form the root of the *samsara.* The multifarious actions during lifetime are various subsidiary roots, those constantly nourish the tree. The *karmas* bind people to various aspirations, hopes, dreams, latencies, and memories in the form of *samskara;* and provide momentum to the cycle of birth, death and rebirth. The *sanchit karmas* initiate the new *karmas;* and in the process of fulfilling new desires, people create many more new births for themselves and are trapped in the ever revolving cycle of the world. The word *mulani* in the second verse stands for the root signifying the actions of men in the world of mortals. In the words of Swami Ramsukdhas, "When a person performs actions inspired by desires, the impressions of these actions accumulate in his mind and force him into the cycle of birth and death. A man has to reap the fruits of actions performed during this life here as well as hereafter. So it is the indisputable fact that the root of the tree of creation are indeed the *karmas* initiated by the past and present *samskara* (memories)". Srī Kṛṣṇa makes it very clear in the second verse saying—Nurtured by the constituent qualities of nature, with sense objects for their tender buds and leaves, the tree of life extends both upward and downward from the roots of thought and latencies; which binds the embodied-soul in all respects.

The world of human beings is considered to be the field of actions. It is through the mutually acting karmic procedures, that the world comes into existence. Everything and everybody inherits the characteristics of one's own previous existence and adjusts to the law of cause and effect. This phenomenon makes the entire creation accountable for the memories, *samskara* and for the actions inspired by the thoughts. In the words of Swami Chinmayananda, "the main root of the tree of *samsara* is lost in the Absolute Reality, High above, the "secondary roots" which spring from it are spread all around, and grow even downward, in the world of men, initiating all actions. Here, secondary roots are thought-channels *(vasanas),* which are created in us, and which propel each one of us towards our own typical actions and reactions in the world. They are the very causes that promote man's evil as well as meritorious activities in the world. Just as the main taproot, while spreading its secondary roots, claws the earth through them and gets the plant well-rooted, so too these *samskaras,* actions and their reactions, both good and evil, bind the individuals fast to the earthy plane".

The expression "*chandamsi yasya parnani yas tam veda sa veda-vit*"—the leaves of this tree of life are the revelation of the Absolute Truth as described in *Vedas.* Anybody who comprehends the nature of this specific tree, he surely understands the nature of the universe. The word *Veda* has been derived from the root-word *vid* means to know. *Vedas* are the repository of all knowledge and wisdom. The *Vedic* knowledge encompasses the knowledge of the whole universe, which covers all the subjects those relate to animate and inanimate. About *Vedas* it has been said "*yada budham bavyam bavishyach sarvam vedaat prasidyati*"—The vedic knowledge envelopes in it the entire wisdom of past, present and future. It is valid for all times in every field of life and for everyone in the universe. The vedic knowledge is the beacon light for proper guidance to humanity in all respects. *Veda* is the word of God and the fulfilment of the vedic order is Dharma. Authority of vedic knowledge is the highest in each and every field, whether religious, social, legal, purely literary and the sciences. The hymns in Vedas have been categorized in three sections. The first part is known as *Samhitas.* The *Samhitas* are four and constitute the *Mantra* portion. The second part is known as *Brahmanas* which deals with the rites, ceremonies and rituals. The third part constitutes the *Aranyakas,* which describes the knowledge of the Supreme-self. The *Upanishads* form the very important part of the *Aranyakas.* The word *Upanishad* literally means to sit nearby devotedly. The *Upanishads* illustrate the knowledge of the Supreme-soul which has been imparted in the form of questions and answers. It is very interesting and very useful for self-realization and God-realization. Out of one hundred and eight *Upanishads,* only eleven have been recommended for general studies. These eleven are—*Isha, Kena, Katha, Prashna, Mundaka, Mundukya, Chhandogya, Brihadaranyaka, Aitareya, Taittiriya* and *Shvetashvatara.* Vedas declare—as the macrocosm so is in the microcosm. Every atom in the material world is some how related to every little molecule in the body. Human mind is a fragment of the cosmic mind and human body is composed of similar elements as the rocks, stars, trees, water, etc. The *Vedas* present guidelines for living a balanced and harmonious life on earth. In this verse Srī Kṛṣṇa declares that the sage who has clearly comprehended the truth, about the tree of life is definitely the knower and the experiencer of the self-revealed knowledge of the *Vedas.* He is indeed *Veda-vid*—means the knower of the *Vedas.*

In the third verse Srī Kṛṣṇa makes it very clear that understanding the tree of *samsara* is very difficult for human beings. It is surely beyond the simple grasp of a person. *Samsara* is the manifestation of various interconnected events. It is indeed very difficult to trace back its origin because every single root has emerged from the preceding one. So the reasonable interpretation can be that there are no specific signs or marks of any beginning of this world., The history of the entire universe is the evolutionary chain of alterations which is being worked out by a specific law of *karma* (cause and effect). The entire process is a continuous flow of renewal and degeneration, evolution and dissolution, birth and death, following each other with an inevitable sequence. Everybody and everything has its heritage in the One which existed before. Srī Kṛṣṇa says that the understanding of *samsara* is very difficult as long as the person remains trapped in pursuing material comforts and sensual pleasures. He suggests to mankind to wake up from the everyday reality and comprehend the truth, which lies veiled behind the perceptual boundaries of the senses. This verse conveys a subtle message that the human beings are not just the passive victims of some unknown destiny. Every person has the ability and insight to awaken the power within and be liberated from the bonds of *karmas.* When the individual feels awakened, he develops affinity with the indwelling Lord. It is only from such revelation that he gradually becomes attached to the Lord and detached from the mundane world. The roots of this tree of creation are firmly entangled around the feeling of 'I and Mine'. With the spirit of self surrender to the Supreme being, when 'I and Mine' is replaced by 'Thou and Thine'; dispassion and detachment from the world takes place naturally and surely.

The expression *asanga-sastrena drdhena chitva*—means cut asunder the roots of this strongly rooted tree with the axe of detachment. Human life is the most privileged one among all the species in creation. Human beings are blessed with subjective awareness and can develop the insight of realizing and experiencing the presence of God within. Human beings are free and independent in the performance of their new actions. Every individual is privileged to make and design his own destiny, while the other species can only follow the dictates of their instinctive nature and are bound to reap the fruits of their actions. Swami Vivekananda has written that '*karma* is the eternal assertion of human freedom'. Every person is absolutely free in the execution of his actions but definitely bound in reaping the fruits thereof. A person entangles himself into the web of bondage in human life; but at the same time it is only in human life wherein he can liberate himself from the bondage also. There is a poem:

> "*Duniya ke moha jal ko, yatno se tor de, sambhand zindagi ka, oos preetam se jor le. succha vypar na kya toe vypar kya kia. Ishwar se pyar na kya to e pyar kya kia.*"
>
> दुनिया के मोहजाल को, यत्नों से तोड़ दे, सम्बन्ध जिन्दगी का उस प्रीतम से जोड़ ले। सच्चा व्यापार न किया तो व्यापार क्या किया। ईश्वर से प्यार न किया तो प्यार क्या किया॥

The expression in verse four indicates that when a person takes refuge in the primordial Supreme-spirit, from where the ancient flow of creativity has streamed forth, he is blessed with experiential knowledge of his own immortality. In the state of revelation the individual becomes free from the false notions of 'I and Mine'. He feels very contented within his own self and his attachment to the worldly desires starts disappearing. A person who feels fulfilled and contented within, he definitely rises above the dualities of life. The realm of transcendental consciousness is self-illuminated. This field of pure effulgence and splendour is within the access of every human being. It becomes distant *(para)* and difficult to experience because of individual's own ignorance in the form of obscured and deluded perception. So when the person surrenders to the Divinity within, he feels awakened once again and experiences the self-illuminated field of pure consciousness. The individual learns to live a life inspired from the unified field of transcendental unity'.

ममैवांशो जीवलोके जीवभूतः सनातनः।
मनःषष्ठानीन्द्रियाणि प्रकृतिस्थानि कर्षति॥ ७॥

mamaivāñśo jīvaloke jīvabhūtaḥ sanātanaḥ
manaḥṣaṣṭhānīndriyāṇi prakṛtisthāni karṣati

(7) An eternal fragment of Myself, having become the embodied-soul in the world of living; draws to itself thc senses with the mind as the sixth, which rests in Prakriti (Nature).

शरीरं यदवाप्नोति यच्चाप्युत्क्रामतीश्वरः।
गृहीत्वैतानि संयाति वायुर्गन्धानिवाशयात्॥ ८॥

śarīraṁ yad avāpnoti yaccāpyutkrāmatīśvaraḥ
gṛhītvaitāni saṅyāti vāyur gandhānivaśayāt

(8) When the soul (as embodied-soul) takes up a body and also when he leaves it, he takes along these (the mind and senses) and goes as the wind carries the perfumes from their seats.

श्रोत्रं चक्षुः स्पर्शनं च रसनं घ्राणमेव च।
अधिष्ठाय मनश्चायं विषयानुपसेवते॥ ९॥

śrotraṁ cakṣuḥ sparśanaṁ ca rasanaṁ ghrāṇameva ca
adhiṣṭhāya manaścāyaṁ viṣayānupasevate

(9) Presiding over the ears, the eyes, the touch, taste and smell as well as the mind; the embodied-soul enjoys the object of the senses.

उत्क्रामन्तं स्थितं वापि भुञ्जानं वा गुणान्वितम्।
विमूढा नानुपश्यन्ति पश्यन्ति ज्ञानचक्षुषः॥ १०॥

utkrāmantaṁ sthitaṁ vāpi bhuñjānaṁ vā guṇānvitam
vimūḍhā nānupaśyanti paśyanti jñānacakṣuṣaḥ

(10) The deluded do not perceive the indwelling-soul, while departing from or dwelling in the body and experiencing the objects of the senses in contact with the modes; but they who possess the eye of wisdom truly see.

यतन्तो योगिनश्चैनं पश्यन्त्यात्मन्यवस्थितम्।
यतन्तोऽप्यकृतात्मानो नैनं पश्यन्त्यचेतसः॥ ११॥

yatanto yoginaś cainaṁ paśyantyātmanyavasthitam
yatanto'pyakṛtātmāno nainaṁ paśyanty acetasaḥ

(11) The striving yogins do perceive the indwelling-soul, established in the Self but the ignorant those have not purified their

hearts; even though endeavouring, do not perceive the indweller.

Commentary—After presenting a detailed description of *samsara* Srī Kṛṣṇa proceeds further to enlighten Arjuna about the essential nature of *jivatma.* Srī Kṛṣṇa declares that *jivatma* is an eternal fragment of Myself in the world of life. The word *jiva* literally *jiv*—a Sanskrit word which means to breathe. *Jivatma*—meaning a fragment of the *Atma* who identifies with *Jiva. Jivatma* is perennially one with the *Atma* (Supreme-soul) but also separate because of its separate assumed identity. As a bubble of water from the ocean appears to be separate because of the air in it, similarly the embodied-soul appears to be separate from the Supreme-soul because of its assumed identity with the body. It is due to the alienation from its real nature, that *Jiva* forms a separate identity. According to the *Samkhya* theory of multiplicity, it is the only one Supreme-soul in the entire creation, which becomes manifested in many modes at many levels. An eternal *amsa* or fragment or part of the Supreme-soul permeates everything. According to Swami Chidbhavananda, "*Jivatma* is never an entity separate or independent of the Paramatma. As a wave is essentially a part of the sea, the individual-soul is eternally a part and parcel of Iswara". In the *Ramayana* the same truth has been described in these words *"Iswar Ansa jiv avinasi, chaitana amal saheja sukhrasi*" In essence the embodied-soul is identical with the universal-soul (Brahman). It is only due to ignorance that the embodied-soul forms a separate identity and feels alienated. In the words of Srī Ramsukdhas, "the soul having assumed its affinity with the body, senses, mind, and life breath, which are the evolutes of nature, has become the *Jivabhutah* which is like an actor in a play". The experience of alienation occurs because of duality; but when the individual-soul dives deep in the subtle layers of consciousness from the gross to the subtlest realms of awareness; it realizes its true identity and feels a part of the Super-soul again. Everyone can experience this truth, that in moments of deep pain and disappointments when the individual turns inward for help, he feels altogether renewed and revitalized by the power of the Indweller. This is exactly like going back to the source of life and experiencing one's own essentiality. It comes to the individual in the form of revelation and total fulfilment.

Swami Vivekananda has said "Each soul is potentially Divine". The real nature of *Jivatma* is *Sat-chit-ananda*. It is due to the ignorance he assumes several *upadhis*—limiting adjuncts and forgets his real nature. Swamiji has given a very good example with the illustration of a story. 'Once a tigress attaçked a flock of sheep. As she sprang on her prey, she gave birth to a cub and died. The cub grew up in the company of sheep. Since the sheep eat grass so the cub also followed their habits. As the sheep bleated; so the cub also bleated like them. Gradually the cub grew to be a big tiger. One day another tiger attacked the same flock of sheep and was totally amazed to see a grass eating tiger. When the wild tiger attacked, the grass eating tiger began to bleat. The wild tiger dragged the grass eating tiger to the water pond and roared : look at your face in the water. It is just like mine. The wild tiger made a big roar and reminded the timid bleating tiger of its true identity. In the beginning it was difficult for the bleating tiger to roar with full strength but quickly it realized the identical voice and roared to the full strength and felt very good about its true identification". Similarly the Supreme Lord reveals Himself to the devotee and makes the individual aware of his true identity as a fragment of the Divine. Sometime the individual becomes blessed with the realization of the Self through the help of saints and sages who help the person to eliminate his *jiva-brahma-bheda bhranti* in the form of inner awakening. In the other half of verse seven Srī Kṛṣṇa explains very clearly how the person remains bound in his separate individuality, saying "An eternal portion of Myself becomes an embodied-self; when he becomes involved in the objects of senses'. The pure consciousness becomes individualized when he is drawn to the five subtle senses of perception along with the mind as the sixth. Srī Kṛṣṇa declares that it is only due to an error, the eternal *amsa* of the Supreme forms a separate individuality. When the individualized-soul identifies with the body, mind, and senses, he gradually becomes involved in the enjoyments of the body and forgets the real identity. The sense faculties are rooted in the mind, that is why the mind has been called the sixth sense. The information from the material world is given to the mind by the organs of perception such as hearing, sight, touch, taste and smell those influence the organs of actions such as tongue, feet, hands, genitals and the organs of defecation. These senses serve as various windows to the world outside to the indweller in the body. The messages are conveyed from the physical body and interpreted by the mind. Mind interprets the data, stores it and also feeds back the physical body with new and old information. It is surely through the senses of perception and mind that the individual-soul relates himself to the field of nature and gains the experiences of pleasure and pain.

The *Kathopanisad* has described this in these words *Atmaindrya yuktem Bhoktetyahur manishrna*. The soul when united with the senses and mind is called the enjoyer by the seers. The self imposed identity of the individualized soul with the mind is very strong, it follows the individual from one life to another. *Jivatma* remains united with the faculty of the sensory perceptions, thoughts and impressions throughout the life-time and also leaves the physical body with their repositories as the wind carries the scents from their blossoms. *Jivatma* packs up all the information of mind and senses while leaving the physical body and also enters into another body with the package. Srī Kṛṣṇa affirms very strongly that every embodied-soul checks into the new body with some luggage of *samskaras* (memories) and checks out with luggage of *samskaras*; with a lot of shopping at every station of life. Swami Chinmayananda has given the interpretation in these words: "at the time of departing from the body, the subtle body gathers itself, from the gross 'dwelling place' and on reaching the new physical structure, it spreads itself out again to use its faculties through the new house of experience.'

At the time of transmigration the embodied-soul carries the conception for the future body in the form of most favourite thoughts and latencies. The procedure of transmigration from one life to another has been called the Jiva's strong urge for expression and fulfilment of certain desires. Each new life is an expression of some memories of past lives. For example, just reflect on the span of present life till today. It exists only in the form of some thoughts; those have gone into the bank of memories and have become merely a memory of yesterday. All cherished moments of life, strong urges and desires, difficult times, favourite times; where are they? The entire past has become a mere idea of mind. The life is a series of thoughts designed in a certain order and the cycle of transmigration is also a series of thoughts which appcar and disappear constantly tumbling over one another. The memory bank is created, maintained and sustained by the embodied-soul. Each and every thought exists because of the conscious involvement of the individual soul with it.

Srī Kṛṣṇa points out in verse ten that the subtle indulgence of the embodied-soul with the mind, senses and body is not perceived by people in general, and that is why people become the victim of their conditioned habits. They experience good and bad times under the spell of sensory enjoyments. Every single movement in life expresses the sufficient reason of bondage and slavery but still hardly anyone comprehends the real cause of slavery. People live their lives in total ignorance and without realizing their legitimate potentials for freedom, liberation and emancipation. Srī Kṛṣṇa has called these ignorant people *vimudha*—those are not sensitive to the presence of the spirit dwelling within their own selves. He tells that the deluded people do not perceive the presence of the indwelling-soul, while departing from or dwelling in the body and experiencing the objects of senses, in contact with the modes; but those who possess the eye of wisdom, they truly see. The transcendental majesty of the Divine is definitely missed by ignorant people but it is distinctly perceived by the men of wisdom. They have the insight to cognize and experience the soul as the knower of the body and make proper efforts for self emancipation. The word *yoginah* in verse eleven stands for the sages those are constantly trying to live in the consciousness of the Supreme Lord. These striving aspirants do conceive the ultimate reality within themselves with constant practice and determination. A clean hearted, highly resolved yogi definitely experiences the majesty of the Divine in the Self but the unintelligent, undisciplined those are impure at heart; they remain unsuccessful inspite of their rigorous efforts. Success in spirituality is accomplished by some dedicated, sincere, pure hearted and fully committed individuals. An aspirant who aims at self-realization has to be fully resolved, genuinely inquisitive, intuitive and diligent. Spiritual progress demands proper endeavour made through the purity of mind, and the clarity of intelligence. The word *Kritat* used in the verse stands for those aspirants who have experienced and perceived the Supreme-soul in yogic unity and are constantly making efforts to maintain that connectedness. These awakened aspirants are totally surrendered to the Divine and continue their yogic practices for self-purification and increased spiritual awareness, they definitely perceive the essential nature of the Supreme-self.

यदादित्यगतं तेजो जगद्भासयतेऽखिलम्।
यच्चन्द्रमसि यच्चाग्नौ तत्तेजो विद्धि मामकम्॥ १२॥

yadādityagataṁ tejo jagad bhāsayate'khilam
yaccandramasi yaccāgnau tat tejo viddhi māmakam

(12) The light of the sun which illumines the whole universe, that which is also in the moon and fire—know that light to be My splendour.

गामाविश्य च भूतानि धारयाम्यहमोजसा।
पुष्णामि चौषधीः सर्वाः सोमो भूत्वा रसात्मकः॥ १३॥

gāmāviśya ca bhūtāni dhārayāmyaham ojasā
puṣṇāmi cauṣadhīḥ sarvāḥ somo bhūtvā rasātmakaḥ

(13) Penetrating the earth I support all beings with my vital energy and nourish all the herbs by becoming the sapful soma (moon).

अहं वैश्वानरो भूत्वा प्राणिनां देहमाश्रितः।
प्राणापानसमायुक्तः पचाम्यन्नं चतुर्विधम्॥ १४॥

ahaṁ vaiśvānaro bhūtvā prāṇināṁ deham āśritaḥ
prāṇāpānasamāyuktaḥ pacāmyannaṁ caturvidham

(14) I am the universal fire (vaishvanara) dwelling in the body of all living beings; and joined with the rhythm of inhalation and exhalation I digest the four kinds of food.

सर्वस्य चाहं हृदि संनिविष्टो,
मत्तः स्मृतिर्ज्ञानमपोहनं च।
वेदैश्च सर्वैरहमेव वेद्यो,
वेदान्तकृद्वेदविदेव चाहम्॥ १५॥

sarvasya cāhaṁ hṛdi sanniviṣṭo
mattaḥ smṛtir jñānamapohanaṁ ca
vedaiś ca sarvairahameva vedyo
vedāntakṛd vedavideva cāhaṁ

(15) I am seated in the hearts of all. I am the source of memory, wisdom and ratiocinative faculty. I am subject to be known through all the *Vedas :* I am the author of Vedanta, as well as the knower of the *Vedas.*

Commentary—Here in these verses Srī Kṛṣṇa declares once again that the entire manifestation has emanated from the Supreme-soul. The well-known scripture *Yogadarsana* describes God as the preceptor and the ancestor of every being and everything in the creation. The illuminating characteristic of the sun, moon and fire is an aspect of the infinite consciousness. The cosmic energy pervades the entire universe and holds it intact. It comes as life energy, enters the earth and sustains all the movables and immovables. The same energy penetrates into the earth in the form of *rasatmakah somah* and nourishes all the juicy vines, medicinal herbs and other healing plants by infusing sap into them. Srī Kṛṣṇa tells Arjuna that the nectarean soma which nourishes the herbs on earth is also a form of Divine energy which emanates from the Supreme-soul. Moon is merely a transmitter of the sapful soma or nectarean elixir. The light of the moon is considered to be the repository of all the savours. The life in the microcosm as well as in the macrocosm is deeply influenced by the light of moon. The ancient Ayurvedic text describes that in the rotation of moon around the earth, there are certain days when the earth and human body are influenced very deeply by the rays (*ojas*) of the moon. At that time the water level in the sea as well as in the human body rises to the peak level. These four special days are the fourth, the eighth, the eleventh and the fifteenth of the lunar calendar. The Ayurvedic tradition recommends that people should observe fast on these days and especially they should avoid to drink water if possible. They should also avoid eating green vegetables because of the high contents of water in them. This austerity is highly recommended for people who suffer from high blood pressure, chronic asthma and sinus problems. The effect of the moonlight is very powerful on the physical as well as the psychological make up of the individual; especially on the full moon day. It is also described in Ayurveda that the child in the mother's womb during the period of nine months, grows in size and weight only in the bright half of the ascending phase of the moon.

The word *Vaishvanara* in verse fourteen stands for the cosmic energy which sustains life on earth. Srī Kṛṣṇa says that taking the role of *Vaishvanara* (the fire of life), I abide in the bodies of living creatures; and joined with inhalation and exhalation, I transform and assimilate the fourfold foods. This energy is also called *jatharagni* means the fire in the stomach that helps in the digestion of food. The fourfold food mentioned in this verse comprises the *bhojya* means that which is chewed with teeth such as bread, rice, grains, fruits etc. The second *peya* that which is swallowed like milk, water, juice etc. The third one is *cosya* that which is sucked and fourth one is *lehya* that which is licked. *Shruti Bhagvati* has also described the digestive power in these words "*Ayam Agni Vaishavanaro Yoamanta Purusha yenedam anyam pachayate*"—that fire is *Vaishavanara* within the man which digests food. Srī Kṛṣṇa declares that the digesting energy in the stomach is only a fragment of the infinite energy which pervades in all the three world. It is indeed very important to understand the truth that it is only one consciousness within and without, transforming and appearing in the various different forms of energy. Everything has emerged from one ultimate reality. There are beautiful lines by Tagore, as written in *Gitanjali* "The same stream of life that runs through my veins, night and day, runs through the world and dances in rhythmic measures. It is the same life that shoots in joy through the dust of the earth in numberless blades of grass and breaks into tumultuous waves of leaves and flowers. It is the same life that is rocked in the ocean-cradle of birth and of death, in ebb and in flow. I feel my limbs are made glorious by the touch of this world of life".

In verse fifteen Srī Kṛṣṇa draws Arjuna's attention from the cosmic body to the human body and says, 'I am also seated in the hearts of all. I am the source of memory, knowledge and ratiocinative faculty'. Earlier in chapter thirteen Srī Kṛṣṇa has declared the human heart to be the shrine of the Lord. Although the Supreme consciousness is the essence of life and resides in each and every little molecule of the body but can be perceived, intimated and experienced only at the heart centre. The realization of the Supreme Lord at the shrine of the heart is easy and most rewarding experience of life. It is easy because the individual is not seeking something distant, not something foreign and alien; it is very much known, familiar and one's own indwelling-self. The contemplation at the heart centre has been highly recommended in almost all the religious traditions of the world. It is indeed in the subtle realms of consciousness at the *Anahat chakra* where the aspirant can perceive and experience the presence of the spirit within. When an ardent devotee concentrates at the heart centre and makes effort to grasp the sound waves of the eternal nada (AUM); he goes into yogic unity with the indwelling-soul.

The spiritual experience of proximity with the Divine at the heart centre prepares the individual for the devotional love of the Lord. The individual mind surrenders to the indwelling Supreme-soul and gradually becomes peaceful. When the mind feels immersed in the affinity of the Lord, there comes a certain sensitivity and alertness which is symbolized by a yogi sitting in perfect lotus position. In yogic unity at the shrine of the sacred heart centre; the aspirant experiences self-expansion and cosmic unity. In the state of self-revelation, the individual is transformed in all respects and accelerates himself from the narrow identities of the individual-self. The grace of the Divine functions through the individual in the performance of his worldly activities. He becomes the embodiment of Bliss and carries that Bliss wherever he goes. This can be observed and seen clearly from the life style of some enlightened aspirants. In the other half of this verse Srī Kṛṣṇa repeats once again the magnificence of the Supreme consciousness saying 'I am the source of memory, knowledge and also the ratiocinative faculty'. The ability to understand anything and to rationalize, surely emanates from the Supreme spirit. It is the grace of the omnipotent Lord that functions through various faculties such as comprehension of knowledge, and also its retention. The act of forgetfulness also takes place with the power of the Divine. The useless and purposeless retention in the memory bank is destroyed by nature in due time; so that people can renounce the past and make a new start at every step for further progress in all respect. Every aspect of human nature emerges from one consciousness only, which creates, supports, sustains and also annihilates. It is one and the only power that has initiated the writings in the *Vedas* and has also made possible the dialogues and discussions in Vedanta. The Supreme-soul encompasses and controls all the movements of each and every field in microcosm as well as in macrocosm.

द्वाविमौ पुरुषौ लोके क्षरश्चाक्षर एव च।
क्षरः सर्वाणि भूतानि कूटस्थोऽक्षर उच्यते॥ १६॥

dvāvimau puruṣau loke kṣaraś cākṣara eva ca
kṣaraḥ sarvāṇi bhūtāni kūṭastho'kṣara ucyate

(16) There are two kinds of purushas in this world, the perishable and the imperishable. All beings are perishable—The unchanging (the soul) is called the imperishable.

उत्तमः पुरुषस्त्वन्यः परमात्मेत्युदाहृतः।
यो लोकत्रयमाविश्य बिभर्त्यव्यय ईश्वरः॥ १७॥

uttamaḥ puruṣas tvanyaḥ paramātmetyudāhṛtaḥ
yo lokatrayamāviśya bibhartyavyaya īśvaraḥ

(17) The Supreme Purusha is yet other than these—called the highest Self; the indestructible Lord. Who enters the three worlds, upholds and sustains them.

यस्मात्क्षरमतीतोऽहमक्षरादपि चोत्तमः।
अतोऽस्मि लोके वेदे च प्रथितः पुरुषोत्तमः॥ १८॥

yaśmāt kṣaramatīto'hamakṣarādapi cottamaḥ
ato'smi loke vede ca prathitaḥ puruṣottamaḥ

(18) Since I transcend the perishable and am even higher than the imperishable; therefore in this world as well as in *Vedas,* I am declared to be the Supreme Purusha.

यो मामेवमसम्मूढो जानाति पुरुषोत्तमम्।
स सर्वविद्भजति मां सर्वभावेन भारत॥ १९॥

yo māmevamasammūḍho jānāti puruṣotttamaṁ
sa sarvavid bhājati māṁ sarvabhāvena bhārata

(19) The undeluded one, who knows Me thus, as the Supreme Purusha, is the knower of all. He worships Me with his whole being (whole heartedly) O' Arjuna.

इति गुह्यतमं शास्त्रमिदमुक्तं मयानघ।
एतदबुद्ध्वा बुद्धिमान्स्यात्कृतकृत्यश्च भारत ॥ २० ॥

iti guhyatamaṁ śāstramidamuktaṁ mayānagha
etad buddhvā buddhimān syāt kṛtakṛtyaś ca bhārata

(20) Thus, this most profound teaching has been imparted by Me, O'sinless one; by understanding this, one becomes self-enlightened and his goal in life is accomplished, O'Arjuna.

Commentary—In these verses Srī Kṛṣṇa explains in detail the concept of '*purushottam yoga*,—which literally means an introduction and communion with the Supreme-self. Purushottam yoga means a union and communion with the transcendental Supreme-soul. The word *ksarah* stands for the perishable manifestations in the world. This includes all the movables and immovables from the grossest to the tiny blade of grass. This is the material world which is composed of five gross elements. Everything which is seen and perceived by the eyes and the senses and comprehended by the mind comes under the vast territory of *ksarah* (perishable). This is the manifestation of the Divine potency in the field of space and time. The perishable creation comes into existence, is sustained for a while and finally goes back to the essential field of the primordial nature. The entire realm of matter is perishable, while the conscious principle that shines through matter is indeed imperishable. The Supreme consciousness manifests itself through light and heat of the sun, through life in the plants, fertility in the earth and consciousness in the body. This is imperishable. The realm of matter is perishable but the Supreme soul which expresses through the matter is imperishable and immutable. When the pure lucid, luminous *atman* (a fragment of the Lord) identifies with the material body, he is called *jivatma;* and appears to be the enjoyer and the experiencer. The *jivatma* is not separate from the Divine purusha. This is an eternal portion of the Supreme-Soul. The *jivatma* is essentially Divine. When *jivatma* accelerates himself above the false identifications and identifies more with the Supreme-Soul; the *jivatma* becomes spiritually enlightened and is called Mahatma. Later in spiritual progression; when the identification with the Supreme-Soul is established more vividly and completely, the *jivatma* rises to the status of *Paramatma.* These are indeed various stages of self-awareness in the evolution of self-revelation. The embodied-soul is only a fragment of the Supreme-Soul. The soul enters into the primordial nature and plays many roles with many temporary veils.

The expression *dvavimau Purushau loke ksaras ca aksara eva ca*—means there are two kinds of purushas in the world, the perishable and the imperishable. The Supreme-Soul which is called the Higher-Self is distinct and stands above the perishable and also the imperishable. The *Uttama purusha* is greater than the mutable and also greater than the immutable. The Supreme power is '*anyah*' means the other than these, which is known and perceived by the senses and mind. That power just observes and witnesses everything which takes place in the ever changing world. The *Purushottama yoga* is the ultimate identification of the embodied-soul with the Supreme-Soul. It is the most difficult status to be achieved in spiritual progression. It is the most enlightened status in which the aspirant perceives the essential nature of both perishable and imperishable quite separately and distinctly. The discovery of the Supreme-Self is the most valuable and most rewarding gift of life. It is the journey from the gross to the subtle levels of consciousness and then to the subtle most centre of the Supreme-Soul. All the other pursuits of life are really very transitory limited to the boundaries of space and time. The real meaningful pursuit is the discovery of the *uttamapurusha* (Higher-Self) within, which transcends both the mutable and immutable. Srī Kṛṣṇa tells in the verse eighteen, since He transcends both the fallible and infallible; therefore He is known as the Supreme-Purusha, both in the world as well as in the hymns of Vedas'. The word uttama in verse seventeen signifies that the Supreme-Soul is indeed unsurpassible, higher than the perishable and beyond the imperishable. Shruti

Bhagvati has stated it very clearly *nityo nityanam cetanas cetananam*—means it is ever luminous and is indeed the essence of the entire universe. Srī Kṛṣṇa suggests Arjuna to look behind the veil of his own self-assumed identity and experience the truth of his own essential nature. It is only through self-exploration—he can discover for himself the misalignment within his own personality and then pursue his decision in the light of the Self. With the exploration of the essential nature the person gains some conscious control over everything in life. The moment one becomes attuned to the experience of the Self within the individual is transformed instantly and transported from less awareness to increased awareness and eventually to ultimate Bliss. The experience of the inner Bliss in yogic unity, eliminates all the dualities of life and the individual can perceive everything very clearly and harmoniously. After the experience of the indwelling Supreme-ṣoul in yogic unity, the person becomes attuned with the entire universe. He is blessed with the insight to perceive the One existing in many and the many existing in the One.

The expression *sarvavit* means the one who understands everything with subtle insight and in great detail. The person who transcends into the realm of the yogic communion with *Purushottma,* he definitely becomes the knower of all existent and nonexistent. The sage Udalaka has expressed this in these words 'one must know that by knowing which everything is known'. It is not merely the intellectual comprehension, it is surely the deep subjective apprehension which makes the experience of the indweller possible. Srī Kṛṣṇa tells Arjuna that the one who has fully identified himself with the Supreme-purusha, he can really comprehend the grandeur of the Lord's magnificence and is blessed with self-realization in due course. Even a momentary experience of eternal Bliss nourishes the mind with spirituality and awakens an immeasurable love for God. Srī Kṛṣṇa tells Arjuna with conformity that when the individual is awakened to the Blissful state of inner tranquillity, he loves to live in that peace for ever. He appreciates and enjoys the proximity of the Supreme Lord, with genuinely aroused devotion and dedication. He worships the Lord from the very core of his being and from the totality of his heart. The word *sarvabhavena* means wholeheartedness. It is indeed a fact that after perceiving the reality of the ultimate Bliss, a person worships the Lord with joy and satisfaction. He feels elevated, exhilarated and exalted every minute of life. The echo of the inner unison helps him to maintain his devotional ecstasy. It keeps the covenants renewed perpetually. An aura of ineffable devotion and dedication prevails over his mind and the entire thinking faculty, which keeps the individual charged with the unique power of yogic communion. The inner Bliss is exhibited spontaneously in each and every word he speaks and every bit of work he undertakes. Such an individual lives his life in perpetual ecstasy of the Supreme Bliss, and carries that Bliss along wherever he goes and shares that Bliss with any one who comes across. The expression *kṛita-kṛityasca* means fully blessed and enlightened in all respects. Such an individual is specially graced from within, with the proximity of the Lord which enables him to achieve the goal of life in the form of self-realization.

In the last verse Srī Kṛṣṇa says that I have imparted to you the most secret doctrine in the realm of spiritual knowledge; having known that a person becomes wise and the knower of all that needs to be known in human life. The knowledge of the Supreme-self is indeed the highest form of knowledge, which gives liberation in due time. The chapter fifteen has been called a *Sastra* by Srī Kṛṣṇa. This chapter presents a complete description of the Supreme-soul as well as the embodied-soul. The very first verse describes the nature of the universe. The next few verses present a description about the nature of the *Jivatma* (embodied-soul) and also the reasons of bondage. The declaration of *Purushottma* combines all the three and assimilates them into a clear and distinct statement. The knowledge of the Supreme-soul, which is the theme of this chapter, has been very clearly indicated in the last verses. Srī Kṛṣṇa has called the knowledge of the *Purusottama Guhyatamam* means the most secret, the most profound doctrine in the realm of spiritual knowledge. This knowledge becomes revealed to the individual from the treasure of his deepest awareness and from the field of pure consciousness. The inner wisdom and intuition unfolds itself in many different ways, and helps the individual in solving the most difficult intrigues of life. The person's love for God blossoms in all respect and also his love for life. The word *buddhiman* stands for the man of wisdom and sincere devotion. Absolute surrender to God is indeed the most reliable and all-sufficing method of God realization. Let the Supreme Lord possess the individual and become the means and the goal simultaneously.

ॐ तत्सदिति श्रीमद्भगवद्गीतासूपनिषत्सु ब्रह्मविद्यायां
योगशास्त्रे श्रीकृष्णार्जुनसंवादे पुरुषोत्तमयोगो
नाम पञ्चदशोऽध्यायः ॥ १५ ॥

'Aum' tatsaditi Śrīmadbhagawadgeetā sūpaniṣatsu
brahmavidyāyām yogaśāstre Śrīkṛṣṇārjunasamvāde
puruṣottamayogo nāma pañcadaśo'dhyāyaḥ

'AUM TAT SAT'—Thus, in the Upanishad of the glorious Bhagawad Geeta, the science of the Brahman (Absolute) the scripture of yoga, the dialogue between Srī Kṛṣṇa and Arjuna—thus, ends the chapter fifteen entitled "Purusottamayoga".

इति श्रीमद्भगवद्गीतासु पञ्चदशोऽध्यायः ॥ १५ ॥

Chapter Sixteen

DEVĀSURSAMPATTIVIBHĀGAYOGA

THE YOGA OF THE DISTINCTION BETWEEN THE DIVINE AND THE DEMONIACAL ENDOWMENTS

श्रीभगवानुवाच

अभयं सत्त्वसंशुद्धिर्ज्ञानयोगव्यवस्थितिः ।
दानं दमश्च यज्ञश्च स्वाध्यायस्तप आर्जवम् ॥ १ ॥

abhayaṁ sattvasaṅśuddhir jñānayogavyavasthitiḥ
dānaṁ damaś ca yajñaś ca svādhyāyas tapa ārjavam

The Blessed Lord said :

(1) Fearlessness, purity of heart, steadfastness in Yoga of knowledge, charity, self-control, performance of yajña, study of the scriptures, austerity and straightforwardness.

अहिंसा सत्यमक्रोधस्त्यागः शान्तिरपैशुनम् ।
दया भूतेष्वलोलुप्त्वं मार्दवं ह्रीरचापलम् ॥ २ ॥

ahimsā satyamakrodhas tyāgaḥ śāntirapaiśunaṁ
dayā bhūteṣvaloluptvaṁ mārdavaṁ hrīracāpalaṁ

(2) Non-violence, truthfulness, absence of anger, renunciation, peacefulness, aversion to fault finding, compassion towards all beings, non-covetousness, gentleness, modesty and absence of fickleness.

तेजः क्षमा धृतिः शौचमद्रोहो नातिमानिता ।
भवन्ति सम्पदं दैवीमभिजातस्य भारत ॥ ३ ॥

tejaḥ kṣamā dhṛtiḥ śaucamadroho nātimanitā
bhavanti sampadaṁ daivīmabhijātasya bhārata

(3) Brilliance, forgiveness, fortitude, purity, absence of hatred, absence of arrogance—These are the marks of the one who is endowed with divine nature, O'Arjuna.

दम्भो दर्पोऽभिमानश्च क्रोधः पारुष्यमेव च।
अज्ञानं चाभिजातस्य पार्थ सम्पदमासुरीम्॥ ४॥

dambho darpoabhimānaś ca krodhaḥ pāruṣyameva ca
ajñānaṁ cābhijātasya pārtha saṁpadamāsurīṁ

(4) Hypocrisy, arrogance, self-conceit, anger, rudeness and ignorance are the characteristics of the one who is endowed with demoniac nature O'Arjuna.

दैवी सम्पद्विमोक्षाय निबन्धायासुरी मता।
मा शुचः सम्पदं दैवीमभिजातोऽसि पाण्डव॥ ५॥

daivī saṁpad vimokṣāya nibandhāyāsurī matā
mā śucaḥ saṁpadaṁ daivīmabhijāto'si pāṇḍava

(5) The divine nature is conducive to emancipation and the demoniac to bondage. Grieve not, O'Arjuna, thou art born with divine endowments.

Commentary—The chapter sixteen opens with the purpose of presenting a marked distinction between the *Devas* and the *Asuras*. *Deva* literally means the one who knows how to give and share. The other word which is used for *Deva* is *Sura*—it is a Sanskrit word. *Sura* as the word itself explains—means the one who is consciously in tune with the Supreme-soul. The *Asura* means the one who is not consciously in tune with the Supreme-soul. *Devas* are endowed with divine traits; their nature expresses the purity, humanity, clarity, honesty, truthfulness and spontaneity of spiritual awareness. On the other hand, the *Asura* are endowed with demoniac traits and their behaviour expresses the conscious misalignment with the Higher-Self. The Divine characteristics are conducive to liberation and attainment of Bliss, while the demoniac traits promote bondage. In the first three verses of this chapter Srī Kṛṣṇa brings forth an exhaustive list of twenty-one divine characteristics. Absolute fearlessness is one of the most vibrant characteristic of an individual who has learnt to live a life in perfect harmony with the Supreme-self. Fearlessness is expressed spontaneously and it indicates the inner security and proper alignment with the higher-self. Faith in God manifests itself as the faith in one's ownself. The nature of the *Devas* is marked by an acme of inner security and fearlessness. In the words of Swami Chinmayananda, "By placing this quality of fearlessness at the head of the list, with the unsung music of sheer suggestiveness, the divine *Acharya* is indicating that true ethical perfection in one is directly proportional to the spiritual evolution attained by the individual."

Purity of heart has been highly emphasized in all religious traditions of the world. "Blessed are the pure at heart for they shall see God." Purity of thought corresponds to the innate nature of the Self which is pure and uncontaminated. People who are pure at heart, are indeed the walking manifestations of God. They impart purity even to the places of pilgrimage. In the words of Roy Eugene Davis, "All our efforts to meditate, study, practice self-discipline, etc., are only for the purpose of clearing the mind, so that the light of the soul can be clearly perceived."

Jñanayogavyasvasthi—means steadfastness in knowledge and yoga. It is perpetual absorption of mind in the knowledge of the Supreme. The yogic unity which is maintained by constant connectedness with the Supreme, it does bless the person with self-reliance and steadfastness. It promotes inner stability, faith and the spirit of detachment. *Daya, dana, daman* and *Yajña* constitute the basis of divine nature. *Daya*—is the quality of love and compassion for others and *dana*—means charity. A person becomes compassionate and charitable only when he learns to live in the awareness of the inner-self and feels himself reflected in others. It is the identification of self with others which promotes the spirit of sharing and charity. It is a great austerity which purifies the 'inner instruments' (*Antahkaran)* and helps the person to live perfectly in tune with his own self and with others. It elevates the individual, from the lower levels of selfishness and possessiveness and initiates him into the virtue of sharing and caring for others. *Dama*—means self-control and self-discipline in all respects. With self-control the physical and psychological energy can be channelized into the higher realm of self-unfoldment and God-realization. *Dama* is a spiritual discipline and a necessity for an aspirant who wants Yogic progress. *Yajña* means selfless service or sacrifice. The expression *Yajña* also signifies, the performance of *Agnihotra* (spiritual worship) for self-purification. The performance of *Yajña* forms the initial step for yoga communication. It is a prayer-cum-contemplation which connects the individual at all the three levels of his existence—physical, psychological and spiritual simultaneously. Oblations of purified butter and herbal mixture of medicinal plants connect the individual to the material world and the cosmic bodies; the chanting of hymns with each offering connects one to the psychological and spiritual-self.

Swadhyaya—are two words—*Swa* means the self and *adhyana* mean study. It is the study of the Self. *Swadhyaya* also indicates the study of the sacred scriptures; which helps the individual in self-realization and God-realization. Self-study inspires the person for the attainment of higher goals in life. '*Tapa*'—literally means to purify. All conscious efforts of living a disciplined and pure life both at the physical and psychological level are called '*Tapa*'. It is a very difficult form of austerity. '*Arjavam'*—is a Sanskrit word which means straightforwardness and uprightness. Spontaneity in conversation reflects the honesty of heart. *Arjavam* is the sincerity and purity which reflects the perfect unison of thoughts, words and deeds in dealing with others. Non-violence is one of the highest forms of austerity, which stands for *manase, vachya, karmana*—means, do not hurt anybody by thought, word and deed. It is a fact that every action which a person performs, and every word which he speaks, is indeed the manifestation of a particular thought which has flashed in his mind. So even to think of harming others is indeed an act of violence. As described earlier in the previous chapters, violence—literally means violating the laws of the Self, or going against the voice of the Self. So non-violence is the obedience to a higher law of *swadharma.* Truthfulness means taking all precautions to speak with the honesty of heart and what has been seen, heard or experienced in utmost awareness. The habit of speaking truth is a great austerity. It makes the person fearless and very confident. As described in *Maundukya Upanisad* the Supreme-Soul is always attainable by truth, austerity, inner wisdom and celibacy. The holy sages who are truthful, pure and illumined in their heart do experience His presence, from moment to moment: In the words of Gandhiji, 'The word *satya* (truth) is derived from *sat,* which means 'being'. Nothing is or exists in reality except Truth. That is why *Sat* or Truth is perhaps the most important name of God. Hence we know God as *Sat-Chit-Ananda,* one who combines in Himself Truth, Knowledge and Bliss. All our activities should be centred in Truth. Truth should be the very breath of our life. When once this stage in the pilgrim's progress is reached, all other rules of correct living will come without effort and obedience to them will be instinctive. But without Truth it is impossible to observe any principle or rule in life. There should be Truth in thought, Truth in speech, and Truth in action. To the man who has realized this Truth in its fullness, nothing else remains to be known, because all knowledge is necessarily included in it. Therefore the pursuit of Truth is true *Bhakti* (devotion). It is the path that leads to God".

Akrodha—means absence of anger. A person becomes angry because of his own personal insecurity, impatience and egoism. Although the waves of anger are very natural in human behaviour, but this emotion must not be allowed to rule one's life. The feeling of anger can be monitored, checked and controlled merely by living in the awareness of the Supreme-self. In the words of Swami Vivekananda, "the process of becoming angry has been described like this: 'Suppose a man says something very harsh to me, and I begin to feel that I am getting heated. And he goes on till I am perfectly angry and forget myself and identify myself with anger. When he first began to abuse me, I thought, 'I am going to be angry'. Anger was one thing and I was another. But when I became angry, I was anger. These feelings have to be controlled in the germ, the root, in their fine forms, even before we have become conscious that they are acting on us." *Tyaga*—means the spirit of renunciation. *Tyaga* is the abandonment of the feeling 'I' and 'Mine' and to work by the gospel of selfless action. *Santi*—means the quietude both at the psychological and the physical level. A person of inner peace keeps his mind very balanced and tranquil even in the middle of all kinds of turmoils, and disturbing situations. *Apaisunam*—means the prohibition of the use of the sarcastic and malicious words. It is an austerity and a conscious inner discipline. It is a progressive realization of the inward harmony.

Daya—means love and compassion for others. The scriptures proclaim. *Daya dharm ka mool hai*—means compassion forms the basis of *Dharma*. The virtue of compassion brings people closer and binds them together with the feeling of caring and sharing for one another. A person can be regarded religious, only if his heart is full of compassion and kindness toward others. *Prajña* and *Karuna*—move hand in hand. *Prajña* is the conscious alignment with the indwelling Lord and *Karuna* is the virtue through which the inner alignment manifests itself. *Aloluptvam*—means non-covetousness. Total absence of covetousness is another important characteristic of the individual who is endowed with divine traits. To the majority of mankind the finer levels of consciousness are not known because they live their lives totally controlled by worldly desires, passions and attractions. The man of sharp insight knows how to practise non-covetousness and how to control passions at the very root from where these emotions emerge. He knows that in every desire, which initiates him to pursue various enjoyments; he actually seeks for the satisfaction, which in the end has to be restored from his own inner resources.

Mardavam—means modesty and softness in thoughts and speech. A person who is established in the serenity of the Higher-Self he exhibits kindness, generosity and modesty naturally and spontaneously in his behaviour. *Hrih*—means a sense of shame in violating the injunctions of the scriptures. A person who is grounded in the nature of the Divine, he always respects scriptures and hesitates to violate the message given by the great seers and sages. *Achapalam*—means absence of fickleness and unsteadiness of mind. A person who is endowed with divine characteristic he is always very steadfast and determined. *Achapalam* also means lack of conscious control on the muscular movement of the body. The unnecessary movement of limbs in the body reflects the restlessness of mind. People who are emotional, imaginative, insecure and indecisive, they make unnecessary body movements, while eating, sitting or working etc. *Achapalam* is the total negation of these habits. *Tejah*—means the special glow which reflects the spiritual radiance and immanence of Divine. It is the spiritual glow and *Halo* of brilliance around the face of a holy person. *Kshama*—means forbearance. It is a very unique characteristic which is shown by a person of inner integrity and serenity. Such an individual is very integrated, bold and very wise. *Kshama* also means forgiveness. The person who is settled in the serenity of the self, he naturally becomes very tolerant and forgiving. *Dhriti*—means fortitude. It is indeed a great virtue which helps the individual to maintain his appropriate balance of mind, in favourable and unfavourable circumstances. It is a fact, that there is no other treasure which is equal to inner contentment and no virtue which is equal to fortitude. *Soucham*—means internal and external purity. It is the purity of thoughts, physical body and also the cleanliness of place where one lives and works. 'There is a famous saying, cleanliness is next to godliness'. *Adroha*—means absence of hatred and any inclination to harm others. A person who lives in unity with the Supreme-Self, he never intends to harm and injure any body. He perceives the presence of the Supreme Lord in everybody and feels himself reflected in others. *Na-ati-manita*—means absence of total egoism. A self-realized and integrated person, never exaggerates his own glory; and does not expect any self-assumed importance. He glorifies the Lord for each and everyone of his achievement and success in life.

In the fourth verse Srī Kṛṣṇa gives a brief description of the demoniac traits also. *Dambha*—means ostentation or hypocrisy. *Dambha* is bragging of one's charitable deeds and spiritual discipline. It is a mixed behaviour of deceit and false show off. It is pretending to be virtuous, compassionate and religious with some vicious intentions in the heart. *Darpa*—means arrogance. An arrogant person struggles constantly and tries to prove others that he is better, more educated and wealthy. He boasts a lot about his learning, wealth and status in the community. He lives in a world of his own self-imagined importance. Since he expects and demands attention from others, he usually becomes exiled from the genuine love of others. Such an individual generally becomes lonely and lives a miserable, isolated and depressed life, in his own imaginative world. *Abhimana*—means egoism. An egoist person lives his life under the notion of 'I' and 'Mine'. Anybody who identifies himself with ego, he loses his connection with the indwelling Supreme-Self and separates himself from the conscious presence of the Divine within. Such an individual makes deadly mistakes in his deluded state of mind and suffers in the long run. *Krodha*—means anger. As described earlier in thc second chapter, verse sixty-three, *Krodhah bhavati sammohah, sammohat smrti-vibhramah, smrti-bhramsad buddhi-naso, buddhi-nasat pranasyati*—. From anger arises the delusion and infatuation, from delusion the confusion of memory, from the confusion of memory the loss of reason and discrimination; from the loss of discrimination one goes to complete ruin. Anger is indeed a very harmful enemy of the individual. An angry man behaves like a furious beast. He does a lot of harm to himself and to others who come in contact with him. *Parusya*—means sternness and harshness. It is the total negation of humility, modesty and lack of manners. Such an individual is very sarcastic and taunting in behaviour. He is also very vindictive, selfish and violent. His life style predominates his personal interests, above everything and everybody else. *Ajnanam*—means ignorance and lack of proper insight. It is also the misconception of one's duties and lack of proper understanding about the right and wrong. An ignorant man becomes involved in forbidden activities without thinking about the consequences. Swami Sivananda gives a very appropriate example in this respect, "Just as a child will put anything it gets in his hands into his mouth, whether it is clean or dirty, so also is the condition of the ignorant man who is not able to discriminate between the real and the unreal, the good and the evil, virtue and vice".

Srī Kṛṣṇa has expounded upon the divine traits in great length and detail in the first three verses of this chapter; but about the demoniacal traits, He has touched very briefly in the fourth verse. Srī Kṛṣṇa, the knower of human psychology, has made the most appropriate use of each and every word. He knows that it is a natural inclination of the individual to listen about the virtuous and good qualities at first and then the rest. It helps to revive the beaten up energies of the individual and energize the fatigued thoughts. This encourages the person for ethical living and promotes the virtuous, pious and spontaneous living. It is surely quite appropriate and advisable to point out, at first towards the virtuous qualities of a person and then enlighten him about his shortcomings. By adopting good qualities with receptive attitude, the individual can easily and very spontaneously abandon the bad qualities. Srī Kṛṣṇa tells Arjuna that the divine qualities have been recognized to be conducive to liberation and emancipation; while the demoniac qualities do become a great obstacle towards the path of liberation. The demoniacal nature becomes the cause of suffering and bondage. These qualities are Satanic in character, conducive to serfdom and slavery. Towards the end of this verse Srī Kṛṣṇa assures Arjuna of his divine endowments. He says "Grieve not, O'Arjuna, thou art born with divine endowments".

द्वौ भूतसर्गौ लोकेऽस्मिन्दैव आसुर एव च।
दैवो विस्तरशः प्रोक्त आसुरं पार्थ मे शृणु ॥ ६ ॥

dvau bhūtasargau loke'smin daiva āsura eva ca
daivo vistaraśaḥ prokta āsuraṁ pārtha me śṛṇu

(6) There are two types of beings in the world : The divine and the demoniac. The divine has been explained in detail, now hear about the demoniac from Me, O'Arjuna.

प्रवृत्तिं च निवृत्तिं च जना न विदुरासुराः।
न शौचं नापि चाचारो न सत्यं तेषु विद्यते ॥ ७ ॥

pravṛttiṁ ca nivṛttiṁ ca janā na vidurāsurāḥ
na śaucaṁ nāpi cācāro na satyaṁ teṣu vidyate

(7) The demoniac people do not know what to do and what to refrain from; neither purity nor good conduct, nor truth is found in them.

असत्यमप्रतिष्ठं ते जगदाहुरनीश्वरम्।
अपरस्परसम्भूतं किमन्यत्कामहैतुकम् ॥ ८ ॥

asatyam apratiṣṭhaṁ te jagadāhuranīśvaraṁ
aparasparasambhūtaṁ kimanyat kāmahaitukaṁ

(8) They say, that the world is without truth, without any foundation and without a God; brought about only by the mutual union with the desire for its cause.

एतां दृष्टिमवष्टभ्य नष्टात्मानोऽल्पबुद्धयः।
प्रभवन्त्युग्रकर्माणः क्षयाय जगतोऽहिताः ॥ ९ ॥

etāṁ dṛṣṭimavaṣṭabhya naṣṭātmāno'lpabuddhayaḥ
prabhavantyugrakarmāṇaḥ kṣayāya jagato'hitāḥ

(9) Holding fast to this view, these ruined beings of meagre understanding and cruel deeds; come forth as the enemies of the world, for its destruction.

कामममाश्रित्य दुष्पूरं दम्भमानमदान्विताः।
मोहाद् गृहीत्वासद्ग्राहान्प्रवर्तन्तेऽशुचिव्रताः ॥ १० ॥

kāmam āśritya duṣpūraṁ dambhamānamadānvitāḥ
mohād gṛhītvāsadgrāhān pravartante'śucivratāḥ

(10) Filled with insatiable desires, motivated by hypocrisy, vanity and arrogance; they hold false values through delusion and work with impure resolves.

चिन्तामपरिमेयां च प्रलयान्तामुपाश्रिताः।
कामोपभोगपरमा एतावदिति निश्चिताः ॥ ११ ॥

cintāmaparimeyāṁ ca pralayāntāmupāśritāḥ
kāmopabhogaparamā etāvaditi niścitāḥ

(11) Obsessed with innumerable anxieties, those end only with their death, they regard the enjoyment of sensuous pleasures as their highest goal of life and are fully convinced that, that is all.

आशापाशशतैर्बद्धाः कामक्रोधपरायणाः।
ईहन्ते कामभोगार्थमन्यायेनार्थसञ्चयान् ॥ १२ ॥

āśāpāśaśatair baddhāḥ kāmakrodhaparāyaṇāḥ
īhante kāmabhogārthamanyāyenārthasañcayān

(12) Bound by hundreds of fetters of expectations, given over to lust and anger; they strive to collect wealth by illegal means for the gratification of their desires.

इदमद्य मया लब्धमिमं प्राप्स्ये मनोरथम्।
इदमस्तीदमपि मे भविष्यति पुनर्धनम् ॥ १३ ॥

idamadya mayā labdhamimaṁ prāpsye manoratham
idam astīdamapi me bhaviṣyati punardhanam

(13) This has been secured by me today and that desire I must fulfil soon. This wealth is mine, and that wealth will also be mine in future.

असौ मया हतः शत्रुर्हनिष्ये चापरानपि।
ईश्वरोऽहमहं भोगी सिद्धोऽहं बलवान्सुखी॥ १४॥

asau mayā hataḥ śatrur haniṣye cāparānapi
iśvaroahmahaṁ bhogī siddho'haṁ balavān sukhi

(14) This enemy has been destroyed by me and others too I will finish soon. I am the master and the enjoyer. I am successful, powerful and very prosperous.

आढ्योऽभिजनवानस्मि कोऽन्योऽस्ति सदृशो मया।
यक्ष्ये दास्यामि मोदिष्य इत्यज्ञानविमोहिताः॥ १५॥

āḍhyo'bhijanavānasmi ko'nyo'sti sadṛśo mayā
yakṣye dāsyāmi modiṣya ityajñānavimohitāḥ

(15) I am wealthy and born in a noble family. Who else is equal to me? I perform sacrifices, give charity and rejoice; thus they are deluded by ignorance.

अनेकचित्तविभ्रान्ता मोहजालसमावृताः।
प्रसक्ताः कामभोगेषु पतन्ति नरकेऽशुचौ॥ १६॥

anekacittavibhrāntā mohajālasamāvṛtāḥ
prasaktāḥ kāmabhogeṣu patanti narake'śucau

(16) Bewildered by many fantasies, entangled in the snare of delusion, addicted to the sensual enjoyments, they fall into the foul hell.

आत्मसम्भाविताः स्तब्धा धनमानमदान्विताः।
यजन्ते नामयज्ञैस्ते दम्भेनाविधिपूर्वकम्॥ १७॥

ātmasambhāvitāḥ stabdhā dhanamānamadānvitāḥ
yajante nāmayajñais te dambhenāvidhipūrvakam

(17) Self-conceited, stubborn, intoxicated with arrogance of wealth, they perform sacrifices which are only for name, with

ostentation and with disregard to the scriptural ordinance.

अहङ्कारं बलं दर्पं कामं क्रोधं च संश्रिताः।
मामात्मपरदेहेषु प्रद्विषन्तोऽभ्यसूयकाः॥ १८॥

ahaṅkāraṁ balaṁ darpaṁ kāmaṁ krodhaṁ ca saṅśritāḥ
māmātmaparadeheṣu pradviṣanto'bhyasūyakāḥ

(18) Possessed of egoism, power, arrogance, lust and anger, these malicious people despise Me, in their own bodies and in those of others.

तानहं द्विषतः क्रूरान्संसारेषु नराधमान्।
क्षिपाम्यजस्त्रमशुभानासुरीष्वेव योनिषु॥ १९॥

tān ahaṁ dviṣataḥ krūrān saṅsāreṣu narādhamān
kṣipāmyajasramaśubhān āsurīṣveva yoniṣu

(19) These cruel haters, the most degraded among men in the world; I hurl these evildoers repeatedly into the wombs of demons only.

आसुरीं योनिमापन्ना मूढा जन्मनि जन्मनि।
मामप्राप्यैव कौन्तेय ततो यान्त्यधमां गतिम्॥ २०॥

āsurīṁ yonimāpannā mūḍhā janmani-janmani
māmaprāpyaiva kaunteya tato yāntyadhamāṁ gatim

(20) Fallen into the wombs of demons, these deluded beings from birth to birth do not attain Me O'Kaunteya. They fall further into the lower state than that.

Commentary—Srī Kṛṣṇa opens the conversation with declaration that there are only two types created beings in this world, the divine and the demoniacal. The divine traits have been discussed at length, now hear in detail from Me of the demoniacal. Although every individual-soul (*Jivatma*) is potentially divine and a fragment of the Supreme-soul; but when the embodied-soul seeks expression of its latencies and memories, he becomes entrapped. When the soul takes upon the human body, he becomes possessed with two strong desires. The individual-soul likes to enjoy everything in the material world;

but being a fragment of the Divine, the embodied-soul likes to remain in the proximity of the Supreme-soul. In human body the embodied-soul becomes confused and enshrouded by various contradictions. The spiritual impulses give warmth, serenity, tranquillity and make the goal of his life spiritually oriented and stable, while the primitive impulses and materialistic desires make him restless, weak and distorted. An individual has the potential to rise to the greatest heights of spirituality in life and work in a copartnership with God but if he becomes enslaved to the material comforts of the world, he falls into the ditches of degradation. He can become the glory of the universe and also a ridicule for himself and for others. He can become the crown of creation, but if he acts against the voice of the Supreme-self, he becomes the scandal of the world. Although all the embodied-souls are essentially spiritual, but the degree of spiritual awareness differs from one person to another. In general, people divide themselves into two categories; the men of divine traits and the men of demoniac traits. This statement of Srī Kṛṣṇa has been also repeated by Viktor Frankl in his book *Man's Search for Meaning.* He writes, "There are two races of men in the world, but only these two—the race of a decent man and the race of the indecent man. Both are found everywhere; they penetrate into all groups of society. No group consists entirely of decent or indecent people". In general, the entire creation falls into these two categories, the *Deva* and the *Asura* or the gods and the Titans. This distinction is quite primordial. The very old scriptures of India and other religious books of the world have described a constant struggle between the gods and their deluded opponents. The master of light and the children of darkness, the celestials and the non-celestials, the good and evil. The religious scriptures of Zoroaster are full of many tales, which illustrate the war between the lower and the higher forces. The story of *Ramayana* illustrates the conflict between the *Deva,*—the God-incarnate and the *Rakshasa* (Demon). Similarly the story of *Mahabharta* describes a perpetual conflict between men of divine traits with high ethical values and men of demoniac characteristics. There are many other illustrations in *Rigveda* those describe the conflict of *Suras* and their deluded opponents the *Asuras.* In description of the demoniac nature Srī Kṛṣṇa says that the deluded people can never distinguish between the right type of activity and the one which is forbidden. They can not see the difference between the right and wrong. The concept of purity, good conduct, truthfulness and cleanliness does not exits for them. These people become consciously disconnected from the Supreme-Self within. Their thinking faculty becomes corrupt and the mind becomes totally impure. The day-to-day dealings of these people are diabolical and devoid of truth. They involve themselves in harmful dealings with others, and create problems for themselves. They take pride in lying and taking advantage of other innocent people. They deliberately pursue immorality, impurity and mendacity. Such people proclaim that the universe is without any basis, without God; which has been brought into existence only by mutual union. These sceptical materialists look upon the world from their own self-assumed point of view; for them nothing else exist beyond the perceptual experience of the sensory organs. They fail to recognize and experience the power of the Divine working as the substratum of the universe. Even when their scientific observations and analytical statements indicate clearly that there is some changeless foundation behind the ever changing world, these atheists deny to accept the omnipresence of the Supreme; as the sustainer of the universe. For them there is no creator, no sustainer and no destroyer as such; it all happens merely by mutual interactions. They deny and defy the laws of *Dharma* (righteousness). These people condemn the religious ceremonies and openly ridicule the wisdom of the saints and the sages. Srī Kṛṣṇa calls these people *Alpabuddhyah* in verse nine and says that these people of meagre intellect and limited understanding get involved in some terrible activities and become the cause of fierce destruction for mankind. They live their lives against the laws of *swadharma* and act as the enemies of the world, those are born to create problems for others. For them to murder someone, in order to acquire wealth or to fulfil the sensual desires is perfectly reasonable. They do heinous crimes in order to satisfy their passionate desires.

A tragic incident that took place in a small town of America explains this truth. A married woman, who was in love with another man, she killed her two little toddlers in order to enjoy her new relationship and pursue her selfish passionate desire. Such heinous incidents are happening quite often everywhere, in almost all the so-called educated and flourishing societies of modern world. People those become enslaved by their insatiable passionate desires; they entertain unholy resolves and become involved in undertaking cruel and sinful actions. For these people, the lust is just a minor vice; like the rest of the seven deadly sins—egoism, envy, greed, anger, lust, sloth and gluttony. The seven sins have been indicated as vices, because these promote actions which are against the voice of the inner-self. The demoniac people those are endowed with clouded and deluded intellect; for them being violent is perfectly OK. They dictate that violence should be perfectly accepted because it is the ultimate solution of solving the status frustration; just as gambling is one of the methods to solve the financial problems. The words such as ethical, religious, moral and honest do not exist in their books. A man of demoniac nature says "let me do anything that pleases me, as long as it does not get in your way". These people do not realize that each and every person is connected with the other in some or the other manner. The whole universe functions with mutual co-opration, depending upon one another. Disrespect to mutual well-being is indeed disrespect to the laws of *swadharma*. For these demoniac individuals the personal hygiene, the environmental cleanliness and the concept of integrated community living, carries no meaning. They pollute the waterways and lakes with harmful waste, destroy the forests for selfish reasons, promote the business of deadly drugs and injurious substances. They are always motivated by insatiable selfish desires and they act with totally impure resolves.

The expression *Asapasatair baddhah*—meaning bound by hundreds of expectations, dreams, worries and aspirations all at once. The people of demoniac traits are usually very restless. They generally drag themselves unknowingly into the hell of confusion and distortion of personality. For them the entire life style becomes a circular pattern of worrying and innumerable anxieties those become resolved only at their death. Enveloped in the net of self-created delusion they become very impure and lead a very degraded life. They are always busy to amass money by all kinds of mixed means. They get involved in committing all kinds of forbidden deeds. Steeped in their ignorance they declare 'Enjoy the world of sensual luxuries, who has seen the next life'. They claim, 'this wealth is mine and there will be more, I am successful, learned, wealthy, powerful and deserve all the respect and attention in society'. These self-conceited individuals regard others merely a worthless straw. They do not treat others with respect and reverence. They say 'I am rich, powerful and successful. I am well born and there is no one who equals my status. I donate lot of money and perform religious deeds, others should consider me as the master and respect me as the lord in society'. These deluded, arrogant people do not respect the learned sages and the offerings they make in the name of religion are only a gesture of ostentation. They ridicule the religious ceremonies and look down upon the holy procedures; they even hesitate to salute the spiritual teachers, monks and elders. Since they hold a very high opinion about themselves they really do not care to learn anything from others. They lack proper manners, humility and meekness. Srī Kṛṣṇa says in verse sixteen, that the people who are blinded by ignorance, they become entangled in the snare of delusion. Their intellect becomes bewildered by innumerable hopes and anxieties, and they fall into very impure, immoral and unhealthy circumstances. Srī Kṛṣṇa calls them self-conceited, stubborn and egoist and says that these malicious people despise Me and ignore Me as the inner controller of all, while dwelling in their bodies. They do not pay any attention to the voice of the indeweller and disregard all the instructions of *swadharma*. These cruel and vilest among men are hurled into the wombs of demons only. They are born again and again to the lower grades of life, which corresponds to their conditioned aptitude. In verse twenty, Srī Kṛṣṇa asserts, that even after successive births if these deluded ones are not awakened to the consciousness of the Supreme-Self, they fall into circumstances those are even lower than before.

त्रिविधं नरकस्येदं द्वारं नाशनमात्मनः।
कामः क्रोधस्तथा लोभस्तस्मादेतत्त्रयं त्यजेत्॥ २१॥

trividhaṁ narakasyedaṁ dvāraṁ nāśanamātmanaḥ
kāmaḥ krodhas tathā lobhas tasmādetat trayaṁ tyajet

(21) This is the triple gate of hell, that leads to the destruction of the embodied-self—'Lust, anger and greed'. Therefore, one must abandon these three.

एतैर्विमुक्तः कौन्तेय तमोद्वारैस्त्रिभिर्नरः।
आचरत्यात्मनः श्रेयस्ततो याति परां गतिम्॥ २२॥

etair vimuktaḥ kaunteya tamodvārais tribhir naraḥ
ācarātyatmanaḥ śreyas tato yāti paraṁ gatim

(22) The man who is released from these three gates of darkness O'Arjuna, he practises, what is good for him and thus goes to the highest state.

Commentary—In verse twenty-one Srī Kṛṣṇa declares desire, anger and greed to be the triple gate of hell; that brings about the degradation of the embodied-soul. The expression '*Kama*' is also used for—lust or the passionate desire of sensual enjoyment. These three—lust, anger and greed, form the gateway of a very unhappy, frustrated and restless life which eventually leads the individual into the dark abyss of hell. These Hi-three are indeed very destructive in all respects and the foremost cause of man's total ruin and disaster. These three traits of human behaviour act in close copartnership with each other and do appear as uninvited comrades. In the words of Swami Chinmayananda, "Where there is desire, anger is a natural corollary. The constant flying of an individual's thoughts towards an object of gratification is called 'desire', and when the steady flow of these thoughts of aggrandizement and possession are deflected by some obstacle, the refracted thoughts are called 'anger'". He further writes, "When a desire gets fulfilled, an insatiable thirst for more and more joy holds the individual, and this endless appetite ruins the mental strength and saps dry the personality-vitality in the individual". The person who is driven by passionate desires he constantly lives under the impulse of acquiring, accumulating and possessing everything within his reach or even something beyond his apprehension. He becomes a helpless victim of greed and starts committing sins, such as robbery, adultery and the sale of the prohibited stuff. Any obstacle and interruption in his plans causes frustration and anger. An angry man is impelled into violence, retaliation and other sinful activities. A most sensational criminal case that took place once, in the city of New York explains this truth. A forty year old multi-millionaire was charged with three contracted killings, tax evasion and fraud. This person had managed to pay thousands of dollars to a gang in order to kill the owners of other businesses, which seemed a threat to his business. Such type of unethical and disastrous activities are taking place almost in all other communities of the world. Any type of passionate desire for woman or wealth, drags the individual into the ditches of degradation and self-disaster. The person becomes involved in lying, cheating, duplicity, thieving, perfidy and other types of immoral and unethical activities. Greed is indeed an insatiable demon. The greedy people always remain unsatisfied, miserable, restless and insatiate. They do not have the insight and time even to enjoy and make proper use of whatever is in their possession. They are always too busy, too involved, too concerned, to accumulate more than ever before. They live a very unhappy and frustrated life here and take nothing worthwhile to the lives hereafter.

The same aphorism has been discussed earlier in detail, in the third chapter verse thirty-six, wherein Arjuna brings forth a question, "O'Kṛṣṇa, By what a man is compelled to commit sin, as if driven by force, even against his will?" Srī Kṛṣṇa has given the answer in these words, it is indeed the desire, later transformed into wrath, which is all-devouring and the most vicious enemy in this respect. As the fire becomes obscured by smoke, an embryo by membrane, similarly the intellect of the individual becomes obscured by the surging waves of a passionate desire. The insatiable desire obscures the understanding of even men of knowledge and delude them into committing serious sins. It is indeed the most vicious and dangerous enemy of a person. 'Desire, anger and greed'—together corrupt the thinking faculty of the individual and lead his life into the dark abyss of hell. In the words of Srī Vinobaji, "Desire, anger and greed are the forces that have set the entire world dancing. Anger and greed spring from desire. When circumstances favour the desire, greed arises; when the circumstances obstruct the desire, anger arises. Again and again Geeta tells us to beware of these three. These are the broad gateways of hell. They are thronged by crowds coming in and going out. The roads to Hell are indeed very wide".

In the verse twenty-two Srī Kṛṣṇa has emphasized upon the elimination of behaviour, which is characterized by these 'Hi-Three' evils. Lust, anger and greed are the human weaknesses; those disrupt and corrupt the *(Antahakaran)* inner instruments. These are very destructive emotions, and have to be renounced and shunned in all respects. Victory over these three gates of hell, prepares the individual for inner enlightenment and liberation. When the darkness of ignorance is dispersed with insight and knowledge, the individual makes his progress in the attainment of *Shreyas (spirituality),* which brings the feeling of completeness, inner-satisfaction and contentment. This has been called the progressive realization, which makes the individual eligible for the attainment of the Supreme goal. The person who can genuinely renounce these three demoniac traits, he can definitely attain the highest goal in the form of God-realization and salvation.

यः शास्त्रविधिमुत्सृज्य वर्तते कामकारतः।
न स सिद्धिमवाप्नोति न सुखं न परां गतिम्॥ २३॥

yaḥ śāstravidhimutsṛjya vartate kāmakārataḥ
na sa siddhimavāpnoti na sukhaṁ na parāṁ gatim

(23) He who abandons the ordinances of the scriptures and acts merely under the impulse of his desire, he does not attain either perfection, or happiness or the Supreme Goal.

तस्माच्छास्त्रं प्रमाणं ते कार्याकार्यव्यवस्थितौ।
ज्ञात्वा शास्त्रविधानोक्तं कर्म कर्तुमिहार्हसि॥ २४॥

tasmācchāstraṁ pramāṇaṁ te kāryākāryavyavasthitau
jñātvā śāstravidhānoktaṁ karma kartumihārhasi

(24) Therefore, let the scripture be thy authority, in deciding what ought to be done and what should not to be done; having known what is declared in the ordinance of the scriptures, you should perform your work.

Commentary—In these verses Srī Kṛṣṇa declares the superiority of scriptural knowledge which should be used as the beacon light for living a balanced and harmonious life. The sacred books describe the exploration in truth, step by step, and also the techniques for self-purification and self-perfection. The four holy *Vedas* and the other scriptures those have been written on the basis of the holy *Vedas,* such as The *Manusmriti,* the *Puranas* and epics; all of these have been called the *Sastras* by learned scholars. The knowledge of these scriptures should be accepted as an authority, and one must perform all his actions as ordained by the scriptures. In the words of Swami Sivananda, 'A man who wants to obtain eternal bliss, he should respect the *Vedas* and the *Smritis* which lay down the code of right conduct. He should readily renounce whatever the scriptures teach him to abandon and accept whatever he is directed to accept. The scriptures restrain us from doing evil and bestow on us the greatest good (liberation or moksha). Therefore treat the scriptures with great respect'.

These scriptures are indeed the *prasada* (grace) of deep research undertaken by the holy scholars. The ordinance of the *Sastras* have been written on the basis of *janan, vijnan* and *prajnan*—means the knowledge, experiential knowledge, and also the knowledge of the indwelling-Self. These are the testimony to guide the people into an ideal style of living. *Shastras* unfold the reservoirs of spiritual experiences and laws of sanctity and purity described by religious teachers. The knowledge of the sacred scriptures provides stability, integrity, sanctity and the concept of morality to the individual, as well as to the community and the country at large. The genuine progress of any civilization depends upon the fact, as to how much people rely upon the wisdom of the ancient books, in relation to the activities of their day-to-day life. The family and society in which the people lose their touch with the teachings of the scriptures, they live in utter confusion. The ethical religious tradition are incentives for harmonious living. The code of conduct helps the individual to tread on the path of virtue, morality and primordial Dharma. The society in which people lose their respect for the holy scriptures; they definitely lose their sense of belongings eventually. The distortion of values and the restlessness of mind which we see in the so-called educated society, is due to the fact that people have lost their respect for the holy scriptures. Disrespect to the sacred books of Dharma, brings chaos in society. The people become selfish, insensitive and forget about their responsibilities of living a harmonious life. It is indeed obedience to the ethical code of conduct which brings people together and unites them into a well-planned family and society. Study of *Sastras* is helpful for the proper growth of the individual as well as for the growth of the society in which he lives. The scriptures have been written in order to guide mankind on the path of righteousness and *swadharma.* In the words of Swami Tapasyananda, "Scripture is held forth before man as the most important help in providing the criteria by which one could determine what should be done and what should not be done. With its help, the growth of demoniac qualities is arrested and the development of divine qualities is helped".

In these verses Srī Kṛṣṇa has highly emphasized upon the necessity of reliance on the teachings of the scriptures. *Sastras* do describe the most appropriate guidelines, for peace, progress and spiritual advancement. In the words of Srī Aurobindo, "*Sastra* is the knowledge and teaching laid down by pure intuition, experience and wisdom, the science and art and the ethics of life, the best standards available to the race. The half-awakened man who leaves the observance of its rules to follow the guidance of his instincts and desires, can get pleasure but not happiness, for the inner happiness can only come by right living". The appropriate mode and conduct of life is determined only when the individual can comprehend the genuine concept of right and wrong, what should be pursued and what must be abandoned. *Sastras* do provide the most experienced and recognized guidelines to the individual with sufficient information. Every human being must follow the instructions of the scriptures at every step in life, until he becomes fully tuned to the voice of the indwelling Supreme Lord. The ancient authentic scriptures should be respected, read intelligently and assimilated very diligently.

ॐ तत्सदिति श्रीमद्भगवद्गीतासूपनिषत्सु ब्रह्मविद्यायां
योगशास्त्रे श्रीकृष्णार्जुनसंवादे दैवासुरसम्पत्तिविभागयोगो
नाम षोडशोऽध्यायः ॥ १६ ॥

'Aum' tatsaditi Śrīmadbhagawadgeetā sūpaniṣatsu
brahmavidyāyām yogaśāstre Śrīkṛṣṇārjunasamvāde
daivāsurasampattivibhāgayogo nāma ṣodaśo'dhyāyaḥ

'AUM TAT SAT'—Thus, in the Upanishad of the glorious Bhagawad Geeta, the science of the Brahman (Absolute) the scripture of yoga, the dialogue between Srī Kṛṣṇa and Arjuna—thus, ends the chapter sixteen entitled *"Daivāsurasampattivibhāgayoga"*.

इति श्रीमद्भगवद्गीतासु षोडशोऽध्यायः ॥ १६ ॥

Chapter Seventeen

ŚRADDHĀTRIYA VIBHĀGA YOGA

THE YOGA OF THE THREEFOLD DIVISION OF THE FAITH

अर्जुन उवाच

ये शास्त्रविधिमुत्सृज्य यजन्ते श्रद्धयान्विताः।
तेषां निष्ठा तु का कृष्ण सत्त्वमाहो रजस्तमः॥ १॥

ye śāstravidhimutsṛjya yajante śraddhayānvitāḥ
teṣāṁ niṣṭhā tu kā kṛṣṇa sattvamāho rajas tamaḥ

Arjuna said :

(1) Those who, neglecting the ordinances of the scriptures, perform yajña (worship) with faith, what is their status O'Kṛṣṇa? Is it *sattva, rajas* or *tamas*?

श्रीभगवानुवाच

त्रिविधा भवति श्रद्धा देहिनां सा स्वभावजा।
सात्त्विकी राजसी चैव तामसी चेति तां शृणु॥ २॥

trividhā bhavati śraddhā dehināṁ sā svabhāvajā
sāttvikī rājasī caiva tāmasī ceti tāṁ śṛṇu

The Blessed Lord said :

(2) The faith of the embodied beings is of three kinds, born of their innate disposition—the *sattvic* (pure) the *rajasic* (passionate) and the *tamasic* (ignorant). Thus thou hear of it.

सत्त्वानुरूपा सर्वस्य श्रद्धा भवति भारत।
श्रद्धामयोऽयं पुरुषो यो यच्छ्रद्धः स एव सः॥ ३॥

sattvānurūpā sarvasya śraddhā bhavati bhārata
śraddhāmayo'yaṁ puruṣo yo yacchraddhaḥ sa eva saḥ

(3) The faith of each person is in accordance with his innate nature O'Arjuna. Man is made of his faith; as a man's faith is, so is he.

यजन्ते सात्त्विका देवान्यक्षरक्षांसि राजसाः ।
प्रेतान्भूतगणांश्चान्ये यजन्ते तामसा जनाः ॥ ४ ॥

yajante sāttvikā devān yakṣarakṣāṅsi rājasāḥ
pretān bhūtagaṇānścānye yajante tāmasā janāḥ

(4) The *sattvic* (pure) men worship the gods; the *rajasic* (passionate) worship the Yakshas and Rakshasas; while others—the *tamasic* (deluded) men worship the ghosts and spirits.

Commentary—This chapter opens with a question by Arjuna. He requests Srī Kṛṣṇa to describe the different modes of *sraddha* (faith). He expresses his desire to know in detail the spiritual status of those people who do not know how to follow the ordinances of the scriptures but perform their worship with ardent faith and devotion. According to Arjuna, the genuine explanation of the scriptural knowledge is not available to everybody. It is very difficult to comprehend, and only a few have the earnest quest and intellectual ability to study and understand. Living in a world which is circumferenced at each step by commerce, anxieties and diverse type of activities; there are only a few in millions who can comprehend scriptural knowledge and plan their religious activities accordingly. It is also difficult to find a spiritual instructor who can actually teach the sacred books. The facilities are very rare and most of the people do not have time and patience to learn anything metaphysical. He desires to know more about the spiritual status of the earnest devotees; those who have very little knowledge of the scriptures but perform their worship with utmost reverence? Srī Kṛṣṇa declares in the second verse that the faith of all the human beings is threefold; because of their inherent disposition—the *sattvic* (pure), the *rajasic* (passionate) and the *tamasic* (ignorant). A person can be graded to be *sattvic, rajasic* and *tamasic,* in direct proportion to the degree of his self-awareness. A person's faith or *sraddha* corresponds to the texture of his *samskaras.* All personal concepts, ideas, thoughts and activities of a person revolve around the type of faith he holds. The faith of an individual expresses itself in his entire personality. It is indeed a well established fact that "As a man's faith is, so is he". The expression *sattvanurupa sarvasya sraddha*—explains that the faith of every person is in accordance with his inner disposition. In the words of Swami Chidbhavananda, "A stone soars up in the sky to the extent momentum is imparted to it. A tree grows up in tune with its inherent vitality. A lotus shoots up along with the rise in the level of the water in the pond. Similarly, a man rises in his worth and attainments corresponding to the *sraddha* with which he is endowed". All the achievements of a person's life revolve around the kind of faith he holds. It is the person's faith and attitude which motivates the entire field of his diverse activities and various kinds of pursuits. It is the faith that colours the entire field of choices he makes, the likings and dislikings, and also the acceptance and rejections. The essential characteristics of faith of an individual are generally determined by the degree of his self-awareness. The quality of faith directly correspond to the innate nature or *swabhava* of the person. *Swabhava*—comprises two words. *Swa* means the indwelling light and *bhava* means the personal thinking. So *swabhava* means the personal thinking of the embodied-self. It also means the individualized comprehension of the indwelling-self. An enlightened person is generally distinguished by his respective adherence to truth and untruth. Srī Kṛṣṇa tells Arjuna that in general, people are influenced by three inherent qualities of mother nature, and categorize themselves in three types of *swabhava*—the *sattvic* (pure), *rajasic* (passionate) and *tamasic* (ignorant). In the fourth verse Srī Kṛṣṇa tells how the innate-disposition (faith) of a person determines the object of his worship. The *sattva* stands for purity, honesty and clarity. The *sattvic* people are spiritually awake and enlightened. They seek inner fulfilment from their inner connectedness with the Divine. They worship the bounties of nature, the gods and goddesses like twelve *Adityas*, eight *vasus,* like sun-god, moon-god, wind-god, fire-god, water-god, *Asvinikumars, Visvedevas* and many others as described in the holy books. The *sattvic* people perform all kinds of worships, merely, for self-purification and for the maintenance of orderliness in life. The people of *rajasic* (passionate) temperament are generally very ambitious. They worship the *Yakashas* and *Rakshasas*. The *yakashas* are the demigods and the brothers of Kubera. Kubera is the Lord of wealth. These people worship the god of wealth in order to accumulate more and more wealth. They are constantly restless and always in pursuit of some material comfort or luxury. For them the accumulation of material wealth forms the greatest happiness of life. The worshipper of *Rakshasas* pursue power, both physical and material. The *tamasic* people worship the evil spirits and the vicious powers for sense-gratifications. These superstitious people are very selfish and seek only their personal comforts while ignoring the laws of *swadharma*. They make impure resolves in their worship in order to fulfil their selfish desires. They perform the *yajña* with the unholy resolves those are against the laws of *swadharma*. The *tamasic* people worship the tombs of the dead men in order to fulfil their heinous desires. Sometime these deluded people engage themselves in forming a cult and do misguide others into committing some heinous crimes. These deluded people of meagre understanding do create a lot of confusion in society and disturb peace and harmony.

अशास्त्रविहितं घोरं तप्यन्ते ये तपो जनाः।
दम्भाहङ्कारसंयुक्ताः कामरागबलान्विताः॥ ५॥

aśāstravihitaṁ ghoraṁ tapyante ye tapo-janāḥ
dambhāhaṅkārsaṁyuktāḥ kāmarāgabalānvitāḥ

(5) Those men, who practise fierce austerities which are not enjoined by the scriptures, being given to hypocrisy and arrogance, impelled by the force of lust and attachment.

कर्षयन्तः शरीरस्थं भूतग्राममचेतसः।
मां चैवान्तःशरीरस्थं तान्विद्ध्यासुरनिश्चयान्॥ ६॥

karṣayantaḥ śarīrasthaṁ bhūtagrāmamacetasaḥ
māṁ caivā'ntaḥśarīrasthaṁ tān viddhyāsuraniścayān

(6) Senselessly torturing all the elements in the body they also hurt Me, who dwells within the body—know them to be of demoniacal resolves.

Commentary—In these verses Srī Kṛṣṇa tells Arjuna that the men, who practise violent austerities, which are not enjoined by the scriptures; they torture their bodies and also hurt Me, who dwells within the body. These deluded egoists, engage themselves in the practice of severe penances, which are against the laws of *swadharma*. They are very ignorant, unwise, disintegrated, stubborn and demoniac. Their goals are diabolic, harmful for their ownselves and also for others. The performance of their austerities reflects the lack of knowledge and proper insight. These people are generally very egoistic and puffed up with their vain glories. They are stubborn and capriciously design their own rules. For example, the austerity of standing in water for months, laying on the thorns or spikes and living without food for days at stretch, sitting before fire and standing only on one leg for days together, these are the deluded type of penances. These difficult austerities are contrary to the ordinances of the holy scriptures. The ignorant people of deluded understanding think that mortification of the body is a penance and usually they torture their bodies merely to get the attention of other people. For them the real penance consist in tormenting the physical body. According to their viewpoint the real austerity means physical mortification, extremism and bodily torture by all means. Such individuals are generally very insecure and distorted, they merely follow the dictates of their passionate desires.

Srī Kṛṣṇa says that these deluded egoists torture their physical body and also the indwelling Lord, who resides within the body. They create disharmony in the organs of the body and interfere with spontaneous flow of the vital force. In general, their approach is very unreasonable and unauthentic. These types of penances have not been approved by the holy scriptures, because these are against the laws of nature and the voice of the inner-self. Srī Kṛṣṇa asserts that self-discipline and self-restraint should not be confused with the physical torture of the body. The practice of self-mortification is painful and unworthy, it should not be followed at all. The expression '*Kamaragabalanvitah*'—means compelled by the force of desire, lust, attachment and power. These people are obsessed with many desires and follow the dictates of their impulsive nature. They engage themselves in austerities which create sufferings for themselves and for other living beings. They are very obstinate and doomed to destruction. Srī Kṛṣṇa calls these people insensitive deluded fools, and their austerities to be totally impure and demoniac.

आहारस्त्वपि सर्वस्य त्रिविधो भवति प्रियः।
यज्ञस्तपस्तथा दानं तेषां भेदमिमं शृणु ॥ ७॥

āhārastvapi sarvasya trividho bhavati priyaḥ
yajñastapas tathā dānaṁ teṣāṁ bhedamimaṁ śṛṇu

(7) The food, which is liked by everyone is of three kinds, so is the *yajña,* austerity and charity. Hear thou the distinction of these.

आयुः सत्त्वबलारोग्यसुखप्रीतिविवर्धनाः।
रस्याः स्निग्धाः स्थिरा हृद्या आहाराः सात्त्विकप्रियाः ॥ ८॥

āyuḥ sattvabalārogyasukhaprītivivardhanāḥ
rasyāḥ snigdhāḥ sthirā hṛdyā āhārāḥ sāttvikapriyāḥ

(8) The foods which promote longevity, purity, strength, health, happiness and cheerfulness, which are tasty, oleaginous, substantial and agreeable are liked by the *sattvic* (pure) people.

कट्वम्ललवणात्युष्णतीक्ष्णरूक्षविदाहिनः।
आहारा राजसस्येष्टा दुःखशोकामयप्रदाः ॥ ९॥

kaṭvamlalavaṇātyuṣṇatīkṣṇarūkṣavidāhinaḥ
āhārā rājasasyeṣṭā duḥkhaśokāmayapradāḥ

(9) The foods which are bitter, sour, saline, excessively hot, pungent, dry and burning are liked by *rajasic;* which cause discomfort, pain and disease.

यातयामं गतरसं पूति पर्युषितं च यत्।
उच्छिष्टमपि चामेध्यं भोजनं तामसप्रियम् ॥ १०॥

yātayāmaṁ gatarasaṁ pūti paryuṣitaṁ ca yat
ucchiṣṭamapi cāmedhyaṁ bhojanaṁ tāmasapriyam

(10) That which is stale, insipid, putrid, discarded and impure is the food liked by the *tamasic.*

Commentary—In these verses Srī Kṛṣṇa proceeds to explain the threefold qualities of food which is generally agreeable to different kinds of people according to their innate disposition. The *swabhava* or the innate-nature of the individual expresses itself in almost all fields of his activities. The physical body is called the "*Annamaya Kosa*"—which means the field that is sustained by food. In verse seven, Srī Kṛṣṇa declares that the food which promotes longevity, purity, strength, health, happiness, good-appetite; which is savoury, oleaginous, substantial and agreeable is liked by *sattvic* people. The milk and milk products, vegetables, fruits, wheat, barley, grams, rice, almonds, cashewnuts, dates and raisins etc., come under the category of *sattvic* food. This group of food produces cheerfulness, purity and emotional clarity; which promotes good health in all respects. It energizes the body and keeps the digestive system in perfect order. Such type of food is highly conducive for intellectual clarity, purity and stability of mind. The foods which are bitter, sour, saline, pungent and dry are liked by people of *rajasic* temperament. These types of foods cause sickness and discomfort in the body and mind. The food which is half-cooked or half-ripe, insipid, putrid and polluted is liked by the deluded people of *tamasic* temperament. This also includes the non-vegetarian foods such as meat, fish, eggs etc. those have been considered totally unfit for human beings. Human teeth are meant for eating vegetarian foods; and also the human intestine which is long and narrow is not designed to digest any type of meat. The undigested meat stinks in the stomach and causes many type of diseases. An ignorant person does not care about the adverse effects of the food which he eats; for him the taste of palate is the first and foremost priority. He does not mind eating the remnants of food and also sharing his dish with others. For example, some people sit together and eat from the same dish or plate and drink juice or water from the same glass. Such habits do promote infections and are not pure. The *shastras* describe that the food which has been partly eaten by someone, it becomes unfit to be taken by another.

The *tamasic* man is usually very careless about the quality and quantity of food he consumes. The type of food which is consumed by the individual, it produces positive and negative effects on the body; it influences the physical body as well as the subtle body, which is a reservoir of thoughts. Food is called *anna* in Sanskrit. *Anna* is related to *prana*—the life breath. *Prana*—the life breath energizes the body and is also very closely connected with *Mana*—the mind. *Shruti Bhagwati* describes at length *Jaisa khave anna, vaisa hove manna*—means the purity of mind is influenced by the purity of diet. The *Taittriya Upanisad* describes *Annam na nindyan tat varatam prano va Annam. Shariramnnandam prane Shariram pritsthatam sharire pranah pratishthitah.* One should respect the food one eats. *Prana* depends upon food which is eaten by the body. The body rests on *prana* and *prana* rests in the body. *Chhandogyopanishad* describes, "that the food which is consumed by the individual, it is assimilated in a threefold process. The coarsest portion becomes the feces; the middle portion becomes the flesh, and the subtlest portion becomes the mind." So it is indeed very important to eat the specific quality of food which can promote the purity of thoughts. Besides it is not just the ingredient of food which influences the state of mind; also the procedure in which the food is cooked and consumed. This is one of the reasons why most of the saints and sages prefer to cook their own meal. For example, when a certain recipe is given to five cooks, they exhibit five different results, because each one of them adds his individual thoughts and feelings into the cooking. Good and positive thoughts in cooking do produce pleasant and enjoyable taste and also affect the temperament and health of the person who eats. Another important factor which influences the mind is the attitude with which the food is consumed.

It is indeed very important for a person to hold good and positive thoughts about the food, both while cooking and eating. Almost all sacred books of the world, do recommend many different kinds of hymns, those should be recited, during the cooking, and before eating the meal. For example, a prayer of gratitude before eating has been emphasized in almost all the religions of the world, such as, *Thank you, God for the world so sweet, Thank you God for the food we eat.* The prayer is a gesture of appreciation and humility towards the benefactor. A simple prayer before eating creates the atmosphere of devotion, love and relaxation for the individual which helps his body in the proper assimilation of food. The holy *Vedas* have also recommended to recite this hymn before eating *Aum annepate annyasaya no dehyan mivasya shushminah, pra pradataram tarisha oorjam no dhehi dvipade chatushpade.* Means, may the food I eat be beneficial for the body in all respect. The holy sages have emphasized that the individual should recite the verse fourteen from chapter fifteen of *Bhagawad Geeta* after he finishes the meal. This verse is recited by placing the middle finger on the naval. *Aham vaisvanaro bhutva praninam deham asrītah pranapansamayukta pacamy annam caturvidham.* Means, having become the fire *Vaisvanara,* I dwell in the bodies of the living beings, and united with *prana* and *apana* (the inhalation and exhalation), I digest the four kinds of food. The recitation of this verse helps in the appropriate digestion and assimilation of the food.

अफलाकांक्षिभिर्यज्ञो विधिदृष्टो य इज्यते।
यष्टव्यमेवेति मनः समाधाय स सात्त्विकः॥ ११॥

aphalākāṅkṣibhir yajño vidhidṛṣto ya ijyate
yaṣṭavyameveti manaḥ samādhāya sa sāttvikaḥ

(11) The *yajña* which is performed selflessly, enjoined by the scriptural ordinance and merely out of the feeling of duty is *sattvic* (pure).

अभिसन्धाय तु फलं दम्भार्थमपि चैव यत्।
इज्यते भरतश्रेष्ठ तं यज्ञं विद्धि राजसम्॥ १२॥

abhisandhāya tu phalaṁ dambhārthamapi caiva yat
ijyate bharataśreṣṭha taṁ yajñaṁ viddhi rājasam

(12) The *yajña* which is performed, keeping in view its reward and also for the sake of mere display, O' Arjuna, know that to be *rajasic* (passionate).

विधिहीनमसृष्टान्नं मन्त्रहीनमदक्षिणम्।
श्रद्धाविरहितं यज्ञं तामसं परिचक्षते॥ १३॥

vidhihīnamasṛṣṭānnaṁ mantrahīnamadakṣiṇam
śraddhāvirahitaṁ yajñaṁ tāmasaṁ paricakṣate

(13) That which is contrary to the scriptural injunctions and performed without the distribution of food, without chanting the holy

hymns, giving gifts and sincere devotion, that *yajña* is said to be *tamasic.*

Commentary—In verse eleven Srī Kṛṣṇa proceeds with the word *Aphalakanksibhiryajno*—means the *yajña* which is performed without desiring any fruit in return and also according to the injunctions of the scriptures, that is considered to be pure and *sattvic.* The expression *Yastavyam*—means ought to be offered. It clearly indicates that the worship such as *Agnihotra* and others should be performed daily as the essentials of day-to-day life. It is the duty of every individual to understand his appropriate role in the world and he should try to live a life in perfect cooperation with others. A *sattvic* person performs *yajña* as a duty and makes all offerings to the gods and goddesses without any desire for reward. For a *sattvic* man, the love of God, and living a life in a most intimate relationship with God is everything. The purpose of his *yajña* is to enhance the love of God within and in the world where he lives. A man of clarity and genuine austerity, performs *yajñas,* chants hymns, studies the scriptures, listens to the sermons, observes fasts, practises meditation and makes offerings only as a gesture of his personal duty towards the creation of the Lord. He perfectly understands the necessity of living in harmony with his inner-self, and with other fellow beings on the planet. He genuinely knows that each and every individual is indeed a very important member of the community, country and the world. Every one should understand his duties as well as his rights in order to live a harmonious life. A *sattvic* person realizes his dignity as a human being and seeks for orderliness in every bit of the work he performs. His attitude is awakened and supportive of universal life. On the other hand, a *rajasic* person makes his offerings in order to seek all kinds of rewards and for merely ostentation. Such an individual is generally preoccupied with the worries of rewards even at the time when the service is being offered. He performs *yajña* and worship not from the sense of duty or appreciation for the Divine, but merely as an act of ostentation. In the performance of *yajña* and charity his aim is to satisfy his ego by showing off his wealth, riches and resources. His act of charity exhibits his hidden desire for name, fame and popularity in society. The performer of such *yajñas* has the motive of increasing his importance or gaining more wealth and riches. Srī Kṛṣṇa tells Arjuna in verse twelve that the *yajña* which is performed with a desire to gain something in return—know that to be *rajasic* (passionate). Any worship which is undertaken with a selfish personal motive that is surely considered to be *rajasic;* instead of bringing peace and tranquillity, it rather brings anxiety and restlessness. The *rajasic yajña,* even though it is performed with the ordinance of the scriptures, it contributes very little towards the goal of self-realization and liberation.

The verse thirteen describes the nature of *tamasic* worship, which is generally performed out of fear and superstition. Such services are not performed in conformity with the ordinances of the sacred books. In such type of *yajña,* the Vedic hymns are not chanted devotedly and the sacrificial fee (*dakshina)* is not paid with respect. Srī Kṛṣṇa says that any ritual which is conducted without proper recitation of the *mantras* and without the offering of *dakshina* (fee) to the learned priest, that is considered to be *tamasic.* In this case the performer does not attain any merit, neither here nor hereafter. He rather lives in constant guilt and shame. The word *sraddhavirahitam*—literally means the service which is devoid of faith, respect and reverence, and which is performed with arrogance, hypocrisy, and for ostentation only.

देवद्विजगुरुप्राज्ञपूजनं शौचमार्जवम्।
ब्रह्मचर्यमहिंसा च शारीरं तप उच्यते॥ १४॥

devadvijaguruprājñapūjanaṁ śaucamārjavam
brahmacaryam ahinsā ca śārīraṁ tapa ucyate

(14) Worship of the gods, learned men, teachers and men of wisdom; cleanliness, straightforwardness, celibacy and non-violence—are called the austerities of the body.

अनुद्वेगकरं वाक्यं सत्यं प्रियहितं च यत्।
स्वाध्यायाभ्यसनं चैव वाङ्मयं तप उच्यते॥ १५॥

anudvegakaraṁ vākyaṁ satyaṁ priyahitaṁ ca yat
svādhyāyābhyasanaṁ caiva vāṅmayaṁ tapa ucyate

(15) The austerity of speech is considered to be the utterance of the words, which do not cause annoyance and are truthful, pleasant and beneficial; also the regular study of *Vedas;* and recitation of the Divine name.

मनःप्रसादः सौम्यत्वं मौनमात्मविनिग्रहः।
भावसंशुद्धिरित्येतत् तपो मानसमुच्यते ॥ १६ ॥

manaḥprasādaḥ saumyatvaṁ maunamātmavinigrahaḥ
bhāvasaṁśuddhirityetat tapo mānasamucyate

(16) Serenity of mind, gentleness, silence, self-control and total honesty of thoughts—this is called the austerity of the mind.

Commentary—In these verses Srī Kṛṣṇa describes the three kinds of penances. The austerity of body includes worship of the gods and goddesses, respect of learned Brahmins and spiritual master; practice of self-discipline, inner purity, straightforwardness, celibacy and non-violence. Living a life which is in perfect harmony with the cosmic forces, is indeed the worship of the gods and goddesses. Srī Kṛṣṇa has described earlier in chapter three verse eleven *Parasparam bhavayantah shreyah paramavapsyatha*—means attain the highest good by fostering one another disinterestedly. By living in harmony with the gods and goddesses in nature the individual is blessed with full cooperation of nature in return. *Dvija*—literally means the twice-born. The person who has been initiated into wearing the sacred thread and also the study of the sacred books. The sacred thread is called the *yagopaveet* in Sanskrit. *Yag* and *upa-veet*—means the over-cover of the subtle body, which helps the individual to be a responsible participant in the performance of various types of *yajñas* (selfless work). The sacred thread reminds the individual of his duties as a member of the family, community and country. It is an initiation into living a balanced life. Giving due respect to the spiritual teacher is also an austerity. Proper respect and service to the teacher is essential.

The *Brahmacaryam*—means control over the sensory organs and total negation of lust in thought, word and deed. *Brahman* is the Supreme Lord and *charya* means the course of conduct. The expression *Brahamani charati ite Brahmachari*—means the one who lives in the consciousness of the Supreme *Brahman* is called *Brahmachari*. *Bramacharya* should be observed at almost all stages of life. It gives a lot of self-respect and helps the individual to develop a sound mind and a sound body. It is indeed a doorway to a decent and respectable life-style. In the words of Gandhiji, "what chiefly distinguishes a man from the beast is that, man from his age of discretion begins to practise a life of continual self-restraint. The conquest of lust is the highest endeavour of a man or woman's existence; without overcoming lust one cannot hope to advance in life both materially and spiritually, outwardly and inwardly. As such it is the royal road to self-realization or attainment of Brhaman". Non-violence as explained earlier—means not violating the voice of the indwelling-self. It is a state of perfect peace and harmony with the indwelling-self and with others. It is a progressive realization of the Supreme-self. It is the goal towards which all mankind moves naturally though unconsciously. In the words of Gandhiji, "Non-violence is necessary for us in our search for absolute truth. Ahimsa and Truth are so inter-twined that it is difficult to disentangle and separate them. They are like the two sides of a coin or rather of a smooth unstamped metallic disc. Nevertheless, Ahimsa is the means, Truth is the end". Non-violence is indeed mandatory for any type of advancement in personal and spiritual progress. The holy scriptures declare *Ahimsa permo Dharma* means non-violence is the first and foremost Dharma of mankind.

In verse fifteen Srī Kṛṣṇa speaks about the austerity of speech. Speaking appropriate words with the knowledge of how to speak, what to speak, when to speak and how much to speak, really involves a lot of self-discipline. Humility, truth and straightforwardness in speech is also important in order to live in peace with others and with one's own self. In the words of Swami Rama, "Teaching and interpersonal communication are carried on mainly through the medium of speech. A great man speaks in accord with the way he thinks and acts; there is a complete coordination in his inward action and speech. He never intends to hurt, harm or injure anyone through his speech".

Speaking truth is an austerity. It is the most honourable virtue. *Satyameva Jaiyate*—means it is the truth that prevails and always wins eventually. Speaking of truth is an austerity which helps the individual to inculcate many more virtuous habits in life, those are helpful in self-realization and God-realization. The name of Yudhistra is still remembered as *Dharam Putra* because of his truthfulness. The principle of speaking truth assists the person to be fearless, straightforward and secure. It gives self-respect and self-confidence. The story of Satyakama Jabali is well-known. He was an earnest student of the great sage Gautama. One day when the sage enquired from him about his parentage and Gotra—he confessed with honesty and told the sage that his mother had many men in her life. So he was not aware of his parentage. The sage Gautma was very impressed by the truthfulness of Satyakama Jabali and accepted him as his disciple. Truthfulness in thought, word and deed is the genuine devotion to the Lord. It purifies the individual and gives him inner strength and stability. In the words of Gandhiji, "Truth is like a vast tree, which yields more and more fruits, the more you nurture it. The deeper the search in the mine of Truth the richer the discovery of the gems buried there in the shape of openings for an ever greater variety of service". The principle of speaking truth is indeed a great austerity which gives inner strength, purity and integrity to the individual. On the other hand, the people who tell lies, they lack self-confidence, self-respect and self-reliance. They become the victims of bad habits and harm themselves more than anybody else. The person who tells lies, he becomes very fearful and suspicious because he remains under the impression that others are also lying. The person who is always suspicious and who does not trust others, he lives in perpetual misery and pain. The people who tell lies they degrade themselves and cheat themselves more than anybody else. About this Emerson has written very beautifully, "Men suffer all their life under the foolish superstition, that they can be cheated. But it is as impossible for a man to be cheated by any body else but himself". Speaking truth and taking pride in it, is indeed a noble penance. It is a very tough ethical discipline but it can be surely accomplished by living in the consciousness of the Divine. There are famous words from the *Bible* "Nothing gives me greater joy than to hear that my children live in the truth".

A daily practice of reciting the hymns of *Vedas* and other prayers is also an austerity of the speech. The recitation of the benedictory notes is very conducive to peaceful and harmonious living. Chanting of the *Vedic* hymns and other prayers with proper intonation is indeed a very sanctifying practice. After the austerity of speech, the next important austerity is mental asceticism. It is the practice to live in perpetual awareness of the Divine. The mind is a very complex field and its operations are very mysterious. Mental asceticism is to be a silent witness of all the sensory experiences—the feelings, the emotions and the latencies of the past and present. In the words of Swami Chidbhavanenada, "Permitting pure thoughts and noble emotions alone to crop-up in the mind is self-control mentioned herein. What is in the mind expresses itself as words and actions. He who has mastery over his mind, he never utters an unwanted word and never does an undesirable action. When a person's temperament is congenial and his attitude felicitous, he is said to be imbued with purity of disposition. Maintaining this benign state of mind under all circumstances is austerity of the mind". The word *Saumyatvam* means the attitude of peacefulness, love compassion, kindness and sympathy for others. There is a verse in puranas—*Saumya saumyo guno patum*—means living a life in the grace of the indwelling-Self; reflects the peaceful majesty of the Self in the behaviour of the individual. *Maunam* is the silence of mind and speech. *Mauni* or *muni* is the one who has learnt to live in the silence of the indwelling-self. It is indeed an austerity of mind and speech. Discipline of speech promotes the silence of thoughts and inner tranquillity. In the words of Gandhiji, "In the practice of maintaining silence, the soul finds the path to a clearer light, and whatever is elusive and deceptive resolves itself into crystal clearness. Our life is a long and arduous quest after truth, and the soul requires inward restfulness to attain its full height." The discipline to practise silence provides an opportunity to listen to the voice of the indwelling-Self and experience inner tranquillity. In general, people are accustomed to talk unnecessarily and hear unnecessary sounds. So in the beginning, one finds it very difficult to remain silent even for a little while; but as the practice grows regular and disciplined, the observance of silence becomes a second nature.

The individual starts liking to be in silence and he finds ineffable peace and tranquillity in its practice. The holy scriptures have declared the auspicious days for observing a fast and also the specific days for observing silence—such as the fourth, eighth, eleventh and fourteenth day of the lunar calendar are considered to be sacred for observing silence. If a person finds it difficult to remain silent on those days he should attempt to observe silence for at least half an hour every day. The *Mauna Vratha* gives an experience of deep relaxation and inner tranquillity. It gives peace of mind, inner quietude and an opportunity for self-study. The '*Atmavinigrahah*'—means self-control which helps the individual to focus his thoughts in the desired direction with constant vigilance. It is the conscious control over the thinking faculty and the power to manoeuvre the quantity, quality and the direction of thoughts. The expression *bhavasamsuddih*—means the purity of feelings and the purity of thoughts in dealings with others. It is the complete negation and elimination of evil propensities like prejudice, partiality, jealousy, anger, greed, arrogance, infatuation and animosity. Purity of mind is experienced by living in the consciousness of the indwelling Lord.

श्रद्धया परया तप्तं तपस्तत्त्रिविधं नरैः।
अफलाकांक्षिभिर्युक्तैः सात्त्विकं परिचक्षते ॥ १७ ॥

śraddhayā parayā taptaṁ tapas tat trividhaṁ naraiḥ
aphalākāṅkṣibhir yuktaiḥ sāttvikaṁ paricakṣate

(17) This threefold austerity, practised with utmost faith by men of steadfast wisdom, without the expectation of a reward, is said to be *sattvic.*

सत्कारमानपूजार्थं तपो दम्भेन चैव यत्।
क्रियते तदिह प्रोक्तं राजसं चलमध्रुवम् ॥ १८ ॥

satkāramānapūjārthaṁ tapo dambhena caiva yat
kriyate tadiha proktaṁ rājasaṁ calamadhruvam

(18) The penance which is practised in order to gain respect, recognition, honour, and with hypocrisy—is said to be *rajasic.* It is unstable and transient.

मूढग्राहेणात्मनो यत्पीडया क्रियते तपः ।
परस्योत्सादनार्थं वा तत्तामसमुदाहृतम् ॥ १९ ॥

mūḍhagrāheṇātmano yat pīḍayā kriyate tapaḥ
parasyotsādanārthaṁ vā tat tāmasamudāhṛtam

(19) The austerity which is practised with deluded understanding and with self-torture or the purpose of causing harm to others, is declared to be *tamasic.*

Commentary—In verse seventeen Srī Kṛṣṇa tells Arjuna that the person who practises these three kinds of austerities with genuine faith and without desiring any reward, his penance is considered to be *sattvic.* The penance which is performed with the object of gaining attention, respect, honour from others that is said to be *rajasic.* This type of austerity becomes very conditional and is considered to be unstable and essentially passionate. Such penances yield only momentary results. The individual who undertakes these austerities is generally very uncertain and unstable about his faith. He expects others to respect him as a man of austerity. A passionate person suffers from lack of faith in God and also in his own resolve. He lacks inner integrity and always lives in fear of losing whatever he has accomplished. In verse nineteen Srī Kṛṣṇa talks about austerity which is practised with misunderstanding and self-torture, promoted by some foolish ideas and aspirations. The austerity which is undertaken in order to harm somebody is considered to be *tamasic.* For example, some people perform black magic under the guidance of some deluded priests with the purpose of being blessed with progeny. These persons undertake severe austerities which are contrary to the ordinance of the holy scripture. They are very obstinate, egoistic, and foolish. They torture themselves and others in order to attain some demoniac powers. They take advantage of innocent people for the attainment of their selfish motives. Such penances are of very low quality and generally create disharmony with the laws of nature. Srī Kṛṣṇa condemns these penances and calls these ascetic the deluded obstinate, and harmful hypocrites. Such austerities eventually degrade the performer bringing pain and sorrow in the long run.

दातव्यमिति यद्दानं दीयतेऽनुपकारिणे।
देशे काले च पात्रे च तद्दानं सात्त्विकं स्मृतम्॥ २०॥

dātavyamiti yad dānaṁ dīyate'nupakāriṇe
deśe kāle ca pātre ca tad dānaṁ sāttvikaṁ smṛtam

(20) Charity which is given with a sense of duty to the one from whom nothing is expected in return, and also at the right place and time to a deserving person—that charity has been pronounced as *sattvic.*

यत्तु प्रत्युपकारार्थं फलमुद्दिश्य वा पुनः।
दीयते च परिक्लिष्टं तद्दानं राजसं स्मृतम्॥ २१॥

yat tu pratyupakārārthaṁ phalamuddiśya vā punaḥ
dīyate ca parikliṣṭaṁ tad dānaṁ rājasaṁ smṛtam

(21) The gift, which is given with the hope of receiving a favour in return or with the expectation of a reward and also given reluctantly, is considered to be *rajasic.*

अदेशकाले यद्दानमपात्रेभ्यश्च दीयते।
असत्कृतमवज्ञातं तत्तामसमुदाहृतम् ॥ २२॥

adeśakāle yad dānam apātrebhyaś ca dīyate
asatkṛtamavajñātaṁ tat tāmasamudāhṛtam

(22) The charity that is given at an inappropriate place and time, to an unworthy recipient with disrespect and contempt is declared to be *tamasic.*

Commentary—There is a famous saying in *Rig Veda Dakshinavanto amritam bhajante*—the blessed are those who can give and share in charity. This is indeed very true, that the virtue of being able to share with others, does bless the individual with the subtlest joy and inner contentment. To give and share means to perceive oneness with others. This is a gesture of spontaneous love, compassion and kindness which arises from the purity of indwelling-self. This is being a participant in the act of sharing the need of others. The spirit of charity arises from the feeling of seeing one's ownself reflected in pain and need of other people. Donation which is given out of honest spirit of sharing and caring for others is considered to be essentially pure. In this case the benefactor does not expect anything in return from the beneficiary. Also the charity which is given to the appropriate recipient, in the appropriate circumstances is said to be *sattvic.* The spirit of giving charity must come from the sincerity and purity of heart without any sign of egoism. The gift which is given with an idea of receiving some favour in return and also in a very reluctant manner, that is held to be *rajasic.* For example, some people make charities in order to receive attention of the public and for some name and fame in society. There are also some people those give donations with the expectation that it is going to be returned to them in the form of increased prosperity and celestial happiness. Any gift which is given grudgingly with some future expectation in mind, that is said to be *rajasic.* In verse twenty-two Srī Kṛṣṇa declares that the donation which is given inappropriately to an unworthy person with contempt—that donation is considered to be *tamasic.* This donation is offered very unwillingly in an egoistic style, without proper respect and sincerity. *Tamasic* people make charity without any feeling of sympathy, kindness, and generosity. They give only out of compulsion and also demand much more in return than whatever they give. They have no sense of respect for the recipient and sometime they humiliate the beneficiary.

ॐ तत्सदिति निर्देशो ब्रह्मणस्त्रिविधः स्मृतः ।
ब्राह्मणास्तेन वेदाश्च यज्ञाश्च विहिताः पुरा ॥ २३ ॥

oṁ tatsaditi nirdeśo brahmaṇas trividhaḥ smṛtaḥ
brāhmaṇās tena vedāś ca yajñāś ca vihitāḥ purā

(23) 'Aum Tat Sat'—this has been declared to be the threefold designation of the Brahman; by that, the *Vedas,* the *Brahmanas* and sacrifices were created in the ancient past.

तस्मादोमित्युदाहृत्य यज्ञदानतपःक्रियाः ।
प्रवर्तन्ते विधानोक्ताः सततं ब्रह्मवादिनाम् ॥ २४ ॥

tasmādomityudāhṛtya yajñadanatapaḥkriyāḥ
pravartante vidhānoktāḥ satataṁ brahmavādinām

(24) Therefore with the utterance of the holy syllable "AUM" the acts of *yajña,* charity and austerity are commenced; as enjoined in the scriptures by the expounders of the *Brahman.*

तदित्यनभिसन्धाय फलं यज्ञतपःक्रियाः।
दानक्रियाश्च विविधाः क्रियन्ते मोक्षकांक्षिभिः॥ २५॥

tadityanabhisandhāya phalaṁ yajñatapaḥkriyāḥ
dānakriyāś ca vividhāḥ kriyante mokṣakāṅkṣibhiḥ

(25) With the utterance of the word *Tat,* without aiming at the fruit; the various acts of *yajña* (sacrifice) austerity and charity are performed by the seekers of liberation.

सद्भावे साधुभावे च सदित्येतत् प्रयुज्यते।
प्रशस्ते कर्मणि तथा सच्छब्दः पार्थ युज्यते॥ २६॥

sadbhāve sādhubhāve ca sadityetat prayujyate
praśaste karmaṇi tathā sacchabdaḥ pārtha yujyate

(26) The word *Sat* is used, to express Realty and that which is good. Similarly O'Arjuna, the word *Sat* is used in the sense of an auspicious act.

यज्ञे तपसि दाने च स्थितिः सदिति चोच्यते।
कर्म चैव तदर्थीयं सदित्येवाभिधीयते॥ २७॥

yajñe tapasi dāne ca sthitiḥ saditi cocyate
karma caiva tadarthīyaṁ sadity evābhidhīyate

(27) Steadfastness in *yajña* (selfless action) asceticism and charity is also called *Sat;* and also the action which is in connection with these, is called *Sat.*

अश्रद्धया हुतं दत्तं तपस्तप्तं कृतं च यत्।
असदित्युच्यते पार्थ न च तत् प्रेत्य नो इह॥ २८॥

aśraddhayā hutaṁ dattaṁ tapas taptaṁ kṛtaṁ ca yat
asadityucyate pārtha na ca tat pretya no iha

(28) Whatever is offered in *yajña,* given as charity, practised as austerity and whatever rite is observed without faith (sincere devotion), is called *asat* O'Arjuna. It bears nothing, neither here nor hereafter.

Commentary—After giving an elaborate description of the trifold penances and charities, Srī Kṛṣṇa quickly draws Arjuna's attention to the subtle power of *Aum-Tat-Sat* which transforms each and every act into the purity of *sattvikta.* These three holy words have some specific spiritual powers, so every type of work should be performed with the consciousness of the Supreme Brahman. It gives sanctity to worship and also it is done with the spirit of respectful dedication. Srī Kṛṣṇa tells in verse twenty-three that *Aum-Tat-Sat*—has been declared to be the trifold designation of the Absolute. *Aum-Tat-Sat*—the three words indicate one or the other aspect of the absolute Divinity. *Aum* as described earlier, is the holy syllable which represents the transcendental Supreme Self. All the hymns in *Vedas* and in almost all other sacred scriptures always start with the holy syllable AUM. In the words of Eugene Davis, "OM is the highest mantra to contemplate in meditation because by merging in OM we can flow our attention back to the field of God. OM can be heard as the background sound of Nature. It is the sound from which all other sound-frequencies emerge and into which they return. OM meditation can be used by devotees of any religion or philosophical persuasion because it is beyond all contrived names or forms of God and beyond all concepts of God".

The holy syllable AUM has been highly exalted in the *Vedas,* the *Upanishads, Geeta* as well as in other scriptures. It is believed that Aum symbolizes the triad in space and time. "A" stands for *adimata* means the beginning, "U" stands for *utkrishta*—means the sustenance; "M" symbolizes the *mitti*—the dissolution. Yet another theory states A to be symbolic of *vac*—means word; 'U' represents *mana*—means mind, 'M' represents *prana*—means the breath According to Mandukya Upanisad, A stands for the conscious leve of wakefulness; U stands for the dream stage; and M for sleep stage The scriptures describe that when the person pronounces these letter in harmony, he catches the energy of the half syllable (*Ardhabindu* which leads the individual into silence. That perfect silence is th fourth stage of consciousness known as *Turyia*. This is the state o union and communion with the indwelling Divinity. According t Joseph Campbell "concentration on the sound of Aum connects th person to the throbbing being—the power which is omniscient and omnipresent. All the vowels have come out of the sound of AUM and all the consonants are the images and the fragments of the sound". AUM is the primordial *nada.* All the notes in music have originated from the vibrating *nada* of AUM-M-M." The sound of AUM has been the primordial sound which was heard in deep meditation by the sages of the antiquity. The great mother Gayatri has been revealed from the holy syllable AUM and from Gayatri has emanated the *Vedas.* In the description of the development of creation in *Rigveda;* it is written *vac* is Brahman. It is the *vac*—the word that envelops the entire creation. *Guru Granth Sahib* also explains that "it is indeed the *shabad* from which has emanated the entire world, it is the *shabad* that sustains all the three worlds". The sound energy of the holy syllable AUM is indeed a connecting link to the cosmos, as well as to the deepest mysteries of the Supreme-Self.

In the performance of any penance or ritual and worship, the individual is suggested to begin the worship with the holy syllable AUM; which initiates the spirit of surrender and essential unity. The significance of beginning the hymn with the holy syllable symbolizes the Lord Himself to be the centre of importance in every act of life. According to Swami Chinmyananda, "To cherish in our mind the divine awareness and the absolute supremacy of the infinite, as expressed in AUM, is to add purpose and meaning to all the acts of sacrifice, charity and austerity. To invoke in mind the divine concept of the Absolute is to free the personality from its limited fields of egocentric attachments. When a mind is thus liberated from its limitations, it becomes more efficient in all austerities, more selfless in all *Yajñas,* and more liberal in all charities". The recitation of the pranava AUM liberates the thinking faculty from its superficiality and the mind becomes settled in the dedicated performance of the *yajña* and penance. The attitude of the person becomes pure and honest, and the act of his penance becomes dedicated, and harmonious. Srī Kṛṣṇa tells in the verse twenty-four that it is with the utterance of AUM, the act of sacrifice, charity and austerity should be undertaken as enjoined in the scriptures. In general, the knowers of the *Vedas* and other holy scriptures, know the techniques of perceiving a very clear and vivid resonance of the sound of AUM in their mind. They always begin the recitation of each and every hymn in worship, with the sacred sound of AUM. Every type of penance, *yajña,* yoga and worship becomes ennobled and sanctified by uttering the holy syllable AUM at the commencement. In the words of Srī Aurobindo, "AUM is the initiating syllable pronounced at the outset, as a benedictory prelude and sanction to all acts of sacrifice and all acts of giving, it is a reminder that our work should be made an expression of the triple Divine in our inner being and turned towards Him in the idea and motive. The seekers of liberation do these actions without desire of fruit and only with the feeling, and *ananda* of the Absolute Divine behind their nature. It is that which they seek by this purity and impersonality in their works, this high desirelessness, this vast emptiness of ego and plenitude of spirit." *Aum Tat Sat*—has been known to be the threefold appellation of the Absolute. These three words stand for pure energy of the Supreme Divinity. The pronunciation of these three together arouses the latent Divinity and the person feels himself to be a part of the universal cosmic energy. The power of creation emanates from this mantra *Aum Tat Sat.* AUM is the primordial sound that envelops the entire creation. The word *Tat* stands for the supreme reality in essence. It expresses the universal truth, the absolute truth in essence. The expression *Aum Tat Sat* denotes that in essence everything is AUM. It is recommended in Sastras, that all types of worship, *yajña,* and austerity should commence with the holy syllable AUM and the completion of worship should be dedicated with the recitation of the trifold phrase *Aum Tat Sat.*

The offering of service with the words *Aum Tat Sat* declares that the Supreme Lord is indeed the substratum of the universe and pervades everywhere in everything. The worship has been initiated by the Supreme Divinity and is dedicated to the service of the Supreme Divinity. The knowers of truth perform various types of austerities and charities, in order to remain united with the indwelling-Lord, and for the sake of living in harmony with the God's creation. The worship and penance which commences with the holy syllable AUM in the beginning and which is dedicated to the Lord with the utterance of

Tat becomes sanctified and a means for emancipation and liberation. Here the word *Tat* signifies Brahman. It is specially uttered with AUM by the performer towards the completion of an offering. In the words of Swami Sivananda, "The immortal Soul which transcends the whole world, the three Gunas, the three bodies, the three states of waking, dreaming and deep sleep, which illumines everything, which is the basis of all, and the source of everything is connoted by the word *Tat*. The sages and the aspirants meditate on *Tat*. They utter the word *Tat* and say, "May all our actions and the fruits of them be in the name of *Tat* (That or Brahman)". The primordial sound of AUM connects the individual to the cosmic reality, *Tat* signifies the experiential knowledge and unity with the Supreme Brhaman and the attitude of service and selflessness; *Sat* stands for the Truth behind everything and also for the work which is auspicious. It is used in benediction and sanction. It means both truth, the absolute reality and goodness. As described earlier in chapter four verse thirty-three that anyone, who performs all actions with the pure spirit of *yajña* (selfless service) he eventually becomes Brahman. The compound words *sadbhave* and *sadhubhave* in verse twenty-six stands for nobility, honesty and purity of attitude in the performance of any worship and austerity. The pure and honest attitude is always conducive to peace, happiness, fulfilment, self-realization and God-realization. Srī Kṛṣṇa glorifies this attitude and has announced it to be genuinely praiseworthy. The expression *Sat* used in this verse signifies both the sense of reality and whatever is good, praiseworthy, auspicious and beneficial. In verse twenty-seven Srī Kṛṣṇa proceeds to explain, that the steadfastness in *yajña,* austerity and charity is also called *Sat* and the work which is performed in relation to these, that has been also announced as *Sat*. In the recitation of *Aum Tat Sat* the worshipper pledges himself to constancy, detachment, truth, beauty and goodness. Srī Krṣna recommends that every type of worship and austerity should revolve around the holy formula *Aum Tat Sat.* Again, in the verse twenty-eight Srī Kṛṣṇa repeats the genuine role of *sraddha* in the progressive realization of the Supreme Divinity. *Sraddha* signifies the earnest faith which proceeds from the unity of devoted love for the indwelling Lord. It is an honest, energetic effort of developing the most intimate relationship with God. He tells Arjuna that anything which is offered in worship and any austerity which is practised without faith, reverence and *sraddha*; that is called *Asat*. It renders no benefit to the individual here or hereafter. It is the attitude or the *bhava* which matters the most in any type of penance. Without faith and genuine attitude of loving devotion, even the most glorious and the most difficult penance is of no avail to the doer in his present life or in the life beyond. The performance of work with dedicated, pure, and honest attitude is indeed mandatory in every field of life. This is an unquestionable truth of life. It is the sincere and selfless attitude in any pursuit that connects the individual with the ultimate reality. It is *sraddha,* the ardent faith and ardent devotion that renders peace, happiness, liberation and emancipation eventually. In the words of Swami Tapasyananda, "*Sraddha* is the wholehearted and sincere acceptance of a supreme Spiritual Principle, which gives meaning and direction to life; combined with a readiness to put into practice what one has accepted with conviction. It is much more than mere belief *(visvasa),* which is mere conventional acceptance of an idea without any conscious intention to put it into practice. The importance of *sraddha* is further emphasized by equating a man's humanity with the *sraddha* he entertains. It means that the stature of a man consists in the loftiness of the ideals and aspirations he sincerely cherishes and tries to practise".

ॐ तत्सदिति श्रीमद्भगवद्गीतासूपनिषत्सु ब्रह्मविद्यायां
योगशास्त्रे श्रीकृष्णार्जुनसंवादे श्रद्धात्रयविभागयोगो
नाम सप्तदशोऽध्यायः ॥ १७ ॥

'Aum' tatsaditi Śrīmadbhagawadgeetā sūpaniṣatsu
brahmavidyāyām yogaśāstre Śrīkṛṣṇārjunasamvāde
śraddhātriyavibhāgayogo nāma saptadaśo'dhyāyaḥ

'AUM TAT SAT'—Thus, in the Upanishad of the glorious Bhagawad Geeta, the science of the Brahman (Absolute) the scripture of yoga, the dialogue between Srī Kṛṣṇa and Arjuna—thus, ends the chapter seventeen entitled *"Śraddhā-triya-vibhāga-Yoga"*.

इति श्रीमद्भगवद्गीतासु सप्तदशोऽध्यायः ॥ १७ ॥

Chapter Eighteen

MOKṢA-SANNYĀSA YOGA

THE YOGA OF LIBERATION THROUGH RENUNCIATION

अर्जुन उवाच

संन्यासस्य महाबाहो तत्त्वमिच्छामि वेदितुम्।
त्यागस्य च हृषीकेश पृथक्केशिनिषूदन ॥ १ ॥

sannyāsasya mahābāho tattvamicchāmi veditum
tyāgasya ca hṛṣīkeśa pṛthak keśiniṣūdana

Arjuna Said :

(1) I desire to know in detail the truth about renunciation *(sannyasa)* and also about relinquishment separately, O'Hrishikesa (Srī Kṛṣṇa).

Commentary—The dialogue opens with a specific questiōn by Arjuna regarding the precise concept of *sannyasa* (asceticism) and that of *tyaga* (renunciation). He expresses his genuine desire to know the essential characteristics of both, relinquishment and renunciation, distinctly and separately. In this verse Arjuna addresses Srī Kṛṣṇa, with three specific attributes such as Mahabaho, Hrishikesa and Kesinisudana. The use of these words indicates Arjuna's intimacy, love, devotion, respect, reliance and strong faith in his Master and his friend Srī Kṛṣṇa. Mahabaho means the Mighty-armed Lord whose arms are being the sinews of war, Hrishikesa means the controller, the ruler and the master of senses, Kesinisudana means the slayer of demon named Kesi.

श्रीभगवानुवाच

काम्यानां कर्मणां न्यासं संन्यासं कवयो विदुः।
सर्वकर्मफलत्यागं प्राहुस्त्यागं विचक्षणाः ॥ २ ॥

kāmyānāṁ karmaṇāṁ nyāsaṁ sannyāsaṁ kavayo viduḥ

sarvakarmaphalatyāgaṁ prāhuṣ tyāgaṁ vicakṣaṇāḥ

The Blessed Lord said :

(2) The sages understand *sannyasa* to be the renunciation of all actions prompted by desire; the learned declare the abandonment of the fruits of all actions to be the *tyaga* (relinquishment).

त्याज्यं दोषवदित्येके कर्म प्राहुर्मनीषिणः।

यज्ञदानतपः कर्म न त्याज्यमिति चापरे ॥ ३ ॥

tyājyaṁ doṣavadityeke karma prāhur manīṣinaḥ

yajñadānatapaḥ karma na tyājyamiti cāpare

(3) Some sages declare that actions should be abandoned as an evil, while others say that the act of *yajña* (sacrifice), charity and austerity should not be relinquished.

निश्चयं श्रृणु मे तत्र त्यागे भरतसत्तम।

त्यागो हि पुरुषव्याघ्र त्रिविधः सम्प्रकीर्तितः ॥ ४ ॥

niścayaṁ śṛṇu me tatra tyāge bharatasattama

tyāgo hi puruṣavyāghra trividhaḥ samprakirtitaḥ

(4) Listen from Me the final truth about the relinquishment, O'best of the Bharatas (Arjuna). The abandonment, O'best among men, has been declared to be of three kinds.

यज्ञदानतपः कर्म न त्याज्यं कार्यमेव तत्।

यज्ञो दानं तपश्चैव पावनानि मनीषिणाम् ॥ ५ ॥

yajñadānatapaḥ karma na tyājyaṁ kāryameva tat

yajño dānaṁ tapaś caiva pāvanāni manīṣiṇām

(5) *Yajña* (sacrifice), charity and austerity are not to be abandoned; these should be performed, for the acts of *yajña,* charity and austerity are the purifiers of the wise.

एतान्यपि तु कर्माणि सङ्गं त्यक्त्वा फलानि च।

कर्तव्यानीति मे पार्थ निश्चितं मतमुत्तमम् ॥ ६ ॥

etānyapi tu karmāṇi saṅgaṁ tyaktvā phalāni ca
kartavyānīti me pārtha niścitaṁ matamuttamam

(6) Even these actions should be performed abandoning all attachments and desire for fruits. O'Arjuna, this is for certain my decisive opinion.

Commentary—Srī Kṛṣṇa opens the conversation with the word *kamyanam*—which literally means the desireful actions. The work which is performed for the attainment of specific personal desires such as wealth, prosperity, progeny, social status name and also other heavenly boons and powers. Srī Kṛṣṇa tells Arjuna that renunciation of the desireful actions have been considered to be *sannyasa* by some sages and saints; while other men of wisdom declare that relinquishment of the fruits of all actions is the renunciation or *tyaga* in essence. The literal meaning of both words *sannyasa* and *tyaga* is to renounce; and both the words are used in the sense of relinquishment, but *tyaga* is slightly different from *sannyasa.* Renunciation is the abandonment of all desire-prompted actions, while relinquishment is the abandonment of the fruits of all ordinary and extraordinary activities. It is the renouncement of all anxieties related to the enjoyment of the fruits of actions. In verse three Srī Kṛṣṇa tells that some men of wisdom do declare that all types of actions should be abandoned as evil (*doshavat*) because every action leads to bondage; while other sages proclaim that actions such as the performance of *yajña,* charities and austerities must not be relinquished even by the men of wisdom.

In the following verses Srī Kṛṣṇa gives His own decisive opinion. He declares that the act of *yajña,* charities and austerities should not be abandoned. These actions are considered to be necessary and ought to be performed. Contemplation, worship and sacrifice (*yajña*), these are associated with the daily life of the individual and these are surely the means of self-purification. The performance of these actions helps the individual to eliminate the negativity of the previous *karmas,* which usually stand as a blockade in the way of attaining Supreme bliss. The performance of these actions educates the individual in the path of self-realization and God-realization—if these acts are performed with an attitude of detachment. These activities do accelerate and purify the thoughts and help the individual to live in harmony with his own inner-self, with other people and with cosmic powers. For example, *yajñas* are performed in order to maintain balance between the living species and the cosmic powers. The *Upanishads* have declared the importance of *yajña* in these words. *Triyo dharmaskandha yajñoadhyam danam iti*—means *yajña,* self-study and charity constitute together the foundation of a religious life and *Asuran yajña udetenatyaam—yajña* eliminates the demoniac tendencies. There are other beautiful lines explaining *Purusho vava yajña*—means the life itself is *yajña.* The performance of *yajña* inculcates the spirit of caring, sharing and giving. It helps in the advancement of a prosperous human society. There is another saying from the *Vedas, Esha ha ve yajño yoaham pavate yadesh yamvidam.* The process that purifies the universe is *yajña. Yajña* marks the summit of giving and receiving—The person who performs *yajña,* he shares its fruits with the entire creation, without the subtlest traces of egoism; also the one who receives its benefit does not have to salute to the giver. It is a silent sharing, giving and receiving that fits most appropriately with the laws of righteousness and the ordinance of the world order. *Vedas* declare—*Yajña dishantoi mitra bhavanti*—which means the spirit of *yajña* creates friendship and eliminates all enmity. For example, the *Gopath Brahaman* describes *Ritu sandhi-shu viyadhirjayate—Ritur sandhishu yajña kriyate*—means at the end of one season and at the beginning of another, *yajña* should be performed for the purification of the air. *Vedas* assert that the entire creation is sustained by the performance of *yajña. Yajñno vishnu prajapati sarve punati tasmedesh eva yajña*—means *yajña* purifies everybody, everyone and everything in all respects. As mentioned earlier in chapter three, verse eleven *prasparam bhavayantah shreyah param avapsyatha.* By fostering one another you shall attain the highest good.

About charity the *Vedas* proclaim *shatahasat samahara, sahastrahasta sankirah*—which means earn with hundred of hands and distribute with thousands of hands. The holy act of charity reflects the love of God for others and promotes the spirit of kindness. *Yajña* and charity are the blessings to the one, who gives and also to the one who receives. The person who has learnt to give and share, he grows and progresses in plenitude and abundance. It is the culmination of the spiritual advancement. The acts of *yajña,* charity and austerity help the individual to maintain his purity and unity with the indwelling-self. There is a famous saying *dakshinavante amritam bhajante*—meaning Blessed are those who can give and share; they attain the state of perfection in due time. These sacred activities do purify both the performer and the beneficiary and also promote the spirit of equanimity and sanctity in the universe; only if these are undertaken with the attitude of non-attachment. A detached attitude forms the foundation and the basis of asceticism and renunciation. When the attitude of detachment is firm and mature then the individual does not have to worry about bondage; he acts spontaneously and skilfully with the spirit of freedom. The person becomes free from all psychological conflicts and he performs every bit of his work with proper understanding and clarity of vision. A genuine renunciate performs all assigned duties in the spirit of *yajña,* in order to maintain the orderliness in the community and society. He attempts every action with zeal and enthusiasm, and offers all the work as a service to the Supreme Lord. The performance of his duties becomes educational for him, which transforms his every activity into *yajña* and helps him to overcome the shackles of all bondage. He always maintains his spirit of *tyaga* through the abandonment of the fruit of actions and gradually attains the tranquillity of *sannyasa.* In the words of Srī Aurobindo, "As a matter of fact, when people talk of *tyaga,* of renunciation, it is considered to be the physical renunciation of the world. The real *tyaga* is the renunciation of desire for the fruits of actions, and that too is the real *sannyasa*". In the up-coming verse Srī Kṛṣṇa explains to Arjuna, how with the practice of a detached attitude the individual can actually comprehend the meaning of *tyaga* and can prepare himself for the serenity of *sannyasa.* It is the process of rising above the limitations of the individual-self and embracing the entire creation in the spirit of cosmic unity with great responsibility and genuine pleasure. In *tyaga* a person lives a full life in the world, and performs all his assigned duties of life, with a heart anchored to the Divine. This type of renunciation brings fulfilment, satisfaction, joy, acceptance and perfection.

नियतस्य तु संन्यासः कर्मणो नोपपद्यते।
मोहात्तस्य परित्यागस्तामसः परिकीर्तितः॥ ७॥

niyatasya tu sannyāsaḥ karmaṇo nopapadyate
mohāttasya parityāgas tāmasaḥ parikīrtitaḥ

(7) The renunciation of an obligatory act is not proper; its abandonment through delusion is considered to be *tamasic.*

दुःखमित्येव यत्कर्म कायक्लेशभयात्त्यजेत्।
स कृत्वा राजसं त्यागं नैव त्यागफलं लभेत्॥ ८॥

duḥkhamityeva yat karma kāyakleśabhayāt tyajet
sa kṛtvā rājasaṁ tyāgaṁ naiva tyāgaphalaṁ labhet

(8) He, who renounces his action, because it is painful or from the fear of physical suffering, his act of renunciation is considered to be *rajasic.* He does not attain the merit of relinquishment.

कार्यमित्येव यत्कर्म नियतं क्रियतेऽर्जुन।
सङ्गं त्यक्त्वा फलं चैव स त्यागः सात्त्विको मतः॥ ९॥

kāryamityeva yat karma niyataṁ kriyate'rjuna
saṅgaṁ tyaktvā phalaṁ caiva sa tyāgaḥ sāttviko mataḥ

(9) He, who performs the obligatory actions, simply because it ought to be done; by abandoning attachment and also the desire for the fruit—that relinquishment is regarded to be *sattvic.*

न द्वेष्ट्यकुशलं कर्म कुशले नानुषज्जते।
त्यागी सत्त्वसमाविष्टो मेधावी छिन्नसंशयः॥ १०॥

na dveṣṭyakuśalaṁ karma kuśale nānuṣajjate
tyāgī sattvasamāviṣṭo medhāvī chinnasaṅśayaḥ

(10) The wise man of renunciation is the one who is imbued with the purity of *sattva,* whose doubts are dispelled, who does not hate the disagreeable work nor is attached to the agreeable one.

न हि देहभृता शक्यं त्यक्तुं कर्माण्यशेषतः।
यस्तु कर्मफलत्यागी स त्यागीत्यभिधीयते॥ ११॥

na hi dehabhṛtā śakyaṁ tyaktuṁ karmāṇyaśeṣataḥ
yastu karmaphalatyāgī sa tyāgītyabhidhīyate

(11) Verily, it is not possible for an embodied being to renounce actions altogether. He, who abandons the fruits of actions—he is said to be the renouncer.

अनिष्टमिष्टं मिश्रं च त्रिविधं कर्मणः फलम्।
भवत्यत्यागिनां प्रेत्य न तु संन्यासिनां क्वचित्॥ १२॥

aniṣṭamiṣṭaṁ miśraṁ ca trividhaṁ karmaṇaḥ phalam
bhavatyatyāginām pretya na tu sannyāsinām kvacit

(12) Disagreeable, agreeable and mixed—threefold is the fruit of action, accruing after death, to those who have not relinquished—but there is none whatsoever for those who have renounced.

Commentary—In these verses Srī Kṛṣṇa declares that renunciation of obligatory actions is not proper. He tells that renunciation of *niyatam karma* merely out of ignorance, is considered to be *tamasic*. The obligatory actions include, both the performance of the daily duties at the individual level and also the special duties which a person is expected undertake as a member of family and society in which he lives. If a person ignores his obligatory duties and refuses to accept his responsibilities in the community which supports his living and protection his renunciation is considered to be *tamasic*. The individual who neglects his obligatory duties he disturbs the continuity of action in nature and brings about a chaos in society. His relinquishment is marked as an escapism from the realities of life. This abandonment, which is undertaken through ignorance, brings in deterioration. Such an individual degrades himself and he becomes a burden for himself and for others in the family and community.

In verse eight, Srī Kṛṣṇa proceeds to tell about the *rajasic* type of relinquishment. He explains to Arjuna, that when a person gives up the performance of actions on account of the fear of physical discomfort and trouble that abandonment is considered to be *rajasic*. Such an individual renounces the performance of work because the ordeal of effort it involves and also because of the fear of loss and failure. When a person abandons his duty out of the fear of physical discomfort, that withdrawal is considered to be ignorant. The feeling of escapism and pessimism originates from the lack of self-reliance, self-respect and the misunderstanding of one's personal duty. In the words of Swami Chidbhavaninda, "There are people who view worldly life as full of troubles and difficulties, and they are not prepared to face those ordeals. Governed by an escape-mentality, they choose to embrace *sannyasa* and live a life of ease and comfort at the cost of credulous people. They do not obtain the Supreme benefit of renunciation". Swamiji further gives the example of Arjuna who comes to the battlefield to wage a war of righteousness and suddenly he becomes overwhelmed with the emotions of *sannyāsa* in the middle of the battlefield. Arjuna's notion of relinquishment clearly shows his deluded notion of escapism. A withdrawal of this type, which is due to lack of discrimination and proper insight, that is indeed the *rajasic* type of renunciation. As a matter of fact no one should abandon the assigned duties out of mere disappointment or on account of the fear of emotional and physical discomfort. This type of renunciation brings more pain than any fulfilment or peace. A genuine relinquishment is that, which guides the individual to the acceptance of higher moral values with greater responsibilities. It leads the individual in to deeper satisfaction, inner fulfilment and towards one's own completeness. A true renunciate is the one who performs all his duties as a husband or wife, as a doctor, teacher, soldier, while renouncing both the desire for reward and also egoistic attitude of 'Mine-ness'. The performance of his work reflects his inner state of tranquillity, devotion and the inclination to serve others. As a business man he aims at making reasonable profits in the field of his business. He himself works very hard, very enthusiastically and also he loves to share his profits with his co-workers and with the rest of the community.

A genuine renunciate perfectly understands the gospel of selfless action, he does his duty to the very best of his ability with an unattached attitude towards rewards. In the words of Swami Sivananda, "When a man does obligatory duties without agency and unselfishness and egolessness, his mind becomes purified, his *antahakaran* (heart) becomes prepared for the reception of the divine light or the dawn of the self-knowledge". There are always some genuine renunciates in every society, those who perform their duties as a service to humanity and as a worship to the Divine. They do not care for name or fame or even to attain the world of celestials. Such dedicated renunciates do help the community in order to maintain harmony with the laws of the Divine. They believe in righteousness and the maintenance of proper ethical values. Their work manifests the love of God, truthfulness and unselfishness. There is an incident from the life of a very dedicated person who genuinely spent almost every minute of her life in the service of others. Occasionally, she accepted the money for the service she performed but she used the one hundred percent of those funds towards the welfare of the community. She gave money to schools and temples. She would buy religious books and distribute them among children of all ages. Once in an interview, she was asked by a reporter, that if she did not use a penny out of the collected funds for herself, why did she accept the money from others at all? To that she answered, that she wanted to teach people the importance of making donations which helps the deserving recipients in so many different ways. The virtue of giving donation promotes the spirit of sharing and giving. To be able to give and share is the greatest joy of life and everyone should get the opportunity to experience it. She further added that the acceptance of the donation, protects her from becoming an egoist and saves her from the feeling of 'I-ness'. A person who abandons the thirst to enjoy the fruits of his actions is indeed a *sattvic* renunciate. A *sattvic* relinquisher is a man of inner integrity and steady wisdom who remains deeply rooted in the awareness of the Supreme Lord, and he becomes blessed with the higher intuitive understanding, called *medhabuddhi* in Sanskrit. The increased awareness and understanding plays a very significant role in spiritual progress.

According to sage Patanjali there are various levels of intuitive wisdom which are experienced by the individual. He describes the names such as *Taraka, Viveka, Jñana, Pratibha, Medha, Prajña, Rtambhara. Taraka*—literally means to reason and speculate. *Viveka*—the general discriminating ability, *Pratibha* and *Medha*—means the increased ability to discriminate. The next one is *Prajña*—which is the highly developed intuitive power; and *Ṛtambhara*—is going into the purest awareness of the Soul, wherein the individual experiences oneness with God and becomes highly enlightened. All these are various steps from less intuitive ability to increased intuitive ability. A genuine renunciate is usually very intuitive; he develops this faculty of increased awareness by living in the consciousness of the Supreme and by performing his duties in the spirit of Yoga. Srī Kṛṣṇa has used the word '*Medhavi*' for such a man of integral wisdom, whose intellect becomes purified. Although, physically he remains an ordinary individual and yet attains the proximity of *sannyasa.* A *sattvic* relinquisher is very bright, sharp, intelligent and very knowledgeable in all respects. According to the holy sages and scholars, intuition is inner wisdom, inner guidance, inner awakening, which helps the person to maintain his proper place in the inner world and also in the material world. It sharpens the discriminating ability and helps the person to differentiate between the real and unreal, the eternal and the transient. It dispels all doubts those are caused by ignorance and enables him to function from the higher planes of enlightened insight. A genuine renunciate has the ability to maintain his peaceful attitude while performing both the agreeable and the disagreeable actions. He neither becomes attached to the pleasant nor hates the work which is unpleasant. He maintains his inner peace and equipoise amidst adversity and prosperity, joy and sorrow and honour and dishonour. He develops a profound and comprehensive understanding of each situation as it occurs and knows very clearly how to deal with it. A *sattvic* person who is always settled at the higher planes of understanding; the performance of his work proceeds from perfect clarity and purity of his intellect. He experiences the Supreme Divinity working through him and thus he performs everything very spontaneously and appropriately. Such an individual is indeed a gem of the society, his life style becomes a role model for others; in order to become inspired into renunciation and selfless service to community.

In verse eleven, Srī Kṛṣṇa glorifies and complements the person who has learnt to relinquish all the desires for the rewards of his actions. He tells Arjuna that it is indeed very difficult for an embodied being to relinquish all actions completely; but the person who abandons the desire for the fruits of actions, is called a man of renunciation. So in order to become a relinquisher, the person has to learn to perform all his work with the attitude of detachment. He has to train himself into the gospel of sclfless action, wherein he performs all his obligatory duties with the attitude of relinquishing the fruits of his actions. He who is able to renounce his affinity to the results of his action is indeed a genuine renouncer, fit for the asceticism. He lives on this planet as a celestial (*Deva*), who simply gives and gives unconditionally. As a matter of fact all actions do lead to some type of reactions, creating a trap for the performer; unless the work is performed with the attitude of detachment and relinquishment for the rewards. As described earlier, actions are merely the manifestations of thoughts, ideas and notions. The thoughts become actions and reactions become the latencies and *samskaras.* Since every thought is influenced and motivated by the three modes (qualities of nature) so every action brings out a psychological reaction in accordance to the attitude of mind.

In verse twelve, Srī Kṛṣṇa declares that in general, there are three types of fruits of every action; undesirable, desirable and also mixed. The reactions of all types of actions are stored in the field of information as latencies for future expressions into the life hereafter. This process of life which is bound in past, present and future, goes on until one learns to renounce the fruit of all actions. The person who is a genuine renunciate, for him actions do not bear any reactions, so he remains free. It is indeed the attitude of selfless action that prepares the individual for total asceticism and renunciation. A true renunciate is always very determined and mature. He performs all his duties very skilfully, faithfully, diligently and intelligently with an attitude of service. His actions become liberating and do not create any bondage in the present life or in the life hereafter. For him the performance of his duty becomes a means for self-realization and God-realization. His life becomes enjoyable, purposeful and meaningful.

पञ्चैतानि महाबाहो कारणानि निबोध मे।
सांख्ये कृतान्ते प्रोक्तानि सिद्धये सर्वकर्मणाम्॥ १३॥

pañcaitāni mahābāho kāraṇāni nibodha me
sāṅkhye kṛtānte proktāni siddhaye sarvakarmaṇām

(13) Learn from Me, O'mighty armed (Arjuna), these five causes as declared in the *Samkhya* philosophy for the accomplishment of all actions.

अधिष्ठानं तथा कर्ता करणं च पृथग्विधम्।
विविधाश्च पृथक्चेष्टा दैवं चैवात्र पञ्चमम्॥ १४॥

adhiṣṭhānaṁ tathā kartā karaṇaṁ ca pṛthagvidham
vividhāś ca pṛthakceṣṭā daivaṁ caivātra pañcamam

(14) The seat of action (body) and likewise the doer, the instruments of various sorts (sense organs and mind) many kinds of efforts and providence (destiny) being the fifth.

शरीरवाङ्मनोभिर्यत्कर्म प्रारभते नरः।
न्याय्यं वा विपरीतं वा पञ्चैते तस्य हेतवः॥ १५॥

śarīravāṅgmanobhir yat karma prārabhate naraḥ
nyāyyaṁ vā viparītaṁ vā pañcaite tasya hetavaḥ

(15) Whatever action a man performs with his body, speech and mind—whether it is right or wrong, these five are its causes.

तत्रैवं सति कर्तारमात्मानं केवलं तु यः।
पश्यत्यकृतबुद्धित्वान्न स पश्यति दुर्मतिः॥ १६॥

tatraivaṁ sati kartāramātmānaṁ kevalaṁ tu yaḥ
paśyatyakṛtabuddhitvān na sa paśyati durmatiḥ

(16) Now, such being the case, the man of impure intellect, who on account of his perverse understanding looks upon himself as the sole agent, he does not see (truly).

यस्य नाहंकृतो भावो बुद्धिर्यस्य न लिप्यते।
हत्वापि स इमाँल्लोकान् न हन्ति न निबध्यते॥ १७॥

yasya nāhaṅkṛto bhāvo buddhiryasya na lipyate
hatvāpi sa imāṅllokān na hanti na nibadhyate

(17) He, who is free from the egoistic notion of 'I-ness'; and whose mind is not tainted—even though he kills these people, he neither slays nor is he bound.

Commentary—Here in these verses Srī Kṛṣṇa presents an analysis of factors which are generally involved in the accomplishment of all actions. The expression *sarvakarmanam* in the verse thirteen indicates the entire field of actions, enjoined by the holy scriptures, and also the ordinary and extraordinary actions. The entire superstructure of innumerable activities is directly connected with these five well-defined causes, as the basic constituents of action. The five factors as described in *Samkhya* (philosophy) system of analytical knowledge (sequential) are *adhisthanam*—means the body, the seat of action. *Karta*—the doer, *karana*—means the instruments, in the form of sensory organs, *cheshta*—meaning the conscious efforts, and the fifth one is known as *daivam* means the destiny. Every type of activity which is performed by the individual, it is expressed through the seat of all actions—the body. The embodied-soul within the body acts as a doer for the performance of all actions. *Shruti Bhagwati* has also confirmed this view in these words *Esa hi drasta srasta* means this is indeed the witness and as well as the doer. The embodied-soul revolves in an ongoing wheel of actions and reactions due to his identification with the body. The *karana* are the sensory organs of action such as hand, feet, mouth, anus and genitals, the five sensory organs of perception are touch, taste, smell, hear and sight. These ten sensory organs combined with mind, intellect and ego together form the inner instruments those become involved in the performance of any activity. The fourth one is *cheshta* means the applied effort. The fifth factor for the accomplishment of all kinds of actions is the *daiva* means the destiny. It is indeed the destiny, which is knowingly or unknowingly the instigator of all actions. Destiny is the software of all impressions, memories and (thoughts) *vasanas,* those are stored in the bank of the informational field known as the subtle body. It is the thought which originates from the reservoir of memories, and persuades the embodied-self into specific type of actions. The doer acts according to the information which is fed by the mind. Every action is indeed a manifestation of the thought which is initiated from the reservoir of *samskaras*. Everyone generates his own external world from his own subconscious depths of memories, and builds his own personality which is wrapped around by his own destiny (thoughts).

The mind recalls the information from the field of stored memories and initiates the body into new actions. This whole process is very orderly and precise. Each and every memory unfolds itself at particular time in life in relation to appropriate. circumstances. The seed-memories instigate the new ideas and new actions.

The impressions from the actions of the past lives and of the present are experienced as the fruits and also in form of some fleeting thoughts, which appear as flashes in the mind. Every embodied-soul has previous *samskaras* in the subconscious mind. The dormant impressions and memories are definitely the chief factor in moulding the character and destiny of an individual. These latencies do remain dormant until favourable conditions instigate them into proper expressions on the surface of the consciousness. The impressions and the latencies of the past are never lost. This storehouse of memories is indeed the destiny of man. The destiny of a person expresses itself in the form of favourable and unfavourable circumstances. Anyone who develops the ability to maintain constant vigil over his mind through meditation, he can actually perceive the *sanskaras* of the past. He can replace old memories with the new ones, and can create a new destiny for himself. The yogis know very well, how the recorded data of the latencies and *sanskaras,* operates in the field of action. In the words of Swami Ramsukhdasji, "Although a thought comes to the mind according to the *prarabhda*—the destiny, the thought of past memories (*Sanchita Karma*) cannot force a man to perform an action. But if there are attachments and aversions, it becomes a *sankalpa* and can force him to act. Destiny forces a man to act in order to get the fruits of past actions. But by applying his discrimination, he should check himself from performing prohibited actions, and he is free in doing so". As long as a man does not realize the supreme power of God within, he definitely lives like a poor victim in the hands of destiny, but at the dawn of self-realization he is awakened to the reality and his conditioned behaviour. The old memories are replaced by new thoughts and dormant latencies are washed by the grace of the Divine. The person becomes very integrated, strong, pure and confident. In the words of Dr. Paul Brunton, "The difficulty lies in the persistence of strong mental habits which we have brought down from former incarnations, habits of false belief and of ignorant thinking which keep us tied to the 'not-self'. We are the creators of those habits; but since we have made them, we can unmake them. If their elimination were dependent entirely upon our own efforts, it might no doubt be a very difficult process to get rid of them, but we have help. The higher power exists. That will help you, but only after you have made strong endeavours of your own". A person has the ability to change the pattern of his *samskaras* by living in the consciousness of the Divine. The play of destiny is within the domain of every individual; the required effort is to be awakened to it.

In verse fifteen Srī Kṛṣṇa tells that any type of action which a person performs with his body, speech and mind, whether it is right or wrong—there are five factors involved in that; the body, the doer, the sensory organs, the required effort and destiny. Every action is indeed only a thought in the initial stage. A thought in the mind expresses itself through speeçh or through other sensory organs and finally becomes an action. A thought becomes a word, and then it is transformed into some kind of performance. This entire mechanism operates in the realm of Nature bound by the three gunas of nature. Now this being the truth, he who looks upon the embodied-self, as the doer, he is for sure of the perverted understanding. He does not perceive the reality about the functioning of nature. In the words of Swami Tapasyananda, "In all actions there are five factors involved—the body, the I-sense of the performer, senses, expression of energy through them, and as the fifth, the unknown and incalculable factor. All these are factors belonging to Prakriti. Behind, it is the pure light of consciousness, the Atman, who is the unaffected witness. In ignorance, this pure witness identifies himself with these factors external to him and their performances, and creates bondage for himself. So, if the actor has no feeling like 'I am doing', and no attachment to the fruits accruing, it can be said that he does not act, even if all the world sees him acting in the physical sense". The hidden message of this statement is, that every individual should educate himself about the truth of the existence of the Indweller who remains the unaffected witness of every action. The feelings and thoughts keep changing from moment to moment but the one who witnesses the entire drama, He remains the same, throughout the innumerable mutations which occur at the gross and subtle levels of consciousness. When the individual beholds only one unchanging, all-blissful reality as the basis and substratum of all activities, his notion of 'I and Mine' starts fading. He becomes free from the egoistic notion of 'I-ness'. He works in a copartnership with God. Since all his thoughts and actions are prompted by the purity of the indwelling Self, he can never harm anybody and is not bound by any activity. Even if he has to wage a war against the wicked, in order to re-establish the ordinance of righteousness, he is not tainted by the evil of killing the enemies. He considers himself merely a soldier, a representative of the Supreme-Lord, who has to fight on behalf of the community for the preservation of peace and morality. He becomes free from the intention of causing any harm to others and his mind remains unstained. He maintains his vigilance in carrying out the orders but still remains aloof from the bondage of good and bad results.

ज्ञानं ज्ञेयं परिज्ञाता त्रिविधा कर्मचोदना।
करणं कर्म कर्तेति त्रिविधः कर्मसंग्रहः॥ १८॥

jñānaṁ jñeyaṁ parijñātā trividhā karmacodanā
karaṇaṁ karma karteti trividhaḥ karmasaṅgrahaḥ

(18) Knowledge, the object of knowledge, and the knower, form the threefold impulse to action; the instrument, the action and the agent form the threefold basis of action.

ज्ञानं कर्म च कर्ता च त्रिधैव गुणभेदतः।
प्रोच्यते गुणसंख्याने यथावच्छृणु तान्यपि॥ १९॥

jñānaṁ karma ca kartā ca tridhaiva guṇabhedataḥ
procyate guṇasaṅkhyāne yathāvacchṛṇu tānyapi

(19) The knowledge, action and the actor are also declared to be threefold, in the science of the gunas, according to the distinction of the gunas. Listen about them also as they are.

Commentary—The verse eighteen describes the *Triputi* the threefold impulse to all types of actions. This is indeed the motivating force behind all actions which a man performs in this world. These three aspects relating to any activity always move together, like the three sides of a triangle. This *'triputi'* constitutes, the knowledge, the object of knowledge and the knower. Similarly the instrument, the action and the doer are the threefold constituents of action. All types of impulses which are involved in the performance of any action, do arise out of this *triputi.* The first one is the *jnanam*—means the knowledge in general, the second aspect is *jneyam*—what is to be experienced and the third one is *parijnata*—means the experiencer. This *triputi* has to move together in order to motivate the idea which is executed by the threefold constituents of action, such as the instruments, the object and the doer. These are the means for the execution of any work.

After describing the threefold impulse for any action and the threefold means of action, Srī Kṛṣṇa proceeds to tell something very important in verse nineteen. He unfolds the mystery, about the variety of results which come from different people for the performance of one and the same type of activity. For example, when the recipe of baking a bread is given to a group of four individuals, the results are always different, while they are given the same ingredients, the same instructions and the same necessary gadgets to bake the bread. This evident difference in results is due to the difference in their personal attitude and psychological makeup. The reason for this diversity is their personal conditioned behaviour which is motivated by the qualities of nature. The trifold qualities of nature do influence the entire field of activity. People act so distinctly because they become influenced by distinct impulses in the performance of their work. This basic difference which occurs in the performance of every activity is because of the difference, in the degree of personal self-awareness. It is indeed so true that the result of every action can be measured by personal attitude of the individual towards the accomplishment of the work. The personal touch of the individual, the personal involvement, the feelings and sentiments are reflected in every kind of performance. The attitude of the individual plays a very significant role in the quality of the work which is produced. As described earlier in the chapter fourteen and seventeen, generally people categorize themselves in three types due to the inherent qualities of nature, *sattvic*, *rajasic* and *tamasic.* The knowledge, the action and the doer have been classified under these categories and a detailed description of these have been given in the following verses.

सर्वभूतेषु येनैकं भावमव्ययमीक्षते।
अविभक्तंविभक्तेषु तज्ज्ञानं विद्धि सात्त्विकम्॥ २०॥

sarvabhūteṣu yenaikaṁ bhāvamavyayamīkṣate
avibhaktaṁ vibhakteṣu tajjñanaṁ viddhi sāttvikam

(20) The knowledge by which one perceives in all beings the 'One' imperishable existence as undivided in the divided—know that knowledge to be *sattvic.*

पृथक्त्वेन तु यज्ज्ञानं नानाभावान्पृथग्विधान्।
वेत्ति सर्वेषु भूतेषु तज्ज्ञानं विद्धि राजसम्॥ २१॥

pṛthaktvena tu yajjñānaṁ nānābhāvān pṛthagvidhān
vetti sarveṣu bhūteṣu tajjñānaṁ viddhi rājasam

(21) But that knowledge which perceives in all beings, the manifold entities of distinct kind, as different from one another—know that knowledge to be *rajasic.*

यत्तु कृत्स्नवदेकस्मिन्कार्ये सक्तमहैतुकम्।
अतत्त्वार्थवदल्पं च तत्तामसमुदाहृतम्॥ २२॥

yattu kṛtsnavadekasmin kārye saktamahetukam
atattvārthavadalapaṁ ca tat tāmasamudāhṛtam

(22) That which is confined to one single act, as if it were the whole, which is without reason, without foundation in truth and is trivial—that is declared to be *tamasic.*

Commentary—In these verses Srī Kṛṣṇa enlightens Arjuna, about the threefold nature of knowledge. The knowledge that deepens the insight, expands the horizon of the out-look, which enhances the perception of truth and initiates the individual into the realization of his cosmic unity with the Supreme-soul is *sattvic* (the pure knowledge). It promotes inward discipline, self-respect, universal love and brotherhood. The *sattvic* knowledge is perceived from the inward connectedness with the source of life. It helps the person to experience the presence of all-pervading imperishable Lord behind the apparent diversity of all beings. A person endowed with (pure) *sattvic* knowledge develops an attitude of tolerance, respect and hospitality towards all the varieties and diversities in different communities, countries and nations. He helps people to develop and maintain spiritual solidarity and integrity. A vedic prayer explains this concept of *sattvic* knowledge. "*Aum sarve bhavantu sukhinah, sarve santu niramayah, sarve bhadrani pasyantu, ma kaschith dhukha bhag bhavveth*"—which means, may every one be happy, may all be healthy, may all enjoy prosperity; and see happiness. May no one be subject to sorrow.

There is another, similar type of prayer, for universal peace and harmony, for everything and everybody in the entire universe. *AUM dyouh shaanti-rantarikshagam, shanti prithavi, shantiraapah, shantiroshadhayah, shantih vanaspatayah, shantir vishve-devaah, shantir brahma, shantir sarvagam, shantih-shantih reva, shantih saa maa, shantih redhi. Aum shantih shantih shantih*—May there be peace and harmony in all the three worlds. Unto the heavens be peace, unto the earth and sky be peace. May there be peace unto the waters; the medicinal herbs and may there be peace unto the trees and shrubs. May there be peace unto the gods and unto the creator Brahma. May the entire world be at peace and May we realize and enjoy that peace". Srī Kṛṣṇa tells Arjuna that this direct, clear, vivid and right perception of the non-dual Supreme-self is indeed the *sattvic* and pure form of knowledge. It is this integral knowledge which helps the individual to comprehend the fundamental cosmic unity which prevails as oneness underneath the apparent diversity. The *sattvic* type of knowledge perceives the wholeness of the Supreme-soul in the entire universe. It promotes understanding into realization of the ultimate truth. On the other hand, the knowledge by which one perceives the manifold entities of different kinds as separate from one another, that knowledge is considered to be the *rajasic*. This type of knowledge separates and disintegrates people initiating them into the achievement of selfish personal goals. This deluded knowledge makes people selfish and greedy. It creates disruption of human relationships. Those who are led by the passionate form of knowledge, they feel themselves pushed into a frenzy of greed and an orgy of envy. The moral values and the ethics of quality living are suppressed and discarded by the man of *rajasic* understanding. He equates everything and everybody merely on the basis of material progress and prosperity. The attitude of selfishness creates social atomization and ethical stagnation. In the words of Srī Aurobindo, "It is a restless kinetic multiple action with no firm governing higher ideal and self-possessed law of true light and power within it". The knowledge that imprisons the individual into his limited self-created boundaries of one particular belief is indeed the *tamasic*. The individual with deluded understanding is very obstinate and pays no attention towards anything that lies beyond his limited circle of comprehension. He clings to one single (idea) concept as if it was the entire truth.

There is a very good incident from the life story of Srī Ramakrishna as described by Isherwood. "At the Dakshineshwar temple, the Durga festival used to be a five-day long worship of the Deity, ending on the evening of the fifth with the immersion of the image, which has been used in the worship. This image is usually made up of clay for one particular festival; then it is consigned to the nearest river, lake or sea. During the five-day worship, the worshipper must evoke the Divine presence from his own heart and transfer that presence to the image. Before the image can be removed from the shrine and immersed, the divine presence must be withdrawn from it again, and reinstalled within the worshipper's heart. The reason for this procedure is very obvious. Mathur, a devotee of Srī Ramakrishna, worshipped the image for five days with great devotion. At the end of the last day of worship when he was told that it was the time for the image to be immersed, Mathur was overwhelmed with grief and then violently agitated. At this strange behaviour of Mathur, Sri Ramakrishna asked Mathur, "Do you really think mother will leave you, just because of her image is immersed in the Ganga? For three days you have been worshipping her in the shrine. But now she is coming to be much nearer to you within your own heart. Finally Mathur understood that his fears had been totally meaningless." It is the *tamasic* type of knowledge that creates fears and all types of insecurities. This knowledge is not based on reason and the person objects to comprehend the reality of things. It is narrow and remains within the boundaries of the self-assumed limited understanding. The person of *tamasic* thoughts does not care to probe into real cause and effect, and sticks to the one and the only one, self-chosen idea. He is very fanatic and egocentric. There is no worst fate than to become trapped into the narrow fanatic boundaries of deluded understanding. A person, who is endowed with *tamasic* knowledge, he ignores the omnipresence of the Divine and treats the faiths and beliefs of other people with indignation and ignorance. Such an individual creates all kinds of troubles in the society, and he becomes a problem for himself and for others.

नियतं सङ्गरहितमरागद्वेषतः कृतम्।
अफलप्रेप्सुना कर्म यत्तत्सात्त्विकमुच्यते॥ २३॥

niyataṁ saṅgarahitam arāgadveṣataḥ kṛtam
aphalaprepsunā karma yat tat sāttvikamucyate

(23) The obligatory action which is performed without attachment, without love or hatred by the one who is not desirous of any reward—that action is called *sattvic.*

यत्तु कामेप्सुना कर्म साहङ्कारेण वा पुनः।
क्रियते बहुलायासं तद्राजसमुदाहृतम्॥ २४॥

yat tu kāmepsunā karma sāhaṅkāreṇa vā punaḥ
kriyate bahulāyāsaṁ tad rājasamudāhṛtam

(24) That action, however, which is performed with great strain by the one who seeks to gratify his desire or is impelled by egoism—that action is declared to be *rajasic.*

अनुबन्धं क्षयं हिंसामनवेक्ष्य च पौरुषम्।
मोहादारभ्यते कर्म यत्तत्तामसमुच्यते॥ २५॥

anubandhaṁ kṣayaṁ hinsāmanavekṣya ca pauruṣam
mohād ārabhyate karma yat tat tāmasamucyate

(25) The action which is performed with delusion, regardless of the consequences, loss, injury and the individual's own ability—that is declared to be *tamasic.*

Commentary—In these verses Srī Kṛṣṇa proceeds to describe the threefold nature of action. Every individual as member of the family, society and community is expected to perform his obligatory duties in order to live a balanced life. Srī Kṛṣṇa declares that the obligatory action, which is performed without the sense of doer-ship and attachment to the fruit is considered to be *sattvic*. A *sattvic* activity is that which proceeds from the purity of heart and is performed with the clarity of proper understanding. It is executed faithfully, skilfully, intelligently, enthusiastically, and righteously. It renders peace and joy to the performer; being the source of fulfilment in itself. A *sattvic* action is always rewarding and blissful. On the other hand, the actions which are performed with great strain, in which the individual is desirous of fruits and seeks self-gratification, those actions are *rajasic* (passionate). A passionate activity creates a lot of tension and mental strain for the doer, such as anxiety, worry, resentment, guilt and annoyance. It has been noticed in modern societies, that people in general, are under stress psychologically, emotionally and physically. The reason for this discomfort and restlessness is indeed the *rajasic* attitude of people—which characterizes greed and envy. It is true that an individual cannot achieve anything without reasonable effort, but when the effort becomes painful, stressful, and harmful to the health; it is considered to be *rajasic.* The activity which is undertaken out of delusion and regardless of the consequences that is considered to be *tamasic*. The execution of this work is initiated and performed in a confused state of mind in which the individual is motivated by the lower instinctive impulses. The performance of this activity is carried on, in a egoistic manner without realizing the capacity which is required to accomplish the task. The *tamasic* attitude drags the individual into self-degradation, disintegration and disappointment. The irresponsible activities such as polluting the environment, dumping the nuclear waste around the farms and orchards, forgery, corruption, theft, gambling and drug-dealing etc. are indeed *tamasic.*

मुक्तसङ्गोऽनहंवादी धृत्युत्साहसमन्वितः।
सिद्ध्यसिद्ध्योर्निर्विकारः कर्ता सात्त्विक उच्यते॥ २६॥

muktasaṅgo'nahaṁvādī dhṛtyutsāhasamanvitaḥ
siddhyasiddhyor nirvikāraḥ kartā sāttvika ucyate

(26) Free from attachment and the feeling of I, who is endowed with determination and enthusiasm, who remains unaffected by success and failure—that doer is said to be *sattvic* (pure).

रागी कर्मफलप्रेप्सुर्लुब्धो हिंसात्मकोऽशुचिः ।
हर्षशोकान्वितः कर्ता राजसः परिकीर्तितः ॥ २७ ॥

rāgī karmaphalaprepsurlubdho hinsātmako'śuciḥ
harṣaśokānvitaḥ kartā rājasaḥ parikīrtitaḥ

(27) The one who is swayed by passion, who eagerly seeks the fruits of his actions, who is greedy, violent, impure and who is easily moved by joy and sorrow—that doer is said to be *rajasic* (passionate).

अयुक्तः प्राकृतः स्तब्धः शठोऽनैष्कृतिकोऽलसः ।
विषादी दीर्घसूत्री च कर्ता तामस उच्यते ॥ २८ ॥

ayuktaḥ prākṛtaḥ stabdhaḥ śaṭho'naiṣkṛtiko'lasaḥ
viṣādī dīrghasūtrī ca kartā tāmasa ucyate

(28) Who is unsteady, vulgar, stubborn, deceitful, malicious, lazy, despondent and procrastinating—that doer is declared to be *tamasic* (ignorant).

Commentary—After giving a detailed description of the three types of knowledge and the trifold nature of every activity, Srī Kṛṣṇa proceeds to enlighten Arjuna about the third important constituent, "the doer". The knowledge, the action, and the doer, all the three move simultaneously into the performance of an action. The doer who is free from attachment and egoism, who is endowed with steadfastness and enthusiasm, who is unperturbed in success and failure—he is said to be *sattvic* (pure). A *sattvic* doer is perpetually connected with the purity of the Supreme-Self. He is highly intuitive and very positive. His projects are always well planned and systematic. His work plans are executed by keeping in mind the welfare of others. He performs his work in a very detached attitude of mind and he is always free from the egoistic feeling of I-ness. The style of his performance is very natural, effortless and spontaneous. He knows how to integrate different impulses and adjust his work according to the changing circumstances of life. He maintains a balanced state of mind, both in success and in failure, loss and gain, and also in pleasure and pain. A *sattvic* doer is very honest, enthusiastic, intelligent, and genuinely dedicated to the performance of his work. The execution of his activities is always accompanied with the moral sensibility and righteousness. On the contrary, the *rajasic* (passionate) doer is the one, who is easily inflated by success and becomes deeply depressed at the slightest failure. It is very difficult for him to maintain his equilibrium in the changing circumstances of his day-to-day life. He is generally very greedy, selfish, egoistic and quite confused about his sense of duty. He is very ambitious, restless and executes his performance with great tension and strain. He moves with his plans like a tornado, and is passionately attached to quick results. His eyes are always set on quick rewards and unreasonable profits. A *rajasic* (passionate) doer is violently desirous of the fruits and pursues his projects very impatiently. He really does not care whom he hurts and how much he hurts in the execution of satisfying his personal demands. Such an individual is led forward by unending greed and envy. His eyes are always set on accumulating, possessing and hoarding the wealth by all kinds of means, ethical or unethical.

The verse twenty-eight describes the characteristics of a *tamasic* doer, who is always unsteady, vulgar, malicious, negligent, lazy and procrastinating. Such a person lives his life under the slavery of his moods, uncultured thoughts and undisciplined habits. His resolves are very wavering and also superficial. His attempts are very fickle and unsteady. He lives in a world of his own dreams and fantasies. A *tamasic* doer of deluded understanding expects other people to take care of his needs and requirements. Sometime he acts like a neurotic and demands unnecessary attention. He is very indecisive, unsteady and very suspicious. The word *'Naishkritikah'* literally means the one who is jealous, suspicious and always bent upon creating quarrels and arguments among friends and other people. He enjoys harboring negativity for others and can be very retaliating by nature. A *tamasic* doer is generally very insecure and malicious and sometimes he becomes very obstinate and stubborn. A man of *tamasic* nature is very unpredictable and unreliable. Since he doesn't care for himself, obviously he doesn't care for others. Despondency and indolence are the other well-marked characteristics of a *tamasic* individual.

बुद्धेर्भेदं धृतेश्चैव गुणतस्त्रिविधं शृणु।
प्रोच्यमानमशेषेण पृथक्त्वेन धनञ्जय॥ २९॥

buddher bhedaṁ dhṛteś caiva guṇatas trividhaṁ śṛṇu
procyamānamaśeṣeṇa pṛthaktvena dhanañjaya

(29) Now hear, O'Arjuna the threefold division of intellect and also of steadiness, according to the gunas; as I declare them fully and scparately.

प्रवृत्तिं च निवृत्तिं च कार्याकार्ये भयाभये।
बन्धं मोक्षं च या वेत्ति बुद्धिः सा पार्थ सात्त्विकी॥ ३०॥

pravṛttiṁ ca nivṛttiṁ ca kāryākārye bhayābhaye
bandhaṁ mokṣaṁ ca yā vetti buddhiḥ sā pārtha sāttvikī

(30) The intellect which determines clearly the path of activity and renunciation; what ought to be done and what should not be done; what is to be feared and what is not to be feared; what is bondage and what is freedom; O'Partha (Arjuna)—that intellect is *sattvic* (Pure).

यया धर्ममधर्मं च कार्यं चाकार्यमेव च।
अयथावत् प्रजानाति बुद्धिः सा पार्थ राजसी॥ ३१॥

yayā dharmamadharmaṁ ca kāryaṁ cākāryameva ca
ayathāvat prajānāti buddhiḥ sā pārtha rājasī

(31) That which gives an erroneous understanding of Dharma and Adharma, and also of what should be done and what should not be done—that intellect O'Partha is *rajasic.*

अधर्मं धर्ममिति या मन्यते तमसावृता।
सर्वार्थान्विपरीतांश्च बुद्धिः सा पार्थ तामसी॥ ३२॥

adharmaṁ dharmamiti yā manyate tamasāvṛtā
sarvārthān viparītānś ca buddhiḥ sā pārtha tāmasī

(32) That which perceives even Adharma to be Dharma; which is enveloped in darkness and reverses every value—that intellect

O'Partha is indeed *tamasic.*

Commentary—In these verses the threefold division of intellect and fortitude have been described. *Buddhi* a Sanskrit word means intelligence. It is the faculty of reason and discrimination. The intellect that grasps the distinction between worldliness and renunciation, ordinance and prohibition, moral and immoral, what ought to be done and what should not be done, what is to be feared and what is not to be feared, what is bondage and what is liberation—that intellect is *sattvic.* It is the purity of intellect which helps the individual to make correct judgements and pursue appropriate goals in life. Pure understanding initiates the person in the pursuit of that work which is beneficial for the individual himself, and also for the society in which he lives. A *sattvic buddhi* which is very sharp and clean, it can grasp the distinction between the work which should be pursued and the one which should be shunned. It is indeed the purity of intellect which gives the ability to understand each situation of life in its clear perspective.

A man of clear vision knows exactly the expectations of the family, and the society in which he lives. He performs all his duties very skilfully, intelligently and diligently. He knows quite clearly the time when he should move forward towards the accomplishment of his project and also when he should refrain from activity. He knows very clearly, the appropriate age and time in life, when he should prepare himself for partial renunciation and for total renunciation. A *sattvic* person structures his life style in such a way that even while he lives in a family and community, he maintains his inner integrity and remains anchored to the Supreme-self. He is well acquainted with the nature of his work and knows exactly what ought to be done and what should not be done. A man of *sattvic* understanding remains conscientious about his involvement in any kind of activity, which is prohibited by the law and interferes with the rights of others. He knows how to respect the code of conduct and he always tries to act in harmony with the laws of Dharma. On the contrary, the intellect that grasps a confused and distorted notion of righteousness and unrighteousness and errs in determining as what ought to be done and what should not be done—that intellect is considered to be *rajasic*. A man of passionate intellect interprets the concept of Dharma and Adharma in a little perverted manner. He makes his own interpretation in accordance with his mixed understanding. His judgements are based upon his own preconceived ideas and notions. In the words of Jaydayal Goyandka, "The intellect which is at a loss to judge, whether a particular course of action is worth adopting or abstaining from, and to decide what should be done and how, also what should not be done, what is *karya* and what is *akarya,* that intellect is *rajasic.*" A man of *rajasic* intellect is generally very restless, anxious and always busy in making new plans and new projects. His mind runs riot, allowing his senses to indulge in all kinds of worldly enjoyments. His greed increases in all respects, so much so that anything which lies beyond the reach of his grasp, that alone escapes his attention. A person endowed with *rajasic* (passionate) intellect goes to the extent of exploiting others and sometimes he ruins the life of even the near and dear ones. The words such as Dharma, truth, honesty and humility are quite foreign to him. A passionate individual takes delight in acting contrary to whatever has been ordained by the authorities or the spiritual men of wisdom. He ridicules honesty and avoids listening to the spiritual and ethical code of Dharma.

The intellect that conceives everything quite opposite and contrary to the *sattvic* is indeed the *tamasic*. Srī Kṛṣṇa tells that the *buddhi* which mistakes adharma to be dharma and interprets everything in a perverted way, that is *tamasic*. Dharma is whatever is enjoined and ordained by the holy scriptures and adharma is whatever is prohibited by them. A man of *tamasic* understanding regards and interprets the immoral to be moral, unethical to be ethical; and thus reverses all values. Such an individual takes delight in disparaging discussions and wastes his time in making fun of others. A man of *tamasic* intellect lives his life under the guidance of a perverted intelligence. He always likes to move against the flow of ethical life. He enjoys to create problems for others and ridicules almost every moral and ethical suggestion. A man of *tamasic* intellect, disregards morality and also makes fun of the simple and straightforward people. He plays dirty games and wastes his time in planning some wicked projects.

Everything that is virtuous appears to be purposeless and useless and every activity which is trivial and sedentary, that appeals to be pleasant and inviting to him. A *tamasic* life style is very slothful, depressed, lonely, undisciplined and irregular.

धृत्या यया धारयते मनः प्राणेन्द्रियक्रियाः।
योगेनाव्यभिचारिण्या धृतिः सा पार्थ सात्त्विकी ॥ ३३ ॥

dhṛtyā yayā dhārayate manaḥ prāṇendriyakriyāḥ
yogenāvyabhicāriṇyā dhṛtiḥ sā pārtha sāttvikī

(33) The unwavering steadiness by which, through Yoga, one controls the activities of the mind, the life breath and the senses—that firmness O' Partha is *sattvic.*

यया तु धर्मकामार्थान्धृत्या धारयतेऽर्जुन।
प्रसङ्गेन फलाकांक्षी धृतिः सा पार्थ राजसी ॥ ३४ ॥

yayā tu dharmakāmarthān dhṛtyā dhārayate'rjuna
prasaṅgena phalākāṅkṣī dhṛtiḥ sā pārtha rājasī

(34) The steadiness by which one holds fast to Dharma (duty), pleasure and wealth; desiring the fruit in consequence thereof—that firmness is *rajasic,* O'Arjuna.

यया स्वप्नं भयं शोकं विषादं मदमेव च।
न विमुञ्चति दुर्मेधा धृतिः सा पार्थ तामसी ॥ ३५ ॥

yayā svapnaṁ bhayaṁ śokaṁ viṣādaṁ madameva ca
na vimuñcati durmedhā dhṛtiḥ sa pārtha tāmasī

(35) That by which a fool does not abandon sleep, fear, grief, depression and conceit as well—that firmness O'Arjuna is *tamasic.*

Commentary—From verse thirty-three onward Srī Krṣṇa gives the trifold description of *Dhriti* means steadfastness, firmness, fortitude or resolve. The undeviating steadfastness by which the functions of mind, the life-force and senses are controlled, that firmness is said to be *sattvic*. This type of resolve helps the individual in all kinds of spiritual progress. It fosters the practice of yogic communion and directs the intellect towards the realization of the higher goals in life.

A firm resolve is indeed mandatory for yogic communion and inner transformation. It helps the individual to establish perfect rhythm between mind and breath, and it enables him to enjoy the one-pointed concentration and exhilarating tranquillity of meditation. It is indeed the perfect coordination of breath with the thinking faculty, which brings harmony between all the faculties of mind and body. The *sattvic* firmness becomes a blessing for the person who has decided to live a spiritual life and who pursues the goal of God-realization. The unwavering resolve of a *sattvic* individual is not the repression or suppression of his senses, it is the intelligent and dedicated surrender, which is directed towards the unity with the Divine. A person of *sattvic* resolve holds a very systematic, natural and sensible approach towards everything in life. His resolves are meaningful, purposeful and are meant to create harmony with his own innerself, with other people and with the powers of nature. The purity of steadfastness is indeed a great virtue.

The resolve, that aims at the fulfilment of certain passionate desires and worldly success only, that firmness is said to be *rajasic.* A person of passionate resolve, moves forward very carefully, cautiously but very fast. He moves forward with the cherished concepts of *Dharma, Artha* and *Kama*—means the faithful performance of obligatory duties, accumulation of wealth and the enjoyment of pleasures. He proceeds in accordance with the scheme of life as outlined by the path of *pravritti*—which means an active life as a member of the family and society. He discharges his duties as a householder and as a citizen very faithfully. He practices Dharma in order to attain worldly pleasures in the present life and in the life hereafter. The performance of his religious activities are always desire-oriented, in the form of *putreshena, lokeshna* and *viteshena. Putreshena*—means the desire for progeny. *Lokeshna*—means desire for name, fame and recognition from others. *Viteshena*—means desire for accumulating riches, wealth and worldly enjoyments. In the words of Swami Chidbhavananda, "To the *rajasic* man, the practice of Dharma is a safe and sure investment. He expects that whatever good he does, is going to be returned to him with compound interest both here and in the life hereafter. He is firm in that belief. Therefore with pleasure he goes on doing a good turn here and a good turn there." While describing the *tamasic* type of resolve Srī Kṛṣṇa has used the word *durmedha*—means a person of meagre intelligence. The firmness with which an imbecile refuses to shake off excessive sleep, unnecessary fears, passivity, negligence, grief, despair, and conceit, that is indeed *tamasic.* Such an individual clings to all types of negativity in life. His vision is very narrow and egocentric. He becomes addicted to excessive sleep and considers that to be a normal way of living. A person of a *tamasic* resolve is perpetually caught in the circular pattern of worrying and does not want to make any effort to be liberated. He complains about his miseries and failures, but avoids listening to any type of useful advice. He lacks patience, proper discrimination and the right kind of perception about the realities of life. A person with a *tamasic* resolve, likes to remain enclosed in his symptomatic habits (behaviour) and takes delight in his arrogance. Such an individual is very arrogant, stubborn and obstinate about his ways of doing work in day-to-day life. The person of *tamasic* resolve creates many troubles for himself and for other people. He is irregular, disoriented, fearful and generally very distorted, both emotionally and psychologically. Cowardliness, arrogance, indolence, timidity, heedlessness, negligence towards the performance of his duties and to the call of Dharma are the most evident characteristics of a man of *tamasic* resolve.

सुखं त्विदानीं त्रिविधं शृणु मे भरतर्षभ।
अभ्यासाद्रमते यत्र दुःखान्तं च निगच्छति॥ ३६॥

sukhaṁ tvidānīṁ trividhaṁ śṛṇu me bharatarṣabha
abhyāsād ramate yatra duhkhāntaṁ ca nigacchati

(36) Now hear from Me, O'Arjuna, the threefold division of happiness—that in which one comes to rejoice by long practice and in which he reaches to the end of his pain.

यत्तदग्रे विषमिव परिणामेऽमृतोपमम्।
तत्सुखं सात्त्विकं प्रोक्तमात्मबुद्धिप्रसादजम्॥ ३७॥

yat tad agre viṣamiva pariṇāme'mṛtopamam
tat sukhaṁ sāttvikaṁ proktamātmabuddhiprasādajam

(37) That which is like poison in the beginning but becomes like an elixir in the end—which is born of a clear understanding of the Self, that happiness is declared to be *sattvic.*

विषयेन्द्रियसंयोगाद् यत्तदग्रेऽमृतोपमम् ।

परिणामे विषमिव तत्सुखं राजसं स्मृतम् ॥ ३८ ॥

viṣayendriyasaṅyogād yat tadagre'mṛtopamam

pariṇāme viṣamiva tat sukhaṁ rājasaṁ smṛtam

(38) That which arises from contacts of the senses with their objects; which is at first like nectar and in the end like poison—that happiness is said to be *rajasic.*

यदग्रे चानुबन्धे च सुखं मोहनमात्मनः ।

निद्रालस्यप्रमादोत्थं तत्तामसमुदाहृतम् ॥ ३९ ॥

yad agre cānubandhe ca sukhaṁ mohanamātmanaḥ

nidrālasyapramādotthaṁ tat tāmasamudāhṛtam

(39) That happiness which at the beginning as well as in the end, deludes the embodied-self, through sleep, sloth and negligence—that is declared to be *tamasic.*

Commentary—Srī Krṣna opens his conversation with the words "Now hear from Me, O'Arjuna, the nature of the threefold happiness". The pursuit of happiness is the universal goal of life. It is the cherished goal of all goals. The happiness is a state of mind wherein the individual feels inner fulfilment, satisfaction and a feeling of one's own completeness. Srī Kṛṣṇa declares that human happiness is of three kinds. The verse thirty-six explains that the state of happiness in which the individual delights through long yogic practice, the experience of inner completeness, in which he finds the end of his pains and sorrows; which is initially like poison but like a celestial (nectar) elixir in its effect,-—that happiness is said to be *sattvic*. This pure happiness generates and springs forth from the placidity of one's own inner resources and comes to the individual like a grace from the Supreme-self. Although the yogic practices are very tough and rigorous but their rewards are indeed very pleasant and immeasurable. When the individual is awakened to the joys of the indwelling self, his search of complete happiness becomes very satisfying and rewarding. The realization and comprehension of this happiness awakens the individual into raptures of inner ecstasy and blissful completeness. It is being happy without any reason, and without any specific object. The *sattvic* happiness, which accrues from the connectedness with the Supreme-Soul; it involves tremendous self-control and withdrawal from the sensual pleasures of mundane world. Although it is difficult to practise self-control in the initial stages of yogic communion but with continued practice, the aspirant begins to experience the raptures of ecstastic love for God and he surely tastes the nectar of never-ending happiness. The expressions *Pariname amrtopamam*—which in effect tastes like the elixir of life, it comes to the individual as *Atambuddhiprasadajam*—in the form of self-revelation with the grace of his own indwelling Self. It is born from the purity of one's own Self in the form of God-realization. The joy that springs forth from the immeasurable, unfathomable reservoirs of the inner resources is indeed *Anant*—means never ending. There is a famous saying *Hari anant Hari ki kripa ananta*—means the Supreme Divinity is immeasurable and inexplicable and so is His grace. His bliss is ever abiding, ever refreshing, ever renewing, joy-enhancing, truth-revealing and *sattvic*. It blesses the individual with inner quietude, clarity, contentment, peace and placidity of mind. The *Ananda*—-means the *sattvic* happiness which springs forth, from the grace of the Supreme-self. It is indeed *Ananta*—means limitless, boundless and never ending. Ananda is the yogic delight of the ultimate unity when the individual rejoices in one's own completeness without any particular reason. On the contrary, the *rajasic* happiness which is experienced from the contacts of the senses is very transitory and fleeting. It has a beginning and an end. It tastes like an elixir in the beginning but it culminates into bitter poison eventually. For example, an excessive indulgence in sensual pleasures can be easily mistaken for perennial happiness but it is indeed very momentary. It may taste like a nectar but it is suicidal, self-stultifying and always ends in bored satiety. It deadens the finer instincts, sensibilities and makes the individual a very selfish sensualist. It does not satisfy the individual by mere repetition, an overstimulating thrill is required every time to experience the pleasure.

Sensual pleasure is indeed like usurer, who wants multiple interest and enslaves the debtor. The pursuit of worldly enjoyments follows the law of diminishing returns. At every step one requires more and more and at last even the maximum fails to render the minimum satisfaction. Every sensual pleasure gradually ends in disillusionment, leaves the bitterest aftertaste.

In verse thirty-nine Srī Kṛṣṇa draws a picture of the *tamasic* happiness, which, at the beginning, as well as in the sequel, deludes the individual in all respects. For example, the habit of excessive sleep ruins the sensitivity of the personality. The individual remains lazy and tired most of the time and he keeps postponing even the obligatory duties of day-to-day life. The habits of negligence and heedlessness degrade him in his own estimation and he sinks into the whirlpool of dejection and desperation. The holy scriptures have described "*alasaya hi manushasya sharirasya, maharipum*"—which means laziness is one of the greatest enemy of man. The *tamasic* form of happiness which an individual seeks in his negligence, heedlessness, indolence and in the enjoyment of sensual pleasures is definitely another form of misery. It deludes the person both at the beginning as well as in the end. For example, a man goes to the bar and orders a couple of drinks in order to forget his mistakes, failures and misfortunes. After a few drinks he thinks that all his worries have disappeared; but unfortunately the moment of his happiness are very transitory and fleeting. His deluded act is surely wrought with misery. It intensifies his pains and miseries more than before. Even after he realizes that the presumed satisfaction was only temporary, he repeats the same act over and over again. Similarly, a person who tries to maintain his social status with loans from the bank, he definitely lives his life in total delusion, frustration, confusion and ignorance. Although he feels thrilled when the loan application is accepted, but he is constantly worried, while he spends that money, and struggles to pay off the loans. Similarly, the passionate love that arouses at the very first sight of a single beautiful glance, from the inviting eyes, is indeed like a fire of straw. It deludes the individual very quickly and also dies very quickly leaving the person in utter depression, shame and guilt. The *tamasic* happiness clouds and enshrouds the mind both in the beginning and at the end. When it is pursued for a long time, it contributes further to increased ignorance and promotes the inculcation of false values.

न तदस्ति पृथिव्यां वा दिवि देवेषु वा पुनः।
सत्त्वं प्रकृतिजैर्मुक्तं यदेभिः स्यात् त्रिभिर्गुणैः॥४०॥

na tadasti pṛthivyāṁ vā divi deveṣu vā punaḥ
sattvaṁ prakṛtijair muktaṁ yadebhiḥ syāt tribhirguṇaiḥ

(40) There is no creature either on earth or in heaven among the celestials, which is free from these three qualities, born of Prakriti (Nature).

ब्राह्मणक्षत्रियविशां शूद्राणां च परन्तप।
कर्माणि प्रविभक्तानि स्वभावप्रभवैर्गुणैः॥४१॥

brāhmaṇakṣatriyaviśāṁ śūdrāṇāṁ ca parantapa
karmāṇi pravibhaktāni svabhāvaprabhavairguṇaiḥ

(41) Of Brahmins, Of Kshatriyas and Vaisyas as well as of Sudras, O'Arjuna, the activities are divided in accordance with their own inborn qualities of nature.

शमो दमस्तपः शौचं क्षान्तिरार्जवमेव च।
ज्ञानं विज्ञानमास्तिक्यं ब्रह्मकर्म स्वभावजम्॥४२॥

śamo damas tapaḥ śaucaṁ kṣāntirārjavameva ca
jñānaṁ vijñānamāstikyaṁ brahmakarma svabhāvajam

(42) Serenity, self-restraint, austerity, purity, forbearance, and straightforwardness; knowledge, wisdom and faith in religion—all these are the duties of a Brahmin; born of his inherent nature.

शौर्यं तेजो धृतिर्दाक्ष्यं युद्धे चाप्यपलायनम्।
दानमीश्वरभावश्च क्षात्रं कर्म स्वभावजम्॥४३॥

śauryaṁ tejo dhṛtirdākṣyaṁ yuddhe cāpyapalāyanam
dānamīśvarabhāvaś ca kṣātraṁ karma svabhāvajam

(43) Heroism, vigour, steadiness, fortitude, dexterity (skillfulness), and also not fleeing from battle; generosity and lordliness—are the

duties of a Kshatriya, born of his inherent nature.

कृषिगौरक्ष्यवाणिज्यं वैश्यकर्म स्वभावजम्।
परिचर्यात्मकं कर्म शूद्रस्यापि स्वभावजम्॥ ४४॥

kṛṣigaurakṣyavāṇijyaṁ vaiśyakarma svabhāvajam
paricaryātmakaṁ karma śūdrasyāpi svabhāvajam

(44) Agriculture, cattle rearing and trade are the duties of a Vaisya, born of his nature; while the work consisting of service is the duty of a Sudra, born of his nature.

स्वे स्वे कर्मण्यभिरतः संसिद्धिं लभते नरः।
स्वकर्मनिरतः सिद्धिं यथा विन्दति तच्छृणु॥ ४५॥

sve-sve karmaṇyabhirataḥ saṅsiddhiṁ labhate naraḥ
svakarmanirataḥ siddhiṁ yathā vindati tacchṛṇu

(45) Sincerely devoted to his own duty, man attains the highest perfection. How he attains the perfection, being devoted to the performance of his own inborn duty; listen to that now.

यतः प्रवृत्तिर्भूतानां येन सर्वमिदं ततम्।
स्वकर्मणा तमभ्यर्च्य सिद्धिं विन्दति मानवः॥ ४६॥

yataḥ pravṛttir bhūtānāṁ yena sarvamidaṁ tatam
svakarmaṇā tamabhyarcya siddhiṁ vindati mānavaḥ

(46) He from whom all beings have evolved and by whom all this is pervaded—worshipping Him, through the performance of one's own duty, a man attains perfection.

श्रेयान्स्वधर्मो विगुणः परधर्मात्स्वनुष्ठितात्।
स्वभावनियतं कर्म कुर्वन्नाप्नोति किल्बिषम्॥ ४७॥

śreyān svadharmo viguṇaḥ paradharmāt svanuṣṭhitāt
svabhāvaniyataṁ karma kurvannāpnoti kilbiṣam

(47) Better is one's own duty, though destitute of merits, than the duty of another well performed—He, who does the duty ordained by his own inherent nature, he incurs no sin.

सहजं कर्म कौन्तेय सदोषमपि न त्यजेत्।
सर्वारम्भा हि दोषेण धूमेनाग्निरिवावृताः ॥ ४८ ॥

sahajaṁ karma kaunteya sadoṣamapi na tyajet
sarvārambhā hi doṣeṇa dhūmenāgnirivāvṛtāḥ

(48) Therefore, O'son of Kunti (Arjuna) one should not abandon one's innate duty, even though it is imperfect; for, all enterprises are enveloped by imperfections, as is the fire by smoke.

Commentary—Srī Kṛṣṇa declares that there is no one on earth in heaven or even among the gods who is free from the influence of the three qualities, of the primordial Nature. The influence of these gunas penetrates into the functioning of everything and everybody in the world. The three characteristics *sattvic, rajasic* and *tamasic,* those are inherent in nature, do manifest themselves very vividly in each and every field of action. The innate nature of every human being, which is a mixture of these three qualities, it expresses itself accordingly and orchestrates the various events of life. In almost every society and community, people usually divide themselves into the choice of four types of activities; in accordance to their inborn disposition. This is indeed a natural and psychological categorization of human beings, which is governed by their own inborn choice of likings and dislikings. It is the inner guidance which directs each and every choice of the individual in the field of his activity and self-expression. Human nature is a mixed weft of knowledge, ignorance, truth and falsehood; which becomes expressed through the *swabhava* of the individual *swabhava tu pravartate*. In olden days when people started living in small groups and started to form small communities, they gradually realized that they had naturally divided themselves into four major categories. This division took place very naturally, for the benefit of society.

Srī Kṛṣṇa tells Arjuna that human beings have always divided themselves into four classes in accordance with their own inborn inclinations. This categorization has taken place merely for the well-being of the society itself. The system of division has helped the community in maintaining mutual integrity, cooperation and perfect fellowship. The four categories have been named *Brahmin, Kshatriyas, Vaisyas* and *Sudras*. This classification into four types of work-order, has been defined as caste system. 'CAST' as the word indicates, means the 'role' or the part one is expected to play in specific life-time for the time being. The specific role which is to be played by the person, that becomes his assigned duty, born of his instinctive nature. For example, serenity, self-control, asceticism, purity, forgiveness, simplicity, uprightness, honesty, knowledge of the scriptures, the knowledge of the Self, and a positive faith in God, these are the characteristics of a Brahmin, born of his innate nature. A Brahmin is an embodiment of *sattvikta* (purity) and is expected to practise internal and external purity in all respects. He serves as a role model of serenity, perfect self-restraint and asceticism. He is expected to guide other people into a pure life style from the example of his own purity of body, mind and speech. A Brahmin is expected to be very learned and well-versed in the study of *Vedas.* He should be acquainted with proper methods and observance of religious rituals. He himself should hold strong faith in God in order to guide others in spirituality. To be pure, honest, austere, self-controlled and to grow into scriptural knowledge, wisdom and self-unfoldment are the mandatory duties of a Brahmin. Brahmin is the one who lives in the awareness of the supreme Brahmana and manifests that purity of the Supreme Self through his thoughts, words and deeds. His behaviour expresses proper alignment with the inner divinity. His life style is expected to be simple and the epitome of renunciation, self-dedication, self-sacrifice and service to the entire mankind. As in the scale of gunas the *sattvic* quality has been considered to be the topmost and the people in society those express this life style are also held with topmost respect. In ancient times the learned scholars, the rishis and the sages used to be on the advisory boards of the kings. The king always consulted these learned scholars in order to run his administration properly. These people have been known as the royal priests and royal sages.

As Brahmin is considered to be an embodiment of godliness, the other class (caste) which is next in scale is the Kshatriya; the embodiment of heroism, splendour steadfastness, dexterousness, firmness in battlefield, generosity and lordliness. *Rajasic* and *sattvic* qualities of the primordial nature, do predominate in the personality of a *Kshatriya.* The word *Kshatriya* is a Sanskrit word. The expression *ksatat trayate ity Kshatriya*—means the one who protects others from *ksati* (the injury) is a *Kshatriya.* The duty of *kshatriya* is to enforce the laws of dharma for the well-being of the society. He should make it sure that righteousness is being upheld in respect and people are doing their duties in the awareness of righteousness. Whenever there is decline of ethical values and the rise of unethical values, a *Kshatriya* (the warrior) class is expected to be alert and fight for the protection of good, for the destruction of the wicked and for the establishment of the righteousness. The protection of a country, society and the community is the first and foremost duty of a *Kshatriya.* To exhibit valour, heroism, steadfastness, skill, promptitude, generosity, compassion, lordliness and firmness in the battlefield are the characteristics of a *Kshatriya*, in accordance with his inborn nature. A *Kshatriya* as ruler acts as an embodiment of dharma, and his life becomes dedicated to the maintenance and the preservation of ethical values. Patriotism, heroism, self-discipline, self-dedication, self-confidence and self-sacrifice are some other hallmarks of a genuine *Kshatriya.* In verse forty-four Srī Kṛṣṇa mentions the duties of a *Vaisya* (a member of the merchant class) and of a Sudra (a member of the labouring class). Agriculture, cattle-rearing and skilful trade are the duties, performed by the *Vaisyas* born of their innate nature; and the work that consists manual service, is the duty of the Sudra in accordance with their inclination. The *Vaisyas* are endowed with more *rajasic* and less *sattvic* type of nature. They are highly inclined towards business and trade. The fourth category is that of the Sudras. The inborn natural disposition of a Sudra, is the mixture of *rajasic* and *tamasic* qualities. As stated earlier in verse forty, there is no being on earth or in heaven, who is free from these three qualities of nature. Everyone and everything is being constantly influenced and ruled by these modes of the nature.

In the words of Dr. Radhakrishnan, "*Varna* rules recognize that different men contribute to the general good in different ways, by supplying directly urgent wants of which all are conscious and by being in their lives and work witnesses to truth and beauty. Society is a functional organization and all functions which are essential for the health of the society are to be regarded as socially equal. Individuals of varying capacities are bound together in a living organic social system. All men are not equal in their capacities but all men are equally necessary for society and their contributions from their different stations are of equal value." In *Manusmriti* there is a description of the four classes of society. For example, an empire needs some scholars for the proper guidance in day-to-day life and when the society is faced with conflict of duties. Every community needs research and scientific development for all kinds of progress and advancement. The muscular strength is essential for the protection of the nation and for the protection of the righteousness. Wealth, food, and trade is also mandatory for the harmonious development and manual labour is definitely required for the proper maintenance of society. Each and every station of duty is very significant and holds its proper importance for the development of the society. Spiritualism, introspectiveness, management and leadership, productivity and service—these are the duties of the four character types based upon their innate natural disposition.

This classification in society has originated and proceeded from the personal *svabhava* of every individual. The word *svabhava* combines the two words *sva-bhava. Sva* means the indwelling self and *bhava* means the thoughts. So *svabhava* literally means the conditioned-self. The reason why different people choose different types of activities in the field of action, is because of their personal thoughts and inclination. Every individual is guided by his own *svabhava* and finds his fulfilment in the particular field of action as initiated by his inborn nature. The psychological makeup expresses itself in the physical makeup of the individual. The outwardness of the personality, reflects the inner inclinations of the mind. This classification in society is psychological and universal. The expression *sahajam karma* in verse forty-eight refers to the work which is initiated by one's own inborn disposition. The words such as *svakarma, niyta karma svabhavaniyata karma svabhavaja karma sahajam karma* means—that which is born with the individual, and that which is natural, inborn and innate. The human evolution has not proceeded in one straight line. It has gone through jerks from side to side with many ups and downs. It has always worked through the inter-twined phases of physical, psychological, intellectual, spiritual and the unknown. In the words of Srī Aurobindo, "There is always in human nature something of all these four personalities developed or undeveloped, wide or narrow, suppressed or rising to the surface, but in most men one or the other tends to predominate and seems to take up sometimes the whole space of action in the nature. And in any society we should have all four types".

There is a hymn in the old scriptures which gives the description of the cosmic man and the origin of society. *Brahminosya mukhamasid bahurajanya kritha, uru thathasya yadvaisya padabhyam sudro ajayatha*—which means the Brahmins from His mouth, the Kshatriyas from his arms, the Vaisyas from the lower middle part and the Sudras from still lower region and the feet. In human body the portion above the neck, especially the brain represents the Brahmin. It is the seat of the Supreme Lord which is represented as the full lotus. The people who are tuned to live in the awareness of the Supreme Lord, they are *sattvic.* They become endowed with the purity of the Supreme-soul and take upon themselves the role of enlightening and guiding the society into spirituality and a decent life style. The heart and the arms in the human body, do perform the duties of a Kshatriyas. The stomach is the Vaisya, who transforms and distributes the food (material wealth) in the body for its proper sustenance and well-being. The lower psychic station and the feet do represent the Sudra, who is constantly involved in service. A similar type of concept has been described by Gerald Heard in his book *Man the Master*. He writes, "it seems that there have always been present in human community four types or strata of consciousness. The Aryan-Sanskrit sociological thought, which first defined and named this fourfold structure of society, is as much ours as India's".

Srī Kr̥ṣṇa declares in verse forty-five and forty-six, that by being devoted to one's own duty, a man attains the highest perfection and the spiritual competency in all respects. The Supreme Lord of the universe should be worshipped through the dedicated performance of one's own duty. It is the attitude of sincere devotion to one's duty which reveals the presence of the Supreme through the execution of work. When the individual conducts his personal duty in the spirit of *yajña* (sacrifice) he becomes blessed with the grace of the Divine. In this context, there is an illustration in the *Mahabharta,* about the life story of a merchant, who actually performed his work as a worship to the Supreme and attained God-realization. The merchant Tuladhara lived in the city of Varanasi. He was a businessman, and also a great ascetic. He conducted his business transactions with honesty and sincerity. His devoted attitude and the perpetual unity with the Divine had transformed his entire business dealings into the service of the Lord. His work became his penance and worship for him. He performed his daily duties with a balanced state of mind and gradually entered into identification with the indwelling Supreme Soul. On the other hand, a Brahmin named Jajali who performed rigorous penance in the forest, he remained confused and deluded for a long time. One day while the old Brahmin was praying to God for inner peace and liberation, a voice from inside addressed him saying "Jajali you are not honest to yourself. You are arrogant and you still lack the inner purity. You must approach Tuladhara a merchant in Kasi for your final lesson in asceticism." Jajali felt very surprised, but still decided to visit the Vaisya trader. He sat by the merchant for few hours and observed the method in which he carried on his business. Tuladhar appeared to be at peace with himself and received the Brahmin very respectfully. He bowed to him and then said: "I have heard about your difficult penances in the forest, you are really great, tell me more about yourself and what has brought you here. How can I help you?" Jajali, the old Brahmin, was really amazed at the remarkable insight of the merchant, and requested him for guidance. Tuladhara spoke very politely and gave a remarkable explanation of dharma and on the performance of one's duty. Jajali heard the entire sermon very attentively and respectfully. After hearing the greatest secret of the Karamyoga, the arrogant Brahmin felt greatly enlightened and at peace with himself.

The performance of a duty definitely becomes a means of inner growth and perfection, when it is determined from within and carried out as an offering to the Divine. When the individual makes himself a conscious instrument in carrying out the work of the Divine in society, he can transmute his work into a means for the highest spiritual perfection and freedom. To worship the Lord through the performance of duty is to transform the whole life into a sacrifice. A genuine renouncer is the one who remains soaked in the nature of the Divine while performing his day-to-day activities of life. He develops an identity with the Supreme-Self and with the community in which he lives. His work itself becomes his worship and qualifies him for higher pursuits in spiritual life. The purity of his attitude transforms each activity into a *yajña* and even the toughest type of work becomes interesting and highly rewarding for him. The place of his work becomes the temple of the Lord, and the manner of carrying his work becomes the sacred mode of prayerful service. He lives very peacefully and conducts all his duties very peacefully. The pure and sincere duty-oriented attitude uplifts the individual and he lives like a yogi in the midst of worldly affairs.

असक्तबुद्धिः सर्वत्र जितात्मा विगतस्पृहः।
नैष्कर्म्यसिद्धिं परमां संन्यासेनाधिगच्छति॥ ४९॥

asaktabuddhiḥ sarvatra jitātmā vigataspṛhaḥ
naiṣkarmyasiddhiṁ paramāṁ sannyāsenādhigacchati

(49) He, whose intellect is unattached in all respects, who is self-controlled and free from all desires—he by renunciation, attains the Supreme state of freedom from action.

सिद्धिं प्राप्तो यथा ब्रह्म तथाप्नोति निबोध मे।
समासेनैव कौन्तेय निष्ठा ज्ञानस्य या परा॥ ५०॥

siddhiṁ prāpto yathā brahma tathāpnoti nibodha me
samāsenaiva kaunteya niṣṭhā jñānasya yā parā

(50) Know from Me, in brief, O'Arjuna, how having attained perfection, he attains to the Brahman—The Supreme consummation of knowledge.

बुद्ध्या विशुद्धया युक्तो धृत्यात्मानं नियम्य च।
शब्दादीन्विषयांस्त्यक्त्वा रागद्वेषौ व्युदस्य च॥ ५१॥

buddhyā viśuddhayā yukto dhṛtyātmānaṁ niyamya ca
śabdādīn viṣayāns tyaktvā rāgadveṣau vyudasya ca

(51) Endowed with the purity of intellect, controlling the mind by steadfastness, relinquishing the external sounds and the other objects of senses; laying aside both attraction and aversion.

विविक्तसेवी लघ्वाशी यतवाक्कायमानसः।
ध्यानयोगपरो नित्यं वैराग्यं समुपाश्रितः॥ ५२॥

viviktasevī laghvāśī yatavākkāyamānasah
dhyānayogaparo nityaṁ vairāgyaṁ samupāśritah

(52) Resorting to solitude, eating but very little, controlling speech, body and mind; always engaged in Yoga of meditation and taking refuge in dispassion.

अहङ्कारं बलं दर्पं कामं क्रोधं परिग्रहम्।
विमुच्य निर्ममः शान्तो ब्रह्मभूयाय कल्पते॥ ५३॥

ahaṅkāraṁ balaṁ darpaṁ kāmaṁ krodhaṁ parigraham
vimucya nirmamaḥ śānto brahmabhūyāya kalpate

(53) Having abandoned egoism, violence, arrogance, lust and anger; who is free from the notion of 'mineness' and is totally at peace within—he becomes worthy of being one with Brahman.

ब्रह्मभूतः प्रसन्नात्मा न शोचति न कांक्षति।
समः सर्वेषु भूतेषु मद्भक्तिं लभते पराम्॥ ५४॥

brahmabhūtaḥ prasannātmā na śocati na kāṅkṣati
samaḥ sarveṣu bhūteṣu madbhaktiṁ labhate parām

(54) Settled in the identity with the Brahman, cheerful in mind; he neither grieves nor desires. Regarding all beings alike, he attains Supreme devotion to Me.

भक्त्या मामभिजानाति यावान्यश्चास्मि तत्त्वतः।
ततो मां तत्त्वतो ज्ञात्वा विशते तदनन्तरम्॥ ५५॥

bhaktyā māmabhijānāti yāvān yaś cāsmi tattvataḥ
tato māṁ tattvato jñātvā viśate tadanantaram

(55) Through devotion, he comes to know about Me, what and who I am in essence; then having known Me in truth, he forthwith enters into Me.

सर्वकर्माण्यपि सदा कुर्वाणो मद्व्यपाश्रयः।
मत्प्रसादादवाप्नोति शाश्वतं पदमव्ययम्॥ ५६॥

sarvakarmāṇyapi sadā kurvāṇo madvyapāśrayaḥ
matprasādād avāpnoti śāśvataṁ padamavyayam

(56) While performing all actions, he who always seeks refuge in Me—by My grace, he attains the eternal, immutable state.

चेतसा सर्वकर्माणि मयि संन्यस्य मत्परः।
बुद्धियोगमुपाश्रित्य मच्चित्तः सततं भव॥ ५७॥

cetasā sarvakarmāṇi mayi sannyasya matparaḥ
buddhiyogamupāśritya maccittaḥ satataṁ bhava

(57) Consciously surrendering all actions to Me, regarding Me as the Supreme goal; resorting to the Yoga of integral wisdom (Buddhi-yoga)—focus your mind constantly on Me.

Commentary—The worship of the Supreme Lord through the dedicated performance of one's assigned duty, purifies the individual in all respects. He experiences the presence of the Lord in the execution of his work and performs that as a worship to the Divine. His attitude of worshipfulness, transforms every bit of his work into the Yoga of action, and prepares the person for the majesty of *sannyasa.* The total dispassion and *sannyasa* is indeed a state of mind. It does not come at some particular age or at the particular time of life; it is a process, which penetrates into the life style of a person, very slowly and gradually. It is the progressive realization of the self, the inner integration, stability and dispassion from the mundane world. A dedicated Karmayogi grows into *sannyasa* even without his being aware of it. Srī Kṛṣṇa declares in verse forty-nine that the one whose intellect is unattached, who has subdued his cravings, whose desires have faded away, he grows into the majesty of renunciation and attains the supreme state of freedom from the bondage of actions.

It is the freedom from the worldly desires, which prepares the person for inner integrity, stability and attachment with the Supreme Self. When the mind intends to avoid the pursuit of transitory thrills, from the gratification of the sensual objects; he automatically learns to enjoy the peace within. The expression *vigatasprhah*—literally means the disappearance of desires, which leads the individual into *naiskarmya siddhim* means the perfection into the gospel of selfless action. When the mind settles in the supremacy of the Divine, it naturally becomes unattached from the objects of the senses; its egoistic individuality is subdued and all the cravings are dissolved. All the angularities of the mind are shaped into one-pointed unity with the Supreme-Self. The expression *Asakta buddhi sarvetra* indicates the attitude of dispassion. It is being unattached from everything else and everybody else, almost everywhere, with a strong alignment to the consciousness of the Divine. This unique attunement into the yogic union, purifies the individual in all respects. His faculty of discrimination becomes purified and his intellect can differentiate between the real and unreal. Such an individual is blessed by the Lord with dispassion, discrimination, integral wisdom and integral knowledge. The same statement has been made by Srī Kṛṣṇa previously in chapter ten, verse eleven with these words *anukampartham aham ajnanajam tamah nasayamy atmabhavastho jnanadipena bhasvata*—Out of my compassion for them, I, dwelling within their self, destroy the darkness born of ignorance, by the luminous lamp of knowledge.

Starting from verse fifty-one onward, Srī Kṛṣṇa outlines the characteristic of a yogi, who has attained perfection. The expression "*buddhya visuddhaya yukto*" indicates the purity of the intellect. When the faculty of reason rests in God, it naturally becomes pure and reflects the truth very clearly and distinctly. A yogi who has resumed his identity with the Brahman, he comprehends everything from the purity of the Brahman. He knows how to withdraw his mind from the worldly objects of sensory pleasures, and to rise above the dualities such as attraction and aversion, love and hate etc. He inculcates the habit of enjoying the serenity of the solitary places. He knows that the solitary spots are very conducive to meditation. The seclusion helps the individual to slip into the solitude of mind and enjoy the serenity in association with the indweller. A desire to be in seclusion is one of the foremost characteristics of an aspiring yogi, who draws relaxation from his association with the indwelling divinity. A self-realized yogi enjoys solitary places and also eats moderately. His spiritual fervour itself contributes a lot to the sustenance of his physical body and so his requirement for food, becomes less than usual. Also, a genuine yogi holds his conscious control over his thoughts, words and speech. He speaks quite sparingly and his words are proper and very well measured.

The silence of speech is very helpful in silencing the waves of mind. To a yogi, *mauna* comes as a natural habit, because of his perpetual connectedness with the inner silence. He enjoys meditating upon the Supremacy of the Lord; and it becomes his favourite past-time. He lives his life in harmony with the rhythm of the inner tranquillity, peace and contentment. The radiance of his contemplated moods, becomes reflected in the field of his activities and manifests his identity with the Supreme Brahman. His yogic unity with the source of life, awakens the soul consciousness and his identification with the body, mind and ego starts fading. The anchorage with the Self becomes redemptive and replaces the feeling of 'I and Mine' with 'Thou and Thine'. When the consciousness of the Self becomes more evidential to him, the more transformative are its effects. The individual's mind becomes purified and more receptive to the truth of the infinite. The attitude of dispassion and renunciation becomes more pronounced and all doubts and fears become extinct. He lives his life with an unflinching faith in God and enjoys the assurance of immortality.

In verse fifty-four Srī Kṛṣṇa tells Arjuna that the individual who feels settled in the tranquillity of the Supreme-Brahman, he becomes identical with the indweller. He enjoys the bliss of inner fulfilment and shares it with everybody and everywhere he goes. Universal brotherhood, friendliness, and the attitude of equanimity radiates through his words, thoughts and deeds. He cultivates the spiritual magnanimity of mind which enables him to perceive the presence of the Lord in every heart and everywhere. His spiritual intimacy with the Divine makes itself evidential in his dealings with other people. By using the expression *'bhaktya mam abhijanati'* Srī Kṛṣṇa makes it very clear that 'through devotion, My devotee, surely comes to know Me'. The realization of the God through ardent devotion is indeed being and becoming one with the Lord. It is the same concept of ardent devotion which has been stated earlier in chapter fifteen, verse nineteen, "The wise man who thus realizes Me, as the Supreme person—knowing all in essence, he worships Me wholeheartedly as the all-pervading supreme being. He works through My grace and guidance."

Srī Kṛṣṇa intends to convince Arjuna that every individual is necessarily incomplete and fragmented until, he resorts to the majesty of the Supreme-Self. The dissipated endeavours of a disintegrated individual are the expressions of his inner turmoil, leaping in various directions, with a repeated search for satisfaction and inner completeness. He moves agitatedly here and there in quest of something not quite clear to his own-self. The performance of his work explains his dissatisfaction, restlessness and inner emptiness. The radical cure for all his problems lies in his conscious reorientation and re-association with the source of life in the form of self-surrender. The love of God helps the individual to comprehend the prime truth in its completeness; it is the blessed experience of the consciousness of the Supreme Lord by the entirety of the being. The faculty of reason deprives the individual from the comprehension of the Infinite, but the loving devotion prepares the individual for blessed experience of the Divinity by willingness, acceptance and total surrender. It is the perennial consciousness of the infinite in thoughts, words and deeds; which makes the realization of truth to be natural and effortless. The Upanishads have declared that mind cannot comprehend the majesty of the Brahman, words cannot describe Him; He can be known only by the self through love and faith in Him. In the ecstasy of devotional love the individual soul experiences unity with the Supreme Lord and perceives that the entire humanity is indeed inseparably connected; then all his services become the services of God and his heart rests in the bliss of eternity. The Supreme Lord who has been experienced in self-surrender is now pursued in the service of mankind. The self-realized devotee pursues only one goal—that is to experience the presence of the Divine through the service of his fellow-beings. His genuine effort remains concentrated into efficient service and loyalty to the call of the indwelling-Lord. The blessed yogic unity and introspection persuades him into the service of his fellow beings. Such an individual cultivates the valuable work-ethics, and through the practice of Karmayoga, he becomes eligible for the majesty of going in complete *sannayasa.*

मच्चित्तः सर्वदुर्गाणि मत्प्रसादात्तरिष्यसि।
अथ चेत्त्वमहङ्कारान्न श्रोष्यसि विनङ्क्ष्यसि॥ ५८॥

maccittaḥ sarvadurgāṇi matprasādāt tariṣyasi
atha cet tvamahaṅkārān na śroṣyasi vinaṅkṣyasi

(58) Focusing thus your mind on Me—by My grace, you will overcome all the difficulties; but, if because of egoism, you will not listen to Me, thou shalt perish.

यदहङ्कारमाश्रित्य न योत्स्य इति मन्यसे।
मिथ्यैष व्यवसायस्ते प्रकृतिस्त्वां नियोक्ष्यति॥ ५९॥

yadahaṅkāramāsritya na yotsya iti manyase
mithyaiṣa vyavasāyaste prakṛtis tvāṁ niyokṣyati

(59) If, in your self-conceit, you think "I will not fight," your resolve is in vain. Nature will compel you.

स्वभावजेन कौन्तेय निबद्धः स्वेन कर्मणा।
कर्तुं नेच्छसि यन्मोहात्करिष्यस्यवशोऽपि तत्॥ ६०॥

svabhāvajena kaunteya nibaddhaḥ svena karmaṇā
kartuṁ necchasi yan mohāt kariṣyasyavaśo'pi tat

(60) O'Arjuna, bound by your sense of duty (karma) born of your own inner disposition; that which from delusion, you do not desire to do, even that, you will do helplessly.

Commentary—Here in these verses Srī Kṛṣṇa declares once again that the person who is united in Yoga with Me; who has trained himself to live in the consciousness of the indwelling-self, he surely overcomes all difficulties and attains to the highest spiritual fulfillment. It is a fact that every human being creates his own limitations, problems, whims and fantasies. Most of these whims are the dictates of mind and ego. When the individual resorts to the Supremacy of the Lord, he learns to go beyond these limitations and comes to the realization that he is much more than his mind, body and ego. He experiences for himself that the notion of his assumed limitations, exists only in the dimension of his psychological and physical body. When he transcends these limited boundaries of false identifications; a miraculous transformation takes place instantly. The individual learns to live in the higher dimensions of self-awareness and his regular life becomes very peaceful and effortless. He becomes very confident and begins to change the self-defeating ideas into more goal-oriented, disciplined and harmonious ones. The faith in his own abilities starts increasing and his fears start evaporating in the light of the integral-wisdom. This is quite an extraordinary experience when the greatest mystery of life becomes revealed to the individual. The expression *Buddhi-yoga* in verse fifty-seven indicates the necessity for perfect alignment with the integral wisdom which unfolds the real nature of the Self, and helps the individual to overcome the conflicts of life. *Buddhi-yoga*—means unification with the purified and integrated wisdom; which enables the individual to negotiate with the changing circumstances of life, quite adequately and peacefully. In verse fifty-eight Srī Kṛṣṇa tells Arjuna to rise above the boundaries of his egoistic-self and seek refuge in the graciousness of the Supreme-Self. The person's identification with body, mind and ego is the notion of I-ness which separates him from the indwelling-Self. It creates fearfulness and disintegration because the individual is forced to disobey the voice of the indwelling Divinity. An egoist becomes consciously disconnected from the voice of the Supreme Self. He can harm others and also himself because of his limited and indistinct understanding. He misapplies his strength, misdirects his ideas and misuses his powers.

In the words of Dr. Paul Brunton, "The inflated personal ego is everywhere—in politics and religion, in art and business—attempting to resist the internal and external forces that would reduce its tyranny and undo its selfishness. It is stubborn, unwilling to budge from its position. No matter what sphere of human activity we look at, there the personal ego may be found perversely defending itself and aggressively clashing with other egos. The human ego must make the first faint beginning to renounce its sovereignty in favour of the divine Overself, or be driven by implacable fate in the same direction. The necessity of a change in thought and feeling as a preface to a change in humanity's tragic fortunes is an absolute condition". It is indeed a fact that the egoistic-self separates himself from the indwelling Supreme-Self and remains in a lingering dissatisfaction and fragmentation until the person seeks help from within. The egoistic behaviour is supported by the conditioned automatic memory of the mind. So, when the egocentric individualized-self surrenders in God; the individual's entire personality becomes transformed. The same person who had been formerly a problem for others he becomes an embodiment of love, compassion, generosity and benevolence. The feeling of hate changes into love and his aloofness into perfect harmony. The person feels integrated, friendly and confident.

The grace of the Divine is an inherent treasure of every individual and it manifests itself whenever it is called out. Srī Kṛṣṇa knows very well that Arjuna's refusal has risen from his egoism, delusion and misunderstanding of the situation. He knows that the moment Arjuna will contact the Supreme-Soul within, he will definitely restore himself to the majesty of his indwelling-Self and will understand the call of his inner disposition and *swadharma.* He makes it very clear to Arjuna that the latter's resolve is futile and meaningless because his inborn nature will compel him to fight. Srī Kṛṣṇa has emphasized the fact, that the strongest desire of every human being is to be able to show and express himself genuinely. It is the manifestation of his inborn disposition which gives him the maximum satisfaction, peace and fulfilment in life. A man who acts in conformity with his innate *Dharma* he attains satisfaction and peace in the present life and into the life hereafter. In the word of Dr. Radhakrishnan, "It is no use employing our minds in the tasks which are alien to our nature. In each of us, lies a principle of becoming, and idea of divine expression.

It is our real nature, *swabhava,* finding partial expression in our various activities. By following its guidance in our thoughts, aspiration and endeavour, we progressively realize the intention of the spirit for us. God lays down the conditions and it is for us to accept them. We should not waste our strength in fighting against the stream. The way in which we can be most useful is by submission to God's choice."

ईश्वरः सर्वभूतानां हृद्देशेऽर्जुन तिष्ठति।
भ्रामयन्सर्वभूतानि यन्त्रारूढानि मायया॥ ६१॥

īśvaraḥ sarvabhūtānāṁ hṛddeśe'rjuna ṭiṣthati
bhrāmayan sarvabhūtāni yantrārūḍhāni māyayā

(61) The Lord dwells in the hearts of all beings, O'Arjuna, causing them to revolve (bound by their karmas) by His illusive power; as if they were mounted on a machine.

तमेव शरणं गच्छ सर्वभावेन भारत।
तत्प्रसादात्परां शान्तिं स्थानं प्राप्स्यसि शाश्वतम्॥ ६२॥

tameva śaraṇaṁ gaccha sarvabhāvena bhārata
tatprasādāt parāṃ śāntiṁ sthānaṁ prāpsyasi śāśvatam

(62) Take refuge in Him alone, with all your being, O'Arjuna. By His grace, you will attain the Supreme peace and the eternal abode.

इति ते ज्ञानमाख्यातं गुह्याद् गुह्यतरं मया।
विमृश्यैतदशेषेण यथेच्छसि तथा कुरु॥ ६३॥

iti te jñānamākhyātaṁ guhyād guhyataraṁ mayā
vimṛśyaitadaśeṣeṇa yathecchasi tathā kuru

(63) Thus, this knowledge, which is the Supreme mystery of all mysteries, has been declared to you by Me. Reflect on it fully, and then act as thou wishest.

Commentary—Here in these verses Srī Kṛṣṇa reminds Arjuna, once again, about the mysterious power of the primordial Nature, and the Supreme Lord who controls that. It is the third time during the dialogue that the prime truth has been declared with conformity in specific words, *Isvarah sarvabhutanam hrddese Arjuna tisthati*—Lord dwells in the hearts of all beings. The same type of expression has been made earlier by Srī Kṛṣṇa Himself; in chapter thirteen verse seventeen *hridi sarvasya visthitam* and also in chapter fifteen verse fifteen *sarvasya ca, ham hridi samnivisto*. The Supreme Lord who is the master and the controller of the entire creation, He surely abides in the hearts of all beings. The seat of the Divine at the heart-centre has been illustrated as *hridayakasha*—means the ethereal space of the heart. According to ancient scriptures, it is at the heart centre, where the spiritual transformation takes place and the individual becomes capable of the vision of the indwelling Lord. The heart centre has been considered as the temple of the Divine, wherein the individual is awakened to the comprehension of the Divine power within. The verse sixty-one explains the subservience of all beings to the command of *Prakriti* (the primordial nature). Every individual lives his life in the world, as if programmed by some mysterious power. Every single event of life rolls in a certain predestined pattern. Pleasure and pain, loss and gain, birth and death—all these events take their turn one after the other, in a very specific style and at the very specific moment. Every single event occurs at the command of the secret power. Plotinus, the great Greek philosopher, has described the same idea in these words 'we perpetually revolve around the God, the principle of all things, but we don't always behold it. A band of singers moving about its leaders, may be diverted to the survey of something foreign to the choir, but when it turns itself to him, it sings well and truly subsists to him; thus also we perpetually revolve about the principle of all things, even when we are loosened from it and we have no knowledge of it; but when we behold it, we are no longer discordant, but form a divine dance about it". The idea is that as long as the embodied-self clings to its separateness and egoist individuality, the person becomes bound to move along with the instructions of his conditioned nature; but when he surrenders to the Lord, he becomes the master. An individual feels helpless and weak as long as he lives under the slavery of his conditioned behaviour, but once he takes refuge in the Lord, then the Supreme power takes care of him. In verse sixty-two Srī Kṛṣṇa suggests to Arjuna for a total surrender to the Lord of the universe. It is only through the grace of the Divine, that the individual becomes acquainted with the secret codes of his programmed life and the programmer. He comes to realize the Supremacy of his own essential nature, and the infinity of his power.

The *swadharma* of human beings, demands from every person to become united with the infinite spirit and experience the grace from within. In the word of Srī Ramanuja, "In the verse sixty-two, both the Supreme way as surrender and Supreme goal as attainment of absolute peace, and life eternal are enunciated in a crisp and clear manner. Unconditioned and eternal blessedness is the gift of the Supreme, the one worshipped through supreme surrender. Both in the realm of bondage and in the realm of freedom, God is the absolute power. The transition from one to the other is affected by His grace, and this grace is His response to the prayerful submission of the finite individual". The individual who seeks refuge in God with the totality of his being, he grows into a consciousness of the presence of the Lord at almost all the facets of his existence. He becomes blessed with the experiential knowledge of the Supreme. He learns to perceive and experience for himself the consciousness of the Divine within himself and in others. The expression *sarva bhavena*—means with the wholeness of his being, mind, speech and action. A genuine devotee reorients his entire personality into the awareness of the Lord and surrenders himself to the purity of love and devotion. He offers his entire life in the service of the Supreme. In this context, Tagore has written very beautifully. "Where can I meet Thee, unless in this my home made thine? Where can I join thee unless in this my work transformed into Thy work? If I leave my home I shall not reach thy home; if I cease my work I can never join thee in thy work. For Thou dwellest in me and I in Thee. In truth, Thou are the ocean of joy, this shore and the other shore are one and the same in Thee. When I call this my own, the other lies estranged; and missing the sense of that completeness which is in me, my heart incessantly cries out for the other. All my this, and that other, are waiting to be completely reconciled in thy love".

After describing the deepest philosophy of life, the wisdom of the integral knowledge of the Supreme, and the sublime truth about the infinite divinity, Srī Kṛṣṇa declares very openly to Arjuna "I have expounded to you the most profound knowledge, reflect upon it and act as you choose." This verse of Geeta has truly moved the hearts of millions all around the world. The words 'Act as you wish' really indicates the freedom of spirit which the vedic lore has advocated all along. Srī Kṛṣṇa asserts that the free spontaneity in thoughts and deeds is the first and foremost right of every individual; even the presiding Lord does not interfere that. Every person is free to decide and choose for himself the course of his action and the style of his life. He is very independent in the performance of any action but very much bound in accruing the fruit which proceeds from his actions. Similarly the grace, the cooperation and help of the Supreme is indeed at the demand of every individual; it is within the access of every human being, but it is received by those only, who make themselves receptive to it. Srī Kṛṣṇa encourages Arjuna to make his own independent decision on the basis of his own individual inner confirmation. He suggests Arjuna to apply his free will and decide for himself the course of his actions; based upon his own realization of the truth. Every aspirant must assimilate the truth, and experience it for himself and seek the appropriate answer for his belief.

The legacy of vedic teachings have always advocated that every individual must seek his own personal confirmation from his own inherent resources. The aspirant should be properly guided and not forced into cooperation. He should be entreated and persuaded but not compelled. The free spontaneity in acceptance should be valued and respected. In the words of Swami Chidbhavananda, "Srī Kṛṣṇa encourages Arjuna, and through him all aspirants, to exercise their power of understanding, enquire into Yoga as daringly and inquisitively as they can and accept and practise those principles about which they are convinced, and are beneficial to them. Laws pertaining to ethical and spiritual life of man are inviolable; they are facets of Truth. They require no defenders, no patrons and protectors."

सर्वगुह्यतमं भूयः शृणु मे परमं वचः।
इष्टोऽसि मे दृढमिति ततो वक्ष्यामि ते हितम्॥६४॥

sarvaguhyatamaṁ bhūyaḥ śṛṇu me paramaṁ vacaḥ
iṣto'si me dṛḍhamiti tato vakṣyāmi te hitam

(64) Listen, once again to My Supreme word, the profound secret of all. Since you are very dear to Me, therefore, I shall tell you, that which is good for you.

मन्मना भव मद्भक्तो मद्याजी मां नमस्कुरु।
मामेवैष्यसि सत्यं ते प्रतिजाने प्रियोऽसि मे॥ ६५॥

manmanā bhava madbhakto madyājī māṁ namaskuru
māmevaiṣyasi satyaṁ te pratijāne priyo'si me

(65) Focus your mind on Me, be devoted to Me, worship Me, and prostrate thyself before Me—you will come to Me alone. I promise you certainly, because you are very dear to Me.

सर्वधर्मान्परित्यज्य मामेकं शरणं व्रज।
अहं त्वा सर्वपापेभ्यो मोक्षयिष्यामि मा शुचः॥ ६६॥

sarvadharmān parityajya māmekaṁ śaraṇaṁ vraja
ahaṁ tvā sarvapāpebhyo mokṣayiṣyāmi mā śucaḥ

(66) Resigning all the Dharmas, seek refuge in Me alone. I shall liberate you from all sins. Grieve not.

Commentary—The compassionate words of Srī Kṛṣṇa in the verses sixty-five and sixty-six have moved the hearts of millions and have aroused a genuine love, devotion and respect for the Supreme. It has been really due to the exceptional love of Arjuna for Srī Kṛṣṇa; that in these verses the Lord reveals once again His personal identity as the Supreme Lord of the universe. He assures his friend with these compassionate and the most intimate words, "O' Arjuna have faith in Me, be devoted to Me, perform all your duties for My sake, I will always take care of you, this is My promise, because you are indeed very dear to Me. O' Arjuna you must rise above all the confusions and concepts about *Dharma,* take refuge in Me alone. Don't worry about anything, I will liberate you from all the sins, because you are dear to Me." Srī Kṛṣṇa gives to Arjuna his definite word of promise and tells him to perceive and receive once again the Supreme revelation. In the words of Dr. Radhakrishnan, "God discloses His nature, His graciousness and love and eagerness to take us back to Him. He is waiting, ready to enter and take possession of us, if only we open our hearts to Him. Our spiritual life depends as much on our going to Him, as on His coming to us. It is not only our ascent to God but His descent to man. God who is ever ready to help, is waiting only for our sincere appeal to Him."

The love of God and the grace of the God is inherent in every individual, it just needs to be revealed to the person. It only needs to be known and experienced. The devotional love of God is the experience of unity with the indwelling Supreme Soul. This love is unique, immeasurable and inexplicable. When the intimacy in devotional love grows in depth, the person becomes more and more devoted in the service of Lord. The aspirant lives with the conviction that God has possessed him and he rejoices in the state of unity. 'I belong to the Lord and Lord belongs to me, is the quintessence of all spiritual disciplines'. Nothing such as eligibility, credibility, capability and scriptural knowledge is equal to the devotional love which arises from the purity of a devoted heart. It is ardent devotion which leads the individual to the consummation of ultimate union with the Supreme Lord. Tukaram, a great devotional poet, has written beautifully about the devotional love of God. He writes "I have discarded for good the formalities of family name and pedigree. I have offered myself to Him, to whom I really belong. I was confined to this world alone; the ego was my barrier, separating me from the Lord, now it is vanquished and I am in a blissful state of union. Far above the fears of birth and death. I rejoice in the blissful freedom of the Self. The supreme state of bliss soars high all over me like a canopy of great shield." The words of Tukaram do indicate his faith and feeling of inner security. He has emphasized the need for a total surrender in God with love and devotion.

The grace of the Lord descends upon the individual who trains himself to live in the consciousness of the Divine. The grace expresses itself through his words, thoughts and deed. The Divinity descends into each and every sphere of his life. He may appear ordinary to worldly people but he himself feels extraordinary, special and peaceful in all respects. The spiritual intimacy becomes a blessing for him and eliminates all the traces of his egocentric whims and ideas. This mystery about the devotional love of God can be comprehended only by an ardent devotee of the Lord. The most profound secret which Srī Kṛṣṇa reveals in these verses is that the individual should become a honest recipient to the silent call of the Divine and make a complete surrender in God. The person should remain soaked in the awareness of the Divine and nothing else. In this manner the dedicated man moves through the various avenues of life, very peacefully. The scenery may change from pleasurable events to the painful ones, but he remains unperturbed being united in love with the Lord. If a person seeks for the God, from the depth of his heart and if his resolve is firm, he definitely remains devoted to the quest, day after day and year after year. If his heart longs for mutual love, the moment of unity comes when the individual is blessed with grace of the Lord and the prime truth is revealed to him.

Srī Kṛṣṇa calls it secretive, because it remains foreign to the individual until a genuine endeavour is made by the aspirant and the acceptance from the Lord becomes possible. Any endeavour which is made with the purity of the heart, unveils the knowledge of the self, and the redemptive process of grace becomes active and available to the individual. When the devotee remembers the Lord incessantly, his mind becomes concentrated on the Lord and he starts identifying himself with the Supreme. When the mutual love is strengthened with the indweller, the spirit of self-surrender arouses automatically. A devoted surrender to the supreme lord is a total letting go of one's individual-self. It is the person's request for acceptance into service. It is an appeal to be awakened. It is indeed a total surrender from the aspirant that leads to a total acceptance by the God. When acceptance with the indweller is confirmed and established, the grace of Lord penetrates into the heart of the individual. The person understands the shallowness of his limited individuality and starts enjoying the connectedness of spontaneity which comes from the intimacy of the transcendent spirit.

In verse sixty-six Srī Kṛṣṇa persuades Arjuna in making a complete surrender to the Lord without any traces of reservations. The words *sarva-dharman parityajya mam ekam saranam vraja* are very reassuring, decisive, precise, compassionate, suggestive and do declare a definite promise of the Lord's grace. This is the most reassuring advice. Srī Kṛṣṇa tells Arjuna that he should liberate himself of all his burdens, concepts and the mixed notions about Dharma. The term Dharma is of complex significance. It encompasses within itself, all the ideals and purposes which represent the general growth of the individual at personal level and also as a member of society. Dharma is the realization of the indwelling Lord in every little wisp of thought and in every little act of life. It is to live a life in the eternal union with the Supreme-Soul. The ideal life style which is enjoined by the laws of Dharma is that which follows the instructions of the Supreme-Self and flows spontaneously from within. The concept of Dharma becomes mixed, confused, complex and frustrating for that individual who becomes consciously disconnected from the indwelling light. In order to be restored to the inner integrity, peace and harmony the person is persuaded to make a complete surrender in God and become reoriented into the concept of his Dharma.

Arjuna has been very confused and disturbed about the real concept of his Dharma all along. In this verse sixty-six Srī Kṛṣṇa gives the answer to the question which has been brought forward by Arjuna in chapter two verse seven, when he appeals for proper counselling. He tells Srī Kṛṣṇa that his mind is confused about the concept of Dharma, and he definitely needs guidance in making appropriate decision about the course of his actions. Arjuna takes refuge in the Lord with willingness, trust and acceptance. When the individual becomes surrendered in God, his different concepts of Dharma, his self-assumed notions about obligations and duties, start blending into one essential Dharma—accept to live in the consciousness of the presence of the Divine and experience one's own immortality. It is the realization of being *Sat-Chit-Anand.* In the words of Swami Chinmayananda, "With this understanding of the term Dharma, we shall appreciate its difference from mere ethical and moral rules of conduct, all duties in life, all duties towards relations, friends, community, nation and the world, all our obligations to our environment, all our affections, reverence, charity, and sense of goodwill—all that have been considered as our Dharma in our books.

In and through such actions, physical, mental and intellectual, a man will bring forth the expression of his true Dharma—his Divine status as the All-pervading Self. To live truly as thc Atman, and to express Its Infinite Perfection through all our actions and in all our contacts with the outer world is to rediscover our Dharma".

The expression *aham tva sarva-papebhyo* literally means that I will liberate you from all the sins—means the removal of all the obstructions; those appear as obstacles in union with the Supreme. Srī Kṛṣṇa instructs and takes the full responsibility of guiding, helping and liberating Arjuna form all the sins. It is for sure a fact that with an honest surrender in God, the individual becomes very receptive to the grace and to the instructions of the Lord from within. He becomes blessed with pure insight which helps him to solve the most difficult problems and to wash away his most hideous sins. The expression 'sin' can be also interpreted as the thought which brings about guilt, shame and emotional disturbance. Every thought and action results in some type of reaction and leaves its shadows on the subtle layers of the mind. When the individual transcends the thinking faculty and mind in yogic union, these lingering marks and prints of guilt and shame are automatically removed and the individual feels liberated from all *samskaras* and latencies. A total surrender in God brings the experience of transcendental unity and the exhaustion of all the sins. The individual feels purified and liberated. In process of *saranagati*—means a total surrender to the Lord, the person is awakened to purity of consciousness which gradually exhausts all the *samskaras.* In *saranagati* when the individual-self discards his individuality, he is blessed with *prapti*—means a total acceptance from the Divine. The expression *aham tva sarva-papebhyo* is a most exhilarating assurance from Srī Kṛṣṇa; it indicates that the Supreme Lord personally takes care of all the problems and the sins of that person; who willingly takes refuge in Him and co-operates unconditionally. In these verses, Srī Kṛṣṇa's love for Arjuna has become more explicit. It is also a fact that the Supreme Lord Himself keeps calling the ones who seek His love devotedly and ardently. There are some beautiful lines written by Tagore about the Divine call from within.

"If I don't call Thee in my prayer,

If I keep Thee not in my heart,

Thy love for me, still waits for my love.

At the immortal touch of Thy hands,

My little heart loses its limits in joy and gives birth to utterance ineffable"

इदं ते नातपस्काय नाभक्ताय कदाचन।
न चाशुश्रूषवे वाच्यं न च मां योऽभ्यसूयति॥ ६७॥

idaṁ te nātapaskāya nābhaktāya kadācana
na cāśuśrūṣave vācyaṁ na ca māṁ yo'bhyasūyati

(67) This should not be told by you to the one, who is devoid of austerities and also who lacks devotion; or to the one who is unwilling to hear and also who finds fault with Me.

य इमं परमं गुह्यं मद्भक्तेष्वभिधास्यति।
भक्तिं मयि परां कृत्वा मामेवैष्यत्यसंशयः॥ ६८॥

ya imaṁ paramaṁ guhyaṁ madbhakteṣvabhidhāsyati
bhaktiṁ mayi parāṁ kṛtvā māmevaiṣyatyasaṁśayaḥ

(68) He, who with Supreme devotion to Me, will teach this Supreme secret to My devotees, shall come to Me, there is no doubt about it.

न च तस्मान्मनुष्येषु कश्चिन्मे प्रियकृत्तमः।
भविता न च मे तस्मादन्यः प्रियतरो भुवि॥ ६९॥

na ca tasmānmanuṣyeṣu kaścin me priyakṛttamaḥ
bhavitā na ca me tasmād anyaḥ priyataro bhuvi

(69) There is none among men, who does dearer service to Me than he; nor shall there be another on earth dearer to Me than he.

अध्येष्यते च य इमं धर्म्यं संवादमावयोः।
ज्ञानयज्ञेन तेनाहमिष्टः स्यामिति मे मतिः॥ ७०॥

adhyeṣyate ca ya imaṁ dharmyaṁ saṁvādamāvayoḥ
jñānayajñena tenāhamiṣṭaḥ syāmiti me matiḥ

(70) He, who will study this sacred dialogue of ours, by him I shall be worshipped through the *yajña* (sacrifice) of knowledge. Such is my conviction.

श्रद्धावाननसूयश्च शृणुयादपि यो नरः।
सोऽपि मुक्तः शुभाँल्लोकान्प्राप्नुयात्पुण्यकर्मणाम्॥ ७१॥

śraddhāvānanasūyaśca śṛṇuyādapi yo naraḥ
sopi muktaḥ śubhāṅllokān prāpnuyāt puṇyakarmaṇām

(71) The man who listens to this with full faith and without scoffing—he too shall be liberated, and shall attain the auspicious worlds of the righteous.

Commentary—In these verses Srī Kṛṣṇa tells Arjuna that the knowledge of the Supreme-Soul should be shared with that person only who is receptive and has legitimately prepared himself for the spiritual progress. The person who is humble, polite, open-minded and devoted to the Lord. The individual who is willing to listen and has a desire to serve the Lord in love and devotion; he definitely becomes eligible candidate for the proper understanding of the mystery and the majesty of the spiritual knowledge. The subject matter of such discourses is abstract and can be comprehended by only those who come forward with willingness and faith. So, it is indeed very important for the instructor to share his message with his genuine recipients only; those who are pure-hearted disciplined, devoted and engaged in the service of the Lord. The expression *na ca mam yo bhyasuyati* indicates very clearly that the integral wisdom, the knowledge of the Divine should not be imparted to the one who cavils at the Lord and finds faults with spiritual teachings. The arrogant individual who does not believe in the existence of God, he lives in his own world of deluded notions and holds no desire to learn. He lacks faith, respect and devotion. His mind is unknowingly closed to all the spiritual instructions.

Srī Kṛṣṇa suggests that it is wise to avoid useless discussions with the one, who is arrogant and resists to learn. People those are heavily involved in the materialistic life are generally devoid of austerities and self-discipline. They are consciously inattentive to the voice of the

Supreme-self. They are egoist and scarcely receptive to such discourses. Similar type of words have been said by St. Mathew, "Everyone that heareth these sayings of mine, and doeth them not, shall be likened unto a foolish man, who builds his house upon the sand". On the other hand, the person who comes forward with willingness and faith, who is prepared to listen and learn; he should be encouraged into the studies of God-realization. It is the duty of the enlightened person to initiate his fellow beings into godliness and help them personally. The individual who is genuinely devoted to the Lord and who shares the knowledge of the Supreme with the devoted, legitimate, and inquisitive aspirants, he is doubtlessly very dear to the Lord. Srī Kṛṣṇa, Himself declares in the verse sixty-nine, "There is indeed none among men, who performs dearer service to Me, than that of imparting the knowledge of the divine to others." The person who is awakened to the knowledge of the inner-Self, he must share it with others, and also encourage them into the spiritual realms of self-realization. When an ardent devotee becomes open to the inner-flow of the divine grace, he serves as a channel of the Lord Himself. He becomes a medium and the other people do feel very receptive to his words. His thoughts, words and actions do become instrumental in initiating and enlightening the lives of others.

In the verse seventy and seventy-one, Srī Kṛṣṇa again glorifies the knowledge of the Supreme-Soul and assures mankind that anyone who will study, practise and propagate the message of this sacred dialogue, he will be considered to be the performer of the *jñana-yajña*—means the assimilation and the sharing of the Divine knowledge for the benefit of others. *Jñana yajña'* is an act of sacrifice in which the individual personally tries to initiate others into higher understanding and the love of God. It is to initiate and enlighten those people who are desirous to listen and learn. Srī Kṛṣṇa declares that the teaching of the Divine knowledge is the highest form of service to the Lord. He further adds that anybody who will listen to the teachings of the dialogue faithfully, and will bring the message into practice; even he will become liberated from delusions and attain a high state of spirituality. The message of the holy dialogue is indeed phenomenal. It is a compendium of spiritual wisdom and the most appropriate guide for living a harmonious life. It presents a profound insight, into the workings of human nature and also provides guidance which is needed in every field of life. The entire message advocates a sincere devotion to the Supreme-indweller with proper understanding and insight. This is a gospel of ardent devotion to the Lord combined with proper performance of actions in the mundane world. The path of complete devotion and dedication has been evaluated to be the highest. The dialogue provides an understanding into the reality of the Supreme-Soul and how an individual can restore himself to the Supremacy of his own essentiality. The message illustrates the majesty of the yogic unity which makes possible to live a life totally grounded in the consciousness of the Lord, while being engaged in the worldly activities. The spiritual dimensions are open to every individual. The message of Srī Kṛṣṇa summarizes the essential teachings of the ancient scriptures and it is addressed to the entire mankind. His message reconciles the Yoga of knowledge, devotion and action into one—The Yoga of total surrender in God. Living a life in the consciousness of the Supreme-soul and to perform all the duties of the world in the consciousness of the Divine is to attain the ultimate perfection in Yoga. Asceticism without the knowledge of the Self is impossible, and the knowledge of the Self and knowledge of Karmayoga is possible only by total surrender to the indwelling divinity.

कच्चिदेतच्छ्रुतं पार्थ त्वयैकाग्रेण चेतसा।
कच्चिदज्ञानसम्मोहः प्रनष्टस्ते धनञ्जय॥ ७२॥

kaccidetacchrutaṁ pārtha tvayaikāgreṇa cetasā
kaccidajñānasaṁmohaḥ pranaṣṭas te dhanañjaya

(72) Have you heard this gospel attentively, O'Arjuna? Has your delusion, born of ignorance been dispelled?

अर्जुन उवाच

नष्टो मोहः स्मृतिर्लब्धा त्वत्प्रसादान्मयाच्युत।
स्थितोऽस्मि गतसन्देहः करिष्ये वचनं तव॥ ७३॥

naṣṭo mohaḥ smṛtir labdhā tvatprasādān mayā'cyuta
sthito'smi gatasandehaḥ kariṣye vacanaṁ tava

Arjuna said :

(73) O'Kṛṣṇa, my delusion is destroyed and I have regained my memory (knowledge of the self) through your grace. Now I am totally integrated and free from all doubts. I shall act according to Thy word.

Commentary—In the verse seventy-two Srī Kṛṣṇa enquires from Arjuna O'Partha, have you heard My message with concentrated attention? Has your ignorance been destroyed? Srī Kṛṣṇa wants to make sure that all the questions of Arjuna have been appropriately answered and all the doubts have been eliminated. In the first part of the question—the word *ekagrena cetsa* has been emphasized—means carefully with concentrated attention. The self-revelation becomes possible to the individual only when he is devoted concentratedly with one-pointed reception of mind. Fixed concentration helps the person in organizing his thoughts. It integrates various faculties of mind and reveals the truth more vividly and clearly. In the reoriented consciousness of mind the individual experiences the process of self-expansion and self-revelation. Srī Kṛṣṇa is very well aware of the process and that is why His immediate next question in verse seventy-two is: "Has your delusion born of ignorance been destroyed?" Arjuna answers in verse seventy-three very naturally and spontaneously. He tells that his delusion has been dispelled, and he has regained his memory. He feels integrated and free from all doubts. He tells Srī Kṛṣṇa that he will act according to His instructions. Arjuna's reply indicates his psychological transformation and inner stability. He feels awakened once again to the consciousness of the Divine. Arjuna feels introduced to a higher truth, wherein his memory returns with a new concept of truth and *swadharma*. He perceives that he has regained his lost memory of his perennial connectedness with the Supreme-Soul. He comprehends the essentiality of his nature and re-evaluates the entire situation. The very first word which he speaks in his answer to Srī Kṛṣṇa is *nasto mohah*—means the delusion born out of attachment, ignorance and false identification has been destroyed. The life that seemed like a useless burden, now feels like a great blessing, to be used in the service of the Lord. Arjuna feels very encouraged and enthusiastic about performing his duties.

The expression *smritir labdha* in the verse seventy-three is very significant. *Smritir* literally means memory—and *labdha* means regained. *Smiritir* is to remember some facts, which have been forgotten for some reason. It is the revelation and the realization of one's essential nature. In the words of Swami Ramsukhdas, "As far as the term *smrti* (memory) is concerned it has been explained to be the revelation of something already experienced. A man forgets the Lord, when he accepts the existence of the unreal world to be real and attaches importance to it. Though this forgetfulness has been since time immemorial, yet it comes to an end. When it comes to an end, the memory of the one's own self is aroused which is called *smrtirlabdha*—means the veil has been removed and the reality is being revealed." Arjuna tells Srī Kṛṣṇa that with His grace, he has regained his memory and realized true identity. When the individual restores his awareness to the Supreme-Soul, he becomes blessed with the experiential knowledge of his own immortality. His doubts are dispelled and his fears are destroyed. The person moves forward without hesitation, quite intuitively, courageously, spontaneously and harmoniously. There are some beautiful words by a Sufi poet—

> *Dariya ki mouj se lehar uthi, aur ulat kar behar se kehne lagi, mai tujh se huei aur tujh mae phana, mai aur nahi tu aur nahi.*
>
> दरिया की मौज से लहर उठी, और उलट कर बहर से कहने लगी, मैं तुझसे हुई और तुझमें फना, मैं और नहीं, तू और नहीं।

—means the isolated identification of the wave, dissolves at the dawn of realizing itself as an integral part of the river.

This is an experience of *atmabodha* means the knowledge of the Self. It is being awakened to one's own completeness. It is the experience of being restored to the wholeness in which the individual-soul resumes his unity with the Supreme-Soul. In the words of Swami Tapasyananda, "The restoration of *smriti* or memory spoken of here is the consciousness of one's being the Immortal Atman and not the perishable body-mind." Arjuna feels totally oriented to an absolutely new concept of life. His entire outlook is changed for the better. He feels confident and integrated in all respects. The words *karisye vacanam tava* indicate the feelings of total acceptance with willingness and faith. Arjuna gives up his separate existence and identifies himself with the work of the Lord. A revelation of this magnanimity is indeed the prerogative of each and every individual. This rediscovery of one's own essential nature is possible for everyone, only if the person surrenders himself to the grace of the indweller. The grace of the Supreme Lord lies perpetually within the various sheaths of one's own awareness. It lies veiled beneath one's own individualized egocentric limitations. In the act of total surrender, when the person resorts to the grace of the Lord, the purity and the essentiality of his own divine nature unfolds itself and becomes available to the individual. The word *tvat prasadat* indicates the feeling of exhilaration and indebtedness of Arjuna. The grace of the Lord can never be described in words, it is inexplicable. This is indeed a fact that when a person focuses his attention on the grace of the Divine, and expands his consciousness in its purity; his delusions and frustrations are eliminated. Arjuna's experience of grace indicates his feeling of inner peace and tranquillity, in contrast to the turmoil of his previous emotions. He feels stabilized, confident, integrated, firm and motivated in carrying the command of Srī Kṛṣṇa.

The expression *karisye vacanam tava* indicates Arjuna's assurance to Srī Kṛṣṇa, that now he will follow His instructions and guidance very devotedly, intuitively and spontaneously. This is indeed an evolutionary awakening when the individual-self merges into the cosmic-self, and the person looks upon himself as the perennial fragment (*amsa*) of the Divine and also a medium, meant to accomplish the desired work in the cosmic evolution. Arjuna speaks these words of surrender from the purity of his heart and from the wisdom of inner unity. There is an identical expression in the *Ramayana, Nath kripa mama gatha sandeha, Ram charan upajehu nava neha*—means the grace of the Lord has eliminated my doubts and delusions, now I feel totally surrendered in the majesty of the Lord. It is a very personal experience of the indwelling Divinity at the exalted level of inner awakening. It is the communication of the 'nara' with his eternal companion 'Narayana'. It is the transcendence of the individual-soul into the majesty of the Supreme-Soul. It is the transmutation of the limited identification into the unbound cosmic identification. In moments of self-revelation the embodied-self that has descended earlier into the limitations of mind and body, now wakes up once again to the majesty of its own infinitude. The individual-self, who was enshrouded earlier in *vishad*—he is now awakened into the blessed state of receiving *prasad.* When the individual-self surrenders into the wholeness of the Divine, the emotional turmoil and the *vishad* is transformed into *prasad* of the Lord. When the embodied-soul becomes awakened into the consciousness of the Supreme-soul his individual *Dharmas* are relinquished into the magnanimous nature of the Divine; for pure, clear and uncontaminated guidance from the indwelling Lord (the primordial *Dharma*).

संजय उवाच

इत्यहं वासुदेवस्य पार्थस्य च महात्मनः।
संवादमिममश्रौषमद्भुतं रोमहर्षणम्॥ ७४॥

ityahaṁ vāsudevasya pārthasya ca mahātmanaḥ
saṁvādamimamaśrauṣam adbhutaṁ romaharṣaṇam

Sanjaya said :

(74) Thus, I have heard this most wondrous dialogue between Srī Kṛṣṇa and the highly enlightened Arjuna, which makes my hair stand on end (genuinely thrilled and blessed).

व्यासप्रसादाच्छ्रुतवानेतद् गुह्यमहं परम्।
योगं योगेश्वरात्कृष्णात्साक्षात्कथयतः स्वयम्॥ ७५॥

vyāsaprasādācchrutavānetad guhyamahaṁ param
yogaṁ yogeśvarāt kṛṣṇāt sākṣāt kathayataḥ svayam

(75) Through the grace of the sage Vyasa, I have heard this Supreme mystery of Yoga as declared in person by Srī Kṛṣṇa himself—the Lord of Yoga.

राजन्संस्मृत्य संस्मृत्य संवादमिममद्भुतम्।
केशवार्जुनयोः पुण्यं हृष्यामि च मुहुर्मुहुः॥ ७६।

rājan saṅsṅṛtya-saṅsmṛtya saṁvādamimamadbhutam
keśavārjunayoḥ puṇyaṁ hṛṣyāmi ca muhur-muhuḥ

(76) O'King, as I recall again and again the most wondrous and the sacred dialogue between Srī Kṛṣṇa and Arjuna I rejoice over and over again.

तच्च संस्मृत्य संस्मृत्य रूपमत्यद्भुतं हरेः।
विस्मयो मे महान्राजन्हृष्यामि च पुनःपुनः॥ ७७॥

tacca saṅsmṛtya-saṅsmṛtya rūpamatyadbhutaṁ hareḥ
vismayo me māhān rājan hṛṣyāmi ca punaḥ-punaḥ

(77) And remembering over and over again, that most magnificent cosmic form of Hari (Srī Kṛṣṇa); greater is indeed my amazement. O'King, I feel thrilled with joy again and again.

यत्र योगेश्वरः कृष्णो यत्र पार्थो धनुर्धरः।
तत्र श्रीर्विजयो भूतिर्ध्रुवा नीतिर्मतिर्मम॥ ७८॥

yatra yogeśvaraḥ kṛṣṇo yatra pārtho dhanurdharaḥ
tatra śrīr vijayo bhūtirdhruvā nītir matir mama

(78) Wherever there is Srī Kṛṣṇa, the Lord of Yoga, and wherever there is Arjuna, the wieldier of the bow; there are always the glory, victory, prosperity and righteousness; such is my firm conviction.

Commentary—In these verses Sanjaya the great narrator, glorifies the phenomenal dialogue between Vasudeva (Srī Kṛṣṇa) and the enlightened soul Partha (Arjuna). He feels overwhelmed with delight and overjoyed with inner fulfilment. He says, O'King remembering again and again the wondrous dialogue between Srī Kṛṣṇa and Arjuna, I rejoice again and again. Also as I recall the most wondrous form of Srī Kṛṣṇa, I do feel overwhelmed with astonishment and I rejoice again and again. The comprehension and actual visualization of the Lord becomes possible to the individual only in the transcendental stage of meditation. The cosmic form of the Supreme Divinity holds in it all the three stages of time, space and causation. The individual observes the wholeness of the Divine and the manifested potency of the Divine enveloping all the possible stages and ages into one unparalleled expression. Anyone who becomes blessed with the cosmic vision of the Lord, remembers that for many lives and rejoices again and again while contemplating on it. Whenever the person recalls his blessed experience of personal communication with the Divine, he goes into ecstasy of inner joy over and over again.

Sanjaya tells the blind King that the moment when he recalls the blessed memory of the Divine vision and the words of Srī Kṛṣṇa, his heart is overjoyed with ecstatic love for the Divine. The exhilarating memory of the most wondrous experience keeps coming back to his mind with ever refreshing and renewed joy. He perceives the echo of the wondrous dialogue being repeated in his mind again and again and he feels totally blessed. The dialogue of Srī Kṛṣṇa and Arjuna is the personal communion and communication of the individual-soul with the Supreme-Soul. It is the communion of Nara with Narayana the eternal companion of man. The message of the magnanimous dialogue is heart captivating, the philosophy is ever refreshing, enchanting and exhilarating. After describing his recollections of the marvellous form of Srī Kṛṣṇa and the greatness of the most mysterious dialogue, Sanjaya concludes his narration with the words that wherever there is Kṛṣṇa, the Lord of Yoga, and wherever there is Arjuna the wieldier of the bow, there are prosperity, victory, glory, happiness and righteousness. Sanjaya vocalizes this Supreme statement from the depth of his integral wisdom. He speaks from the experiential knowledge of his unity with the transcendental Supreme-Self. His words are honest, genuine, profound, impressive, optimistic and suggestive in appraisal. Sanjaya concludes that wherever there is the contemplative wisdom and the yogic power of Srī Kṛṣṇa, and the practical efficiency of Arjuna in performing the work; there are success, victory, glory, unfailing righteousness and indeed everything else. The implementation of the yogic power, and the contemplative wisdom under the guidance of the Higher-Self is surely required for any kind of success and victory. Every type of success is based upon the faith and guidance of the indweller. When the individual-self becomes united with the Supreme-self; then the yogic power of the Lord descends upon the individual and blesses him with the inner poise and appropriate balance of mind. It gives the capacity to work with a consolidated attitude of mind and with immovable faith in one's own Self. It initiates, enlightens and inspires the individual to act in a copartnership with the indweller. The yogic power assures victory, spontaneous well-being, morality and the establishment of Dharma. It is the experience of inner unity with the master of Yoga which assures unfailing integrity and success to the individual. When a person performs all his work in perfect conformity with the grace of the Supreme Lord, the results are definitely rewarding and spontaneously beneficial.

The performance of the action is only a medium for the revelation of the Divine power and the yogic integrity. The victory, success and the glory are the expression of the Divine grace, kindness and generosity. A profound faith in the Divine sovereignty is indeed the most cherished blessing and the most rewarding gift of the Supreme Lord. Excellence in the performance of every action lies in direct proportion to the connectedness of the individual in yogic unity. The individual who resorts in the yogic unity of the Supreme-self, and performs all his actions with the guidance of the infinite Divinity, he is rewarded with excellence in work and liberation in life here and hereafter. The concluding word of the dialogue is *mama* while the opening word has been *Dharma*; The message of the entire dialogue is enclosed in these two words *Mama Dharma*—means my Dharma. The life on earth becomes peaceful, prosperous and instrumental for liberation only if the individual understands the meaning of—my Dharma. Dharma of every individual is to remain united with the indwelling Divinity and perform all activities in perfect harmony with the voice of the Supreme-Self. Living in Yoga, and working through the uninterrupted consciousness of the Supreme is indeed the Dharma of mankind. Let the grace of the indwelling Lord be perceived and expressed in everything we think, speak and perform.

Srī Kṛṣṇa Arpanam Astu
Śubham Bhūyāt
ekam śāstram devakīputra gītam
eko devo devakīputra eva
eko mantrasya nāmāniyāni
karmaya eko tasya devasya sevā
Hari Aum Tatsat, Hari Aum Tatsat, Hari Aum Tatsat
Aum Śānti—Śānti—Śānti

ॐ तत्सदिति श्रीमद्भगवद्गीतासूपनिषत्सु ब्रह्मविद्यायां
योगशास्त्रे श्रीकृष्णार्जुनसंवादे मोक्षसंन्यासयोगो
नाम अष्टादशोऽध्यायः ॥ १८ ॥

'Aum' tatsaditi Śrīmadbhagawadgeetā sūpaniṣatsu
brahmavidyāyām yogaśāstre Śrīkṛṣṇārjunasamvāde
mokṣasannyāsayogo nāmāṣṭādaśo'dhyāyaḥ

'AUM TAT SAT'—Thus in the Upanishad of the glorious Bhagawad Geeta, the science of the Brahman (Absolute) the scripture of yoga, the dialogue between Srī Kṛṣṇa and Arjuna—thus ends the eighteenth chapter entitled *"Mokṣa-sannyāsa-Yoga"*.

इति श्रीमद्भगवद्गीतासु अष्टादशोऽध्यायः ॥ १८ ॥
श्रीमद्भगवद्गीता समाप्ता ॥

SHLOKA INDEX

First Line of the Verses	Chapter	Verse
Abhayaṁ sattva-saṁśuddhiḥ	16	1
Abhyāsepy asamarthosi	12	10
Abhisandhāya tu phalam	17	12
Abhyāsa-yoga-yuktena	8	16
Ābrahma-bhuvānal-lokāḥ	8	8
Ācāryāḥ pitaraḥ putrāḥ	1	34
Acchedyoyam adāhyoyam	2	24
Adeśakāle yad dānam	17	22
Adharmā'bhibhavāt kṛṣṇa	1	41
Adharmaṁ dharmam iti yā	18	32
Adhaś ca ūrdhvaṁ prasṛtās tasya	15	2
Adhibhūtaṁ kṣaro bhāvaḥ	8	4
Adhiṣṭhānaṁ tathā kartā	18	14
Adhiyajñaḥ kathaṁ kotra	8	2
Adhyātma-jñāna-nityatvam	13	11
Adhyeṣyate ca ya imam	18	70
Āḍhyobhijanavān asmi	16	15
Ādityānām ahaṁ viṣṇuḥ	10	21
Adṛṣṭapūrvaṁ hṛṣitosmi	11	45
Adveṣṭā sarva-bhūtānām	12	13
Agnir-jyotir-ahaḥ śuklaḥ	8	24
Aham ātmā guḍākeśa	10	20
Ahaṁ hi sarva-yajñānām	9	24
Ahaṁkāraṁ balaṁ darpaṁ	16	18
Ahaṁkāraṁ balaṁ darpaṁ	18	53
Ahaṁ kratur ahaṁ yajñaḥ	9	16
Ahaṁ sarvasya prabhavo	10	8
Ahaṁ vaiśvānaro bhūtvā	15	14
Āhāras tvapi sarvasya	17	7
Ahimsā samatā tuṣṭiḥ	10	5
Ahimsā satyam akrodhaḥ	16	2
Aho bata mahat-pāpam	1	45
Āhus tvāṁ ṛṣayaḥ sarve	10	13
Ajñaścāśraddadhānaś ca	4	40
Ajopi sam avyayātmā	4	6
Ākhyāhi me ko bhavān	11	31
Akīrtiṁ capi bhūtāni	2	34
Akṣaraṁ brahma paramam	8	3
Akṣarāṇām akārosmi	10	33
Amānitvam adambhitvam	13	7
Amī ca tvāṁ dhṛtarāṣṭrasya	11	26
Amī hi tvāṁ surasaṅghāḥ	11	11
Anādi madhyāntam ananta.	11	19
Anāditvān-nirguṇatvāt	13	31
Anantaś casmi nāgānām	10	29
Ananta-vijayaṁ rājā	1	16
Ananyacetāḥ satatam	8	14
Ananyāś cintayanto mām	9	22
Anapekṣaḥ śucir dakṣaḥ	12	16
Anāśritaḥ karmaphalam	6	1
Aneka-bāhūdara-vaktra-netram	11	16
Aniṣṭam iṣṭaṁ miśraṁ ca	18	12
Aneka-vaktra-nayanam	11	10
Aneka-citta-vibhrāntāḥ	16	16
Annād bhavanti bhūtāni	3	14
Antakāle ca mām eva	8	5
Antavanta ime dehāḥ	2	18
Antavat tu phalaṁ teṣām	7	23
Anubandhaṁ kṣayaṁ hiṁsāṁ	18	25
Anudvegakaraṁ vākyam	17	15
Anye ca bahavaḥ śūrāḥ	1	9
Anye tvevam ajānantaḥ	13	25
Apāne juhvati prāṇam	4	29
Aparaṁ bhavato janma	4	4
Apare niyatāhārāḥ	4	30
Apareyam itas tvanyām	7	5
Aparyāptaṁ tadasmākam	1	10
Aphalākāṅkṣibhir yajño	17	11
Api ced asi pāpebhyaḥ	4	36
Api cet sudurācāro	9	30
Aprakāśopravṛtiś ca	14	13
Āpūr yamāṇam acala-pratiṣṭham	2	70

First Line of the Verses	Chapter	Verse
Āruruksor-muner-yogam	6	3
Asakta-buddhiḥ sarvatra	18	49
Asaktir anabhiṣvaṅgaḥ	13	9
Asaṁśayaṁ mahābāho	6	35
Aśāmyatātmanā yogo	6	36
Āśāpāśa-śatair-baddhāḥ	16	12
Aśāstra-vihitaṁ ghoram	17	5
Asatyam apratiṣṭhaṁ te	16	8
Asau mayā hataḥ śatruḥ	16	14
Āścaryavat paśyati	2	29
Asmākaṁ tu viśiṣṭā ye	1	7
Aśocyān anvaśocas tvam	2	11
Aśraddādhanāḥ puruṣāḥ	9	3
Aśraddhayā hutaṁ dattam	17	28
Āsurīṁ yonim āpannāḥ	16	20
Aśvatthaḥ sarva-vṛkṣāṇām	10	26
Atha cainaṁ nitya-jātam	9	26
Atha cet tvam imaṁ dharmyam	2	33
Atha cittaṁ samādhātum	12	9
Athaitad apyaśaktosi	12	11
Atha kena prayukto 'yam	3	36
Atra śūrā maheṣvāsāḥ	1	4
Athavā bahunaitena	10	42
Athavā yogināṁ eva	6	42
Atha vyavasthitān dṛṣṭvā	1	20
Ātmasaṁbhāvitāḥ stabdhāḥ	16	17
Ātmaupamyena sarvatra	6	32
Avācya-vādāṁś ca bahūn	2	36
Avajānanti māṁ mūḍhāḥ	9	11
Avibhaktaṁ ca bhūteṣu	13	16
Avināśi tu tad viddhi	2	17
Āvṛtaṁ jñānam etena	3	39
Avyaktādīni bhūtāni	2	38
Avyaktaṁ vyaktim āpannam	7	24
Avyaktād vyaktayaḥ sarvāḥ	8	18
Avyaktokṣara ity uktaḥ	8	21
Avyaktoyam acintyoyam	2	25
Ayuktaḥ prākṛtaḥ stabdhaḥ	18	28

First Line of the Verses	Chapter	Verse
Ayaneṣu ca sarveṣu	1	11
Ayatiḥ śraddhayopeto	6	37
Āyudhānām ahaṁ vajram	10	28
Āyuḥ-sattva-balārogya	17	8
B		
Bahir antaś ca bhūtānām	13	15
Bahūnāṁ janmanām ante	7	19
Bahūni me vyatītāni	4	5
Bāhya-sparśeṣvasaktātmā	5	21
Balaṁ balavatām asmi	7	11
Bandhur ātmātmanas tasya	6	6
Bhaktyā mām abhijānāti	18	55
Bhaktyā tvananyayā śakyaḥ	11	54
Bhavān bhīṣmaś ca karṇaś ca	1	8
Bhavāpyayau hi bhūtānām	11	2
Bhayād raṇāt uparatam	2	35
Bhīṣma-droṇa-pramukhataḥ	1	25
Bhogaiśvarya-prasaktānām	2	44
Bhoktāraṁ yajña-tapasām	5	29
Bhūmir āponalo vāyuḥ	7	4
Bhūtagrāmaḥ sa evāyam	8	19
Bhūya eva mahābāho	10	1
Bījaṁ māṁ sarva-bhūtānām	7	10
Brahmabhūtaḥ prasannātmā	18	54
Brāhmaṇa-kṣatriya-viśām	18	41
Brahmaṇo hi pratiṣṭhāham	14	27
Brahmaṇy ādhāya karmāṇi	5	10
Brahmārpaṇaṁ brahma haviḥ	4	24
Bṛhatsāma tathā sāmnām	10	35
Buddher bhedaṁ dhṛteś caiva	18	29
Buddhir jñānam asammohaḥ	10	4
Buddhi-yukto jahātīha	2	50
Buddhyā viśuddhayā yukto	18	51
C		
Cañcalaṁ hi manaḥ kṛṣṇa	6	34
Cāturvarṇyaṁ mayā sṛṣṭam	4	13
Caturvidhā bhajante mām	7	16
Cetasā sarva-karmāṇi	18	57

First Line of the Verses	Chapter	Verse
Cintām aparimeyāṁ ca	16	11
D		
Daivam eva apare yajñam	4	25
Daivī hyeṣā guṇamayī	7	14
Daivī sampad vimokṣāya	16	5
Dambho darpobhimānś ca	16	4
Daṁṣtrā-karālāni ca te	11	25
Daṇḍo damayatām asmi	10	38
Dātavyam iti yad dānam	17	20
Dehī nityam avadhyoyam	2	30
Dehinosmin yathā dehe	2	13
Deva-dvija-guru-prājña	17	14
Devān bhāvayatā'nena	3	11
Dharma-kṣetre kuru-kṣetre	1	1
Dhṛṣṭaketuś cekitānaḥ	1	5
Dhṛtyā yayā dhārayate	18	33
Dhūmenāvriyate vahniḥ	3	38
Dhūmo rātris tathā kṛṣṇaḥ	8	25
Dhyānenātmani paśyanti	13	24
Dhyāyato viṣayān puṁsaḥ	2	62
Divi sūrya-sahasrasya	11	12
Divya-mālyā'mbaradharam	11	11
Doṣair etaiḥ kulaghnānām	1	43
Dravya-yajñās tapo-yajñāḥ	4	28
Droṇaṁ ca bhīṣmaṁ ca	11	34
Dṛṣṭvā tu pāṇḍavānīkam	1	2
Dṛṣṭvedaṁ mānuṣaṁ rūpam	11	51
Drupado draupadeyāś ca	1	18
Duḥkham ity eva yat karma	18	8
Duḥkheṣva'nudvigna-manāḥ	2	56
Dūreṇa hy avaraṁ karma	2	49
Dvau bhūta-sargau loke	16	6
Dvā imau puruṣau loke	15	16
Dyāvā-pṛthivyor idam	11	20
Dyūtaṁ chalayatām asmi	10	36
E		
Eṣā brāhmī sthitiḥ pārtha	2	72
Eṣā te'bhihitā sāṁkhye	2	39
Etac chrutvā vacanam	11	35
Etad yonīni bhūtāni	7	6
Etair vimuktaḥ kaunteya	16	22
Etāṁ dṛṣṭim avaṣṭabhya	16	9
Etāṁ vibhutiṁ yogaṁ ca	10	7
Etan me saṁśayaṁ kṛṣṇa	6	39
Etān na hantum icchāmi	1	35
Etāny api tu karmāṇi	18	6
Evaṁ bahuvidhā yajñāḥ	4	32
Evaṁ buddheḥ paraṁ buddhvā	3	43
Evaṁ etad yathattha tvam	11	3
Evaṁ jñātvā kṛtaṁ karma	4	15
Evaṁ paramparā-prāptam	4	2
Evaṁ pravartitaṁ cakram	3	16
Evaṁ satata-yuktā ye	12	1
Evaṁ ukto hṛṣīkeśa	1	24
Evaṁ uktvā hṛṣīkeśam	2	9
Evam uktvā'rjunaḥ saṅkhye	1	47
Evaṁ uktvā tato rājan	11	9
G		
Gāmāviśya ca bhūtāni	15	13
Gāṇḍivaṁ sraṁsate hastāt	1	30
Gata-saṅgasya muktasya	4	23
Gatir bhartā prabhuḥ sāskṣī	9	18
Guṇān etān atītya trīn	14	20
Gurūn ahatvā hi	2	5
H		
Hanta te kathayiṣyāmi	10	19
Hato vā prāpsyasi	2	37
Hṛṣīkeśaṁ tadā vākyam	11	2
I		
Icchā dveṣaḥ sukham	13	6
Icchā-dveṣa-samutthena	7	27
Idaṁ adya mayā labdham	16	13
Idaṁ jñānam upāśritya	14	2
Idaṁ te nātapaskāya	18	67
Idaṁ tu te guhyatamam	9	1
Idaṁ śarīraṁ kaunteya	13	1

First Line of the Verses	Chapter	Verse
Ihaikastham jagat kṛtsnam	11	7
Ihaiva tair jitaḥ sargaḥ	5	19
Imam vivasvate yogam	4	1
Indriyāṇām hi caratām	2	67
Indriyāṇi mano buddhiḥ	3	40
Indriyāṇi parāṇy āhuḥ	3	42
Indriyārtheṣu vairāgyam	13	8
Indriyasye-ndriyasyā'rthe	3	34
Iṣṭān bhogān hi	3	12
Iśvaraḥ sarva-bhūtānām	18	61
Iti guhyatamam śāstram	15	20
Iti kṣetram tathā jñānam	13	18
Iti te jñānam ākhyātam	18	63
Ity aham vāsudevasya	18	74
Ity arjunam vāsudevaḥ	11	50
J		
Janma karma ca me divyam	4	9
Jarā-maraṇa-mokṣāya	2	29
Jātasya hi dhruvo mṛtyuḥ	2	27
Jitātmanaḥ praśāntasya	6	7
Jñanam jñeyam pari-jñātā	18	18
Jñanam karma ca kartā ca	18	19
Jñāna-vijñāna-tṛptātmā	6	8
Jñāna-yajñena ca'py anye	9	15
Jñānena tu tad ajñanam	5	16
Jñeyaḥ sa nitya-sannyāsī	5	3
Jñeyam yat tat pravakṣyāmi	13	12
Jyāyasī cet karmaṇas te	3	1
Jyotiṣām api taj jyotiḥ	13	17
K		
Kacchinnobhaya-vibhraṣṭaḥ	6	38
Kacchid etacchrutam pārtha	18	72
Kair liṅgais trīn guṇān etān	14	21
Kālo'smi loka-kṣayakṛt	11	32
Kāma eṣa krodha eṣa	3	37
Kāmais tais tair hṛtajñānāḥ	7	20
Kāma-krodha-viyuktānām	5	26
Kāmam āśritya duṣpūram	16	10
Kāmātmānaḥ svargaparāḥ	2	43
Kāṅkṣantaḥ karmaṇām	4	12
Kāmyānām karmaṇām	18	2
Karma brahmodbhavam viddhi	3	15
Karmajam buddhi-yuktā hi	2	51
Karmaṇaḥ sukṛtasyāhuḥ	14	16
Karmaṇaiva hi samsiddhim	3	20
Karmaṇo hyapi boddhavyam	4	17
Karmaṇy akarma yaḥ paśyet	4	18
Karmaṇy eva'dhikāraste	2	47
Karmendriyāṇi samyamya	3	6
Kārpaṇya-doṣopahataḥ	2	7
Karśayantaḥ śarīrastham	17	6
Kārya-kāraṇa-kartṛtve	13	20
Kāryam ity eva yat karma	18	9
Kasmāc ca te na nameran	11	37
Kāśyaś ca parameṣvāsaḥ	1	17
Katham bhīṣmam aham saṅkhye	2	4
Katham na jñeyam asmābhiḥ	1	39
Katham vidyām aham yogin	10	17
Kaṭvamla-lavaṇā'ty-uṣṇa	17	9
Kavim purāṇam anuśāsitāram	8	9
Kāyena manasā buddhyā	5	11
Kim karma kim akarmeti	4	16
Kim punar brāhmaṇāḥ puṇyāḥ	9	33
Kim tad brahma kim adhyātmam	8	1
Kirīṭinam gadinam cakrahastam	11	46
Kirīṭinam gadinam cakriṇam	11	17
Klaibyam māsma gamaḥ pārtha	2	3
Kleśo'dhikataras teṣām	12	5
Krodhād bhavati sammohaḥ	2	63
Kṛpayā parayā'viṣṭo	1	28
Kṛṣi-gaurakṣya-vāṇijyam	18	44
Kṣetrajñam ca'pi mām viddhi	13	2
Kṣetra-kṣetrajñayor evam	13	34
Ksipram bhavati dharmātmā	9	31
Kulakṣaye praṇaś yanti	1	40
Kutas tvā kaśmalam idam	2	2

First Line of the Verses	Chapter	Verse
L		
Labhante brahma-nirvāṇam	5	25
Lelihyase grasamānaḥ	11	30
Labhaḥ pravṛtir ārambhaḥ	14	12
Loke'smin dvividhā	3	3
M		
Mac-cittaḥ sarva-durgāṇi	18	58
Mac-cittā mad-gata-prāṇāḥ	10	9
Mad anugrahāya paramam	11	1
Mahābhūtāny ahankāro	13	5
Maharṣayaḥ sapta pūrve	10	6
Maharṣīṇāṁ bhṛgur aham	10	25
Mahātmānas tu māṁ pārtha	9	13
Mamaivā'mśo jīva-loke	15	7
Mama yonir mahad-brahma	14	3
Māṁ ca yo'vyabhicāreṇa	14	26
Māṁ hi pārtha vyapāśritya	9	32
Māṁ upetya punarjanma	8	15
Manaḥ-prasādaḥ saumyatvam	17	16
Mānāpamānayos tulyaḥ	14	25
Man-manā bhava mad-bhakto	18	65
Man-manā bhava mad-bhakto	9	34
Manuṣyāṇāṁ sahasreṣu	7	3
Manyase yadi tac-chak yam	11	4
Mā te vyathā mā ca	11	49
Mat karmakṛn mat paramo	11	55
Mātrā-sparśās tu kaunteya	2	14
Mattaḥ parataraṁ nānyat	7	7
Mayā'dhyakṣeṇa prakṛtiḥ	9	10
Mayā prasannena tavā'rjunedam	11	47
Mayā tatam idaṁ sarvam	9	4
Mayi cā'nanya-yogena	13	10
Mayi sarvāṇi karmāṇi	3	30
Mayyāsakta-manāḥ pārtha	7	1
Mayyāveśya mano ye mām	12	2
Mayyeva mana ādhatsva	12	8
Maghāśā mogha-karmāṇo	9	12
Mṛtyuḥ sarvaharaś cā'ham	10	34

First Line of the Verses	Chapter	Verse
Mūḍhagrāheṇātmano yat	17	19
Mukta-saṅgo'nahamvādī	18	26
N		
Nabhaḥ-spṛśaṁ dīptam aneka	11	24
Na buddhi-bhedaṁ janayet	3	26
Na caitad vidmaḥ kataram no	2	6
Na ca māṁ tāni karmāni	9	9
Na ca mat-sthāni bhūtāni	9	5
Na ca tasmān manuṣyeṣu	18	69
Nādatte kasyacit pāpam	5	15
Na dveṣṭy akuśalaṁ karma	18	10
Na'haṁ prakāśaḥ sarvasya	7	25
Na'haṁ vedair na tapasā	11	53
Na hi dehabhṛtā śakyam	18	11
Na hi jñānena sadṛśam	4	38
Na hi kaścit kṣaṇam api	3	5
Na hi prapaśyāmi	2	8
Nainaṁ chinadanti śastrāṇi	2	23
Naiva kiñcit karomīti	5	8
Naite sṛtī pārtha jānan	8	27
Naiva tasya kṛtenā'rtho	3	18
Na jāyate mriyate vā	2	20
Na kāñkṣe vijayaṁ kṛṣṇa	1	31
Na karmaṇām anārambhāt	3	4
Na kartṛtvaṁ na karmāṇi	5	14
Namaḥ purastād atha pṛṣṭhataḥ	11	40
Na māṁ duṣkṛtino mūḍhāḥ	7	15
Na māṁ karmāṇi limpanti	4	14
Na me pārthā'sti kartavyam	3	22
Na me viduḥ suragaṇāḥ	10	2
Na'nto'sti mama divyānām	10	40
Na'nyaṁ guṇebhyaḥ kartāram	14	9
Na prahṛṣyet priyaṁ prāpya	5	20
Na rūpam asyeha tathā	15	3
Na'sato vidyate bhāvaḥ	2	16
Na'sti buddhir ayuktasya	2	66
Naṣṭo mohaḥ smṛtir labdhā	18	73
Na tadasti pṛthivyāṁ vā	18	40

First Line of the Verses	Chapter	Verse
Na tad bhāsayate sūryo	15	6
Na tu māṁ śakyase draṣṭum	11	8
Na tveva'haṁ jātu nā'sam	2	12
Nā'tyaśnatas tu yogo'sti	6	16
Na veda-yajñā'dhyayanaiḥ	11	48
Nehā'bhikramanāśo'sti	2	40
Nihatya dhārtarāṣṭrān naḥ	1	36
Nimittāni ca paśyāmi	1	30
Nirāśīr yata-cittātmā	4	21
Nirmāna-mohā jita-saṅga-doṣāḥ	15	5
Niścayaṁ śruṇu me tatra	18	4
Niyataṁ kuru karma tvam	3	8
Niyataṁ saṅga-rahitam	18	23
Niyatasya tu sannyāsaḥ	18	7
P		
Pañcaitāni mahābāho	18	13
Pāñcajanyaṁ hṛṣīkeśo	1	15
Paraṁ bhūyaḥ pravakṣyāmi	14	1
Paraṁ brahma paraṁ dhāma	10	12
Paras tasmāt tu bhāvo'nyo	8	20
Paritrāṇāya sādhūnām	4	8
Pārtha naivesa na'mutra	6	40
Paśyādityān vasūn	11	6
Paśyaitām pāṇḍu-putraṇām	1	3
Paśyā me pārtha rūpāṇi	11	5
Paśyāmi devans tava deva	11	15
Patraṁ puṣpaṁ phalam toyam	9	26
Pavanaḥ pavatam asmi	10	31
Pita'hamasya jagato	9	17
Pitā'si lokasya carcarasya	11	43
Puṇyo gandhaḥ pṛthivyāṁ ca	7	9
Purodhasāṁ ca mukhyaṁ maṁ	10	24
Puruṣaḥ prakṛtistho hi	13	21
Puruṣaḥ sa paraḥ pāriha	8	22
Pūrvābhyāsena tenaiva	6	44
Prahlādaś cā'smi daityānām	10	30
Prajahāti yadā kāmān	2	55
Prakāśaṁ ca pravṛttiṁ ca	14	22
Prakṛteḥ kriyamāṇāni	3	27
Prakṛter guṇa-sammūḍhaḥ	3	29
Prakṛtim puruṣaṁ caiva	13	19
Prakṛtim svām avaṣṭabhya	9	8
Prakṛtyaiva ca karmāṇi	13	29
Pralapan visṛjan gṛhṇan	5	9
Prāpya puṇya-kṛtāṁ lokān	6	41
Prasāde sarva-duḥkhānām	2	65
praśānta-manasaṁ hy enam	6	27
Praśāntātmā vigatabhīḥ	6	14
Pravṛttiṁ ca nivṛttiṁ ca	16	7
Pravṛttiṁ ca nivṛttiṁ ca	18	30
Prayāṇa-kāle manasā'calena	8	10
Prayatnād yatamānaṣ tu	6	45
Pṛthaktvena tu yaj jñānam	18	21
R		
Rāga-dveṣa-viyuktais tu	2	64
Rāgī karma-phala-prepsuḥ	18	27
Rājan saṁsmṛtya saṁsmṛtya	18	76
Rajasi pralayaṁ gatvā	14	15
Rajas tamaś cā'bhibhūya	14	10
Rājavidyā rāja-guhyam	9	2
Rajo rāgātmakaṁ viddhi	14	7
Raso'ham apsu kaunteya	7	8
Rṣibhir bahudhā gītam	13	4
Rudrādityā vasavo ye ca	11	22
Rudrāṇām śaṅkaraś cā'smi	10	23
Rūpaṁ mahatte bahu-vaktra	11	23
S		
Sad-bhāve sādhu-bhāve ca	17	26
Sā'dhibhūtā'dhidaivaṁ mām	7	30
Sadṛśaṁ ceṣṭate svasyāḥ	3	33
Sa evā'yaṁ mayā te'dya	4	3
Sa ghoṣo dhārtarāṣṭrāṇām	1	19
Sahajaṁ karma kaunteya	18	48
Sahasra-yuga-paryantam	8	17
Saha-yajñāḥ prajāḥ sṛṣṭvā	3	10
Sakhetī matvā prasabham	11	41

First Line of the Verses	*Chapter*	*Verse*
Saknotīhaivā yaḥ soḍhum	5	23
Saktāḥ karmaṇy avidavāṁsaḥ	3	25
Sama-duḥkha-sukhaḥ svasthaḥ	14	24
Samaḥ śatrau ca mitre ca	12	18
Samaṁ kāya-śiro-grīvam	6	13
Samaṁ paśyan hi sarvatra	13	28
Samaṁ sarveṣu bhūteṣu	13	27
Saṁniyamye-ndriya-grāmam	12	4
Śamo damas tapaḥ śaucam	18	42
Samo'haṁ sarva-bhūteṣu	9	29
Śanaiḥ śanair uparamet	6	25
Saṅkalpa-prabhavān kāmān	6	24
Saṅkaro narakāyaīva	1	42
Sāṅkhya-yogau pṛthag bālāḥ	5	4
Sannyāsaḥ karma-yogaś ca	5	2
Sannyāsas tu mahābāho	5	61
Sannyāsasya mahābāho	18	1
Santuṣṭaḥ satataṁ yogī	12	14
Sargāṇām ādir antaś ca	10	32
Śarīraṁ yad avāpnoti	15	8
Sarīra-vāṅ-manobhir yat	18	15
Sarva-bhūtāni kaunteya	9	7
Sarva-bhūtastham ātmānam	6	29
Sarva-bhūta-sthitaṁ yo mām	6	31
Sarva-bhūtesu yenaikam	18	20
Sarva-dharmān parityajya	18	66
Sarva-dvārāni saṁyamya	8	12
Sarva-dvāreṣu dehe'smin	14	11
Sarva-guhyatamaṁ bhūyaḥ	18	64
Sarva-karmāni manasā	5	13
Sarva-karmāṇy api sadā	18	56
Sarvam etad ṛtaṁ manye	10	14
Sarvāṇī-ndriya-karmāṇi	4	27
Sarvasya cā'haṁ hṛdi	15	15
Sarvataḥ pāṇi-pādaṁ tat	13	13
Sarva-yoniṣu kaunteya	14	14
Sarvendriya-guṇābhāsam	13	14
Satataṁ kīrtayanto mām	9	14

First Line of the Verses	*Chapter*	*Verse*
Sa tayā śraddhayā yuktaḥ	7	22
Satkāra-māna-pūjārtham	17	18
Sattvaṁ rajas tama iti	14	5
Sattvaṁ sukhe sañjayati	14	9
Sattvā'nurūpa sarvasya	17	3
Sattvāt sañjāyate jñānam	14	17
Śauryaṁ tejo dhṛtir dākṣyam	18	43
Sīdanti mama gātrāṇi	1	29
Siddhiṁ prāpto yathā	18	50
Sparśān kṛtvā bahir bāhyān	5	27
Śraddhāvān anasūyaś ca	18	71
Śraddhāvān labhate jñānam	4	39
Śraddhayā parayā taptam	17	17
Śreyān dravya-mayāt yajñāt	4	33
Śreyān svadharmo viguṇaḥ	3	35
Śreyān svadharmo viguṇaḥ	18	47
Śreyo hi jñānam abhyāsāt	12	12
Śrotrādīn indriyāṇyanye	4	26
Śrotrāṁ cakṣuḥ sparśanaṁ ca	15	9
Sruti-vipratipannā te	2	53
Sthāne hṛṣīkeśa tava	11	36
Sthita-prajñasya kā bhāṣā	2	54
Śubhā'śubha-phalair evam	9	28
Śucau deśe pratiṣṭhāpya	6	11
Sudurdarśam idam rūpam	11	52
Suhṛn-mitrā'ry-udāsīna	6	9
Sukha-duḥkhe same kṛtvā	2	38
Sukham ātyantikaṁ yat tat	6	21
Sukhaṁ tv idanīṁ tri-vidham	18	36
Śukla-kṛṣṇe gatī hyete	8	26
Svabhāvajena kaunteya	18	60
Svadharmam api cā'vekṣya	2	31
Śvaśurān suhṛdaś caiva	1	27
Svayam evātmanātmānam	10	15
Sve sve karmaṇy abhirataḥ	18	45
T		
Tac ca saṁsmṛtya saṁsmṛtya	18	77
Tad buddhayas tad ātmānaḥ	5	17

First Line of the Verses	Chapter	Verse
Tad itya'nabhisandhāya	17	25
Tad viddhi praṇipātena	4	34
Tamas tva'jñānajaṁ viddhi	14	8
Tam eva śaraṇaṁ gaccha	18	62
Taṁ tathā kṛpayāviṣṭam	2	1
Tam uvāca hṛṣīkeśaḥ	2	10
Taṁ vidyād duḥkho-saṁyoga	6	23
Tān ahaṁ dviṣataḥ krūrān	16	19
Tāni sarvāṇi saṁyamya	2	61
Tapāmya'ham ahaṁ varṣam	9	19
Tapasvibhyo'dhiko yogī	6	46
Tasmāc chāstraṁ pramāṇaṁ te	16	24
Tasmād ajñāna-saṁbhūtam	4	42
Tasmād asaktaḥ śatatam	3	19
Tasmād om ity-udāhṛtya	17	24
Tasmād yąsya mahābāho	2	68
Tasmān ņā'rhā vayaṁ hantum	1	37
Tasmāt praṇamya praṇidhāya	11	44
Tasmāt sarveṣu kāleṣu	8	7
Tasmāt tvam indriyāṇy ādau	3	41
Tasmāt tvam uttiṣṭha	11	33
Tasya sañjanayan harṣam	1	12
Tataḥ padaṁ tat	15	4
Tataḥ sa vismāyāviṣṭo	11	14
Tataḥ śaṅkhāś ca bheryaś ca	1	13
Tataḥ śvetair hayair yukte	1	14
Tat kṣetraṁ yac ca yādṛk ca	13	3
Tatraikāgraṁ manaḥ kṛtvā	6	12
Tatraikasthaṁ jagat kṛtsnam	11	13
Tatraivaṁ sati kartāram	18	16
Tatrā'paśyat sthitān pārtha	1	26
Tatra sattvaṁ nirmalatvāt	14	6
Tatra taṁ buddhi-saṁyogam	6	43
Tattvavit tu mahābāho	3	28
Tejaḥ kṣamŚ dhṛtiḥ	16	3
Teṣām ahaṁ samuddhartā	12	7
Teṣāṁ evā'nukampārtham	10	11
Teṣāṁ jñānī nitya-yukta	7	17
Teṣāṁ satata-yuktānām	10	10
Te taṁ bhuktvā svarga-lokam	9	21
Traiguṇya-viṣayā vedāḥ	2	45
Traividyā māṁ somapāḥ	9	20
Tribhir guṇa-mayair bhāvaiḥ	7	13
Trividhā bhavati śraddhā	17	2
Trividhaṁ narakasyedam	16	21
Tulya-nindā-stutir maunī	12	19
Tvam ādidevaḥ puruṣaḥ	11	38
Tvam akṣaraṁ paramam	11	18
Tyājyaṁ doṣavad ity eke	18	3
Tyaktvā karma-phalā'saṅgam	4	20
U		
Uccaiḥśravasam aśvānām	10	27
Udārāḥ sarva evaite	7	18
Udāsīnavadāsīnaḥ	14	23
Uddhared ātmanātmānam	6	5
Upadraṣṭā'numantā ca	13	22
Ūrdhvaṁ gacchanti sattvasthā	14	18
Utkrāmantaṁ sthitam	15	10
Utsanna-kula-dharmāṇām	1	44
Utsīdeyur ime lokāḥ	3	24
Uttamaḥ puruṣas tvanyaḥ	15	17
Ūrdhva-mūlam adhaḥ-śākham	15	1
V		
Vaktrāṇi te tvaramāṇā	11	27
Vaktum arhasya'aśeṣeṇa	10	16
Vasāṁsi jīrṇāni yathā	2	22
Vāyur yamo'gnir varuṇaḥ	11	39
Vedāhaṁ samtītāni	7	26
Vedānāṁ sāmavedo'smi	10	22
Vedā'vināśinaṁ nityam	2	21
Vedeṣu yajñeṣu tapaḥsu	8	28
Vidhi-hīnam asṛṣṭānnam	17	13
Vidyā-vinaya-sampanne	5	18
Vihāya kamān yaḥ	2	71
Viṣayā vinivartante	2	59
Viṣayendriya-saṁyogāt	18	38

First Line of the Verses	Chapter	Verse
Vistareṇātmano yogam	10	18
Vītarāga-bhaya-krodhāḥ	4	10
Viviktasevī laghvāśī	18	52
Vṛṣṇīnaṁ vāsudevo'smi	10	37
Vyāmiśreṇeva vākyena	3	2
Vyāsa-prasādāc chrutavān	18	75
Vyavasāyātmikā buddhiḥ	2	41
Y		
Yac cā'pi sarva-bhūtānām	10	39
Yac cā'vahāsārtham asatkṛtaḥ	11	42
Yadā bhūta-pṛthag-bhavam	13	30
Yadāditya-gataṁ tejo	15	12
Yad agre cā'nubandhe ca	18	39
Yad ahaṅkāram āśritya	18	59
Yadā hi nendriyārtheṣu	6	4
Yad akṣaram vedavido	8	11
Yadā saṁharate cā'yam	2	58
Yadā sattve pravṛddhe tu	14	14
Yadā te moha-kalilam	2	52
Yadā viniyatam cittam	6	18
Yadā yadā hi dharmasya	4	7
Yodi hy ahaṁ na varteyam	3	23
Yodi mām aprotīkāram	1	46
Yadṛcchā-lābha-saṁtuṣṭo	4	22
Yadṛcchayā co'papannam	2	32
Yad yad ācarati śreṣṭhaḥ	3	21
Yad yad vibhūtimat sattvam	10	41
Yadyapy ete na paśyanti	1	38
Ya enaṁ vetti hantāram	2	19
Ya evaṁ vetti puruṣam	13	23
Yaḥ sarvatrā'nabhiṣnehaḥ	2	57
Yaḥ śāstra-vidhim utsṛjya	16	23
Ya idaṁ paramaṁ guhyam	18	68
Yajanṭe sāttvikā devān	17	4
Yaj jñātvā na punar moham	4	35
Yajña-dāna-tapaḥ-karma	18	5
Yañārthāt karmaṇo'nyatra	3	9
Yajña-śiṣṭā'mṛtabhujo yānti	4	31

First Line of the Verses	Chapter	Verse
Yajñasiṣṭāśinaḥ santo	3	13
Yajñe tapasi dāne ca	17	27
Yaṁ hi na vyathayanty ete	2	15
Yām imāṁ puṣpitāṁ vācam	2	42
Yaṁ labdhvā cā'paraṁ lābham	6	22
Yaṁ sannyāsam iti prāhuḥ	6	2
Yaṁ yaṁ vā'pi smaran bhāvam	8	6
Yā niśā sarva-bhūtānām	2	69
Yānti devavratā devān	9	25
Yasmān nodvijate loko	12	15
Yasmāt kṣaram atīto'ham	15	18
Yas tvindriyāṇi manasā	3	7
Yasya nā'haṅkṛto bhāvo	18	17
Yasya sarve samārambhāḥ	4	19
Yataḥ pravṛttir bhūtānām	18	46
Yatanto yaginaś cainam	15	11
Yatato hy api kaunteya	2	60
Yātayāmaṁ gatarasam	17	10
Yatendriya-mano-buddhiḥ	5	28
Yathā dīpo nivātastho	6	19
Yathaidhāṁsi samiddho'gniḥ	4	37
Yathākāśasthito nityam	9	6
Yathā nadīnāṁ bahavo	11	28
Yathā pradīptaṁ jvalanam	11	29
Yathā prakāśayaty ekaḥ	13	33
Yathā sarvagataṁ saukṣmyāt	13	32
Yat karoṣi yad aśnāsi	9	27
Yato yato niścarati	6	26
Yatra kāle tvanāvṛttim	8	23
Yatra yogeśvaraḥ kṛṣṇo	18	78
Yatroparamate cittam	6	20
Yat sāṅkhyaiḥ prāpyate	5	5
Yat tad agre viṣam iva	18	37
Yat tu kāmepsunā karma	18	24
Yat tu kṛtsnavad ekasmin	18	22
Yat tu pratyupakārārtham	17	21
Yāvad etān nirīkṣe'ham	1	22
Yāvān artha udapāne	2	46

First Line of the Verses	Chapter	Verse
Yāvat sañjāyate kiñcit	13	26
Yayā dharmam adharmam ca	18	31
Yayā svapnaṁ bhayaṁ śokam	18	35
Yayā tu dharma-kāmārthān	18	34
Ye caiva sāttvikā bhāvāḥ	7	12
Ye hi saṁsparśajā bhogāḥ	5	22
Ye me matam idam nityam	3	31
Ye'py anya-devatā bhaktāḥ	9	23
Yeṣām arthe kāṅksitaṁ no	1	33
Yeṣām tvantagataṁ pāpam	7	28
Ye śāstra-vidhim utsṛjya	17	1
Ye tu dharmyā'mṛtam idam	12	20
Ye tu sarvāṇi karmāṇi	12	6
Ye tvakṣaram anirdeśyam	12	3
Ye tvetad abhyasūyanto	3	32
Ye yathā māṁ prapadyante	4	11
Yoga-sannyasta-karmāṇam	4	41
Yogasthaḥ kuru kaumāṇi	2	48
Yoga-yukto viśuddhātmā	5	7
Yoginām api sarveṣām	6	47
Yogī yuñjīta satatam	6	10
Yo mām ajam anādiṁ ca	10	3
Yo mām evam asammūḍho	15	19
Yo māṁ paśyati sarvatra	6	30
Yo na hṛsyati na dveṣṭi	12	17
Yo'ntaḥ sukho'ntarārāmaḥ	5	24
Yotsyamānān avekṣe'ham	1	23
Yo'yaṁ yogas tvayā proktaḥ	6	33
Yo yo yāṁ yāṁ tanuṁ bhaktaḥ	7	21
Yudhāmanyuś ca vikrāntaḥ	1	6
Yuktāhāra-vihārasya	6	17
Yuktaḥ karmaphalaṁ tyaktvā	5	12
Yuñjann evaṁ sadātmānam	6	15
Yuñjann evaṁ sadātmānam	6	28

—:o:—

WORD INDEX

A

Ajna Chakra - 176, 193, 255, 257
- as eye of intuition-176
- as the sixth psychic station-193
- beeja mantra, lord and deity-194
- point of spontaneous meditation-194

Abhiman - 496

Abhimanyu - 2
- mother-5

Abhyas - 210

Absolute Truth-379

Achapalam (meaning)-495

Achyut - 6

Action - 548
- factors accomplishing it-548
- its 3 fold impulse basis-552
- Sattvic, rajasic, tamasic-557
- seat-548

Adharma (unrighteousness)-12, 24

Adhibhuta - 240, 242, 243

Adhidaivata - 240, 242, 243

Adhikarani - 140

Adhisthanam- 549

Adhiyajna - 24, 242, 243

Adhyatma - 243, 244
- Yoga-436

Adhyayan (study)-39

Adi Shankar- 28, 135, 179, 204, 443
- on immortality of soul-28, 29; samskaras-29
- on inaction in action-135; yogi-180; worthy man-70
- on origin of creature-247
- on spiritual inheritance-214

Adimata - 226, 256
- Utkarsha and Mitti-438

Aditya - 130, 288, 313
- as 12 months of the year-314
- the details-288; names-314

Adroha (meaning)-496

Agni - 130, 236, 249

Agnihotra - 283, 493
- its performance-283

Ahankar - 263

Ahimsa - 304
- Gandhi's view-304, 416, 524

Airs (names)- 288

Airavata - 319, 325

Ajnanam (meaning)-497

Akara 'A' - 329, 331
- Ukara-Makara-256

Akirtikaam (no worldly fame)-20

Akrodhah (meaning)-494

Akshar Brahma Yoga-243

Aksharateet - 366

Aloluptam (meaning)-495

Alpabuddhyah (meaning)-503

Amavasya - 327

Amritam (divine nectar)-193

Anahat Chakra-192, 255, 257, 258, 424, 483
- meaning and location-192
- as focal point of emotional and psychological maturity-192
- its beej mantra, lord and deity-193
- as star of David-193
- colour and element-193

Anahat Nad - 257

Anando Brahmeti Vyajanti (meaning)-246

Anant - 325
- i.e. Sri Krishna-366
- Nag as seat of Vishnu-327

Anantvijaya - 4

Ananya Bhakti- 259

Ananya Bhava- 291

Anarya (not noble)-20

Angira - 130, 319

Anirudha - 321

Anna - 519
- in Shruti Bhagawati, Taittreya/Chhandogya Upanishad-519

Annamaya Kosha-518

Anshuman - 119

- Parva-320

Antahakaran (mind)-140, 382, 492, 508, 544

Anukampayartham (meaning)-308, 434

Anumanta (meaning)-430

Apana - 144, 520

Apaisunam(meaning)-494

Apara Prakriti-222, 223

Aranyakas - 472
- formed by Upanishadas-472

Archira Path (significance)-269

Ardhabindu - 532

Arjavam (meaning)-417, 493

Arjuna - 2, 4, 5, 15, 24
- and a parallel story of Christ, Ramakrishna Paramahans-357
- acts as anarya-20; his gurus-22, 24
- as Purusharbha (the most heroic)-30
- as sole viewer of vishwarupa-367, 368
- bound by Karma-122 i.e. as a jivatma-122
- comes to realize Sri Krishna-310, 311
- declares Sri Krishna above all-362-365
- delusion dispelled-342; compulsion to fight-584
- dilemma-6, 7, 9, 14; inner conflict-10, 121, 375
- fearful fascination for Sri Krishna-349-355, 361-365
- gets enlightened by 'vishwarupa' of Sri Krishna-346, 347, 348-355
- hears what he wants to-156
- his dance guru-324
- his escapism-15; total mind control-207, 208
- his flag-ensign-5; 'kirti'-361
- his nagging question-156; queries-211, 243, 512
- his swadharma-15, 45; true battle-15
- his sympathy and consequences towards Kauravas-24
- killed Kala and Khanja-361
- as Nara, and Sri Krishna Narayan-337
- queries about the man who transcends 3 gunas-460
- seeks difference in Sanyas and Tyaga-537
- sees Krishna as incarnation of Vishnu-375
- shows signs of Rajasic Sanyas-544
- Uvach (saidto Krishna)-6, 7, 22, 23, 61, 80, 112, 121, 156, 243, 310, 311, 342, 348-355, 361, 370, 375, 459, 512, 537, 599
- various names-4, 5, 6, 19, 30, 45
- virtues-18; repents for taking liberty with Krishna-364, 365

Arthaveda - 285, 286

Arya - 20
- meaning-20, 21; as soldier-21

Aryama (god of justice)-131

Aryaman - 325
- as deity of ancestors-327

Asanas - 189

Asat - 531

Asura (demon)-490, 491, 502
- characterics-491
- ntaure leads to bondage-491

Aswatha (Peepul)-318
- according to Aurobindo, Kathopanishad-468
- and mythological Igdrasil-469
- as embodiment of Vishnu-323, 467
- its leaves as Vedas-466
- significance in ayurveda-323
- significance-466, 467; literal meaning-468

Aswathama - 3

Atharva Veda-130
- its subject matter and upveda-285
- later interpolation-286
- on powers of resolution-210

Atiratra (meaning)-332

Atithi yajna - 87

Atma - 37, 200
- and Jivatma-485
- Kripa-148; Bodha-309; Bhavastho-308

- the root and in Rig Vedas-200
Atmaupamya (meaning)-206, 207
Atmavan - 54
Atmavinigrah-418
Aum - 224, 255-257, 424, 425, 440, 531
- according to Bhartrihari-225
- and turiya awastha-226; nada-227
- as beeja mantra-224; origin of vedas-225
- as Omkar Brahma-256, 284
- as worship of Saguna and Nirguna both-256
- in Mandukya Upanishad-225, 226, 284, 321
- in Taittreya Upanishad-225; Chhandogya-321
- in Vedas; Upanishadas-256
- in Verse 11 and 13 (Ch.8)-254-255
- in words of Aurobindo-226; Eugene Davis-532
- known as pranav-256; reveals Gayatri-533
- significance of A, U and M-256, 257, 321, 532, 533
- significance of Ardhabindu-532
- sounds heard during various levels of meditation-257, 258
- the sound and philologists' views-226
- various interpretations-256, 257, 318, 532-534
Aum - Tat-Sat-17, 79, 117, 155, 177, 242, 271, 300, 341, 374, 402, 465, 402, 465, 489, 511, 534, 536, 607
- delineating the three-530, 531, 532-536
Austerity - 515, 516, 520, 521, 526-528
Avasam (meaning)-277
Avash - 262
Avidya - 173
Avyaktam (meaning)-410
- as Mahad Brahma-410
Avyayam (meaning)-468
Ayan (meaning)-268
Ayurveda - 285
- describes Patanjali Yoga Sutra and Charak Shastra-285

B

Balivaisvadeva Yajna-87, 90
- also known as Bhuta Yajna-90
Banyan Tree- 469, 470
- and the samsar-470
Bhagawad Geeta-17, 79, 117, 155, 177, 242, 271, 300, 341, 374, 402, 465, 402, 465, 489, 511, 534, 536
- its message-92; mantra for food-intake-520
Bhakti - 48, 494
- Yoga-48
Bhaktya mam abhijanati-583
Bharat - 122, 152
Bharta - 430
Bhavo - abhavah (meaning)-304
Bhima - 2, 3
Bhishma - 3, 6, 22, 23, 238
- as grandsire-3
- how loses his respect-24
Bhojya - 482
Bhokta - 430
Bhrigu - 245, 318
- the greatest of seers-318, 320
Bhrumadhya- 190
Bhur Bhuvah Svaha-288, 289, 333
- as being, becoming and bliss-289
Bhuta - 90
- Yajna-90
- Prathagbhavam-438
Bible - 525
Binduj (meaning)-306
Birth Sign - 315
Bliss - 488
Body (physical and subtle)-405-414
Book of Wisdom-36
Brahma - 191, 236, 243, 244, 260, 262, 326
- Nirvan-76, 171, 172, 174; Sutras-405
- Vijnan Sadhana-246; adhyatma-246
- as a symbol of embodied self-263
- as defined in Taittreya Upanishad-245
- as mother Nature-491

- as perceived in Vedas-248
- as Sanatan principle-245
- as the creator; presiding deity of mooladhar-191
- as womb of Sri Krishna-441
- called Hiranyagarbha in Vedas-443
- His day and night-260
- jnani-94; Yajna-87, 88
- Kalpa nad Pralaya-261; Vidya-88
- the medium of one imperishable reality-245
- the root-263; and Brahman-262

Brahmachari- 418, 523, 524

Brahman (Absolute)-17, 53, 78, 79, 401, 407, 421, 422
- as neither Sat nor Asat-439
- in the eyes of a worldly mortal-75
- who-573; beyond comprehension of mind-583

Brahmanas - 472

Brahmarandhra-193, 256
- as seat of Brahman-469
- as tenth gate of the body-256

Brahmisthiti (meaning)-75, 78

Breath (significance)- 200
- as manifestation of the Supreme Self, atma-200

Brihaspati (Jupiter)-130, 319
- chief of priests-318; the great scholar-319, 320
- in Rigveda-319; and Kumbha Celebration-319

Brihatsama - 332
- as unique hymn of Samaveda-332

Buddha - 36
- and grieving mother's story-39
- defines a man of wisdom-150
- on conquering ones own self-67
- on wheel of birth-death and rebirth-77

Buddhi - 50, 55, 263, 303
- as dealt in holy scriptures-62
- i.e. intelligence-50
- sattvic, rajasic and tamasic-561
- Yoga-580, 585

C

Calvin Coolidge-402

Carl Jung - 111

Chandra - 131

Chhandogya Upanishad-41, 97, 423
- and the fruit of nyagrodha tree-140
- on transcendental state of consciousness-41

Chaturyugi - 262, 277

Chetna - 316

Christopher Isherwood-65, 206

Commentary - 8, 18, 20, 23
- on a devotee dear to Krishna-391-403
- on a man's rise or fall-68, 167
- on action with some desire-51
- on apara and para prakriti-222
- on Arjuna's craving to know more of Krishna-311, 312
- on Arjuna's inner conflict-8, 10, 11, 13, 14, 15
- on avoiding extremes-196
- on concentration of mind-198, 202
- on demoniac ways-501, 504, 505
- on deva-asura characteristics-491
- on difficulties during meditation-432
- on Divine manifestation, unmanifested, Brahma and beyond-222, 264
- on Divine vision-345; dramatization of self pity-18
- on eco cycle-93; world order-94, 170
- on feeling and touching the god, the supreme self-204
- on finite and infinite senses-41
- on four stages of life-418; on human life-233, 234
- on helplessness-263; ideal self control (discipline)-72, 67, 208-210
- on how kings lived; tax collection those day-120

- on immortality of soul-27, 33
- on incarnation of Krishna and his omniscience-125
- on Jatila Madhusudan story-128
- on Jivatma-476-479
- on Kalpa and Pralaya-276
- on kama, iccha, spriha, trishna and conquences-64, 114
- on Kama, Krodha and Lobha-506-508
- on karma, akarma and vikarma-134, 135
- on Krishna's perception of Arjuna-20
- on Krishna's teaching-34;
- on Krishna's various roles-128
- on law of Karma-213, 214; maya-228
- on losing self-confidence-111
- on magnificence of Karmayoga-95
- on meditation and nirvikalpa meditation-186-190
- on misconception of worshippers-131, 279
- on modern education; society then and now-111
- on necessity and right way of action-84
- on nine gates of the body-165
- on real renunciation-159, 179; renunciates-545
- on righteous person who fails in yoga-213
- on sankhya and yoga of action-159
- on Saptarishi and 14 manus-306
- on Sat and Asat-31; Gayatri-332
- on Sattva, Rajas, Tamas-451-457; 567-570
- on sensory pleasures-170, 173
- on Shabda Brahma-215
- on social ramification of Arjuna's wavering satnd-46
- on Solar and Lunar dynasty-119
- on speaking the truth-303
- on Sri Krishna as best in all forms of existence-225, 319-340
- on state of inaction in action-135
- on swabhava and swadharma-45, 132
- on tradioin of Jnan Karm Yoga-119
- on transmigration of soul-35
- on tuition and intuition-60
- on various ways of performing sacrifices-143
- on Vishad-16
- on ways for God-realization-432
- on what makes a man angry-69
- on why people suffer-134
- on worshipping Him-293; types of worshippers-231-233, 298
- on Yogakshemam Vahamyaham-291
- on yogayukta-161, 163, 165
- on yogic communion-153; natural ways-196
- signifying action over worship-131

Concentration-198
- helps in Self attainment-203
- practice and advantage-198, 199
- significance of breathing-200

Cosmic Powers-88
- its interplay-88
- perceived as devata-88

Cosya - 482

Creation - 92
- and evolution-92
- its root; wheel-92

D

Dadhichi - 326

Daivam - 549

Daksha - 395

Dakshina (meaning)-267, 522
- vanto Amritam Bhajante-529, 540

Dakshinayan-267
- the period-268

Dale Carnegie-57
- and frustration of the business-man-57, 58

Damah - 303, 492

Dambh - 496, 496
Danam - 304, 492
- sattvic, rajasic, tamasic-529
Darp - 496, 496
Dasarath - 119
Daya - 492
- as root of Dharma-495
Death - 36
- and god realization-250-254
- as a mere transition-213
- in Uttarayan-266; Dakshinayan-267, 269, 270
- influence of the Sun and the Moon-268
- the process detailed-255
- views of Sri Krishna and Tagore-36
Dehabhiman- 381
- as a curtain between Nara and Narayan-382
Dehelideepakaanya (meaning)-64
Demon - 490, 491
- characteristics-491
- ways and consequences-498-501
Desire - 112, 113
- as dealt in Manusmriti-116
- views of Sri Krishna-113, 114; Sri Ram sukhdas-116
Devadatta - 45, 144
Devala - 310, 312
Devasurampattivibhagyoga (meaning)-490
Devata (Deva)-88, 547, 490, 491, 502
- Arjuna has this character-491
- Asur, the universal concept-502
- characteristics-490
- nature conducive to emancipation-490
Devotee - 390-403
Devraj Indra- 249
- the story of Vajra-326; Kala and Khanja-361
Dev Yajna - 87
Dhananjaya - 45, 222, 276
- as Krishna-335
- as a function of vital force-144
Dhanurveda - 285
Dhar - 123, 317
Dharma - 111, 123, 131, 215, 224, 272, 279, 327, 402, 403, 495, 510, 561, 603
- and Adharma-125; Putra-525
- as fulfillment of Vedic order-472
- as the golden message-123; a way of victory-338
- a complex concept-594
- the larger social scope-124
Dharmaraj - 131, 131
Dhee - 62
- its relation with Buddhi, Medha and Prajna-62
- meaning of dheemahi-62
- significance of Gayatri-62
Dhristadyumna-5
Dhritrashtra - 5, 14
- and sons shown rushing into Krishna's mouth-353
- his sons-5, 6, 9, 13, 14, 22
- said (Uvach)-1
- as a descendant of Bharat-6; selfish king-14
Dhriti - 496
Dhruv - 317
Dhumah - 269
Dhyan Yoga-178
- as the yoga of meditation-178
Dileep - 119
Divine - 19, 48, 49, 51, 151, 200, 582, 586
- knowledge-151; purush-245
- manifest and unmanifest-222
- nature and its elements-492
- Vision-345, 360, 372
Dr. S. Radhakrishnan-15, 111, 164, 586, 587, 591
- on commitment-111; Arjuna's plight-16
- on introverts and extroverts-82
- on Reality-379; Varna System-574, 575
- on satisfaction of man-164
Drashta - 458
Draupadi - 5, 238
Dravya Yajna-145
Durga - 19
- her blessings to Arjuna-19
Duryodhana- 14, 23, 24
- as durbhuddhi-14

- selfish attitude-14
Dvandva - 331
Dvija - 523

E

E F Schumacher-69, 173
- on materialistic viewpoint-173, 174
Einstein - 409
Ek se aneka - 247
Ekam Sadvipra Bahudha Vadanti-382
Embodied - self-32
Embodied - soul-35
Emerson - 182, 525
- and the washer-woman episode-182, 183
- on concentration versus dissipation-198
Esa hi drashta srashta (meaning)-549
Equinoxes - 268
Eugene Davis- 382
- emphasis on purity-492

F

Feminine Virtues-330
Fichte - 228
Fitzgerald - 400
Five elements that accomplish a work-548
- the details-549
- Tapasyanand's views-551
- belong to Prakriti-551
Food - 480, 519
- as dealt in Shruti Bhagawati, Taittreya, Chhandogya Upanishad-519
- sattvic, rajasic, tamasic-517, 518
- the mantra before its intake-520
Footprint (the story)-291
Four - fold work order-129, 132, 572
- yet exists as a democratic setup-132

G

Gandharva - 324
- as the celestial musician-324
- the Chitrarth-324
- Veda-324
Gandiva - 7
Ganga (the river)-329
- as one of Krishna's attributes-329
Garuda - 325
- as vehicle of Vishnu-327
Gayatri - 62
- as Savitri-333
- evolution-321, 533; the mantra-332
- maha mantra-334; interpretations-333
Geeta - 49
Gerald Heard- 576
Ghee - 283
Gitanjali - 127, 287, 332
God - 16, 588, 599
- as Viswa-283; abode-424, 588
- as Vyakti and Avyakt-242
- attainment and honesty-434
- in the form of five elements-248
- realization and various ways-432
Gospel of John-171
Govinda - 8
Great devotees-233, 597
Grihastha - 418
Gudakesha - 6, 313
Guhya (Hridya)-425
Gunas - 129, 447, 454
- as trifold nature-228
- in harmony with each other-447, 449, 450
- the details-447; views of Aurobindo-450
- transcending them-458
Gunateet - 462
- one alert about predominance of gunas-463
Gunatriya Vibhagyoga-441
Guru Govind Singh-463, 464

H

Hanuman - 378, 379
Haridwar - 329
- footprints of Sri Hari-329
Harishchandra-120
Havankunda- 143

Heat of the Body-267, 269
Hemisphere - 268
Herbal Plants-283, 284
Himalaya - 323
Hirankshyipu-328
Hiranyagarbha-443
- his concept of tattvomasi-379
How To Stop Worrying And Start Living-57
Howard Thurman-73, 291, 292
Hridaya - 425, 425
- Akasha-425; Kosha-426, 588
Hridayantar Jyoti-425
Hrih - 495
Hrishikesha - 6, 537

I

I and Mine - 16, 77, 165, 277, 373, 382, 392, 406, 409, 552
- and Thou and Thine-382, 392, 473, 582
- and tyaga-494
- as Dehabhiman-381: Abhiman-496
- view of Omar Khayyam-382
Ida - 194
Idam na mama-143
- meaning-145
Ikshvaku - 118
Indra - 45
- his gifts to Arjuna-45
Indraprastha- 21
Indriya (senses)-113, 316, 410
Indweller Soul (various roles)-425-431
Intuition - 193, 194
- in the words of Swami Abhedananda-194
Isha - 193
Ishwara - 96
- dwelling-587, 588
- sarvabhutanam hridese Arjuna tisthati-587
- as the cosmic father-444
Ishwaram idam sarvam (meaning)-206

J

Jaap Yajna - 318
- significance-322, 323
Jahnavi - 325
Jajali - 96, 577
Jal - 131
Jayadayal Goyandaka-31, 37, 58, 176, 249, 377, 392, 452
- on Bhrigu-320; Vyas-337; devotee-392
- on sacrifice and swadharma-90
- on sat-asat-31; Vedas-51
Jesus Christ - 357, 402, 416
Jiva - 123
- and divine-124; its fall-123
- brahma bheda bhranti-477
- literal meaning-476; in Ramayan-476
- mukta-459; bhutah-476
Jivatma - 123, 163, 281, 428, 488, 501
- how falls from Swadharma-445
- i.e. embodied soul and its formation-444, 485
- synonyms-428, 429
- the real nature-477
- to Mahatma-279, 280, 486
- to Paramatma-430
Jnan (knowledge)-220
- as spiritual knowledge-220
- Nishtha-85; Yajna-598
- sattvic, rajasic, tamasic-554
- vijnan-220; Yajna-281
- Yoga and karma Yoga-85, 118
Jnana Karma Yoga-118, 599
- comes to Arjuna-118
- its tradition and disappearnce-118

K

Kakini - 193
Kala - 328
- as the demon-361
- the running time-288; Chakra-261
Kalidas - 120
Kaliyuga - 262
- beginning and duration-262
Kamdhenu - 325, 326
Kapila - 159
- as a siddha-324; the perfect sage-318, 324

- parantage-324
- reverence for Samkhya Philosophy-324

Karan - 140, 549
- sa organs-428

Karishye Vachanam Tav-599, 600, 602
Karma - 410
- Sanyasa Yoga-156, 158, 160
- vivek-474

Karm Yoga - 47, 80, 85, 129, 140, 160, 433
- as an art of living-56; yoga of action-80
- its root-47; and sanyas-580
- leading to supreme soul-58

Karmanyevadhikaraste (Verse 47, Chapter 2)-55
Karpanya - 24
- doshophata swabhavah-24
- meaning-24

Karta - 140, 549
- sattvic, rajasic, tamasic-559, 560

Kartikeya - 318
Karuna - 392, 470
Kathopanishad-42, 239
- on abode of God-424
- on all pervasive Supreme Soul-422
- on Atma-425;aswattha-468
- on heart and arteries-255; silence-339
- on limited comprehension of soul-42

Kauravas - 24
Kaunteya - 113, 208, 223, 245, 276, 292
Kesava - 8, 61, 31, 604
Ketu - 131
Khanj - 361
King Drupad- 5
- the Rajrishi-96

King Janak - 65, 95
- as Videha-66, 96

King of Kasi- 5
King Yudhisthir-4, 5
Klaibyam (unmanly)-19
Knowledge (three fold)-554
Krikala - 144
Kripa - 148
Kripacharya - 23
Kripanah Phalhetavah-58
Kritanjali - 366, 367
Kshara Bhava-247, 366
Kshatriya - 570
- who-573, 574; duty-570, 574

Kshetra (field)-404, 409, 468
- and Kshetrajna Samyoga-404, 405, 434, 442,
- as forces-408, 409
- Kshetrajna Vibhagyoga-404

Kuber - 317
- in Bhagwat Purana-317
- lord of yaksha, Raksha and wealth-317

Kuladharma - 13
Kumaras - 306
- as mana, buddhi, chit and ahankar-307
- origin-307

Kumbhaka - 146
Kundalini - 191
- its root word-191;Shakti-327
- and Vasuki-327

Kunti - 4, 238
- her sons-4

Kurma - 144
Kurus - 6, 24
- family-23

Kurukshetra - 370
Kush - 188
- grass cushion-188

L

Lakini - 192
Law of Karma- 213
Lehya - 482
Light - 267
- and fire-267, 269
- forms archira path-269

Lobhah (greed)-505, 506
- leads to hell-506

Lalana Chakra-193
Lokeshna - 565
Lord - 584, 585, 591
- dwellings-587
- remembering Him-593

Love - 229
- as a natural instinct-299, 300

M

Madhava - 9
Madhusudana-18, 129
Madhusudan Saraswati-76, 140
- on still water runs deep-76
- on five constituents of a sacrifice-140
Mahabaho - 157, 208
Mahabharat - 39, 160, 229
- on a real renouncer-160
- on creator-337
- on Saptarishi, 4 Kumaras and Manus-307
- Shanti Parva-307, 320
Mahakala - 359
Maharishi Mahesh Yogi-24, 59
Mahatma Gandhi-78, 96, 147
- on Brahman-524; non-violence-416, 524
- on fasting and prayer-148
- on Karmayoga-96; maun-401; truth-525
- on moksha and the way leading to it-78
Mahayajnas - 145
Mahayuga - 262, 277
Mahesh - 236, 430
Mam Dharma- 606
Mamanusmaran (meaning)-256
Man (Mind) - 75, 263, 316, 443
- 6th sense-477
- maun vrata-338, 527
- maun and mauni-75, 582
Man the Master (book)-576
- supports four-fold society-576
Manasa Vachya Karmana-304, 416, 493
Mandalas - 285
Mandukya Upnishad-148, 256
- on Aum-321;attainment of supreme soul-493
- on necessity of spiritual guidance-148
Mangala - 131
Manipur Chakra-192
- location, colour, elemental quality, lord and deity-192
Manipuspaka- 4
Mantra - 199, 284
- definition; jap and how it helps-199
- jap and significance-322, 323
- siddhi-338
- source-284; in Vedas-285
- views of Vashishtha-323
Manu - 97, 118
- fourteen Manus -306
Manusmriti - 14, 394
- its base-509
- on four fold division of society-575
- on killing a desparado-14
Mardavam - 495
Margshirsa - 330
- significance of the month-334
Marichi - 313, 314
- as glow of all Maruts-315
Maruts (wind Gods)-314, 315
Matter - 444
- as twisted rope of 3 gunas-445
Maturity - 396
Max Mueller- 130
- and Rig Veda-130;
- The sacred books of the East-130
Maya (divine illusion)-227, 229, 241, 279, 440
- as observerd by Sri Krishna-228, 229;
- evading its trap-229
- in Upanishad; Ramayan-229
- in Yaksha-Yudhistir samvad-229
- its creator-227
- views of Ramanuja-228; Sivanand-229
Medha - 545, 546
- buddhi-545
Meerabai - 265
- her unalloyed devotion-265
Meru - 313, 317
- the peak of God and self realization-318
- in Puranas-317; i.e.spinal cord-317
Mithila - 96
Mitti - 256
Moksha - 96, 509

- Gandhi's views-78
- Ekadashi-334; Sanyas Yoga-537
Mooladhar Chakra-191
- as first psychic station of Sushumna Nadi-191
- beej mantra and presiding deity-191
Moon (Soma)- 289, 290
- and Psycho-somatic changes-481, 482
- significance-481
Mozart - 36, 37
Mrigchhala (deer skin)-188
Mudha - 230
- as they see Lord Krishna-278, 279
Muni - 74, 443, 526
- who is a muni-74, 324, 337, 443
- related analogy of day and night-74
- as dealt by Sri Krishna-75

N

Na ati manita (meaning)-496
Nada - 284, 321, 424
- Yoga-258
Nadaj (meaning)-306
- as thoughts embodied-306
Nai Atman balheen labhyah (meaning)-20
Nakshatras - 314, 315
- number and names-315
Nakul - 4
- his conch-4
Nara - 366, 603
- and Narayana-366, 382, 470, 603, 605
Narad - 310, 312, 324
- Bhakti Sutra-324
- as glory of God-324
Naradhipa - 325
Narak Dwar - 505, 506
Nashto Mohah-599, 600
Nirdwandva - 157
Nirguna - 377, 378, 380
- as the difficult path-380, 381
Nirvana (meaning)-78, 185, 260
Niti - 338
Nitya Varina- 116
Nityakarma (meaning)-85
Nityasthwastho (meaning)-5

O

Omar Khayyam-277
Omkar - 226
- as combination of akara, ukara and makara-226
Origin (cosmic man and society)-576

P

Padmasana - 189
- i.e. full lotus posture-189
Pandavas - 24
Pandit Lekhramji-298, 299
Pandu - 5
Paramhamsas (meaning)-239
Parantap - 19, 118, 121, 240
- i.e. scorcher of enemy-19, 21
Parityagi - 396-398
Paroksha Jnan- 220
Paropkar - 145
Partha - 19, 21, 219, 224, 280
Parusya - 497
Patanjali - 60, 159
- describes various stages of inner awakening-60, 61
- Yoga Sutra-191, 285
- on various levels of intuitive wisdom-545
Paul Brunton- 77, 550, 551
- on ego-77, 585, 586
Pavak (fire) - 317
- as divine attribute of sri Krishna-317
- in first hymn of Rigveda-317
Peya - 482
Pindodak (rice-ball and water)-12
Pingla - 194
Pitar(ancestor)- 12
Plato - 403
Plotinus - 588
Prabhasa - 317
Prabhu Kripa- 148
Prahalad - 325
- as the very self of Krishna-327

- his ordeal-325
- the demon king-cum-devotee-327

Prajapati - 249
- on Nadaj-306

Prajna - 62, 545
- meaning-62; and Karuna-495

Prakriti (Nature)-54, 215, 227, 426, 439, 588
- as attributes bound by 3 gunas-458
- as real doer-437; Mahad Brahma-443
- without beginning-426

Pralaya - 222, 223, 261, 263

Prana - 144, 236, 256, 520
- as a form of yajna-144
- five pranas-289

Pranayanam - 146
- advantages-146
- as inaction in action-146
- control of puruka, kumbhaka, rechaka-146

Prasad - 73, 120, 509, 603

Pratibha - 545

Pratijanti name bhaktah pranasyati (meaning)-298

Pratyakshavagamam (meaning)-273

Pratyusha - 317

Pravritti - 468

Prayan (death)-240, 253

Prayaschitta - 39

Pritha - 21

Prithvi - 131

Psalmist - 73

Pundarika (meaning)-425

Puranas - 131, 320
- on Vajra-326; Meru-317
- their base-509

Puruka - 146

Purush - 248, 253, 426
- and Prakriti Sanyas Yoga-436
- details-248; kinds-484
- without any beginning-426

Purushottam- 249, 342, 343
- Yoga-466, 485, 486; Guhyatamam-488

Putreshna - 565

R

Rabindra Nath Tagore-28, 165, 173, 393, 395, 426, 482, 589
- endlessness of life in Geetanjali-28
- love of man and love of god-127
- the story of Guru Govind Singh-463, 464

Rahasyam hyetaduttamam (meaning)-121

Rahu - 131

Rajasic - 116, 204, 445, 447
- characters lead to action-446
- attitude and colour-449, 455, 456
- buddhi-561; person-513, 565
- happiness-566, 567; worship-513, 515
- passion-116, 204, 445
- qualities and death-451; source of attachment-446
- renouncement-542-544; action-557
- yajna-520; food-517, 518; Dhriti-564

Rajguhyam - 272

Rajvidya - 272

Rajvidya Rajguhya Yoga (meaning)-272

Rakini - 192

Rakshasas - 502

Ramayan - 476, 502, 602

Rechaka - 146

Renunciation- 82
- and hypocrisy-83; ideal way-83
- sattvic, rajasic, tamasic-542, 543-547
- Swami Prahupad's view-82
- Swami Satyaprakash Saraswati's view-85

Richastuto - 285

Righteousness- 122

Rigveda - 34, 130, 200, 282, 288, 289
- defines Atma-200; theme-315
- Name, Composition, Number of hymns and its Upveda-285
- on living in harmony with universal soul-34
- on Supreme Soul-422; Dana-529

Rishi Udalaka-220

Rishi Yajnavalkya-65

Ritambhara - 545
Rituraj - 335
Rudras - 131, 192, 288, 313
- as lord of Manipura Chakra-192
- as Pranas in microcosm-131
- names, and bestower of personal desire-317
- their lord-317
Rumi - 439

S

Sacrifice (Yajna)-86
- as milch cow for desire fulfillment-86
- its significance, lack and conquences-86, 87
- Sri Krishna's views-91
- Swami Ram Sukhdas's views-91
Sadguru - 149
Sagar - 119
Sages who believed in Saguna-Nirguna-380
Saguna - 377
- and Nirguna-378
- Sri Krishna's view-380
- the concept of Ideal and Idol-378
- views of sages-379
Saha - yajna-90
Sahadeva - 4
- his conch-4
Sahaj karma- 572, 575
Sahasrara - 194
- as a lotus of thousand petals-194
- as holder of all chakras-194
- can be perceived and visualized-194
- colour and element-195
- the spot of spiritual energy-194
Sakam Upasana-290
- side effects-290
Samadhi - 141
Samah - 303
Samana - 144
Samashti - 306
Samasparsha- 204
- perception of Adi Shankar, Ramanuja and Srinivas-204
Samata - 304
Samhita - 472
Samkarsan - 321
Samkhya - 159
- Philosophy and 24 tattvas-410
- Philosophy and accomplishing any action-548
- and Yoga integration-159
- Yoga-41, 47, 79, 159, 41, 47, 79, 443
Sampradan - 140
Samsara - 314, 468
- and Banyan tree-470
Samskaras - 29, 166, 233, 234, 262, 277, 410, 454, 455, 469, 547, 549
- 16 in number-54; literal meaning-54
- carried by soul-29; past ones-168
Samveda - 130, 258, 313
- seven Swara-258; devotional music-315
- view of Dayanand saraswati-316
- the famous hymn-316
- its upveda-285, 324; mantras-285
- on Trikala Sandhya-288
- quintessence of all Vedas-315
Sanjay - 15, 605
- blessed with divine vision-369
- can see divine Krishna and relate the same to Dhritrashtra-347, 348
- Uvach (Said)-1-6, 15, 16, 25, 346, 3447, 361, 369
Sankalp and Vikalp-201, 409, 443
Santusht - 393
Sanyas (asceticism)-157, 537, 584
- and Tyag-537; Sanyasi-296
- as 4 th stage of life-418
- as expounded by Sri Krishna-157
Saptrishi - 305, 306
- origin-305, 307; names-306
- in the form of five senses, intellect and I-307
Saraswati - 335
Sarvabhavena (meaning)-487, 589
Sarvadharmana parityajaya maamekam (meaning)-591, 593, 594
Sarvavit (meaning)-487
Sat-Asat - 31, 286, 421, 494
- as seen by Sri Jnaneshwari-32

- perception of Sri Jayadayal Goyandaka-31
- views of Ramanuja and Tibaut-286, 287
- views of Sri Krishna-31, 286

Satpatha Brahmana-131
Sattvic - 52, 227, 228, 448, 450, 452, 455, 456, 512, 542, 545
- action-557; buddhi-561; qualities-445
- as the rising Sun-451
- binds imperishable spirit to the body-445
- dhriti (firmness)-564
- happinesss-445, 446, 566, 567
- person-512; food-517; vritti-448
- predominance-450, 452, 455, 456; death-451
- renouncement-542, 545, 546
- yajna-521; worship-513, 514

Satyaki - 5
Sat Chit Anand-31, 281, 594
- as original nature of jivatma-477
- signifies God-494

Satyamev Jayate-524
Satyuga - 262
- beginning, duration-262

Scriptures - 508-510
Seer - 437, 440, 475
- and seen-440

Seven deadly Sins-504
Shanti (significance)-494
Sharir - 35, 405
- i.e. embodied soul-35

Shastra (Scripture)-508
- Kripa-148; leads to Swadharma-510
- significance-508, 509
- views of Sri Aurobindo-510

Shaucham - 496
Shava - 317
Shesh Naga - 327
Shiva - 317
- as consciousness in the body-317
- and Shava - 317
- His abode - 323

Shokasamvigna Manasah-15
- meaning-16

Shradha - 153, 217, 218, 535, 536
- details-218
- and Samskar-513
- Triya Vibhagyoga-512

Shreya - 508
Shridhara - 171
- concept of Sampresana-171

Shruti Bhagawati-47, 220, 549
- on Sahashra Shirsha Purush-422
- on vaishwanar-482; food-519

Shrutipranayah (meaning)-434
Shubhadra - 5
- her son-5

Shudra - 570
Shukra - 131
Shukracharya-335
- the teacher-338; Kavi and Usana-338
- on Shukraniti-338
- Snjivini mantra, mantra Siddhi-338

Siddhasana - 189
Sikhandi - 5
Sitoshna sukhadukhesu samah sang vivarjitah-399
Small Is Beautiful (the book)-69
- on consequences of greed-69

Smriti - 14
Smritir labdha-599-601
Socrates - 37, 402, 408
- related anecdote-37; poisoning episode-408
- views on soul-37

Solar Dynasty-119
- the origin-119
- well known kings-119, 120
- as described by Kalidas-120

Solomon - 36
Solstice - 268
Soma - 287, 289, 317
- as a medicinal plant; in Charak Shastra-289
- in Rigveda; soumya-290

Soul - 29
- Song-459
- as interpreted in Atharva Veda-29
- in Kathopanishad-32
- its transmigration-36

- various interpretations (Verse 18-30)-32, 33, 35, 38, 40
- as Ajah, Nityah, Swatah, Purnah

Sri Aurobindo-66, 239, 556, 576
- cites tortoise to explain self-control-66
- on Maya-239; Tyag-Sanyas-541
- on Varna system-576

Sri Chinmayanand-74
- on inactivity and consequences-85
- on self-centredness-162
- on sense-control-74, 172

Sri Jnanesharji-72, 278
- cites example of tortoise-72

Sri Krishna - 7, 9, 11, 14, 20, 24, 25
- about 'I', 'You' and 'These'-28
- advises Arjuna to know Him-219
- alerts Arjuna about conditioned experiences of the senses-30
- the devouring flame in his mouth-352-355
- as 1000-armed Universal Being-365
- as a mighty wind-274; seed of all living beings-336, 441
- as all devouring Kala (Time)-358, 359
- as author of Vedanta and Knower of Vedas-481
- as beginning, middle and end of every thing-313, 317-319, 330, 335
- as lord of Yoga-603
- as omnipresent force-222, 223, 274, 282, 301, 302, 339
- as origin and annihilation of the universe-222, 274, 304, 305
- as the sun, soma and vaishwanar-480
- as virility in man-224; dyuta-335; Mahatma-234
- calls jnan karma yoga primordial-118
- defines one who qualifies for immortality-30, 458
- delineates Sanyas and Tyaga-538, 539
- describes techniques of pranayam-146
- describes the characteristics of four varnas-570-571
- details about demoniac beings-498-501
- emphasises on a balanced life for yoga (verse 16, 17 Ch. 6)-195
- emphasizes on worship of His manifest form-377, 381, 382
- exhorts Arjuna to become a true yogi-218
- glorifies Aum-257, 531, 532
- governing his own Nature-122
- his divine form as revealed by Sanjay-346, 347
- his eight-fold Prakriti, and two-fold Nature-221
- His supreme Abode-264; that of God's-424
- holds yoga of action superior-83, 157
- main cause of incarnation-125
- manifest and unmanifest-123
- not bound by Karma-122
- on senses, mind, intellect, indwelling self-113, 114
- on 7 rishis and 14 manus-305
- on a devotee who resorts to other Gods-234, 235, 292, 293
- on a prosperous life-96; Brahmasthiti-78
- on a true Karmayogi-83; dear devotee-390, 596-598
- on abhyas and vairagya for self control-210
- on action and inaction-129; mysterious nature of action-133
- on Brahma, Adhyatma, Karma, Adhibhuta, Adhidaivat and Adhiyajna-244
- on death-36; with sattva, rajas, tamas background-451
- on delusion at the time of birth-240; ideal wishes during death-244, 245
- on desire as enemy-113, 114
- on desolation and confusion of

Arjuna-21, 25
- on existence of a man-26, 27
- on high sounding speech, pleasure and power-50, 51
- on how Mahatma seeks Krishna-280
- on ignorance, knowledge and attainment of Brahmanism-167, 168
- on karma, akarma and vikarma-133
- on Kshetra and Ksherajna-404, 405
- on moksha in lifetime-127, 172, 174
- on muni-75, 443; brahamana-139, 169; yogi-171, 185
- on one who has transcended 3 gunas-460, 461
- on plight of septics-152, 154
- on pre- and post-life of a being-28
- on real and unreal (Verse 16)-31
- on righteous ones who fail in yoga-212, 213
- on sankhya yoga of action-158, 159
- on self mortification for Tap-515, 516
- on self-27, 181, 182; self-less action-55
- on several births of Arjun and himself-121, 122
- on significance of smile-25, 26; yoga-152, 153
- on swadhaya-146; transitory feelings-29
- on types of people who worship Him-230, 231, 296, 297, 498
- on various ways of performing sacrifice-141, 142
- on who is a hypocrite-85; wise (yogi)-134, 136
- on why people leave swadharma-112
- on why royal sages used to enlighten kings-119
- on yogic communion with Supreme Self-197, 201
- opening dialogue (Verse 11)-26
- origin and characteristics of Sattva, Rajas and Tamas-227, 557, 445, 446, 450, 451, 455, 456
- other names-8-10, 12, 13, 18
- reveals supreme secret-119, 120
- sees Arjun as merely instrumental-358, 359
- shows his Viswarupa to Arjun-348-355
- signifies knowledge-150-152; knowledge sharing-596, 597
- suggests a way of meditation-175, 185, 186
- suggests alternative ways to attain Him-384, 385, 458
- suggests Arjuna for total surrender-588, 590
- tells when yogis don't take rebirth-266, 267, 427, 458
- visvatomukham-283

Sri Mahadev Desai-56

Sri Ram - 119, 126, 325
- and Hanuman episode-378, 379
- and his dearest being-126
- as incarnation of Vishnu-328
- as Jnan Yoga Karma exemplified-120
- as lord Vishnu incarnate-119

Sri Ramakrishna-125, 136, 217, 259, 299
- on mere book reading-217; Purush and Prakriti-429
- on character of a Divine purush-214, 215
- cancer episode-139; Deoghar episode-206, 207
- Tamasic disciple Mathur episode-556
- on ferocious form of the Ganga-357
- on inaction in action-136
- on incarnation-125; inherited spirituality-214
- pearl oyster episode-149; divine vision-357

Sri Ramanuja- 37, 228, 228
- on eternity of soul-37

- on manifestation and non-manifestation-40
- on performance of ritual-52; divine vision-372
- on predominance of Rajas-453
- on superiority of karmayoga-85
- on total surrender-589

Sri Ram Sukhdas-11, 91, 128, 138, 550
- on absolute and apparent reality-27
- on Arjuna's delusion-11
- on desire-116; Aum-321
- on existence (or non-existence) of Lord-421
- on past Karmas and present samskaras-471
- on expectation that leads to frustration-69
- on homely saints-138; spirit of sacrifice-91
- on cosmic day and night-263
- on perishable object, persisting desire-277

Sri Satvalekar-136
Srimad Bhagawad Geeta-17
St. Marcus - 425
Sthir Mati (meaning)-402
Sthitaprajna - 61, 62
Subramaniam-320
Subtle Body - 263
Sudras - 297
Sughosha - 4
Sukham - Dukham (meaning)-304
Sukhasana - 189
- asana for beginners-189

Sukritino - 231
Suktas - 285
Sun, the - 118, 314
- as Yogi Raaj-314
- worship in Vedas-314
- as the first created object-119

Supreme Consciousness-28, 578, 579
Supreme Peace-75
Supreme Purush-484, 485
Supreme Self- 16, 17, 25, 30, 45, 49, 53, 61, 583, 586
- and individual identity-30
- as a holographic entity-423
- views of Shruti Bhagawati, Rigveda, Kathopanishad, Krishna-422, 423

Supreme Soul-27, 42, 43, 48-51
- signifies Purna as in Vedas-27
- being one with it-578, 579
- its omnipresence-28

Sur - Asura-502
Sushmana Nadi-256, 257
Swabhav - 132, 587
- and swadharma-132
- as basis of caste system-132, 514, 575
- types and details-514

Swadharma - 20, 25, 45, 46, 46, 85, 90, 91, 111, 123, 124, 145, 275, 356, 403, 452, 493, 503, 504, 510, 515, 586, 589
- as an institution of sacrifice-90
- what it demands-90

Swadhisthan Chakra-191
- as second psychic station-191
- literal meaning-191
- location, colour, element-192

Swadhyaya - 145
- details-146
- swa and dhyaya-145

Swami Chhidbhavanand-91, 296, 590
- on Vasuki and Kundlini Shakti-327
- on attributes of Krishna-340
- on man of Yajna-91; rajasic dharma-565
- banyan tree and samskar-470
- escapism and sanyas-544

Swami Chinmayanand-36, 383, 428, 478
- on Samsar-471; fearlessness-492
- on Kama and the train episode-114, 115
- on reincarnation-36; Dharma-594

Swami Dayanand Saraswati-148
- explains Gayatri-333
- his guru-148
- Karma samadhi-141
- total surrender to guru-148

Swami Prabhupad-82, 195, 422
- on peace within-153
- on preconditions of renunciation-

82
Swami Satya Prakash Saraswati-88, 89
- on environmental pollution-88
Swami Shivanand-30, 229, 443
- on a man's discriminatory power-497; obligatory duties-544
- on dwandva (dilemma)-30
- on mrigachhala-188
- on rebirth-431
- on sattva and jaap-452
- on supreme consciousness-421, 422
- on Vedas and Smritis-509
Swami Tapasyanand-49, 252, 373
- on Karmayoga-49; Maya-229
Swami Virajanand-148
- guru of Swami Dayanand Saraswati-148
Swami Vivekanand-135, 233, 378, 476
- bewilderment at the sight of cosmic unity-370
- born with all the 18 character of divine power-214
- on homely saints-138; inherited spirituality-214
- on inaction in action-135; Karma-166, 474
Swara - 315
Swarupa - 264
Swati - 149
Swetaketu - 220
- son of Udalaka-423
Symbolic Representation of Gods and Goddesses-248

T

Taittreya Upanishad-519
- on food-519
Tamas (ic) - 227, 228
- binds through ignorance-446
- food-517, 518
- happiness-567; predominance-450, 451, 456
- person-449, 454, 512, 513; action-557; buddhi-561
- yajna-522; dhriti-564
Tapascharya (austerity)-39, 304, 493
- Sattvic, Rajasic, Tamasic-527, 528
- through torturing the body-515, 516
- various parts-520, 521
- with passionate desire-516, 526
Tapovan - 65
Tat (meaning)-534
Tat tvam asi (meaning)-408
Tatha manapamanayoh (meaning)-398
Tejah - 335, 495
The Life Story of Ramkrishna-65
The Tao of Physics-173
Thomas Kempis-78
Thou and Thine-77, 382, 392, 473, 582
Titan - 502
Tolstoy - 93
Transmigration of soul-36
- as per book of Wisdom-36
- supported by sages and scholars-36
Trataka - 199
Treta Yuga - 262
- the beginning; duration-262
Trikala Darshi-240, 360
Trikala Sandhya (meaning)-288
Trimurty - 170, 248, 262, 288, 359
- the three-fold manifestation of the supreme-288
Trividya - 288, 289
Tropic of cancer, Capricorn-268
Tukaram - 295, 592
Tuladhar - 96
- Jajali episode-96, 577
Tulsidas - 380
Tulya ninda stutir mauni (significance)-400
Turiya - 257
Tusti - 304
Tyaga - 210, 537
- true sense-543

U

Ucchaisrava-319, 325
Udalaka (rishi)-487
- his son-220, 423
- on key to all knowledge-487
Udana - 144

Udasino - 396
Unrighteousness-12
Upanayan samskar-332
Upanishad - 79, 583
- on immanence of God-314
- recommended for studies-472
- total number-472
Updrashta - 429
- as indwelling Supreme-429, 430
Uttam Purush- 486
- as described in Shruti Bhagawati-486, 487
Uttarayan - 266, 314
- the beginning-314; Period-268

V

Vac (word) - 256, 533
- as Shabda; Brahman-320, 533
- sustains all the three worlds-321
Vadah (logic)-329
- samvad and vivad-331
Vairagya - 210
Vaishwarnar-482
- as jatharagni-482
- in Shruti Bhagwati-482
Vaishya - 570
- duty-574; features-571, 574
Vaivasvata - 97
Vajra - 325
- creation as indestructible weapon-326
Vanprastha - 418
Varnas (caste)-12, 570, 571
Varsnyeya - 12, 112
Varuna - 130, 236, 325
- as lord of water-327
Vasanas - 428, 471, 549
Vashishtha Smriti-14
- on killing a felon-14
Vasu - 131, 288, 313, 514
- abodes of 8 vasus-288
- names-317
Vasudeva - 19, 335, 604
- as father of Sri Krishna-336, 337
- vasudevah sarvam iti-231, 234
Vasuki (Nag)-325, 327
Vayu - 130
Vedas - 23, 50-53, 130, 224, 225, 284, 286, 287, 313, 540
- as divine revelation and cause-130
- emphasize that Supreme Soul is formless-375
- essence-130; hold a person for his rise and fall-167
- meaning-51, 284, 472; limitation-368, 372
- names of various Gods and their significance-130, 131
- on abode of God-424; Yajnas-540
- ordains five mahayajnas-143
- personification of Gods-130
- prayers for universal well-being-555
- recitation and outcome-51
- revealed to rishis-130, 284
- samskaras-53, 54; Calander-315
- three sections of hymns-472; recitation-527
- tradition of guru-disciple-23
- Upangvedas-285
Vibhuti Yoga- 301
Victor E Franklin-400, 502
Videh - 66, 96
Vijnan - 220
- as aparoksha Jnan-220
Vikhyad - 331
Vimudha (meaning)-479
Vina - 258
Vinobaji - 14, 39
- on Karmayogi-96
- on Karmnyevadhikaraste-57
- on life cycle-39
- prescribes the way for moksha-299
Virat - 5, 130
Virgil - 36
Visarjan - 378
Vishad - 16, 17, 603
- as a blessing-17; Yoga-16
Vishakha - 262
Vishnu - 314, 359
- announces the beginning of Uttarayan-314

- as the sustainer-359
Vishuddhi Chakra-193
- meaning, beej mantra, presiding deity-193
- location, colour and element-193
Viswa - 130
- its root-283
- Rupa Darshan Yoga-342
Viteshna - 565
Vivasvan - 97
- as Sun God-118
Vyakti - 242
Vyana - 144
Vyas - 160, 286, 310, 335, 603
- authored Brahma Sutra, Puranas, Bhagwat
- describes a real renouncer-160
Vyashti - 306

W

Withdrawing Senses-65-67
- Sri Krishna, Sri Auobindo, Buddha, Mahesh Yogi-66-68
- instance of Janak-66

Y

Yada Yada hi dharmasya (meaning)-122
Yajna - 86, 87, 92, 94, 131, 287, 578
- and Havanakunda-143
- and its spirit-87; types-87, 520-522
- as a spiritual discipline-120; Physical-Psychological discipline-493
- as a term of Vedic tradition-87
- as described in Vedas, Upanishads-540
- B G Tilak's opinion-92
- dan and tap not to be renounced-538
- in words of Gandhi-87; Sri Krishna-87
- its root-131; literal meaning-143
- limitation-368
- provides sustenance-249
- what all it expresses-91, 92
Yajnavalkya- 94
- views on a sanyasi-160
Yajnopaveet- 523
Yajur Veda - 130, 285, 289
- its upaveda and subject matter-285
Yaksha - 39
- Yudhisthir samvad-39
Yama - 325
- as lord of death-327
- description in kathopanishad-327
Yatatma dradhischaya (meaning)-393
Yathechhasi tatha kuru-587, 590
Yoga - 47, 48, 81, 82
- as a skill in action-55
- as an art-81; various types-48
- Chittravriti Nirodhah-48
- difference from Samkhya method-48
- Karmasu Kausalam (meaning)-59
- leading to sanyas-203
- of action as suggested by Sri Krishna-82
- of action-81; wisdom-55
- preconditions and benefits-195
- through mantra-199
- various stages dealt by Patanjali-61
Yogadashan - 481
Yogakshemam Vahamyaham-290, 291
Yogayukta (meaning)-160, 161
- in the words of Sri Krishna-160; Swami Chinmayanand-162
Yogi - 49
- knows bright/dark paths of the world-267
Yudhisthir - 525
Yug - 261
- four yugas-261, 262
Yuj - 47
- meaning-81